MW00785541

THE DEFINITIVE GUIDE TO
PLANTING
FOOD PLOTS

ACCOLADES FOR *THE DEFINITIVE GUIDE TO PLANTING FOOD PLOTS*

"Peter Fiduccia is one of the rare individuals who has truly 'been there, done that' when it comes to whitetail tactics and food plot and wildlife management. His expertise on planting food plots and deer hunting strategies spans decades. The insights found within the pages of this book will not only help you provide optimum nutrition for the whitetails roaming your ground, but they will also help you shorten your learning curve to growing bigger bucks and healthier deer."—**Daniel E. Schmidt, Editor-in-Chief/VP,** *Deer & Deer Hunting*

"Fiduccia has taken decades of real food plot experience and put it all into one, easy to understand volume. Anyone looking to understand what it really takes to engineer the right food plots to draw in bucks, this is the book."—**David E. Dirks, Producer & Host,** *DirksOutdoors*

"I can't express the appreciation for your thorough response about planting my 10 Dunstan Chestnut trees. Guess I shouldn't be surprised, you always do great work and seem like a great guy."—**Mike Mondelli, Schoharie, New York**

"When I want reliable food plot information, I don't turn to the web, magazine articles, or chat rooms. I email Peter Fiduccia. He is approachable and friendly. The "Doc's" information is always spot on. He has helped me grow better food plots and his deer hunting advice is unmatched!"—**Ben Sandro, Dry Ridge, Kentucky**

"When I started a food plot program, I referred to Peter's first book, *The Shooter's Bible Guide to Planting Food Plots*, for guidance. I was very happy with the success of my plantings and the increased deer sightings. That deer season we took three adult bucks on opening day! I expect the information in this new book will help take my food plot program to the next level."—**Leo Somma, Hampton Bays and South New Berlin, New York**

THE DEFINITIVE GUIDE TO
PLANTING
FOOD PLOTS

Plant it *Right* and They *Will* Come

Peter J. Fiduccia

Skyhorse Publishing

Copyright © 2023 by Peter J. Fiduccia

All rights reserved. No part of this book may be reproduced in any manner without the express written consent of the publisher, except in the case of brief excerpts in critical reviews or articles. All inquiries should be addressed to Skyhorse Publishing, 307 West 36th Street, 11th Floor, New York, NY 10018.

Skyhorse Publishing books may be purchased in bulk at special discounts for sales promotion, corporate gifts, fund-raising, or educational purposes. Special editions can also be created to specifications. For details, contact the Special Sales Department, Skyhorse Publishing, 307 West 36th Street, 11th Floor, New York, NY 10018 or info@skyhorsepublishing.com.

Skyhorse® and Skyhorse Publishing® are registered trademarks of Skyhorse Publishing, Inc.®, a Delaware corporation.

Visit our website at www.skyhorsepublishing.com.

10 9 8 7 6 5 4 3 2 1

Library of Congress Cataloging-in-Publication Data is available on file.

Cover design by Kai Texel
Cover photo credit: © Mikael Males | Dreamstime.com

Print ISBN: 978-1-5107-5901-5
Ebook ISBN: 978-1-5107-7169-7

Printed in China

Disclaimer: All seed data provided, as well as all the other planting information reflects the author's earnest efforts to interpret a complex body of scientific research, and to translate it into useful wildlife food plot planting practices and guidelines within this compendium. Following the guidance provided throughout this volume does not assure the reader any or all the information written by the author will imply any steadfast assurances of planting success. As with any farming practice, the planting, management thereof, and successful growing of plants are totally dependent on weather conditions, soil fertility, and many other factors.

Dedication

I devote this book to all those who enjoy playing in dirt. May your soils be fertile, your crops successful, your nut and fruit trees heavy with bounty, and your fields and woods thick with deer and other wildlife. I hope you reap the benefits from what you sow as a wildlife food plot enthusiast and land guardian.

▲ Photo: PCFImages

▲ Planting a variety of late-dropping fruit trees is a sure-fire tactic for any successful food plot program. Credit: Huntingplots.com

Contents

▲ The flowers of phacelia are highly attractive to honeybees and other types of bees. Credit: Go Seed

Foreword

Everything great begins with a simple dream or a vision of what the future could be like.

When I began hunting around the age of twelve or so, I commenced upon a lifetime passion for everything outdoors. Time spent afield was supplemented by reading stories of hunting and fishing. As a youngster I had a dream of having my own hunting and fishing paradise, with the finest opportunities for big bucks, wild turkeys, and pheasants. Of course, there would be great fishing too.

My overriding motivation to acquire and build this ultimate outdoors paradise drove me to become an entrepreneur at a young age, as it seemed to me the quickest way to afford the property I desired in the shortest time possible.

This journey into various businesses was incredibly time-consuming, but I always made time to hunt and fish. I also made time to learn as much as possible about the outdoors to help me be successful when my dream would become reality.

Dreams need to be shaped and brought into focus. This is where people who are great at what they do can be a huge help if they choose to share their experiences and knowledge. It was during this period in my young life when I discovered a man who truly talked to deer, *in their language*, and that man was Peter Fiduccia. Peter not only talked to deer, but in fact had a high degree of success in having deer respond the way he intended. I was hooked and wore that old VHS tape out, studying and practicing talking to deer. Please understand that this was long before calling deer became popular, actually.

I found that Peter's instruction worked and allowed me to become more successful. I considered this skill as a gift and continue to apply many of his ideas today. His tips have stood the test of time. After nearly three decades of managing and enjoying my Illinois farms, I reflect upon the people who helped me obtain my goals, and Peter Fiduccia is one of these folks.

I did my best to emulate the "pass it on" philosophy through my best-selling DVD QDM series, *Building Whitetail Paradise*, my book, many magazine articles, seminars, and television work.

Decades later I would have the pleasure of getting to know Peter personally, while working together on his *Woods N' Water* TV series. While in New York visiting Peter and his wonderful wife Kate, I saw firsthand his impressive knowledge of everything related to deer, including habitat and food plots. Peter's deep experience and practical delivery of information is suitable for a novice or a professional wildlife manager.

I encourage you to apply his solid ideas in *The Definitive Guide to Planting Food Plots* to your hunting property. As with everything my friend Peter does, this book is a gift of his experience that will help bring your dream to reality!

Bob Coine
Heartland Studios, Inc.
Creator of the *Building Whitetail Paradise* DVD series

▲ Photo Courtesy Bob Coine

▲ Bob Coin is the creator and producer of a game management DVD series dedicated to portraying solid food plot management practices and land stewardship. Credit: *Building a Whitetail Paradise*

▲ Deer eat both the leaves and the seeds of sunflowers. Other animals that heartily devour sunflowers include bear, wild turkeys, many upland birds, some waterfowl, and small game. Credit: © Kokoroyuki | Dreamstime.com

Acknowledgments

I have always been blessed with the good fortune of having other people within the outdoor industry extend a helping hand to me along the way. Without their support and input, I would never have reached the point I have today as a full-time outdoor communicator. Therefore, one of the most important and fulfilling parts of any book I have written is here in the acknowledgments section. It is where I can genuinely thank people that have contributed their assistance in this volume.

When it comes to planting wildlife food plots, Kate and Cody, my wife and son, are the two people who are always at my side in the field providing their much-needed help and input. Therefore, anywhere in this book where I have written "I" when it comes to food plots, most often "I" means "we."

Aside from my family, my gratitude starts with you, a valued reader of my latest book. Thank you for your support, I genuinely appreciate it. You have allowed me to take an extraordinary journey over the last thirty-seven years. Therefore, within this space, I want to formally extend a personal acknowledgment of my sincere gratefulness to you. I am, and always have been, humbled by such support.

Keeping to the confines of the subject matter in this book, I want to extend my gratitude to the many people who have contributed their assistance to help make this book more complete and helpful to its readers. They have shared their wisdom, astuteness, sharp insights, and generosity of their time.

Amy Wallander, Sales & Marketing Administrator, Brillion Farm Equipment/Landoll Corp.

Arthur Stephens, Lab Manager, Matson Labs

Ayshea Heckman Marketing Assistant, Ernst Conservation Seeds

Becky Russell and the late Ed Russell, Preferred Seed

Bill Cousins, General Manager, Whitetail Institute of North America

Bob Coine, Founder, Building Whitetail Paradise

Bryan Guercioni Marketing, Pawnee Buttes Seed

Chris and Melissa Rogers and family, River Refuge Seed

Corinne Burgess. Sr. Manager of Creative Projects, Pennington Seed

Dan Schmidt, Vice President / Editor-in-Chief/VP, Deer & Deer Hunting magazine

Daniel Welter, Co-Owner and President; James Welter, Co-Owner and Vice President; Les Welter, Co-Owner and Vice President; Karen Knepper, Co-Owner and Secretary/Treasurer, Welter Seed & Honey Co.

Dawn and Jeff Zarnowski, Z's Nutty Ridge, LLC.

Deb Girardin, Arrow Seed Co., Inc.

Devon Johnk, Food Plot Sales Manager, Arrow Seed Co., Inc.

Don Honcoop and Angela V., Founders/Owners, Maple River Farms

Dustin Porcher, Wildlife Seed Sales, Merit Seeds

Ed Starzec, Territory Manager, Landoll Company, LLC

Ernie Grimo, Founder and Owner; Linda Grimo, Grimo Nut Nursery

Gage Reeves Digital Marketing Intern, Barenbrug USA

Greg Latorre President/Owner, Deer Out®

Iain & Dunstan Wallace, C.E.O. and C. F. O., Chestnut Hill Outdoors

Jacob Wiggins, Seedworld USA

Janie Walters, Marketing-Hunting Division, Pradco Outdoors

Jared Wiklund, Public Relations Manager, Pheasants Forever

Jason McKellar, Marketing Manager, Promotions Mossy Oak/ Dudley Phelps R&D

Jason R. Snavely, Founder and Owner, Drop-Tine Seed Co.

Jay Cassell, Editorial Director, Outdoor Books, Skyhorse Publishing

Jeremy Flinn Co-Founder/Chief Executive Officer DeerGro by AgriGro

Jerry Hall, President and Director of Research, GO Seed

Jim Wall, Marketing Manager, CropCare Equipment

John and Kelly Barsody, Owners, Frigid Forage, Inc.

Jon Cooner, Director of Special Projects, Whitetail Institute of North America

John Stoltzfus, Owner & Founder, Hunting Plots.com & Thunder Ridge Outdoors

Jonathan Rupert, Manager, Smith Seed Services

Kenneth Smith, Owner, Sinclairville Seed Company

Les Welter, V.P.; Jamie Meier, Corey Hyde, Landoll Corporation

Luther Wannamaker, Owner, L.B. Wannamaker Seed Corporation

Morgan and Jake Butler, Buck Forage Products & Arkansas County Seed Co., Inc.

Oleg Vasertriger, Marketing Director; Joel Hagen, Sales Manager, Deer Creek Seed Company

Patricia and Paul Kester, Kester Wild Game Nursery

Paul Zimmerman, Principal and Founder, Esch No-Till Drills

Paula Kastor, V.P. Marketing, Kasco Manufacturing Co., Inc.

Peggy Mogush, Inside Sales and Consulting, Ernst Conservative Seeds

Ray Scott (deceased), Steve Scott, and Wilson Scott, Whitetail Institute of North America

Risa Demasi, Co-Founder, GO Seed

Ryan Hayes, Founder/Owner, Blue Hill Wildlife Nursery

Steve Cummins—Cummins Nursery

Steve Roed, Marketing, Scales Advertising

Steve Tillman, Research and Development, Plantra, Inc.

Ted Rose, Wildlife Photographer

The Nerd Gang: P. Cody (Deputy Dawg) Fiduccia, Eric (Piano Man) Schultz, Alex (Big Orange) Brozdowski; Dr. Victor (Beaker) Schultz; Andrew (Pi) Melchionna and William (Number One) Schultz

Todd Stittleburg, Founder, Antler King

Tony Lyons, Founder, President, and Publisher, Skyhorse Publishing

William Cousins, General Manager, Whitetail Institute of North America

▲ I am especially grateful for the food plot help I receive from the "Nerd Gang" (plotheads one and all). From left to right: Dr. Peter C. Fiduccia, MBA, MPA, - Associate Director, Data Strategy & Partnerships, Merck Pharmaceuticals, Dr. Victor L. Schultz, MS - Senior Scientist, Chemical Engineering, Merck Pharmaceuticals, Eric R. Schultz, MPA, Fulbright Scholar - Project Director, US Department of State, Alex J. Brozdowski, BS - Consulting Manager, Deloitte, and Lieutenant William Schultz - US Navy. Not pictured here - Andrew M. Melchionna, MMath - Doctoral Candidate, Cornell University, Devin T. Martin, MPA - Project Manager, Changeis, Inc., and Daniel Valliere, BS – Senior Accountant, Hypertherm. Credit: PCFImages

About the Author

In 1964, I was in my senior year at Fort Hamilton High School in Brooklyn, New York. Like so many seniors, I struggled with the question, "Where do I go from here?" Continue my education? Join the workforce? I also considered a third option: A potential career in the outdoor industry as a writer. At the time, I had a profound desire to see my name as a by-line in a magazine.

However, there were two fundamental issues I had to grapple with. First, I had to convince my parents a writing career was a viable financial choice. At the time, most people staunchly believed the adage that artists and writers are bound to starve to death. The second issue was much more daunting: I did not have a firm idea concerning what I could write about. Obviously, that hurdle was an enormous stumbling block, the reality of which began to deflate my writing musings.

While attending the New York Institute of Technology, I shared my thoughts and concerns with a professor. To the best of my recall his advice was straightforward, "You must first consider changing your course of study. To address your more prevalent problem, only consider writing about subjects that you know best. The subject matters will come to you, instead of you seeking them out." It was good advice, but in the end, I decided to continue with my business courses.

About a decade later, I was hunting deer in Sterling Forest which encompassed 16,000 private acres in Orange County, New York. About an hour into my hunt, as I was sitting on a flat slab of rock at the end of a ridge overlooking the valley below, I was mentally surprised to see a buck appear in the *exact* spot I had predicted that I would see a buck.

The following day, I mulled over why I was so amazed a buck showed up precisely where I thought it would. I started to think that since junior high school, I had fervently read countless magazine articles and books about deer tactics, anatomy, biology, and behavior. And for the past ten years, I had gained considerable experience hunting deer in several states. So, at that exact instant, I remembered the words of the professor, "Write about what you know best." Then and there I understood. What I knew best was deer behavior, and deer hunting strategies.

Not long after that I wrote an article about antler rattling tactics to attract bucks. I sent the piece to the *New York Sportsman* magazine. To my good fortune, the publisher, the late Paul Keesler, accepted the story. From that point on, I have been extremely fortunate to have written numerous magazine articles. They have appeared in leading outdoor publications like *Deer and Deer Hunting, Outdoor Life, Field & Stream, Sports Afield,* and many others. I even founded a deer hunting magazine and licensed it to Harris Publications. Some of you may remember it: *Whitetail Hunting Strategies.* It was a successful and popular publication for many years. Additionally, I have authored thirteen books, and co-authored three others.

As I write this, I feel lucky and immensely blessed. I realize how privileged I have been to achieve my aspiration to be a writer. Fortunately, I accomplished it without starving to death.

▲ Photo: PCFImages

Introduction

I wrote this book with the intent to not target professional biologists or highly experienced agricultural land managers. Therefore, it doesn't contain complicated and hard-to-decipher information. It specifically addresses straightforward methods for anyone who wants to plant crops to attract deer and other wildlife to their property, and who also inevitably strive to become better stewards of their land.

My foremost undertaking was to share my approach to planting consistently successful wildlife food plots. Consequently, when it comes to my personal methods for planting food plots and my deer hunting strategies, my principal goal has always been to keep the information credible, down-to-earth, and free of advertising propaganda. Thus, as I have done in all written and electronic media I cover, this volume is a practical guide presented in a common-sense way that provides reliable information. When you finish reading this book, you will have gained the ability to take your food plot skills and knowledge needed as a food plot manager to the next level.

Essentially, this book is meant to help the typical deer hunter grow wildlife food plots successfully time and again. Within the following pages I share wide-ranging advice and information about what it requires to consistently keep your resident deer from searching for food items on other properties much less often, and how to attract neighboring deer to come to dinner on your land much more frequently.

If I were a betting man, my wager would be that your chief reason for purchasing this book was because your principal goal is to kill bucks with larger antlers on the lands you hunt. And, that you want to see deer the most during the daylight hours of the hunting season. Therefore, you will also find I have included no-nonsense information to help you take your food plot plantings, deer sightings, and hunting skills to a higher level of success. Whether you have less than one acre or dozens of acres or more of land to sow, you will find helpful, up-to-date information to assist you in planting successful food plots, year after year.

The background for this book is based on my first food plot book, *Shooter's Bible Guide to Planting Food Plots*. Since it was published in 2013, it went through two printings. Since then, modern technologies, plant varieties, and many other aspects of food plot planting have evolved. All of this led to me writing this title with the newest information available.

Hence, I have included chapters that cover everything from the basics to advanced information about planting food plots to help you become the best possible food plot manager you can be. Additionally, you will find more than fifty different plant species profiles for your consideration. To my knowledge, this book has more plant listings than any other food plot book. Most important, I have included many winter-hardy plantings that will attract deer during the hunting seasons from September through January.

I made sure to discuss other subjects that go hand-in-hand with planting wildlife food plots, like how to attract deer from neighboring lands, creating a genuine refuge, plantings for other wildlife, deer aging through tooth analysis, a detailed glossary containing more than 200 listings, a comprehensive resource of seed company listings, where to buy late-dropping fruit trees, where to find nut tree nurseries, a chapter on the vital importance of weighing deer you take, the importance of keeping accurate records, and much more.

Equally important, the information will also help you to become more successful stewards of the property you manage. Furthermore, I want you to know that I clearly understand not everyone reading this book plants large acreages of food plots. Nor is it necessary to do so. Whether you have one acre, a few acres, or hundreds of acres, the information within this book will help you plant successful food plots when you want deer eating them most—during hunting season.

In conclusion, within the pages of this volume, I genuinely enjoyed sharing with you all the experience

I have acquired over the last thirty-five years regarding planting wildlife food plots to nutritionally benefit and attract all *species* of deer and other wildlife. It doesn't matter how much ground you are planting. My best advice about a wildlife food plot program are my two favorite phrases: Plant it *right*—and they *will* come, and *Reap what you sow*. I trust this book will help you to do just that.

Peter J. Fiduccia
South New Berlin, NY

A personal note from the author—
Throughout this book I mention company names and product brands, including some that I use. I did not include them to suggest in any way that readers should purchase any of the brands cited. I strongly believe the choice of buying products is left solely up to the reader and should not be swayed by any unintended influence by me. To my best ability I tried to be fair by including a variety of brands, companies, and products most often by alphabetizing them.

▲ When a food plot of corn is close to a woodlot, it is not uncommon for an adult buck to bite off an ear and return to the woodlot to eat it. Photo: Jim Cummin/Dreamstime.com

▲ By implementing a well-planned food plot and deer management program, hunters will improve their chances of taking mature bucks like the one seen here. Credit: © Mikael Males | Dreamstime.

Chapter One

The Genesis of the Food Plot Industry

Before the mid-1980s, the idea of planting food plots and managing wildlife habitats for white-tailed deer and other wildlife was essentially nonexistent. At that time, there were places in Texas and some other states that did practice several types of deer management. For instance, back then most Texas hunters believed that all spike bucks should be killed as their antlers would never develop into anything more than small antlered bucks. Now we know better than that. The planting of diverse types of clovers, other legumes, brassicas, grains, grasses etc., to enhance the health of a deer herd, improve antler development, and to attract deer to specific plantings was an unexploited, foreign concept within the overall hunting fraternity four decades ago. Moreover, the specific terms "food plots" and "deer nutrition" and "Food Plotters" (and many other food plot terms that came to be) were totally alien to the deer hunter's vocabulary.

Enter stage right—noted bass angler, Ray Scott. Ray is the founder and architect of the Bass Anglers Sportsman Society (B.A.S.S.) and Bassmasters—two entities that became household monikers for millions of anglers throughout North America and across the globe. In the late 1960s, Ray started the bass fishing tournaments that were the genesis of a multibillion—that's billion starting with a "B,"—dollar industry. They are even more popular and successful today. It's no wonder that Ray has been likened to noted Aldo Leopold, and even Teddy Roosevelt. Ray is acknowledged as one of a handful of famous individuals "who has made a difference" in the American outdoors within the past century.

Ahh, but being the founder and creative force of everything related to B.A.S.S. and Bassmasters wasn't

▲ Whitetail Institute of North America founder, the late Ray Scott. Ray has been acclaimed as an individual who has made a difference in the American outdoors within the past century. Photo Courtesy: Whitetail Institute of N.A.

enough for Ray Scott. Why? Because Ray was also a fervent and dedicated white-tailed deer hunter. Like most hunters in Alabama, Ray's home state, he planted and hunted green fields. Green fields are basically properties planted in traditional small grains like wheat, rye, and oats. But Ray, being Ray, was not satisfied with settling for the status quo. He planted all types of forages in a quest to discover which plants produced the best results as nutritious, palatable, and digestible forages. Among the extensive list of plantings was a clover that consistently produced better results in attracting and keeping deer coming to his properties than the other forage varieties.

That forage was a clover variety that possessed characteristics that repeatedly attracted deer. That's all it took to start Ray's wheels turning. It didn't take long for a hypothesis to take shape. Ray felt that whatever deer-attracting characteristics this clover variety had, once they were identified, they could be further enhanced. Ray surmised the clover's genetics held the answers to these questions. That's when he contacted one of the leading plant clover geneticists in the country, Dr. Wiley Johnson. Dr. Johnson was responsible for helping develop the specific clover type that Ray was testing. Both Ray and Dr. Johnson began a research project that would eventually conclude in the development of the first-ever wildlife clover forage variety that was specifically genetically designed for white-tailed deer. They named the clover Imperial Whitetail Clover. This would be primarily responsible for launching an entirely new industry, including manufacturing and selling everything related to planting wildlife food plots. And Ray was a certified genius at selling ideas, concepts, and products. There's an adage attributed mostly to Arthur "Red" Motely, "Nothing happens until someone sells something."

Others were also quick to recognize Ray Scott as the father of launching the entire food plot industry. John Zent, the Editorial Director for the National Rifle Association magazines, said, "that whitetail deer hunting has been enriched by a nationwide proliferation of food plots and plantings can't be overstated, but in fact the domino effect set in motion by Whitetail Institute goes much further than that." Zent went on to say, "Innumerable species—everything from songbirds to black bears—are now thriving in habitats enhanced purely through private initiative. In addition, this DIY conservation ethic has helped to generate its own real estate boom as hunters make a commitment to become land and wildlife managers. America's wildlife has benefited, and so too has the economy of many rural communities."

With the advancement of Imperial Whitetail Clover, an innovative company was crafted; a business founded upon stringent requirements, acknowledged research, and time-tested results. In 1988, Ray kicked off the christening of Whitetail Institute of North America. Like B.A.S.S. and Bassmasters, Whitetail Institute of North America soon became the go-to name for countless deer hunters to buy Imperial Whitetail Clover. There is absolutely no doubt Whitetail Institute of North America was the first and only company at that time whose sole purpose was researching and developing forages and forage blends specifically designed for white-tailed deer. Moreover, a new term was coined as well. No longer was planting a forage referred to as a green field. Now hunters were planting what was designated as a "wildlife food plot."

During the years of research and development of Imperial Whitetail Clover, it was determined that clover's protein content greatly influenced its attraction to deer. The higher the protein content, the more deer sought out Imperial Whitetail Clover. At that time, protein was a little-understood and seldom-used word in deer hunting circles. However, researchers at the

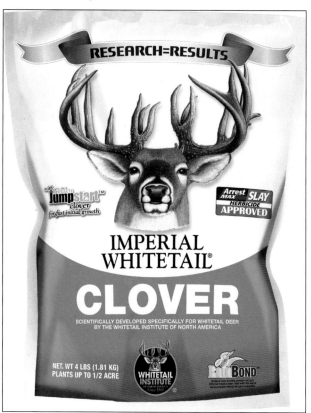

▲ Ray Scott created and launched the deer nutrition industry in 1988. Over three decades later his mantra—"*research equals results*"—has kept Whitetail Institute a leader in the food plot industry. Photo Courtesy: Whitetail Institute of N.A.

Whitetail Institute quickly learned of the vital role protein plays in a deer's life, including antler growth, lactation, and muscle and bone growth. This knowledge led to the concept that not only could you attract more deer with Imperial Whitetail Clover, but because of its high protein content, Imperial Clover would also provide improved nutrition resulting in a better conditioned and healthier deer herd. The combination of nutrition and attraction resulted in a planting that was truly a food plot.

Not long after launching Whitetail Institute, Ray's two sons—Steve and Wilson—came on board. The two shared Ray's passion for deer hunting, deer research, and deer management. At that time, however, Whitetail Institute was still a fledgling company. But Ray, Steve, and Wilson had an undaunting vision to make the company a leader in providing food plot and deer nutritional products to hunters across the country.

According to Wilson Scott, "When we first began testing clovers in the 1980s, other seed types—both annuals and other perennials—were included in the testing. While our focus was on finding and developing clovers that met the high standards we were searching for, we knew that in certain circumstances other forages also had a place in a deer hunter's management plans." He went on to say, "The early research identified certain other forages that deserved follow-up research. We expanded our testing locations to cover all of North America to be sure the products we offered were the absolute best forages available and could thrive in both the harshest cold northern climates as well as the hot and dry Deep South. This research, which continues today, is what sets the Whitetail Institute's products apart."

Steve Scott commented that "All Whitetail products go through an exhaustive research program before ever reaching the marketplace. First, they go through initial testing at various Whitetail Institute facilities, and if they make it through that stage, then they have to make it through expanded testing at satellite research facilities all over North America.

If they make it through the next stage, then they are tested in the real world with field testers across the country. These field testers are just regular guys who love hunting and enjoy being involved in helping test and evaluate potentially the next great thing or things. They use their own equipment and plant the various products exactly the same way that hunters across America will eventually do if the product makes it through this last research stage. This research is expensive and most often a long process, but it all goes back to Ray Scott's vision—'no product will carry the Whitetail Institute brand unless it has proven to be the absolute best.'"

Thirty-two years of business is unquestionably a milestone to celebrate in any company. But thirty-two years in a firm that launched an entire new industry is without a doubt a proclaimed testament to the leaders of the company, the knowledgeable employees, and the value of the products that they produce. The fact is, a company requires all the pieces of the puzzle including longevity, foresight, vision, demanding work, and a commitment to the customers served to flawlessly fit with one another. These elements are what made Ray Scott's Whitetail Institute the consistently successful enterprise it has been throughout the years. Ray Scott's mantra of thirty-two years ago still stands, "Never be content with the status quo."

And so, through the genesis of this one company, today there are literally countless businesses within the outdoor industry and outside of it that produce a mind-bending variety of related food plot products.

Some of the products include minerals, vitamins, flavored attractants of all types, trail cameras, ATV planting implements, soil analysis kits, soil testers, wide-ranging types of planting implements, hand-held seed spreaders, herbicides, inoculants, fertilizers, habitat hooks, electronic fencing, harrow fence rakes, portable back sprayers, deer aging kits, fruit and nut trees specifically designed to attract deer, and an unimaginable list of different types of seeds. All credited to one man with an unstoppable vision—the late Ray Scott.

▲ Applying strict rules of only shooting 3½ -year-old bucks or older gives a buck like this time to develop an even more impressive rack.
Credit: Ted Rose

Chapter Two

Food Plots: The Key to Better Deer and Deer Hunting

If one hundred deer hunters were each asked to list five hunting topics that most interested them, it's a good bet half of them would reply planting food plots. Since the mid-eighties, the interest of all subjects related to planting food plots has steadily increased. Over the last decade, the allure of planting food plots has grown exponentially.

It has become a widely accepted and extraordinarily popular topic of deer hunters throughout North America.

Today the topic has been regularly and prominently showcased in countless outdoor magazines, books, television shows, radio programs, podcasts, YouTube, the web, internet chat rooms, DVDs, in seminar halls,

▲ Planting wildlife food plots to enhance deer health and better deer hunting, has grown exponentially over the last thirty years. This field of forage soybeans will provide top-quality nutrition for deer and other wildlife. Photo: PCFImages

and in other forms of print and electronic media. The subject even dominates conversations at deer camps, at hunting club meetings, sport shows, and within circles of friends who stalk white-tailed deer.

Countless companies now manufacture innumerable amounts of food plot seed and other products. It has spawned an entirely new and successful segment within the outdoor industry.

The coverage, development, and sale of products related to planting food plots appears to be never-ending, mostly because the media and the marketplace are reacting to the insatiable demand for more information and more products.

FINE POINTS TO PLANTING FOOD PLOTS

For those who plant food plots for deer and other wildlife, the one factor that can be counted on and trusted is this: Hunters who grow food plots attract deer to their lands. Creating food plots is a principal factor to a hunter's overall hunting success. Therefore, the availability of adding nutritious, palatable varieties of different plants, fruits, nuts, and other foods enhances a deer's chances of reaching maturity in better health and with larger antlers. Planting winter-hardy foods is a key to better deer survival. Plants capable of cold to frigid winter conditions include winter-hardy clovers, brassicas, the small grains, and many other cold-hardy plantings.

Food plot and deer managers should also include other elements in their programs. This includes the availability of sufficient water sources, shelter from weather and predators, good bedding areas and, particularly, an ample supply of winter foods, especially in northern regions with severe winters.

Winter, when food is harder for deer to find, is the critical time when they must have more energy to survive. This is when food plots play a vital role in helping deer make it through this difficult period. Most, if not all, deer managers do so primarily to improve their day-to-day hunting experiences of seeing more deer on each outing and taking adult bucks with larger antlers.

Therefore, today more hunters than ever before have come to understand that nutrition is a manageable aspect when it is tied to developing a food plot and wildlife management plan. By doing so hunters influence at least three elements on their properties: the

▲ During winter, nutritious food items are difficult for a deer to find. This leaves them no choice but to eat mountain maple, dogwood, elderberry, willow, and so on. Photo Courtesy: T. Rose

buck-to-doe ratio, nutritional factors, and the overall age of the deer. But first you must know what draws them to certain areas, what types of food plot plantings they prefer, and when deer prefer them. This is particularly important from September to the end of December. Having all this information will help you use your planting equipment to attract more deer to your property and keep resident deer from searching for foods on other lands more often.

KEY FACTORS

Of the millions of hunters who own and/or lease small or large tracts of land, many strive to increase the numbers of deer they see, especially bucks, during the hunting season. Secondly, many of them want to improve their kill ratio success from season to season.

▲ These three bucks were taken in different food plots on our property on opening day. The spike was taken by William Schultz. It was his first buck. Photo Courtesy: PCFImages.

[A quick side note: In all the media I cover, I use the words kill, take, bag, or shoot instead of using the word *harvest*. In my mind's eye, hunters *kill* game, they don't harvest it. It may not be the politically correct term to some, but it is *the* realistic description of hunting game.]

There are many other important positive elements food plots and habitat management plans provide to both deer and deer hunters. Female deer benefit from the protein and a host of other nutrients they receive from a variety of plantings. They pass the nutrients on to their fawns by providing them with wholesome top-grade milk, allowing for high fawn survival rates. Once weaned, fawns also have access to healthier food stuffs, which helps them develop healthier bodies more quickly. Buck fawns benefit not only by increasing their health, but also by improving their physical condition, and helping them to develop optimum antler size earlier in their lives. Food plot plantings provide a wide range of other nutritional benefits to deer.

WHY PLANT FOOD PLOTS
Very few food plotters would work as hard, diligently, and tirelessly to develop and maintain food plots if they couldn't reap the benefits of seeing and bagging more deer. Hence the phrase I often use, *Reap What You Sow.*

It is because food plots enable hunters to see and bag more deer that numerous deer hunters throughout North America plant countless tons of seeds, including clovers, legumes, small and large grains, brassicas, grasses, millets, and other plantings into the soil. All for the sole purpose of achieving better deer and deer hunting on their lands.

By no stretch of the imagination should the undertaking of establishing a wildlife food plot program and deer management plan be considered anything less than a dedicated commitment. But once a well-thought-out decision is made to plant food plots and manage deer, you will realize an immense enjoyment and euphoric feeling of satisfaction and accomplishment. These are feelings that are difficult to describe to anyone who has never grown and seen the benefits from successful food plots.

You will also increase deer sightings and deer hunting opportunities by ten to the tenth power—or at least tenfold. Food plots will also increase health benefits and sightings of other wildlife including wild turkeys, bears, waterfowl, upland birds, small game, and many non-hunted species of animals. As I have said for many years, "Plant it right, and they will come! Reap what you sow."

▲ For a buck to grow antlers like these, it requires good genetics and reaching adulthood. It also entails access to nutritious, palatable varieties of different high-protein plants, fruits, true nuts, acorns, and other plantings. Only a well-rounded food plot program can offer these elements to wildlife. Photo courtesy: Ted Rose

▲ When a deer management program offers good nutrition, it helps male deer to develop larger antlers at younger ages. Credit: Canstock Photo

Chapter Three

Nutrition and Deer

The proverb "you are what you eat" could certainly apply to deer. The fact is deer essentially do live and die by what they eat. That is why it is so important for anyone who plants wildlife food plots to better understand some of the nutritional needs of white-tailed deer.

Nutrition is a fickle element to deer. It varies from one habitat to another and from one plant to another. Therefore, there are many components that fluctuate nutritional values. That's unfortunate because when deer have a diet that provides them with quality nutrition, their health and bodies are more apt to be in top physical condition. To develop your food plot management program to its apex function, the plantings should include forages to provide deer with quality nutrition.

NUTRITION

Exactly what does nutrition mean and what is it? According to the Missouri Department of Education, MU Extension and the Missouri Department of Conservation, "Nutrition can be defined as the process

▲ This buck is eating Imperial Whitetail Clover, the clover that single-handedly motivated countless hunters to plant food plots to provide deer with quality nutrition. Photo Courtesy: Whitetail Institute of N.A.

by which an animal sustains its physiological functions through the foods it eats." Physiological functions are described as bodily processes that maintain a deer's health. Bodily processes include circulation, reproduction, and respiration. Adequate nutrition affects physiological activities such as growth, pregnancy, and as most of you reading this are most interested in, antler development.

That is why it is important that any food plot program include a wide variety of plantings that are ripe and available to deer throughout various parts of the seasons. High-protein plants are most helpful and necessary for deer year-round.

As an example, consider that all the summer and winter small grains are packed with beneficial quantities of protein. Triticale has 20 percent to 25 percent, wheat has 15 percent to 25 percent, rye has 12 percent to 25 percent, and oats have 10 percent to 25 percent protein. Corn has a low protein rating of only 5 percent to 8 percent. What it lacks in protein corn makes up for with 4 percent fat and 75 percent in carbohydrates, other elements deer need. All grains are highly palatable to deer as well.

Therefore, making summer and winter small grains available to your deer from early spring through late winter helps to provide them elevated levels of protein for a long period of time. Higher levels of protein aid female deer in developing healthier fetuses and producing quality milk for their fawns after birth. Milk with higher protein levels helps fawns develop healthier bodies to increase their survivability rate.

While protein helps deer (and all other mammals) build and grow muscle tissue, it is also the major contributing component to help bucks of all age classes develop larger antlers throughout their lives (if they continue to have access to significant amounts of protein).

As a side note, when I discuss what "I" plant or on "my" property, a more accurate reference would be "we" and "our," as both my wife Kate and son Cody are integral parts for the planting and maintaining of our food plot programs.

Although we plant most of the small grains in summer for the above reasons, we also make sure to plant the winter varieties of small grains to provide high protein levels to deer during the deer season and throughout

▲ Fall/winter oats provide a very palatable, high-quantity forage containing up to 25 percent protein. They can be seeded in late July or early August. Varieties like Buck Forage, Naked Oats, and Buck Magnet are cold tolerant. Photo Courtesy: PCFImages.

the remaining winter months. I also include some brassica plants that are high in protein: Canola—33 percent, kale—18 percent to 25 percent, forage rape—15 percent to 18 percent, and turnips—12 percent to 15 percent. All these plants deliver their protein from September to late winter. Augmenting your plantings to provide a variety of different high protein forages will work to fulfill the dietary necessities of deer throughout all the seasons.

White-tailed deer rely on a variety of foods for other important nutrients to support their physiological functions and nutritional requirements. Other crucial additional influences on the overall health and antler development of deer include age and genetics.

Deer eat more than 600 plant species. Research has evaluated the specific nutrients found in many of these forages. The current research declares that a deer's nutritional necessities can vary depending on if the deer is a buck or doe, if it's an adult, yearling or fawn, the deer's physiological condition, its bodily needs to grow antlers, develop fetuses, and more. Nutritional requirements for deer are also factored in by something as mundane as the elements, wind, snow, temperature, ice, or frigid conditions. These factors affect the quantity and kinds of foods that are obtainable from a specific area.

Additionally, as if the above weren't enough, soil quality is a crucial factor in influencing the nutrients available within forages deer eat. However, poor soils and healthy soils vary from one location to another (hence the importance of lime and fertilizer). For example, deer that live in the heavily wooded areas of New York's Adirondack Mountains, and in other woodlands in my home state of New York, have access to a plentiful crop of white or red oak fat-producing acorns, especially when the trees produce bumper crops. But

▲ This is a planting of Deer Creek forage soybeans. Managers with enough acreage should include a soybean planting. Deer and other wildlife relish eating the entire plant, not just the pod. Photo Courtesy: PCFImages

they don't have access to nutritious forages that grow in the rich soils found in farmlands.

The deer that live in the woodlands that include open farmlands in New York have fewer acorns to browse but a much more varied plant diet containing crops such as alfalfa, corn, and soybeans. These are major traditional plantings in New York and other parts of the country. So, you can see how in just one state, the differences in the soil's composition and nutritional values changes from one locale to another, and how some deer have different access to several types of nutrition. These regional diet differences make the intricacies of how deer select foods at any given time much more difficult to understand for some deer hunters.

NUTRITIONAL REQUIREMENTS OF DEER

Whitetails often concentrate on eating the tender tips of plants, as they are typically succulent and the most nutrient-rich portion of many forages. But no single food dominates a white-tailed deer's diet throughout the year because its food selection depends on a food's availability and palatability, during various times of the year.

To support a healthy deer population, food plots should include adequate amounts of diverse and nutrient rich food sources throughout the entire year. The nutritional requirements of white-tailed deer are relatively similar throughout the deer's range. Although they change seasonally as does the nutritional content of the vegetation they consume. These requirements include protein, energy, minerals, vitamins, and the one element that is often not given much thought, water.

ENERGY

Food plot managers usually focus on the virtues of protein levels in plantings. And they should. But they should give equal importance to the energy content forages provide deer.

Although researchers and biologists state "energy" is generally not classified as a nutrient, they do say that "energy levels of deer are a direct result of nutrient levels in the foods deer consume." Deer get their energy from the digestion of fats and carbohydrates. It is said, though, that excess protein can also be used as an energy source. Deer require energy for body maintenance,

▲ Acorns are abundant in nutrients. They contain substantial amounts of protein, carbohydrates, fats, minerals, calcium, phosphorus, potassium, and the vitamin niacin. Acorns provide deer with ample amounts of energy. Photo Courtesy: T. Rose.

other types of food plots have high levels of carbo-hydrates or sugars. This is why deer seek them out so enthusiastically in the fall.

Not surprisingly, whitetails have even higher energy requirements in winter. Research has shown that in winter deer select foods that are rich in energy over foods high in protein. This is simply because the winter is when energy is primarily needed to keep the deer's body temperature regulated to keep it warm. The elevated level of stress during the rut can cause bucks to lose up to 20 to 30 percent of their body weight. Because of the dramatic weight loss, they need to eat forages rich in energy. These elements are essential for a buck's body to recover. In winter fawns have a dire need for a high-energy diet because they have low body reserves, making them highly susceptible to severe winter conditions, especially prolonged single-digit temperatures.

▲ Deer seek out high energy foods in winter. One such food source is leftover soybeans, like the deer in this field are eating. Photo Courtesy: Bob Coine

reproduction, and growth. They also need it for normal day-to-day activities, including social interactions with other deer, escaping a coyote, a hunter, or other predator, and even to adjust their body temperatures. Energy requirements of deer are directly correlated to each deer's body size. The larger the deer, the larger its energy requirements. Other conditions that affect a deer's energy requirements include its physiological activity, weather, and something as mundane as its hide.

During the fall, deer seek out foods with elevated levels of carbohydrates or sugars which are stored in the body as fat reserves (a.k.a. lipogenesis). Fat reserves are a source of energy during the rut and especially during the stresses of winter. Corn, chestnuts, acorns, small and large grains, some late-dropping fruits, and

Again, pregnant does have high energy requirements during the summer once they have dropped their fawns and are lactating. Does spend about 20 percent of their total energy to keep their fetuses viable during pregnancy and the remaining 80 percent to provide quality milk for the fawns. The best milk production generally happens between ten to thirty-eight days after does drop their fawns.

MINERALS

Minerals make up about 5 percent of a deer's body. However, the complete list of specific minerals and amounts required by white-tailed deer are currently being studied. The two most prevalent and studied minerals by researchers are calcium and phosphorus.

Deer require these two minerals for bone and antler growth, milk production, and general metabolism.

Calcium and phosphorous make up 80 to 90 percent of a deer's skeletal frame. Researchers from the University of Missouri Extension say that hard antlers are made up of about 22 percent calcium and 11 percent phosphorus. Bucks with diets that don't offer these levels of minerals will sometimes display delayed antler growth and shedding of their velvet. In healthy soils, calcium and phosphorus are readily available. Phosphorus, though, is less accessible, particularly in acidic soils with a low pH level. Again, this is the reason to pay particular attention to your soil's pH value and adjust it accordingly. Liming soil as needed to make sure it remains at a healthy level, generally 6.0 to 6.5, is imperative not only for your plant's health, but your deer's well being too. Calcium and phosphorus are stored in a deer's skeleton until they are needed elsewhere by the body. Once a deer's skeleton has fully grown and reached its maximum potential, then these nutrients are diverted to the buck's antler growth.

OTHER NUTRIENTS

There is a moderate amount of information available about the nutritional requirements deer need from other types of minerals. There are, though, some minimal dietary concentrations that have been documented for a couple of trace elements. The negligible dietary concentrations include iodine and selenium. The complete list of the macronutrient group of elements as well as the micronutrient group of trace elements can be found in an upcoming chapter.

SALT

Sodium, a.k.a. salt, is another mineral deer need. Deer get sodium from natural sources found in the soil. Researchers have documented that female deer require twice the amount of sodium as bucks.

VITAMINS

Vitamins are important nutrients. However, to date, it is not known just what amounts of vitamins are needed by deer. According to general research, vitamin deficiencies in deer rarely happen.

WATER

Ahh, water. The magical liquid that keeps all life roll-

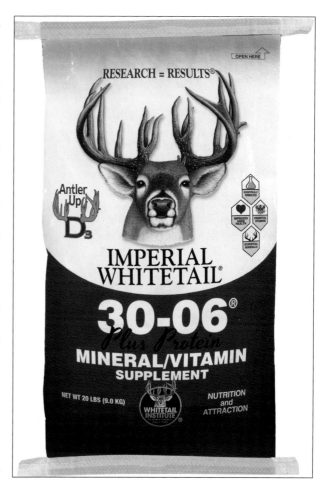

▲ One period of the year when deer seek minerals is winter. Many companies including Antler King, Deer Cane, Mossy Oak, Trophy Rock, TruCare, and Whitetail Institute have minerals specially designed for different seasons. Photo Courtesy: Whitetail Institute

ing on. The fact is water should be called asteroid juice. The geochemical evidence shows that water was packaged and delivered to Earth some 4.6 billion years ago by countless impacts, particularly during the Late Heavy Bombardment (LHB) period by icy planetesimals that have been found to be like the composition of today's asteroids that dwell in the outer edges of the asteroid belt. As hunters and food plot managers we can toast with a glass of asteroid juice to deer who enjoy the benefits of water, as it is to all life on earth, a critical nutrient component.

The water requirements for deer are also available from the moisture within vegetation they eat, although this source doesn't provide all their water needs. Most of the asteroid juice deer get is from ponds, lakes, streams, depressions in the soil, small potholes, springs, and surface water. Deer are said to drink about three to six quarts per day. Drinking that amount of water would keep a deer's nephrologist happy.

Unlike an adult human's body that is made up of about 60 percent water, a deer's body is made up of about 70 to 75 percent water. Deer continually urinate throughout a twenty-four-hour period and so they replace the loss by drinking three to five quarts of water per day or so to stay healthy.

SPRING
During spring, the new growth provides moist palatable forage that is rich in protein and other nutrients. New growth in spring food plots also provide nutrient-rich forages. Controlled burning, timber stand improvement (TSI), selective timber harvests, and disking encourage new growth, and the availability of natural succulent forage with prominent levels of important nutrients.

SUMMER
Annual and perennial forbs, agricultural plantings, natural vegetation, woody browse, fruits, clovers, other legumes, and plantings in food plots are some of the food items deer eat over the summer months.

FALL
At this time of year, soft and hard mast are important food sources for white-tailed deer. Deer will also actively seek out and eat agricultural crops. Other important foods for deer in the fall and winter include winter-hardy clovers, small grains, brassicas, soft mast from fruit trees, and so on.

Now is the time when deer build up their fat reserves for the rigors of the rut and winter. They begin eating chestnuts, acorns, other nuts, corn, and other vegetation that is high in carbohydrates. Therefore, these food sources are preferred fall foods in areas where they are available.

WINTER
During the winter, deer greatly benefit from cool- and winter-hardy food plots. Winter-hardy annuals include brassicas like forage rape, kale, swede, turnips, canola, and radish, and grains like winter rye, oats, triticale, wheat, and barley. The winter-hardy perennials,

▲ Too often deer managers focus on providing calcium and phosphorus because they are needed for antler development. However, it is important to provide minerals that include many other macro and micro minerals. Photo: PCFImages

▲ Winter nutrients can be obtained from mineral licks, protein pellets, supplements, etc. Managers can provide deer vital micro and macro nutrients via plants including grains, brassicas, winter-hardy clover, and legumes. These deer are browsing on leftover soybeans. Photo Courtesy: Bob Coine

although they are not at the peak of their nutritional value during winter, are still important food sources for deer during this time of year. They include several white and red clovers like Frosty Berseem, FIXatioN Balansa, Kura, Ladino, and Alice. All of these provide a source of high protein when planted alone, or when they are planted as a mix with other winter-hardy grains and brassicas (I plant both). All of these make attractive, sought-after food plots at a time (winter) when foods containing elevated levels of protein, carbohydrates, and sugars are generally unavailable. Deer can also obtain sugars in winter from late-dropping fruit— some of which can hang on the trees until January.

It should be said that food plots are important additional plantings meant to complement natural food sources on a property. Winter-hardy food plots offer palatable, digestible, nutritious, healthy, and beneficial plantings for deer—when they need it most.

What does deer nutrition come down to? Basically, food plot plantings must be compatible with the nutritional demands of your deer herd. Although general guidelines are universal, each region is unique. It's always a wise idea to get a little help from the experts. Consult a biologist or your local ag extension to obtain a better idea about the nutritional requirements of the deer in your area.

For more detailed information on how nutrition, age, and genetics affect antler and body size, refer to MO Extension publication G9480, "Implementing Quality Deer Management on Your Property."

Age	Activity	Protein level
Fawn	Average growth	14 to 18 percent
Fawn	Excellent growth	16 to 20 percent
Yearling	Maintenance	11 percent
Adult	Maintenance	6 to 10 percent
Adult (female)	Late pregnancy	11 to 15 percent
Adult (female)	Lactation	14 to 22 percent
Adult (male)	Antler development	15 to 16 percent

Source: University of Missouri and the Missouri Department of Conservation

▲ To improve a buck's antler size, you'll need a well-thought-out food plot program with nutritious plantings high in calcium and phosphorous as well as lesser quantities of potassium, magnesium, iron, and zinc. Credit: Ted Rose

Chapter Four

Setting Your Goals

Whether you own, lease, or hunt public land, there are ways to improve the food sources for deer, turkey, bear, waterfowl, and other wildlife. You must begin with a good understanding of what types of plants work best to nourish and attract deer. It is also important to think realistically about the time involved and money, and your willingness to work. Planting food plots and enhancing natural vegetation will improve the overall health of your deer herd and deer sightings, and, most important for most deer managers, the harvest rate of deer on your land.

Before you start to plant, do you want to develop a program that is more designed to attract deer during deer season? Not surprisingly, most hunters tell me they want to plant food plots to improve their hunting opportunities during the deer season. To accomplish this, the best plan is to include the important benefits of a goal to plant warm, cool, and cold-season plantings that provide food plots for deer from late spring through the hunting seasons. This type of plan provides the nourishment female deer need for better fawning, quality and reliable lactation, better bone

▲ This buck was taken in a sugar beet plot adjacent to the corn. We concentrate on winter plantings to provide deer with high energy nutritional forage. Photo Courtesy: PCFImages

development, and better fawn development. It helps bucks by supplying the nourishment they need for better health, body weight, stronger skeletal development, and better antler growth.

Planning for a warm, cool, and cold season food plot program assures you that deer will be using your property from spring, summer, and more important, when you want them there the most—during hunting season.

As I mentioned earlier, developing a successful, long-term food plot and habitat management program mandates you create a well-thought-out mental and written blueprint of all the aspects involved before making the final commitment to become a food plotter. This is a must-do undertaking whether you have a small or a large tract of property you plan to plant. Jumping in without considering all the elements, both negative and positive, will be the genesis of the prompt termination of your food plot program. Trust this: Any hunter who thinks planting food plots is nothing more than scattering some seeds in the ground, covering them up with soil, and watching them grow to attract deer, is on the road to Disappointmentville . . .

followed by Igiveupville. This is especially so if they also believe in the "throw and grow seed planting" concept.

The first and foremost essential element is to make sure many of your plantings attract deer during the archery and firearm seasons. Frankly, the decision is relatively easy if two crucial elements are addressed. First, warm-season plantings are crucial when they are combined with fall-winter plantings. This works best if you live on the property full time, but to some extent it also is achievable for food plotters who do not reside on the food plot property.

THE FRAMEWORK

A wildlife food plot program consists of a combination of essential fundamentals, all of which are needed to build a solid foundation for long-term success. Some principal elements include improving habitat; population management; protecting yearling bucks; managing the numbers of female deer; and guidelines for taking antlered bucks. It also requires carefully monitoring all aspects of your program.

▲ A field of standing corn will attract deer well into November and even December. Once they have eaten all the corn off the cobs, deer will scour the ground for corn kernels like the buck seen here is doing. Photo Courtesy: Bob Coine

DECIDE ON YOUR GOALS

More than likely, you fall within the majority of hunters who want a food plot program designed to attract deer during hunting season. Not surprisingly, many deer hunters claim they want to plant food plots solely to "attract more deer" to regularly use their land and to improve their habitat of their property. Some have said they want to "create a whitetail utopia." Both are doable.

Over the years, I have asked countless hunters what they expect to benefit from by planting food plots. The following is a list in their order of preference. Some are revealing, others expected, and one is totally unachievable (holding bucks on their lands).

1. Larger antlered/heavier bodied bucks
2. Holding bucks on the land
3. Having deer use the property regularly
4. Seeing more deer during the hunting season
5. Shooting older bucks
6. Better nutrition for deer
7. Better tasting venison
8. Improving deer cover
9. Planting fruit trees
10. Creating a sanctuary
11. Controlling weeds
12. Better fawn survival
13. Habitat improvement
14. Woodland management

Most of these items are achievable when correctly planting food plots, although I am sure about number two, as no food plot will "hold" a buck permanently on your land. It will keep bucks on the property significantly more often, but during the rut, all bets of keeping a buck on your land for any long length of time are off the table. At first, I thought number seven was surprising. But after thinking about it, it's insightful. Food plots indeed provide more nutritious foods, thereby having a considerable effect on enhancing the overall tenderness and flavor of deer meat. Number eleven was humorous. I guess you do benefit learning how to control weeds by planting food plots.

THE LAND

Once you have done all your homework and you are confident that you have all the elements needed to

▲ To draw bucks into your food plots during late hunting season include plantings of winter-hardy varieties of clovers, brassicas, and winter grains, to name a few. Photo Courtesy: Bob Coine

▲ This drone image shows about one-third of dozens of food plots we plant annually. Plot sizes range from 50 x 100 feet to multi-acres, and everything in between. When we first began our food plot plan, we used topo maps and boots on the ground to decide where each plot should be placed. Now we include drone footage too. Photo Courtesy: PCFImages

▲ This is Finger Field Plot. It is slightly larger than one acre. Originally, it attached to a five-acre field. The pines were planted to offer more seclusion to adult bucks. We often see deer in this plot throughout the day during hunting season. Instinctively, deer know they can escape into any of the three sides in seconds. Our refuge is on the right. Five stands cover this plot to take advantage of wind, access, and egress. Photo Courtesy: PCFImages

begin a deer and wildlife food plot program, it is time to make some additional decisions. You should start by scrutinizing either an aerial photo (it depicts existing vegetation) or a topographical map, which illustrates where level ground can be located. Both will describe possible places that are suitable areas to plant your food plots.

Then it's time to put boots on the ground. Begin by analyzing the information from the topo map and the aerial photo to confirm or refute the potential suggested areas that may be planted. If you have agricultural land, check out the fields and identify and mark with plastic posts which spots are most beneficial to plant. Some areas in fields can be better suited to plant at various times of spring, summer, or fall.

It is also advisable to investigate overgrown fields, second-growth areas, abandoned fields covered in briars, brush, or low growing vegetation that can be simply reclaimed by brush hogging the areas. Overgrown fields are prime areas to reclaim as they require a lot less work than clearing out a wooded area to plant.

Other potential areas to plant are trails, old farm lanes, logging roads, and the berms of ponds. All are easy to clear and prepare for seeding.

Naturally, the best food plot locations are in currently used or even idle agricultural fields. They are easily accessed and can be planted with a tractor and implements or with an ATV and its smaller equipment (ATVs are ideal for getting into small, secluded areas to plant). Keep in mind the best food plots planted in fields will be those locations where deer, particularly bucks, feel totally comfortable feeding during daylight hours.

That requires establishing some plots that are close enough to woodlots or other types of cover to enable deer to escape any potential danger with no more than a few jumps. If deer can't seek cover from a field plot within several seconds, it will curtail the chances of adult bucks from entering the food plot in daylight. Instead, they will feed in it at dusk, the twilight of dawn, and at night—that is, until the rut. Then a buck may be following a doe as she heads to what she knows is a luscious food plot ripe for the eating. This can happen any time of the day.

Food plots planted along the edges of woods must be planted far enough away from the trees to avoid being shaded out. If a plot is created inside a woodlot, it will be necessary to clear out twice the size of the area that you want the size of the plot to be. That could lead to a lot of cutting down of trees and removal of surface roots. Again, this prevents over shading from the leaves of trees, and it prevents the seeds planted in the plot from having competition from tree roots, particularly from young trees.

Other potential ideal planting spots include old clearings, clear-cuts, recently abandoned log loading sites, forsaken homesites, and electric company or gas company rights-of-way (where permissible). You would be surprised how easy it is to get permission from these companies to plant food plots in these areas, particularly if they are on your property.

No food plot should EVER be planted bordering neighboring properties (or even close to). It only creates a very enticing situation for someone to shoot across the property line. I also avoid this problem because I don't want a buck (or doe) shot by us to run across the line onto the neighbor's land.

Finally, when establishing your plot locations, remember that the plots you designate as hunting plots must be in areas deemed as good hunting spots. That means placing the plot where you can access it from a few separate locations and wind directions.

Also keep in mind of the rising and setting sun. Our burning star emits most of its radiation in the form of energy of photons. The photons (light) from our sun, even though its 93 million miles away most times, are enough to temporarily cancel any possibility of seeing a deer approach or leave a food plot. We have one such plot on our land. It is a hot spot for seeing deer coming into the plot from the west. It is such a good spot for bucks and does that I can't abandon the blind. The solution? I wear an extra-long-billed cap to block the sun.

▲ When hunting from our treestands Hot-Stuff or Stratosphere, the setting sun can often create difficulty in watching deer emerge into one of our food plots from the west. Since the plot offers so much deer activity, I have learned to tolerate the problem. Photo Courtesy: PCFImages

▲ This buck's body frame, lanky legs, facial features, and light weight suggests it is a young buck. His antlers, however, suggest otherwise. Credit: © Mikael Males | Dreamstime.com

Chapter Five

Matching Equipment to Your Land

Matching the proper equipment to the type of land you plant is the key to better food plot planting success. Basically, a better term for planting food plots, is farming for deer and other wildlife. Using a large tractor with heavy-duty attachments to plant a small plot in the woods, or a half-acre plot in a field, is overkill and not practical. It would also not be reasonable to use an ATV when planting a ten-acre field of corn.

The type and size of equipment needed to farm for wildlife should be coordinated with the total amount of acres you will be planting. The most popular types of equipment used to plant food plots are ATVs with accessories and medium sized tractors with larger implements. Therefore, equipment requirements for food plotters varies. The equipment must be carefully planned to match the current amount of land you

▲ It is important to match your equipment to the size and needs of the property you plan to plant. Photo Courtesy: PCFImages.

intend to plant and the possibility that you may expand your food plot management agenda in the future. An equally important factor is to realistically evaluate your budget in order to avoid emptying the piggy bank.

EQUIPMENT DECISIONS

ATVs and tractors are used from breaking ground to planting, to the general maintenance of small to extensive size food plots. The fact is to grow consistently successful food plots using ATVs or tractors, you need the right types of additional machinery to complete the projects properly and conveniently. The type and size of the ATV, tractor, and other equipment needed should be fine-tuned to your planting plans. Be as attentive and precise in your decision as violinists are when tuning their instruments. That statement shouldn't be taken lightly. That is, unless you don't mind wasting money, time, energy, and you enjoy getting frustrated, tired, and not growing the best wildlife food plots you possibly can.

Often, food plot managers do not consider the possibility of expanding their management program when they first buy their planting equipment. Although they may have more ground to plant, they begin slowly by only planting a portion of their property. When they realize how well food plots draw deer to their lands, they begin thinking about increasing their acreage to plant. In doing so, novice food plotters are lightning struck by the realization that they don't have the proper equipment to expand their project.

Therefore, perceptive food plot managers should treat their first equipment purchases like a game of chess. A successful chess master plans his or her next several moves well in advance of the next move. Consequently, if your total plantable acreage offers more available land to plant than you're thinking of starting with, if the budget can tolerate it, purchase more equipment than you need at first. Then you will be prepared and able to work more land than originally planned. If you don't expand your planting area, you can always sell the additional equipment or even rent it out.

▲ The first purchase of equipment we made was a utility tractor, with only a few important implements like the Land Pride Compactor seeder seen here. We should have considered that we would expand our planting acreage. It would have saved us time, money, and work. Photo Courtesy: PCFImages.

If you only have a specific amount of property with no possibility to expand, then buy only what you need but maybe upgrade one or two pieces of equipment. For instance, if you're planning to buy a tractor, instead of purchasing a heavy duty offset disk harrow (that is pulled behind a tractor), consider buying a PTO-driven box tiller. The box tiller will cut your disking time by two-thirds, and it will disk the soil at more easily adjustable levels and break it up finer as well. Upgrading can sometimes be the better option than buying both the disk harrow and the box tiller. With that said, only if the budget can afford it and there is enough plantable land to make it practical, having both pieces of equipment creates a safety net. Should one or the other break down, you have a replacement at the ready.

Over the thirty-five years I have been planting food plots for deer and other wildlife, I have had my share of successes and mistakes—lots of them. One such lesson was to underestimate my purchases of a tractor, implements, and other equipment needs. Not once,

but twice, I bought less than what I needed to plant more acreage. It was a costly and somewhat frustrating mistake each time. When it comes to developing a successful food plot plan, I have learned the hard way that it is always better to have more equipment than less.

SMALL-SCALE PROPERTIES

Small-scale food plot programs are what I consider planting from one acre up to a few acres. These size plots are ideal for large ATVs with quality implements. ATVs are especially handy when it comes to planting in small, tight, hard-to-get-at areas or remote places that tractors cannot reach. Today, manufacturers offer food plotters a complete line of ATV implements including disk-harrows, multi-tined plows, attachable rotary seed spreaders, cultipackers, disc harrows, sprayers, and spreaders. These implements will provide any small-scale food plotter a complete line of planting products that will get the job done.

▲ For smaller acreage that has little to no options of expanding, an ATV and ATV-type equipment will do the job well enough. The key is to be certain the ATV engine is 550 to 700 cc and the implements are matched to the engine size of the ATV. Photo Courtesy: PCFImages

MICRO FOOD PLOTS

Properties that contain less than a half-acre of plant-able land require specialized planting tools. Pocket-sized plots are generally located in residential areas where backyard trophy class bucks often reside. Most of these types of properties are usually in woods, but they also have a few small open areas which, after some proper ground preparation, can be planted as food plots. Generally, using a tractor or even a small lawn tractor to prepare the ground in these plots is not possible. Therefore, when planting these types of miniscule food plots, it's almost always necessary to plant them either with a small ATV with implements or, when the plots are tiny, by using hand tools.

Anyone who plants micro-size food plots will achieve more planting success when they commit to undertaking proper ground preparation methods. This is accomplished by using well-matched plant-ing implements for the limited size of micro plots. In some instances, the arduous work put into these types of plots can be downright backbreaking. It should be noted, though, the more work put into a micro-plot, the more planting success you will get out of it. This is particularly true when developing a micro-plot in a wooded area. These types of plots and their locations can be extremely attractive to deer. Many times, hunt-ers end up killing dandy bucks over miniature-size wildlife food plots in suburban areas.

Begin by thinking through everything you will need to make the micro plot grow to its maximum potential. A selection of necessary tools includes the following:

- Garden tiller/cultivator
- Leaf blower or sturdy leaf rake
- Stout garden rake with metal teeth
- Heavy four-pronged pitchfork
- Sharp, pointed spade-shovel
- Flat-bladed shovel
- Heavy-duty pinch bar
- Large sharp pair of pruning shears
- Small handheld pair of pruning shears
- Chainsaw with safety chaps, ear protection, gloves, glasses, gas, chain sharpening file, and bar oil
- Handheld or push broadcast spreader (Chapin International or Scott's® Elite Spreader)

- Seed compacter (or a chain-link fence with cinder-blocks to weigh it down)
- Soil test kit
- Fertilizer and lime

▲ Some properties, many of which are in suburban areas, are smaller than one acre. Planting acreage of that size can be done with a small 500 cc ATV and light implements. Planting a couple of micro-sized suburban plots calls for using hand tools—a combination of which are seen here. Photo Courtesy: PCFImages

THE REALITIES

The realistic issue with using an ATV and implements is that they were not manufactured to be tractors. That doesn't mean ATVs made today can't do most of the work needed to plant a couple of acres. They can have pull-behind mowers to cut light to moderate plots of clovers, low grasses, chicory, and similar plants. It is wise, however, to always consider the manufacturer's suggested recommendations regarding the weights of equipment that an ATV can pull when compared to its engine size. For instance, an ATV towing a forty-four-inch-wide disk that weighs four-hundred-plus pounds requires at least a 750-cc engine. The long and short of it is, when planting more than a few acres, it's time to buy a tractor.

LIGHTWEIGHT SUB-COMPACT TRACTORS

There are three types of tractors designed to work well when planting food plots. They include the sub-compact, the compact, and large, heavy-duty farm tractors. The utility tractors and their light implements are a viable choice if you plant no more than five acres or so. These lighter weight units cost less than larger tractors and usually have 19 hp to 24 hp. But keep in mind that they don't provide as many options as mid-size tractors do. In the event you want to start a food plot program and plan to plant up to ten acres or more to start with, but have five or more that you may want to plant in the future, a sub-compact tractor would not be a good decision to buy. It would quickly be overworked.

MID-SIZED "COMPACT" TRACTORS

Mid-sized, a.k.a. compact, 30 hp to 50 hp tractors are defined as small agricultural tractors equipped with a 540-rpm Power Take Off (PTO) and a three-point hitch designed for Category 1 implements. Compact tractors generally have a mass less than 4,000 pounds and use less than 40 PTO hp to run their attachments. They are the bread-and-butter tractors for hunters who plant for wildlife. As a rule, most of the compact tractors are the ideal matchup for any planting job needed for properties with five to twenty acres of plantable food plots.

A compact tractor is usually equipped with a bucket loader, a three-point hitch, and PTO. Implements suggested for long-term food plotters include a sixty-inch PTO-driven box tiller, a heavy-duty six- to ten-foot brush hog, a cultipacker, a PTO-driven heavy-duty plastic spreader, a heavy-duty disk harrow, and, perhaps as a bonus, a PTO-driven three-point post hole digger. A post-hole digger can be an important implement when including fruit, nut, and other trees in your program.

Another equipment option, one that eliminates other implements, is a no-till drill. No-till drills for large ATVs or medium-size tractors cost between $5,000 to $15,000. But when you consider they eliminate most of the other equipment needed, they can be well-worth the money. The fact is, no-till drills not only reduce the planting work substantially, but they all but guarantee that planting everything from corn to clovers will generally produce more successful crops. Kasco manufacturing (www.kascomfg.com) makes an affordable and rugged line of no-till drills including the Eco-Drill (for ATVs) and Plotter's Choice (tractors). Other choices are the Esch no-till drills (www.eschdrills.com) or The Firminator G3 (www.thefirminator.com).

You don't have to get everything listed above the first year, but it would be beneficial to add as many as possible to your list of needed implements.

BUYING PRE-OWNED EQUIPMENT

First-time food plotters with a limited budget can start out with the implements that are most needed. There are many websites that sell all the equipment mentioned above, both new and pre-owned. Just remember to buy with your eyes wide open.

LARGE FARM TRACTORS

The last group of tractors includes the heavy-duty group used primarily by farmers. There are some food plot managers who own extensive properties of hundreds to even thousands of acres. When the time comes to plow, disk, plant, and harvest large acreage

▲ Our mid-size tractor is equipped with our must-have Brillion™ Food Plot Seeder (a Landoll product). It plants everything from tiny clover seeds to corn. Photo Courtesy: PCFImages

▲ A no-till drill is the best way to plant food plots, but most food plotters don't own one. Kasco offers an affordable no-till drill called the Plotters Choice. It is designed to use with an ATV or tractor. Photo Courtesy: Kasco Mfg. Co.

of this size, the logical choice of equipment is traditional farm machines and heavy-duty planting equipment. These large tractors are scary expensive. Some of them can easily cost more than $50,000, and the equipment can cost several thousand dollars each. The fact is 99.9 percent of those reading this book have no need for tractors of this size. 'Nuff said!

A CONSIDERATION
One last thought about tractors. My first compact tractor was basically an open-air version. It came with just a polyethylene canopy. It did not protect me from dust, dirt, biting bugs, rain, scorching hot days, and the cool to colder elements during early fall (a time when I plant winter grains and cut the leftover corn stalks to the ground). I finally made the decision to trade it in. I bought a tractor with an enclosed cab, a slight increase in horsepower, air-conditioning, and a few other small upgrades. It not only provides an amazing amount of comfort, but it also enables me to stay out working longer, and under weather I would otherwise have to stop working in. My point? Just a suggestion that if your budget can afford it, get a tractor with an enclosed cab!

TRACTOR MAINTENANCE
Keep in mind that owning an ATV, tractor, and their implements requires a land manager to be somewhat mechanically inclined. Moreover, there is the absolute necessity to make routine maintenance and, at times,

minor repairs to tractors and equipment. Failure to maintain planting equipment is the leading cause of frustration when planting food plots. A good maintenance program starts with storing your equipment, particularly the implements, out of the weather during the winter months when they are not in use. In the end, however, keeping tractors and implements well cared for will assure you that the tractor will continue to shorten the workload.

IMPORTANT NOTE
Before doing any maintenance to your equipment, ALWAYS check the manufacturer's manual first. Follow the guidelines and recommendations regarding all levels, types of oil to use, etc., and use the manual's recommendations. Keeping up a well-planned equipment maintenance program will ensure that the motorized equipment and other gear and tools will provide you with reliable service season after planting-season.

Take the time to think through what you need in the way of planting equipment before making any purchases. This may sound like common sense advice, but I cannot tell you how many times I have seen equipment mismatched for the land being planted. It will save you a lot of time, money, and frustration if your plan is well thought-out.

▲ When purchasing a tractor, consider your comfort needs like an enclosed cab with air conditioning and heat. Remember the adage, *take care of your equipment and it will take care of you.* Photo Courtesy: PCFImages

▲ Another implement option is an Esch Drill. It is a heavy unit that requires a tractor with at least 45 horsepower. Photo Courtesy: PCFImages

▲ For male deer, the minerals in the soil are the genesis of helping bucks develop better size antlers. Credit: Ted Rose

Chapter Six

Get the Bang on Dirt

I wanted to include a brief geological history about how Earth's soil came to be. After reading this, you may, like me, find a new appreciation for dirt. There were points in time when Earth almost came close to not developing soil, as it was nearly destroyed—several times after its original formation of becoming a planet. Knowing how Earth's soils eventually came into existence can provide food plot managers with a deeper knowledge of the soil in which they plant.

So, how did Earth's crust evolve over billions of years to become the soil that is our planet today? The short answer is that our planet had to undergo an over-*extended* cooking time in the oven of our solar system, and deal with several near-Earth-ending catastrophes. Each event left a trail of devastation and other ruinous forces in its wake. Ultimately, every disaster drastically transformed the course of Earth's crust and its evolution. The entire process took about 4.5 billion years.

▲ The Theia Impact Event was the genesis of Earth creating its soil. Photo: © Pitris | Dreamstime.com

THE GIANT IMPACT HYPOTHESIS
(a.k.a. the Splash or Theia Impact Event)

The giant-impact premise, based on scientific computer simulations, suggests a collision between the proto-Earth, then called Gaia (the primordial goddess who personified the Earth in Greek mythology), and a Mars-sized planet called Theia (named after a mythical Greek Titan). It was Earth's most devastating catastrophe, almost entirely obliterating the young planet. It turned the entire Earth into a liquid ocean of magma. Had the collision been a head-on impact with Earth, I would not be writing this, you would not be reading it, and hunters would not be planting food plots on it [Earth].

Geologists believe Earth eventually cooled and the heavier, denser materials from Theia sank to the center. The lighter materials rose to the top, which became the Earth's crust, the layer we live on. The crust is the most widely studied and understood of Earth's three layers.

The next several Earth cataclysms also eventually affected the endgame of the soil. They included the Late Heavy Bombardment (LHB) event. Most theories claim Earth was most likely covered with a global ocean of magma for the second time in its development. The Mass Glacial Extinction Event: Glaciers moved slowly and steadily over the earth and pushed, dragged, crushed, and deposited debris and rocks, some said to be as tall as mountains, along the way. The mass grinding and meshing resulted in them being ground down to fine materials (soil) and minerals. This was the third event to further change the composition of the crust.

The next calamity was the Chicxulub Impact Event. Sixty-six million years ago, a six-mile-long asteroid slammed into Earth, causing a 100-million-megaton blast that devastated what is now known as the Gulf of Mexico. It produced a shock wave and blast of air with

▲ The Late Heavy Bombardment event brought both water and material to Earth that would contribute to the soil. Photo: © Petrovich11 Dreamstime. com

▲ Glaciologists state the first glaciers deposited crushed rocks and other debris over the entire planet. Photo: © Wissanu Sirapat - Dreamstime.com

winds of 620 mph that swept across the oceans and deep into the interior of what is now North America.

Here's the noteworthy part: The pressure pulse and winds scorched soils, shredded and set afire to all vegetation, and killed 80 percent of all animals. All the dead animals and vegetation added untold amounts of organic matter to the land. What started as a terribly dreadful day, however, eventually ended with the leftover burned organic material absorbed into the Earth as high-grade fertilizer, improving the soil dramatically.

Geologically speaking, Earth's soil hasn't been around that long. Although Earth is 4.54 billion years old, the rich sediments we call soil only appeared 450 million years ago. Today, Earth's dirt makes it distinct from the other three lifeless rocky planets (without organic matter there is technically no soil). The correct term for the loose material on the other planets (and our moon) is regolith.

SOIL TYPES

There are twelve soil types, or orders, in the United States. These are further divided into suborders, great groups, subgroups, families, and series, resulting in more than 100 distinct types of soils. As food plotters, there is no need to understand the 100 different types of soil. There are, however, twelve important soil orders to keep in mind. The five most

▲ The Chicxulub Impact Event created incalculable amounts of organic matter over the entire planet. It returned immeasurable amounts of dead plant and animal material into Earth's early soil. The decomposed matter provided nutrients and habitat to organisms living in the soil, enriching it immensely. Then and now, organic matter binds soil particles into aggregates and improves the water holding capacity of soil. Photo: © Elena Duvernay | Dreamstime.com

important prevalent soils are found within the eastern and central portions of the country. As noted by the USDA, these five soils are commonly used soils for planting.

Alfisols: Alfisols form in semi-arid to humid areas and are mostly found under the canopy of a hardwood forest. They are a clay-enriched subsoil and relatively high in native fertility. The "Alf" portion depicts the aluminum (Al) and represents iron (Fe)—as both are listed in the Periodic Table of Elements.

Andisols: Andisols are young soils formed in volcanic ash and contain high proportions of glass and amorphous colloidal materials, including allophane, imogolite, and ferrihydrite. They are rich in nutrients and hold water well because of their volcanic ash content.

Aridisols (a.k.a. desert *soils*): They are the primary soils of dry shrublands. Aridisols contain an incredibly low absorption of organic matter. It is why most vegetation is lacking within such dry arid soils.

Entisols: These soils are mostly found in sheer, rocky locations. Entisols found in large river valleys and shore deposits offer vast croplands and habitats throughout the world. Entisols are the most extensive of the soil orders, found in about 18 percent of Earth's ice-free land area. In the United States, entisols cover about 12.3 percent of the land area.

Gelisols: Are soils frozen in permafrost for no less than two years, or they contain evidence of permafrost within the soil's surface. Gelisols are found in the Arctic and Antarctic.

Histosols: Histosols are composed mostly of organic materials. They form in low, wet places, like the bogs, swamps, and marshes. The organic matter collects below the water table and decomposes more slowly than it accumulates.

Inceptisols: Inceptisols form quickly through alteration of parent material. They are young soils generally

▲ Alfisols are moderately aged soils. They were formed on old glacial deposits. They contain a high mineral base content, making them beneficial for growing many types of crops. Photo: USDA

INCEPTISOLS

Inceptisols are soils of semiarid to humid environments that generally exhibit only moderate degrees of soil weathering and development.

Inceptisols have a wide range in characteristics and occur in a wide variety of climates.

INCEPTISOLS MAKE UP ABOUT 17% OF THE WORLD'S ICE-FREE LAND SURFACE.

▲ Inceptisols are referred to as Earth's young soils. They have the faintest appearance of layers created by soil-forming factors. Inceptisols are the most abundant soils on Earth, sustaining agriculture over prolonged periods of time. Loamy types are mineral rich, conversely, sandy types are generally mineral poor. Photo: USDA

less than 10,000 years old. They are mostly found in river bottoms, sheer mountains, and in recent ocean deposits within the eastern and midwestern U.S. With no accumulation of clays, iron oxide, aluminum oxide, or organic matter, Inceptisols are more developed than Entisols.

Mollisols: Mollisols are the soils of grassland ecosystems. They are rich, black topsoil with a high mineral

MOLLISOLS

Mollisols are soils that have a dark colored surface horizon relatively high in content of organic matter. The soils are base rich throughout and therefore are quite fertile.

Mollisols characteristically form under grass in climates that have a moderate to pronounced seasonal moisture deficit. They are extensive soils on the steppes of Europe, Asia, North America, and South America.

MOLLISOLS MAKE UP ABOUT 7% OF THE WORLD'S ICE-FREE LAND SURFACE.

◄ The topsoil of Mollisols is naturally dark and rich with organic matter, making it very fertile. In the Black Dirt Region of the onion fields of New York, the soil is predominantly Mollisols. The region is mostly located in my former hometown of Warwick, and the hamlets of Pine Island and Florida. The Black Dirt Region takes its name from the dark, extremely fertile soil left over from an ancient glacial lake bottom. They are prime soils for planting. Photo: USDA

SPODOSOLS

Spodosols formed from weathering processes that strip organic matter combined with aluminum (with or without iron) from the surface layer and deposit them in the subsoil. In undisturbed areas, a gray eluvial horizon that has the color of uncoated quartz overlies a reddish brown or black subsoil.

Spodosols commonly occur in areas of coarse-textured deposits under coniferous forests of humid regions. They tend to be acid and infertile.

SPODOSOLS MAKE UP ABOUT 4% OF THE WORLD'S ICE-FREE LAND SURFACE.

▲ Spodosols are ashy gray, acidic soils that are moderately aged. Their suitability for planting crops is restricted to acid-tolerant crops like some brassicas and other forage plants. However, that is only if sufficient lime and fertilizer are applied. Photo: USDA

content and often a neutral pH. Mollisols are considered the most essential and prolific agricultural soils worldwide. Throughout the country, they are the most prominent of the soil orders, covering about 21.5 percent of the land.

Oxisols: Oxisols are weathered soils in intertropical regions. They are often rich in iron (Fe) and aluminum (Al) oxide. Most nutrients in Oxisol ecosystems are found in the standing vegetation or decomposing plant material. Despite their low fertility, Oxisols can be productive with the proper amounts of lime and fertilizers.

Spodosols: These moderately aged soils are acid soils characterized by a subsurface accumulation of humus that is complexed with aluminum and iron. Spodosols develop in mature coniferous forests in cool, moist climates. They are acidic and therefore infertile. Because of this, Spodosols require lime to be productive in food plots. Sandy Spodosols are mineral poor.

Ultisols: Ultisols are acidic forest soils with relatively low fertility. They are found in humid temperate and tropical areas on older, stable landscapes. They are between 100,000 and a million years old and have a low mineral content. Intense weathering has caused the primary minerals like calcium (Ca), magnesium (Mg), and potassium (K) to have been leached from these soils. Ultisols have a subsurface in which clays have accumulated, often with strong yellowish or reddish colors resulting from the presence of iron (Fe) oxides. The red clay soils are dominant in the southeastern United States and are excellent examples of Ultisols. They have a relatively low ability to retain lime and fertilizer. Because of the favorable climates in which they are usually found, Ultisols often support productive forests. The high acidity and relatively low quantities of plant-available Ca, Mg, and K associated with most Ultisols make them poorly suited for continuous use in food plots without the proper use of fertilizer and lime. With these adjustments, though, Ultisols can be *very* productive soils for food plot plantings.

Vertisols: These soils are clay-rich and shrink and swell with changes in moisture content. During dry periods, the soil volume shrinks and deep wide cracks form. The soil volume expands as it becomes wet. This

ULTISOLS

Ultisols are soils in humid areas. They formed from fairly intense weathering and leaching processes that result in a clay-enriched subsoil dominated by minerals, such as quartz, kaolinite, and iron oxides.

Ultisols are typically acid soils in which most nutrients are concentrated in the upper few inches. They have a moderately low capacity to retain additions of lime and fertilizer.

ULTISOLS MAKE UP ABOUT 8% OF THE WORLD'S ICE-FREE LAND SURFACE.

▲ Ultisols are among Earth's oldest soils, formed more than a million years ago. They are reddish, clay-rich, acidic soils. They have a low mineral content. They can be made agriculturally productive with the proper applications of lime and fertilizers, but even then, the soil has a nominal capability to retain amendments of lime and fertilizer, unless it is applied consistently year-to-year. Photo: USDA

shrinking and swelling process creates some issues in agricultural plantings. Vertisols occupy about 2.0 percent of the land area and occur primarily in Texas.

When it comes to planting food plots in different soils, there are general guidelines about understanding what soils provide the best beds for growing plants. The most beneficial soil will always be a well-drained topsoil that has at least several inches of loamy material with a subsoil layer of loam to clay. Soils that are poorly drained or heavy clay with compacted layers and deep-seated sandy soils all provide less than ideal conditions for plant growth. These types of soils need amendments of lime and fertilizer. Only then will they have the soil fertility needed for healthy plants.

▲ Here are the twelve orders of soil as described by the USDA. Photo: USDA

▲ Healthy soils and plants contain copious amounts of macro and micro minerals. Antlers are made mostly of calcium and phosphorous and lesser quantities of potassium, magnesium, iron, and zinc. When such minerals are available to bucks it can result in quality antler growth. Credit: © Twildlife | Dreamstime.com

Chapter Seven

Understanding Soil pH Values

Working with soil pH levels is like a high wire "Wallenda" balancing act. Just like the human body can be too acidic or alkaline, so can soil. As the pH rises above 7.0 it becomes too alkaline (or "basic"). As the pH falls below 7.0 it is referred to as being slightly acidic. Hydrogen (H+) has a positive charge, and hydroxide (OH-) has a negative charge; therefore, the two react with other elements to shape various compounds, thereby regulating the volume of a plant nutrient in a usable form. Consequently, with a higher pH reading, there are fewer H+ present and more OH- are on hand. When a pH reading is at 7.0 the two ions cancel one another out and the 7.0 pH level is considered or rated as being neutral. When the pH level drops, however, the quantity of hydrogen intensifies by ten times for every pH component (the 'H' in pH stands for the element hydrogen). Moreover, just one unit of change represents a tenfold change in acidity. As a striking example of this, if a pH reading of 7.0 drops to a reading of 6.0, it represents a change

▲ The pH value of the soil in this plot tested at 6.4. The seed being compacted was canola (rapeseed). Canola will tolerate a pH between 5.5 to 7.5. It grows best, however, in a pH above 6.0, making the pH in this plot a good match. Photo Courtesy: PCFImages.

in the soil chemistry that has become 10 times more acidic.

WHY SOIL BECOMES ACIDIC

Acidic soils are common in areas with a lot of precipitation of rainfall. Most soils east of the Mississippi River and in the Pacific Northwest are acidic (but not those found over limestone). Slightly acidic soils (keeping in mind anything below 7.0 is considered acidic) of 6.1 to 6.5 are conducive for most plants. Most wildlife forages, though, will tolerate and grow in pH levels of 5.8 to 6.5, with 6.5 considered the optimum value. Many of the brassicas grow in slightly acidic soils. For example: Kale 5.5 to 6.5, forage rape 5.3 to 6.8, turnips 5.9 to 6.5.

Therefore, only *extremely* acidic soil (1.0 to 3.5) is considered a curse when growing successful food plots. Extremely low pH readings, though, sharply reduce the activity of soil microbes. Keep in mind, as demonstrated above, each plant has different pH needs. That is why it is wise to know as much as you can about all the pH requirements needed by *each* plant species you will grow, as pH has a large effect on soil chemistry.

Acidity is caused by a variety of things, including the amount of hydrogen ions present in soil, organic matter, and fresh plant residues from crops being turned under the soil at the end of the growing season. By microbial decomposition, rainwater leaching away basic ions (calcium [Ca], magnesium [Mg], potassium [K], and sodium [Na]), decomposing roots of stems, organic matter of wildlife, overuse of pesticides. Decaying leaves make up a sizable portion of decomposing matter. Additionally, deer and other wildlife can affect the soil acidity. How, you ask? By eating the very plants that were seeded for them. Wildlife absorbs the plants' alkalinity properties and redeposits it back into the soil via urine.

In very acidic soils (or very alkaline soils), most nutrients dissolve slowly or not at all. In turn, they may form insoluble mineral compounds that lock up nutrients so that plants can't use them. Therefore, if your soil is too acidic or alkaline for nutrients to dissolve easily, you will waste a lot of money buying tons of lime and fertilizer to correct the problem.

Acidic soil is often referred to as "sour soil" because matter that is acidic often tastes sour. Alkaline soil is commonly called "sweet soil" because it is the opposite of acidic soil, but it does not taste sweet; in fact, it tastes bitter. All of this is just another reason why it's critically important to test and correct the pH of your soil *before* adding lime or fertilizer.

The soil pH scale ranges from 0 to 14. A pH of 7.0 is considered neutral. Values greater than 7.0 are more alkaline (or sweet). Rates of 6.1 to 6.5 are considered *slightly* acidic (sour). From 5.6 to 6.0 they are rated as being *moderately* acidic. Any pH value between 5.1 to 5.5 is considered strongly acidic. Preferably,

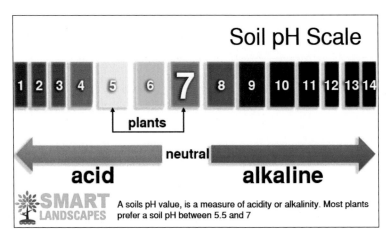

▲ This chart demonstrates the range of pH values and what pH levels most plants prefer. Photo Courtesy: MS Extension

though, most forage wildlife crops do best at pH values between 5.8 and 6.5. Adjusting soil pH within the optimal range of forage crops maximizes growth and increases yield, fertilizer efficiency, palatability of forages, and even herbicide effectiveness.

SOIL ACIDITY (pH)

Lime (a mixture of calcium and magnesium compounds) is used to diminish acidity. The speed at which lime works to neutralize the acidity in soil is dependent on the condition of the elements in the lime used and, more particularly, to exactly how acidic the soil is. The smaller the particles are in the lime, the faster it will be absorbed into the soil.

PELLETIZED LIME

The benefits of applying a lime soil amendment are a result of lime's ability to correct soil acidity. Lime

▲ In plots of an acre or less that have a pH tested at 6.0 to 6.5, applying 300 to 400 lbs./acre of lime, as is being done here, is sufficient. Photo - Fiduccia Ent.

applications neutralize the acidity of the soil, allowing plants to absorb previously "locked-up" nutrients. Consequently, a better soil environment is created when using lime, allowing plants to yield the lime's beneficial results.

WHEN IS TOO MUCH LIME—TOO MUCH?

Consider the old proverb that life is better when "everything is in moderation." That's true about lime and fertilizer. Applying too much lime to a plot may be as bad as adding too little. The exact amount of lime required can only be *accurately* determined by a soil test. It takes a lot of lime to correct an acre of soil with a low pH level. Usually, most soil requires anywhere from 300 to 400 lbs./acre. However, a soil test will give you a much more accurate figure of how much lime you will need. The soil test will even describe the type of lime that should be applied for your specified crop planting intentions.

Lime is available in many forms, including crushed limestone, finely ground powder, granules, and pellets. Although each food plot manager will have a preference as to the type of lime used, over the last several years I have exclusively used pellets mostly because they have less lime dust as compared to pulverized lime. They are a little more expensive, but they are cleaner to handle and easier to apply into the soil. They also don't require a lot of cleanup time.

Powdered lime adjusts the pH levels the fastest, however. For some who need to eliminate acidic soils, powdered lime may be a better choice. Its finer texture gets absorbed into the ground quickly. However, there are some downsides when using powdered lime. It's always best to apply it on windless days. If it is applied on windy days, some of the lime will be blown away—wasting time and money. When handling powdered lime, even with gloves on, it can cause irritation to the skin, eyes, and even worse, the lungs. It also gets all over clothing, machinery, and anything else near it, making it a chore to clean up. It is also a good idea to wear a respirator mask when applying powdered lime.

For best results when applying pellet or crushed lime, spread it as evenly as possible throughout the plot on the surface of the soil, then plow the lime under the soil. Lime can be purchased in the forms mentioned above from any farm supply stores like Tractor Supply,

Lowes, and Home Depot. It usually comes in forty- to fifty-pound bags, making it easier to calculate exactly how much per acre is needed. For the fastest absorption of lime into your soil, apply it when you know there will be a predicted rainfall within twenty-four to forty-eight hours.

One last reminder about lime. Contrary to what some food plot managers think, lime does not act immediately, or even quickly, to amend soil acidity. It can take a month or more to correct a low pH level. The best time to spread limestone is fall, because as I mentioned, it takes time to become available in the soil.

▲ When liming large plots or areas, a lot of lime is needed. Generally, apply surface lime at no more than two and one-half tons per acre per year. The best way to do this is by hiring an ag-company to spread the lime by the truck load, like this truck is doing on our farm. Photo Courtesy: NRCS

AMENDING ALKALINE SOIL

Before amending alkaline soil, test the soil's pH. Values of 7.5 and above need to be corrected sooner rather than later. Alkaline soil generally contains a lot of sodium, calcium, and magnesium. Because alkaline soil is less soluble than neutral or acidic soil, the availability of nutrients to plants can often be limited. Because of this, stunted growth and nutrient deficiencies are common results of alkaline soil.

WHY SOILS BECOME ALKALINE

Alkaline soils are most common in dry climates and therefore found most often in western and especially in southwestern states. Alkaline soil is mostly a result of low amounts of yearly rainfall. They are mostly found in arid or desert areas where rainfall is slim to none. But soils in the East are not immune to having alkaline soil. In places where there are very dense forests, the soils are also inclined to be alkaline. There are several products that can be used (in bulk bags) to amend alkaline soils. These include elemental sulfur, aluminum sulfate, iron sulfate, acidifying nitrogen, and organic mulches.

▲ Taking a soil sample requires taking a few samples of dirt per plot to get the best average pH reading. This is the fourth sample we took in a half-acre plot, the pH tested at 6.3. Photo Courtesy PCFImages

NUTRIENTS

Acidity of soil is one of the most crucial factors behind high-quality soil fertility. It affects all soil properties including the chemistry, biological activity, and structure. Correcting soil acidity or alkalinity will dramatically improve food plot plantings. All plants need thirteen elements to grow well. The elements are divided into two groups: macronutrients and micronutrients. Each group contains certain elements in either greater or lesser amounts. Most nutrients come from weathered rocks that have become resulting soil. Organic matter supplies many of the same nutrients plus nitrogen, which hardly ever occurs in mineral form. Organic matter develops from the remains of plants and animals that hold many different chemical elements in their cells. As the organic matter is broken down by microorganisms, the elements are returned to the soil.

Nutrients can also be commonly applied to the soil as fertilizer and limestone. Nutrients must dissolve in the soil water before plant roots can absorb them. The macronutrient group requires the most amounts of elements including Nitrogen (N), Phosphorus (P), Potassium (K), Calcium (Ca), Magnesium (Mg), and Sulfur (S). The micronutrient group includes small or trace amounts of elements that are also important to healthy plant growth. They include Iron (Fe), Manganese (Mn), Copper (Cu), Zinc (Zn), Boron (B), Molybdenum (Mo), and Chlorine (Cl). All plant growth requires these elements in various degrees in the soil to grow well.

FERTILIZER BASICS

When it comes to planting a wildlife food plot, it is important to know the basics of fertilization to get the maximum yield out of your intended crops. There are numerous blends of NPK fertilizers. Each provides a plant with different benefits. Knowing what NPK mixes do can help you make the right selection.

Many food plotters are familiar with the acronym NPK. For those who aren't, NPK is the scientific buzzword to measure key ingredients in fertilizer. Here is a brief explanation of the breakdown:

N—Stands for Nitrogen. This nutrient is what develops the stem and leaf and adding this will get things growing fast. This is perfect for leafy plants like brassicas, sugar beets, kale, etc.
P—Stands for Phosphorus. This nutrient is valuable for developing the fruit of any plant. It also helps roots take quickly to the soil around them.
K—Stands for Potassium. This nutrient promotes healthy root systems and helps the plants resist disease.

FERTILIZER TYPES

The two types of fertilizer are complete and incomplete. An incomplete fertilizer is a product that does not supply all three of the major nutrients but only one or two. A complete fertilizer is one that provides all three nutrients (NPK).

◄ This bag of complete fertilizer is a mix of 16-18-19. I use this mix to fertilize corn. Photo: PCFImages

Another way to break down fertilizer types is general and special-purpose fertilizers. If the fertilizer contains equal amounts of each major nutrient or has just a slightly higher variation of nitrogen than phosphorus or potassium, then it is a general fertilizer. On the opposite side of the coin, special-purpose fertilizers are formulated for specific needs. For example, a special-purpose fertilizer is 46–0–0. This is used to give a boost of nitrogen to a corn plot that absorbs a lot of nitrogen from the soil.

FERTILIZER INFORMATION

10–10–10 Fertilizer

Triple 10 fertilizer is an all-purpose fertility enhancement for perennial plants. It helps an established plot of perennials and other legumes put out new growth in the spring.

12–12–12 Fertilizer

Triple 12 fertilizer will create a healthy blade, stem, and root structure. With stronger roots, you will not need as much water since the vegetation can absorb more moisture. This is a well-balanced fertilizer. A well-balanced triple 12 fertilizer is recommended at planting to ensure that your new plants get all three essential nutrients.

16–16–16 Fertilizer

Triple 16 (a.k.a. T-16) fertilizer is a general-purpose fertilizer for use on most shrubs, trees, and brassica vegetables. It contains a fast-acting form of nitrogen which plants use, even in cool weather, to help develop a rich green color. This triple 16 fertilizer is especially effective on clay and sand.

19–19–19 Fertilizer

Triple 19 (a.k.a. T-19) fertilizer is a more acidic fertilizer, making its absorption by the leaves more efficient. T-19 helps the general growth of crops and increases disease resistance. Triple 19 also prevents deterioration of soil texture. T-19 can be used on most wildlife food plot plantings.

20–20–20 Fertilizer

Brassicas and corn crave nitrogen in substantial amounts. A fertilizer that meets those needs is Triple-20 (T-20). It also helps to green-up the leaves of corn and brassicas.

0–20–20 Fertilizer

This is a zero-nitrogen fertilizer that is used when legumes and clovers provide enough nitrogen to a planting but still needs phosphorous and potassium.

6–24–24 Fertilizer

This fertilizer is a beneficial supplement for soils low in phosphate and potash. This is best for plants that

▲ This bag of fertilizer contains a complete fertilizer of 19-19-19 (a.k.a. T-19). T-19 is an excellent general fertilizer for almost all food plot plants. Photo courtesy: PCFImages

already give off considerable amounts of nitrogen such as clovers and legumes.

10–20–20 Fertilizer

This fertilizer is used when a plant requires less nitrogen and more phosphorous and potassium.

46–0–0 Fertilizer (Urea)

Urea is 46 percent nitrogen, so its analysis is 46–0–0. The best way to use urea is prior to a predicted rainfall. It is best used with corn to provide the soil a good dose of nitrogen that is quickly used by the corn plant. It mixes well with phosphorus and potassium products.

0–0–60 Fertilizer (Potash)

Potash is an enriched source of the mineral potassium for balanced leaf and root growth. Potash should be

▲ This is a bag of urea which is 46-0-0. Urea is mainly used to provide plants with nitrogen to promote green leafy growth and make the plants look lush. Photo courtesy: PCFImages

applied prior to planting for it to reach the root zones of future plants.

Most seed ag stores also offer a service of making a custom NPK mix. This requires that the food plotter has a keen knowledge of what plants need and which mixes of fertilizers will benefit them best. Better yet, talk to your ag store about their recommendations. Many times, they have developed NPK mixes other than the standard varieties. For instance, I buy an NPK mix of 16–18–19 from my local ag store McDowell Walker. This mix is recommended as a better option for my plantings than 19–19–19.

LIQUID FERTILIZERS

There is another option to fertilize food plots and enhance soil. Most food plotters commonly use traditional granulated fertilizers. While granulated fertilizers do their job, they have some drawbacks. The bags can weigh sixty pounds or more, making them heavy to lift, bulky to handle, expensive to buy (particularly when gas prices rise), and are irritating to the eyes and skin. Granulated fertilizers can also severely rust metal spreaders and eat away at plastic types as well. They also need to be applied at certain times for best results, which generally means putting it down prior to a rainfall. Additionally, pelletized fertilizer can burn plants if used too heavily or when it is applied in extended dry, hot weather. Moreover, when applying granular fertilizers, granules must dissolve into the soil before the plant can utilize the fertilizer.

Another option to fertilize plantings is liquid fertilizers. They negate all the above-mentioned shortcomings of granular fertilizers. My favorite benefit of using liquid fertilizers is that they eliminate the back-straining chore of lifting heavy fertilizer bags. Liquid fertilizers are also considerably easier to apply, are absorbed into the soil much faster, and they last for a couple of months. They are easily applied using a backpack- or ATV-type sprayer. Using liquid fertilizers will also cut down on the time it takes to fertilize a food plot/s.

Most liquid fertilizer companies state that when using liquid fertilizer on food plot plants, they help in making the plants more palatable (better tasting) to deer and other wildlife. Equally important, unlike the granular minerals, liquid fertilizer ensures the consistency of providing an equal amount of nutrients. This consistency allows plants to absorb the nutrients more quickly and efficiently through leaves, stems, and blooms. This process makes the nutrients immediately available.

In the end fertilizers, be they granular or liquid, are important elements in food plot management. If plants lack nitrogen, phosphorus, potassium, and micronutrients, they will not be as healthy or beneficial to deer and other wildlife. When looking over the different process and benefits of the two fertilizers, I feel liquid fertilizer offers more benefits. I am at the age where lifting and toting sixty-seven-pound bags of granular fertilizer is inviting a hernia.

CONCLUSION

To conclude this chapter, I suppose the key phase is DON'T TREAT YOUR SOIL LIKE DIRT! Instead take as good care of it as possible by following the above fertilizer and lime guidelines. There are many companies that offer liquid fertilizers from which to choose. Some include DeerGro, Plot Start™ and PlotBoost™, Whitetail Institute Impact Soil Amendment, AgroThrive™, Great Days Outdoors, Clark's Plots Nutrients, Plot Max, Big Z& J, and Power Grow. There are many different types of fertilizers that serve different purposes depending on the nutrient requirements needed. Before applying granular or liquid fertilizer it is important to know your soil and the nutritional needs of your food plot plants to adjust their requirements with different limes and fertilizers.

TALE OF TWO FERTILIZERS

PlotBoost™ is a spray for use on food plots, crops, vegetables, trees, and lawns. Developed by an American company that is a thirty-year veteran of the agricultural industry, PlotBoost's™ unique mix of complex carbohydrates, amino acids, and micronutrients NOT found in *traditional fertilizers* allow your plantings to reach their maximum potential. Made in the U.S.A., **PlotBoost™** affects both the plant and the immediate soil environment to maximize effectiveness.

PlotStart™ is a calcium-based spray for use on food plots, crops, vegetables, trees, and lawns. PlotStart™ provides instantly soluble and available calcium PLUS a unique mix of complex carbohydrates, amino acids, and micronutrients not found in *traditional fertilizers* that allow your plantings to explode from seed to plant and begin to grow at full potential. PlotStart™ targets the soil, providing the most beneficial growing environment possible.

▲ Liquid fertilizers like the ones shown here from DeerGro, are growing in popularity due to their ease of application. Photo courtesy: PCFImages

▲ To achieve the absolute best results from your plantings, always get a pH test of the plot's soil first. Credit: Antler King, WINA

To grow bucks with antlers like this, make sure your soil pH levels are at their proper values before planting. Credit: Ted Rose

Chapter Eight

Make Your Soil Tests Mandatory

This chapter could be many pages long and contain a lot of scientific gobbledygook about the many essential, but scientifically intense, aspects of soil and soil fertility. Most of the information about the science behind soil fertility is what very few of you reading this need to become immersed with. In the end game, taking a soil test is the most important aspect of planting successful food plots. Unfortunately, it is often overlooked despite it being so incredibly important. Soil problems are responsible for most food plots either not performing up to par or failing entirely.

Instead of loading you up with a lot of the scientific aspects about soil, I will cut to the chase about soil and its partner fertility. If you want to grow the type of food plots you see on outdoor television programs, in magazines, like the images and videos seen on food

▲ To grow food plots like the soybeans seen here, it is vital to make sure your soil is fertile. Fertile soil equals healthy plants. Photo Courtesy: PCFImages

plot company websites, heed this: Consistently successful food plots start and end with good soil and soil fertility. Keep in mind that the chief difference between rich, fertile soil and paltry infertile soil is all about mineral structure. Your food plot plant's palatability and nourishment are mostly grounded (pardon the pun) on the soil minerals that are available and not the amount of nitrogen, phosphorus and potassium (NPK) that is applied within an overall food plot program or in any one food plot.

SITE SELECTION

Choosing the right sites is the first step in ensuring you will create productive food plots. One of the most common mistakes is planting in wet, bottomland areas. The key word in that sentence is wet. Bottomland plantings can be greatly beneficial if the area is not consistently wet. Most forages of wildlife seeds require well-drained soils to grow best.

SUNSHINE

Another commonplace error is planting seeds in areas that are too shady. Like the song "Aquarius," by the Fifth Dimension, repeatedly said, *"Let the sunshine in."* To grow your plants *right*—hum that tune while planting them. Maximize direct sunlight exposure to grow great looking, healthy food plots. If you ignore this point, I assure you will it will result in minimal forage production. Plots that are oriented east to west will receive an upper limit of more hours of direct sunlight per day.

TEST YOUR SOIL!

Here is the absolute *crucial* factor in growing the best food plots—test your soil. Never skip this first step if

▲ The tools seen here are all that is needed when taking soil samples from a limited number of food plots. Keep a record of each sample taken: name of land, plot name, and sample number. Photo Courtesy: PCFImages

you want your food plots to look like the plots "wild-life pros" grow. Always test your soil before planting a single seed. Nothing, and I mean nothing, in food plot planting is more important than taking soil tests. Why? Because a soil test report will provide a baseline from which a food plotter can make educated decisions about the types of nutrients, based not on guesswork, but on a laboratory report. Food plotters will know what they need to apply for the types of crops planned

to sow. Hence, the guesswork in amending the soil in your food plot is eliminated.

PH OF SOIL

Soil tests provide an accurate index of the level of available nutrients in the soil in each food plot. Soils can differ widely, even within a single plot. A soil test reveals the degree of the soil's nutrients, be they lacking, or sufficient. While a soil test effectively demonstrates if the soil is nutrient deficient, it also provides the soil's pH value and the soils fertility. As mentioned before, depending on the pH value, chemical reactions in the soil can cause nutrients to form compounds that do not easily dissolve. This process essentially locks nutrients out of the plant's reach. The pH value of soil has a big effect on soil chemistry. Either acidity or alkalinity can bind up many nutrients at once. Therefore, improper pH is the most common reason for nutrients present in soil to be locked out of the soil solution resulting in them being out of reach of the plant's roots.

▲ Take a few samples from each plot. Mix the samples from each plot thoroughly to get an average pH value for a particular plot. The objective of soil analysis is to inventory the soil's levels of nutrients and chemical composition. Photo: © Microgen Dreamstime

NUMBER OF SOIL SAMPLES

Many food plot managers are surprised to discover soil samples may differ considerably from one location to another. In fact, there can be a change in a pH value reading from one sample taken in a plot to another sample taken only yards away. To get the most accurate reading from a food plot, take a few soil samples from various locations within the plot and place them in a bucket. Mix the soil thoroughly. This will give you an average pH of the soils you are testing from the plot you are analyzing.

The most effective way to take multiple soil samples is with a quality stainless-steel soil sampler probe. There are many brands and styles available. Prices range from $49 to hundreds of dollars. A quality soil sampler that withstands the rigors of taking soil samples should cost about $100. You can find them at Barn Door www.barndoorag.com, A.M. Leonard–www.amleo.com, and Mid-South Ag Equipment www.shopmidsouthag.com. Other tools that come in handy for taking soil samples include a small bucket, old soup spoon, indelible black felt pen, and several small zip-top bags (to label each sample). Remember the best test results will be from submitting dry soil; avoid taking soil samples when the soil is wet.

WHERE TO SEND SAMPLES

Once you have taken your soil sample, the best way to get an accurate reading is by sending it out to a reliable soil test facility. Most states have coop extension programs that provide basic fertilizer and lime requirements from the samples you send in. There are also many laboratories that test soil. Fees at soil testing laboratories range in price depending upon what services you order. A basic pH test is the least expensive, but most labs offer more detailed testing for additional fees.

▲ Taking soil samples from multiple plots, particularly large plots of an acre or more, requires a professional sturdy soil probe. It makes the job easier and quicker. It also takes a better sample. If your soil's nutrients are off their baseline, your food plot crops will suffer or even fail to grow properly. Photo Courtesy: NRCS

Moreover, a soil test that demonstrates a deficiency will suggest an effective solution about how to make the appropriate decision as to what nutrients need to be added to amend the soil. If you want to be on top of your game, though, spend a few extra dollars to have the lab include a more detailed soil analysis that will include not only soil pH, but percentages of organic matter, nitrogen, phosphorus, and potassium. It will also include a micro-nutrient analysis of calcium, magnesium, boron, manganese, zinc, and sulfur for the additional charge. The three other elements plants also require are carbon, hydrogen, and oxygen. Plants get all they need of these elements, though, from the air and from water.

A soil test can also provide you with recommendations for the right amount of fertilizer and lime applications to properly amend the soil. Properly amended soils result in healthier soils for your plants to grow in.

Most laboratories recommend that soil tests be done every three to five years. I like to do it every other year because I can track my soil's characteristics and performance more accurately.

When taking soil tests remember to allow enough time prior to planting to receive your sample information and recommendation/s back from the laboratory. It is also best if you provide the lab with the length and width of the plot/s being tested, the crop or vegetation currently in the plot, and what you intend to seed the plot with. When a lab has that kind of information, it will test the sample accordingly and provide a report that will instruct a food plotter to add specific amounts of inputs (fertilizer and lime) for each intended plot/s.

Soil tests are commonly performed by local cooperative extension offices. State universities also provide affordable soil testing services through their cooperative

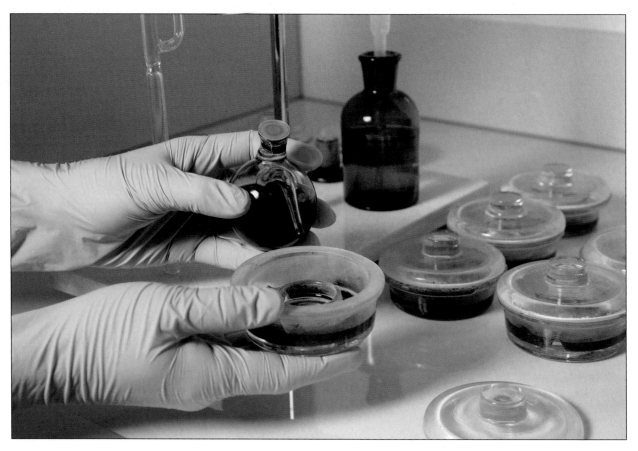

▲ This tech is testing for nitrogen. To get the best scientific analysis of your soil tests, let the lab know the crop history of what was planted last year, and what you plan to plant in the plot this season. Photo: © Chernetskaya | Dreamstime

extension service. In most cases you will get both soil testing and fertilizer and amendment recommendations based on the test results for what you intend to grow.

▲ When taking soil samples, take notes indicating from which areas of fields samples are taken. This reference will come in handy when results are returned and when taking samples the following year. Photo: © Microgen | Dreamstime

SOIL TEST DIGITAL METERS

Digital soil test meters have come a long way over the last decade. The more expensive models generally cost about $75 or more. However, most are designed for gardeners. For food plotters, especially those planting multiple plots, using soil test meters may provide a

▲ Soil meters are okay to use, particularly if your food plot budget is limited. They are not nearly as accurate as a sample analyzed by a laboratory. Photo Courtesy: PCFImages

reasonable reading, but they do not provide the type of accuracy and information a soil testing laboratory can offer.

CONCLUSION

Knowing your soil's nutrient information will allow you to make amendments in soils that are more accurate than just liming and fertilizing without knowing what your soil needs. Not only does this lead to better plant growth, health, and nutrition, but it also helps you grow the healthiest bucks and does possible.

SOIL TEST ANALYSIS SOURCES

Easy-to-use food plot soil test services or soil test kits and meters are available from ...

OUTDOOR INDUSTRY SOIL TESTING SOURCES
Agassiz Seed Company—**www.agassizseed.com**
Antler King—**www.antlerking.com**

Building Whitetail Paradise—**www.heartlandillinois.com**

Deer Creek Seed—**www.deercreekseed.com**

Extreme Custom Food Plots—**www.extremecustom-foodplots.com**

Frigid Forage—**www.frigidforage.com/soil-test-kits**

Thunder Ridge Outdoors' - **www.huntingplots.com**

Whitetail Institute—**www.whitetailinstitute.com**

▲ Nearly all, if not all, seed companies provide soil test kits. Simply return the soil sample to the seed company for testing. Photo Courtesy: Whitetail Institute

SOIL TESTING SITES AT STATE UNIVERSITIES ACROSS THE COUNTRY

AL—Auburn University Soil Testing Laboratory

AK—Soil Testing Labs

AZ—University of Arizona Cooperative Extension— Soil Testing Labs

AR—University of Arkansas System—Soil Testing and Research Laboratory

CO—Colorado State University—Soil Testing

CT—University of Connecticut—Soil Testing Program

DE- University of Delaware Soil Testing Program

FL—University of Florida Cooperative Extension—Soil Testing Services

GA—University of Georgia Cooperative Extension— Soil Testing

HI—University of Hawaii at Mānoa—Soil Testing

ID—University of Idaho—Soil Chemical and Physical Analyses

IL- University of Illinois Extension—Soil Testing Labs

IN- Purdue University Soil Sampling & Testing

IA—Iowa State University—Soil and Plant Analysis Laboratory

KS—Kansas State University Agronomy Soil Testing Lab

▲ A laboratory tech filtering soil samples. For a few extra dollars labs will provide much more than just a pH test. They can test for macro and micronutrients, organic matter, base saturation percentages, pesticide residue, heavy metals, microbiology, and more. Photo: © Chernetskaya | Dreamstime

KY—The University of Kentucky College of Agriculture—Cooperative Extension Fayette County

LA—Louisiana State University—Soil Testing & Plant Analysis Lab

ME—The University of Maine—Cooperative Extension Publications Soil Testing

MD—University of Maryland Co-Op Ext Soil Testing Services

MA—University of Massachusetts Soil Testing Program

MI—Michigan State University—Soil Testing

MN—University of Minnesota—The Soil Testing Laboratory

MS—The Mississippi State University—Soil Testing

MO—University of Missouri Extension—Soil Testing & Plant Diagnostic Services

MT—Montana State University Extension—Soil Testing Information and Labs

NE—University of Nebraska-Lincoln—Soil Testing Information and Labs

NV—University of Nevada Las Vegas—Environmental Soil Analysis Laboratory

NH—University of New Hampshire Cooperative Extension—Soil Testing

NJ—Rutgers University Cooperative Extension Office Soil Test Program

NM—New Mexico State University—Soil Testing Labs

NY—Cornell University Cooperative Extension

NC—North Carolina Department of Agriculture—Soil Testing Services

ND—North Dakota State University Soil Testing Lab

OH—The Ohio State University—Soil Testing Resources

OK—Oklahoma State University—Soil Testing

OR—Oregon State University Central Analytical Laboratory—Soil Testing

PA—Penn State Soil Testing Services

RI—University of Rhode Island Soil Testing Program (in conjunction with UMass)

SC—Clemson University Cooperative Extension—Soil Testing

SD—South Dakota State University—Soil Testing Labs

TN—University of Tennessee Soil, Plant, and Pest Center

TX—Texas AgriLife Extension Service Soil, Water, and Forage Testing Service

UT—Utah State University Soil Testing Laboratory

VT—University of Vermont Soil Testing

VA—Virginia Tech Soil Testing Lab

WA—Washington State University Soils and Soil Testing

WV—West Virginia University Soil Testing Laboratory

WI—University of Wisconsin Soil & Plant Analysis Laboratory - https://uwlab.soils.wisc.edu/

WY—University of Wyoming—Soil Testing Laboratory - http://www.uwyo.edu/wrrc/resources-soil-kits.html

In cases where the university doesn't directly perform soil testing, it recommends information about other options.

▲ Laboratories test hundreds of soil samples per day. A professional lab uses the latest methods for testing agricultural soil samples. Photo: © Chernetskaya | Dreamstime

▲ A lab technician checks a flask of soil. Labs perform many other tests other than just pH values. Photo: © Chernetskaya | Dreamstime

▲ The elemental analysis of soils is of vital importance not only for your food plots, but also from an environmental perspective of your land. Photo: © Microgen |Dreamstime

▲ Proper seeding rates yield healthier food plots. By following suggested rates, you won't have plantings competing with one another due to overcrowding and competition for nutrients. Credit: Ted Rose

Chapter Nine

Measuring Your Plots for Better Success

T his chapter shares information and advice that should not be ignored. It will help you to grow more successful, sumptuous-looking food plots. One of the most overlooked aspects of planting food plots is to precisely measure the size of each plot. Knowing what a food plot's measurements are will help you quickly establish the accurate amounts of lime, fertilizer, herbicide, and seed that you will need to apply, plant, and manage each of your food plots.

Taking the exact measurements of a food plot does not require managers to be rocket scientists; all it requires is adding a few minutes of time. The process can be done with the help of another person, or it can be done alone. Either way, determining a plot's accurate dimensions can be done quickly and easily using any one or a combination of the following methods:

- Pad and/or cell phone to take note of the plot name and measurements.
- A 200-hundred-foot measuring tape.
- The calculator on your cell phone.
- A rangefinder.
- GPS unit.
- Something as hi-tech as the distance ruler on Google Earth or the hunting GPS app OnXMaps.com.
- Something as antique as a pad and pencil.

MEASURE EACH PLOT ACCURATELY

One of the chief causes of food plots not growing to expectations, or even potentially failing, is that many times they suffer from too much or too little lime, fertilizer, herbicide, and *most* often—way too much seed. Most of the time this happens simply because the food plotter either did not think measuring the plot was important enough to do or did not realize it was a necessary step to successful plot management. The reality is that when food plots are not measured precisely, they will almost always get over-seeded. Planting too much seed in a food plot is always worse than under-seeding it. When a plot is over-seeded, all the plants

▲ Measuring a food plot accurately will help save money when buying the correct amounts of herbicides, fertilizer, and lime. Photo Courtesy: PCFImages

▲ One quick and easy method of measuring plots is to use a rangefinder. Photo Courtesy: PCFImages

result in not providing the plants with enough minerals needed for maximum growth. It can also lead to lock out from oversaturation of nutrients.

If you neglect to accurately determine the overall dimensions of each food plot, not only will the plantings suffer, but you will also waste quite a bit of valuable time, work, and money. It can also result in frustration when the plots do not perform as expected. I strongly suggest that you take the time to measure each plot accurately. Do not skip this major step.

▲ This image shows some of the food plots we plant each year. It also depicts one of our fruit and nut tree orchards planted with eighty-five trees. Photo Courtesy: PCFImages

are in competition with one another. Generally, this ends up with plants with stunted growth. A classic example is when turnips are over-seeded and end up growing much smaller than they should. Many times, it results in tiny bulbs. As the adage goes, "Everything in moderation."

This is particularly valid when it comes to preparing and planting a food plot. If too much herbicide is applied to a food plot, for example, the excess herbicide can either result in the plot's inability to grow a crop properly or, worse, render the soil of the plot dormant for extended periods of time. Placing either too much or too little lime in a plot inadvertently results in the pH levels becoming either too acidic or too alkaline. Putting too much fertilizer down can end up burning the plants. Not applying enough fertilizer can

HOW TO CALCULATE A PLOT'S SIZE

An important figure to keep in mind when measuring food plots is the overall dimension of an acre of land, which is 43,560 square feet. Since most plots are square or rectangular in shape, simply measure the length and width of the plot to get its precise overall size. To determine what percentage the plot size is as it relates to an acre, take the plot's overall dimensions, and divide it by 43,560. This will provide you with the fraction figure or percentage of an acre that is related to each plot. For example: Let us say your plot is 125 feet by 125 feet. Multiply 125 by 125; it is 15,625 square feet. Next, divide 15,625 by 43,560, and you get 0.36—or slightly more than one third of an acre.

This formula can also be used to determine the size of irregularly shaped plots. It takes a little more math work in measuring and calculating asymmetrical plots, but it is still an essential step in the overall land manager's food plot program. It is worth the extra effort. Measure all sides of lopsided plots individually, then apply the same calculations to reach a close approximation of the overall size of the plot.

RECORD THE MEASUREMENTS

To eliminate having to recalculate food plots every season, store the plot's name, location, and its dimensions either on a computer, your cell phone, or in a handwritten logbook for future reference. It will help eliminate unnecessary work the following year, leaving you only to calculate the size of new plots that are created. To eliminate confusion, each food plot should be given a *name* rather than a *number*. The dimensions should then be applied to that plot to prevent the final measurements from being confused with another plot. Obviously, if the size of a plot is extended or reduced, the plot needs to be measured again and the new dimensions re-entered into the log. Knowing the exact dimensions of all your plots will save you lime, herbicide, fertilizer, seed, money, time, and, most important, the frustration and grief of a plot not growing as well as you hoped it would.

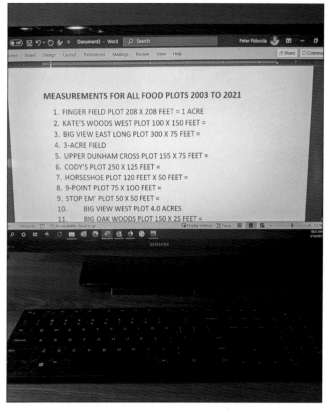

▲ We record each food plot's size. If the size of a plot is altered, it is easy to make the change on the computer. It prevents having to guess at what each plots size is from year-to-year. Photo Courtesy: PCFImages

▲ In this photo it is easy to see how deer can overbrowse a food plot. Using deterrents like Deer Out or other preventive brands will increase the production of your plantings. Credit: Huntingplots.com

▲ Most of us expend a lot of time and effort in developing a food plot and deer management program all in a desire to improve our deer herd's health. Our secondary goal is to attract adult bucks, particularly during the daylight hours of the hunting season. Credit: Deposit Photos

Chapter Ten

Creating a Proper Seedbed

Failure to follow good seedbed preparation protocols is a surefire way to ensure a food plot that is destined to fail. In my first food plot book, the *Shooter's Bible Guide to Planting Food Plots*, I emphasized one of the most common mistakes by food plotters, particularly novices, is not properly preparing a seedbed. A poorly made seedbed can be considered a misstep second only to not taking a soil test. Both are primary reasons for food plots to fail. Focus on and frame these goals in a manner so that you develop procedures based on your land's unique situations.

NEW SITE SELECTION

Preparing a new seedbed first requires choosing a proper location. Choosing a spot for a food plot is important and requires some careful considerations. Some factors include the plot's elevation, security it offers to deer, drainage, security it offers to deer, soil conditions, security it offers to deer, and convenience of getting planting equipment to the plot. The repeated phrase in the last sentence is not a mistake. A plot's location also helps to determine which type of forage seed is best to plant. As far as hunting goes, site selection should also take into consideration the many factors that are related to hunting over a food plot.

All food plot plantings begin by knowing the pH values of your soil in *every* food plot that is planted, even from year-to-year. A pH level not only indicates the amount of alkalinity or acidity in the soil, but it also measures moisture content. The range of pH starts at zero and goes to 14, with 7.0 being a neutral reading. A pH reading of less than 7.0 indicates acidity, and a pH higher than 7.0 indicates a base. A pH of 6.5 is considered ideal for an overwhelming majority of plants. A pH level is nothing more than a measure of the comparative amount of free hydrogen and hydroxyl ions in water. When a soil is acidic, forage seeds have

▲ This is an example of a food plot with its location planned out. It borders our refuge on the right. It also illustrates a well-prepared seed bed. It is clear of all large rocks, limbs, sticks, and other debris. The soil has also been worked to accept seed. Photo: PCFImages

a harder time absorbing nutrients, hampering their growth. Also, knowing a pH level will help you correct soil issues *before* you plant. For example, low soil pH can be amended by applying lime. If a pH reading is too high, or alkaline, then an adjustment is also called for prior to planting the plot. To lower a soil's pH (make it more acidic), use products like sphagnum peat, elemental sulfur, aluminum sulfate, iron sulfate, or acidifying nitrogen.

REMOVE WEEDS

Generally, when preparing a site that was planted previously, or a new plot, the plot will have weeds and other unwanted vegetation. It is vital to remove them with an herbicide by either using an ATV with an attached herbicide sprayer or a backpack sprayer. Both will work to kill the competing weeds and other plants. It is crucial when working with herbicides, wear a long-sleeved shirt, work gloves, eye protection, and a ventilator mask. Once the vegetation is dead, it can be removed by hand, burned, or dug up with a york rake.

▲ This field illustrates a well-prepared seed bed. We are using the Brillion seeder to plant a plot of triticale (a hybrid grain of wheat and rye). Photo: PCFImages

Once the weeds and other vegetation are cleared from the plot, it will be easy to see what other matter should be removed prior to working the soil so the seedbed is prepared correctly. Whether you are going to plant the plot by broadcasting seed or using machinery, the next step should be to clear the site of as many softball sized and larger rocks as is practical, large twigs, branches, and other debris. The goal is to make sure the plot will be as free of debris as possible to make it easier to disk. It can be disked using a disk harrow or a PTO-driven rotary tiller. You can use an ATV if the unit meets the requirements to pull a heavy set of disc-harrows to lightly disk

the ground and a drag chain harrow to prepare the seedbed.

A tractor or ATV and the appropriate implements will make short work of working the soil to the right texture. Remember, not preparing a good seedbed for the seed being planted is a crucial mistake. Disking a food plot is a step that should never be skipped or rushed. Generally, to achieve a better textured soil, it takes several passes using a disc to establish a top-notch seedbed. Take your time and it will be done correctly. The best time to disk a plot is when the soil is dry. The goal is to achieve a fine-textured soil that will enable you to accomplish good seed-to-soil contact.

SMOOTH AND LEVEL

Once you have properly disked the soil, the next objective is to make the plot as level and smooth as is practical. This is best accomplished by using a drag-type harrow, sometimes called a chain harrow, attached to a farm tractor or an ATV (500 cc or, better yet, a 700 cc with four-wheel-drive). Drag the food plot as many times as is necessary to break up small clods of soil. While doing this you may drag up some additional weeds, rocks, and other natural debris. They should be cleared away. The benefit of using a chain harrow is that it will also help level the plot, aerate the soil, and help to quickly dry a damp plot. If you don't have a drag harrow you can make one from a section

▲ Drag chain harrows are multi-use implements. They cover seed, smooth rough soil, or expose rocks and other rubble that should be removed prior to sowing and compacting a plot. Photo: PCFImages

of chain link fence with a flat heavy piece of metal at the front end. Then use plastic ties to secure bricks and a four- by four-foot post to the chain. The harrow can then be secured to a trailer hitch using a six- to eight-foot heavy chain.

A word of caution: When using a chain harrow in preparing a new food plot, it takes more time to prepare the seedbed. When it is done, though, the seedbed you have created will be clean, level, and fine-textured. You will have assured yourself that the seed you plant will grow to its maximum capability because you have created a well-prepared seedbed.

LIME AND FERTILIZER

Once you have finished preparing the soil of your fine-textured food plot, this is the time to amend it if necessary. Your soil test (you did take one, didn't you?) will determine if the plot requires lime or fertilizer. If you need one, or both, use a seeder on a tractor, ATV, or

▲ All spreaders must be properly calibrated to deliver the right amounts of seed, fertilizer, or lime. Without calibration, the product can either be applied too heavily or lightly. Moreover, proper calibration will ensure better seed growth. It saves money by not wasting product. Photo: PCFImages

even a hand-held unit to spread the lime or fertilizer. If the plot was limed or fertilized, it is important to thoroughly wash out any type of seeder used (hand-held, three-point hitch, or a pull-along). The residue left from lime and fertilizer contains powerful chemicals that will quickly rust out metal seeders.

DO NOT OVERSEED

This one mistake is a major cause of a planting not performing to its best ability. In fact, on the other end of the spectrum, it can cause total plot failure. Over-seeding will cause severe competition of the plant sowed. In most cases, the plot ends up with stunted plants. I learned this lesson more than thirty years ago. There were times when I planted turnips, sugar beets, or swede only to discover that I used too much seed for a given plot. The result was extremely frustrating. The bulbs of each plant were tiny, and the leaves and stems never grew properly enough to attract deer. It is far better to under-seed than to over-seed. That is why it is so important to calibrate a seeder to the manufacturer's instructions. It will go a long way to distributing the proper number of seeds at the recommended rate for the given measurements of a food plot. Take this to the deer hunting bank: Too few or too many seeds per acre will result in a poor-quality food plot. Take your time and do it right.

PLANTING DEPTH

Sowing a seed too deeply is also a common gaffe made by some food plotters. Different seeds require different soil depths for the seed to germinate properly. If they are planted too deep, or too shallow, it can cause the plant not to germinate at all. Generally, tiny seeds like clovers and brassicas should be planted at one-eighth inch and never more than one-quarter inch (they can also be successfully top-seeded).

I have also had excellent success in top-seeding tiny seeds of clovers and brassicas on top of a well-prepared seed bed. For best results, you can scratch the surface lightly prior to top-seeding it or simply hand-seed the plot directly over the prepared soil. However, make sure there is good seed-to-soil contact by culti-packing the plot to lightly press the seed into the soil.

The above methods will be enhanced if they are planned when you know there is a rainfall predicted within twenty-four to forty-eight hours after you have planted the plot. While I have heard that some folks plant and compact the clovers and brassicas during a rain, I have not had success with that method, as sometimes the seed gets so wet that it is picked up by the roller or cultipacker. But that is not to say others have had the same problem.

The larger seeds of legumes are mostly planted at a depth of three-quarters to one-inch deep. The grains, like corn, oats, and sorghum, should be planted from one to one-and-one-half inches deep and never more than two inches. Always check the proper seed depths prior to sowing any seed. If push came to shove about how deep to plant a seed, I would opt to plant seed shallower than too deeply.

Using a cultipacker behind a tractor, or a drag harrow behind an ATV, will help finish off a properly prepared seedbed by compacting the sown seed for good seed-to-soil contact. Proper seed-to-soil contact is critical for a high germination rate. Again, cover the seed according to the seed company's recommendations. It is worth repeating that most times when seed is covered too deeply it will not germinate. But here is the crux of the matter: Seed that is not covered properly will fall victim to being eaten by wild turkeys, crows, and a host of other seed-eating animals. This is the drawback when top-seeding plots with seeds larger than the tiny seeds of clovers and most brassicas.

When it comes to planting seeds in food plots, there are options. They can be sown using a hand-held seeder, a pull-behind ATV seeder, or three-point hitch seeder on a tractor. All work well when calibrated properly. Other options are to use till-and-seed-type equipment like those made by Brillion, Esch, Firminator, Northern Tool, and Land Pride.

In the end, site preparation and planting can all be done well by using a variety of methods including a no-till drill, a disk harrow, or a PTO- driven box tiller, a handheld broadcast spreader, tractor, and cultipacker. Or you can use a top-sowing method with little cultivation of the soil, proper disking, and matching depth to seed. But none of these methods are going to give you the best germination and success rate alone. To grow successful food plots, all methods require that you have made sure your seed has good seed-to-soil contact.

▲ When walking and seeding, both the pace of your walk and the seeder's opening should match how much seed is being spread. Photo: Fiduccia Ent

BRILLION FOOD PLOT SEEDER

The Brillion Food Plot Seeder (FPS) is designed to operate under a wide variety of conditions and will plant everything from clovers, legumes, small grains, and other blends and mixes. The Brillion FPS is my go-to unit to plant corn, cereal rye, and other grains. The FPS Series has the features to provide the necessary proper seedbed preparation, seed metering and placement, as well as seedbed finishing, all of which will provide a state-of-the-art food plot. Many of these units are affordable, and they all combine a heavy-duty disk harrow, a true agricultural grade cultipacker with a precision ground-driven seed system capable of planting clovers, brassicas, wheat, oats, soybeans, and seed blends. Other similar implements include LandPride's 3P500 & 3P500V Compact Drills, The Firminator G3, and Remlinger's 2300 Series No-Till Drills. For pull-behind ATV units, some include Kasco's line of No-Till Drills, The Dew Drop Drill, and Jordan Engineering's Super Sow-Lite seed drills.

Other options for sowing food plots is to use no-till drills. Generally, they are quite expensive and can range from $15,000 and up. However, Kasco makes quality drills meant to plant food plots at very reasonable prices. Kasco produces the most comprehensive line of food plot drills that are focused on food plot management.

▲ Using the proper equipment goes a long way in helping a food plotter prepare a top-notch seedbed. Photo: PCFImages

▲ Many varieties of noxious weeds need to be controlled. However, not all weeds are bad. Deer and other critters eat many types of weeds.
Credit: Ted Rose

Chapter Eleven

Weeds—The Bane of Every Food Plotter

Weeds are to wildlife food plots, like an empty rifle chamber is to a hunter being charged by a grizzly . . . deadly. Like the infamous organization "Murder for Hire," weeds will ultimately "whack" crops, sending food plotters' desires to grow healthy, nourishing plants up in gun smoke.

Weeds grow everywhere, mostly where they are never wanted. Often, when a food plot fails, it is usually lost to uncontrolled weed growth. Weeds effectively compete with wildlife plantings for nutrients, light, space, and *water.*

Even when edible weeds like dandelion, plantain, purslane, wood sorrel, and others are left to grow unrestrained, they become overbearing in food plots. Pennsylvania Smartweed, sumac, poison ivy, and other similar emerged weeds can be controlled by

▲ While smartweed (a.k.a. knotweed) is indeed a weed; it is one that ducks, deer, rabbits and other game eat. The point being, not every weed is bad-to-the-bone. Photo: kesternursery.com

tillage. This option though can only be addressed prior to planting the plot. Even then, it is not the best of choices for controlling weeds as they will emerge again.

Some of the most common weeds are listed below, including those that deer, waterfowl and other wild game eat. The italicized weeds are some of the most *nefarious* weeds . . .

Amaranth, Annual Ragweed, Annual Fleabane, Albus, *Bermudagrass,* Buckhorn Plantain, Butter & Eggs, Canada Thistle, *Cocklebur,* Chickweed, Common Couch, Common Mallow, *Common Mullein,* Crabgrass, Creeping Charlie, *Curly Dock,* Dame's Rocket, Dandelion, Early Whitlow Grass, Field Bindweed, *Foxtail, Garlic Mustard,* Goldenrod, *Horsenettle, Johnsongrass, Lambsquarters,* Milkweed, *Morning Glory,* Mugwort, Narrow Leaf *Plantain,* Nutsedge, *Pigweed,* Oriental Bittersweet, Pennsylvania Smartweed (actually a great weed for waterfowl), Poison Ivy, Poison Oak, Pokeweed, Purple Dead Nettle, Purslane, *Queen Ann Lace, Quackgrass, Ragweed,* Red Sorrel, Ribwort Plantain, Shepherds Purse, Swallowwort, *Sicklepod, Yellow Nut Sedge, Thistle, Velvetleaf,* and Yellow Wood Sorel.

I recommend reading all you can on weed control and the identification of weeds. I found the following books to be excellent sources: *Invasive Plants* by Sylvan Ramsey Kaufman and Wallace Kaufman; *Weeds of the Northeast* (Comstock books) by Richard H. Uva; *Common Weeds of the United States* by the U.S. Department of Agriculture; and, for the more "green-minded" food plot planter, *Weeds: Control without Poisons* by Charles Walters—all available on Amazon. The web is also a source for more detailed information on weeds and their control. It is also a good place to get further information on the safe and effective use of all types of chemical herbicides.

MOW PATROL CONTROL

Controlling or eliminating weeds from overtaking any food plot can be a frustrating and challenging problem. Luckily, a lot of weed problems can be evaded by using something as basic as the proper site selection and preparation. And when weeds do rear their ugly heads in perennial plots, they can be somewhat controlled with mowing at least a few times over the growing season. Mow the plots just high enough so that it prevents the weeds from getting taller than the forage plants. Luckily, most annual weeds grow upright, allowing for easier mowing.

Mowing some perennial plots will go far to keep them lush and nutritious for deer and other wildlife. What mowing accomplishes is preventing the forage plants from using a lot of their energy to flower and produce seed. Another way mowing aids to keep perennials lush and robustly growing is by promoting more foliage at lower levels of the plant.

DISKING TOO DEEPLY

One factor that initiates weed growth is disking the soil too deeply when cultivating a plot. The deeper the soil is disturbed, the more the weed bed is agitated, creating a surge of new weed growth.

HERBICIDES

Even after using weed control practices, there are

▲ Mowing weeds keeps them low and helps prevent them from overtaking a food plot planting. Photo: PCFImages

◄ Surfactants are added to herbicides to break the surface tension of the herbicide and leaf surface. In so doing, the herbicide kills the target plant more effectively. Photo: PCFImages

▲ While at the Continental, John Wick uses a heavily customized reverse two-tone Kimber Super Carry 1911 fitted with a compensator. When it comes to killing weeds, using herbicides is more effective than a Kimber pistol. Photo courtesy: Kimber

times when weeds can become so problematic the only viable solution is herbicide treatment. There are several types of herbicides to fit different types of weed control. While there are many herbicides on the market, food plot managers will get by using the most common and popular ones.

GLYPHOSATE—"I'll KILL THEM ALL."

At the end of the movie *John Wick: Chapter 2*, after Winston tells John his life is in "forfeit," Jonathan replies, "Winston, tell them. Tell them all. Whoever comes, whoever they are, I will kill them. I will kill them all." With a smirk, Winston replies, "'Course you will." Departing farewells ensue, "Winston." "Jonathan."

That is the type of John Wick philosophy that food plotters, a.k.a. plotheads, should embrace when weeds threaten to kill their food plots. The best herbicide choice to kill grasses, sedges, broadleaves, and other types of weeds down to their roots, will be to 'kill them all' using *glyphosate,* and *not* John Wick's Kimber 1911 .45 ACP.

Glyphosate is the main component of Roundup® and is *the* most used herbicide when planting food plots. It is a *non-selective* herbicide, which means it is meant to kill any plant it comes in contact with. Roundup®, FarmWorks, Big-N'-Tuff®, and many other generic glyphosate herbicides include surfactants. Surfactants are a helpful supplemental adjuvant (a surfactant is any substance within herbicides to improve herbicidal activity or application characteristics). They are added to herbicides to break the surface tension of the herbicide and leaf surface, so the herbicide kills the target plant more effectively. Brand name and generic glyphosates have surfactants in their formulations. Most generic brands cost less than noted brands and they work equally well.

Glyphosate is a viable choice for killing the existing unwanted vegetation in a food plot *prior* to planting the plot. Glyphosate is a systemic herbicide, meaning it is absorbed by the plant leaves and carried to the root system, thereby killing the entire plant. The weeds must be a few inches tall prior to killing them. If glyphosate does not contact the leaves, stem, and other parts of the plant, it will not kill it. Glyphosate does not remain active on bare soil, so it will *not* prevent new weeds under the surface from germinating and emerging.

After spraying weeds, read the directions regarding how long to wait before planting the plot. It is generally seven to ten days, but check to be sure. Killing the weeds will allow the seeds you plant to germinate and

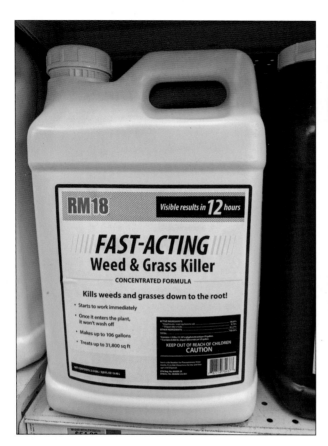

▲ Glyphosate is termed a broad-spectrum systemic herbicide and drying agent. It is a phosphonate (organic molecules related to phosphorus). It is generally used to kill weeds like broadleaf weeds and grasses. Photo–PCFImages

▲ Dow AgroSciences LLC developed genetically modified crops to withstand heavy exposure to 2,4-D. It kills plants by triggering the cells in the tissues to divide and grow without stopping. Herbicides that do this are called auxin-type herbicides. Photo: PCFImages

get a jump on any new weeds. Once the plants grow at least six inches, they can shade out slower emerging weeds. This process will provide a food plot that is mostly weed free.

Glyphosate is also well-liked because it can be used on Roundup® Ready (RR) crops. Some of these crops include Roundup® Ready corn and soybeans. Roundup Ready® plantings allow managers to spray glyphosate directly over the growing corn or soybeans, killing the surrounding weeds and not harming the soybeans or corn. Make sure, however, the bag of corn or soybeans clearly states they are Roundup Ready® varieties.

THE TROUBLESOME BROADLEAVES

2,4-D Herbicide
Persistent *broadleaf* weeds and grasses can quickly alter a lush food plot into a plot dominated by broadleaves. In grass family plots of cereal rye, oats, triticale, wheat, barley, Wild Game Food (WGF) grain sorghum, or corn, and there is a broadleaf weed issue, then 2,4-D is the right herbicide choice. Other brand names for 2,4-D include, Butoxone® 200, and Butyrac® 200, 2–4-D. A popular herbicide to use with the above grains is called Deadbolt®. This is another post emergent herbicide for broadleaves in plots of wheat, barley, oats, rye, and triticale.

At this point most novice food plotters may be asking, "Hey, wait a minute here. What the heck is he talking about? Those are all grains, not grasses." Well, the long and short of it is this: A corn stalk and cob of corn certainly do not look like a green grass, but corn is a member of the grass family. Furthermore, the same holds true for oats, barley, rye, wheat, WGF grain sorghum, and triticale, all of which are considered annual or perennial grasses by botanists and biologists. I know; go figure.

The herbicide 2,4-D is a common selective herbicide that specifically targets and controls broadleaf weeds without harming grasses (including small and large grains). That is only true, however, when it is used exactly as the label states, which as mentioned already, holds true when using any herbicide. The herbicide 2,4-D can be bought from many farm supplies stores, like Tractor Supply, Agway, and others. Like the other herbicides, 2,4-D is a systemic herbicide. The broadleaves should be actively growing and at least a few inches tall (not higher) before they are sprayed. While 2,4-D breaks down relatively quickly, it can remain active in the soil for one to four weeks. Keep that in mind when using it.

2,4-DB Herbicide

Do not confuse 2,4-D with 2,4-DB (a.k.a. Butyrac™). The "B" is important. While it is like 2,4-D, there is a vital distinction: 2,4-DB will not eliminate certain legumes species of clover and alfalfa when applied. This makes it a terrific choice for controlling broadleaf weeds in plots of pure or mixed stands of clovers. It will also work equally well when used in mixed stands of clovers and cereal grains. Do not use 2,4-DB if the mix contains brassicas, chicory, or other broadleaf forbs, as they will likely be damaged or killed.

Sethoxydim Herbicide

Sethoxydim herbicide is commonly known by the trade name Poast® but is also sold under an assortment of other names: Over-The-Top II Grass Killer, Poast® Plus, Vantage®, and Sethoxydim G-Pro. Unlike glyphosate, sethoxydim is a selective herbicide. It only affects specific weeds. Sethoxydim targets grasses. It will not kill broadleaf plants. Like other systemic herbicides, it must be sprayed on young growing grass weeds about three inches or so. Always read the label for proper suggested heights. Sethoxydim does not remain active in the soil after spraying. It is commonly used to control grasses in food plots of legumes and brassicas.

Clethodim Herbicide

Clethodim is also like sethoxydim because it too is a grass-specific, selective herbicide. Its more popular brand names include Whitetail Institute Arrest Max™, Arrow®, and Select®. It functions in the same way

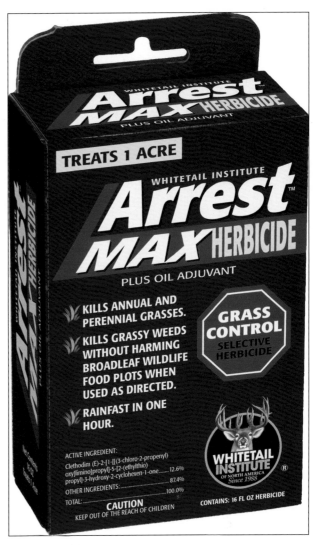

◄ Arrest Max™ is a selective grass herbicide. It controls a wide range of annual and perennial grasses. By spraying grasses in their early growth stage, it can eliminate follow-up herbicide applications. Arrest Max is said to work within an hour and is rain-fast in an hour as well. Photo: Whitetail Institute

sethoxydim does. Some say clethodim appears to do a better job of controlling the dreaded johnsongrass, which is considered among the world's ten worst weeds!

Both sethoxydim and clethodim are known to be slow herbicide killers. It can take up to several weeks for them to entirely kill the grasses in a food plot. So, do not become frustrated if you don't see quick obvious results within a week or so. Be patient—they will do the job.

NOT EVERYTHING COMES UP ROSES

After applying any herbicide, there can be a multitude of unintended herbicide effects on wildlife food plots. For example, generally after eight to ten days after spraying either Clethodim or Butyrac® 200 on a clover plot, you might see some clover leaves starting to wilt. Herbicide damage does happen at times. The most usual form of herbicide damage in both corn and soybeans is known as "yellow flash." Glyphosate can suppress the formation of nitrogen nodules, resulting in a shrinkage in nitrogen and in the yield of the plot. The worst result from herbicide damage is that your food plots can possibly experience a drop in nutrients, protein levels, and production, all important elements deer seek out in plantings. Therefore, it is critical to apply herbicides correctly to avoid the above pitfalls.

Controlling weeds in food plots is an age-old problem. This issue often needs a multi-layered approach to help food plotters gain the best results from their plantings. The key is to know the nuisance weeds that are common on your land and have a strategic plan of attack ready to go when the issue of weeds arises. While the herbicides mentioned above will help to manage a lot of customary food plot weed problems, there are countless other herbicide options to consider. And I can't repeat this enough: when applying herbicides, always follow the recommended rates, application directions, and all safety guidelines *exactly* as written on the herbicide label.

APPLYING HERBICIDES

One way to get a large tract of land (like 5 or more acres of corn or soybeans) free of weeds is to hire a spray truck from a local ag-store, farm supply, or co-op. The truck usually has long boom-arms for dispensing the herbicide over a wide area. It will cost more than doing it yourself, but it will save a lot of time, work, and effort on your part. A more affordable way is to spray the weeds yourself. This is particularly the case for smaller food plots. Some food plotters only plant an acre or two. In this case, it is feasible to spray herbicide yourself and save some money. For small plots of a half-acre or less, a backpack sprayer will do the job nicely too.

Whether you are planting a couple of acres or several acres, I highly recommend a fifty-gallon trailer sprayer

▲ The herbicide being sprayed over the white clover and chicory is a selective grass herbicide. A spray tank low to the ground and with long boom arms allows more herbicide to reach the weed plants being killed. Photo: PCFImages

that attaches to an ATV. Trailer sprayers have bars that are close to the ground, enabling the herbicide to effectively saturate the weeds and kill them. When buying sprayers, look for the ones that have the longest retractable bars. The longer the bars, the faster you will be able to cut time off this task. A particularly critical point about using sprayers is to calibrate them. If you skip this vital process, you won't be able to manage your weeds effectively. As a safety precaution, always wear a long-sleeved shirt, safety glasses, work gloves and a respirator mask when spraying herbicides.

NOT ALL WEEDS ARE EVIL

Not all weeds are totally bad. In fact, some are edible for both deer and humans. For example, the broad leaf plantain is chock full of protein, and the dandelion is considered one of the healthiest and most versatile weeds on earth; the entire plant is edible. Eating dandelion leaves is like taking vitamin pills, as they contain copious amounts of vitamins A, C, and K. Purslane is another weed that is said to be not only tasty, but also tops the list of plants containing Omega-3 fatty acids, the healthy fat found in salmon. Lamb's quarters (a.k.a. goosefoot) is like spinach, except it is healthier and tastier than spinach. Or at least that's what is said—I haven't tried eating them. However, it is highly recommended to not eat any dying, dead, or diseased-looking leaves on Lamb's quarters. So, if weeds are edible to humans, it isn't farfetched that many more weeds are edible and even healthy for deer to eat.

▲ Goldenrod is often considered a weed, but it is natural browse for deer. It is low in nutrients, but deer eat it. In fact, during a year, it makes up a significant portion of a deer's diet. Again, not all weeds are evil. Goldenrod can be an extremely invasive plant. Photo: ernstseed.com

Therefore, it should be noted that not every weed has to be eradicated from your land. Many weeds are a principal element within a deer's overall diet. Some weeds that deer regularly consume include giant ragweed and pigweed. Pigweed is a weed that deer eat, particularly in the summer. That is why educating yourself about the native weeds on your property is vital.

Deer feed four to six times per day (every four to six hours), actively seeking out a wide variety of food sources. Recent studies have documented deer eat more than 600 distinct species of plants. Some of these plants are weeds. Deer also eat sumac and poison oak. My point is, while weeds are evil in a food plot, some weeds do play a vital role in a deer's diet, making them an important food source, if they are only growing outside of your food plot plantings, however.

CONCLUSION

Eradicating or even reducing weed problems in food plots is a never-ending battle. It is not an easy problem to control, especially without the proper use of herbicides. You can get an upper hand on weed management by mowing. However, there is no doubt that the proper and safe use of chemicals is by far the most effective way to eliminate or severely reduce weeds in food plots. Be forewarned again, though, that it is essential to completely understand what each type of

herbicide is best to apply on the distinct types of weeds you are meaning to kill. No matter what type of weed, grass, broadleaf, etc., you want to eliminate, there is a chemical made to kill it.

▲ Always, and I mean always, read the entire label on all herbicides. It will help in understanding how to use it correctly and provide the user with vital safety information. Photo: PCFImages

Important Closing Note: Using herbicides requires a serious understanding of how to use chemical herbicides safely and effectively. Therefore, the instructions on the labels should *always* be read carefully and they should *never* be ignored.

Warning: Food plot managers should never plan to plant fruit or nut trees anywhere near traditional food plots. When herbicides are used to control weeds in crops like RR corn, soybeans, etc., just the slightest drift of herbicide carried in the air will kill nearby fruit or nut trees, especially young trees, lickety-split. Instead, plant trees ONLY in herbicide-free zones.

▲ Occasionally rotating crops is a good farming practice. When it comes to planting brassicas, though, rotate them yearly. Credit: © Michael Males | Dreamstime

Chapter Twelve

The Importance of Crop Rotation

No matter what management advice or tips you have read or heard about for improving your food plot program, it's hard to beat crop rotation as a management practice. According to Merriam-Webster's dictionary, crop rotation is "the practice of growing different crops in succession on the same land chiefly to preserve the productive capacity of the soil."

HISTORY OF CROP ROTATION

Agriculturalists have long recognized crop rotations like planting spring crops in place of grains, made it possible to restore nutrients to maintain productive soil. Ancient Egyptians, however, practiced crop rotation in 6,000 B.C., probably without ever really understanding the chemistry behind crop rotation but using it to improve their harvests. Crop rotation is even mentioned in the Bible. In Chapter 25 of the Book of Leviticus, the Israelites are told to heed the *"Sabbath of the Land":* every seventh year, they should not plow, prune, or even manage the insects.

Rotating crops significantly helps to improve soil structure and nutrient levels. Another practice called "deep root shallow root" is also used when alternating between crops. One season a plot is seeded with plants that have deep root systems (like forage radish or alfalfa) and the following year it is seeded with plants that have shallow root systems (like white clovers). Another example of crop rotation is if you were to plant a food plot of corn, which draws a lot of nitrogen from the soil, the following year you should plant beans or other legumes that will put nitrogen back into the soil.

Another important reason for crop rotation from one year to another is to deter diseases and soil-borne insects, parasitic nematodes, weeds, and plant

▲ Crop rotation is an important element in any wildlife food plot program. It should not be ignored, particularly when rotating crops of brassicas. Credit: Fiduccia Ent.

pathogens from getting a foothold in soils. Moreover, if crops are not rotated, insect pests that feed on a crop and spend their larval state in the soil become more abundant because their food source remains available to them. Each following year, the pests become harder to manage as their population increases, sometimes exponentially. In the end, they must be eliminated for the soil to recover.

Additionally, when certain crops are planted in the same piece of ground year after year, the soil structure begins to slowly deteriorate because the same nutrients are being used repeatedly. All the soil's nutrients have been drawn out of the soil. After a few years, the soil becomes unhealthy because it has been depleted of specific nutrients. Rotations are an important part of any sustainable food plot program. Yields of crops grown in rotations are typically 10 percent higher than those of crops grown in single crops in normal growing seasons and are much higher in droughty growing seasons.

There is another option other than replanting the plot with a new type of seed to restore the nutrients the soil has lost. It can be left fallow for a time. Fallow ground (a.k.a. unsown, unplanted, or dormant) is the farming word used to describe any idle soil. By leaving the plot fallow, the soil's nutrients will begin to get restored and the soil will become more fertile ground again. The option of leaving a plot unsown for a while will enable a food plotter to gain most of the traditional crop rotation methods of planting the plot with another type of seed, which will restore nitrogen and other minerals back into the soil from the new planting.

WHEN TO ROTATE CROPS

Ascertaining if a crop rotation is called for is rather a straightforward basic process. It generally begins when the crop that is currently growing in the plot isn't performing as it has in the past. It isn't as tall, it doesn't look as green, and the crop might start to look spindly. This can be evident even if you have made pH adjustments, fertilized, and limed the plot. You will also notice the leaves of the current crop don't look as healthy as they used to. Another way to determine if the present crop needs to be rotated is to pull up a few plants with their roots and inspect them. It should be easy to see if there is any disease or insect problems. The roots should feel firm and look fleshy. There will, however, be some root decay even in a healthy stand. But if most or all the plants examined show signs of root problems, then it is time to rotate the plot and sow an entirely different plant variety for at least one season.

WHAT TO SOW

When you have determined it is time for a food plot crop to be rotated, begin by selecting the forage you want to replace the old planting with. When it comes to forages for revitalizing the soil, choose wisely. If the old planting drew nitrogen from the soil, sow the plot with plants that contribute high contents of nitrogen back into the soil. A terrific way to rotate a perennial legume field such as clover or alfalfa that is beginning to get thin and has run its course is to plant heavy nitrogen-loving plants like corn, cereal grains,

▲ The time to rotate a crop is easy to determine. One sign is when the current crop isn't performing up to par. Other red flags are when the plant looks pale green or is stunted. Photo: © Lightpoet | Dreamstime

or brassicas behind it. The nitrogen that is available on the root nodules of the decaying legume will be a great fertilizer for the new crop. The nitrogen left behind by the legume is available in a natural, time-released state and provides a slow and steady supply through the growing season.

BRASSICAS

When it comes to brassicas, it is highly recommended they not be planted in the same food plot more than one or two years in a row, without rotating the plot. Once the plot shows signs of needing to be rotated, the brassicas will begin to turn purple or burgundy. This usually happens because of a few important reasons. First, the plot was likely over-seeded. Second, the plants are showing signs of soil deficiencies or insect infestation. Third, the burgundy-colored plants may also be indicating a lack of phosphorus. Should this happen to your brassicas, consider planting buckwheat as a follow-up crop. Buckwheat has an excellent "rotational effect." Root residues make phosphorus more available to the follow-up crop, and they also return considerable levels of phosphorus to the soil. This is a classic example of how crop rotation works to enhance your overall food plot program.

To revitalize brassicas, or what is often referred to as "cleaning" the soil, the best course of action is to sow the plot with an entirely new forage seed. This can include any clovers or other legumes that will provide high protein and fix nitrogen in the soil. Legume choices include Austrian winter pea, burgundy bean, cowpeas, Lablab, and soybeans. Many mixed seed plantings from companies like Antler King, Frigid Forage, Mossy Oak's BioLogic, and Whitetail Institute offer plantings that have these types of mixed legumes.

BENEFITS OF CROP ROTATIONS

Implementing a crop rotation management plan in your food plot program, no matter if your plan is 1 acre or 100 acres, will enhance your food plot soil's nutrition, as well as improve the soil's ability to grow healthier crops that harbor fewer insects. Other benefits include:

- Improved crop yields
- Improved workability of the soil
- Reduced soil crusting
- Increased water availability for plants
- Reduced erosion and sedimentation
- Recycled plant nutrients in the soil
- Reduced fertilizer & insecticide inputs

▲ This image depicts fields grown in strip crops. The pathogens and pests that can build up in the soil when crops are not rotated can be decreased quickly by planting even strip crops from different plant families that have different nutrient needs and systematic make-up. Photo: © Martingraf | Dreamstime

▲ With the proper nutrients, minerals, plantings, and deer management, growing bucks like this one can be achievable for dedicated food plotters. Credit: © Michael Males | Dreamstime

Chapter Thirteen

Frost Seeding

The definition of the term frost seeding is as basic as it can be. It's a down-to-earth, real-world seeding practice. Essentially, frost seeding is a quick and economical method of creating a new or improving an existing food plot by broadcasting the seed on frozen bare ground or over a one-half to three-quarters of an inch of snow cover. In the North, it is best done in mid-March but can be done later if the ground is frozen. In the South, it can be done if, and when, the ground is frozen prior to spring. As the ground freezes and thaws, it opens and closes, allowing the seeds to fall into tiny cracks in the soil. This keeps the seeds from germinating until there is an ample moisture supply in early spring. The process provides the planting with particularly good seed-to-soil contact.

To some food plotters, the term frost seeding is an alien term that sends chills down their spines. However, frost seeding is an age-old farming practice. Basically, it's Mother Nature's way of getting her Old Man Winter to help food plotters to reduce the amount of planting work they do in late spring and summer. The best time to begin frost seeding is solely dependent on where you live. The ideal time to frost seed, however, is in early spring.

NEW SITE SELECTION LOCATIONS

When it comes to successful frost seeding of new plots, it is important to select the best locations for plot sites. Basically, that means staying away from areas that present a high possibility of runoff from melting snow or rain that will wash seed away. For example, slightly sloped plots are a better choice than fields with high sloped sides. Essentially, you want to avoid frost seeding any area that can have substantial runoff and/or collect standing water. Even plots on mostly level ground should be carefully selected to make sure they don't have deep dips, low places, or poor drainage within them that will collect puddles of water.

▲ Ideally, the best method to frost seed is over frozen bare soil. The heave-and-ho of the ground will set the seed below the surface. Seeds will sprout as soon as ground temperatures warm up in the spring. Photo: PCFImages

A little caution goes a long way, because one never knows how much snow or spring rain Old Man Winter and Mother Nature will send your way. The truth be told, there are many variables that can affect how successful frost seeding is in a given situation. Therefore, it is difficult and impractical to list a set of specific conditions in which frost seeding will always be successful. I tend to stick with one specific set of rules, however. Select as flat a piece of ground as is practical and that has good drainage and good soil. Frost seedings work best on loams and clay soils or other soils that have natural moisture into early summer.

EQUIPMENT

Frost seeding requires little equipment. It is often done with an ATV, a tractor and spreader, or a hand-held broadcaster like an EarthWay 2750 or similar type seeder. The equipment will depend on the size of the plot you're intending to frost seed. For larger plots, especially when the ground is frozen well enough to support a tractor without rutting up the soil, you can use a tractor and PTO-driven spreader to seed a new plot or existing plot. Medium-size plots can be done with an all-terrain vehicle (ATV) with an attached broadcast spreader. For smaller plots, another option is to puts boots to the ground using a hand-held spreader.

SELECTING SEEDS

Red, white, and some other varieties of clovers work best for frost seeding. Some ideal choices are the winter-hardy varieties like Red Marathon, Alice White, Frosty Berseem Clover (it can tolerate -14°F) or FIXatioN Balansa Clover (can tolerate 0 to 5°F). These varieties of clovers are sold pre-inoculated. Frost seeding is the best method of planting perennial clovers. These improved varieties provide better established plots. Other good legume choices include trefoils like Bulls, birdsfoot, Bruce, or Norcen. The birdsfoot trefoils mentioned have high seeding vigor and good winter hardiness, making them more conducive for good stand establishment. But don't mix trefoil with red clover. Research has shown red clover significantly reduces trefoil seed establishment.

The clovers mentioned above are more vigorous and hardier than the average red and white clovers, establish better, and last three or more years instead of two. I have planted mixed seeded stands of red and white clovers and birdsfoot trefoil in a plot we call "The Three-Acre Field." At the point of this writing the field has provided three years of top production that regularly attracts ten to twenty deer five out of seven days a week from mid-May through December. The birdsfoot

▲ The best time to frost seed is on bare frozen ground or on frozen ground that may still have thin patches of snow here and there. Frost-seeding can also work when there is one inch or less of snow. Credit: © Ansar Kyzylaliyeu | Dreamstime.com

trefoils mentioned have high seedling vigor and high winter hardiness making them more conducive for good stand establishment.

Other seeds that can be frost seeded include cool-season legumes such as alfalfa, chicory, and cool-season annuals like oats, rye, wheat, and other small grains. When frost seeding, use the recommended broadcast seeding rate for each of the crops you are planting. Chicory should be the last seed to frost plant as it likes warmer soil temperatures as soon as they become available. I try to seed it at the end of March to mid-April. I live in upstate New York, and at that time of year we may still have some frozen ground—but not for much longer than that. Chicory will get a jump start on upcoming weeds when frost seeded. That alone will enable the chicory to establish itself much better than planting it in spring or later. It also enables a food plotter to fertilize the plot earlier. I like frost seeding a stand-alone plot of pure chicory. But it can also be frost seeded with red and white clovers and even a mix of clovers, small grains, and a brassica. For me, though, a pure stand of frost-seeded chicory is magical.

Seeding Practice. Broadcast only inoculated clover seed and trefoil on bare frozen ground before spring grass begins to thaw. Because of the location and elevation of our farm, we have found that it is okay to frost seed on a shallow snow cover, about one-half-inch deep. A benefit to broadcasting over snow allows you to easily see where you have spread your seeds,

▲ One advantage of frost seeding over snow is that it is much easier to sow the seed. That helps in not missing any spots. Photo: PCFImages.

▲ The author frost seeds on frozen ground that still has thin patches snow here and there. Credit: © Ansar Kyzylaliyeu | Dreamstime.com

therefore helping you to avoid missing spots in the spreading pattern. Snow, along with the later frosts, also considerably aids to settle the seed into the cracks of the soil. Don't broadcast on a snow that is a few inches or more deep. You take a risk that a sudden fast thaw can cause a significant run-off, and that event will thoroughly wash your broadcasted seed away.

If the conditions are ideal, a light covering of snow (one-half inch or less) on frozen ground will allow for good heaving of soil; especially if you are broadcasting a stand-alone (pure) plot of Marathon Red clover, use about six to seven pounds per acre. If the snow is absent and you are broadcasting the seed over frozen bare ground, use about eight to nine pounds per acre. White clover should be seeded at a rate much lower than red clover. Generally, it is recommended to only broadcast two to four pounds/acre. On frozen bare ground, you could raise that rate to three to five pounds/acre.

Fertilization Practice. Generally, wait until the snow has melted, the ground is not frozen, and the seed has germinated and has grown to a couple of inches in height before fertilizing the plot. It is also advisable to wait until you know there will be a predicted rainfall before fertilizing. Fertilize with T 19–19–19 at 350 to 400 lbs./acre.

CONCLUSION

Frost seeding should be a more popular planting technique method than it is among plotheads. It will significantly improve the long-term life of clovers and other plots. It is also a terrific method of rejuvenating old plots post-haste. Frost seeding is also very inexpensive and, when done correctly, it has an excellent rate of success. Frost seeding will improve any wildlife manager's food plot plan. Try it. I think you will like the results.

SOME FROST SEEDING BENEFITS

- Cost of frost seeding is relatively low compared to traditional seeding methods.
- The ability to plant a forage in a plot without disking.
- Reduces time, labor, and energy during spring and summer plantings.
- Excellent method to enhance a spotty food plot.
- Terrific way to give a shot in the arm to a clover plot that has become worn-out over time.
- Reduces herbicide cost, labor, and need, as plantings usually get a jump start over weeds.
- Enables deer to begin feeding in plots earlier in spring.
- Provides female deer with high protein levels prior to dropping their fawns.

▲ Ensure that any variety of clover and/or other types of legumes are inoculated. Planting without the proper live bacteria strain for each particular plant will result in a poorly growing crop. Or, even crop failure. Credit: © Mikael Males | Dreamstime

Chapter Fourteen

Inoculants—What Are They Good For?

If you are a fan of the television series *Seinfeld*, you may recall that in the seventy-eighth episode, "The Marine Biologist," Jerry jokingly says to Elaine that the novel *War and Peace* was originally called *War: What Is it Good For?* Later in the episode, Elaine shares that information with a noted Russian writer, Yuri Testikov. Her comments to Testikov cause a hullabaloo between Elaine, Mr. Lipman (her publishing boss), and Testikov. The Russian author promptly digresses into a frenzied tirade about the nonsensical title *War: What is it Good For?*

▲ *Seinfeld* was unquestionably one of the best sitcoms ever produced. I borrowed a part of a line from episode No. seventy-eight, replacing the word "war" with the word inoculants, for the title of this chapter. Photo: EW

I have always wanted to use "what is it good for" as a chapter title in one of my books. Mission accomplished. But what is it good for?

When it comes to inoculating seeds, "what is it good for" is an important question. Merriam Webster defines inoculation of clovers and other legumes as "the inoculation of legume seeds with a specific culture of bacteria that multiply in the roots of a legume plant forming nodules where the bacteria fix atmospheric nitrogen for the nutrition of the plant." Clovers and other legumes convert atmospheric nitrogen to usable ammonia nitrogen for the plant. Inoculation is the method of introducing commercially prepared rhizobia bacteria into the soil. Each specific clover or legume species needs a type of rhizobia to form nodules and fix nitrogen. An inoculant in finely ground peat moss acts as a transport agent for the Rhizobium bacteria. Inoculants that include an adhesive to hold it to the seed are better than inoculants without an adhesive. The adhesive helps to keep the bacteria alive in dry soil. Clover seed inoculation is especially important when a clover or other legume species is planted in a new area.

Clovers and other legumes require inoculation to achieve their best growth. Among wildlife food plot plants, the clovers and other legumes are well known for being able to obtain nitrogen from three sources: the atmosphere via biological nitrogen fixation (BNF), the soil, and from fertilizers. Food plotters who can maximize the amount of nitrogen plants draw from the air will be able to reduce the amount of fertilizer they need to buy.

Once again, symbiosis comes to the forefront. Clovers and legumes have the capability to form a symbiotic relationship with rhizobia bacteria to change atmospheric nitrogen gas to ammonia nitrogen, a form which they use. This takes place in special root tissues termed nodules. Therefore, nitrogen fertilizer is generally not needed. Nitrogen-fixing bacteria are also found naturally in soil in microorganisms called diazotrophs.

▲ There are numerous types of inoculants. Each is developed to explicitly inoculate specific types of plants. Photo: PCFImages

I refer to clovers and other legumes as such, because even though they are different in some ways, they both belong to the family *Fabaceae*. Legumes, whether they are annuals, biennials, or perennials, are plants that contain one to several or more seed pods which split open. There are more than 300 clovers called Trifolium or trefoil. All clovers typically have leaves that have three leaflets on them.

Additionally, for the purpose of wildlife food plots, most clovers are grown as forages for wildlife. Most legumes are generally grown for agricultural purposes. Therein lies the differences of clovers compared to legumes and why I generally refer to both as "clovers and other legumes," even though the term legumes is meant to cover clovers as well. I feel that lumping clovers and legumes together can be a bit confusing, particularly to novice food plotters.

To assure that an adequate amount of Rhizobium bacteria is present in the soil to benefit the crop, a food plot manager should apply different inoculants to different legumes and clover seeds before planting. This step is not necessary when a seed is pre-inoculated. When acquiring inoculants, it is important to know that the symbiotic relationship between legumes and Rhizobium bacteria is specific. Although most Rhizobium bacteria will work with most clovers and legumes, if optimum nitrogen production is desired, the selected plants should be inoculated with specific Rhizobium bacteria. The number of nodules present on the root system is related to the amount of nitrogen fixation that occurs. The greater the number of nodules, the greater the potential for nitrogen fixation.

Nearly all clover seed can be purchased pre-inoculated. There are some instances when the seed is not inoculated. Not to worry. The process of inoculating seed is not difficult. However, it needs to be done correctly for the inoculant to work as it is meant to. Should the inoculation be done improperly, the plants will not grow to their fullest capability.

There are many different companies that offer inoculants, but they will all have virtually the same species of inoculants for certain types of legumes and clovers. Always follow the manufacturer's recommendations regarding the special strain of Rhizobium bacteria and the amount to be added to the clovers or other legume

seed. The inoculant package will list the appropriate plant species. Due to the different formulations and carriers used in developing the inoculant, each manufacturer has a different requirement for the amount needed.

▲ Exceed Superior Legume Inoculant is used to improve legume yields. The inoculant helps the plants convert nitrogen in the air into a usable form for the plant, allowing the plants to create their own fertilizer. Credit: Fiduccia Ent.

There are many distinct types of inoculants. N-Dure™ is one of the most economical inoculants on the market to improve a plant's nitrogen intake. N-Take™ is a premium liquid inoculant for legumes that improves their nitrogen uptake. Prevail™ is a true clover inoculant that contains a blend of beneficial rhizobia that are specific to certain plant species, like alfalfa. Trifolium Spec 3, WR Strain, Trifolium incarnatum, Trifolium subterraneum, Trifolium resupinatum, and Trifolium repens are yet other types of specific inoculants.

Listed below are some of the more popular legumes and clovers and their designated inoculants. Fortunately, most clovers also come pre-inoculated. Some do not. So, it is wise to ask if the clover you are buying is pre-inoculated. If it does not come pre-inoculated, ask what proper strain Rhizobacteria should be used. In the list below, pre-inoculated clovers are designated as such. However, all pre-inoculated seed does not always come marked.

PROPER INOCULANT RHIZOBACTERIA STRAINS—LEGUMES
Name: Inoculant Type
Alfalfa: A (or PreVail™)
American Jointvetch: Strain EL
Austrian Winter Pea: Strain C or EL
Birdsfoot Trefoil: Strain K
Burgundy Bean: Sold Pre-Inoculated and Coated
Cowpeas: Strain EL
Crownvetch: Strain N-Dure
Hairy Vetch: Strain C (all three other vetches also take Strain C)
LabLab: Strain EL
Lupines: Strain H
Soybean, wildlife: Strain S
Sunn Hemp Strain EL
Sweetclover: Strain A

PROPER INOCULANT RHIZOBACTERIA STRAINS—CLOVERS
Name: Inoculant Type
Alsike: Strain B
Arrowleaf: Strain O
Crimson: Strain R
Kura Strain: Trifolium Spec 3
Ladino Clover: Strain B
Durana White Clover: Strain B
Red Clover: Strain B
Subterranean Clover: WR Stain
Alice Clover: EL
Sainfoin Strain: F
Alyce Strain: EL
Crimson Strain: R
Common Lespedeza, Korean Lespedeza: EL (all other 5 species of Lespedeza are also EL)

▲ There are three colors of lupine blue, yellow, and white. White is the most winter-hardy, but Sweet Blue lupine is low in alkaloid and is recommended for deer and wild turkey. Lupines must be inoculated to grow best. At planting, inoculate lupines with Rhizobium bacteria (Strain H). Photo: H. Hickman

INOCULANT APPLICATION METHODS

Inoculants are available in three forms: dry, granular, or liquid. It is critical that the inoculant adheres to the seed. If not, the entire process may be useless.

The Slurry Method

The inoculant is mixed with a liquid sticker. The resulting slurry is mixed with the seed. Immediately after coating the seed with the mixture, spread the seed out on a clean, dry tarp and allow it to dry in a cool, shady area before planting. This method is generally considered to be the most effective.

▲ For best results, it is important when mixing inoculant with seed to make sure the inoculant sticks to the seeds. Photo: PCFImages

Dry Sprinkle Technique

A dry inoculant is sprinkled over the seed and thoroughly mixed in a container or seed hopper. This may be a quick way to inoculate seed, but it is not considered as effective as the slurry method because the inoculant does not adhere as well to the seed.

Stickers

A commercial "sticker" should be used to stick the inoculant to the seed. Some sticking agents contain gum Arabic, which is recommended for its ability to hold high numbers of bacteria onto the seed. Homemade stickers can be created with 10- to 20-percent solutions made from gums and/or sugars that are mixed with water. Some people have used soda or pop as a sticker. However, this may not be the best method, dependent upon the type of bacteria. The reason why you may not want to use cola or soda pop as a sticker is because the pH in most soft drinks is low and the acid solution may kill the bacteria.

I strongly recommend eliminating that homemade method and instead suggest buying any of the commercially made sticker products that are available on most seed company websites. Tacky products like stickers help the inoculant attach itself firmly onto the seed, ensuring that the inoculant remains on the seed before planting it.

EXPIRATION

Inoculants have a shelf life. The expiration date will be on the package. If they are not going to be used within

▲ New or leftover inoculants can be stored in a refrigerator at a temperature of 39°F. They will remain effective at that temperature for several months. Photo: PCFImages

a reasonable time, it is best to keep them refrigerated until you are ready to use them. However, they cannot be kept for extended periods of time in a refrigerator. For instance, soybeans should never be inoculated more than four days before they are ready to be planted. Soybean inoculant has a short shelf life. Once oxygen contacts the inoculant, it will only last a few days. Many inoculants require the seeds to be planted as soon as possible after the inoculant is applied.

INOCULANT/SEED MIXING METHODS

Always mix seed and inoculant in a shady area. One way to mix the inoculant and seed is to use a small, clean (spotlessly clean) cement mixer. It is an efficient and effective technique to mix inoculants and seed. But be practical. If the mixer is dirty, you'll waste a lot of time and money, as it will not provide the clean environment needed to inoculate seed. Another more practical method is to use a clean five-gallon plastic bucket. Place the seed inside the pail, add your inoculant as directed, and thoroughly mix the two together. After mixing, place the seed on a clean drop cloth or plastic tarp in the shade. Spread the seed out evenly across it and let the inoculant dry.

CAUTION

The Rhizobia bacteria in commercial inoculants are living organisms. They should not be exposed to heat, direct sunlight, excessive moisture, or other adverse conditions. Never leave a package of inoculant

▲ The best way to make sure the inoculant adheres to the seed properly is to use a commercial type "sticker." Here, I am making a slurry-type sticker. Photo: PCFImages

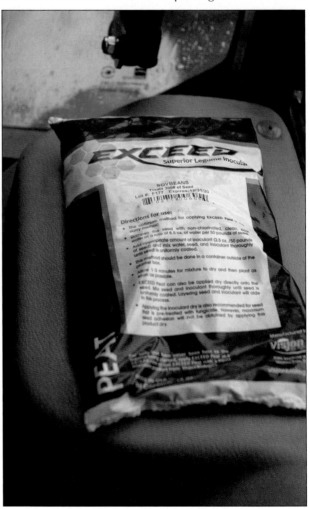

▲ N-Dure™ is one of the most economical seed inoculants on the market for obtaining nitrogen fixation. But that does not mean you should leave it on the dashboard of the tractor instead of refrigerating it. Photo: PCFImages

(Rhizobia bacteria) on anything that is hot—including the dashboard of a tractor, ATV, or any warm or hot surface while getting seed ready to inoculate. These types of conditions can create excessive heat rather quickly and the heat will be harmful to the Rhizobia in the inoculant. To safeguard the maximum effectiveness of the inoculant, keep it in a shady area until you are going to mix it. If it was kept in the refrigerator, remove it, and let it acclimate to the temperature of the place where it will be mixed with the seed.

Again, you can't leave inoculants for extended periods in the refrigerator, as they are living organisms. It is as harmful as letting the inoculant become too hot. Some seed companies say you can store inoculants for about six months, others say for one planting season (about three months), and still others recommend shorter periods than that.

▲ To achieve the best growth for all clovers and other legumes, they must be inoculated with the proper strain rhizobium bacteria prior to planting in order to fix atmospheric nitrogen. Photo: PCFImages

▲ Small secretive food plots, particularly those in suburban areas, are sure bets to attract adult bucks. Credit: Ted Rose

Chapter Fifteen

Small Plots—Big Dividends

During a crossbow hunt a few years ago, I was comfortably sitting in an enclosed blind called Big View that was near a half-acre plot of kale. The temperature was in the low teens, so I thought about turning on the heater, when a sixth sense told me to check the surrounding area first. I began to look over the edges of the woods and didn't see anything. I glanced at my watch. It was 11:00 a.m. As I turned my head, I caught movement from a lower secluded field called Finger Field. I studied the spot intensely and within a few seconds I could make out the antlers of a buck. Seconds later, I saw its head and neck. The buck was standing motionless at the very edge of the brush in that field.

It was Tuesday, November 14, 2017, and the big chase phase of the rut was at its apex. Earlier that morning I saw several bucks chasing does in the surrounding woods and through the fields. For several minutes, the buck remained frozen in place with its entire body hidden in a thicket. Then, as if the buck were checking traffic before crossing a street, he lifted his head, lip-curled (flehmen), then turned his head quickly from one side to the other—twice. He was obviously making an olfactory and visual assessment

▲ This photo is representative of my description of the happenings on the opening morning of New York's regular 2017 firearm season. Photo: © Mikael Males | Dreamstime

to see if there was an estrus doe in the small food plot, or if there was one that was about to enter the plot from the woods across from where he stood.

My rangefinder placed the buck at 305 yards from me—not a perfect crossbow shot, I sarcastically whispered to myself. As I glassed the buck with my binoculars, I could see it had a heavy set of 8-point antlers. "Geez Marie," I whispered. The antlers really sent my adrenaline flowing. I became more frustrated with each passing second. My annoyance grew because the buck was standing broadside about twenty-five yards from another enclosed blind called Instant Doe at the bottom of Finger Field. I had *almost* decided to hunt from Instant Doe that morning. Instead, as Murphy's Law clearly states, "Whatever can go wrong, will go wrong" came into play. Murphy, the dog that he is, sent me to Big View instead.

After a few minutes of the buck checking the food plot, it seemed as if the odor wafting from the beets and greens was more than he could take. He stepped into the small plot and began to chow down in earnest. To my surprise, a micro-second later a larger antlered buck followed him boldly into the food plot. He came into the plot from nearly the identical spot the first buck was standing in. While I was watching the first buck, the thick brush must have totally hidden the second larger antlered buck from my view. I did not get time to count his points, but during the five or so seconds that I saw him, I was reasonably sure it was a 10-pointer.

But here is the most interesting part about sighting these two adult bucks that morning. It confirmed that a small, well-concealed, easy-to-escape-from food plot can attract two adult bucks in broad daylight, without an estrus doe luring them out. Both bucks walked out of our 26-acre sanctuary and were scent checking for estrus does. When they did not see any, they stepped from cover, and it seemed as if their brains immediately switched from thinking about receptive does to food. After about fifteen minutes, without any apparent reason, both bucks zoomed back into the refuge at a warp speed of 9.9. Most likely, while they were eating, they picked up the enticing aroma of an estrus doe. If that was the case, that is all it took for them to break from the spell the food plot cast on them and to run off.

The south side of this small three-quarter-acre food plot is blocked off visually by a double row of closely

▲ Food plots like our Finger Field help deer, especially adult bucks, feel safe, secluded, and close to an escape route. They promote more daytime use even under heavy hunting pressure. Photo: PCFImages

planted twenty- to twenty-five-foot-high white pine trees. We planted them in 2008 to separate the small plot from a much larger 5-acre field to the south of the pines. The pines were specifically planted to offer total seclusion to the small field and to block the upper 5-acre field from the view of deer. The pines have worked flawlessly to that end. The three other sides of the little plot also offer ample amounts of cover. Two sides have inside corners (an inside corner is any place that has a change in terrain that offers deer cover). The remaining side is a thick stand of second-growth woods and mature pines. With all this cover, the food plot appears to be a super-secretive place for deer to feed in safety, and for bucks to locate does during the rut. All these features help to make this small plot a superlative food plot to deer, particularly skittish adult bucks. The fact is that deer instinctively know they can quickly escape to cover from any one of three sides.

SIZE DOESN'T MATTER

The point of this anecdote is this: Never believe that there is such a thing as a small food plot that would not be effective in attracting deer. As sure as you are reading this, the size of a food plot is not what is most important. Like a successful restaurant, a food plot's

▲ This is a "stopper" plot. It is only thirty-five by seventy-five feet. It was made in an area near a bog (in front of the ATV). The area is heavily used by deer. They leave the wetland and stop briefly to eat in the small plot before heading to our larger food plots. We've taken a lot of deer over this tiny plot. Photo: PCFImages

success is principally related to location, location, location. That is *the* most critical factor to a small food plot's success. But the question may arise, as to what size should a small food plot be. I like to keep many of my small food plots no smaller than one-eighth to no larger than one-half of an acre. With that said, most of my small food plots are one-quarter acre. Another factor to keep in mind is the shape of the plot. While rectangular small plots (like Lower Finger Field) work well, one that has an "S" or "L" shape or even a slight angle to it can look more inviting to a deer.

Another principal element in creating a small food plot is to place it near where you have seen buck rutting sign (like rubs or scrapes) or activity that has taken place in the past. You must also consider the type of terrain that surrounds the plot. Another point to think about is how well can the plot be made to be totally concealed from a deer's point of view. In other words,

always limit what a deer can see from a small food plot.

The next consideration, and it is an important one, is to judge how rapidly a deer can escape from the plot and back into cover. An ideal distance for a deer to escape from a small food plot is two to three "deer leaps" away. Lastly, and probably the most vital of the other elements, is the type of seed or seeds you choose to plant. Remember that summer plantings do not work for killing bucks in small plots during hunting season. Brassicas, grains, and other winter-hardy blends will draw does and bucks to them when you want them there the most, during the daylight hours of hunting season.

No matter which way you twist or turn it, small food plots are the ideal hunting plots, as they are meant to be instinctively attractive to does and bucks during the rut and into the winter. If Murphy had not interfered with my thinking processes that morning, I would have been set up in the blind overlooking that small plot and would have at least had an opportunity to take a quality shot at one of those two bucks. But as fate would have it, I did not. In fact, over the remaining crossbow season and throughout the firearm season, I never saw either buck again. But my wife Kate did. More about that story later.

DEER ARE DRIVEN BY THEIR STOMACHS

As any savvy whitetail hunter knows, find the deer's current food sources and you will find the deer. That can be a little problematic when hunting big woods. Food plots help to focus deer feeding activities; that is a fact. Small hidden plots limit the peering eyes of predators, including uninvited hunters. Small plots fit that bill perfectly. But keep in mind nothing about hunting deer is written in stone. Many adult bucks are killed in large, multi-acre, agricultural fields and food plots.

This is often the case in mornings during the rut, when bucks are winding up their nighttime patrols of cruising for estrus does. Experienced bucks, a.k.a. adult bucks, know they can locate does more readily in areas where does regularly feed. Small, secluded food plots are magnets to does seeking food in secure places. Therefore, while does are drawn to larger food plots, both does and bucks are more attracted to smaller plots that are well concealed, whether the plot is one-eighth to a half-acre or even more.

Not all concealed food plots have to be small. They can be an acre or more if the surrounding area limits a deer's view and offers thick cover for a quick escape. Concealment is *King* when it comes to food plot placement. A well-concealed food plot will improve daylight deer activity ten-fold.

Additionally, during the rut, bucks are even more instinctively drawn to cruise into a well-concealed, isolated food plot to check for does, or to scent check if any have been there. They may repeat the pattern

▲ I have found that planting clovers, or chicory, either alone or in mixes, is ideal for small food plots. It is difficult for deer not to stop and grab a few bites even when heading to a larger plot of a much more preferred planting like corn, soybeans, sugar beets, and so on. Photo: Whitetail Institute

▲ This plot is only one-hundred by fifty feet. It is in a secluded area surrounded by woods. There is a transition area behind the blind from bedding to larger food plots a few hundred yards away. Deer, especially bucks, often pause to eat in this small plot because of its feeling of security. Photo: PCFImages

a few times throughout the day. In well-hidden food plots, does figure out the safety factors quickly. Once they do, female deer will often enter smaller plots *earlier* in the afternoon and leave from them later in the mornings. During the rut, this makes bucks even more vulnerable.

The overall attractiveness rating of a food plot climbs significantly when each of the following elements is included:

- Concealment (ample surrounding cover along the plot's borders)
- Limited visibility from the deer's point-of-view (POV)
- A deer's feeling of security
- Nearby rapid escape routes alongside the plot
- Nutritious and winter-hardy plantings

These factors go a long way to drawing deer into small food plots when you want them there the most—(yup, you got it)—during the daylight hours. When any one or more of these factors are left out, the food plot's attractiveness rating drops accordingly.

LACKING COVER? NO PROBLEM

If you want to create a small food plot (or even a large one), but it doesn't offer concealment on a side or two, there are forages that many seed companies carry that will create a barrier of cover. To my knowledge, the first seed product created was Frigid Forage's "PlotScreen." Today, there are many other companies that offer cover type blends that create barriers, including Biologic's "Barrier Blend," Whitetail Institute's Imperial "Conceal," Deer Creek Seed's "Silver Screen," Antler King's "Barricade," Arrow Seed's "Green Screen," and The Cisco Companies' "Safe & Tasty" or a grass called Gigantus miscanthus. These are but a few companies that offer blends meant to provide fence-type concealment with natural forages. By planting these barrier types of seed mixtures as borders in food plots where cover is lacking, you will create a total feeling of security for deer, encouraging them to feed in the plot in daylight.

These natural forage fences can be used for a wide variety of other reasons too. They will:

- Give cover for deer along travel routes.
- Offer additional cover in funnels.

▲ Many seed companies have created mixes that grow high and thick enough to provide hunters concealment to get to their stands. This is a plot of Imperial Whitetail Conceal; many other seed companies like Antler King, Frigid Forage, and others make comparable products. Photo: Whitetail Institute

- Create deer travel corridors across open ground.
- Connect two points of woods.
- Hide hunters from deer as they go across open areas to and from stands.
- Conceal small food plots from larger food plot areas.
- Block food plots from being seen from roads.
- Keep neighbor's prying eyes off your food plots (and deer).
- Provide cover for ground stands.

At one time or another, most of us have had issues with snooping neighbors, hunters who spotlight fields, even folks who just like to stop and watch wildlife. I have had experience with this. A certain group of hunters, and I use that word guardedly, used to stop and spotlight one of my fields along the road. Their routine got so bad that it eventually led to an extremely uncomfortable and dangerous confrontation. This was before screen plots were available and I did not know about a shield-type plant called *Gigantus miscanthus*. My best choice was to put up some wooden four- by eight-foot

fencing to block the view of my field. It was costly and it took a lot of time to build.

Over the years, several repairs have had to be made to the fence—what my son and wife refer to as "The

▲ The fence at the top of the photo blocks the view of deer in the three-acre field from the road. Generally, this food plot is planted with winter rye mixed with a winter clover like Frosty Berseem or FIXatioN balansa clover. Photo: PCFImages

Great Wall of Fiduccia." After many years now, the fence has seen better days. My plan now is to use a natural fence. I want to plant two rows of the perennial *Gigantus miscanthus* with an annual natural screen planting behind the *Gigantus*. These natural screen-type fencings should be planted at least six feet wide, "Nice and thick makes for a neat fence trick."

Any of the barrier-type plantings mentioned above are a quick and easy solution to prevent the above negative issues, or to use for general hunting purposes on your property. Many of these seed products can grow ten to twelve feet high.

SMALL PLOT WINTER-HARDY PLANTINGS

Some terrific plantings that work well in any size food plot, especially in small plots, are brassicas, winter

▲ This is a warm-season small planting of cereal rye mixed with clovers. As a warm-season planting it helps divert deer from over browsing other types of food plots. Cereal rye and cool/winter-hardy clovers and chicory make excellent small stopper food plots. Photo: PCFImages

grains, winter-hardy clovers, chicory, and winter-hardy mixes. As I have mentioned, when I refer to winter-hardy plantings, I am referring to plants that are capable of providing deer nutrition from November through January and sometimes longer). See the key below for the way I define the different seasons. they are the same seeds that are often referred to by others as "cool-season" plantings. Since they are viable into late winter I have no idea why they are called cool-season instead of winter-hardy, but, eh, whatever.

Winter-hardy stand-alone or blended seed mixtures are a clever idea for any size food plot. However, they work very well in small plots too. Here are a few companies that have blended seed offerings that fill the bill as ideal plantings for small food plots. A more comprehensive list of seed companies can be found in the Food Plot Seed Company Sources appendix.

- **Antler King** offers a very cold-tolerant mix called Fall/Winter/Spring Food Plot Blend. This unique mix of fall rye and winter peas can grow six to eight inches in just ten days. It should be planted *only* in the fall. It will attract deer through January. It will still be green and provide food, energy, and protein, well after everything else is dead or dormant.
- **Frigid Forage** offers a winter-hardy blended mix of a brassica called Big-N-Beasty. It contains sugar beets, turnips, Daikon radishes, and three varieties of forage rape. According to Frigid Forage, it should be planted in late summer. Deer eat the large nutritious leaves first. When the leaves are gone, deer will paw the turnips and radishes out of even frozen ground.
- **Huntingplots.com** offers a winter-hardy blend called Ridgeline Rage to build soils, attract and feed deer for early season through late season. Ridgeline Rage is a blend of winter rye, triticale, crimson clover, radish, turnips, and other brassicas that attracts whitetails.
- **Mossy Oak's BioLogic** offers a terrific blend called Winter Bulbs & Sugar Beets, which is designed to be a late-season attraction with brassica bulbs and sugar beets. This is a combination of bulbs (roots) that can consistently attract deer.
- **Whitetail Institute** offers a wide variety of late-season mixed blends. One annual called Imperial

Winter-Greens is a proprietary blend of brassicas designed for late-season food plots and late-season hunting. It can withstand extremely cold temperatures and stands tall even under snow, so that deer will find it when everything else is either dead or buried.

Since this chapter is about the success of small plots, I must emphasize that small food plots with certain legumes can be over-browsed rather quickly. This can happen when these types of plants are sown in less than three to five acres. They should not be used in small plots. Plants like corn, or legumes like soybeans and other beans, peas, lablab, lupine, and some others, need to be planted in multi-acre sized food plots. Unless they are planted in mixes. The fact is while these plantings can get wiped out quickly in plots less than a few acres, any small food plot planting is also vulnerable to being eliminated by deer. The key for growing successful small food plots is to use plants like winter-hardy clovers including Frosty Berseem, FiXatioN Balansa, and others along with chicory and winter grains. They can better tolerate heavy browsing. However, by fencing them off, or by using a liquid deer deterrent, you will ensure they don't become over-eaten. Here are some options.

LIQUID REPELLENTS
One option to keep deer away from your small food plot while it is growing is a liquid deer repellent like

▲ This is one type of product that can be used to deter deer from over browsing your food plots. There are many other brands to choose from. Photo: Deer Out

Milorganite®. According to a study done at Warnell School of Forestry Resources at The University of Georgia, Milorganite® is a slow-release, organic fertilizer that is produced from human sewage. If using a repellent made from human poop does not appeal to you, there are other repellents to use including Deer Out®, Liquid Fence Deer and Rabbit Repellent, Deer Scram, Deer Stopper, and others. Using liquid repellents is just the first step, however, in protecting any small food plot from being eaten to the ground by deer.

FENCE OPTIONS
Physical fencing options include Buck Forage's Dr. Deer's Deer-Resistant Electric Fence System (Dr. Deer is Dr. James Kroll, not me, The Deer Doctor), PlotSaver's Deer Barrier System; and a variety of metal, poly, plastic, and electric fencing options from DeerFencing. com. Electric fencing can get expensive; however, it works very well to deter deer.

So, there you have it. Growing small food plots is not something that should be seen negatively. They

▲ Another option for preventing deer overbrowsing a food plot is to use fencing (not like the fencing I used along a road). Some options include Buck Forage's Dr. Deer's Deer Resistant Electric Fence System, PlotSaver's Deer Barrier System, or homemade fencing systems. Photo: Buck Forage

can be successful for hunters who plant food plots with limited acreage. If you pay attention to the plot's location, shape, concealment, escape routes, and, most important, the type of plants, you will have success. Remember, tiny plots can provide big results.

Oh, let me get back to the story about the two adult bucks. On opening day of firearm season, again at 11:00 a.m., a large-bodied, heavy-beamed buck chased a doe from our refuge into a section of woods called Kate's Woods. The doe left the woods through a field to the east, quickly eluding the buck who inadvertently exited the woods in the opposite direction to the west at the end of the secluded small plot in Finger Field.

Seemingly somewhat confused, he started trotting through Finger Field's food plot heading to another section of woods when Kate used a doe blat to stop him. Her 192-yard shot found the middle of his front shoulder. The buck staggered, ran off, and collapsed only 20 yards away in the woodlot.

I was hunting from the same blind (Big View) earlier that morning. At 8:00 a.m., I shot an 8-point buck that was in the same small food plot—the same one that Kate's buck would be in three hours later. My buck's antlers, however, were not nearly as large as Kate's buck's. Two bucks both killed in the same small, secluded, ¾-quarter-acre food plot, just three hours apart. Need I say more about the benefits of creating small-sized, sheltered food plots? I think not.

▲ Adult bucks feel particularly comfortable eating in small, well-concealed food plots. These types of food plots draw deer, even adult bucks, during daylight hours, like Finger Field did to Kate's buck. Photo: PCFImages

▲ All varieties of white clovers are nutritious and palatable for deer and other wildlife. They are fast-growing and offer outstanding nitrogen-fixation capabilities. Equally important, they offer excellent persistence under heavy grazing by wildlife. Credit: © Twildlife | Dreamstime

Chapter Sixteen

White Clovers

ithout question, the white, red, and other varieties of clovers are the most popular seeds sown by food plot managers for wildlife. One of the most often-asked questions about clovers, however, is what is the difference between them? Essentially, red clovers grow tall and erect, require more seed per acre, and have a shorter life cycle. Conversely, white clovers are shorter, they spread laterally, are more tenacious growers, and can reseed themselves even under persistent grazing conditions. The category often referred to as "other clovers" has distinctive features that are discussed in that grouping.

Whether clovers are planted in mixes or alone, it's hard to beat them as attractive and super nutritious wildlife crops. There are many reasons clovers are embraced by food plotters, especially since red, white, and other clovers are easy to grow and have a high-quality production value. They are well suited as forage for deer from spring into winter. They can also be sown to complement grasses like timothy,

▲ White clover is considered a bio-mass plant. It provides an abundance of tonnage even during deer season. A well-cared for plot can be three feet high. Clover like seen here can produce more than 300 lbs./acre of nitrogen. Photo: PCFImages

perennial rye grass, and Kentucky Blue grass. Or they can be terrific companion partners with white, red, and other clovers. They can also be successfully mixed with other plants including other clovers, chicory, lupines, other legumes, vetches, all small and large grains, and some brassicas. In other words, clovers are extremely versatile with most other companion plants.

Many clovers won't put a big dent in the piggy bank, as nearly all of them are quite affordable. They are abundantly available, straightforward to plant, and there is a wide variety of white, red, and other clover types to choose from. Clovers also tolerate the widest kinds of climates and flourish in the broadest types

of soils. Furthermore, when clover plots are managed properly, they can often last for a few years or longer. That is why I often say that clovers should be known as "food plotter's best friends."

What many novice food plotters may not realize about clovers is that there are various types of red, white, and other types which are bred to withstand cool, and even downright frigid, winter temperatures, and still be nutritionally sustainable to deer. Warm-season spring and summer clovers need no explanation. Clovers that are rated or referred to as cool-season are those that have adapted to climates with considerably cold temperatures. They generally thrive at temperatures of 15° to 20°F. Some will even tolerate

▲ Three of the most top-rated winter-hardy clovers were developed by GO Seed: AberLasting, FiXatioN and Frosty Berseem. GO Seed functions as a seed breeder, producer, and provider. It evaluates more than 4,000 unique lines of multiple species annually. AberLasting can endure temperatures of -4°F to -22°F, FiXatioN Balansa can tolerate temperatures of -14°F, and Frosty Berseem can withstand 5°F and lower. This photo is of Frosty Berseem. Photo: GOSeed.com

0° to -15°F. They are described as "cool-season forages" by seed companies, agronomists, biologists, and even food plot pros. To me, the term "cool-season" is misleading. In my mind's eye 15° to 20°F certainly cannot be viewed as being "cool," I think "cool"—as far as weather—would be temperatures ranging from 40° to 50°F.

On the other hand, a few seed breeders characterize some cool-season clovers as *cold-hardy* varieties. This term is somewhat more accurate, but it, too, misses the point. The clovers labeled cold-hardy can tolerate frigid winter temperatures from 14°F to -15°F. That's not just cold, it is winter-frigid cold. Again, I can't justify classifying clovers that can endure temperatures of 14°F to -15°F as just being cold-hardy. Therefore, I restricted my reference to cold-hardy clovers in this book, and instead referred to these types of clovers and other plants that tolerate negative temperatures as winter-hardy varieties. Why? Because whether you are a novice or veteran, knowing what type of clovers can be planted to be nutritionally viable to deer from October through January (depending upon what part of the country where they are sown) is a particularly key point. Knowing this, at a quick glance, you will be able to select and plant clovers you can count on being nutritious to deer during the time when you want them there the most: the colder part of the hunting season.

When it comes to all types of clovers, the long and the short of it is they are extremely versatile wildlife forages. When clover seeds are planted correctly in fertile soil and on properly prepared seed beds, they often sprout within three to five days. No matter where you live in North America, or what type of species of deer you hunt (whitetails, mule deer, blacktails, Coues, elk, moose, etc.), there are many different types of varieties of clovers to plant that will attract all species of deer.

Moreover, clovers are excellent deterrent plantings. This means they are often included with other plants to significantly reduce browsing pressure by deer on a primary plant in the plot. This is particularly true when clovers are planted alongside or with other legumes like soybeans, lupines, lablab, birdsfoot trefoil, and all types of peas.

Following are many different brands of white clovers available from seed companies. Clovers include a considerable number of varieties; I have named some that I have had many years of experience with and some that are popular among most food plotters.

WHITE CLOVERS (*Trifolium repens*)

Clovers are classified in three general groups: small, intermediate, and large. The small low-growing white clover (Dutch clover) is referred to as wild-growing white clover. A substantial portion of white clovers available to food plotters belongs to the intermediate group (Ladino, Patriot, and Regal clovers). The group referred to as large clovers includes leaf types that are two to four times larger than the intermediate or small white clovers. An example of this is Jumbo II Ladino. Large clover varieties include Regal, Patriot, Merit, Pilgrim, Grassland Huia (formerly known as New Zealand) and Tillman. This group is commonly referred to as "ladino

▲ Food Plot Clover White from la Crosse Seed. White clovers are among the most nutritious and palatable clovers. A well-cared for plot of white clover can fix 100 to 150 lbs./acre of nitrogen per year. Photo: La Crosse Seed

clovers." Most of the large white clovers derived from the "Ladino Gigante Lodigiano" of Italy. Apart from their differences in size, all three groups of white clovers can be difficult to distinguish from one another.

The intermediate and large varieties of white clovers are prime plantings to choose from, each having its own unique aspects. The white clovers are nutritious and palatable plants. They are fast-growing, offer outstanding nitrogen-fixing capabilities and most have excellent persistence. The extensive root system's capabilities of white clover prevent soil from running off, thereby keeping key soil nutrients in place.

White clovers are often less expensive than other clovers and legumes, and they don't require as much maintenance. Consequently, several types of white clovers should be sown as mixed stand and as stand-alone plots. Furthermore, when developing a food plot and deer management program, and you have sufficient tillable acreage, you should include both mixed plots and pure stands of clovers. Many wildlife seed companies offer quality clover seeds and mixes.

I am a big devotee of planting many of the different warm-season and winter-hardy varieties of white, red, and other types of clovers. Some of them can withstand and even flourish, in very frosty winter temperatures from 0°F down to -22°F. You read that correctly, MINUS 22°F. Nonetheless, I feel some warm-season clovers are equally important to plant. With that said, though, the truth is that most of you reading this book are more than likely looking to sow plants to attract deer throughout the hunting season—during the daylight hours—and the different winter-hardy clovers mentioned above fit the bill.

▲ Although clovers are primarily planted to attract deer and other big game, many game animals including upland birds, some waterfowl, rabbits, and some small game are attracted to all clovers as well. Credit: Ted Rose

ARROWLEAF (*Trifolium vesiculosum Savi*)

Arrowleaf is a winter-hardy perennial white clover. It must be inoculated prior to planting and is generally available pre-inoculated. Otherwise, it must be inoculated with Rhizobium bacteria Strain O. Arrowleaf has a deep taproot that can penetrate more than four feet into the soil, allowing it to have good drought tolerance. Its leaves are non-hairy and are shaped like the tip of an arrow. The leaves can be up to two and a half inches long. Most often its arrow-shaped leaves have a characteristic large, white V-mark, but not always. Arrowleaf produces large flowers (about two inches) that start off white and eventually turn pink later in the season. Its stems bend upward and reach a height of two to four feet and sometimes higher.

areas where it receives at least eighteen to twenty-five inches of yearly precipitation.

To best establish Arrowleaf, managers should prepare a smooth, clean seedbed free from large rocks, limbs, and other debris. For best seed emergence, the soil should be compressed using a cultipacker or heavy drag, before and after seeding the plot. Sow the seed no deeper than one-quarter to one-half-inch deep. Plant at a rate of 10 to 15 lbs./acre. As with all plantings, a soil test should be taken prior to fertilizing. However, in lieu of a soil test, at planting apply about 300 lbs./acre using 0–20–20 or a similar mixture. Arrowleaf will endure a soil pH between 5.0 and 7.5. For best results, however, the pH should be between 5.8 and 6.5.

▲ Arrowleaf is a winter-hardy clover. It can stand temperatures between 0° and 10°F. Arrowleaf is a dependable reseeding annual clover. For hunting season, plant the late maturing variety called Meechee. Photo: Cooper Seed

▲ This is a field of arrowleaf clover. When stressed, arrowleaf's leaves turn a distinctive purplish-red color. Apache and Blackhawk varieties have virus disease resistance. Photo: USDA

Arrowleaf seeds are large, about twice the size of other white clovers. The hard seed requires scarification to provide excellent quality germination. It is mostly grown throughout the Midsouth and southeastern United States. Arrowleaf will tolerate moderately acidic to mild alkaline soils that are reasonably well-drained. It is not suited to droughty soils with low fertility or poorly drained, wet soils. Additionally, it is also slightly sensitive to salinity. Arrowleaf does best in

Arrowleaf is an excellent clover as a companion plant to any of the small grains. It contains a high crude protein content of 15 to 24 percent. Arrowleaf clover is a reseeding cool-season annual legume that is often planted with small grains or ryegrass. It has good drought tolerance and starts rapid growth following rain. Arrowleaf forage quality is high (16–20 percent protein) and digestible dry matter content is particularly high (80 percent) at the peak of vegetation. Its greatest limitation is its high susceptibility to viruses and fungi (more about this later).

Arrowleaf is another clover that does best when planted with a blend of other clovers, legumes, or small grains. If planted with grains, the seeding rates of the grains must be reduced accordingly. As with all mixture plots, a blended plot helps to reduce the risk of over-browsing of a pure stand, and it guards against a particular plant undergoing a complete crop failure. When blending arrowleaf, use a winter-hardy red clover like Marathon Red clover, fall oats, or grain rye. Be careful not to use too much of the oats or rye as they will shade out the clovers.

There are a few varieties of arrowleaf clover including Amclo, Meechee, and the most often used variety, Yuchi. Other varieties like Apache or Blackhawk are varieties that are available at www.smithseed.com and other seed companies.

CONDENSED RECAP

- **Temperature Tolerances:** Cold tolerant. From Texas to Georgia, it is rated as winter-hardy withstanding temperatures from 0°F to 10°F.
- **Inoculant:** Comes pre-inoculated. Otherwise inoculate with Rhizobium bacteria Strain O.
- **Planting Times:** Sow in early September in more northern climates and early to mid-October in the south.
- **Seeding Rates:** In a pure stand, 12 to 15 lbs./acre. Better yet, in a blended stand 10 lbs./acre.
- **Planting Depth:** ¼- to ½-inch deep.
- **Companion Plants:** Red clovers like Marathon, small grains like rye, wheat, barley, triticale, or cold-season oats.

- **pH Levels:** 5.8 and 6.5. Tolerates 5.0 to 7.5. It will not endure acidic soils below 5.0.
- **Soil Preferences:** Well-drained loam or sandy loam soils; but does well on well-drained clay soils.
- **Germination:** In fertile soil, emerges within three to seven days. All clovers take less than a week to germinate when temperatures are around 59°F.
- **Fertilizer:** At planting 300 to 350 lbs./acre of 0–20–20.
- **Crude Protein Content:** 18 to 24 percent.
- **Total Digestible Nutrients (TDN):** 80 percent.
- **Nitrogen Fixation:** Yes. A fertile stand of arrowleaf fixes 100 to 150 lbs./acre nitrogen per year.
- **Overgrazing Concerns:** Not an issue once established.
- **Extends Grazing Season:** In the North, extends grazing into November; later in the South.
- **Sunlight:** Prefers full sun.
- **Pollinator Friendly:** Yes. Rated as a top honeybee attractive clover.
- **USDA Hardiness Zone:** Check your local USDA zone.
- **Advice:** To maintain a productive plot, keep mowed to about a four-inch height.
- **Caution:** Requires well-drained soil.
- **Level of Maintenance:** Low to medium.
- **Note:** Arrowleaf needs sufficient rain to grow best. At least eighteen to twenty-five inches of yearly precipitation.

DURANA WHITE CLOVER (*Trifolium repens*)

Durana, a.k.a. Patriot, is a cool-season intermediate perennial white clover that has smaller, more abundant leaves than large-leaved tall ladino clovers, but it produces more runners (a.k.a. stolons). It was developed by the University of Georgia plant breeder Dr. Joe Bouton. Durana competes assertively with weeds and grasses. It is productive, persistent, aggressive, and when managed properly can be a *very* long-lived clover. Durana is also a heavy producer of flowers and over prolonged periods of time, it will reseed itself more reliably. With the proper management, a Durana clover plot can last from 5 to 8 years as it is a very dependable re-seeder.

Durana was crossed with a virus-resistant ladino clover to form a variety known as Patriot. However, Patriot white clover (the close cousin of Durana) has better production but less persistence. Durana is a tough ol' clover. It is more drought tolerant, better able to compete with weeds and grasses, and more tolerant of acidic pH values, can deal with cold better than some other varieties of clovers, and still perform well. Durana is one of the few clovers that tolerates shady conditions—but not full shade. It needs at least 4 to 6 hours of full sunlight per day.

It is regarded as a top planting for production, nutrition, and attraction for deer. Durana white clover can do very well in the Northeast, Southeast, and Midwest. It has also adapted well to the Pacific Northwest and the Rocky Mountain states.

Durana should be mowed periodically to maintain its productivity and palatability. When mowing it, don't remove more than one third of the top of the plant. All clovers quickly benefit and recover from this type of mowing which generates succulent and nutritious new growth. Mowing also helps to reduce weed growth within the plot.

▲ Durana white clover is a large-leaf clover. It can last three times longer than other ladino white clovers. It is persistent, cold-hardy, and tolerates heavy grazing. As I mentioned in my first food plot book, Sergeant Joe Friday of the 1951 T.V. series *Dragnet* was fond of saying "Just the facts, Ma'am, just the facts." That's what I just gave you about Durana—the facts. Photo: HS Pro Staff

Durana is an excellent plant for wildlife. It is grazed by white-tailed deer, elk, mule deer, bears, and wild turkey. Its seeds are eaten by almost all upland birds, and some waterfowl.

Durana clover is pricey at about $6 to $9 per pound. Like most clovers and brassicas, Durana's seeds are tiny and should not be planted more than ⅛- to ¼-inch deep. I have found it can be top-seeded prior to a rainfall in a well-prepared seed bed and compact it lightly to achieve good seed-to-soil contact. It can also be drilled or frost-seeded. Durana requires a minimum of a week or two to germinate. Durana White Clover is available at www.pennington.com and other seed companies.

CONDENSED RECAP

- **Temperature Tolerances:** Rated as a cool-season plant, it is cold-hardy to 15°F.
- **Inoculant:** Sold pre-inoculated with Rhizobium bacteria (Strain B).
- **Planting Times**: In the North, as a *cool-season* planting sow after the danger of frost (May or June); in the South, September or October.
- **Seeding Rates:** Alone broadcast at 5 lbs./acre, drill at 3 lbs./acre, frost-seed at 4 lbs./acre.
- **Planting Depth:** ⅛- to ¼-inch, no deeper. Stand failures usually result from planting too deeply.
- **Companion Plants:** Red clovers, any of the small grains, chicory, or rape.

▲ Durana is highly competitive when mixed with grasses or other aggressive plants. It is also persistent, productive, and long-lived. A healthy well-cared for plot can last several years. Photo: © Nela Petria | Dreamstime

- **pH Levels:** Does best in 6.0 to 6.5; tolerates 5.4.
- **Soil Preferences:** Tailored to the Southeast, Northeast, and Midwest on all soils other than deep sands.
- **Germination:** In fertile soil at 50°F and above will sprout in 7 to 15 days.
- **Fertilizer:** If a soil test wasn't taken, use 300 lbs./acre of 19–19–19 or 16-18-18. In September, top-off using 300 to 350 lbs./acre of a no-nitrogen type fertilizer like 0–20–20 or 0–20–30.
- **Crude Protein Content:** 25 to 30 percent.
- **Total Digestible Nutrients (TDN):** Up to 80 percent.
- **Nitrogen Fixation:** Yes, can fix from 75 to 150 lbs./acre per year.
- **Overgrazing Concerns:** Not an issue, persists under continuous grazing.
- **Extends Grazing Season:** From spring to late November.
- **Sunlight:** At least 4 to 6 hours of full sun. Durana tolerates some shade.
- **Pollinator Friendly:** Yes. Highly desirable pollinator plant to honeybees.
- **USDA Hardiness Zone:** All across the lower 48; check with your local cooperative extension.
- **Advice:** Because the seeds are tiny, be vigilant not to overseed.
- **Caution:** Does not do well planted in sandy soils.
- **Level of Maintenance:** Medium. Durana must be mowed occasionally to help productivity and keep weeds and grasses controlled.
- **Note:** Patriot white clover is a first cousin of Durana. It offers more production than Durana but is not as persistent. When planting Durana, a wise owl would use a mix of half Durana with half Patriot. This option would provide the best of both plantings.

▲ Durana is an adaptable clover. It has a tolerance for shade, an ability to endure weather extremes, and heavy grazing pressure from deer and other wildlife. Durana is a proven plant as a top-choice perennial forage for any wildlife food plot management program. Credit: Pennington Seed

DUTCH WHITE CLOVER (*Trifolium repens*)

Dutch white clover, a.k.a. white Dutch clover, is categorized within the small group of the three types of white clovers. It is often referred to as a wild growing plant. Dutch is a slow-growing perennial strain of white clover. It is adapted to North America. Dutch is a vigorous and aggressive clover plant which has a creeping pattern forming low dense mats. Depending on soil fertility, Dutch white clover will reach about 2 to 4 inches in height and it will continuously spread *indefinitely*—most times to a *fault*. Dutch white clover will flower with white petals that can reach about ¾- to 1-inch during the summer.

Dutch white clover will grow best in moist, well-drained soils. It also requires a neutral soil pH of 7.0 to reach its full growth potential. Once established, Dutch white clover grows rapidly. **Warning:** It can become a very invasive clover to other plants and can often behave like a weed. If planted, Dutch white clover should be sown in early spring or late summer before mid-August.

In a food plot program, Dutch white clover is usually used as ground cover and erosion control. Due to its glabrous trifoliate leaves, Dutch clover acts as a suitable food source for many species of gamebirds and small mammals. Dutch contributes some nitrogen to soil, which can help the growth of other foliage. However, because of its invasive tendency it should be planted alone or in mixes, with the understanding of its aggressive potential. Dutch white clover is available at www.deercreekseed.com or other seed companies.

CONDENSED RECAP

- **Temperature Tolerances:** Cool season. Will tolerate 40°–50°F. From Texas to Georgia, it is rated as winter-hardy.
- **Inoculant:** Comes pre-inoculated.

▲ Dutch white clover is often seen growing wild. It is aggressive and can be hard to control. Used mostly by food plotters as a ground cover, cover crop, erosion control, and in pasture mixtures. Usually matures around 8 inches tall. Photo: © Wirestock | Dreamstime.

- **Planting Times:** Fall plant from mid-August to mid-September. In spring, plant as early as possible.
- **Seeding Rates:** Broadcast at 7 to 14 lbs./acre.
- **Planting Depth:** ¼- to ½-inch deep.
- **Companion Plants:** Not recommended to be planted alone. Mix with other red clovers; do not mix with other white clovers.
- **pH Levels:** Prefers a pH of 6.0 to 7.0.
- **Soil Preferences** Well-drained soil.
- **Germination:** Will emerge within 10 days.
- **Fertilizer:** At planting use 150 lbs./acre of 5–10–5, which is high in phosphorous.
- **Crude Protein Content:** 8 to 12 percent.
- **Total Digestible Nutrients (TDN):** 70 to 80 percent.
- **Nitrogen Fixation:** Yes, albeit lower than other white clovers.
- **Overgrazing Concerns:** Not an issue once established.
- **Extends Grazing Season:** In the North into October, later in the South.
- **Sunlight:** Prefers full sun but tolerates some shade.
- **Pollinator Friendly:** Yes, but not rated as a high honeybee attractant.
- **USDA Hardiness Zone:** Check your local USDA zone.
- **Advice:** Mow close to the ground to prevent the plants from making seed, thereby limiting Dutch's ability to become too invasive.
- **Caution:** Can be very invasive. Recommend using as erosion control and along trails.
- **Level of Maintenance:** Low.
- **Note:** Tolerates shade and wet growing conditions.

▲ During the summer, many food plotters hone their shooting skills by stalking woodchucks that are focused on eating them out of house and home. Woodchucks are heavy users of clover plants. Credit: © Thorvis | Dreamstime.com

JUMBO II LADINO (*Trifolium repens*)

Jumbo II ladino white clover is rated by seed companies as a winter-hardy clover. It is a fast-growing, giant-leafed ladino known for its behemoth leaf size and robust growth habit. It is immensely popular in deer mixes or as a stand-alone food plot. Jumbo II is an excellent nitrogen builder and soil enhancer. It is also a nutritious and high-yielding clover. Because of these accolades, Jumbo II ladino has earned its way of becoming an exceedingly popular giant-leafed ladino-type clover. Jumbo II is very palatable to deer and other game animals. Its aggressiveness provides a dense canopy of forage. All types of tall, long-stemmed big leaf ladinos work well for deer and other wildlife; because deer primarily eat the leaf.

Jumbo II is an extremely popular clover as a stand-alone food plot and is also exceptionally popular in deer mixes containing several types of seeds. It is an excellent choice when used in mixes that aim for a stand of ⅓ clover to ⅔ grasses like annual or perennial ryegrass or timothy. When mixed with grasses, it is recommended to plant approximately 5 lbs. of coated clover seed to 25 lbs./acre of grass seed.

Jumbo II can be used with all the annual grains like wheat, triticale, rye, barley, and oats. It also works well when mixed with grasses like timothy, perennial rye grass, or SucraSEED® high-sugar grass (HSG). If mixing Jumbo II ladino with other clovers, good choices include winter-hardy varieties of red clover like Marathon, Persist, and Mammoth, and any of the extremely winter-hardy white clovers mentioned above. Jumbo II can also be mixed with some of the legumes like cowpeas, hairy vetch, or Austrian winter peas.

If a soil test is not taken, fertilize the above mixes but keep the nitrogen levels lower than 60 lbs./acre to discourage grass from competing with the mixed plots. Use plenty of phosphorus and potassium. You can use either 300 lbs./acre of 8–24–24 or 300 lbs./acre of 19–19–19 (a.k.a. T-19).

Your best results when using Jumbo II ladino (or the intermediate size leaf ladino) is to control grass and weed growth within the plot. When planting Jumbo II or other ladinos with perennial grasses, the plot should be mowed at least 2 to 3 times per summer, with a last mowing in late August; just don't mow it to the ground then. Finally, fertilize it again in September using 300 to 350 lbs./acre of 0–20–30. All the information provided with Jumbo II can be applied to ladino clover. Jumbo II ladino is available at www.meritseed.com and other seed companies.

CONDENSED RECAP
- **Temperature Tolerances:** Is rated as a winter-hardy plant; can tolerate early winter temperatures.
- **Inoculant:** Usually is pre-inoculated with live Rhizobium bacteria (Strain B).
- **Planting Times:** Spring and fall, can be frost-seeded.
- **Seeding Rates:** Stand-alone, use 2 to 4 lbs./acre. Blended mix, use 1 to 3 lbs./acre.

▲ Jumbo II ladino was developed from a selection of Jumbo plus clover. It received superior tiller density and disease resistance from the parent plant. Its aggressive tillering provides a dense canopy of forage for wildlife. Photo: Tecomate

- **Planting Depth:** No deeper than ¼-inch. Cultipack soil lightly before and after planting.
- **Companion Plants:** Timothy, perennial grasses, red clovers, legumes, small grains, and chicory.
- **pH Levels:** Prefers pH between 6.0 and 6.5. Tolerates 5.9 to 6.7.
- **Soil Preferences:** An ideal soil bed is moist, fertile, and firm.
- **Germination:** In temperatures of 59°F in a fertile, well-prepared seedbed, sprouts in a few days.
- **Fertilizer:** In lieu of a soil test, use either 300 lbs./acre of 19–19–19 or 8–24–24. In September, fertilize using 300 to 350 lbs./acre of 0–20–30.
- **Crude Protein Content:** 17 to 33 percent.
- **Total Digestible Nutrients (TDN):** 65 to 80 percent.
- **Nitrogen Fixation:** Yes. Provides 100 to 150 lbs./acre per year.
- **Overgrazing Concerns:** Generally, not an issue after it is established.
- **Extends Grazing Season:** In the North, from late October to early November.
- **Sunlight:** Prefers full sun.

- **Pollinator Friendly:** Yes.
- **USDA Hardiness Zone**: Check your USDA location for winter-hardiness zone accuracy. Or consult with local ag-soil, water, and conservation departments.
- **Advice:** I have found on our farm that deer somewhat prefer the large leaf varieties like Jumbo II over the intermediate variety.
- **Caution:** White clovers can be affected by viruses. Peanut stunt virus, alfalfa mosaic virus, and clover yellow vein virus are all transmitted by insects like aphids or thrips.
- **Level of Maintenance:** Low to Medium. Must be mowed to prevent bolting.
- **Note:** White clovers are more tolerant of 2,4-D herbicide applications than other clovers. But the effectiveness of herbicides is dependent on weather and maturity of the type of weeds being controlled. Clover is exceptionally sensitive to dicamba (Weedmaster, Banvel), picloram (Grazon P+D) and triclopyr (Remedy). These chemicals normally eliminate existing clover.

▲ The large leaves of Jumbo Ladino are like hitting the lotto for a rabbit. Rabbits can do substantial damage to a small food plot of clover. Credit: © Eichelbergerr023 | Dreamstime.com

LEGACY WHITE CLOVER (*Trifolium repens*)

New Legacy white clover has excellent winter-hardiness. It is a large-leafed variety. It is an exceptionally high-yielding perennial with a tall growth habit. Legacy was bred for greater persistence and improved production. It also provides high stolen density. Legacy can be planted from spring to fall and can provide viable forage throughout the year. It is said to maintain its persistence and production for about 3 years.

Legacy is an ideal white clover to sow in wildlife food plot programs as either a pure stand or in a mixed clover seed blend. It is a broadly adapted large leaf white clover for deer to browse into November and December. It has terrific ground cover ability under a wide range of climatic conditions. In only its second year, Legacy's yields are outstanding when compared to other white clover varieties. Legacy is coated and pre-inoculated for improved establishment and growth.

Like all plants, a soil test should be taken prior to planting Legacy to help identify the amounts of nutrients such as phosphorus, sulfur, and potassium that may be needed. A soil test will also identify if the pH is too high or low. Legacy large leaf white clover can be sown in spring or autumn. When planted in a mixed seeded food plot, Legacy performs best when it is sown with erect growing species like perennial ryegrass or timothy.

Legacy white clover can be grazed continuously without fear of the plot being overeaten by deer. It can be grazed to a height of about 1 inch without seriously damaging the crop. If browsed under 1 inch, however, grazed plants must be allowed to recover.

Most seed companies say Legacy large-leaf white clover has replaced Kopu II white clover. Kopu II was selected for stolen density, persistence under heavy grazing by wildlife, high yield, and its large leaf. Legacy surpasses all the benefits that Kopu II provides. Buy Legacy white clover at www.welterseed.com, www.deercreekseed.com and other seed companies.

CONDENSED RECAP
- **Temperature Tolerances:** Rated as a winter-hardy plant.
- **Inoculant:** Comes pre-inoculated with Rhizobium bacteria (Strain B).

▲ Legacy is an exceptionally high-yielding, large-leafed clover that grows tall. Its tall growth enables Legacy to compete very well when mixed with grasses. Legacy's vigorous growth also improves its tolerance to clover root weevil. Photo: WGG Wrightson Seeds

▲ Marmot are a PITA for western food plotters. They will browse clover plots heavily and bring the family with them too. Credit: © Shayne Kaye | Dreamstime.com

- **Planting Dates:** In the North, from spring to September. In southern areas, as late as October or November.
- **Seeding Rates:** Alone, broadcast at 2 to 4 lbs./acre. In a mix, use 1 to 3 lbs./acre. Can also be frost-seeded.
- **Planting Depth:** Plant ¼-inch deep in a moist, fertile, and firm seedbed.
- **Companion Plants:** Red clovers, chicory.
- **pH Levels:** Best in 6.0 to 7.0; tolerates as low as 5.8.
- **Soil Preferences:** Prefers well-drained soil but will endure moderately drained soil.
- **Germination:** In fertile soil, sprouts in 3 to 5 days.
- **Fertilizer:** Use a low nitrogen mix of NPK like 0–20–20, 0–10–10 or 20–60–20.
- **Crude Protein Content:** 29.5 percent.
- **Total Digestible Nutrients (TDN):** 60 to 70 percent.

- **Nitrogen Fixation:** Fixes 100 to 150 lbs./acre a year on fertile soil and growing conditions.
- **Overgrazing Concerns:** Can withstand heavy grazing.
- **Extends Grazing Season:** In most northern zones, during the hunting season.
- **Sunlight:** Prefers full sun; tolerates moderate shade.
- **Pollinator Friendly:** Yes, pollinator friendly to honeybees.
- **USDA Hardiness Zone:** Zones 4–8, check with your local cooperative extension.
- **Advice:** Legacy does best when planted with grasses or red clovers.
- **Caution:** Do not use a heavy nitrogen fertilizer.
- **Level of Maintenance**: Medium. During hot or dry conditions, do not mow frequently.
- **Note:** Legacy's robust growth improves its tolerance to the root weevil.

RENOVATION WHITE CLOVER (*Trifolium repens L.*)

Renovation clover is a cool season plant with wide leaves, much like ladino-type clovers. This results in more forage and less pressure even under heavy grazing. It was specifically bred for increased stolon density utilizing a combination of long-lived Southern Plant ecotypes and disease-resistant ladino varieties resulting in increased persistence, even when it is heavily grazed by deer and other wildlife. It also has an early growth habit that is better than other white clovers.

Renovation should reach a mature height of about 8 to 10 inches and will maintain that height if it is not mowed. It is a viable choice to improve and maintain healthy productive wildlife food plots. It provides high protein, is a long season attractant, and contributes nitrogen to the soil and surrounding plants.

Renovation works extremely well when planted with companion plants like small grains, especially rye. It also does well with grasses including timothy, perennial ryegrass, chicory, peas, red clovers, turnips, forage rape, and kale. Its seeding rates when planted with companion plants must be adjusted accordingly, however. As a cool season clover, Renovation needs time to establish before harsh weather arrives. It can be planted in northern areas and can withstand temperatures ranging from 15° to 20°F. It also works very well when planted in the southern zones of the country.

Renovation is often available as a pre-inoculated coated seed to ensure better establishment.

▲ Renovation is an ideal clover for wildlife food plots. It provides high protein, acts as a seasonal attractant, and contributes nitrogen to surrounding plants. Renovation has wider leaves, resulting in less weed pressure, even under grazing. Photo: Brian Motes

It does best in soils within its preferred pH values. Renovation tolerates semi-acidic soils. It will grow best on moist, well-drained, fertile soil. Once established and effectively managed, Renovation can provide protein-rich food for deer and other wildlife. It is an excellent choice to improve and maintain productive food plots whether it is planted in a mix or alone. In the end, Renovation makes a terrific wildlife food plot mostly because of its early growth and its ability to withstand heavy grazing which enables it to be available to deer for longer periods of time. Buy Renovation white clover at www.seedland.com or other seed companies.

CONDENSED RECAP

- **Temperature Tolerances:** Cool season. Will tolerate some cold temperatures but not for long periods.
- **Inoculant:** All Renovation clover is Nitro-Coated® with a high level of the leguminosarum biovar trifolii rhizobium.
- **Planting Times:** In the North, plant from spring to late summer. In the South, plant in spring or late fall. Can also be frost-seeded.
- **Seeding Rates:** Alone, plant 4 to 5 lbs./acre. In a mix, reduce to 2 to 3 lbs./acre.
- **Planting Depth:** 1/8- to 1/4-inch. Risk of total plot failure if planted too deep. Cultipack before and after seeding.
- **Companion Plants:** Small grains, chicory, other clovers, timothy or perennial ryegrass, peas, kale, rape.

- **pH Levels:** Prefers 6.0 to 6.5 but will endure as low as pH 5.0.
- **Soil Preferences:** Performs best on fertile, moist, well-drained soils.
- **Germination:** In a well-prepared fertile seedbed, will sprout in 3 to 7 days.
- **Fertilizer:** In the absence of a soil test, use 300 to 350 lbs./acre of 19-19-19.
- **Crude Protein Content:** 25 to 30 percent.
- **Total Digestible Nutrients (TDN):** 65 to 80 percent.
- **Nitrogen Fixation:** Yes, it can fix 100 to 150 lbs./acre of nitrogen per year.
- **Overgrazing Concerns:** Not a concern because of its ability to withstand heavy grazing.
- **Extends Grazing Season:** From October to November.
- **Sunlight:** Prefers full sun. Will tolerate light shade.
- **Pollinator Friendly:** Excellent pollinator for honeybees to easily access the nectar in Renovation's short florets.
- **USDA Hardiness Zone:** Check your local USDA Hardiness Zone or local Ag Soil and Water departments.
- **Advice:** As with any plant, perform a soil test prior to planting.
- **Caution:** Seeding Renovation into deep sandy soils is not recommended.
- **Level of Maintenance:** Medium.
- **Notes:** Its ability to aggressively spread also makes it perfect for erosion control and slope stabilization. Renovation is also ideal for use as living mulch in small fruit or nut orchards, or vineyards.

SUBTERRANEAN CLOVER (*Trifolium subterranean*)

Subterranean clover is a cool season clover that is best suited to areas having mild winters. It offers a range of low-growing, self-reseeding clovers with high nitrogen contribution, excellent weed suppression, and strong persistence as a wildlife food plot. Subterranean clover, a.k.a. subclover, is an ideal clover for food plotters with shade problems. Researchers in Louisiana found it a very suitable variety of clover for planting in shady areas, even in stands of pine trees. As clovers go, subclover's best attribute is its ability to grow in shade. In one study, subclover demonstrated that it could produce about 90 percent of its growth potential in 50 percent of shade. That's notable if you have shady places in which you want to grow a clover plot. Subclover's shade tolerance also makes it popular with many managers who use it for food plots in wooded areas. It is often used throughout the Northeast and New England as a clover to plant in the shade.

Other benefits of subterranean clover include its ability to withstand heavy grazing, its resistance to acidic soil conditions, its excellent seeding vigor, and its rapid germination. Equally important, it is a highly nutritious clover. Subclover will tolerate winter temperatures to 15°F, but not much lower than that. On the flip side of that coin, however, subterranean does have its drawbacks. Subclover is an unreliable reseeder, it can have low production, and it is intolerant of drought.

Subclover is also often planted in western states, particularly along the coast, and used as a rangeland legume in western Oregon and California. In fact, subclover mixtures are used on thousands of acres of California almond orchards. It is also popular in the South and along the Atlantic Coast. It can be seeded in the fall from September to October. Subclover needs to be inoculated. It can be planted as a stand-alone plot, but it can also be planted in a mix with traditional small grains including rye, triticale, oats, wheat, and barley. It will also do well when planted with white clovers and even vetches.

Do not plant subclover more than ½-inch deep. When thinking about planting it, select among the many cultivars that fit your climate and your cover crop food plot goals. There are several recognized varieties or subspecies of subterranean clover *Trifolium subterraneum: T. subterraneum, T. subterraneum L. ssp. brachycalycinum,* and *T. subterraneum L. var. yanninicum.* For instance, *T. yanninicum* cultivars are best adapted to water-logged soils. *T. subterraneum* are the most common cultivars that thrive in acidic to neutral soils (pH between 5.5 and 7.5). Other more common varieties include Nangeela, Mt. Barker, Tallarook, Oregon, and Woogenellup.

▲ Subterranean (a.k.a. subclover) clover is very tolerant and suitable to plant in shade, especially in thinned-out stands of pine or hardwoods. Subclover is considered a reseeding winter-hardy annual plant. Photo: USDA

Subterranean clover is an ideal planting for managers who have more areas of wet bottomlands, semi-wet woods, shady woodlots, and thin stands of pine than they do open fields. However, subclover planted in very thick stands of pines or mature hardwoods are less likely to be successful. Subclover develops differently than other clovers and legumes. After it is pollinated, the flowers develop a burr. The burrs weigh down the stems and by doing so they deposit seeds into the soil, allowing for continued grazing to occur without limiting seed production. Surprisingly, seed production is reduced if the subclover is not kept tightly grazed to heights of 2 to 4 inches. The stoloniferous growth habit of subterranean clover makes it an ideal plant for the close-type grazing of deer. Subclover is available at www.seedworldusa.com and some other seed companies.

CONDENSED RECAP
- **Temperature Tolerance:** Will winter-kill at 20 to 30°F.
- **Inoculant:** Specific subclover inoculant (WR Strain).
- **Planting Times:** Should be planted in late August or early September before a predicted rain.
- **Seeding Rates:** Broadcast at 15 to 20 lbs./acre. Drill at 10 lbs./acre.
- **Planting Depth:** Not more than ½-inch deep.
- **Companion Plants:** All small grains, white clovers, and even corn and sorghum.
- **pH Levels:** Optimum at 6.5; tolerates 5.5- 7.5.
- **Soil Preferences:** A wide variety of soils, other than extended standing water or flooding.
- **Germination:** Sprouts in 5 to 7 days in fertile soil.
- **Fertilizer:** At planting, use 300 to 350 lbs./acre of 8-24-24.
- **Protein Content:** 16 to 30 percent.
- **Digestibility:** 80 percent.
- **High Nitrogen Fixation:** Yes.
- **Over Grazing:** Not a problem when established.
- **Extends Grazing Season:** Generally, into mid-November.
- **Sun:** Grows best in full sun but will tolerate areas that receive up to 50 percent shade.
- **Pollinator Friendly:** No. Because the flowers of subclover are mostly found under the leaves, they are low in nectar, making access both difficult and unappealing for bees.
- **USDA Hardiness Zones:** Zones 7 or warmer, check your local ag department for your zone.
- **Advice:** Very suitable for planting in thin stands of pines, but not in dense, mature pines or hardwoods.
- **Caution:** Do not plant in dense shade or in areas of heavy leaf fall.
- **Level of Maintenance:** Low.
- **Avoid:** Do not let it exceed 5 inches in height. Keep it mowed or grazed at 2 to 4 inches.

▲ Although sub clover does best in full sun, it performs well in areas that get up to 50 percent shade per day. Credit: G.D. Carr

ALICE CLOVER (*Trifolium repens*)

Alice white clover is ranked as being a very winter-hardy, long-lived, herbaceous, large-leafed, perennial clover. It should not be confused with Alyce clover, which is primarily adapted to the Gulf Coast area. Alice white clover is a popular variety for food plotters. It is high-yielding, a vigorous producer, aggressive grower, and has terrific drought tolerance. Alice has greater stolon density than most ladino-type clovers, allowing for better persistence under intense grazing by deer. Most important for wildlife managers is that Alice white clover has excellent winter-hardy survivability. Deer will paw it up even when it is covered with snow.

Alice was the first white clover variety to successfully combine production and persistence when interplanted with grass. In addition, it produces its own nitrogen through nitrogen fixation, a symbiotic process in which Rhizobium bacteria in the root nodules "fix" nitrogen.

Alice is exceedingly high in protein, vitamins, and minerals. It was also specifically developed to provide exceptional palatability to deer. Its vigorous spring and summer growth make it a very good choice as a food plot for deer and other wildlife from spring to winter.

Alice prefers well-drained soil, but it will adapt to a wide variety of other types of soils. Alice blooms from May to June. Its flowers are white with a slightly pinkish hue. Like all clovers, Alice requires some proper maintenance. Stands of clover should not grow too tall or go to flower, though. If they do, they become much less palatable to deer. Mowing management will help reduce the risk of plant bolting. Alice clover is available at www.welterseed.com and other seed companies.

CONDENSED RECAP
- **Temperature Tolerance:** Exceptionally winter-hardy.
- **Inoculant**: Generally available pre-inoculated w/ Rhizobium bacteria (Strain B). Check with seller to be sure.
- **Planting Times:** Best planted in late June or early September.
- **Seeding Rates:** Alone at 3 to 4 lbs./acre. In a mix, 1 to 3 lbs./acre. Frost seed at 4 to 5 lbs./acre.

▲ Alice is a popular clover variety mainly because it is extraordinarily winter-hardy. It is also exceptionally palatable to deer, elk, and other wildlife. It is aggressive enough to compete in mixed plots of grasses. Photo: © Hannu Viitanen | Dreamstime

- **Planting Depth:** ⅛- to ¼-inch. Can be top-seeded in a prepared seedbed prior to a rainfall.
- **Companion Plants:** Can be mixed with any clovers, chicory, some other legumes, any of the small grains, timothy, or ryegrass.
- **pH Levels:** Will tolerate 6.0 but prefers an optimum pH of 7.0.
- **Soil Preferences:** Prefers medium to heavy soils but will tolerate a wide range of soils other than wet soil.
- **Germination:** Under ideal conditions, will emerge in a week.
- **Fertilizer:** 350 to 400 lbs./acre of 19-19-19 or 16-18-19. In September, use 400 lbs./acre of 0-20-30 or 0-20-20.
- **Crude Protein Content:** 25 percent or higher.
- **Total Digestible Nutrients (TDN):** 60 to 80 percent.

- **Nitrogen Fixation:** Yes, reduces need for nitrogen-heavy fertilizer.
- **Over-Grazing Concerns:** Once established, tolerates heavy grazing by deer and other wildlife.
- **Extends Grazing Season:** Into hunting season.
- **Hours of Sunlight:** Prefers full sun but can tolerate some light shade.
- **Pollinator Friendly:** Yes, Alice's flowers attract honeybees.
- **USDA Hardiness Zone:** Zones 1–6.
- **Advice:** Alice white clover is a perfect companion with most cool-season perennials.
- **Caution:** Do not plant in flood-prone areas or drought-type soils. Avoid over-seeding.
- **Level of Maintenance:** Medium. Generally, Alice only requires weed management and mowing.

▲ Whether you live in the east or west, horses, mules, and donkeys, wild or domestic, seek out clovers wherever they can find them. This mule's laughter is your forewarning. Credit: PCFImages

▲ Red clovers are one of the fastest establishing legumes and are an excellent source of nitrogen. They also have a high nutritional value with excellent digestible protein. Credit: Ted Rose

Chapter Seventeen
Red Clovers

R ed clover (*Trifolium pratense L.*), Red clover, a.k.a. June, peavine, and cow clover, is an introduced short-lived perennial that lasts from 2 to 3 years. In the botanical sense, the term "short-lived" refers to the life expectancy of a plant. For instance, in many areas, especially when planted on acidic soil, red clover is short-lived. This is due to a combination of issues including insect pests, diseases, and nutrient balance; often referred to as "clover sickness." When crop rotation is managed properly, red clover will grow healthier and with gusto.

▲ Red clovers are the most broadly adapted of the true clovers. They can withstand winter type temperatures. Red clovers are ideal for attracting deer during the hunting season. Photo: PCFImages

Red clover is a herbaceous species of flowering plant in the bean family *Fabaceae*. Herbaceous plants do not have woody stems. Red clovers are native to Europe, western Asia Minor, and northwest Africa. There are two types of red clover: medium red, a.k.a. double-cut, and mammoth red, a.k.a. single-cut. Red clover grows from crowns. The plants have hollow, hairy stems, and branches. Medium red and Mammoth red varieties have stem lengths that can average from 1½ to 3 feet. The leaflets are often marked with a white "V." Oddly enough, its mostly pinkish flowers are not colored red. Instead, they range from pink to violet. This peculiarity can often lead to red clover being confused with crimson clover, a cool-season annual with deep reddish flowers. The flowers grow in clusters that bloom usually from June through August.

Red clovers are one of the fastest establishing clovers and an excellent source of nitrogen. They can fix good amounts of nitrogen into the soil (70 lbs./acre) that benefits a follow-up crop like corn, grain sorghum, and other plants that are heavy nitrogen users. Red clovers also have a high nutritional value and elevated levels of digestible protein that are a beneficial component in pasture mixes for deer and other wildlife. Medium red clover is the most common. It is quicker to establish than mammoth and grows back well after being mowed.

Red clovers grow best throughout the Northeast, New England, and other northern and central parts of the United States. Under good management practices, it can be planted in the upper northern regions of the South. It is not an ideal clover in the deep southern zones of the US. It is somewhat drought tolerant but not for extended periods. Red clovers tolerate soil acidity down to a pH of 5.5 but prefer and do much better in pH values of 6.0 to 7.2. Red clovers do not do well when planted in wet soils. Red clover, like alfalfa, needs sulfur and micronutrients. It doesn't need a lot of boron, but it does need low amounts of micronutrients like manganese, medium amounts of copper, zinc, and molybdenum.

When buying any red clover variety, look for good disease resistance and proven persistence types. Current varieties have been bred for better persistence and, with proper management, will provide 2 to 3 years of production after establishment. When selecting for disease resistance, varieties chosen should have resistance to northern anthracnose and powdery mildew. Varieties like Arlington and Marathon have proven disease resistance and persistence. For more current information on variety performance for your area, consult your local NRCS Field Office or your local Cooperative Extension Service office. Try to avoid seed that is labeled "common" or "common red clover." These varieties are said to have little disease resistance and persistence.

▲ A healthy planting of Rackup Red clover. It is a variety of red clover that is very productive, fast growing, and provides high levels of protein. Photo: Tecomate

Red clover is a dependable, cool season mainstay within much of the US (hardiness Zone 4 and warmer). Of the two types of red clover, Medium and Mammoth, there are many other varieties of the two types, with each having its own attributes. Some of the more popular types include Marathon, Persist, Medium, Alta-Swede, Cinnamon Plus, Mammoth, Starfire II, Freedom! MR, Kenstar, Bulldog, and Cherokee. Each variety of red clover performs differently from region to region. Therefore, investigate what types of red clovers grow best in your area.

The one thing for sure about all red clovers is that they are workhorse-type plants. They germinate quickly, grow fast, put nitrogen into the soil, enhance soil fertility, are heavy producers of forage, and provide nutritious protein-packed palatable food for deer and other wildlife into hunting season. Red clovers are also readily available and are inexpensive. I would not go without planting red clovers on our property. They can be planted as a stand-alone crop or, better yet because they are winter-hardy, they can be mixed with other winter-hardy grains, like cereal rye, wheat, triticale, or winter oats. Red clovers also do well when blended with other white clovers, some legumes, perennial grasses, and chicory.

Let me end this by putting to bed an old wives' tale about red clover. Red clovers have long been coupled with the advice or old axiom that they should be planted *only* for cattle and other domestic farm animals, due to their excellent hay production. Consequently, they are referred to as "cattle clovers." That term led to some food plotters avoiding red clovers. That is too bad. The indisputable fact is red clovers are a top-notch clover for deer and other wildlife. Cold season red clovers are fairly tolerant of temperatures in the mid to low twenties (20°F - 25°F) making them viable in the winter. 'Nuff said.

MAIN ATTRACTION (*Trifolium pratense*)

This is a red clover mix that is highly attractive to deer. Because it contains six percent chicory, it could have been included in the "Advantages of Planting Mixed Seeded Plots" chapter. This red clover mix was discovered as an experimental planting. Ryan from Blue Hill Wildlife Nursery planted this new mix next to white clovers (which are commonly found in food plot mixes) and a soybean plot. He noticed greater numbers of deer browsing in this mix more than any of the other clovers. In fact, this plot's attractiveness was comparable to the soybeans, but able to handle much greater browsing pressure. For this reason, Ryan named this deer forage clover formula "Main Attraction." Ryan told me, "This will provide an attractiveness comparable to soybeans, with more versatility and ease of planting." Main Attraction has the capability to reach 3 feet in height, but the deer keep it mowed. Ryan recommends this product be planted in the fall, but it can also be frost-seeded or spring-seeded on a firm prepared seed bed. This mix also contains six percent chicory. Deer Forage Clover, a.k.a. Main Attraction, is available only at www.bluehillwildlifenursery.com.

DYNAMITE RED CLOVER (*Trifolium pratense*)

Dynamite is a cool season red clover that is listed as very winter-hardy. It is a short-lived perennial that is a high-yielding, double-cut clover. It is ideal for use throughout the United States. It has both improved disease resistance and forage production. Dynamite exhibits early spring growth and abundant regrowth after it is cut, which improves the overall life of the stand.

Dynamite clover is less fibrous and is highly digestible, which can lead to an increase in doe milk production. When a combination of Dynamite red clover and high-sugar grasses are planted, deer receive synergistic benefits from the two. The high-sugar allows female deer to convert more of the protein of the clover into high quality milk. Dynamite clover has outstanding forage yields. Its persistence and palatability are rated as excellent. Dynamite has terrific drought tolerance as well.

Its ease of establishment is rated excellent. Planted alone, use a seeding rate of 6 to 9 lbs./acre. When mixed with other plantings, sow at 4 to 6 lbs./acre. The seeding depth should be $1/8$- to $1/4$-inch and not deeper. In a well-prepared food plot, it generally takes Dynamite about 7 to 14 days to germinate. Its coated seeds are pre-inoculated.

Dynamite red clover offers it all to deer from high yields to high digestibility, and twice the protein of

▲ This is a field of Dynamite red clover developed by GO Seed. Dynamite is very winter-hardy, and it extends the growing season though November and longer. It establishes quickly and is very compatible when used in a mix with other plants. Photo: GO Seed

grasses. It also needs little nitrogen fertilizer, and the seed is inexpensive. It is shade tolerant and is good for weed suppression. Dynamite red clover is available from Preferred Seed Co. (www.preferredseed.com) and a few other seed companies.

CONDENSED RECAP

- **Temperature Tolerances:** Winter-hardy.
- **Inoculant:** Live bacteria Rhizobium Strain B.
- **Planting Times:** For a fall/winter plot, plant 8 weeks prior to a freeze.
- **Seeding Rates:** Alone, 6 to 9 lbs./acre. In a mix, 4 to 6 lbs./acre.
- **Planting Depth:** Sow at ⅛- to ¼-inch deep.
- **Companion Plants:** Plant with small grains, grasses, other legumes, and chicory. Because it is shade tolerant it can even be used effectively as a cover crop under corn.
- **pH Levels:** Does best in 6.0–6.5.
- **Soil Preferences:** Moderate to well-drained soils.
- **Germination:** Sprouts in 7 to 14 days.
- **Fertilizer:** Needs little to no nitrogen. In September top-off with 300 to 350 lbs./acre of 0-46-0.
- **Crude Protein Content:** From 20 to 30 percent.
- **Total Digestible Nutrients (TDN):** 65 to 75 percent.
- **Nitrogen Fixation:** Fixes nitrogen at 100 to 150 lbs./acre.
- **Overgrazing Concerns:** Not a problem once established.
- **Extends Grazing Season:** From July throughout the hunting season.
- **Sunlight:** Prefers full sun.
- **Pollinator Friendly:** Yes. Attractive to honeybees.
- **USDA Hardiness Zone:** Can be planted in most northern areas of the country.
- **Advice:** To attract deer from fall to winter, plant by mid-June to August.
- **Caution:** Does not need nitrogen fertilizer.
- **Level of Maintenance:** Low.
- **Note:** Keep Dynamite clover mowed to prevent bolting.

▲ Here's yet another uninvited dinner guest. Not all animals that eat clovers have to be herbivores. Believe it or not, red fox will dine on your lush clovers. Who would of "thunked" it? Credit: © Klomsky | Dreamstime.com

FREEDOM! MR RED CLOVER

Freedom! MR red clover, exhibits improved winter hardiness as well as improved heat and drought tolerance. Red clovers are rated as cool-season perennial legumes. Freedom! was selected for its increased dry matter production. It has finer stems and fewer hairs on the stem which causes the plant to dry out faster. Freedom! was named as such because of its freedom from pubescence (non-glandular hairs). It is one of the more recent red clovers developed.

▲ Freedom! red clover was developed at the University of Kentucky. It is high yielding, palatable, and nutritious for deer and other wildlife. It has improved winter-hardiness and persistence. Photo: River Refuge Seed

Freedom! has a strong taproot allowing it to use subsoil moisture in summer and during droughts. It produces excellent yields of highly palatable, nutritious forage. Freedom! is a persistent variety. It is a rapid-establishing high-quality red clover, well-adapted for heavy grazing. Freedom! MR red clover can be sown as a pure food plot crop. It also performs well in a mixed seeded food plot.

For a fall/winter food plot crop, wait at least eight weeks before a killing frost to sow Freedom! It can also be frost-seeded in early spring. Freedom! does well in wet, acidic soils with pH values between 5.5 and 6.5. Freedom! red clover is available at www.forageseeds.com and other seed companies.

- **Temperature Tolerances:** Improved winter-hardiness to 20°F.
- **Inoculant:** Available pre-inoculated with N-Dure.
- **Planting Times:** As a fall/winter plot, plant 8 to 10 weeks before a killing frost.
- **Seeding Rates:** Alone, 15 to 20 lbs./acre. When sowing with grass, 8 to 10 lbs./acre.
- **Planting Depth:** Sow ¼-inch deep.
- **Companion Plants:** Timothy, perennial ryegrass, all small grains, white clovers, and chicory.
- **pH Levels:** Prefers 6.0 to 6.5 but tolerates 5.5 to 7.6.
- **Soil Preferences:** Performs best in moderate to well-drained soils.
- **Germination:** Emerges in 7 to 15 days when minimum soil temperatures reach 42°F.
- **Fertilizer:** Little to no nitrogen. Use 300 lbs./acre of 0-46-0 in September.
- **Crude Protein Content:** 16 to 22 percent.
- **Total Digestible Nutrients (TDN):** Highly palatable for deer and other wildlife.
- **Nitrogen Fixation:** Fixes a minimum of 75 to 150 lbs./acre.
- **Overgrazing Concerns:** Tolerates grazing but reduced when mixed with other seeds.
- **Extends Grazing Season:** Extends grazing from October into December.
- **Sunlight:** Likes full sun, but will endure partial sun, and even light shade.
- **Pollinator Friendly:** Yes, it is attractive to honeybees.
- **USDA Hardiness Zone:** 2 through 10.
- **Advice:** Sufficient levels of calcium, phosphorous, and potassium are vital to its success.
- **Caution:** Do not use nitrogen fertilizer.
- **Level of Maintenance:** Low.
- **Note:** Red clover varieties are the most widely grown of all the true clovers.

MAMMOTH RED CLOVER (*Trifolium incarnatum*)

Mammoth is a cool season red clover that is tolerant of temperatures in the low to mid-twenties. It is a herbaceous biennial short-lived clover. It is frequently grown as a single forage, or in a blended plot of other plants, particularly the small grains. It can do very well when planted with winter oat varieties, or other winter small grains like cereal rye, wheat, triticale, and barley. Mammoth red clover is also an ideal cover crop. In agriculture, cover crops are planted to protect soil rather than to be harvested. Cover crops act to control soil erosion, manage soil fertility, soil quality, weeds, pests, diseases, water, and so on.

Mammoth red clover has long tap roots that loosen soils and mine phosphorus and other nutrients from deep soil. As a soil nitrogen fixer, it can also add as much as 200 lbs./acre of nitrogen per year. It helps protect soil from erosion and improves soil tilth tremendously. It can be sown from April or May to August or September. It can also be frost-seeded in the late winter. With its fast establishment, Mammoth clover is ideal for providing copious amounts of organic matter to the soil. Compared to medium red clover, Mammoth matures about 2 weeks later and is a much larger plant, reaching 2 to 3 feet in height at maturity. In regions where soil pH or fertility is low, Mammoth red clover has a higher forage yield than alfalfa; so, it does much better than alfalfa as a forage crop for deer and other wildlife.

Mammoth red clover is a fast starter, is fast growing, highly productive, and more persistent than older common types of red clover. Mammoth has higher TND (digestibility) than alfalfa and considerably more undegradable protein. Mammoth food plots should be mowed at least 2 times per season if the clover

▲ Mammoth red clover is taller and coarser than medium red clover. It is often used as a plow-down or cover crop to build organic matter into the soil. Photo: © Lauraganz | Dreamstime

height gets too high. It should be kept down to about 3 to 4 inches to prevent bolting and other problems. Mammoth red clover is available at www.ernstseed.com and many other seed companies.

CONDENSED RECAP

- **Temperature Tolerances:** Rated as a cool-season clover that can tolerate winter temperatures in the low to mid-twenties. It is cold-hardy in most northern regions of the US.
- **Inoculant:** Available pre-inoculated or inoculate with a live bacteria culture Rhizobium (Strain B).
- **Planting Times:** In the North, in August. In the South, October.
- **Seeding Rates:** Alone, 10 to 12 lbs./acre. Mixed, 3 to 6 lbs./acre.
- **Planting Depth:** 1/8- to 1/4-inch deep. No deeper. Can be successfully frost-seeded.
- **Companion Plants:** Small winter grains, grasses, alfalfa, white clovers, and chicory.
- **pH Levels:** Prefers 6.0 to 7.0. Will tolerate 5.8 to 7.2.
- **Soil Preferences:** Well-drained to moderately drained soils.
- **Germination:** In fertile soil, sprouts in 5 to 7 days.
- **Fertilizer:** Soil test recommended. In fall, fertilize with 100 lbs./acre of 0-46-0.
- **Crude Protein Content:** Ranges from 15 to 30 percent depending on the season.
- **Total Digestible Nutrients (TDN):** From 15 to 16 percent.
- **Nitrogen Fixation:** Fixes up to 70 to 110 lbs./acre.
- **Overgrazing Concerns:** Not an issue. Mammoth tolerates heavy grazing.
- **Extends Grazing Season:** From October through November.
- **Sunlight:** Full sun, tolerates part shade.
- **Pollinator Friendly:** Yes, honeybees are attracted to Mammoth.
- **USDA Hardiness Zone:** Zones 1 to 6.
- **Advice:** Responsive to phosphorus and potassium; apply once a year in September.
- **Caution:** Do not plant deeper than recommended. Could result in plot failure.
- **Level of Maintenance:** Low to medium.
- **Note:** Mammoth produces a significant biomass. Best sown with small grains or cool-season grasses. Mammoth is later flowering than medium red clover, but it does not recover as well after being mowed.

▲ Mammoth red clover produces a significant biomass and is best grown with grains or grasses.
Credit: Johnny Seeds

MARATHON RED CLOVER (*Trifolium pratense*)

Marathon red clover is yet another winter-hardy clover. It is a tall, strong, 3- to 4-year perennial red clover cultivar. A cultivar is a plant that is produced and maintained by growers but does not produce true-to-seed; whereas a variety is a group of plants within a species that has one or more distinguishing characteristics and usually produces true-to-seed. The botanical meaning of true-to-seed simply means the offspring plant is genetically the same as the parent (a clone). Marathon Red Clover was developed by the University of Wisconsin.

As a winter-hardy variety, Marathon remains palatable and nutritious to deer and other wildlife well into December, particularly if it is covered in snow. Like most red clovers, it has a USDA Winter Hardiness Zone ranking in much of the US of 4 and warmer. A well-cared for stand of red Marathon clover can produce 2 to 3 tons of dry matter per acre and fix 75 to 150 lbs./acre of nitrogen annually. As mentioned, there are two general types of red clover commonly planted in the northern regions of the country. Medium red clover (a.k.a. double-cut) is a multi-cut clover which will recover nicely after each mowing. It is also a good choice for under-seeding with any of the winter small grains: Cereal rye, triticale, wheat, barley, and winter-type oats.

Marathon is resistant to bean yellow mosaic virus and northern anthracnose. It is adapted to the northern half of the United States. As a red clover, Marathon is a fast-establishing legume. It can be grown on more acidic soils than other white and some red clovers. Marathon can be sown as a pure stand, or with a blended mix of one or more companion crops. Broadcast at about 10 lbs./acre in a pure plot. Mixed with other seeds sow at 2 to 5 lbs./acre. It can also be successfully frost-seeded. The tiny seeds should not be planted more than ⅛- to ¼-inch deep. It is vital to plant

▲ Marathon is a strong re-seeder developed by the University of Wisconsin. It is a very winter-hardy clover that is resistant to bean yellow mosaic virus and northern anthracnose. It is best adapted to the northern half of the US. Photo: GO Seed.

Marathon in a well-prepared, firm seed bed for the seed to make good seed-to-soil contact. When planting all clovers including Marathon, it is a wise practice to minimize the depth of the tillage before seeding. It will help to reduce the disturbance of the weed bed and avoid soil moisture loss.

Marathon (and all red clovers) fixes atmospheric nitrogen with Rhizobium bacteria in root nodules. So, additional nitrogen fertilizer is generally not required. Be sure the seed is treated with the proper inoculant before planting. If your soil is very acidic (pH 5.5 or lower), nodulation may be reduced, and extra nitrogen may be necessary prior to planting. Marathon is available pre-inoculated with an OMRI Listed inoculation for improved establishment and growth. The OMRI Listed® seal assures the suitability of products for certified organic production, handling, and processing.

When planting Marathon and other red clover cultivars, select planting sites that have had some prior weed control management. All clover seedlings do not compete well with established weeds. Maintaining a dense pure stand or a mixed stand of Marathon will prevent most weed issues. Regular mowing can kill or at least suppress annual and biennial weeds. However, Marathon will only regrow as high as it was cut. There are a few herbicide treatments available for mixed clover and grass combinations. Be careful, though, as red clover is sensitive to the soil residues of atrazine and some other herbicides that fall into the Group 2 herbicides. I have found that spot spraying is often the best and safest choice for scattered weed incursions.

Marathon and other red clovers are excellent crops to attract and nourish honeybees. Some food plotters plant red clovers primarily for that reason alone. Marathon red clover is available at www.welterseed.com, www.alliedseed.com and many other seed companies.

CONDENSED RECAP

- **Temperature Tolerances:** Graded as a winter-hardy variety.
- **Inoculant:** Available pre-inoculated with OMRI listed inoculation.
- **Planting Times:** Sow in August/September in the North, later in the South.
- **Seeding Rates:** Stand-alone, 10 to 12 lbs./acre. In a mix, 3 to 6 lbs./acre.
- **Planting Depth:** Plant at $1/8$- to $1/4$-inch deep with good seed-to-soil contact.
- **Companion Plants:** Includes alfalfa, timothy, orchard grass, white clovers, some other legumes or chicory.
- **pH Levels:** Best at 6.0. Will tolerate up to 6.5.
- **Soil Preferences:** Medium-textured soils.
- **Germination:** Sprouts in 10 to 15 days.
- **Fertilizer:** In absence of a soil test, fertilize at planting with 150 to 250 lbs./acre of 20-60-20 or 20-60-40.
- **Crude Protein Content:** Maximum of 27.7 percent.
- **Total Digestible Nutrients (TDN):** 55 to 65 percent.
- **Nitrogen Fixation:** Fixes 70 to 100 lbs./acre annually.
- **Overgrazing Concerns:** Not a concern once established.
- **Extends Grazing Season:** From October to December.
- **Sunlight:** Prefers full sun; will tolerate partial shade.
- **Pollinator Friendly:** Yes, Marathon is very pollinator friendly to honeybees.
- **USDA Hardiness Zone:** Zones 5 to 9.
- **Advice:** For best results, plant with small grains. Does particularly well with cereal rye and winter-type oats.
- **Caution:** Needs at least 6 weeks of growth after germination to survive the winter.
- **Level of Maintenance:** Low.
- **Note:** Handles wetter soils, lower fertility, and lower pH than most other red clovers.

PERSIST BRAND RED CLOVER (*Trifolium pratense L.*)

Persist Brand Red Clover is a cool-season blend of premium three- to four-year red clover strains selected for their persistence and longevity. Persist also has a wide range of disease resistance. It does very well in deer and other wildlife food plots. It is a red clover variety that is long lasting and one that deer relish.

Red clovers are one of the fastest establishing legumes and can even be grown on more acidic soils. Persist Brand red clover is pre-inoculated with an OMRI-listed inoculant for improved establishment and growth. Red clovers use soil or top-dressed phosphorus or potassium more efficiently than alfalfa. This is due to red clover's more extensive surface rooting system.

It is best to grow red clover like Persist in combination with a grass that deer like, such as timothy or perennial ryegrass. Agronomically, mixes are most always stronger than stand-alone seedings. Red clover also pairs well with other clovers and legumes. Mixing in grass will also greatly reduce concerns about overgrazing that come along with pure stands of many legumes. Seeded in the spring, it can be grazed in early summer. In places with heavy deer densities, grazing should be trimmed back in mid-September through the first frost. The best way to achieve this is to plant it in a mix so that grain plants, like oats or rye, will take the pressure off the red clover. This will help to develop the red clover's root reserves needed for winter survival and disease resistance.

Like all red clover, Persist is widely adapted to different soil and climatic conditions and is tolerant of soil acidity. It also tolerates dry conditions quite well, and it is one of the best yielding clovers available. Research has documented that during low rainfall years, red clover plots' measured dry-matter production rated at more than 6,500 lbs./acre per year. The crude protein level in Persist clover is akin to many red clovers. It

▲ Persist clover does very well as a wildlife food plot. It is a brand of red clover selected for persistence and longevity. It also has a wide range of disease resistance. Photo: USDA

typically ranges from 20 to 30 percent depending on soil quality and the time of year.

Persist red clover is easy to establish and can either be broadcast at a rate of 10 to 12 lbs./acre or drilled at 8 to 10 lbs./acre. If broadcast, prepare a smooth, firm seedbed free of large rocks, branches, and other debris to ensure optimal germination and seedling establishment. Its seeds, like other red and white clover seeds, are tiny, so be sure the field is free of deep furrows from disking and large clods of soil to prevent covering the seed too deeply. When planting tiny clover and brassica seeds, it is always best to cultipack before and after sowing the seed. It will go a long way to assist with achieving a good seedbed, seed-to-soil contact, and it will help with having the clover emerge more quickly. Persist red clover is available at www.merit-seed.com.

CONDENSED RECAP

- **Temperature Tolerances:** A cool-hardy clover. It will tolerate some early winter temperatures but not for extended periods.
- **Inoculant:** Live bacteria culture Rhizobium Strain B.
- **Planting Times:** Spring through summer. Plant in July for a fall food plot.
- **Seeding Rates:** As a pure plot, use 10 to 12 lbs./acre. In a mix, sow 3 to 6 lbs./acre.
- **Planting Depth:** Sow at ¼-inch deep.
- **Companion Plants:** Sow with small grains, white clovers, chicory, and grasses.
- **pH Levels:** 6.0 and 6.5 for best results.
- **Soil Preferences:** An ideal soil bed is moist, fertile, and firm.
- **Germination:** In fertile soil, 7 to 10 days.
- **Fertilizer:** In September, use 100 lbs./acre of 0-46-0.
- **Crude Protein Content:** From 20 to 30 percent.
- **Total Digestible Nutrients (TDN):** 16 to 16.5 percent.
- **Nitrogen Fixation:** Yes.
- **Overgrazing Concerns:** Tolerates grazing soon after emerging.
- **Extends Grazing Season:** From October to December.
- **Sunlight:** Prefers full sun.
- **Pollinator Friendly:** Yes, is a copious attractor of honeybees.
- **USDA Hardiness Zone:** Consult your local NRCS field Office or your local Cooperative Extension Service office.
- **Advice:** Best sown with small grains or grasses. Also does well mixed with white clovers.
- **Caution:** Do not use a heavy nitrogen fertilizer.
- **Level of Maintenance:** Medium.

OTHER RED CLOVERS

There are not nearly as many varieties (brands) of red clovers as there are white types of clovers. The remaining red clover varieties in this section have remarkably similar accolades and information to the red clover types listed above. Listing more would necessitate including much of the same detail and data and it would become redundant. Other varieties include types like Alta-Swede Mammoth Red Clover, Cinnamon Plus, Bulldog, Kenstar, Kenland, Cherokee, etc. Below are abbreviated overviews of these red clovers.

NOTE: Most of the red clover varieties below can be planted at 10 to 12 lbs./acre. In a mix use 3 to 6 lbs./acre. Plant at ¼-inch deep.

ALTA-SWEDE MAMMOTH RED CLOVER
(*Trifolium hybridum*)

Alta-Swede Mammoth is a very winter-hardy red clover and is a tall, quick-growing single-cut clover. Alta-Swede is taller and coarser than medium red clover and is about two weeks later in maturity. It is considered a single-cut perennial due to its slow regrowth, and is consequently used primarily as a green manure crop.

Alta-Swede does well in most soils and growing conditions. It is pre-inoculated with an OMRI listed inoculation for improved establishment and growth. An ideal soil bed is moist, fertile, and firm. A soil test is recommended for proper plant establishment and growth. Alta-Swede red clovers can be broadcast or frost-seeded successfully. Alta-Swede Mammoth red clover will fix up to 80 to 100 lbs./acre of nitrogen. It has a long tap root which can loosen soils and mine phosphorus and other nutrients from deep within the soil. Alta-Swede can be planted in the spring or 8 weeks before the first heavy frost and grow in acidic soil with pH values of 5.0–6.0 but prefers 6.0 and higher. Alta-Swede Mammoth Red Clover

▲ Alta-Swede Mammoth Red Clover is extremely winter-hardy. Deer eat clovers most when they are lush and green and do not usually eat the stems. Keeping clovers mowed to about 6 inches in height is ideal to keep them most palatable to deer. In most cases that means preventing clovers from flowering. Photo: USDA

is available at www.welterseed.com and other seed companies.

CHEROKEE RED CLOVER (*Trifolium pratense*)

Cherokee Red Clover is yet another clover or other legume that is inappropriately referred to as a "cool-season" plant. Most often cool-season references actually mean the plant can withstand winter-type temperatures. For instance this clover is winter-hardy in USDA hardiness Zone 4, which means it survives throughout the winter in Pennsylvania, most of New York and other Northeast states. It was developed in Florida and is specifically selected for an earlier spring production. Cherokee has a higher nematode resistance than other red clovers. It can be one of the better deep southern types of clover crops if managed correctly. Plant Cherokee at 8 to 20 lbs./acre depending on the method used to sow the seeds. Never sow Cherokee seeds in hot, dry soil. Wait for some moisture from rainfall, or plant it early in the morning while the dew point is higher. Don't apply nitrogen unless starting a new planting with other seeds, and then only small amounts. Cherokee is available at www.seedland.com and many other seed companies.

CINNAMON PLUS RED CLOVER (*Trifolium pratense*)

Cinnamon Plus is adapted to and intended for use in the east-central and north-central United States. It has been tested in Kentucky, Michigan, Pennsylvania, Tennessee, and Wisconsin. Cinnamon Plus is a diploid medium red clover. Its flower color ranges from light to dark pink. Approximately 75 percent of the plants exhibit leaf markings. Cinnamon Plus is highly resistant to northern and southern anthracnose and powdery mildew. It is a high-quality red clover variety that can be planted with confidence. Vigor and persistence are two top characteristics food plotters want and can expect from this red clover seed for wildlife plots. Cinnamon Plus was selected for persistence under intense grazing pressure and excellent seeding vigor. Available at www.clarkseeds.com and other seed companies.

KENLAND RED CLOVER (*Trifolium pratense*)

Kenland red clover is a cool-season clover. It is a short-lived herbaceous biennial clover that builds nitrogen

▲ Cinnamon Plus Two is an improved variety. It is bred for persistence under intense grazing pressure, making it an ideal clover for wildlife food plots. It does best in a pH of 6.0 or higher and can be grown in most soils. Photo: Dreamstime–© Ruud Morjin

and organic matter. Kenland establishes quickly in the fall and grows slowly through the winter. It is sold as pre-inoculated seed with a life expectancy of 2 to 3 years. It is a single-crown, fast-growing clover that can reach 2- to 2½-feet in height. Kenland has some disease resistance. It prefers fertile soils and a pH value of 5.5 to 6.0 and tolerates a pH from 5.5 to 7.6. Kenland has superior yields to other red clovers and is longer lived. It tolerates most soil types from loam to clay. It does not tolerate drought well. Kenland can fix up to 100 lbs./acre of nitrogen. If seeded in a pure stand, use 15 to 20 lbs./acre. In a mix with grasses or small grains, use 8 to 10 lbs./acre. Kenland can also be frost seeded using 10 to 12 lbs./acre. It tolerates grazing better by deer once it reaches 6 inches or more. Kenland can be grown anywhere in the north-central, Northeast, or New England areas. It is also adaptable to the Midwest, eastern mountains and Piedmont, and the Atlantic and Gulf Coastal plains. Kenland prefers full sun. It has good resistance to southern anthracnose (common in the southern corn belt) and a few other fungal infections. It has striking purple to magenta flowers that are highly attractive to honeybees. To me, a food plot of Kenland clover's deep purple and magenta flowers is more striking than a field of deep red crimson clover. Kenland is available at www.hearneseed.com and other seed companies.

▲ Kenland is tall growing and has pinkish purple to magenta-red flowerheads. It is recommended that this red variety should be sown in the late summer or early fall. It prefers a pH of 6.0 and higher. It tolerates most soil types from loam to clay. It can fix up to 100 lbs./acre of nitrogen per year. Photo: © Lidija Jankulov | Dreamstime

KENSTAR RED CLOVER (*Trifolium pratense*)

Kenstar should not be confused with Kenland. It is a newer variety of medium red clover released by the University of Kentucky. It is a cool-season clover remarkably like Kenland in its area of adaptation and its resistance to southern anthracnose and powdery mildew. However, Kenstar's yield ability is slightly enhanced compared to Kenland. Kenstar's biggest advantage over Kenland is its ability to persist and produce during its third year. Kenstar is available at www. seedland.com and other seed companies.

STARFIRE II RED CLOVER (*Trifolium pratense*)

Starfire II is a relatively new cool-season red clover. It combines several positive aspects including high yield, improved persistence, and strong disease resistance. It is a top-choice for food plotters to attract deer and other hunted game. Starfire II can be sown at ¼-inch

▲ Starfire is a long-lasting clover variety that provides three to four years before having to be replaced or overseeded. One reason for its longevity is because it has excellent resistance to disease. Photo: © Monner | Dreamstime

deep in a firm, moist seedbed. Cultipack the plot before and after seeding it to ensure good seed-to-soil contact. When used in a mix, use 4 to 5 lbs./acre. Best companion plants are small grains, alfalfa, white clovers, or chicory. Available at www.ernstseed.com and other seed companies.

▲ All red clovers are known for their fast establishment. Better yet, they are recognized for their digestible protein, high nutrition, palatability, and ability to provide copious amounts of nitrogen into the soil. Photo: © Milllda | Dreamstime

▲ There are some clover varieties that don't fall into the categories of red or white. They are referred to by most seed companies as "other clovers." Many of these varieties have special attributes including extreme winter-hardiness, shade and acidic soil tolerance, or endure long standing wet or even flooding conditions and more.   Credit: Ted Rose

Chapter Eighteen
Other Clovers

ABERLASTING CLOVER (*Trifolium repens*) is a cool-season red clover that is exceptionally winter-hardy. What also makes AberLasting clover attractive to food plotters is that it has demonstrated superb tolerance for frigid and freezing temperatures. It can withstand overnight exposure to harsh winter from -4°F which will kill off 70 percent of plants of the most tolerant varieties of white clover. According to Deer Creek Seed Co., it survive to an unbelievable -22°F. This is a classic example of why referencing this plant as cool-season clover is in my mind's eye totally inaccurate.

▲ AberLasting clover is a long-lived perennial hybrid developed by GO Seed and available from many retail seed companies. With its stolons above ground and rhizomes below, AberLasting can make a fast recover after heavy grazing by deer, elk, and other wildlife. Photo: GO Seed

Aberlasting is a long-lived hybrid perennial that was developed by crossing Kura (caucasian) clover with white clover. A distinguishing feature of Caucasian clovers is their strong underground root systems, consisting of a dense network of rhizomes and taproots. They are persistent and have good nitrogen-fixing capabilities. AberLasting is drought tolerant because it can maintain its leaf water content far longer than conventional white clovers. This is a good asset for a plant in places where water may be limited or in drier areas. It also shows a strong tolerance to clover root weevil.

AberLasting does best in full sun as long as it gets at least 6 hours per day. However, it can also grow in areas of low light (partial shade). Once any clover reaches 8 to 10 inches tall, including AberLasting, it will have to either be grazed or mowed to about 3 to 4 inches. AberLasting clover is available at www.deercreekseed.com, www.welterseed.com or www.meritseed.com. It can be a bit difficult to find AberLasting clover seed.

CONDENSED RECAP

- **Temperature Tolerances:** Is exceptionally winter-hardy. Tolerates -4°F to an incredible -22°F.
- **Inoculant:** Is available as a pre-inoculated clover.
- **Planting Times:** Best planted at temperatures 52°F and above.
- **Seeding Rates:** Alone plant AberLasting 8 to 12 lbs./acre. In a mix plant at 2 to 3 lbs./acre. Can be frost-seeded.
- **Planting Depth:** Sow at 1/8- to 1/4-inch deep.
- **Companion:** Can be planted alone or in a mixture with other clovers, grasses, or grains.

- **pH Levels:** Prefers 5.8 to 7.0
- **Soil Preferences:** An ideal soil bed is a well-drained moist, fertile, and firm soil.
- **Germination:** Fast. Sprouts in 5 to 7 days. However, emergence is dependent on soil moisture.
- **Fertilizer:** In lieu of a soil test, use 300 lbs./acre of 19-19-19. In September use 300 lbs./acre of 0-20-20.
- **Crude Protein Content:** From 25–30 percent.
- **Total Digestible Nutrients (TDN):** Like most clovers, the TDN is rated high: 75–82 percent.
- **Nitrogen Fixation:** Can produce 150 to 200 lbs./acre per year.
- **Overgrazing Concerns:** It is rated to tolerate severe grazing—negating any concerns about being over-browsed.
- **Extends Grazing Season:** Well into winter.
- **Sunlight:** Prefers full sun; tolerates partial shade.
- **Pollinator Friendly:** Yes.
- **USDA Hardiness Zone:** Check the USDA Hardiness Zone in your area. However, AberLasting is winter-hardy enough to not worry about planting it in the North.
- **Advice:** Exhibits only limited persistency under more extreme environmental stress.
- **Caution:** Without snow cover, can only withstand temperatures from -4° to -22°F for a few days.
- **Level of Maintenance:** Medium.
- **Note:** In areas with heavy deer densities, AberLasting makes an excellent planting because of its ability to tolerate heavy grazing.

ALSIKE CLOVER (*Trifolium hybridum*)

Alsike Clover is another, winter-hardy annual or biennial clover which is adapted to northern climates and cool summers. This is a perfect plant for all northern regions. Alsike clover is a true species despite its name, which originally implied that it was a hybrid of white clover (*T. repens*) and red clover (*T. pretense*). It is an introduced, non-creeping clover with a growth habit like red clover. Alsike is often used under abnormal planting conditions, like very wet soil. But when needed, it's ideal for the job when those conditions include poorly drained and acidic soils. Alsike prefers wetter soils over droughty soils. It will tolerate lengthy spring flooding and completely waterlogged soil, but not for long extended periods. In these conditions, alsike can still provide quality forage for multiple years.

however, has little tolerance for shade. It is often sold pre-inoculated with Rhizobium bacteria Strain B. But when buying pre-inoculated seed, it is always wise to check with the seller that it is indeed pre-inoculated.

Alsike is commonly used for soil improvement. Its relatively shorter growth height (compared to other clovers) makes it desirable for food plotters as a stand-alone plot, or in wildlife mixtures. Alsike is best established in April or early May when the moisture content in soils is most favorable. It can also be planted in late summer in areas that receive adequate rainfall.

Alsike's small seeds should not be planted too deeply—no more than $\frac{1}{8}$- to $\frac{1}{4}$-inch. It can be broadcast at 8 to 12 lbs./acre and drilled at 4 to 6 lbs./acre. Plant alsike in a well-prepared seedbed that has been

▲ Alsike is the go-to clover for food plotters. It has excellent attributes. It is extremely winter-hardy, withstands excessive soil moisture and even flooding, it is more adaptable to a variety of soil types, and is exceptionally easy to grow. It does not tolerate drought or shade, however. Photo: PCFImages

Alsike is a semi-erect perennial that reaches heights of 1 to 3 feet with white and pink flowers. Alsike can withstand low pH levels. It is a legume that is more adaptable to a variety of soil types and is extremely easy to grow in almost any condition. It can easily be established with a minimum of soil preparation, but it must not be seeded deeply. It can be grown throughout the United States and in most of Canada. Alsike,

▲ Big N' Tuf is an effective herbicide to kill grass and broadleaf weeds. It is carried in Tractor Supply and other farm stores. Photo: PCFImages

well disked and has been killed with an appropriate glyphosate herbicide like FarmWorks, Roundup, Whitetail Institute's Slay, Arrest Max, or Big N' Tuf.

Alsike can be planted as a pure stand, or with grasses like timothy or perennial ryegrass, small grains like wheat, barley, rye, oats, triticale, or with birdsfoot trefoil. When mixing alsike, the seeding rate for the small grains should be 50 lbs./acre mixed with 6 to 8 lbs./acre of alsike. In lieu of a soil test, which is always preferable to get before planting any seed, fertilize a pure stand of alsike with 350 to 400 lbs./acre of 8-24-24. In mixed plots, fertilize alsike with 300 to 350 lbs./acre of 16-18-19 or T-19 (19-19-19). Once established, alsike will tolerate heavy grazing by deer. Alsike's highest production generally takes place from May to September. Fertilize it again in August with 200 to 250 lbs./acre with a non-nitrogen fertilizer like 0-20-30. Alsike should be mowed about 2 times per year: once in June and again in late July.

Alsike is a top-notch seeding in areas that are too wet to plant other types of clovers, brassicas, or other types of plantings that cannot tolerate wet soil. I have successfully grown alsike in wet areas. I have even seen it tolerate flooding—but not more than about 6 weeks. It is also an excellent choice for northern areas that experience cold winter temperatures, as alsike is winter-hardy. Alsike white clover is available at www.deercreekseed.com and other seed companies.

CONDENSED RECAP

- **Temperature Tolerance:** Rated by seed companies as extremely winter-hardy.
- **Inoculant:** Not usually sold pre-inoculated. It must be inoculated with the proper strain—*Rhizobium leguminosarum biovar trifolii.*
- **Planting Times:** Plant in spring or late summer. Can also be frost-seeded in late winter.
- **Seeding Rates:** Broadcast at 8 to 12 lbs./acre.
- **Planting Depth:** No more than 3/8-inch deep. It can be drilled at ¼-inch deep.
- **Companion Plants:** All the small grains (rye, oats, wheat, triticale, barley), grasses like timothy or ryegrass, and birdsfoot trefoil.
- **Preferred pH:** It will tolerate a soil pH as low as 5.1 prefers 6.0 to 6.5., will also tolerate alkalinity.
- **Soil Preference:** Prefers wetter soils over droughty soils. Can tolerate limited flooding of about a few weeks or so.
- **Germination:** When correctly planted most times, it will emerge in under a week.
- **Fertilizer:** In lieu of a soil test, use 300 to 350 lbs./acre of either 16-18-19 or 19-19-19.
- **Protein Content:** About 20 percent.
- **Digestibility:** Rated at 65 percent.
- **High Nitrogen Fixation:** Yes, alsike clover fixes nitrogen.
- **Over Grazing:** Once established, grazing is generally not an issue.
- **Extends Grazing Season:** Yes, well into November.
- **Sun:** Prefers full sun.
- **Pollinator Friendly:** Alsike's flowers are particularly attractive to honeybees for the nectar and pollen.
- **USDA Hardiness Zone:** Zones 3–8.
- **Advice:** This plant is an excellent choice for lands with wet soils. Will not tolerate hot summers.
- **Caution:** For best production, mow once in June and again in July.
- **Level of Maintenance:** Low.
- **Note:** Alsike does not tolerate shade. It grows well on cold, wet to acidic or alkaline soils.

CRIMSON CLOVER (*Trifolium incarnatum L*)

Crimson clover is a cool-season clover that is primarily winter-hardy in the South and a spring/summer annual in the North. Crimson clover is highly productive, attractive, and nutritious to deer and other wildlife. Crimson clover should not be confused with the perennial red clover, which belongs to the family *Fabaceae* (the bean family). They are two separate plants with the latter belonging to the red clovers. Crimson clover is usually categorized as part of the "other" types of clovers. It is an exceedingly popular annual clover among wildlife managers, particularly throughout the southern parts of the country, where it can be grown as a beautifully colored winter-hardy planting. It can even do well as far west as the Pacific Coast, where winters are also mild. In the North, crimson clover can be planted throughout the Northeast and New England as a warm-season summer and very early fall crop. It will not tolerate winter-hardy temperatures in northern areas and will winter kill soon after the first hard frost.

Depending on soil fertility, crimson clover plants grow to a height of about 1 to 3 feet and produce stunningly brilliant, deep-red crimson flowers. Crimson clover is also a top-notch clover to attract honeybees. It is more acidic tolerant than some other clovers and can endure a pH range as low as 5.5 and up to 7.0, but prefers a pH range from 6.0 to 6.7. Crimson clover grows best on well-drained, fertile, loamy soils, but is also adapted to sandy to clay soils of moderate acidity.

▲ This is a field of a variety of crimson clover called Kentucky Pride Crimson clover. Crimson is cool-season annual that most deer species, wild turkey, upland birds, and small game are all decidedly attracted to. Photo: GO Seed

In the North, Crimson is best planted either in spring or early summer. In the South, where snow and cold temperatures are not common, it can be planted from April through October and even later in the deep South. Plant it in a well-prepared seed bed and culti-pack it to ensure good seed-to-soil contact.

Prior to planting, crimson must be inoculated. It usually comes pre-inoculated, but if it is not, use Rhizobium bacteria (Strain R). Seeds can be drilled in at 10 to 15 lbs./acre. Planted as a stand-alone plot, broadcast seed at a rate of 20 lbs./acre. For best success, cultipack the plot prior to planting and again after it has been sown. As a legume, it is not necessary to provide considerable amounts of nitrogen to crimson. However, the fertilizer should contain adequate amounts of potassium and phosphorus. If a soil test is not taken, a good fertilizer mix would be low in nitrogen like 8-24-24. When sown with other plants, fertilize crimson at planting with 300 lbs./acre of 16-18-19 or 19-19-19.

Good companion plants for crimson include all the cereal crops such as rye, triticale, wheat, barley, or cold season oats. The grains should be kept at no more than 50 lbs./acre. It will also do well when planted with other clovers and some legumes. Crimson clover forage is highly nutritious, providing more than 25 percent crude protein levels and 80 percent digestibility.

Crimson clover is not tolerant of extreme drought and extended heat. In some areas it will not tolerate prolonged cold spells. It is inexpensive, easy to grow, and productive after planting. It is very palatable to deer.

▲ Kentucky Pride Crimson Clover was developed by GO Seed. It has a deeper shade of magenta red (reddish-purple) flowers than I have ever seen on other crimson varieties. GO Seed is a valuable resource for information, education, and advocacy. It functions as a breeder, producer, and provider of a wide range of seed products and knowledge. While they develop many product lines in house, they also access some of the finest research and development programs around the world. Photo: Goseed. com

I plant a half-acre of crimson clover as a single seed plot mostly to enjoy the aesthetics of looking at the incredibly beautiful deep, brilliant flowers. My other plots of crimson are planted either as a primary crimson plot mixed with other plantings, or a plot of some other primary seed with a smaller amount of crimson included. Crimson clover is available at www.johnny-seeds.com and many other seed companies.

▲ Most seed companies sell crimson clover pre-inoculated with rhizobium bacteria Strain R. However, it is always wise to check first before buying. If it's not pre-inoculated, you will need to inoculate the seed yourself. Photo: PCFImages

CONDENSED RECAP

- **Temperature Tolerances:** Winter-hardy in the South and deep South. Best used as a summer planting in northern zones. It will winter-kill after a couple of hard frosts.
- **Inoculant:** Available pre-inoculated. Otherwise inoculate with Rhizobium bacteria (Strain R), which is a different strain of bacteria than many other varieties of clovers.
- **Planting Times:** Plant in late April or May. In the South it can be planted from August to early November, later in the deep South.
- **Seeding Rates:** Alone, plant at 10 to 15 lbs./acre. In a mix, plant at 10 lbs./acre.
- **Planting Depth:** Plant no more than ¼-inch deep.
- **Companion Plants:** Red clovers like Marathon red and small grains (rye, wheat, barley, triticale, or cold-season oats) and some legumes.
- **pH Levels:** Prefers a pH of 5.8 and 6.5. Will tolerate a pH of 5.0 and 7.5. It will not endure acid soils.
- **Soil Preferences:** Productive when grown on well-drained, fertile, loamy to sandy clay soils.
- **Germination:** In fertile soil, it generally sprouts in 2 to 3 days.
- **Fertilizer:** When sown with other plants, fertilize crimson at planting with 300 lbs./acre of 19-19-19. Alone, at planting use 300 lbs./acre of 8-24-24.
- **Crude Protein Content:** Has a crude protein level of up to 25 percent.
- **Total Digestible Nutrients (TDN):** Rated at 80 percent.
- **Nitrogen Fixation:** A fertile stand of crimson will fix 70 to 150 lbs./acre of nitrogen.
- **Overgrazing Concerns:** Crimson can withstand heavy grazing.
- **Matures:** In 70 to 90 days.
- **Extends Grazing Season:** In the North, can extend grazing into early October; later in the South and deep South.
- **Sunlight:** Prefers full sun.
- **Pollinator Friendly:** Yes. Rated as an excellent honeybee attractive clover. Crimson clover has relatively short florets, making the nectar relatively easy for honeybees to attain.
- **USDA Hardiness Zone:** Zones 6–9.
- **Advice:** Plant millet, corn, or sorghum in plots where crimson was sown.
- **Caution:** Crimson requires inoculation. Always follow the instructions carefully. Poor inoculation can cause crop failure.
- **Level of Maintenance:** Low to Medium.
- **Note:** Crimson establishes better when mixed with a companion crop of a small grain. Keep grains to 50 lbs./acre.

FIXatioN BALANSA CLOVER (*Trifolium michelianum savi*)

If you are looking for a bio-massive and an *extremely* winter-hardy clover, take a look at FIXatioN (a.k.a. fixation) Balansa clover developed by the breeder GO Seed. FIXatioN Balansa is an annual white clover that is exceptionally winter-hardy. It ranks second in winter-hardiness to AberLasting (which can tolerate up to -24° F). FIXatioN Balansa is capable of withstanding temperatures down to -14° F. That's seriously cold for a clover or any food plot plant for that matter. It will survive and be nourishing to deer even if it is covered under snow. FIXatioN Balansa clover has been shown to be a highly nutritious planting that is a favored food source for deer, elk, upland birds, and waterfowl.

This is an exciting and revolutionary clover. FIXatioN Balansa clover is somewhat of a newcomer to the deer food plot scene, but its many unique qualities make it an excellent choice as a deer forage.

Balansa grows well in a wide variety of soil types and can be planted throughout the United States. Its root system is capable of 18 inches of growth in just 45 days. FIXatioN draws water and nutrients from well below surrounding plant roots. It is also tolerant of dry conditions because of its large tap roots that can access soil moisture. Additionally, one of the best attributes of FIXatioN Balansa is its ability to thrive in poorly drained soils and periodic standing water; very few quality deer forages have this ability. FIXatioN provides an excellent option for hunters and food plotters

▲ To grow healthier deer and large antlered bucks, stop reading this and order FIXatioN. It produces copious amounts of nitrogen and its roots support vigorous XL large leaf growth that offer protein levels of 22 to 30 percent. Its key benefit is that it tolerates winter temperatures of 5°F without snow cover. With snow cover, it has survived sub-zero temperatures as low as -14°F! Photo: Goseed.com

whose properties have occasional soggy bottomlands during winter. It also tolerates heavy grazing by deer.

FIXatioN Balansa is a small seeded annual legume that produces exceptional quantities of nitrogen (it can set more than 200 lbs. of nitrogen per acre). It can grow up to 3 feet in height with stems growing up to 8 feet long. These long stems suppress weed growth by shading out competing weeds for water and nutrients. FIXatioN also does well in wet soils, including short periods of flooding. It is also tolerant of heat and drought. FIXatioN Balansa grows well in mixes with other cover crops, although it is not a good partner with soybean cyst nematodes. It is also a terrific re-seeder. Its serrated leaflets are variable, with about 45 percent having markings. Finally, FIXatioN seed may be more expensive per pound when compared to the cost of other annual clovers. However, as a highly attractive, nutritious, and extremely winter-hardy clover, FIXatioN Balansa is well worth the extra cost. FIXatioN will continue to produce substantial amounts of highly nutritious forage long after hunting season is over. This leads to larger, healthier deer and better deer winter survival.

Additionally, with the ever-declining populations of honeybees, FIXatioN is a clover that helps support honeybee populations. FIXatioN flowers can range from white to pink and are especially attractive to pollinator insects. Its pollen contains 27–29 percent protein (dry weight), producing a light-colored honey with a very distinct and pleasing flavor. The pollen produced by FIXatioN Balansa clover has been documented to meet all the dietary needs of European honeybees, one of the few clover species to do so. FIXatioN Balansa Clover is available at www.welterseed.com, www.outsidepride.com and many other seed companies.

CONDENSED RECAP

- **Temperature Tolerances:** FIXatioN is *extremely* winter-hardy. Withstands temperatures down to -14°F. It is the second most cold-tolerant of annual clovers.
- **Inoculant:** Available as pre-inoculated seed with a specific strain of live rhizobia bacteria (Prevail) contained in the coating of FIXatioN.
- **Planting Times:** In the North, plant as early as May or as late as June. In the South, plant either in March or June. Can also be frost-seeded.
- **Seeding Rates:** Broadcast at 8 lbs./acre. When planted with any grain use a rate of 4 to 5 lbs./acre. Drill at 3 lbs./acre.
- **Companion Plants:** Forage rape, all grains like cereal rye (5 lbs./acre FIXatioN and 20 lbs./acre rye grain), chicory, and other clovers. Its small seed size and hardiness enable it to be successfully broadcast and established with many existing forages.
- **Planting Depth:** 1/8- to 1/4-inch. Sow in a well-prepared, smooth, clean seedbed that has been cultipacked prior to a predicted rainfall.
- **pH Levels:** Prefers 6.5 but can be successful in pH levels ranging from 4.5 to 8.0.
- **Soil Preferences:** Grows well in a wide variety of soil types. Also tolerates poorly drained soils with moderate salinity. Can performs well in wet soils including soils with short periods of flooding.
- **Germination:** Can sprout in 3 to 5 days, depending upon soil temperature and moisture.
- **Fertilizer:** In lieu of a soil test, use 350 to 400 lbs./acre of 19-19-19 (a.k.a. T-19).
- **Crude Protein Levels:** Excellent. Between 25 and 30 percent.
- **Total Digestible Nutrients (TDN):** Rated extremely high in digestibility and deer preference.
- **Nitrogen Fixation:** Yes, capable of setting more than 100 units of nitrogen per acre.
- **Overgrazing Concerns:** Once established, tolerates heavy grazing pressure by deer and other game.
- **Hours of Sunlight:** Prefers full sun but has good shade tolerance with 4 to 6 hours of sunlight.
- **Extends Grazing:** Will remain a nutritious plant well into the winter months.
- **Pollinator Friendly:** Yes, its white to pink flowers are attractive to bees.
- **USDA Hardiness Zones:** Zone 6B to -14°F.
- **Advice:** Plant either as a stand-alone winter-hardy crop or with other winter-hardy grains.
- **Caution**: Not a host for soybean cyst nematodes. Do not plant in areas of extended flooding or standing water.
- **Maintenance Level:** Rated as medium. Should be mowed to prevent bolting.

FROSTY BERSEEM CLOVER (*Trifolium alexandrinum*)

Frosty berseem is an annual clover. At the outset, let me say that Frosty Berseem is a more recent variety of berseem clover and the only variety that is rated as very cold-hardy, as it can survive temperatures down to 10°F, and even in the low single digits. It should not be confused with other types of warm-season berseem clovers, which are highly susceptible to winter kill. Frosty berseem was bred to provide more nutritional value than other berseem varieties of clovers. Therefore, it will be a nourishing and viable clover that lasts well into December and longer. That changes the way food plotters once thought of berseem clovers.

Deer absolutely savor Frosty berseem and seek it out enthusiastically. Thankfully, Frosty berseem is also very tolerant of heavy deer browsing. Nutritionally, Frosty has excellent palatability for deer and other wildlife including high crude protein levels. It is rated as a fast-growing annual clover. Frosty berseem clover has oblong-shaped leaflets that are considered large when compared to many other clovers. It can reach 2 to 3 feet tall but rarely does because deer graze it so heavily.

Frosty can be broadcasted, drilled, or frost-seeded. It can be planted in a mix or as a stand-alone plot. Cultipacking the plot prior to sowing the seed will help with accomplishing the ideal flat seedbed, which in

▲ My second favorite to FIXatioN, is Frosty berseem clover. It is an improved variety that is tolerates cold temperatures better than other berseem varieties. It has survived temperatures down to 10°F. FYI: The dog's name is Stormy; he is a Mountain Feist. I hope Stormy doesn't eat clover. Photo: GO Seed

turn will help quicker germination. If planted in loose soil, it will reduce germination.

Frosty prefers well-drained to moderately drained soils with a pH (greater than 6.0). It grows well in all soil types except deep sands with low moisture retention. It is tolerant of dry conditions, and high soil moisture. One of the best assets is that it germinates very quickly when compared to other types of clovers. Frosty berseem clover is available at www.seedbarn.com and many other seed companies.

CONDENSED RECAP

- **Temperature Tolerance:** Able to tolerate freezing temperatures of 10°F for an extended period of time.
- **Inoculate:** Available pre-inoculated with live Rhizobium bacteria (Strain R). Check first, however.
- **Planting Times:** In the South, seed in fall. In the North, seed in July or early August for a fall crop.
- **Seeding Rates:** Broadcast at 25 lbs./acre, mix at 12 to 16 lbs./acre. Drill at 15 lbs./acre.
- **Companion Plants:** Can be mixed with some brassicas, all grains, chicory, and other clovers. Its small seed size and hardiness enable it to be successfully broadcasted and established with many existing forages.
- **Planting Depth:** ¼-inch deep.
- **pH Levels:** Prefers 6.0 to 6.5, will tolerate higher 6.6 to 7.0.

- **Soil Preference:** All soil types except deep sands that do not hold moisture well.
- **Germination:** In ideal conditions, will emerge quickly.
- **Fertilizer:** In lieu of a soil test, use 350 to 400 lbs./per acre of a 19-19-19; better yet, 16-18-19. In September, use 400 lbs./acre of 0-20-30 or 0-20-20.
- **Crude Protein Content:** Frosty has a crude protein level of 18 to 28 percent.
- **Total Digestible Nutrients (TDN):** Rated as particularly good to excellent.
- **Nitrogen Fixation:** Yes. Reduces the need for nitrogen-heavy fertilizers.
- **Overgrazing:** Once established, will tolerate heavy grazing by deer.
- **Sun:** Prefers full sun but can tolerate part shade.
- **Extends Grazing Season:** Into December.
- **Pollinator Friendly:** Yes, highly attractive to honeybees.
- **USDA Hardiness Zone:** Hardy to about 15°– 20°F.
- **Advice:** For quicker germination, sow into a well-prepared, clean, smooth seedbed prior to a predicted rainfall if practical.
- **Caution:** Do not mix up Frosty berseem with older types of berseem clover.
- **Level of Maintenance:** Medium. Plot should be mowed twice to prevent plant bolting.

▲ Pheasants prefer corn, sorghum, and other grains. However, as omnivores, they will eat anything they can peck at, including clovers. Credit: Ted Rose

KURA CLOVER (*Trifolium ambiguum*)

Kura is a winter-hardy clover. It is a long-lived, high-quality perennial clover, although it is sometimes referred to as a legume. Kura spreads by rhizomes rather than stolons. The leaves have three leaflets with a crescent or watermark on the upper surface of the leaf and sawtooth leaf edges. The flowers are white to pink and a little larger than other white clovers.

Kura clover blooms once per season and only after being induced by low winter temperatures. It will grow in a variety of soils, but it generally does well in clay and silt soils in humid areas. It grows well on droughty soils. In fact, it is the only clover known to grow in a drought. But it does not tolerate poor drainage. Kura clover's dense rhizomatous root system penetrates the soil to a depth of two feet. These deep roots give it the ability to not only survive in a drought, but also grow.

Kura is a terrific choice when a food plotter is looking for a pure stand of clover that is incredibly

▲ Kura clover is yet another very winter-hardy clover. I also like it for its ability to tolerate heavy grazing. Much better than red clovers or alfalfas. Grasses and weeds must be controlled during its first six weeks of growth. Kura can be expensive. Photo: NC

winter-hardy. Like FIXatioN Balansa, Frosty berseem, and Alice clover, Kura can tolerate temperatures in the low single digits. It is a very winter-hardy clover that has survived severe northern winters when other clovers and legumes like alfalfa, birdsfoot trefoil, arrowleaf, Durana, crimson, and other ladino types of clovers have not.

Kura is a high-quality forage that is an excellent attractant for white-tailed deer, elk, mule deer, other big game, wild turkeys, other upland birds, and even some small game. It can also withstand intense heavy grazing. Kura is a top-notch clover to attract deer during the hunting seasons from late October throughout December. Deer will paw up all the above-mentioned clovers from under a few inches of snow.

There are three varieties of Kura available in the country: Cossack, Endura, and Rhizo. There are also many different VNS varieties. A VNS variety is a seed that has not been researched and certified; it instead is sold as an uncertified seed under the label Variety Not Stated (VNS).

Kura, however, does have some limitations. First off, it is very iffy about its availability. In some years it is difficult to find; other years it is not. Whenever you can locate it, it is among the most expensive clovers. It can cost $10 or more per pound. Lastly, it has poor seeding vigor and is slow to establish. Consequently, Kura should be grown by itself the first year. But it is important to note all the other positive points about Kura far outweigh the few negatives. Kura clover is available at www.interlakeforageseeds.com, www.welterseed.com and some other seed companies.

CONDENSED RECAP
- **Temperature Tolerances:** Very winter-hardy.
- **Inoculant:** Available pre-inoculated w/Rhizobium bacteria (strain Trifolium Spec 3).
- **Planting Times:** Best planted in May or early June for a fall crop. Frost-seeding kura is risky and not recommended.
- **Seeding Rates:** Alone, 6 to 8 lbs./acre. In a mix, 1 to 3 lbs./acre.
- **Planting Depth:** ¼-inch deep in a well-prepared seedbed.
- **Companion Plants:** Does best when planted alone in its first year. It can be mixed in following years

with other clovers, chicory, small grains, timothy, or ryegrass.

- **pH Levels:** Prefers 6.0 to 7.0.
- **Soil Preferences:** Clay and silt soils in humid areas.
- **Germination:** Slow to establish.
- **Fertilizer:** 350 to 400 lbs./acre of 19-19-19 or 16-18-19. In September, use 400 lbs./acre of 0-20-30 or 0-20-20.
- **Crude Protein Content:** From 22 to 25 percent.
- **Total Digestible Nutrients (TDN):** Average digestibility is 83 percent.
- **Nitrogen Fixation:** Yes, reduces need for nitrogen-heavy fertilizer.
- **Overgrazing Concerns:** Once established, will tolerate heavy grazing by deer.
- **Extends Grazing Season:** From late October throughout December.
- **Hours of Sunlight:** Prefers full sun.
- **Pollinator Friendly:** Kura is an absolute favorite of honeybees.
- **USDA Hardiness Zone:** Since Kura is a relatively new clover, there is no official USDA winter-hardy listing for it at this writing.
- **Advice:** Planting Kura later than June is not advised for a fall crop.
- **Caution:** Slow to establish. Susceptible to being shaded out by weeds/grass.
- **Level of Maintenance:** Medium—requires mowing to keep it palatable for deer.
- **Note:** Kura is expensive. If not purchased in April or May, it can be difficult to find.

▲ Kura clover is one of the hardiest winter clovers. Credit: GoSeed.com

▶ Legumes are highly attractive plantings for deer and other wildlife. They include the more popular varieties like soybeans, lablab, cow peas, burgundy beans, lupine and several others. Credit: Ted Rose

Chapter Nineteen

The Legumes

There can be some confusion between clovers and legumes. All clovers are legumes but not all legumes are clovers. To keep it simple, many times when clovers and legumes are referred to, they are correctly called clovers and *other legumes*. The group known as "other legumes" is a cluster of plants that are well-known forage and agricultural crops grown for humans, domestic animals, deer, and other wildlife. Of the thirteen *other legumes*, some include alfalfa, soybeans, peas, beans, vetches, lupines, and trefoil. Therefore, most times when they are written about, the two categories of legumes are separated into "clovers" and "other legumes." Hence, this chapter includes only *other legumes*.

Every resident deer on your property needs between 1 to 2 tons of nutritional food per year. If they cannot get it on your land, they will seek it elsewhere. That is why many biologists and food plot experts recommend a minimum of 5 to 6 percent of any property should have nutritious food plots. Large properties of hundreds or thousands of acres can include much larger

▲ Alfalfa is an excellent forage plant for deer and other wildlife. But it is not a miracle plant. Because it is dormant by November, it is not a top choice to plant to draw in deer during hunting season. It is expensive and difficult to establish and requires plenty of farming experience and equipment to grow well. Additionally, it is not practical to plant it in fields less than 3 acres. Photo: PCFImages

percentages. These food plots can consist of traditional plantings as well as fruit trees, nut trees, and enhanced natural vegetation.

Of that 6 percent, set aside what you feel is an appropriate percentage for warm-season plantings. Vary the plots not only in size but also shape. Some plots can be long and narrow, others square or oval, and still other plots can be imaginatively shaped like the letter "Z," for example. The key is to be creative about the shapes of your food plots. However, it is crucial that all plots, despite their size and shape, do not exclude sunlight.

I generally allocate about 15 percent of my food plots to warm plots. Most years, I plant about 35 plots ranging in size from 100 x 50 feet to a few acres, and everything in between. Therefore, there are always about 5 to 6 warm-season plots within the 35 food plots planted. The remaining 30 food plots are devoted to winter-hardy plantings. That's not accounting for non-traditional food plots like chestnut trees, a wide variety of late-dropping fruit trees, our "real" nut trees like almonds, and the other non-conventional food plots.

As I have said, the abundance, nutrition, and condition of deer and other wildlife is related directly to soil fertility. Soil fertility can vary widely from one area to another only 75 yards away. Most often higher fertility will generally be located near areas that were seeded with warm-season forages particularly in drainages and low-lying areas. These areas will often produce the best warm-season forage sites, since they are both fertile and generally hold moisture better during the hot summer months. Remember, like clovers, all other legumes—be they warm, cool, or winter-hardy—must be treated with the proper inoculant before and/or at the time of planting.

A Sidenote: Before discussing the warm, cool/winter-hardy season legumes, I want to make sure you understand that I'm not advocating that you plant just late-season plantings. Warm-season plantings have a significant role and place in a food plot management program, particularly, if you have an ample amount of acreage. When planting only a couple of acres or less, however, it is wise to keep your plantings focused mostly on cool-season winter-hardy plantings, as they will be the best plants to draw deer to your plots during

▲ I plant at least 15 acres or more in food plots. The plots seen here are a total of about 3½ acres, not including one of our small fruit and nut tree orchards (upper right). When you have enough acreage, it is more practical to dedicate more of it to planting spring and summer forages. Photo: PCFImages

the hunting seasons from October through December. For land managers who plant large acreages from two to several acres or more, it is much more practical to include summer plantings, too. For instance, if you have only one acre to plant, allotting one-fifth of the that acre to a warm-season plot may not be as beneficial as adding an extra cold-season plot to attract deer when you want them there the most—during hunting season. Of course, the choice, however, is up to each individual food plotter. A fix to such a problem may be to include a plot or two that includes both warm and winter-hardy plantings.

Because I plant a total of about 15 to 20 acres of food plots, I can justify including up to 20 percent of them as warm-season legumes such as Alyceclover, lablab, sweetclover, etc. They provide quality nutrition in early spring when the pregnant does could use some extra nutritious forage. Warm-season legumes are also used heavily by fawns after they are weaned. Many warm-weather legumes (and clovers) can tolerate heavy spring and summer grazing. The main purpose of planting warm-season legumes and clovers serves another crucial function other than providing spring and summer forage to wildlife on our farm. We also want to attract honeybees so they can help pollinate our fruit trees and other plantings. Honeybees gather and eat a wide variety of sweet items including, but not limited to, nectar, pollen, sugar, juices from fruits, and syrups. Pollen is one of the purest and richest natural foods, containing all the nutritional requirements of a honeybee: sugar, carbohydrates, protein, enzymes, vitamins, and minerals. Each honeybee colony collects more than 60 pounds of pollen per year. Nectar is the sweet fluid found in flowers.

Honeybees collect pollen and nectar from a variety of flowering plants, including legumes, clovers, fruit trees, and other plantings as well as from a variety of weeds like milkweed, dandelions, and goldenrod. So naturally it is highly beneficial for us to plant legumes that attract and help hold wild honeybees on our land. Human beings have recognized the important value of honeybees in agriculture for thousands of years. Honeybees are the single-most effective pollinators of plants in the world. They are an irreplaceable resource to agriculture productivity. To that end, I rent at least one beehive a year from a local beekeeper. Honeybees will significantly bolster the overall health and productivity of all your plantings. This simple strategy will quickly encourage wild honeybees to set up homes on your land and help in your pursuit of a more productive food plot program. Consider renting a beehive for a couple of seasons. To encourage wild bees into your plots, plan to include some of the warm-season legumes in your management program that are mentioned below.

COOL and WINTER-HARDY LEGUMES

Legumes are usually listed as either warm-season or cool-season plants. While these designations are correct, I prefer to divide legumes (and clovers) as a more

▲ To attract and hold honeybees on your property, it is important to plant warm-season clovers, fruit trees, and other legumes. The bees repay you by pollinating all your plantings. Photo: NRCS

self-explanatory groupings: warm-season, cool-season/ and winter-hardy. Each of the categories accurately describe legumes and clovers based on how well they fare under different weather conditions. The cool-season rated plantings are diverse enough to double as both warm-season and cold-season plantings. Both the cool-season to winter-hardy groups can be mixed with other winter-hardy plantings, including small grains like winter cereal rye, winter wheat, oats, sorghum (milo), triticale, and even corn. Some of the extremely winter-hardy legumes can be planted as stand-alone plots due to their ability to withstand extreme winter temperatures. These legumes are for managers who have hunting properties in cold, northern areas who want legumes and clovers to be viable during deer hunting seasons.

WARM SEASON ANNUAL LEGUMES

ALYCECLOVER (*Alysicarpus vaginallis*)

Alyceclover has a name that can be somewhat misleading. One would think it is a true clover (having a trifoliate leaf), but it is not. Instead, alyceclover is a warm-season, thin-stemmed, erect annual legume. It has rounded leaves and its flowers can range from bright pink to a deep reddish purple. Alyceclover is mostly planted as livestock forage and is rated as a quality forage for deer. It can tolerate persistent grazing well. Alyceclover performs well when planted in a variety of soils and can even tolerate drought conditions, but not for extended periods.

Alyceclover production does particularly well when it is planted in well-drained sandy loam or clay soils, but not heavy clay. It is mostly tailored to the Gulf Coast zone but will also perform well from the mid-Atlantic to the eastern parts of the United States.

While Alyceclover is relatively easy to plant and grow, it is not always said to be a highly preferred food source for deer. With that claim made, though, alyceclover's nutritional quality is regarded as "excellent." In well-managed food plots having quality soil fertility, alyceclover can produce elevated levels of protein and digestibility.

Alyceclover is slow to germinate and has a slow-going growth habit. Once it is established, however, it is exceptionally productive, often producing notable 2 to 3 tons of forage (dry weight) per acre throughout its growing season. Furthermore, as mentioned, alyceclover is quite resistant to grazing pressure, making it a rather good legume for food plotters to plant, particularly in areas with high deer densities. Alyceclover will produce well from June to September, still being palatable to deer in a time of year when other plants are stressed by the summer's heat to the point of providing lower quality food stuffs.

▲ Alyceclover is not a true clover but a warm-season legume. It can supply abundant amounts of high-quality forage for deer, elk, wild turkey, et-al. It is a quality forage for nursing does and their growing fawns. Credit: © Hguerrio | Dreamstime

Another advantage of Alyceclover is that it can be successfully established by top-seeding it on a prepared seed bed. Kill the existing vegetation with glyphosate at least ten days prior to planting, then broadcast the seed prior to a forecasted rainfall.

CONDENSED RECAP

- **Temperature Tolerances:** Warm-season plant.
- **Inoculant:** Most times it comes pre-inoculated. The proper strain is Rhizobium bacteria (Strain EL).
- **Preferred pH:** Will tolerate some soil acidity from 5.5 but prefers a pH value of 6.0 to 6.2.
- **Planting Time:** Should be planted in mid-May to June in warm soils above 60°F.
- **Soil:** Will withstand clay soils but prefers well-drained sandy loam soils.
- **Seeding Rates:** Planted as a stand-alone plot, use 15 to 20 lbs./acre. Drill at 12 lbs./acre.
- **Seed Depth:** Sow from ¼- to ½-inch deep. Do not plant deeper than ½-inch. Can also be top-seeded only in a well-prepared, clean seed bed that is appropriately cultipacked.
- **Germination:** Slow to germinate.
- **Fertilizer:** In lieu of a soil test, apply 3 lbs./acre of 8-24-24 at planting. Alyceclover does not need nitrogen fertilizer since it produces its own.

However, it responds well to phosphorus and potassium for optimal growth, nutritional quality, and attraction.

- **Maturity:** This plant is slow to reach maturity.
- **Crude Protein Content:** In terms of crude protein, it typically contains 20 to 30 percent protein.
- **Total Digestibility (TDN):** Regarded as high.
- **Companion Mixes:** Alyceclover does well mixed with American jointvetch. Plant each at 10 lbs./acre. Plant with cowpeas or other perennial legumes, or clovers.
- **Overgrazing:** Rated as being grazing resistant.
- **Extends Grazing Season:** From summer to late September.
- **Advice:** Plant alyceclover in a mix with jointvetch to provide a more high-quality summer forage for deer than practically any other annual mix.
- **Caution:** Do not confuse alyceclover warm-season legume with Alice clover and/or alsike clover; both are cool- to cold-season clovers and are different plants.
- **Pollinator Friendly:** Yes.
- **Sun:** Full sun.
- **USDA Hardiness Zones:** Not applicable as a warm-season annual legume.

AMERICAN JOINTVETCH (*Aeschynomene americana*)

American Jointvetch, a.k.a. jointvetch, is a warm-season annual legume native to the southeast. It can be grown quite successfully in the eastern half of the country. It is also a legume that reseeds itself. Don't be confused by its name, however. American Jointvetch is not a vetch nor is it rated as a cool-season forage as are the genuine vetches. It is also called aeschynomene, jointvetch, shyleaf, forage aeschynomene, deervetch, and other nicknames. It is a warm-season annual legume that is an exceptional summer forage for whitetails. Jointvetch can also provide terrific rearing habitat for wild turkeys and some other upland gamebirds. American jointvetch is also an excellent choice for waterfowl hunters as it will grow on wet sites and can be flooded 18 to 24 inches for ducks.

Under appropriate management, American jointvetch performs well in a variety of soil types. It prefers sandy loam to clay soils and will grow best when planted in them, often reaching heights of 5 to 6 feet, depending on soil fertility and deer browsing pressure. It can also tolerate low soil fertility. It is often recommended to plant jointvetch in low-lying sites with high soil moisture. American jointvetch can also perform well on upland pasture sites.

It can be mixed with other warm-season plantings. One such mix is 10 lbs./acre American jointvetch, 10 lbs./acre of Alyceclover, and about 20 to 25 lbs./acre of cowpeas. Can also be mixed with grain sorghum if the sorghum rate is kept around 5 lbs./acre. Can also be mixed with buckwheat or warm-season perennial grasses. It does well when mixed with other plants including Alyceclover, grain sorghum, if the seeding rate of the sorghum is kept at about 5 lbs./acre.

When it comes to forage production, American jointvetch ranks high, producing up to 3 to 4 tons of dry matter per acre during the entire growing season.

▲ Hairy Vetch, a.k.a. sand vetch, is the most winter-hardy vetch. It can be fall-seeded to reach maturity the following July. It cannot be grown successfully in the extreme northern states of the US. Photo: © Yorozu Kitamura | Dreamstime

This type of growth compares to some of the more popular summer legume forages, including soybeans, sanfoin, cowpeas, lablab, and burgundy bean. In a study conducted in Louisiana to examine jointvetch as a deer forage, researchers found that it comprised nearly 33 percent of the dry matter in deer diets on the 2,500-acre study area during summer.

In most of the South, American jointvetch can be planted as early as April. Throughout the entire eastern part of the country, it can be planted from May to June. American jointvetch is not drought tolerant.

CONDENSED RECAP

- **Temperature Tolerances:** Warm-season planting.
- **Inoculant:** Seed must be inoculated with Strain EL.
- **Preferred pH:** Tolerates low fertility pH of 5.5 but optimal production and attraction to deer takes place when the pH is between 6.0 and higher.
- **Planting Time:** In the South, plant in April to June. In northern regions, planting dates can be extended to May and June.
- **Soil:** Performs well in a variety of soil types but grows best in sandy loam to clay soils.
- **Seeding Rates:** Planted alone, broadcast 20 lbs./acre or drill 10 to 12 lbs./acre.
- **Seed Depth:** Plant at a maximum depth of ½- to 1-inch.
- **Germination:** A negative point about American jointvetch is that its initial germination and growth is rated as slow.
- **Fertilizer:** Like other legumes, it does not need nitrogen fertilizer as it produces its own. Phosphorus and potassium are important for optimal growth, nutritional quality, and attraction, though. In lieu of a soil test, apply 300 lbs./acre of 0-20-20 or 0-10-20 at planting.
- **Maturity:** Matures at different rates according to soil fertility.
- **Crude Protein Content:** Has a crude protein level exceeding 20 to 25 percent.
- **Total Digestibility (TDN):** Its TDN value is rated as "excellent," because it has an acid detergent fiber (ADF) below 25 percent, meaning it is highly digestible to deer.
- **Companion Mixes:** Can be mixed with other legumes, buckwheat, perennial grass, and grain sorghum.
- **Overgrazing:** Not an issue; American jointvetch can withstand heavy grazing pressure.
- **Extends Grazing Season:** Can provide outstanding early-season hunting opportunities.
- **Advice:** Avoid planting in sandy soils.
- **Caution:** Must be properly inoculated to grow healthy and produce well.
- **Pollinator Friendly:** Yes.
- **Sun:** Prefers sun but is also very shade tolerant.
- **USDA Hardiness Zones:** Not applicable as a warm-season planting.

BURGUNDY BEAN (*Macroptilium bracteatum*)

They gave this plant the right name, as the beans are colored a rich dark burgundy. It is a warm-season legume that is native to South America. It is generally considered an annual planting throughout the country, excluding parts of the deep South. Burgundy bean is best adapted to the central and southern states, where it grows well in warm soil temperatures over 60°F, after the last frost has occurred.

This is not a plant to sow in plots smaller than a few acres, because deer will quickly eat the plant to the ground. It may require using repellents like Deer Out® or even fencing with a product like PlotSaver for a month or two until the young emerging plants get established. The most inexpensive commercial deer fencing is the 8-foot-tall plastic mesh. The 8-foot-high metal wire deer fencing is stronger and more durable, but also more expensive. If you plant burgundy beans in August, they will deliver nutritious forage until the first couple of frosts. In well-maintained plots, burgundy beans can produce 2 to 3 tons/acre in dry weight in southern zones. Burgundy beans are somewhat tolerant of drought, but not for extended periods. They also require good drainage and do not do well in excessively moist soils. They do not compete well with weeds.

To give burgundy beans the best chance of survival, they should be planted in a mix to avoid crop failure by deer totally eating them. A good mix planting is burgundy beans, corn, or grain sorghum.

CONDENSED RECAP

- **Temperature Tolerances:** Warm-season planting. Will grow in temperatures lower than many other subtropical and tropical legumes, however. Tops are killed by frost.
- **Inoculant:** Most often sold as pre-inoculated, coated seed, which is a specific inoculum Strain CB1717.

▲ Burgundy Beans are palatable and high in protein. As a perennial it can last two to three years and longer. Its greatest asset to food plotters is that burgundy beans will withstand foraging much better than soybeans. Photo: © Barmalini | Dreamstime

- **Preferred pH:** Tolerates slightly acidic soil to alkaline soil fertility pH of 5.5 but ideal pH levels are 6.0 to 6.5.
- **Planting Time:** Can be sown in spring or summer depending on moisture availability and soil temperatures of 65°F.
- **Soil:** Performs well in a variety of soil types but grows best in sandy loam to clay soils.
- **Seeding Rates:** Planted alone broadcast 20 lbs./acre or drill 10 to 12 lbs./acre.
- **Seed Depth:** Plant seeds at 1 to 1½ inches deep.
- **Germination:** Seeds will sprout in about 8 to 16 days. Germination problems usually stem (pun intended) from planting burgundy beans too early, particularly when the soil is cold. Young seedlings grow rapidly but do not compete well with weeds.
- **Fertilizer:** Like other legumes, it does not need nitrogen fertilizer as it produces its own. In place of a soil test, use 100 to 200 lbs./acre of 0-46-0.
- **Maturity:** Reaches maturity in about 50 to 55 days depending on soil fertility and temperatures.
- **Crude Protein Content:** Burgundy bean has a crude protein level of about 20 percent.
- **Total Digestibility (TDN):** Its TDN value is rated as very high.

- **Companion Mixes:** It is recommended to plant burgundy beans with corn or grain sorghum. The vines use the corn and sorghum stalks as climbers. A good mix would be 5 to 6 lbs./acre of burgundy bean, with 12 lbs./acre of corn or 8 lbs./acre of grain sorghum. Burgundy can also be planted with grasses, and low seeding rates of cowpeas, soybeans, or even buckwheat.
- **Overgrazing:** Rated as extremely high. To avoid overgrazing, plant in 2- to 3-acre or larger food plots. Once beans get past 45 days, they are more resistant to grazing.
- **Extends Grazing Season:** Can provide outstanding early-season hunting opportunities.
- **Advice:** In small plots that are less than one acre, it is highly prudent to fence burgundy beans off for at least 45 days.
- **Caution:** Do not use nitrogen when fertilizing burgundy beans.
- **Pollinator Friendly:** Yes.
- **Sun:** Prefers sun.
- **USDA Hardiness Zones:** Not applicable, it is a warm-season planting that winter kills after a frost or two.

▲ When it comes to quail, they simply love eating clovers. Credit: Ted Rose

SOYBEANS (*Glycine max*)

Ask any experienced food plot manager to name the top five warm-season annual legumes, and soybeans will most assuredly be at or near the top of the list. Soybeans place exceedingly high on whitetail and other deer species preferred food items. Many upland birds, waterfowl, and a host of other huntable and non-huntable critters all chow down on soybeans. Therefore, when planting them, keep in mind any animal that walks, flies, hops, jumps, or crawls, will come to dinner at your soybean food plot.

▲ This is a plot of Wallhanger Soybeans. While all the vegetation was long devoured by hunting season, deer were still drawn to eating the leftover beans into December. Photo: Sinclairville Seed Co., LLC

There are literally thousands of soybean varieties, and many of them are Roundup Ready (RR) varieties. But if the truth be told, deer won't really care what variety they eat. Any land manager who plants soybeans would be extremely hard-pressed to find a variety that deer will not eagerly devour.

Of the more than 2,500 varieties of soybeans, some of the top choices are Bobwhite, Tyrone, Laredo, and Quail Haven. You can research more forage varieties at the Natural Resources Conservation Service Plant Materials Center in Coffeeville, Mississippi.

RED ALERT–A bit of *Star Trek* trivia about Red Alert: Lt. Malcom Reed was the armory officer of the U.S.S. Enterprise. He created the term "Reed Alert" as a ship's warning of impending danger. Eventually, Reed Alert became Red Alert.

Continuing on–RED ALERT! Deer really, *really* like eating soybeans, and they eat them with gusto.

Therefore, don't be fooled into believing you can successfully plant soybeans in small food plots and expect to still have soybeans there when hunting season rolls around. Small plots under 5 acres get eaten by deer very quickly. If you believe you can, be forewarned, you are setting yourself up for disappointment. If you do not have at least 5 to 10 acres for planting soybeans, they are most likely not your best warm-season food plot choice.

▲ If you ever wondered why any soybean plot less than several acres is over-browsed, this is your Answer! According to the Dept. of Agriculture, deer and a plethora of other animals that eat soybeans cause upwards of $4.5 billion to soybean and corn crops annually. Photo: Sinclairville Seed Co., LLC

In the preliminary stages of growth, soybeans have extraordinarily *little* resistance to overgrazing pressure by deer. Consequently, large food plots are *the* key to growing soybeans successfully. Their low tolerance to overgrazing, is unfortunately a *genuine* drawback for most hunters who plant soybeans. If you have adequate acreage to dedicate to soybeans, you have hit the food plot lottery. By all means, plant forage soybeans.

Soybeans are easy-peasy to establish and, if managed properly, they epitomize the meaning of growing a true year-round food plot. They can provide quality forage from spring through November and even longer. Deer will be drawn to soybeans to eat the grain and whatever left-over beans are still in the pods. Now that's what you call a true, year-round food plot.

With all that said, soybeans are an amazing plant to grow to draw in deer. All is not lost for those food

▲ This photo demonstrates how the best way to plant soybeans (or any other plant) is with a drill. The perfect rows are also helpful in spotting deer walking through the plot. Some affordable choices of drills include Kasco Plotters Choice, Woods® drill, and Firminator G-3. Photo: Sinclairville Seed Co., LLC

▲ When using liquid deer repellent, read the label carefully, not only to use the product correctly, but to also evaluate the differences between each brand. It pays to do your homework. Photo: Deerout.com

plotters who only have a limited amount of acreage to grow soybean plots. There is a way to plant them on a small acreage, but it involves a lot more work and money. To have soybeans available during hunting season, some critical steps must be taken.

LIQUID REPELLENTS

Liquid deer repellents like Milorganite® will help keep deer from wiping out small plots. Repellents like Deer Out®, Liquid Fence, Deer Scram, and Deer Stopper are top choices as well. Using liquid repellents is just the first step, however, in protecting a small soybean food plot (or any other wildlife food plot you want to protect from being over-browsed by deer).

FENCE OPTIONS

You will also need fencing. Fencing options include electric fencing, reversible fencing, wire, or plastic fencing to protect soybeans or other plants from being over-browsed. Electric fencing can get expensive; however, it works very well to deter deer. For other choices, visit Buckforage.com, PlotSaver.com, and DeerFencing.com.

BLENDED PLOTS

Another option to preserve soybean plots is to plant them with one or more companion crops. To be frank, this applies to all the other legume plantings. By planting soybeans with other plants, it helps divert deer from eating young seedlings, providing them a better opportunity to grow. Once the beans mature, the other mixed plants act as a diversion to deer. Deer won't concentrate on eating just the soybeans, which allows for greater soybean survival into the hunting season.

One high-quality option is Whitetail Institute's Imperial Whitetail PowerPlant. It's a blend of specially selected annuals that are specifically designed to provide deer with massive tonnage during the antler growing, fawning, and lactating times of late spring and summer. Additionally, this seed is approved to use Whitetail Institute's Arrest Max herbicide. Taking this route will save a lot of time and money, and up the ante for improved success of a blended soybean planting. An equally excellent choice is Mossy Oak™ Biologic™ Game Changer Forage Soybeans. Game Changer Forage Soybeans are glyphosate tolerant, have good height, great stress tolerance, and excellent disease resistance. There are other seed companies that also sell soybeans mixed with other seeds. No matter which product you choose, the one thing that remains constant about soybeans is this: they make for a top-notch food plot.

▲ This is a multi-acre planting of soybeans on our farm. At this height, soybeans are most susceptible to over-browsing by deer and other wildlife. Photo: PCFImages

CONDENSED RECAP

- **Temperature Tolerances:** Although soybeans are rated as a warm-season annual legume, there are cold-hardy varieties available.
- **Inoculant:** If they are not inoculated use the appropriate Rhizobium (Strain S) inoculant.
- **Preferred pH:** Soybeans usually do best at soil pH levels between 5.8 and 7.0. However, an ideal level for soybeans is between 6.3 and 6.5. This range amplifies nutrient accessibility and biological nitrogen fixation. It also limits soybean cyst nematode (SCN) population growth.
- **Planting Time:** In the lower South, plant soybeans in April. They can be planted in May or as late as June in the North.
- **Soil:** Soybeans tolerate a wide range of soil types throughout the country. They prefer well-drained, medium-textured soils such as sandy loams and clay loams.
- **Seeding Rates**: Broadcast 50 lbs./acre and cover ½-inch deep. Drill at 30 lbs./acre. Plant in a well disked, firm seedbed.
- **Seed Depth:** It is recommended to plant soybeans from ½- to 1-inch deep. Each plant can produce up to eighty pods and about 160–200 seeds.
- **Germination:** Soybeans emerge amazingly fast. It commonly takes a soybean seed about two days to germinate. The plant itself doesn't emerge from the ground until about a week.
- **Fertilizer:** In the absence of a soil test, use 300 lbs./acre of 0-20-20. Soybeans do not need a fertilizer with nitrogen.
- **Maturity:** It usually takes soybeans 45 to 65 days to reach maturity. Dry soybeans require 100 or more days to mature. Soybeans all reach maturity at the same time.
- **Crude Protein Content:** Ranges from 25 to 30 percent and higher. While soybeans are a terrific source of protein, most of the nutritional value of a forage soybean, in fact the majority, is in the leaf and stem mass that the deer consume throughout the growing season.
- **Total Digestibility (TDN):** The total digestible nutrients (TDN) run about 77 to 84 percent.
- **Companion Mixes:** Available as a blend, or home-made mix with R.R. corn, tall sorghum, other

beans, sunflowers, cowpeas, and other warm-season legumes.

- **Overgrazing:** Very vulnerable to be over-eaten by deer and most other wildlife, particularly in small plots.
- **Extends Grazing Season:** Rated as an excellent summer and early fall food plot. Cold varieties can last into November and later.
- **Advice:** In small plots, plant commercial or home-made blends with soybeans to deter heavy over-browsing by deer.

- **Caution:** Do not use a nitrogen fertilizer on soybeans.
- **Pollinator Friendly:** Soybeans are self-pollinating. While honeybees are not essential to pollinating them, new research shows that bee pollination helps to boost yields.
- **Sun:** Soybeans prefer full sun.
- **USDA Hardiness Zones:** Predominately a warm-season planting, but some new cold-hardy varieties are available.

▲ Like all species of deer, wapiti will eagerly seek out and eat their fill of clover. Credit: © Riekefoto | Dreamstime.com

COWPEAS (*Vigna unguiculata*)

Cowpea is a warm-season annual legume that is also known as iron-and-clay pea and black-eyed pea. Cowpeas are heavily browsed by deer, as well as wild turkeys, other upland birds, and most other critters. Deer love to eat cowpeas. Like sugar beets, the cowpea is considered an "ice-cream" plant for deer. It is ill-advised to plant cowpeas in plots smaller than one acre. Deer will immediately overgraze them. Practical and successfully planted cowpeas are those planted in plots of at least 3 acres. When sown with other plantings, cowpeas get additional insurance from being totally decimated by deer that overgraze small plots.

Cowpeas can be grown throughout the country. Like other warm-season legumes, warm soil is required for cowpeas to germinate. Like some other legumes, cowpeas are somewhat tolerant of drought, soil acidity, and low soil fertility. They thrive best in pH levels of 5.5 to 7.0. They are sensitive to wet soils and do best in soils with ample drainage. The best planting times are from May to August. August plantings generally survive long enough to be attractive plots during September and early October archery seasons.

Like soybeans, cowpeas planted in small plots will benefit from liquid repellents or fencing options. Some varieties include Blue Goose Crowder Cowpea, Big Boy Southern Pea, Black Crowder Southern Pea, Thorsby Cream, Tory, Wilcox, Iron Clay, and Catjang.

CONDENSED RECAP

- **Temperature Tolerances:** Cowpeas are a warm-season annual that die off after a few hard frosts.
- **Inoculant:** The (Strain EL) type inoculant is recommended for use with cowpeas as well as for Alyceclover, American Jointvetch, Lablab, Lespedeza, Hairy Indigo, Mung Beans, and Partridge Peas.
- **Preferred pH:** Will tolerate a wide range of pH values between 5.5 and 7.0. Ideally, cowpeas do best in a pH range of 5.5 to 6.5.
- **Planting Time:** Plant from May to August. August planted cowpeas will provide good attraction through most of the bowhunting season from September to October.
- **Soil:** Cowpeas work well in a wide variety of soils and soil conditions but perform best on well-drained sandy loams or sandy soils.
- **Seeding Rates:** Broadcast rates are 60 to 90 lbs./acre. Drill at 40 to 60 lbs./acre.
- **Seed Depth:** Plant 1 to 2 inches deep directly into warm soil (60°F).
- **Germination:** Seedlings emerge in 10 to 14 days depending on soil and weather conditions.
- **Fertilizer:** Use 200 to 250 lbs./acre of T-19 (19-19-19).
- **Maturity:** Cowpeas take about 3 months to mature.

▲ Cowpeas have all the same over-eating issues that soybeans have. They, too, must be planted in large 5-acre or larger plots. Or they can be sown in smaller plots with other mixed seeds to divert the deer from eating the cowpeas to the ground. Photo: © Vnikitenko | Dreamstime

- **Crude Protein Content:** Cowpea's protein range is between 25 to 28 percent.
- **Total Digestibility (TDN):** Digestibility is about 50 to 56 percent on a whole-plant basis. The leaf is much more digestible than the stem. Leaf parts have 60 to 75 percent digestible dry matter (DDM), while stems have 50 to 55 percent DDM.
- **Companion Mixes:** Mixing with other plants considerably helps stave off crop failure caused by deer overgrazing the cowpeas. Cowpeas can be mixed with other annual peas, Peredovik sunflowers, buckwheat, lue lupine, oats, Browntop millet, and corn. Reduce cowpea rate when mixing with other plants.
- **Overgrazing:** Highly susceptible to being overgrazed in plots smaller than 2 to 3 acres.
- **Extends Grazing Season:** From early September to mid-October.
- **Advice:** To get cowpeas past mid-October, plant with winter-hardy forage oats, marathon red clover, and FIXatioN Balansa clover.
- **Caution:** This is not a crop for food plot managers with small acreage.
- **Pollinator Friendly:** Yes.
- **Sun:** Full sun.
- **USDA Hardiness Zones:** Not applicable as a warm-season plant.

▲ A field of cow peas is not only highly attractive to deer and other animals, but they also add a beautiful element of color. Credit: © Anne Laure Affre | Dreamstime.com

LABLAB (*Lablab purpureus*)

Lablab is one of the top-tier warm-season annual legumes planted for deer. It is widely adapted to a variety of soils and weather conditions throughout the United States.

It is tolerant of low fertility and soil acidity. Lablab does not tolerate wet soil conditions, however. The flowers are white, pink, or purplish. Like most legumes, lablab must be inoculated. Lablab can tolerate dry conditions. It is also extremely productive and can produce more than 7,000 pounds of quality forage/acre (in dry weight) throughout its growing season. Lablab holds up somewhat well to grazing pressure. Deer, especially in high density areas, can obliterate a small 1- to 2-acre plot of lablab—lickety-split. A good option for its survival is to use liquid repellent or fencing. Lablab produces and survives best when planted in two to three acres or more.

▲ LabLab is yet another legume that requires large acreage to avoid being overgrazed by deer and other wildlife. Good companion choices are corn, grain sorghum, and wheat. Photo: Tecomate

Like all the other warm-season annual legumes, lablab does not require a lot of nitrogen fertilizer, as it makes its own nitrogen. Lablab does get a benefit from phosphorus and potassium, which help it to produce ideal nutritional value, growth, and to maintain palatability attraction to deer. As with any plant, it is always wise to take a soil test before planting lablab to determine the appropriate NPK amount needed.

Broadcast lablab in a well-prepared, smooth, firm planting surface free of large rocks and heavy clumps of soil to ensure the best possible germination. The most practical way to plant lablab, particularly in smaller plots, is to plant them with other legumes or grains to allow young lablab plants to establish themselves. There are a lot of companion choices to plant with lablab including, but not limited to, grain sorghum, millet, cowpeas, Egyptian wheat, and Peredovik sunflowers, or corn. The lablab vines will wrap around and grow up the stalks of these plants, allowing both plants to thrive and provide abundant forage to animals.

Inoculated seed will always result in a more productive and attractive stand, as it ensures excellent nitrogen fixation. Thus, it increases protein levels, which enhances body and antler development, as well as milk production in does.

The entire game plan for growing lablab completely revolves around getting it past the deer herd for at least

▲ When planting lablab, your goal is to get it past the deer herd for at least 30 to 45 days. If that can't be done, don't waste time or money planting it. Photo: © Yogesh More | Dreamstime

30 to 45 days. If that can't be done, this section about planting lablab is moot. The options to accomplish this include using repellents like PlotSaver's Liquid Deer Repellent or Milogranite, electric fencing like James Kroll a.k.a. Dr. Deer's Deer-Resistant Electric Fence, other less expensive fencing options, or the best option: planting a large 3- to 5-acre plot of lablab.

CONDENSED RECAP

- **Temperature Tolerances:** Warm-season planting (spring, summer, and early fall).
- **Inoculant:** Inoculate with Strain EL.
- **Preferred pH:** Grows in a wide range of pH from 5.5 to 7.5. However, it prefers a pH of 6.0 to 6.5. Like all plants, a pH of 6.5 is optimal.
- **Planting Time:** In southern zones, plant in April. In northern zones, plant in May or June. In both zones, plant only after all danger of frost has ended.
- **Soil:** It is extremely tolerant of soil textures, growing in deep sands to heavy clays provided there is ample drainage. It is quite drought tolerant when established, but it will not grow in wet soils.
- **Seeding Rates:** When broadcasting lablab, plant about 25 lbs./acre. Drill seed at about 15 lbs./acre.
- **Seed Depth:** Recommended ranges can vary from ½ to 2½ inches deep. I plant lablab no more than 1-inch deep.
- **Germination:** In properly cared for soil, large lablab seeds germinate quicky.
- **Fertilizer:** Use a low nitrogen fertilizer mix with 250 to 300 lbs./acre of 0-20-20.

- **Maturity:** The game plan is to keep grazing pressure off the young, tender succulent seedlings until enough of a root system can be produced to withstand grazing pressure. Lablab generally matures in 30 to 60 days.
- **Crude Protein Content:** With a protein range between 25 to 30 percent, LabLab is a high quality warm-season forage choice for summer food plots, especially during a time when antler development is critical.
- **Total Digestibility (TDN):** Is considered as very high.
- **Companion Mixes:** Can be planted with other warm-season annual legumes, corn, grain sorghum, Egyptian wheat, forage millet, cowpeas, and Peredovik sunflowers.
- **Overgrazing:** Is highly susceptible to overgrazing, particularly in plots smaller than 1 acre.
- **Extends Grazing Season:** From spring, summer, and into early October.
- **Advice:** For maximum success and production, plant lablab in plots of 2 to 3 acres or more and use electric fencing (especially on small plots of one acre or less). Better yet, plant it in a mix.
- **Caution:** Do not use a fertilizer high in nitrogen.
- **Pollinator Friendly:** Yes.
- **Sun:** Prefers full sun.
- **USDA Hardiness Zones:** Not applicable as a warm-season food plot.

COOL SEASON LEGUMES

The following legumes are all rated as cool-season to cold-hardy.

SWEETCLOVER (*Melilotus spp.*)

Sweetclover is a biennial legume that is available in three varieties: 2 yellow and 1 white clover, which all grow quickly. The root system can reach depths of 5 to 8 feet, making sweetclover one of the most drought and heat tolerant plantings. More beneficially, sweetclover is an extremely winter-hardy legume.

Both yellow and white sweetclover can adapt to clay or loam soils. However, they do not perform well in acidic soils. Sweetclover needs a high pH level. Seed can be planted in spring or autumn and must be inoculated.

Sweetclover contributes substantial amounts of nitrogen (80 to 100 units per acre) and organic matter into the soil, which is highly beneficial to plants that

▲ First-year plants of sweetclover are rarely other than vegetative growth. During their second season they will develop a strong taproot which can grow up to 5 inches deep below the soil. Photo: Deposit

are sown in future plots. Yellow blossom sweetclover is highly attractive to honeybees.

White sweetclover is also a high nitrogen-producing biennial legume. Their stems can grow 3 to 8 feet tall. White sweetclover generally blooms about 2 weeks later than yellow blossom sweetclover. Like the yellow variety, white clover is rated as excellent for honey production.

In the North, at planting, sweetclover can be blended with cool-season grain sorghum and corn, any of the winter-hardy grains, or clovers. I have found that sweetclover can be successfully mixed with cereal rye. Using winter-hardy red or white clovers adds another level to help sweetclover tolerate lower temperatures, particularly in early spring.

Sweetclover produces best in May to August. It can be sensitive to heavy early grazing. However, grazing in late spring and fall is helpful to both the plant and the roots. It produces more vegetative growth the first year than other legumes. During sweetclover's second year, their taproots can reach amazing depth of 50-inches or more. This accounts for its excellent capacity to deal with severe drought.

Sweetclover also provides very nutritious forage for deer and other wildlife, but only if it is managed properly. Like alfalfa and other legumes and clovers, it is high in protein. When sweetclover is controlled from getting too tall with heavy stems, it is easily digested by deer and is a reliable source of energy. It also provides good food for mule deer, elk, and antelope and good nesting habitat for pheasants, grouse, and other upland birds. Sweetclover is extremely attractive to pollinators such as honeybees. In fact, its scientific name, *Melilotus,* comes partly from the Latin word *Mel,* which means "honey."

CONDENSED RECAP

- **Temperature Tolerances:** Sweetclover is ranked as a "very winter-hardy" biennial.
- **Inoculant:** It should be inoculated with (Strain A).
- **Preferred pH:** This plant prefers pH levels ranging from 6.5 to 8.0. It requires a high level of fertility (Phosphorus and Potassium) for high production.
- **Planting Time:** From May to August.
- **Soil:** Sweetclover will grow on most any type of soil but is best adapted to a deep, well-drained, loamy soil.

- **Seeding Rates:** Alone, plant at 12 to 15 lbs./acre. When mixed, plant at 2 to 6 lbs./acre. Use higher rates when broadcasting, lower rates when using a drill like any of the Kasco or other drill models designed for this type of purpose. When frost seeding sweetclover, use 25 percent more seed on frozen ground.
- **Seed Depth:** Plant no deeper than ¼-inch.
- **Germination:** On a well-prepared seedbed, sweetclover emerges quicky, usually 7 to 10 days, which helps to shade out weeds, particularly when planted with grains like corn or grain sorghum a.k.a. milo.
- **Fertilizer:** In the absence of a soil test, adding 1 to 2 tons of agricultural lime and adding phosphorus, and potassium is recommended. A standard fertilizer recommendation of 200 to 300 lbs./acre of 0-20-30 would be a good starting point.
- **Maturity:** It emerges relatively quickly but grows slowly the first 60 days.
- **Crude Protein Content:** Sweetclover has a crude protein content of 15 percent (of dry matter).
- **Total Digestibility (TDN):** It has a digestible crude protein level of over 30 percent.
- **Companion Mixes:** Corn, grain sorghum, other grains, and clovers.
- **Overgrazing:** New seedlings are sensitive to heavy grazing pressure.
- **Extends Grazing Season:** From spring to well into November and later.
- **Advice:** Do not use nitrogen in a fertilizer mix.
- **Caution:** Sweetclover does not like acidic soils.
- **Pollinator Friendly:** This is an ideal plant to attract honeybees.
- **Sun:** Full sun.
- **USDA Hardiness Zones:** Sweetclover plants have evolved contractile roots, which pull the plant crown down into the soil in the fall, allowing the plant to survive cold winter temperatures.

▲ Sweet clover is a popular food plot planting throughout the western mountain states making it a prime attractant for mule deer, elk, moose, and whitetails. Kate took this mule deer in a grass and clover pasture in Wyoming. Credit: Fiduccia Ent

ALFALFA (*Medicago sativa*)

Alfalfa has long been a prime perennial legume of farmers and deer managers alike. It provides top-quality forage that is highly sought after by deer, elk, mule deer, and all other types of grazing animals, domestic and wild. It is a palatable and nutritious crop. It is rich in protein, vitamins, and minerals. Many varieties have been bred to withstand cold temperatures, resist heavy grazing, and are insect-resistant.

As a food plot planting, alfalfa is a demanding and finicky crop. It needs to be mowed to the ground at least a few times per growing season. And the cuttings should be removed so as not to smother new growth. This fact alone makes alfalfa difficult for many food plotters. With that said, in areas with a high density of deer, 1- to 2-acre plots of alfalfa can be kept at manageable heights by the deer.

▲ Alfalfa needs a lot of TLC. Even experienced farmers agree it is difficult to grow and maintain. Photo: PCFImages

Even long-time experienced farmers say alfalfa is a difficult crop to maintain. Furthermore, like corn, alfalfa is an expensive seed. A 50-pound bag of alfalfa can range from $125 ($2.50/pound) to $286 ($5.72/pound). It is susceptible to poor soil drainage and it is overly sensitive to competition when mixed with other plantings, including clovers and other legumes, even when the seeding rates are reduced. Choosing the correct variety of alfalfa can be daunting as there are innumerable types available.

Although grazing-tolerant varieties have recently been developed, alfalfa does best when planted in plots of at least 2 acres. I have planted alfalfa several times on our farm in plots ranging from ½- to 1-acre. Each time the plots were quickly eaten to the ground by deer and other critters.

Alfalfa requires vigilant management, including careful attention to pH levels and soil fertility. It is a heavy user of plant nutrients. Weeds can cause severe problems when planting alfalfa. Preparing a weed-free seedbed is critical. As mentioned, alfalfa must be mowed a few times a year and the cuttings should be removed for new growth. When you grow alfalfa, you're developing a long-term relationship with the plant. And, like any lengthy relationship, it demands a lot of attention and obligations.

Let's just say that unless you have already planted alfalfa successfully, you may want to exclude it from your plantings and replace it with another cold-hardy annual or perennial legume that is easier to grow productively. Instead of planting alfalfa, a good suggestion is birdsfoot trefoil (a.k.a. the poor man's alfalfa) or a legume like sainfoin. Both these alternate plantings can better withstand winter temperatures than alfalfa. If you do plant alfalfa, select varieties that will produce forage for deer into winter. Most seed companies provide information that will help you to choose the best winter-hardy types for your USDA Hardiness Zone.

Alfalfas have different ratings from the Association of Official Seed Certifying Agencies (AOSCA) and the National Alfalfa Variety Review Board (NAVRB) report. The two most important ratings are the Winter-Survival Index (WSI) and the Fall Dormancy (FD) rating. The WSI rates the alfalfas on how well they will survive winter by a 1–6 rating. The lower the rating, the more winter-hardy a particular variety is. The FD rating

▲ If you grow alfalfa, be prepared to take care of it. It must be sprayed to eliminate weeds and mowed at least a few times per season. The cuttings should be removed as well. Photo: PCFImages

denotes how soon the alfalfa will do dormant in the season. The lower the number, the earlier in the season the alfalfa will enter dormancy. The higher the number, the later the alfalfa will grow into fall. This is important information for food plotters who want their alfalfa varieties to be viable during the hunting seasons. You can also visit www.alfalfa.org for more detailed ratings and information. Many seed vendors, like Welter Seed and Honey Co., and Preferred Seed, Inc. include these ratings in their catalogs.

A closing thought about planting legumes (and corn). If you have enough acreage and do not have the equipment or time to plant large plots, a key would be to hire, if practical, a local farmer to plant these crops. Once any of the legumes are planted in multi-acre food plots, it eliminates the need for liquid repellents, fencing, or even mixing the seeds to deter deer from eating the primary plant. A downside to hiring a farmer is that they generally charge for their time and

fuel. This can be a significant amount. The fee can get higher if you need to pay the farmer for seed, fertilizer, and herbicide. There are times, though, when a barter can be struck where you provide the farmer free acreage to plant and harvest such crops in return for not charging him a lease fee.

CONDENSED RECAP
- **Temperature Tolerances:** Dependent of varieties. Winter-hardy types can be viable forage into the hunting season.
- **Inoculant:** Alfalfa is available as a pre-inoculated seed. Otherwise inoculate with (Strain A).
- **Preferred pH:** Alfalfa requires a soil pH between 6.5 and 7.0 for optimal production.
- **Planting Time:** In the northern-most areas, plant alfalfa if you have land available in mid-July, preferably just prior to a predicted rainfall. Optimal seeding dates are July 15 through August in the

upper Midwest. For food plotters in warmer southern climates, seed up to early September.

- **Soil:** Alfalfa, like sainfoin and birdsfoot trefoil, prefers a well-drained soil rather than wet, heavy clay soils.
- **Seeding Rates:** For a stand-alone plot, use 18 to 20 lbs./acre. For mixed stands, reduce the rate to 15 to 16 lbs./acre. When broadcast, seeding rates should be increased by 10 to 20 percent.
- **Seed Depth:** The suggested seeding depth for alfalfa is ¼- to ½-inch deep. It is advisable to plant alfalfa shallow rather than too deep.
- **Germination:** Early planting time combined with good soil fertility, weed control, and correct seeding depth are the keys to spring alfalfa establishment and quick germination.
- **Fertilizer:** Since alfalfa seed is expensive, soil tests are highly recommended. In lieu of a soil test, phosphorus and potassium should be broadcast into soil prior to planting. Nitrogen application is not needed, but if it is used keep the rate below 40 lbs./acre.
- **Crude Protein Content:** The protein levels can range from 15 to 20 percent.
- **Total Digestibility (TDN):** High in palatability and digestibility. Early-bloom alfalfa has more total digestible nutrients (TDN) and crude protein (CP) than mature alfalfa. Fiber content is 20 to 28 percent.
- **Companion Mixes:** Can be mixed with other cold-hardy clovers but keep rates low to avoid the risk of early competition.
- **Overgrazing:** Is generally only an issue in small plots under an acre or two.
- **Extends Grazing Season:** Winter-hardy types can produce forage into November.
- **Advice:** When choosing alfalfas, buy varieties that are both winter-hardy and have good fall dormancy ratings.
- **Caution:** Alfalfa is a heavy user of nutrients. Preparing a weed-free seedbed is essential.
- **Pollinator Friendly:** Yes, absolutely. Alfalfa nectar has been reported to be a major food source for honeybees.
- **Sun:** Prefers full sun.
- **USDA Hardiness Zones:** Totally dependent on the varieties chosen to plant. Check your area within the USDA hardiness zones and select a variety to match it.

▲ Falcata alfalfa is a variety that has some differences from the purple-flowered alfalfas. Falcata works best when planted in grass mixtures like Timothy or perennial rye grass. What's to say about any variety of alfalfa other than it is a top-shelf planting for deer and a variety of other wildlife. Credit: GO Seed

AUSTRIAN WINTER PEA (*Pisum sativum*)

Austrian winter pea is an annual legume that ranks way up on a deer's preferred list of food sources. Austrian winter pea, a.k.a. black pea, is another plant referred to as the ultimate winter-hardy ice cream plant. Austrian winter pea is a viny type of legume plant that grows low to the ground. It can fix more than 200 lbs./acre of nitrogen in well-cared-for food plots. Its succulent stems are hollow, slender, and about 3 to 4 feet long. It has showy flowers that range in color from pink to light red and purple.

Obviously, its name denotes its ability as a terrific winter-hardy pea. However, it can't undergo prolonged frigid temperatures below sub-zero. But that is cold-hardy enough for any food plotter who wants to attract deer during the hunting season. It is also a nutritious plant to offer deer throughout the summer.

In the North, Austrian winter pea can be planted in early August. In the South, it can be planted as late as October. Like all legumes, because they are so nutritious and palatable, young Austrian winter pea plants are susceptible to being overgrazed. In addition, they are slow to establish and are vulnerable to overgrazing by deer and every other animal that walks, crawls, flies, skips, hops, jumps, or tunnels underground.

Consequently, Austrian winter peas must be planted in plots of at least 3 acres or more. Even then they should not be planted alone, but rather planted in a mix. They do nicely when combined with cold-hardy clovers, other legumes, all grains, particularly oats or cereal rye. This is a crop that can be extremely helpful for managers who intend to hunt over their winter-hardy food plots and, therefore, winter peas can be essential to a cold-season planting program.

Soybeans, lablab, cowpeas, and burgundy bean are classified as warm-season plantings and, as such, are excellent food plot choices to enhance lactation, fawn survival, and antler development. They, too, can be

▲ Peas are also vulnerable to overgrazing, especially in small plots. It isn't practical to plant them alone; don't waste your time or money trying to. Plant them in a mix with grains like rye, oats, and some clovers. Credit: © Xookits | Dreamstime.com.

quickly overgrazed by land managers who do not have enough large acreage to plant these legumes successfully. Austrian winter peas, cowpeas, burgundy bean, and soybeans, et al., need plots from 3 to 5 acres or more each to escape being devastated by deer before they can mature. By now you know the drill. The only way to get most of these legumes past your deer herd is by using liquid repellents, different fencing. Better yet, plant them in blended mixes to divert deer from overgrazing them.

The food plot will benefit from the many choices of other plantings that can be mixed with Austrian winter peas. This includes many of the winter-hardy red and white clovers, the warm-season clovers, all the grains, and chicory. When winter peas are planted with small grains, the grains will act as a nurse crop, but again, only in large fields. This will help the Austrian winter peas to dodge being overgrazed.

There are several varieties, but for a wildlife food plot it is hard to beat Austrian winter peas. For food plotters with enough acreage, Austrian winter peas should be included as a top-choice in your planting program.

CONDENSED RECAP

- **Inoculant:** Inoculate with rhizobium bacteria specific to peas which is (Strain C).
- **Preferred pH:** Does best in pH levels between 6.0 and 7.0.
- **Planting Time:** Early August in the North, October in the South.
- **Soil:** Austrian winter peas do best on loam or clay loam soils that are well-drained.
- **Seeding Rates:** Broadcast at 50 lbs./acre. Drill at 30 lbs./acre. Be sure to follow up with light compacting for good seed-to-soil contact.

- **Seed Depth:** Cover the seed approximately ½- to 1-inch deep.
- **Germination:** Emerges in about 21 days or so providing the soil temperature is 40°F. At temperatures of 65 to 70°F the seeds will sprout within 7 to 14 days.
- **Fertilizer:** If planted alone, use a low nitrogen fertilizer mix like 0-20-20. If planted with grains etc., use 300 lbs./acre of triple 19.
- **Maturity:** About 30 to 45 days. Once established, they can produce quality forage for a period of 7 to 8 months.
- **Crude Protein Content:** Protein levels can range from 25 to 30 percent.
- **Total Digestibility (TDN):** On 100 percent dry matter, the TDN is about 85 percent.
- **Companion Mixes:** Clovers, small grains, and chicory.
- **Overgrazing:** Young plants are vulnerable to overgrazing, particularly in plots that are 1- to 2-acres in size.
- **Extends Grazing Season:** Peas will be available to deer throughout the deer season (October through December).
- **Advice:** Plant in 3-acre or larger plots. Use fencing, liquid repellents. Better yet, plant with other companion seeds.
- **Caution:** Do not plant in small plots alone or in mixes without fencing and repellents.
- **Pollinator Friendly:** As a bonus, winter pea's bright red flowers provide much-needed pollen and nectar for pollinators and other beneficial insects in spring.
- **Sun:** Prefers full sun.
- **USDA Hardiness Zones:** Winter-hardy in USDA zones 6 and above.

BIRDSFOOT TREFOIL (*Lotus corniculates*)

If you are looking for a plant that attracts deer as well as alfalfa, look no further than birdsfoot trefoil. It ranks remarkably high as a deer preference food and can be a better choice to plant than alfalfa for the average food plotter. In fact, birdsfoot trefoil is often referred to as the "poor man's alfalfa." It is among my favorite perennial legumes, especially to replace fussy alfalfa.

What is even more attractive about birdsfoot trefoil is that it can endure severe winters and extended cold temperatures. There are specific varieties bred to be adapted to the northern states and Canada. The Empire brand trefoils are better tailored as wildlife food plots.

Other practical reasons for food plotters to plant trefoil instead of alfalfa, is that it is superior to alfalfa in both production and quality—even when planted in soils with marginal fertility, particularly low pH readings. birdsfoot is also a lot less expensive than alfalfa, it is easier to care for, and it can *reseed* itself.

Some flatter growing varieties (Leo, Dawn, Empire, Fergus, and AU Dewey) are high yielding and endure better with heavy weed competition. They are also better suited to withstand extended grazing by deer. Birdsfoot trefoil winter-hardy varieties are adapted to the northern United States, the Midwest, and even Canada. Leo is a variety specifically developed with an exceedingly high degree of winter-hardiness. It is an excellent choice for food plots in northern areas that undergo frigid cold winters. You can buy Leo birdsfoot trefoil seed from www.riverrefugeseed.com. It's a variety I recommend.

Birdsfoot trefoil should be an integral part of any cold-season food plot planting program. It will be even more of a highly attractive planting when mixed with other winter-hardy clover, chicory, and grains like cereal rye or oats plantings for deer, turkey, and other wildlife.

CONDENSED RECAP

- **Temperature Tolerances:** Does well in northern areas. Some varieties (like Leo) were developed to withstand extreme winter-hardiness.
- **Inoculant:** If it doesn't come pre-inoculated, use the proper Strain K of Rhizobium bacteria to inoculate it prior to planting.
- **Preferred pH:** For establishment it prefers a pH range of 6.0 to 6.5. It will tolerate a pH range of 5.5 to 7.5.
- **Planting Time:** Trefoil may be seeded in late winter, early spring, or fall. Winter-hardy varieties can be planted in August or September in the North and in October in the South.
- **Soil:** Birdsfoot trefoil is suited to low and moderately fertile soils. It does best in areas that receive 20 inches of precipitation or more per year. It adapts to poorly drained soil or soils with low pH levels.
- **Seeding Rates:** In stand-alone plots, broadcast 10 lbs./acre. I use a Brillion No-Till Seeder/cultipacker, which cuts the rate in half to 5 lbs./acre. When mixed with perennial grasses, use 10 lbs./

▲ Birdsfoot trefoil, a.k.a. "the poor man's alfalfa," will attract deer equally and sometimes even better than alfalfa. It is also much less expensive, much easier to grow, less finicky, and requires a lot less maintenance than alfalfa. Credit: © Philip Stewart | Dreamstime.com

acre of birdsfoot, 5 lbs./acre of timothy, and 15 lbs./acre of perennial ryegrass.

- **Seed Depth:** Plant trefoil at ¼-inch deep and cover lightly.
- **Germination:** One fault of trefoil is its weak seedling vigor when stands are first established. It will germinate quicker in plots that have been well-prepared and free of competitive weeds.
- **Fertilizer:** At establishment, use 300 lbs./acre of 0-20-30 that is well mixed into the soil at planting. Spring planted plots should be fertilized in September with 300 lbs./acre of 0-20-30.
- **Maturity:** In well-prepared and cared for plots, about 60 days.
- **Crude Protein Content:** Ranges from 10.5 to 15 percent.
- **Total Digestibility (TDN):** In a third study in Pennslyvania State University (Hall and Cherney), it was reported the total digestible nutrient (TDN) concentration of birdsfoot trefoil was 63 percent compared with 54 percent for alfalfa.

- **Companion Mixes:** Can be mixed with grasses such as timothy and perennial ryegrass, or other cold-hardy clovers.
- **Overgrazing:** Like all legumes, birdsfoot is vulnerable to over-grazing.
- **Extends Grazing Season:** Spring through summer and fall plantings from August to December.
- **Advice:** Birdsfoot is less aggressive than most plants. As seedlings develop over the first 60 to 90 days, competition from other plants must be controlled.
- **Caution:** There are over two dozen varieties of birdsfoot trefoil. Select a winter variety like Leo if you want to have it available to attract game during the deer season.
- **Pollinator Friendly**: Honeybees will forage on birdsfoot trefoil's bright yellow flowers frequently, mostly observed for pollen.
- **Sun:** Prefers full sun.
- **USDA Hardiness Zones:** Check the USDA Hardiness Zone in your area.

▲ Birdsfoot trefoil is tolerant to a wide range of soils and can endure in wet or acidic areas. Trefoils are commonly used in mixes with grasses and other legumes. Credit: © Olaf Speier | Dreamstime.com

HAIRY VETCH (*Vicia villosa*)

Hairy vetch, a.k.a. winter vetch or sand vetch, is an annual or biennial legume. It is widely adapted and rated as the most winter-hardy of all the vetches. It can be grown in all but the most extreme northern United States.

Hairy vetch is a top nitrogen provider. It is also rated as a consistently high producer of forage production. It produces dense, pea-like flowers that range in color from reddish purple to violet and white. Flowers develop into oblong seed pods, which produce small, black, round seeds that are irregular in size. Hairy vetch is somewhat drought tolerant.

It is possible to top-seed vetch in late summer to early fall. However, it is important that if it is planted on heavy or firmly packed soils, particularly infested with weeds, the soil must be disked thoroughly prior to planting. Hairy vetch must be properly inoculated using Mycoapply, True Leaf Market Legume, or N-Dure.

Plant vetch in the North in August and in the South in September. When planted as a stand-alone plot, vetch, like all clovers and other legumes, does not need a lot of nitrogen fertilizer. What makes vetch an ideal planting for deer is that it can consistently reseed itself and fix substantial amounts of nitrogen (50 to 140 lbs./acre or more) for use with any follow-up crop, especially corn, grain sorghum, and even millet.

One negative aspect with hairy vetch is that it is an intense competitor, particularly in spring. It can lay down a mat that can easily eradicate other good competition plantings. Hairy vetch can also become exceedingly difficult to mow or plow under.

▲ Hairy vetch is a vigorous winter annual. It can be seeded with my favorite grain (used as a cover crop) cereal rye in the fall. When I have planted it in mid-August, hairy vetch was 3 feet tall the following May. Photo: Smithseed.com

CONDENSED RECAP

- **Temperature Tolerances:** This is a very winter-hardy planting.
- **Inoculant:** Use the proper Strain C fresh inoculant.
- **Preferred pH:** Will tolerate a soil pH of 5.9 to 6.5. Prefers 6.0 to 7.0.
- **Planting Time:** Hairy vetch is normally planted in the fall.
- **Soil:** Prefers sandy soils but is adapted to all soil textures.
- **Seeding Rates:** The recommended planting rate is 20 to 25 lbs./acre.
- **Seed Depth:** Plant 1-inch deep.
- **Germination:** Sprouts in 10 to 14 days.
- **Fertilizer:** In lieu of a soil test, at planting use 300 lbs./acre of 0-20-30.
- **Crude Protein Content:** Hairy vetch forage is high in protein, ranging from 19 to 30 percent.
- **Total Digestibility (TDN):** Crude fiber is in the 17–28 percent DM range.
- **Companion Mixes:** Plant with cereal rye, oats, or other winter grains for improved winter survival.

Wheat and triticale are best suited in combination with hairy vetch. In the South, plant with crimson and/or arrowleaf clover

- **Overgrazing:** Generally, not an issue once established.
- **Extends Grazing Season:** Plants will be viable and draw in deer well into the winter months.
- **Advice:** Hairy vetch is a fierce competitor; hence it can choke out other plantings.
- **Caution:** Vetches can be at risk to several diseases and nematodes, including funguses, gray mold, downy mildew, and others. It can also become a weed in annual rotations.
- **Pollinator Friendly:** Of all the vetches, the pink to purple flowers of hairy vetch and crown vetch are among the two most popular as bee-attracting cover crops.
- **Sun:** Hairy vetch needs at least 6 hours of sunlight per day.
- **USDA Hardiness Zones:** Hardiness Zones 4 and into Zone 3 (with snow cover).

▲ A field of hairy vetch in the west. Some varieties of vetches are winter hardy to -20°F which makes it a perfect plant for food plotters in northern areas. Credit: Smith Seed

LUPINES (*Lupinus perennis*)

The lupine genus contains both annual and perennial herbaceous species. Lupines used for deer forage are erect-growing winter annuals that can reach heights of 3 to a maximum of 6 feet. They are members of the pea family. They are also classified as both warm- and cool-season plantings. The three most common varieties available are white, blue, and yellow flowered lupines. The most winter-hardy variety is white lupine, although Blue lupine is rated as the hardiest and most edible for deer.

Lupines produce excellent high-quality deer forage from spring to fall. They provide excellent seed production for all types of upland gamebirds and waterfowl. Blue lupine is highly palatable and provides a protein rich forage for deer, elk, moose, and all other grazing wild game. It is preferred by wild turkeys and both eastern and western gamebirds.

Planted alone, broadcast lupine at about 100 lbs./acre. Lupine seeds can also be drilled but the seeding rate should be cut in half (50 lbs./acre). Plant lupine seed in a well-prepared seedbed at ½-inch deep. They should be covered with a cultipacker (or drag), as they require good seed-to-soil contact to properly germinate.

Seeding vigor is rated as good. However, lupines establish rather slowly. Therefore, they do not withstand heavy grazing until about six to eight weeks after being planted. As with other legumes, planting lupines in a mix with other nurse crops can help deter heavy grazing. Good companion plants are winter-hardy red clovers, winter-hardy white clovers, and oats. When mixed with plants where nitrogen is needed, use a fertilizer of 19-19-19. The plant makes beautiful flowers that are 4 to 10 inches long.

They can be planted in the North in April and May, earlier in the South. Lupine can be mixed with grains,

▲ Deer are especially attracted to Blue lupine. These erect-growing winter annuals not only provide a nutritious and palatable food plot for deer, but they are also a beautiful, picturesque planting. Lupine can be somewhat hard to find. They are available from Wannamaker.com. Photo: H. Hickman

clovers, and even chicory. Avoid planting lupine varieties that are high in alkaloids, as deer and other wildlife will avoid grazing them because they have a bitter taste.

Therefore, selection of lupine varieties ends up being a crucial starting point. I plant a variety called Sweet Blue lupine, which is low in alkaloid. However, Sweet Blue lupine can be overgrazed by deer, especially in plots less than one acre. As mentioned with most legumes, lupines do best in plots that are 3 acres or larger. In smaller plots, they will require liquid repellents and fencing. Better yet, simply plant them in a blend with other clovers, grains, or chicory to divert over-grazing by deer.

If your deer have never been exposed to lupine, it may take them a season to discover that they are edible. Once they do, however, they will become addicted to eating Sweet Blue lupine. A good source for purchasing lupine is from Wannamaker Seed Co. www.wannamakerseed.com. I have not found another seed company that provides this seed at the affordable rates found at Wannamaker.

CONDENSED RECAP

- **Temperature Tolerances:** According to plant researcher Professor Barbacki (1960), annual lupine species are capable of enduring severe frost. They are also rated a winter-hardy to about 10°F.
- **Inoculant:** Inoculant is needed prior to planting. Use an H type inoculant for Blue lupine.
- **Preferred pH:** Lupines are tolerant of a wide range of pH levels from 5.5 to 7.0. A pH level of 6.0 to 6.5 is considered an optimal pH range for lupines.
- **Planting Time:** Plant in the North in May or June and in the South in March or April. Can also be planted in the fall.
- **Soil:** Lupines will tolerate moderately acidic soils but do best in loamy soils. Both types of soils require good drainage, however.

- **Seeding Rates:** Plant alone at 100 lbs./acre.
- **Seed Depth:** Plant lupines from ¼- to ½-inch deep.
- **Germination:** Usually, under good soil fertility, expect germination in 14 to 30 days.
- **Fertilizer:** Planted alone, lupines do not require nitrogen. In lieu of a soil test, use 200 to 300 lbs./acre of 0-20-30; 300 lbs./acre of 0-20-20 or 5-10-10. Inadequate phosphorous is the major cause of limited lupine growth.
- **Maturity:** Generally, about 30 to 45 days under ideal conditions.
- **Crude Protein Content:** In tests, lupines foliage has been found to provide from 25 to 30 percent crude protein.
- **Total Digestibility (TDN):** Digestibility is rated as being high: 75–80 percent.
- **Companion Mixes:** Other legumes, clovers, grains, and chicory.
- **Overgrazing:** Vulnerable in early development.
- **Extends Grazing Season:** Can provide quality forage into November.
- **Advice:** For best results plant in large plots mixed with other plantings to divert overgrazing issues.
- **Caution:** Avoid planting lupine varieties that are high in alkaloids because they have a bitter taste to deer.
- **Pollinator Friendly:** Most lupine varieties have proven to be excellent attractions for bumblebees. Lupines also attract butterflies.
- **Sun:** Lupines prefer full sun but will tolerate some partial shade.
- **USDA Hardiness Zones:** Most lupine species grow in U.S.D.A. Hardiness Zones 4 through 8, although a few cultivars grow in USDA zones 3 to 7 and 9a.

SAINFOIN (*Onobrychis*)

Sainfoin, a.k.a. Holy Clover, is a perennial cool-season legume that can be used successfully as a popular wildlife food plot. This deep-rooted perennial legume arises from a branching root crown. Sainfoin flowers are pink, white, or purple and tightly arranged in a compact cluster of 20 to 50 flowers per head. It is a forb plant with erect stems that can reach up to 39 inches in height. Stems are hollow and appear coarse but are quite succulent. They have deep, branched taproots; the main taproot is very sturdy. The seed itself is large, kidney-shaped, and greenish-brown.

For many years, sainfoin was used mostly by cattle ranchers in the western parts of the country. But it has gained popularity as a food plot planting in the eastern part of the United States. Sainfoin is a disease-free cool-season perennial legume that is highly nutritious,

▲ Sainfoin is a legume that places high on the "like to eat list" of deer, elk, and other wildlife. It has good winter-hardiness, is drought tolerance, and is resistant to alfalfa stem nematode. Photo: Deposit Photo

and very palatable for deer and other wild animals. It contains an elevated level of the major and micronutrients and, as such, provides excellent high-quality forage for deer, elk, mule deer, and all grazing species. One short-coming of sainfoin is that frequent and severe grazing will quickly diminish a sainfoin stand, especially when grazed in its vegetative stage.

Sainfoin likes well-drained, dry sites not subject to long-term wet conditions, especially flooding. Well-drained soils are ideal for growing sainfoin. In addition, soils should have pH levels ranging from neutral to alkaline and be moderately fertile. Sainfoin is very drought-resistant and is more drought tolerant than alfalfa. Sainfoin is strikingly like alfalfa, which makes it a perfect choice, along with birdsfoot trefoil, as a replacement. Sainfoin is taller than alfalfa, but it is shorter-lived. It will also bloom a few weeks earlier than alfalfa. Moreover, sainfoin is resistant to the alfalfa weevil and the root-rot phase.

Before planting sainfoin, create a well-prepared soil bed. Make sure the seeds make good seed-to-soil contact by compacting the soil after seeding it. Though sainfoin has large seeds compared to other forage legumes, it needs to be seeded shallow, no more than 3/4-inch deep. Avoid fields that will make soft seedbeds as they are more difficult to pack; it also reduces the seed-to-soil contact. Inoculate sainfoin with the correct rhizobia species before seeding to allow nodules to develop. Sainfoin can be seeded before the end of June. Late-autumn seeding has also been successful when planted after October 1. A planting of sainfoin will last for years if the plot is well-maintained and managed.

Because sainfoin has an extended period of flowering, it is extremely attractive to honeybees. Bees readily take the nectar from its beautifully colored flowers. This can lead to high yields of honey; also, it can provide a habitat for wild bees that are currently threatened with extinction. Therefore, it is considered a very environmentally friendly plant.

CONDENSED RECAP

- **Temperature Tolerances:** Sanfoin is ranked as a cold-season legume, meaning it can tolerate cold temperatures of fall and early winter. Newer varieties like Shoshone and Eski were selected for their winter-hardiness.

- **Inoculant:** Is usually sold as pre-inoculated. Otherwise get an inoculant specific to sanfoin.
- **Preferred pH:** Prefers a pH value of 6.5 to 7.5.
- **Planting Time:** Can be planted in the spring or fall.
- **Soil:** Prefers well-drained soils, or sites not subject to flooding at the root zone are ideal for growing and performance. It is overly sensitive to acidic soils.
- **Seeding Rates:** In a stand-alone plot, broadcast 20 to 30 lbs./acre. When planted in a blended plot with other cold-hardy legumes, grains, or grasses, use 10 to 25 lbs./acre.
- **Seed Depth:** Plant ½- to ¾-inch deep. Do not exceed ¾-inch.
- **Germination:** Seedlings are not competitive. Consequently, sanfoin germinates well, but establishes slowly, with spring-seeded sainfoin normally well established by fall.
- **Fertilizer:** Sainfoin does not require a lot of nitrogen fertilizer because it has nitrogen-fixing capabilities. Use 300 lbs./acre of 0-20-20 or 5-10-10.
- **Maturity:** Matures within 30 to 45 days.
- **Crude Protein Content:** Sainfoin delivers excellent protein values; between 20 to 30 percent when soils are fertile and well-managed.

- **Total Digestibility (TDN):** All deer prefer sainfoin over alfalfa. TDN about 60 percent.
- **Companion Mixes:** Sainfoin does not compete well when mixed with other forages. Hence, blending sainfoin with other cool-season or winter-hardy legumes or grasses can be a trial-and-error proposition.
- **Overgrazing:** Sainfoin that undergoes severe grazing will quickly diminish, especially when grazed in its vegetative stage. Overgrazing is not an issue as soon as young plants become established.
- **Extends Grazing Season:** Winter varieties will extend grazing well into December or longer.
- **Advice:** Do not plant in consistently wet areas.
- **Caution:** Young plants can be quickly over-browsed; use other deterrent methods to prevent over-browsing of young plants.
- **Pollinator Friendly:** Sainfoin is extremely pollinator friendly to honeybees.
- **Sun:** Prefers full sun.
- **USDA Hardiness Zones**: Zones 3a to -40 °F with snow cover.

▲ Sanfoin is a deep-rooted perennial, making it a very drought-resistant plant. Credit: © Laurentiu Iordache | Dreamstime.com

PEANUT (*Arachis hypogaea*)

Peanuts, a.k.a. ground nuts and goobers, are not actually nut trees; they are classified as a legume. Deer are highly attracted to peanuts. As a legume plant, I included them in this section as a plant that grows from 12 to 20 inches tall. If you live in a zone where peanuts can grow, they are worth considering as a wildlife planting. Peanuts are high in protein and fat, making them a top food source for deer and other wildlife. This combination is especially important during the post-rut, when both does and bucks need to replace weight lost during the breeding season. In the southern states, where peanut crops are common, it has been reported that white-tailed deer go "nuts" over peanuts.

Peanuts like the sandy loam type soil found in this area. Peanuts are limited to specific areas, and they can be an expensive wildlife food plot to establish. The USDA Plant Hardiness Zones for peanuts are 5b through 10b; but peanuts are said to be adaptable to a range of climates. While it is safe to say they prefer warm weather, surprisingly peanuts are frost tolerant and they can grow in areas with an average low winter temperature of -15°F. Peanuts reach their peak growing performance in soil temperatures between 70° and 80°F.

▲ Deer savor eating forage peanuts. They provide high protein and fat, making them a terrific crop for deer. Forage peanut plants grow best in the South. Unfortunately, peanut plants generally do not survive in northern states. Photo: © lovelyday12 | Dreamstime

▲ The two most popular grains for wildlife are rye and winter oats. Other varieties include triticale, barley, and wheat. Brm1949/CanstockPhoto

Chapter Twenty
Large and Small Grains

Among some of the most attractive, healthy, and palatable of wildlife food plot plantings are the small and large cereal grains. Cereal grains, a.k.a. true *grains*, are members of the *Poaceae*, grass family, which includes summer and winter varieties of rye, wheat, triticale, barley, oats, corn, and sorghum. Other popular grains planted for deer, ducks, upland birds, and turkeys are rices and millets. All cereal grains work well to attract deer, whether they are sown for summer or winter-hardy plantings.

Do not underestimate the benefit of planting cereal grains as attractive food plots. They are high quality plantings that benefit deer in both summer and winter. All the cereal grains provide deer with high protein, palatability, and digestibility. They are resistant to being over-eaten and they can be available forage for deer from May to January. Moreover, other than corn, the other cereal grains are easy to grow, do not require a lot of babysitting, and they are very affordable. As if that isn't enough, cereal grains also have drought hardiness, adaptability to a wide variety of soils, and they can withstand heavy grazing. Equally important, white-tailed deer, mule deer, elk, and other big game love the taste of cereal grains. Lastly, and most important to food plotters, all the small cereal grains (rye, triticale, wheat, barley, and winter variety oats like Buck Forage Oats) make excellent winter-hardy plantings. The large cereal grains, corn, and grain sorghum are nearly impossible to beat as fall and early winter plantings.

Cereal grains that are sown in spring and summer provide excellent forage for deer. However, I will mostly address the benefits of planting winter grains as winter-hardy plots to attract deer during hunting season.

All the cereal grains will draw in deer like a super massive black hole draws in matter. In order of my

▲ I regularly include barley as one of the grains I plant. It is excellent fodder for deer. Barley is high-yielding and can be used as a grazing food plot or as a cover crop. Photo: Hancockseed.com

preference, the go-to winter grains are cereal rye, oats, triticale, wheat, and barley.

As with all wildlife food plots, a healthy plot always begins with good soil. As I have mentioned in earlier chapters, soil is the base, or foundation, of what makes a food plot effectively flourish. This is particularly true when planting any of the cereal grains. The reason is as plain as the nose on a deer's face. Plants thrive in good quality soils. However, they rarely, if ever, reach

▲ Triticale is a cross of wheat and rye. It is another regular on our farm. It is a highly versatile hybrid as a forage for deer and other wildlife, as it offers deer high protein and digestibility. Photo: Deposit Photo

their full potential of growth, or produce their best nutritional capabilities, when planted in inferior quality soils.

The formula for healthy, quality producing plants is basic. Take care of your soils—and they will take care of your plantings. While it is important to keep this point in mind about all plantings, when it comes to planting winter-hardy grains, it is even more important to have quality soils to provide plants the best nutrients needed for them to grow, do well, and survive the winter.

The one negative aspect about the small cereal grains is that if they start to grow too tall, they will become unpalatable to deer. This is a problem that happens with summer-planted small grains. If this occurs, mow the grains to about 2 to 3 inches to create new, tender growth. Winter-planted small grains are kept from growing tall because they are so attractive to deer, that the deer keep them neatly mowed.

CORN (*Zea mays*)

I want to set the record straight about my feelings about planting corn. In my 2013 book, *The Shooter's Bible Guide to Planting Food Plots*, I wrote a couple of negative points about planting corn. Although I clearly stated it is an important crop, I also emphasized that corn is not a crop to be planted by *all* food plotters. Some readers took what I said the wrong way, thinking I advised corn is not a good crop to plant for deer. Evidently, I didn't make myself clear. My apologies.

Factually, corn ranks extremely near the top, if not at the top, of a deer's preferred food. It fills their need for fat-building carbohydrates as winter approaches. I *strongly* believe corn is a top-notch plant for a food plot and I *absolutely* think it should be planted. But here's the fly in the ointment. While corn is a highly attractive and nutritious planting for deer, it can only be grown successfully when its needs are taken into consideration.

Grain corn is an annual warm-season crop that can withstand fall temperatures. It is not a winter-hardy planting. However, when the stalks are left standing into November, its corn cobs are a very enticing food for deer and other wildlife. These factors make corn one of the most effective and attractive food plot crops for deer.

Plant corn in the best soil available, preferably on level ground. Well-drained bottomlands are ideal areas. In lieu of that, flat higher ground will work. In either case, corn is sensitive to drought conditions, so it is vital to select planting areas with good soil moisture.

In the North, corn is planted in May or June, and in March or April in the South. Sow corn when soil

▲ If you know the words to the song "Hair," by the Cowsills, change the second verse by removing the word hair and replace it with corn. That is what every food plotter should sing when they plant corn. A planting of corn left standing is an A++ crop to attract deer into the firearm season. Photo: PCFImages

▲ A heavy beamed buck adult buck checking a corn planting for any leftover corn cobs, fallen corn, or perhaps an estrus doe. Note his barrel-shaped chest and overall body size. Photo: © Lynn Bystrom | Dreamstime

root growth prevents the uptake of phosphorus. When leaves are purple, dig up a seedling and examine the roots. Even cold water from a thunderstorm filtering into the soil can cause seedlings to become deformed. So, when planting corn it is wise to take soil temperatures seriously. It pays to be prudent.

Corn growth and high yield cob production will be stunted by weeds. Roundup Ready (RR) varieties are the best choice. Prior to planting, kill noxious weeds with an appropriate herbicide, and wait about 10 days before planting. Corn plants develop well when spaced about 6 to 12 inches apart and in rows 30 to 36 inches away from each other. This converts to be about 6 to 10 lbs./acre. Broadcast rate is about 12 to 18 lbs./acre. Corn is typically in bags with about 80,000 kernels. A bag weight can vary from about 35 to 65 pounds. One bag of corn will plant about 2 to 2½ acres. When the RR corn reaches about 24 to 36 inches, spray the crop for weed control. It is important to read the directions of the herbicide beforehand.

A key factor for planting corn as a food plot is having enough land to plant more than 1 acre. Small plots, particularly in areas with heavy deer densities, rarely, if ever still have corn cobs left on the stalks into the firearm seasons. Why? Simply because deer and countless other animals relish eating corn.

temperatures reach 60° F. The best way to be sure about a soil's temperature it to use a soil monitor to accurately get a reading at a depth of one inch. Early morning is the best time to take a reading.

Corn emergence is referred to as Vegetative Emergence (VE). As corn emerges from the soil the seedling is exposed to above-ground weather conditions. As mentioned earlier, corn sprouts and grows best when the soil temperatures are above 60°F. It has been undoubtedly documented by botanists that cold air temperatures after emergence can significantly have a negative effect on corn seedling development. Moderately cold temperatures can retard growth (warm temperatures can increase growth). Very cold or very hot temperatures can be stressful to newly emerged corn plants. Such conditions can even result in plant death. Should you see leaf discoloration after cold weather, it pays to visually inspect a plant. Purplish leaves can develop when retarded

▲ A young buck on our farm rummaging through corn for dropped kernels in late November. Most if not all the corn cobs had been eaten, leaving only kernels for deer to pick through. Photo: PCFImages

According to biologists, corn is eaten by more than 100 different animal species. Corn-loving wildlife includes bears, rabbits, raccoons, foxes, woodchucks, wild turkeys, all upland birds, waterfowl, squirrels, opossums, songbirds, hawks, blackbirds, pigeons, crows, beavers, and about 80 other corn-eating critters. It becomes easy to understand how quickly a 1-acre plot (or smaller) can be wiped out. The reality is that if you plant corn, plant at least 2 acres and preferably 3 acres or more.

It helps to have the type of farm implements that make planting corn easier and successful. The best corn planting method is with a drill. However, farm drills are expensive. They also require a larger tractor to operate them. Generally, these farm drills cost about $20,000 or more. This price point is out of reach for most food plotters. The good news is that there are drills specifically made for planting food plots for wildlife. The unwelcome news, though, is they, too, are somewhat expensive, generally selling between $8,000 and $12,000. There are less expensive drills, but they often encounter mechanical problems, especially when they are used on grounds that have rocks and hard soil. Do your homework when considering buying a drill. Some drill manufacturers include Kasco (www.kascomfg.com) and Zimmerman Farm Service (www.zimmermanfarmservice.com). Another choice is a Brillion Food Plot Seeder www.brillionfarmeq.com or a 2- or 4-row John Deere corn planter www.ebay.com.

With that said, food plotters can also plant corn by simply broadcasting the seed. But broadcasting corn requires creating a well-prepared seedbed. Plant

▲ I like to check our corn in late September prior to the bowhunting season. I look for insect damage and if wildlife has started to browse it. Photo: PCFImages

the seed at 1½ to 2 inches deep. Broadcast the seed by hand or mechanically. By hand you can use an EarthWay, Solo, or similar brand hand seeder. Or use a seeder that can be attached to either an ATV or a tractor. A crucial point, however, is no matter how the seed is planted, it must be well compacted into the soil.

Corn requires plenty of fertilizer. Therefore, it is necessary to take a soil test prior to planting corn. In lieu of a soil test, use 300 to 400 lbs./acre of T-19 (19-19-19) at planting. About 4 weeks later top-dress it using 150 lbs./acre of ammonium sulfate (34-0-0), or urea (46-0-0).

Botanists and biologists have well documented corn's nutritional value. It only provides 5 to 8 percent levels of protein. But it makes up for that deficiency by providing deer about 75 percent in carbohydrates and about 5 percent in fat. These are two vital nutrients that deer need during the rut and to survive the harsh winter months.

There are numerous corn hybrids available. Talk with your local seed dealer about hybrids adapted to your specific region. Stay away from "silage" corn hybrids. Hybrids produce more forage and less grain. You can select between early- and late-maturing varieties. For hunters, the late-maturing varieties of corn are going to be most productive as food plots that will draw in deer. Be sure, though, to plant late-maturing corn early enough for it to mature before the growing season ends.

CONDENSED RECAP

- **Temperature Tolerances:** Can withstand fall temperatures.
- **Inoculant:** Not applicable.
- **Planting Times:** Plant when soil temperatures reach at least 60° F.
- **Seeding Rates:** Drill corn at a rate of 8 to 10 lbs./acre. Broadcast at about 10 to 15 lbs./acre depending on the size of the seed and the variety.
- **Planting Depth:** In a well-prepared seedbed plant at 1½ to 2 inches deep, and thoroughly cultipack after planting.
- **Companion Plants:** Tall, bird-resistant grain sorghum, forage soybeans, cowpeas, Lablab, and even clovers to restore nitrogen into the soil.

- **pH Levels:** The optimum range is 6.0 to 7.0. Fertilize according to a soil test.
- **Soil Preferences:** Corn grows best when planted on fertile, well-drained, loamy soils.
- **Germination:** Corn seeds planted in warm soil, germinate within 6 to 10 days. In cold, wet soil seeds are unlikely to germinate successfully.
- **Fertilizer:** Depending on soil fertility, use 300 to 400 lbs./acre of 19-19-19 at planting. A month later top-dress the corn with either 150 lbs./acre of ammonium sulfate (34-0-0), or urea (46-0-0).
- **Crude Protein Content:** Corn provides 5 to 8 percent protein, 4 percent fat levels, and 75 percent of carbohydrates.
- **Total Digestibility (TDN):** Corn contains around 90 percent TDN, and most of the energy comes from starch.
- **Nitrogen Fixation:** No, just the opposite: corn is a heavy user of nitrogen.
- **Overgrazing Concerns:** Will undoubtedly occur in small 1 acre or less plots. Plant at least 2 to 3 acres of corn.
- **Extends Grazing Season**: Extends grazing into November.
- **Sunlight:** Full sun.
- **Pollinator Friendly:** No.
- **USDA Hardiness Zone:** Corn will do well in most northern or southern areas across the country and into Canada. Check exact USDA Hardiness Zones for corn.
- **Maturity:** Depending on variety, matures from about 75 to 112 days (some varieties mature slightly later).
- **Advice:** Only plant Roundup Ready (RR) corn. Spray corn with RR to prevent weed growth and competition.
- **Caution:** Do not plant sweet corn for deer.
- **Level of Maintenance:** Medium to High.
- **Note:** Small plots of one acre or less will be eradicated by deer and other wildlife long before firearm season. Larger plots at 2 to 3 acres and more, will draw deer into late November.

GRAIN SORGHUM (*Sorghum bicolor*)

Grain sorghum, a.k.a. milo, is a highly versatile crop for deer. Like its cousin corn, it is also a member of the grass family. Sorghum is one of the top five grain crops that can be grown as grain forage. Unfortunately, grain sorghum is often overlooked as a top-tier grain for deer and other wildlife by some food plot managers. This is most likely due to the fact that it is not well-marketed as a top choice grain for food plot managers. With that said, it should be. Interest in growing grain sorghum, though, has increased in many eastern and southern areas of the country due to its many advantages. Grain sorghum is very drought tolerant, has a wide adaption to soils, and features versatile planting dates.

Sorghums are classified into four groups: grass sorghums, grain sorghums, broomcorn, and sorgos. The grain sorghums are typically planted for deer and other wildlife because of their ability to produce grain, making them the most beneficial of all sorghum varieties. Grain varieties of sorghum are generally short-growing and have large seed heads unlike the taller syrup, silage, and hay varieties. The sorghums that should never be planted for deer are cane, Sudan, and sweet sorghum. The red selections are more attractive to deer than the lighter colored varieties are. Taller varieties tolerate weeds better than shorter varieties of grain sorghum.

Grain sorghum can be grown almost anywhere within the United Sates, if the growing season allows it to mature before the first frost occurs. Grain sorghum needs about 3 to 4 months to reach maturity. It makes an excellent substitute for corn. Plant grain sorghum

▲ Wild Game Food (WGF) Sorghum is a terrific summer and fall food plot for deer and elk. The longer it stands, the more it loses tannic acid, making it most palatable to deer through the fall. Photo: lacrosseseed.com

for deer in May in the central part of the country, in early June in the North, and in April in the most southern portions of the U.S. Plant sorghum when soil temperatures reach 60 to 65°F for at least a few consecutive days, which generally occurs about a month after the last frost.

Grain sorghum doesn't like exceptionally low acidic soils but will tolerate soils from 5.7 and higher. It prefers a pH between 6.0 to about 7.5. Planting depth is from 1 to 2 inches deep on a firm, well-drained seedbed. Do not plant sorghum deeper than 2 inches. Grain sorghum can be drilled at 5 lbs./acre, broadcast alone at 10 lbs./acre. Do not use more than 10 lbs./acre or the plot will produce spindly seed heads. A starter fertilizer is an option but is necessary if planting seed with a no-till drill. In lieu of a soil test, use 400 to 450 lbs./acre of T-19 (19-19-19). Grain sorghum is a heavy user of nitrogen. Adding a top-off of an additional 100 lbs./acre of nitrogen will help the plant produce better. For heavy clay soils, increase the nitrogen by 20 to 30 lbs./acre. Splitting nitrogen is also an option; apply one third at planting and the remainder when plants are in the 4- to 6-leaf stage.

Grain sorghum can be planted alone or as a mixture. It can be combined with other plants including any of the beans, peas, even Jointvetch (a.k.a. *aeschynomene*). When including other plants with sorghum, broadcasted sorghum rates should be reduced to about 7 lbs./acre. I plant my grain sorghum alone and use a mix of clovers along one side of the planting and a blend of other legumes on the other side. The deer will feed actively on the clovers and legumes, and overlook the sorghum seed heads, until fall when they are more attractive and beneficial to deer.

Deer prefer the seed head of sorghum, and they will occasionally begin to feed on it as early as August. However, deer make the most use of sorghum after the plant matures and feed on the seed heads from fall to late winter depending on the type of grain sorghum planted.

In June 2020, Alta Seeds released a new herbicide-tolerant grain sorghum. The companion herbicide IMIFLEX was EPA approved in December 2020. Food plotters can now plant grain sorghum from Alta Seeds and use IMIFLEX, the first non-GMO herbicide resistant technology to control weeds.

▲ Sorghum is an exceptional crop for wild turkeys, quail, doves, pheasants, and all other upland birds. It is also sought after by many types of ducks and geese. Photo: Deposit

There is another variety of sorghum that is beneficial to deer called WGF (Wild Game Food) sorghum. It is a shorter variety that grows to about 3 feet tall. Weeds should be killed prior to planting this variety and controlled while it grows.

CONDENSED RECAP
- **Temperature Tolerances:** Withstands fall temperatures until the first frost.
- **Inoculant:** Not applicable.
- **Planting Times:** Grain sorghum should be planted in soil temperatures of 60 to 65°F. North–June; Central–May; South–April. Later plantings can lead to decreased yields.

- **Seeding Rates:** Broadcast it alone at 10 lbs./acre. Drill it at 5 lbs./acre.
- **Planting Depth:** Plant grain sorghum 1-inch deep in heavy clay soils. Broadcast it at 1 to 2 inches deep.
- **Companion Plants:** Plant with corn, soybeans, clovers, or peas. Can also be strip-planted next to clovers and other legumes to deter deer from eating the seed heads.
- **pH Levels:** It doesn't like low acidic soils but will tolerate soils from 5.7 and up. Grain sorghum *prefers* a pH between 6.0 to about 7.5. Like all plants, the optimum pH is 6.5.
- **Soil Preferences:** Grain sorghum is tolerant of a wide range of soil types. It prefers medium-textured soils for best growth, but with good management, sandy and very heavy soils can produce high yields as well.
- **Germination:** Depending on soil temperatures and weather conditions, the number of days for sorghum to sprout can take 7 to 25 days.
- **Fertilizer:** In lieu of a soil test, at planting use 350 to 400 lbs./acre of 19-19-19. Top dress with about 100 lbs./acre of urea (46-0-0).
- **Crude Protein Content:** Contains 7 to 8 percent.
- **Total Digestibility (TDN):** It has with total digestible nutrients (TDN) of 65 percent (about 50–60 percent of the plant's dry matter remains in the field after harvest).
- **Nitrogen Fixation:** No. It is a heavy user of nitrogen.

- **Overgrazing:** Generally, overgrazing grain sorghum by deer is not an issue.
- **Extends Grazing Season:** While grain sorghum is planted during the warm months, it provides a food source for deer and other wildlife during the late fall and winter. Deer generally do not eat the plant while it is in the early stages of development.
- **Sunlight:** Prefers full sunlight.
- **Pollinator Friendly:** Sorghum is a wind-pollinated plant. However, honeybees do occasionally visit sorghum plants.
- **USDA Hardiness Zones:** Adaptable to USDA Plant Hardiness Zones: 4, 5, 6, 7; 8 and 12 temperate zones are transitional. Check your USDA Hardiness Zone for more information.
- **Advice:** Bird-resistant varieties with red seed heads are more attractive to deer than the lighter colored varieties.
- **Caution:** Do not plant cane, sudan, or sweet sorghum grasses for deer. Tall-growing varieties are better than shorter ones for better tolerance of weed problems.
- **Level of Maintenance:** Low.
- **Maturity:** Depending on the variety, grain sorghum matures from about 90 to 120 days.
- **Note:** For best results, plant grain sorghum with clovers along one side and other legumes on the other side.

▲ Sorghum, like corn, is attractive to big game and many gamebirds. It requires a soil temperature of 60°F for several days prior to planting. Credit: © Sofiaworld | Dreamstime.com

RYE (*Secale cereale*)

Rye is also known as cereal rye, grain rye, and winter or spring rye. If push came to shove and I had to make a choice to plant just a few types of food plots, one of my top choices would unquestionably be cereal rye or *Secale cereale*. Be careful not to mistake cereal rye with annual or perennial ryegrass; they are entirely different plants. There is absolutely no doubt that cereal rye offers a wide array of benefits to both deer and hunters who plant food plots for wildlife. That may seem like somewhat of an overstatement, but it is not. When cereal rye is scrutinized, it quickly becomes clear it should be the "go-to" plant for food plotters who want to draw in deer to their food plots from spring green up to the frigid winter months by planting either winter or spring varieties of cereal rye. Whether you plant a ¼-acre plot or less, or a couple of acres or more, winter cereal rye will turn out to be one of your best decisions. Plant it and they will come.

CEREAL RYE'S VIRTUES

When it is too late to plant anything else, winter rye can be planted in the North as late as mid-September or October in the South. Spring-planted cereal rye, a.k.a. rye, should be planted as early as possible, generally April in the North and February or March in the South. As with all the grains, cereal rye can be grown either as a warm-season food plot or a winter-hardy planting. It is even more cold tolerant than winter varieties of oats

▲ When planting wildlife food plots, cereal rye should very rank high as a planting to attract deer during the hunting season. Photo: © Geothea Dreamstime

and even winter wheat. But that's not all. This plant can tolerate low fertility, acidic soil, and a wider range of ecological conditions better than most other food plot plants including all the other small winter grains.

Cereal rye is widely considered by most land managers as the hardiest of cereal grains. It can be seeded later than other cover crops and still provide considerable amount of dry matter. Cereal rye is also an unbelievably valuable and efficient manufacturer of organic matter (OM). Organic matter is made up of organic compounds that derive from the remains of living organisms, including plants and animals and their waste products left in the environment (organic molecules are also made by chemical reactions that end up having nothing to do with life).

Rye is the best cool-season cereal cover absorbing unused soil nitrogen. Cereal rye does not have a taproot, but its quick-growing, fibrous, soil-holding, extensive root system can take up and hold as much as 100 pounds of nitrogen. Its main root digs very deeply into the soil, and it has a web of smaller, tributary-like roots too. All of these enable rye to go dormant when temperatures drop below freezing and trigger it back to life when temperatures warm up again. The significance of that statement should not be lost. Moreover, rye reduces soil erosion, and enriches water penetration and retention.

WEED SUPPRESSOR

A significant point about cereal rye that is worth tattooing on your brain is it is one of the best cool-season crops for reducing and/or severely limiting competing weeds, such as dandelions, thistle, pigweed, and foxtail. Rye also suppresses many weeds allelopathically which *Merriam Webster* defines as "the suppression of growth of one plant species by another due to the release of toxic substances." Rye has been shown to impede germination of some triazine-resistant weeds. A study done by Midwest Cover Crops Council (mccc.msu.edu) showed that "Rye reduced total weed density an average of 78 percent when rye residue covered more than 90 percent of soil in a Maryland no-till study, and by 99 percent in a California study." So, in addition to its other attributes listed so far, cereal rye can release a natural chemical herbicide that helps to significantly reduce weed problems. It has been documented that rye

▲ Remember this about winter-hardy cereal rye: when it is too late to plant anything else, plant rye. Rye can be sown from mid-September (late-September in a pinch). It is a more winter-hardy grain than winter oats, wheat, or triticale. Photo: PCFImages

reduces total weed biomass by 60 to 95 percent when compared to controls with no residue. Therefore, rye residues modify the physical and chemical environment during seed germination and during the plant's growth cycle.

However, do not expect rye to eliminate all weeds. There may be a time when some additional weed management measures may be required. But I have not found that to be necessary yet, and I have been planting cereal rye for 35 years.

PEST SUPPRESSOR

Rye is susceptible to the same insects that attack other cereal grains. However, serious infestations are rare. Cereal rye reduces insect pest problems and attracts significant numbers of beneficial insects like lady beetles. Fewer diseases are said to affect rye than other cereal grains. Rye can also help reduce root-knot nematodes and other harmful nematodes.

SOIL ENHANCER

If so far all this is not impressive, here is another attribute about cereal rye. As I have mentioned throughout this book, when it comes to growing healthy, nutritious food plots that reach their maximum potential, soil is the foundation that is the genesis of all successful plantings. Here, rye comes into its own. It increases the concentration of exchangeable potassium near the soil's surface by bringing it up from lower in the soil's profile. Rye's rapid growth (even in cold fall weather) helps trap snow in winter, further aiding in its winter-hardiness. When you want to improve a poor soil, turn your attention to Mother Nature's top-shelf soil enhancer—cereal rye.

Depending on the variety, soil fertility, and grazing pressure by deer and other wildlife, cereal rye grows from 2 to 4 feet tall. Rye grows taller and faster than wheat. It can also help as a windbreak and trap snow or hold rainfall over winter. Rye overseeds readily into other crops and resumes growth quickly in spring. Rye can be mixed with hairy vetch (a winter annual legume) to help offset its tendency to tie up soil nitrogen in spring. Furthermore, cereal rye is exceedingly easy to establish. You can grow it even if you have the dreaded disease of "black thumb." It also outperforms all other cover crops on fertile, infertile, sandy, acidic soil, or on poorly prepared land. It is widely adapted to many different types of soils, weather conditions, pH levels, and temperatures, but it grows best in cool, temperate climate zones.

Like other grains, rye can be planted in spring as a warm-season plot, late August, or early fall as a winter-hardy plot that provides excellent nutrition for deer. Are you still not impressed? Here is a fact you can't ignore. Deer are highly attracted to cereal rye's tender, nutritious foliage. They enthusiastically seek it out in spring and particularly in late fall and winter. And why not? Cereal rye offers 12 to 25 percent crude protein levels. Even better is its ability to withstand extra cold temperatures. That point alone is why many hunters who plant food plots for deer should be focused on planting cereal rye. If I were limited to one sentence

▲ Cereal rye (*Secale cereale*) is a cereal grain. It is a high preference forage for whitetails, elk, mule deer, antelope, bears, and other game. They all savor the tender nutritious (12 to 25 percent) protein especially in fall and winter. Rye is very cold-hardy and can be grown anywhere in the US. Photo: PCFImages

to write about cereal rye, it would be this: Plant it and deer will come!

There are dozens of cereal rye varieties available. Some have been developed specifically as forage crops. As such, they are the best choices for planting for deer and other wildlife. Some of the forage winter and spring rye varieties include Aroostook, Maton, Bates, Brasetto, Winter King, Wheeler, Dacold, Elbon, FL401, Guardian, Hazlet, Maton II, Merced, Oklon, Wheeler, Wintergrazer 70, Wrens Abruzzi, and Rymin. Varieties with high forage production can produce significant amounts of dry matter. Some are said to produce 3 or more tons of forage per acre, in dry weight, and up to 80 bushels per acre of grain in healthy soils and under careful management practices.

CONDENSED RECAP

- **Temperature Tolerances:** Very winter-hardy.
- **Inoculant:** Not applicable.
- **Planting Times:** Plant winter rye in August or September in the North and October in the South. Plant summer rye in early spring.
- **Seeding Rates:** Broadcast at 90 to 120 lbs./acre. Drill at 45 to 60 lbs./acre. When planting in mixes, use no more than 60 lbs./acre.
- **Planting Depth:** Rye is hypersensitive to seeding depth. Plant it 1½ to 2 inches deep, but not deeper than 2 inches.
- **Companion Plants:** Very compatible with triticale, wheat, hairy vetch, winter-hardy clovers, chicory, and other legumes. When mixed, plant rye at a reduced rate of about 60 lbs./acre when broadcast.

- **pH Levels:** Cereal rye widely adapts to pH levels. Optimum pH levels are above 6.0. However, rye can tolerate 4.5 to 7.0.
- **Soil Preferences:** Does best on well-drained loamy soils but can handle heavy clay and sandy soils.
- **Germination:** Depending on soil temperatures and moisture (rain), rye emerges in 3 to 7 days.
- **Fertilizer:** Rye will often respond to a modest application of nitrogen fertilizer. In late winter add 100 lbs./acre of nitrogen (34-0-0) if needed.
- **Crude Protein Content:** Cereal rye can provide from 12 to 25 percent levels of crude protein.
- **Total Digestibility (TDN):** TDN is rated at 53–63 percent.
- **Nitrogen Fixation:** Average to above-average.
- **Overgrazing:** Not an issue.
- **Extends Grazing Season:** Will be a viable winter food plot well into December or later.
- **Sunlight:** Prefers full sun.
- **Pollinator Friendly:** No. Grains are flowering plants that are wind-pollinated. Since they do not need to attract pollinators, the plants do not expend energy to produce colorful petals, nectars, or attractive odors.
- **USDA Hardiness Zones:** Seed in late summer to mid-fall in Hardiness Zones 3 to 7. Seed in fall to midwinter in Zones 8 and warmer. In the upper Midwest and cool New England states, seed cereal rye 2 to 6 weeks earlier than a wheat to ensure maximum fall, winter, and spring growth.
- **Advice:** Always include winter cereal rye in at least one of your food plots.
- **Caution:** Do not confuse cereal rye with annual or perennial ryegrass. They are entirely different plants.
- **Level of Maintenance:** Low.
- **Maturity:** Rye grain germinates readily even at low temperatures (40°F). Generally, rye emerges within 5 to 7 days.
- **Note:** To attract deer during the hunting seasons, plant winter rye with winter clovers no later than August in the North and October in the South.

▲ Geese, like other game animals, are highly attracted to grain rye. Credit: River Refuge Seed

OATS (*Avena sativa*)

There are countless land managers who agree that warm- and fall-season oats may very well be the best deer attractant within the family of grains (corn, grain sorghum, rye, oats, triticale, wheat, and barley). I, too, think oats are a terrific food plot within the winter-hardy small grains (cereal rye, triticale, wheat, oats, and barley). If oats are not the best deer attractant, they are most certainly among the top three of favorite grains of land managers (cereal rye, corn, and oats).

Without question, warm-season or cold-season oats are highly attractive to deer. Early oat plantings are remarkably successful when moisture is advantageous. Oats sown in late August or early September, however, while still attractive to deer, do not last well into November or longer. In upstate New York, we get some bone-chilling temperatures as early as late October and into November. It is not uncommon for us to have frigid cold weather, where temperatures do not climb above 10° to 15°F, for extended periods in late November. Oats, even the winter-hardy varieties, are characteristically vulnerable to cold temperatures. Most varieties, including the winter varieties, will winter kill between 10° to 20°F. That is why I still rank cereal rye as a number one winter-hardy grain choice.

In a recent research study, plant physiologist David P. Livingston, with the USDA's Agricultural Research Service Plant Science Research Laboratory and plant breeder Paul Murphy at North Carolina State University, reported their findings about fall grain crops and cold temperatures in the journal Crop Science. "Among fall-sown grain crops, oats are much less winter-hardy

▲ Winter oats are popular cereal grains. Buck Forage, Naked Oats, Arctic Forage, Buck Magnet, and other winter-hardy varieties are terrific sources of forage for deer and other big game. Oats can be sown with winter rye, brassicas, and even winter-hardy legumes. Photo: PCFImages

than wheat, barley, and rye. Sustained temperatures at or below 20°F usually result in yield losses." With that said, though, winter oats planted in late August or the first week of September have been attractive and had good yields on my land, before winter-kill in mid-November. But the oats consistently had good yields and drew in deer during October to mid-November.

Oats are best seeded using a drill at 1 to 1½ inches deep. When drilled, the optimal seeding rate for oats is about 90 to 100 pounds. The recommended broadcast rate can range from 100 to 120 lbs./acre to allow for variable seed placement. If seeded as a mixed plot, the seeding rate is 60 to 90 lbs./ acre. It is best to plant oats and other small grain seeds in moist soil. Oats can also be frost-seeded.

Oats perform very well in mixtures with other forages like winter-hardy balansa, frosty berseem, and kura clovers (all winter-hardy), or lupines, chicory, and winter peas. Planting oats in a mixture with ryegrass will produce more total forage over a longer grazing season than planting oats as a stand-alone crop. Deer will heavily use food plots mixed with clovers, legumes, and chicory. These other plantings extend the life while oats are growing and even after oats mature. They also benefit by putting nitrogen into the soil that is beneficial for oats. As oats begin to mature and produce seed, palatability and digestibility are substantially reduced.

Oats are slightly slower than other grains to sprout. Seeds will germinate at 40°F. However, like most plants, oats will germinate faster as soil temps increase. The goal is to balance an early planting date with biological limitations and the potential for seed predation issues (wild turkeys and crows can decimate a newly seeded plot of oats). Early planting dates usually mean higher yield. Deer will begin foraging in the plot soon after the oats and other plantings germinate. Once they germinate, they establish very quickly, and the rapid

▲ Winter oats provide high-sugar forage that deer and other big game will flock to in late fall and beyond. Oats will also attract wild turkeys and upland birds as well as geese and ducks. Photo: H. Hickman

growth rate will help suppress weed pressure naturally. Some weed control methods may be warranted in some cases. It has been my experience that a plot of warm-season oats will mature by the middle to the end of summer. By that time, deer, turkeys, squirrels, and a host of other critters have eaten the mature oat seeds. The fat content of oats increases their energy content.

WINTER OATS

As a rule, the hardiest winter oat varieties include Buck Forage Oats by Arkansas County Seed and Arctic Forage Winter Oats by Deer Creek Seed (two of my favorite varieties). Other oats include Ram Forage Oats, Wintok, Norline, Kenoat, and Buck Magnet. However, in the southern US, winter oats will usually survive most winters and produce high yields of forage (4-8T/Ac). Like barley, winter oats must be seeded in mid-September to be well established before cold weather arrives. Winter oats are best adapted to well-drained clay and sandy loam soils. They do not perform as well as wheat and rye do under extremely dry or wet conditions. Winter oats produce a high-quality silage; however, lower yields are common compared to the other small grains.

CONDENSED RECAP

- **Temperature Tolerances:** Use winter varieties to attract deer. Some oats are sensitive to cold temperatures and will winter kill at 10° to 20°F.
- **Inoculant:** Not applicable.
- **Planting Times:** Plant spring oats in early spring. Plant fall oats in early August/September in the North and September/October in the South.
- **Seeding Rates:** Depending on planting methods (drilled, broadcast, or frost seeded), about 90 to 120 lbs./acre. Use 60 lbs./acre when mixed with other seed.
- **Planting Depth:** Plant oats about 1 to 1½ inches deep.
- **Companion Plants:** Can be mixed with red or white winter-hardy clovers, or chicory.
- **pH Levels:** The recommended optimum pH level is 5.8 to 7.0. Some varieties tolerate soil pH as low as 4.5.

- **Soil Preferences:** Prefers well-drained to moderately drained soils.
- **Germination:** Oats germinate quickly, generally in 3 to 5 days.
- **Fertilizer:** When it comes to fertilizing and liming oats, it is highly recommended that a soil test be done prior to planting. Oats require more specific NPK mixes than many other plantings do. In lieu of a soil test, however, use 200 to 250 lbs./acre of 13-13-13.
- **Crude Protein Content**: 10 to 28 percent crude protein.
- **Total Digestibility (TDN):** Excellent digestible energy—75 to 77 percent.
- **Nitrogen Fixation:** Does not fix nitrogen.
- **Overgrazing:** Not an issue if planted with clovers, other legumes, etc.
- **Extends Grazing Season:** Summer oat plots provide forage until August. Winter oat plantings provide forage into late fall.
- **Sun:** Full sun, tolerates partial shade.
- **Pollinator Friendly:** No. Grasses are flowering plants that are wind-pollinated. Since the grasses do not need to attract animal pollinators, the plants do not expend energy to produce colorful petals, nectars, or attractive odors.
- **USDA Hardiness Zones:** Check your area with the USDA Hardiness Zone maps.
- **Advice:** Plant oats in mixes for best results.
- **Caution:** Do not apply more than 20 lbs./acre as urea (46-0-0) with the drill. Do not place ammonium thiosulfate (12-0-0-26s) in direct contact with the oat seed. Ammonium thiosulfate contains 12 percent nitrogen and 26 percent sulfur. Do not place fertilizers containing boron in direct contact with the seed. Avoid buying inexpensive winter oats like Bob oats that have little or no winter tolerance or oats labeled as Variety Not Stated (VNS).
- **Level of Maintenance:** Medium.
- **Note:** Oats will tolerate heavy grazing.
- **Maturity:** Oats take up to 60 to 75 days of growth to mature. Summer seeded oats mature slowly and may require an additional 10 days or so.

WINTER WHEAT (*Triticum aestivum*)

Winter wheat is said to be the "mother" of fall cereal grain forage food crops. It is the most planted grain within the United States. Wheat is used in countless foods for humans. Deer eagerly eat wheat as well, and will eat wheat in spring, early fall, and especially during the winter months. Like most of the other grains, deer will browse on wheat's tender and nutritious foliage as soon as it becomes available to them. Wheat provides 15 to 25 percent (and more) protein levels.

As a winter-hardy forage grain for deer, wheat deals with cold temperatures better than winter oats, but it is not nearly as tolerant of cold winter temperatures as cereal rye. But then again, cereal rye is the most cold-hardy of all the grains. Winter wheat is generally planted in September in the North and October in the South. It can be planted in the spring as well. When planted alone, broadcast about 100 to 120 lbs./ acre. If wheat is planted in a mix, reduce the amount by half, to 50 to 60 lbs./acre. Wheat sprouts before freezing

▲ All grains like this warm-season planting of wheat and crimson clover can be planted with companion crops. When planting winter-hardy grains, make sure the companion plant/s are also a winter-hardy variety. Photo: meritseed.com

occurs, then becomes dormant until the soil warms up in the spring. The wheat grows and matures until ready to be harvested by early July. Deer find winter wheat irresistible. Wheat likes a soil pH of 6.0 and higher and will produce best under these conditions. Fertilize it with about 300 to 400 lbs./acre of 19-19-19 when it is planted.

Winter wheat is compatible with a variety of red or white clovers and other legumes, including Austrian winter peas, birdsfoot trefoil, and chicory. The clovers and legumes also help the wheat by fixing nitrogen in the soil—which the wheat uses. As with other grains, when seeding wheat, first firm the plot using a culti-packer behind an ATV or a light drag. Broadcast the seed evenly across the food plot. Don't cover the seed more than 1- to 1½-inches deep. To ensure success-ful establishment of wheat or any grain, make sure there is good seed-to-soil contact. As with all seeds, the best time for planting is just prior to an expected rainfall. There are many varieties of wheat from which to choose. Many wheat varieties have been designed as forage selections which are the most appropriate varieties for deer.

CONDENSED RECAP

- **Temperature Tolerances:** Cold-hardy, will remain winter-hardy if crown temperatures remain below about 32°F.
- **Inoculant:** Not applicable.
- **Planting Times:** Late August or early September.
- **Seeding Rates:** Alone, 90 to 120 lbs./acre; mixed, 60 lbs./acre.
- **Planting Depth:** 1 to 1½ inches.
- **Companion Plants:** Other grains, winter-hardy clovers, and other legumes, birdsfoot trefoil, and chicory.
- **pH Levels:** Prefers 6.5, will tolerate 6.0 to 7.0.
- **Soil Preferences:** Clay loam or loamy texture.
- **Germination:** Takes place in 4 to 5 days.
- **Fertilizer:** At planting, 300 to 350 lbs./acre of 19-19-19.
- **Crude Protein Content:** 15–28 percent.
- **Total Digestible Nutrients (TDN):** 80 percent.
- **Nitrogen Fixation:** Low to moderate.
- **Overgrazing Concerns:** Not an issue, particularly when planted with companion crops.
- **Extends Grazing Season:** Well into winter.
- **Sunlight:** Prefers full sun.
- **Pollinator Friendly:** No.
- **USDA Hardiness Zone:** Grows in most northern areas of the country, check your local ag extension department.
- **Advice:** Some varieties have been bred for forage production and are most suitable for deer.
- **Caution**: Do not plant "combine-run" (not inspected) wheat. It can contain noxious weeds.
- **Level of Maintenance:** Low.
- **Note:** Wheat planted side-by-side with oats and cereal rye has proved to be an excellent planting on our land.

WINTER TRITICALE (*Triticosecale rimpaui*)

Triticale is a hybrid cross of wheat and rye grain. The newer varieties combine winter-hardy wheats (as parent plants), and rye which helps significantly to produce triticale with particularly good winter-hardiness. These newer varieties are most suitable to plant for deer. I have had considerable success planting triticale as a winter-hardy food plot on our farm. Triticale is a grain that can also be planted as a warm-season crop. Triticale's young tender growth can yield protein levels between 20 to 30 percent. When managed, triticale's forage yields can produce 3 tons or more per acre.

Winter triticale can be planted earlier than winter wheat, generally in mid-August or early September in the North, and in September and October in the South. I plant triticale mostly as a fall/winter food plot. It's terrific forage for deer, turkeys and other upland birds, and waterfowl. We have planted at least one warm-season plot and two winter-hardy plots of triticale on our property almost every year for the last 20 years.

Triticale is rated higher than wheat by many wildlife managers. Once the ground is ready to plant in spring, I put in triticale usually by mid-May. Planted by itself, triticale can be planted at 90 to 100 lbs./acre. When it is mixed with other plants, sow it at about 50 to 60 lbs./acre. When triticale is planted using a no-till drill, cut the seeding rate in half. In general, triticale has

▲ Triticale is a hybrid of wheat and rye grains. Its origin can be traced back to the late 1880s where it was first bred in laboratories in Germany and Scotland. Triticale usually has larger seed heads than wheat. Photo: © Jaboticaba | Dreamstime

superior drought resistance compared to barley, wheat, and oats.

Some land managers claim that triticale is not a winter-hardy grain. That may have been true years ago, but today there are several varieties of triticale that are sold as winter-hardy types. For instance, Forage FX 1001 is rated as an "excellent winter-hardy" forage. Other winter-hardy varieties include Trical® 719, Deer Creek Seed's Winter Triticale, Argee, Charmany, Tritigold-22, and WB UW26. While triticale has come a long way to becoming a much more winter-tolerant grain, it is less winter-hardy than winter wheat and the most winter-hardy grain–cereal rye. Deer are attracted to both warm- and cold-season plots of triticale.

Triticale also does well when it is planted in a mix with other grains like oats, and barley. Better yet, I have found that planting triticale with winter-hardy clovers and legumes helps it considerably. Good companion winter-hardy clovers include Marathon Red, Alice White, Ladino, Frosty Berseem, and FIXatioN Balansa. All are very winter-hardy clovers. Winter triticale can also be mixed with other winter-hardy legumes like Austrian Winter Peas, Hairy Vetch, birdsfoot trefoil, and Blue lupine. When mixing triticale with clovers and legumes, reduce its rate accordingly. Generally, that means planting about 30 lbs./acre of triticale with perhaps 30 lbs./acre of oats or wheat, 2 clovers at about 10 lbs./acre, and 2 legumes at about 10 to 15 lbs./acre.

Triticale will provide its best production when pH levels are between 6.2 and 6.7. In place of a soil test, use 400 lbs./acre of 13-13-13 or 300 lbs./acre of 19-19-19. In late winter add about 150 lbs./acre of nitrogen (46-0-0) to your planting. But do NOT apply nitrogen fertilizer when planting triticale with clovers and legumes; they will provide all the needed nitrogen triticale needs. As with any planting, it is always advisable to get a soil test done at a certified lab prior to prescribing any general fertilizer/s. There are a lot of triticale varieties to choose from. Some varieties have been created particularly for fall and winter production.

Don't overlook triticale as a worthwhile winter-hardy planting. Remember it is a hybrid born of two top winter-hardy grain parent plants—cereal rye and wheat. Triticale has few of the diseases that its wheat parent

▲ Winter triticale is commonly planted as wildlife forage. It displays desirable traits from each of its parent species (wheat and rye). It is a midmaturity winter annual in comparison with rye and forage winter wheat. Photo: © Jaboticaba | Dreamstime

has, but it is slightly more prone to diseased than its cereal rye parent plant. For example, the main diseases triticale are susceptible to include the three rusts (leaf, stem and stripe rust), crown rot, Barley Yellow Dwarf Virus (BYDV), and nematodes. Like all grains, triticale must deal with its share of problem insects. However, many studies have documented those insects that attack triticale do not end up causing any significant crop losses.

Many times, I plant grain crops as standalone plots. When I do plant them as mixed plots, one of my choice mixed varieties includes 50 lbs. /acre of triticale, 30 lbs./acre of winter oats, 12 lbs./acre of Marathon red clover, and 15 lbs./acre of Frosty berseem. Another desirable choice is 50 lbs./acre of triticale, 30 lbs./acre of barley, 20 lbs./acre of Austrian winter peas, and 8 lbs./acre of FIXatioN Balansa clover.

Often, others recommend mixing triticale with wheat. Since triticale is a hybrid cross of rye and wheat, I skip planting it with cereal rye and replace it with a grain like barley, and winter peas and winter-hardy clovers.

One more interesting point about triticale is that it has recently been discovered in several triticale research projects that winter triticale, like winter cereal rye, has an additional benefit. Triticale has demonstrated it has some "allelopathic" effects in the soil that

▲ Triticale is a great crop fall food plot. It is very versatile, deer love it, and it can assist the growth of other crops, such as winter peas or other companion plants. As a hybrid of winter rye and winter wheat, triticale is more stress resistant and disease resistant. Photo: © Dariusz Leszczynski |Dreamstime

can hinder germination of small weed seeds. However, triticale's allelopathic abilities are not as strong as the allelopathic effects of winter cereal rye. But some weed limiting abilities are better than none.

CONDENSED RECAP

- **Temperature Tolerances:** Winter-hardy varieties of triticale will tolerate winter temperatures through November and sometimes December, depending on the depth of snow.
- **Inoculant:** Not applicable.
- **Planting Times:** In the North, mid-fall to early winter. In the South, late mid-fall or early to mid-winter.
- **Seeding Rates:** Alone, average 75 to 100 lbs./acre. Drill at half that rate. In mixes, reduce seeding rate to about 25 to 30 lbs./acre.
- **Planting Depth:** Sow at 1 to 2 inches deep, not deeper than 2 inches.
- **Companion Plants:** Winter oats, all small grains, winter-hardy clovers, and legumes.

- **pH Levels:** Prefers 6.2 to 6.5, will tolerate a pH range of 6.0 to 7.0.
- **Soil Preferences:** Favors well-drained to moderately drained soils.
- **Germination:** In well-prepared plots, will germinate in 5 to 7 days.
- **Fertilizer:** In place of a soil test, fertilize at planting with 400 lbs./acre of 13-13-13, or 19-19-19. In late winter, top dress with 46-0-0. Do not use 46-0-0 if triticale is mixed with clover or other legumes.
- **Crude Protein Content:** Protein range of 20 to 25 percent.
- **Total Digestibility (TDN):** 52 to 54 percent.
- **Nitrogen Fixation:** Low.
- **Overgrazing Concerns:** Generally not an issue after established.
- **Extends Grazing Season:** Extends deer browsing into late November and longer.
- **Sunlight:** Prefers full sun. It will tolerate part sun and shade but needs at least 5 hours of full sun for best results.
- **Pollinator Friendly:** No.
- **USDA Hardiness Zones:** Rated as good winter-hardiness.
- **Advice:** When planting triticale to provide forage for deer during the hunting season, plant only the winter-hardy varieties.
- **Caution:** Avoid using a nitrogen fertilizer like urea (46-0-0) or an all-purpose nitrogen like 34-0-0 when the triticale is planted with clovers and other legumes.
- **Level of Maintenance:** Low.
- **Note:** Fewer diseases affect triticale than wheat. Triticale can hinder the growth of some small weed seeds.
- **Maturity:** Winter triticale matures about 5 days later than winter wheat and about 2 weeks later than fall rye under similar growing conditions.

BARLEY (*Hordeum vulgare L*)

Barley is one of the world's most ancient crops. It was cultivated from wild barley some 10,000 years ago. Barley heavily contributed to the development of agriculture and currently is the fifth most important grain crop worldwide. Barley is used primary as forage feed for cattle; however, barley receives its highest market value from the malting and brewing industries. I'll raise a beer to that!

▲ Barley is yet another winter-hardy grain that attracts deer into late hunting season. Unfortunately, it does not get the fanfare its winter-hardy small grain cousins do (rye, oats, wheat, triticale). It is, however, a grain that deer are very much drawn to on our land. Photo: NRCSWA

Barley, like all the grains, is a member of the grass family. This grain is an inexpensive sweet cereal grain that grows quickly and can be planted in spring or winter. Winter barley cover crop seed is an upright, cool-season annual cereal grain known for its quick growth and low water use. Winter barley cover crop seed is often used on soils where reclamation and/or rapid soil recovery is the goal. Unfortunately, as deer forage, winter barley does not get a lot of attention from food plot managers. It could be said that barley is often ignored because of lack of press. Another reason is because it has been claimed that fall barley does not winter well. In the past, winter barley did *not* winter well, and had less winter-hardiness than rye or wheat. Today, however, there is good news about barley. There are now vastly improved varieties that are available with considerably better winter-hardiness than ever before, especially under grazing pressure. Many of the newer varieties also produce more forage than older varieties. Barley produces palatable growth rapidly in the fall under favorable conditions. It is considered superior to other cereals for fall and early winter pasture; but wheat, triticale, and rye provide better *late winter* and *spring* grazing. Barley also has excellent drought and heat tolerance. Winter barley forage is typically the most palatable of all the other small grain cereals; its feed quality is the highest, as well.

Winter barley can best be seeded as a winter plot from mid-September and can even be planted as late as early October. I plant winter barley no later than mid-September.

I have planted barley with considerable success. It can be planted earlier than wheat. It seems to provide more yield than wheat as well. Deer start eating barley in the fall. They eat it so heartily that they keep it cropped down like a Marine's crew cut. They hit it so hard that I tend to keep it away from my fruit and chestnut orchards to prevent deer from eating the fruits and nuts instead of the barley. I also don't like to plant any of my grains, particularly barley and cereal rye, in areas where my fields border public roads; it helps to keep prying eyes away.

Like most of my food plots, I don't like to plant many plots larger than 3 acres. It has always been my plan to spread many more smaller food plots on our property that range in size from 100 by 100 feet (stopper plots) to a couple of acres. Generally, I end up planting between 30 to 35 plots of all different sizes on our land every year. Deer usually won't be attracted to food plots outside their home ranges, which is about 640 acres for bucks and 250 acres for does. Spreading many different varieties of food plots across your

▲ Barley has the potential as a commodity crop for food plotters with large acreage. It can be used for fuel ethanol, feed, and food production. Or you can just let your deer and other game eat it. Photo: © Perolsson | Dreamstime

property maximizes your chances of keeping your resident deer from searching for food on other lands more often. Of course, during the rut, all bets are off.

As I have stated, I have grown barley successfully over the last 7 years, and the deer, turkeys, and other wildlife on my land have found it an attractive food source. In conversations with local farmers in Otsego County, New York, where I live, farmers that grow barley have told me that deer readily feed in their barley plots. Barley has more protein than other cereal grains commonly planted as wildlife food plots. Starch is the chief element in barley kernels. In fact, Montana Fish, Wildlife & Parks reports that barley is "utilized by big game," including both mule and white-tailed deer, elk, and even moose. Winter barley, like winter wheat, grows best in areas of moderate moisture with cool weather. Planted in fall, winter barley will become dormant in late winter and then it begins to grow again in spring. Besides green browse for deer, barley grains become available to all upland and most waterfowl birds in late fall. Barley, like rye and wheat, also provides fall roosting sites for pheasants and other gamebirds.

A few barley varieties include Conlon, Foxtail, Robust Spring, Valor Winter, and my favorite variety from Preferred Seed, Thoroughbred Winter Barley. Check Preferred Seeds website at www.Preferredseed. com.

CONDENSED RECAP

- **Temperature Tolerances:** Can tolerate winter temperatures, although barley dies if the temperature drops below 17°F for extended periods of time.
- **Inoculant:** Not applicable.
- **Planting Times:** Winter barley can be planted as early as mid- to late August. Spring barley can be planted April through May.
- **Seeding Rates:** Alone, broadcast barley at 90 to 120 lbs./acre. Drill at 50 lbs./acre.
- **Planting Depth:** Barley should be planted 1 to 1½ inches deep.
- **Companion Plants:** Grains, all winter hard clovers and legumes, and chicory.
- **pH Levels:** Barley grows well when pH values are between 6.0 and 6.5.
- **Soil Preferences:** Grows best in well-drained, fertile loams or light, clay soils.
- **Germination:** Emerges in 6 to 8 days.
- **Fertilizer:** In lieu of a soil test, 300 lbs./acre of 19-19-19 at planting.
- **Crude Protein Content:** Barley offers 7.5 to 18 percent crude protein levels.
- **Total Digestible Nutrients (TDN):** Barley offers a TDN value of 62–66 percent.
- **Nitrogen Fixation:** Minimal.
- **Overgrazing Concerns:** Deer graze on barley soon after it emerges. But barley withstands heavy grazing well.
- **Extends Grazing Season:** Winter barley is available to deer from October to December.
- **Sunlight:** Full sun.
- **Pollinator Friendly:** No.
- **USDA Hardiness Zones:** Winter barley prefers cool, dry growing regions and is hardy to USDA growing zones 8 or warmer. Check with your local ag extension departments.
- **Advice:** Don't overlook barley as a productive, nutritious, palatable, attractive food plot for deer.
- **Caution:** Barley is very susceptible to barley yellow dwarf virus caused by aphids.
- **Level of Maintenance:** Low.
- **Note:** Does best when mixed with nitrogen-fixing clovers and legumes.
- **Maturity:** Spring barley ripens in 60 to 70 days. Fall-planted barley matures in about 60 days.

▲ When cold weather arrives, the starches in brassica leaves turn to sugars and deer will feed on them more heavily. Brassica leaves will remain green even under some snow cover. Photo Credit: CanstockPhoto

Chapter Twenty-One
The Incredible Edible Brassicas

Brassica oleracea is a plant species that includes many common cultivars that belong to the mustard family. The group of brassica forages commonly planted by food plotters for deer and other wildlife includes kale, rape, turnips, canola, swede, and radishes. They all belong to the brassica family, which also includes cabbage, mustard, cauliflower, choy sum, Brussel sprouts, broccoli, collards, kohlrabi, rutabaga, parsnip, and other brassicas that are often thought of as vegetables. The entire family of brassicas fall into the category of plants known as cold-season annuals. It is important to note that all brassicas are mostly sown as winter-hardy plantings. However, many varieties of brassicas can also be planted as wildlife food plots in northern regions in the spring or early summer.

Not all the types of the brassicas mentioned above are commonly planted by food plot managers. Many of the latter are grown almost exclusively by farmers for human consumption. Some brassicas, though, are among the favorite plantings by food plotters as forage crops for deer and other wildlife. They include all the different varieties mentioned above.

According to many seed companies, the three most frequently planted brassicas are rape, kale,

▲ The most common wildlife food plot brassica plants include kale, forage rape, turnips canola, swede, radishes, and sometimes mustard. Of this group, forage rape is the most popular and most planted variety. Photo: PCFImages

▲ Deer generally begin heavily feeding on brassica crops mid- to late October and throughout November. Stand-alone brassica plantings are one way to virtually guarantee deer will be feeding in your food plots during the hunting season. This photo was taken on our farm in mid-November. Photo: PCFImages

and turnips. About 90 percent of these plants are rated as being highly digestible and contain 15 to 20 percent protein in the leaves and another 8 to 10 percent protein in the plant's roots. These 3 brassicas are excellent palatable food sources from early fall through winter.

As brassicas grow, they start out with a very bitter taste, allowing them to go mostly untouched (uneaten) by deer and other wildlife during the first couple months of the growing season. As brassicas undergo a hard frost or two, the starches in the plant's leaves quickly convert to sugars, making them much sweeter and more palatable. This is when deer begin to feed on them in earnest. Additionally, brassicas will remain green and upright throughout the winter, even under some snow cover. Deer can visit brassica plots a few times a day during late winter to dig up the plantings that are covered by snow, making brassicas excellent late-season forage options for mid-fall to late winter. It is brassica's winter-hardiness that makes them ideal food plot plants to be used for hunting season, as brassicas remain highly active food sources for deer when hunters want them in their food plots most.

Another benefit of brassicas is that they can be planted alone or in mixes with other plants like chicory, winter-hardy clovers, mustard, small grains and other brassicas. I have had success with brassicas grown in plots of corn. For instance, kale and rape are ideal to plant along with chicory and clovers. Turnips, on the other hand, are best planted with other brassicas like swede or radishes. They key factor, though, is whenever a particular brassica is planted along with another crop, its seeding rate must be reduced accordingly.

Be careful choosing the companion plants, as brassicas are big leafy plants that can shade out other crops. Moreover, each variety should have different maturity times to ensure that a mixed seeded plot is a long-lasting winter food plot that will attract deer throughout the hunting season. The reason for this is different brassicas will mature and provide nutrients and palatability at a different time than other brassicas.

Brassicas help combat weeds because many of the brassicas grow large leaves that can quickly shade weeds out. For example, a kale leaf can reach 1 to 2 feet tall and wide. Brassicas also can control some harmful plant pests. Additionally, some brassicas,

▲ This is a plot of mixed beets and greens. Note the plot is long and narrow with cover on both sides, giving deer, particularly adult bucks, a false sense of security. To get the deep green color and lush growth seen here requires healthy soil, lime, and fertilizer. Photo: Whitetail Institute

particularly radishes, are terrific soil enhancers. All these attributes make the incredible and edible brassicas among the top choices for food plotters to help attract and nourish their resident deer. Brassicas will also help to limit resident deer from seeking food sources elsewhere.

Most brassicas used in deer food plots are planted as cool-season (winter-hardy) crops, which makes planting dates important. It should be noted that planting dates for brassicas can vary from planting them as early as late June to early August. This is necessary so that each plant's maturity date comes as close to the time that you want them in the plot the most: October through December. Another reason that planting dates are important is that it gives the plant enough time to reach its maturity to get well-established.

The amount of time required for brassica plants to reach maturity depends mostly on the *varieties* planted. Many brassicas can be seeded between 60 and 90 days prior to the first expected killing frost. Forage kale and swede, though, are known to be slow-growers. Both can take from 110 to 130 days or more to mature. Consequently, they need extra time to grow to maturity to provide better nutrition and the maximum amount of forage tonnage. Precise planting dates also vary.

According to seed growers, agronomists, biologists, and many food plot authorities, brassicas can be

▲ This plot has been well-prepared for seeding. All large debris has been removed and the soil is lightly disked. Note the "L" shape of the plot. Creating different shapes of your food plots will result in seeing more deer. Photo: Antler King

grown in a wide range of diverse types of soils. They prefer loamy, fertile, and slightly acidic soil with a general pH of 6.0 to 6.5. A couple of brassicas even prefer pH values of 5.8 to 5.9. They will grow satisfactorily in heavy clay but will not tolerate wet or poorly drained soils. For best results, the soil preparation must provide a smooth, firm seed bed free of large softball-size rocks, large twigs and branches, clumps of clod, and other similar debris.

As a group, brassicas are high in levels of crude protein, with typical levels reaching from about 15 to 32 percent or more. For instance, the tops of turnips can provide from 16 to 25 percent crude protein, while the roots and bulbs averagely contain 12 to 20 percent protein. Properly cared for plots of forage rape can provide 18 to more than 30 percent crude protein in its leaves

and have a total digestive nutrient (TDN) value of 70 percent or more. And so, brassicas are hard to beat as deer and other wildlife forage offerings, particularly regarding high protein levels and excellent digestibility.

Well-maintained brassica plots are extremely productive plantings, and they can produce anywhere from 6 or more tons of forage per acre. The volume of production again substantiates further why brassicas are such an ideal choice as food plot plantings.

Brassicas also require less work to maintain than other warm-season clovers and legumes, which necessitate mowing, fertilizing, and other care. They can be easily grown in tiny or small plots (less than ¼-acre) to much larger multi-acre plots.

If neighboring food plotters, nearby farmers, and hunting clubs are planting brassicas, they are most

▲ The mixed planting of brassicas seen here is what I refer to as a "stopper" plot, a plot that is intentionally small and placed where deer can stop and feed in it securely, before moving on to larger food plots (in this case corn). Stopper plots increase buck sighting significantly. Photo: Wildlife Perfect

likely growing common Purple Top turnips. In this case, you should concentrate on planting the different varieties of turnips like appin, Barkant forage, or Pasja turnips, canola, or swede, because these brassica varieties are rarely planted. Therefore, you will be providing a unique group of brassicas. But by no means am I suggesting that you should limit your brassica plantings by not also including kale, mustard, radishes, or Purple Tops.

If you're limited to planting only a few different varieties of plants, this tactic becomes even more crucial to consistently draw neighboring deer to your land. This single maneuver will also significantly improve your chances of enticing and keeping your resident herd of deer from occasionally seeking out food sources elsewhere. Equally important, it will attract deer from other more distant properties to visit your

land more frequently. You can deposit that advice to the deer-hunting bank!

When it comes to the winter-hardy brassicas, there is no doubt that during the hunting season deer will turn lush green plots of big-leafed brassicas into cleanly stripped, leafless stalks. Your plots can look like the forest of Tunguska in Russia 112 years ago. This is where a massive explosion by a 330-foot stony meteor 3 to 6 miles above the earth attributed to an air burst that left 80 million trees flattened and stripped bare over 830 square miles. That is how deer will make your rape, turnips, swede, mustard, and other brassicas look after they finish eating the leaves. But if that's not convincing enough for you, the deer will then eat the brassica stems. If the brassica has a bulb, they will dig up the bulbs and roots leaving the plot looking like a mine field.

Brassicas, however, should not be thought of as a silver-bullet-type planting by food plot managers. To this point, everything I have said about brassicas may have you thinking that just planting brassicas is the only way to go. It is not. Brassicas have their downsides too. For example, if deer have never been exposed to the different varieties of brassicas, it may take them a year or two to discover that brassicas are good to eat. I know this for a fact, as it took the deer on my property a full season to become familiar with mustard and canola. These were two brassicas I had never previously planted. But once deer discover all brassicas are good to eat, they quickly become a high priority food sources for them. From that point on, deer become hooked on brassicas and they are drawn to brassicas like a honeybee is drawn to pollen.

Planting brassicas must include some forethought about their location. Brassicas should not be planted in the same place more than 2 consecutive years to deter diseases and soil-borne insects, parasitic nematodes, and plant pathogens from getting a foothold in the soil. Moreover, if crops are not rotated, insect pests that feed on a crop will spend their larval state in the soil and then become more abundant because their food source remains available to them. Each following year, the pests become harder to manage as their population increases, sometimes exponentially. In the end, insect pests must be eliminated for the soil to recover.

▲ When planting brassicas, always be mindful that they need to be rotated the following year. Photo: Antler King

One sign of a brassica food plot that needs to be rotated is the brassica's leaves will begin to turn a deep purple or burgundy. This usually happens for 3 reasons. The first, and often the most common, is due to over-seeding the plot. Over-seeding results in plant competition, which ends in high stress levels for each plant. A second red flag is when the plants show signs of soil deficiencies or insect infestation. Lastly, plants will turn a burgundy color due to other stresses like drought, excessive heat, and so on.

Most often, leaves that turn a burgundy color indicate a lack of phosphorus. If this happens, consider planting buckwheat as it has an excellent "rotational effect." It's root residues make phosphorus more available to any follow-up crop, and it also returns considerable levels of phosphorus to the soil. But the group of brassica's positive points far outweigh its negative aspects. So, they are high-quality, incredibly attractive, winter-hardy food plot plantings, that are sure to increase meat in the freezer and antlers on the wall.

I would like to make an important point at this juncture about planting winter-hardy brassicas and other winter-type plants. In addition to cold-hardy brassicas, it's important to keep in mind that a well-rounded food plot program also includes some warm-season plantings for the following reasons. Including quality nourishment during spring and summer goes a long way to having a deer herd in good physical condition. It helps considerably with adult does having better reproductive rates and higher quality lactation, fawn survival, improved fawn growth, antler enhancement in buck fawns, and more. After weaning, fawns require 15 to 20 percent or more of protein to just maintain average growth. They need 20 percent or more protein levels to significantly increase their growth rate. The point most hunters are interested in, though, is that good nutrition is also the key element needed to improve optimum antler growth.

▲ This adult buck has received the type of nutrition and protein that allowed it to reach the physical condition it is in. Food plots play a substantial role in deer achieving healthier bodies. Photo: Antler King

THE BRASSICAS

FORAGE RAPE (*Brassica napus*)

When food plot managers are looking for a brassica that is a top attraction to deer, they shouldn't overlook the annual rape cultivars. Forage rape provides food plotters with very quick-growing, high-yielding, quality forage. There are several varieties of forage rape. Some were developed for seed and oil production, while other types were developed for forage tonnage. Rape is a forage that has been used extensively in Canada, New Zealand, Europe, and Australia for both food plots for deer and other wildlife. Do not

▲ Cody Fiduccia checks a young plant of forage rape for potential insect damage and overall plant health. Photo: Fiduccia Ent

make the mistake of confusing forage rape with oilseed rape or canola. Currently, seed companies say that forage rape is the most common brassica planted as a food plot for deer. Why not? It has a lengthy list of advantages to support that claim.

Forage rape is a short-season leafy brassica with stems and leaves that can be browsed 30 to 90 days after it is planted. It can be seeded almost anywhere within the United States or southern Canada (other than semi-tropical areas). Like all brassicas, forage rape should not be planted more than 2 successive years in the same place, to avoid root and insect issues. Forage rape is multi-tolerant of cold to very cold temperatures, heat, and drought. This makes it a quality food source over other plantings that are less tolerant of one or more of these types of conditions.

Rape grows well in soils with pH levels between 5.5 to 6.7, albeit 6.0 to 6.5 is better. For rape to yield its best production and its highest quality forage, it absolutely needs to be planted in an area with good soil drainage. Rape does not do well on poorly drained sites that stay wet. It also requires attention to being fertilized properly. Rape has high fertility requirements to maximize forage production and nutritional quality to be more attractive to deer.

Thus, before planting any wildlife food plot plant, a soil test should be conducted to determine exactly how much lime and fertilizer is needed to make sure soil fertility and pH are in the desired range for each plant. If these factors are paid attention to, forage rape can produce 2 to 4 tons of quality forage per acre (dry weight) in a short amount of time. The leaves are wide, thick, fleshy, lobed, and the plant can reach a height of about 12 to 18 inches, depending on soil fertility and planting density. Food plotters need to be careful not to overseed rape. Forage rape produces a small yellow flower in the spring.

Rape is rated as a cool-season winter-hardy annual forage. It is an extremely versatile forage and has adapted to a wide range of climatic conditions across the entire United States and southern Canada. As an exceptionally cold-weather brassica, rape's leafy greens can draw deer to food plots from October through January.

Over the 35 years I have been planting food plots, I have found forage rape to be an easy seed to grow.

▲ I planted this plot of rape for a food plot client. It was intentionally set up near the end of a cornfield. The forage rape plot was only 40 by 100 feet. Photo: PCFImages

It germinates quickly and is easy to maintain. Deer browse the rape leaves during the summer, but they really don't eat the plant aggressively until it undergoes a few hard frosts in late fall. Forage rape is one of many winter-hardy plantings that can extend a deer's grazing season well into winter.

When preparing a seedbed for planting forage rape, make sure the surface of the soil is smooth, free of large debris, and firm before broadcasting seed. Once it is seeded it should be compacted to assure good seed-to-soil contact. These steps will promote ideal germination and growth that will help considerably to develop a healthier food plot that can better withstand tough weather conditions, diseases caused by insects, grazing pressure, and troublesome weeds. If you use a no-till drill take an extra step and kill the existing vegetation with glyphosate a few weeks prior to drilling or top-sowing to eliminate weed competition and create bare ground for good seed-to-soil contact.

When planting forage rape alone, which I often do, broadcast the tiny seed at 5 to 9 lbs./acre. It can be planted as early as late June or early July in the North. In the South, wait until September before planting it. It is important to plant rape and other brassicas earlier than most forages to allow at least a couple months of growth and development for them to reach maturity before the first hard frost. Rape can also be spring planted in the North after soil temperatures reach about 55°F.

Although I typically plant forage rape alone, there are times, when I plant it in mixtures with other brassicas to aid in maximum forage production. As

▲ Forage rape is easy to grow, it sprouts very quickly, it responds well to fertilizer, and it attracts deer into late November and longer (depending on the size of the plot). Photo: PCFImages

mentioned, because rape develops quickly with tons of leafy biomass, it can overcrowd and suppress lower growing or smaller forages. Therefore, when mixing rape with other non-brassica type plants, such as clovers, chicory, or a winter variety of oats, it is vital to reduce the planting rate to 2 to 4 lbs./acre. There is rarely a season in which I do not include forage rape plantings in one or more of my food plots.

There are several different varieties of forage rape from which to choose. One is Dwarf Essex rape seed, which was designed to be a lower growing rape plant. Another is Bonar rape seed, which is a newer high-yielding, late-maturing variety, specifically bred for improved palatability and higher leaf-to-stem ratio. Conversely, brassica forage rape seed is an early-maturing forage rape with high yields and excellent cold tolerance.

Another ideal way to plant rape is to strip plant it. Plant winter-hardy clovers on one side of a rape strip and winter-hardy grains on the other wide of the rape. This tactic takes the browsing pressure off the rape and allows it to establish its best growth.

Forage rape is available at www.deercreekseed.com and other seed companies.

CONDENSED RECAP

- **Attraction:** High to very high.
- **Temperature Tolerances:** Endures winter-type temperatures very well.
- **Inoculant:** Not applicable.
- **Planting Time:** Mid July to early August in the North and September in the South; best before a predicted rainfall.
- **Seeding Rates:** Alone, 6 to 10 lbs./acre; drilled rate, 2 to 6 lbs./acre. In a mix, 3 to 6 lbs./acre.

- **Planting Depth:** Plant at ⅛- to ¼-inch deep but never deeper than ¼-inch. Can be successfully top-sown in a well-prepared seedbed.
- **Companion Plants:** Can be mixed with brassicas, winter-hardy clovers, legumes, chicory, and cold-season oats. When used as mixed reduce the seeding rate appropriately.
- **pH Levels:** Soil pH of 6.0 to 6.5 is ideal. Can tolerate pH levels as low as 5.5 to 6.7.
- **Soil Preferences:** Can grow in most soils but prefers light loam and good drainage.
- **Germination:** In ideal conditions, rape emerges in 2 to 4 days; otherwise, 7 to 10 days.
- **Fertilizer:** In lieu of a soil test, planted alone, use 300 to 350 lbs./acre of 19-19-19 or 16-18-19. Top dress with 100 lbs./acre of ammonium sulfate (34-0-0).
- **Crude Protein Content:** Rape leaves provide from 18 to 30 percent protein.
- **Total Digestible Nutrients (TDN):** About 70 percent. A high quality, highly digestible forage.
- **Overgrazing Concern:** Deer generally don't browse brassicas hard until after the first hard freeze. Therefore, overgrazing is usually not an issue.
- **Extends Grazing Season:** From October into January.
- **Sunlight:** Prefers full sun.
- **Pollinator Friendly:** Yes.
- **USDA Hardiness Zones:** Can grow anywhere in continental U.S. but check the USDA Plant Hardiness Zone Map for your area.
- **Advice:** Plant early enough for rape to reach full maturity by deer season.
- **Caution:** Do not confuse forage rape with oil-seed canola rapeseed.
- **Level of Maintenance:** Low.

▲ When it comes to planting rape, there are several varieties from which to choose. The most cold-tolerant variety is Barsica forage rape seed. Credit: © Valdorf | Dreamstime.com

FORAGE KALE (*Brassica oleracea*)

There are two types of kale varieties: Scotch types that have grey-green and very curled or crinkled leaves, and Siberian types with green-blue leaves that are less curled. Kale is available in both tall and dwarf-type varieties. However, among food plotters, the dwarf types seem to be preferred.

Kale is rated as a cold-hardy green that is high in nutrition. It is one of the top fall forage brassicas chosen by food plotters. As a winter-hardy "green," kale provides high nutritional value to wildlife with crude protein levels ranging from 20 to 28 percent. Dry matter yields of kale can range from about 4,500 to more than 7,000 lbs./acre.

Kale is a slower growing plant than most other brassicas. If you plant kale, you must allow at least 4 months for it to grow to maturity, or about 100 to 150 days. Generally, that means planting kale in early May in the North, and August in the South. When practical, plant kale (or any plant) when the forecast calls for rain within 24 to 48 hours. Kale produces best in the North because it prefers cool summers. Kale is not adapted to hot weather, particularly extended periods of high temperatures.

Kale grows best when planted in soils with good drainage. The best pH levels will be between 5.6 and 6.5. If the pH gets too high, the leaves will begin to molt. Plant kale seeds about ¼-inch deep. Forage kale should be broadcast at rates between 4 to 5 lbs./acre. At planting, fertilize kale with 300 to 400 lbs./acre of 19-19-19 or 16-18-19. For best results, remember that kale requires a little more fertilizer than most brassicas

▲ Kale is a highly preferred forage for deer. It is loaded with vitamins and up to 25 percent protein. It comes in either curled or less curled varieties like the one seen here, planted on our land. Deer relish kale and it will attract deer as late as December or longer. Photo: PCFImages

including 2 to 4 lbs./acre of boron, 50 to 120 lbs./acre of magnesium, and about ⅛ to ⅕ lbs./acre of copper and zinc (trace amounts) but only when a soil test suggests they are necessary.

There are many types of forage kale available, including Siberian, Improved Vates, Premier, Kestrel, Rangi, Fora, Wairoa, and Maris. A new variety is Bayou which is high-yielding, has high digestibility, medium maturity and good winter-hardiness (ideal for extending the winter grazing season).

However, there are specific species of forage kale that deer prefer over other varieties, one of which is the Siberian Kale variety. It tastes sweeter than other kale varieties and tends to have more sugar after a hard frost or two. Siberian kales are also strong growing and will do well in a variety of soils. In northern areas, Siberian favors a milder winter but will still grow well and produce forage well into the hunting season from November through December.

When I planted it early enough, I had good success with it as a standalone plot. However, kale can be mixed with other brassicas. When mixing other plants with kale, it is best to plant kale with brassicas like Appin turnip or Barsica rape. Both are early maturing plants that will help assure the survival of your kale planting, as deer will concentrate on the turnip or rape before they browse the kale. This will allow the kale leaves to reach their maximum growth of about 24 inches. As soon as there have been a couple of deep freezes, deer will march into your kale stand with a serious intent to eat as much as they can.

I have had my best success when planting kale in large plots of an acre or more. I have had good success with planting smaller plots (one-half acre or less) if it is fenced off. I'm never disappointed by how kale attracts deer. Once you plant kale, it will quickly become a favorite brassica planting for you.

Kale is available from www.welterseed.com, www.seedworld.com, and other seed sellers.

▲ This is what is referred to as course curled kale. Deer could not care less about what the leaves look like. They eat both curled and less curled equally enthusiastically. Photo: La Crosse

CONDENSED RECAP

- **Attraction:** Medium to high.
- **Temperature Tolerances:** To 10°F.
- **Inoculant:** Not applicable with brassicas.
- **Planting Time:** Best planted in mid-June or no later than early July. In multi-acre plots, plant in May. In the South, August.
- **Seeding Rates:** Alone, broadcast 8 to 10 lbs./acre in a properly prepared firm, moist seedbed. When planted in a mixed plot, reduce the seeding rate by half.
- **Planting Depth:** Plant no deeper than ¼-inch below the surface. Kale can be top-seeded successfully when good seed-to-soil contact is made.
- **Companion Mixes:** Can be mixed with other brassicas, winter-hardy clovers, and chicory.
- **pH Levels:** Prefers a pH of 5.5 to 6.5. In soil with a higher pH, its leaves will molt.
- **Soil Preferences:** Prefers well-drained sandy loams to light clay.
- **Germination:** Kale seeds germinate in 5 to 10 days in warm soil that has received adequate moisture. Optimum soil temperature for planting kale is 60° to 65°F.
- **Fertilizer:** At planting use 350 to 400 lbs./acre of 19-19-19 or 16-18-19.
- **Crude Protein Content:** When planted in ideal soil conditions, 20 to 28 percent; and in less favorable soil, 15 to 17 percent.
- **Total Digestible Nutrients (TDN):** High—80–85 percent.
- **Overgrazing Concerns:** Once kale establishes itself, overgrazing is less of an issue.
- **Extends Grazing Season:** Well into December or later.
- **Sunlight:** Full sun; but will tolerate some partial shade.
- **Pollinator Friendly:** Yes. Attracts honeybees.
- **USDA Hardiness Zones**: Can grow anywhere in the continental U.S. but check the USDA Plant Hardiness Zone Map for your area.
- **Advice:** In a strip plot of kale, split the plot in half. Plant one side with kale. On the other side, plant rape, turnip, chicory, and a winter-hardy red clover. This will ensure survival of the kale plot. Deer will browse on everything other than the kale, helping it to reach maturity.
- **Caution:** Planted alone, allow enough time after planting kale to reach its full maturity—generally 5 to 6 months.
- **Level of Maintenance:** Medium.

▲ Kale is a slow-growing brassica that needs about four months to grow to maturity and it prefers cool summers. Credit: Millborn

TURNIPS (*Brassica rapa*)

When it comes to planting brassicas, the first plant that pops up in the minds of most hunters who plant food plots is the Purple Top turnip. There are a few other varieties of turnips to choose from as well. Each type offers a range of different specialties.

All varieties of turnips are excellent sources of forage during fall and winter for deer and other wildlife. Turnip leaves offer the highest concentration of protein and yield of any leaf. They are closely related to rutabagas. Like other brassicas, turnips are classified as excellent cold-weather plantings. Deer will eat the turnip leaves from mid-September until January, adding to their value for early-fall bow hunters. The leaf tops can provide between 15 to 25 percent crude protein content. Even the plants' bulb and roots contain 10 to 15 percent protein. Deer fervently feed on the bulb as soon as the plant undergoes a few hard frosts.

An acre of turnips can provide a crop anywhere from 1 to 5 tons per acre of dry matter, which includes the turnip bulb as well. In rare cases it may take a season for deer to discover what turnips are. But once they do, they quickly become addicted to them and will seek them out enthusiastically as soon as falling temperatures cause a few hard frosts. All varieties of turnips are excellent choices as food plot plantings, particularly for the colder northern regions of the United States and southern Canada.

Turnips are also drought tolerant. They can be planted as late as July or early August. In the southern regions, turnips can be planted in August or September. I find that planting them no later than the July 4th weekend gives them a longer growing period and helps them to fully mature, which usually takes about 75 to 90 days. This will be beneficial toward managing the grazing pressure until the first frosts, allowing for maximum growth of the bulbs.

▲ I shot this buck during the late muzzleloading season (December 19th at 11 a.m.). The buck followed a doe into a food plot of turnips. The buck was fifty yards away from the blind in the background. Photo: PCFImages

All varieties of turnips can tolerate slightly acidic soil but prefer a pH level between 6.0 and 6.5. I have had most success when I plant them in deep loamy fertile soil. They will not do well, however, in wet ground or heavy clay soils. Forage turnip seeds are exceptionally tiny. Because of the miniscule size of the seed, turnips can be top sown on a smooth compact bed of soil using a quality hand-operated spreader like a Harvest Broadcast Spreader. They can also be drill seeded with quality made drills like a Kasco Plotters' Choice or an Esch No-Till Drill.

Unfortunately, if the deer graze on the turnips before then (like Purple Tops), the browsing can hurt the production of both the tops and bulbs. So, it is always better to plant turnips in larger plots rather than smaller ones, when feasible. That is why I like to plant other turnip varieties (Barkant and Appin) that mature quicker than Purple Top, and have significantly higher proportions of leaf yield, vigorous establishment capabilities, and regrowth potential.

I will also often plant strip plots of chicory, winter-hardy clovers, and even other brassicas near my turnips. The other crops help to distract and deflect the deer from eating the turnips, as I want them to be in prime condition from November to January, when I'm hunting deer.

All varieties of turnips make an extraordinary crop that will prove to be an integral part of your winter-hardy planting program. Once the deer begin to eat them, they won't stop until they are gone. Like all the other brassicas, turnips should not be planted in the same plot more than 2 consecutive years. There are a lot of different forage varieties to choose from. Once you discover how well turnips draw in deer during the hunting season, you will be as addicted to them as the deer are.

▲ This is a food plot of Barkant turnips. They have a tankard shaped bulb. Barkant provides 30 percent protein and 80 percent TDN. Deer on our land like them more than Purple Top turnips. Photo: Tecomate

PURPLE TOP TURNIPS

Purple Top turnips make terrific food plot plantings for deer and other wildlife. They are not only high in available protein and highly digestible; they can produce up to 6 to 8 tons of forage per acre. Purple Top turnips are not affected by light frosts. In fact, turnip palatability increases after cold weather arrives because the young leaves are somewhat bitter at first but turn sweeter as they mature with cooler temperatures. Deer will preferentially eat both the leafy green tops and the big round bulbs, tubers, and roots of all turnips.

Some varieties of turnips produce more leaves than roots, whereas Purple Top turnips are known more for their traditional large bulbs. The name Purple Top derives from the fact that the shoulders of the round roots stick out above the soil line and turn purple, while the below-ground root stays white. The protruding purple tops are a boon for deer as they stick out above the ground, allowing deer better access to graze

▲ Chris Roberts is holding two gigantic Tecomate Turbo Turnips. A planting of these mega turnips should not only draw in deer big time, but also any local dinosaurs as well. Photo: Tecomate.com

not only on the tops, but also the roots of the plants. Late into winter, deer will continue to seek out turnip roots (which includes the bulb).

Purple Top turnips can be grown alone or in a mixture and require minimal growing effort with excellent results. They are adaptable to a wide range of growing conditions, but prefer fertile, loamy soils with a pH range between 6.0 to 7.5. Purple Top turnips, however, do not grow well in heavy clay soils, wet, or poorly drained soils, especially when they are getting established. Purple Top turnip seeds germinate at temperatures above 45°F. Under ideal growing conditions, they'll grow extremely fast and can reach maturity in 50 to 55 days. The best time to plant them is July or early August in the North or October and November in the South. Both times are ideal for Purple Top turnips to be ready for deer to eat during hunting seasons.

When planted alone, the recommended broadcast seeding rate is 3 to 6 lbs./acre or drill at 1½ to 2½ lbs./acre. In a mix with other brassicas, plant 1 to 3 lbs./acre. When seeded, fertilized, and limed according to a soil test, Purple Top turnips will grow large and quickly shade out unwanted vegetation.

Keep in mind that turnip seeds are tiny. A little bit of seed goes a long way. It is always best to not overseed as the plants will crowd each other, causing stunted leaf and bulb growth. Always exactly follow the recommended seed rate. Because of their small size, turnip seeds can be planted at ⅛-inch and seeded into an existing plot with little or no tillage. When broadcast, it is always best to drag and/or cultipack after planting to ensure good seed-to-soil contact and germination.

At planting, fertilize turnips with 400 lbs./acre of 19-19-19 or 16-18-19. For best results, about 6 to 8 weeks after planting, top-dress turnips with about 100 to 200 lbs./acre of ammonium sulfate (34-0-0), which will help to increase the production of the plant and bulb. When the plant gets to be about 10 inches high, deer will start eating the leaves.

Purple Top turnips included in your food plots will not disappoint. They are easy to grow and manage and provide a great crop for deer to browse from October to November and even into January if there are any still available. They are a terrific starter crop when first experimenting with food plots and are a wonderful addition to previously established plots that are thinning out. If you're short on time or just want a "one-stop-shop" kind of plant, Purple Tops are a good choice.

▲ This is a planting on our land of the most traditional and known turnip, Purple Top turnips. The one drawback of Purple Top turnips is that fawns and yearlings have trouble eating the large bulbs. Photo: Deer Creek Seed

Purple Top turnips and Royal Crown turnips have larger bulbs but less top growth (leaf growth). There are many forage varieties of turnips, including Barkant, Appin, Star, All Top, Rondo, Dynamo, and Forage Star, all of which have more leaf growth (top growth).

If Purple Top turnips have a negative aspect to them, it is the size of their bulbs. Their bulbs can reach softball sizes and larger. These large bulbs are difficult for fawns and yearlings to eat. Anyone who has ever grown Purple Top turnips has had a chuckle or two watching young deer struggle while trying to bite off bits of the bulb. Other than that, there is no other negative aspect of Purple Tops.

Purple Top turnip seed is available at many seed companies.

CONDENSED RECAP

- **Attraction:** Can range from low to very high, depending on whether deer are familiar with them.

- **Temperature Tolerances:** Temperatures of 15° to 20°F can burn the foliage but will not kill turnip bulbs. Bulbs will freeze at 5°F but are still edible.
- **Inoculant:** Not applicable with brassicas.
- **Planting Times:** In the North, plant in July or early August. In the South, October to November. Turnips mature in 50 to 80 days.
- **Seeding Rates:** Broadcast alone, 3 to 6 lbs./acre; drill, 1½ to 2½ lbs./acre; mixed, 1 to 3 lbs./acre. It is best to top sow on bare ground prior to a predicted rainfall.
- **Planting Depth:** ⅛- to ¼-inch deep; never deeper than ¼-inch.
- **Companion Mixes:** Does very well when planted alone. Can be mixed with other brassicas like forage rape, swede, or other varieties of turnips.
- **pH Levels:** Tolerates soils with a pH of 6.0 to 7.5. Does best in 6.5.
- **Soil Preferences:** Turnips prefer fertile, loamy soils.
- **Germination:** Turnips generally germinate in 3 to 10 days at about 70°F. Longer in colder soil.
- **Fertilizer:** At planting, use 350 to 400 lbs./acre of 19-19-19, 16-18-19 or an all-purpose fertilizer of 12-12-12; 30 to 60 days later, top dress with 100–150 lbs./acre of ammonium sulfate (34-0-0).
- **Crude Protein Content:** Tops provide about 17 to 25 percent protein, bulbs/roots contain from 12 to 15 percent protein.
- **Total Digestibility (TDN):** The roots (bulb) of turnips have an 80 to 85 percent digestibility rate.
- **Overgrazing Concerns:** Is generally not an issue after establishment.
- **Extends Grazing Season:** October to January. Deer will paw up bulbs from under several inches of snow.
- **Sunlight:** Prefers full sun.
- **Pollinator Friendly:** Yes. Their yellow flowers attract honey bees.
- **USDA Hardiness Zones:** Zones 2–9.
- **Advice:** Do not exceed recommended seeding rates as this will stunt the growth of the plants and the bulbs.
- **Caution:** Do not plant in poorly drained soils or heavy clay.
- **Level of Maintenance:** Low.

BARKANT FORAGE TURNIPS

Barkant turnips are a newer, improved variety of turnip with a distinctive tankard-shaped bulb and high leaf-to-stem ratio. These turnips produce high yields with good top growth. Barkant is a diploid variety, with good resistance to bolting and exceptionally good disease resistance. This variety can produce up to 4 to 6 tons/acre of dry matter. Crop maturity occurs in about 60 to 90 days. They make an excellent strip of turnips planted next to other brassicas like forage rape, kale, and swede. The Barkant will attract deer earlier, thereby reducing grazing pressure on other brassica crops. They are an excellent choice to plant in addition to Purple Top turnips. The Barkant bulb is smaller and sweeter than Purple Tops so it is easier for fawns and yearlings to eat. Barkant turnips are a superior quality energy source well suited for food plots.

Barkant turnip seed is available from www.meritseed.com, www.welterseed.com and other seed sellers.

▲ This image shows the unique shape of Barkant turnips. We plant Barkant, as it helps fawns and yearling deer to eat the turnips more easily than they can eat Purple Top turnips. Photo: Merit Seed

CONDENSED RECAP

- **Attraction:** Once deer discover what they are, attraction is high.
- **Temperature Tolerances:** Temperatures of 15 to 20°F can burn the foliage but will not kill turnip bulbs. Bulbs will freeze at 5°F but are still edible.
- **Inoculant:** Not applicable with brassicas.
- **Planting Times:** In the North, plant in July or early August. In the South, August to September.
- **Seeding Rates:** Alone, 6 to 8 lbs./acre, drill at 3 to 5 lbs./acre. Can be topsown on a well-prepared seed bed prior to a predicted rainfall.
- **Planting Depth:** Best at ⅛- to ¼-inch deep; never deeper than ¼ inch.
- **Companion Mixes:** Does well when planted alone. Can be mixed with other turnips, rape, and swede.
- **pH Levels:** Barkant turnips prefer *slightly* acidic soil with a pH of 6.0 to 6.5.
- **Soil Preferences:** Turnips prefer moist, fertile, loamy soils.
- **Germination:** Turnips generally germinate in 3 to 10 days at about 70°F; longer in colder soil.
- **Fertilizer:** At planting use 350 lbs./acre of 19-19-19. Thirty days later, top dress with 100 to 150 lbs./acre of urea (46-0-0).
- **Crude Protein Content:** Tops provide about 17 to 25 percent protein; bulbs/roots contain from 12 to 15 percent protein.
- **Total Digestibility (TDN):** The roots (bulb) of turnips are 70 to 80 percent.
- **Overgrazing Concerns:** Is generally not an issue after establishment.
- **Extends Grazing Season:** October to January. Deer will paw up bulbs from under snow.
- **Sunlight:** Prefer full sun.
- **Pollinator Friendly:** Yes.
- **USDA Hardiness Zones:** Zones 2–9.
- **Advice:** Do not exceed seeding rates as overseeding will stunt the growth of the plants and the bulbs.
- **Caution:** Do not plant in poorly drained soils.
- **Level of Maintenance:** Low.

APPIN FORAGE TURNIPS

Appin turnip is yet another excellent standalone food plot choice, particularly as a second plot of another variety like Purple Top. What makes Appin such a good choice is that this turnip was specifically bred for fast, vigorous establishment and quick maturity. Appin turnips mature in about 12 to 14 weeks. Additionally, Appin has a significantly higher proportion of leaf yield compared to other varieties of turnips. Appins are also multi-crowned, meaning they have several growth points that provide improved regrowth potential. I have planted Appin turnips for a few years now and can attest to the fact that they live up to all their marketing claims. More important, we have seen deer enthusiastically seek them out.

Appin turnip seed is available at www.antlerking.com, www.hancockseed.com, and other seed companies.

▲ Shown here is an Appin turnip planting. The bulbs are more rounded than other turnips. Appin has a significantly higher proportion of leaf yield compared to other turnips. Photo: Welter Seed

CONDENSED RECAP

- **Attraction:** Very high.
- **Temperature Tolerances:** Temperatures of 15 to 20°F can burn the foliage but will not kill turnip bulbs. Bulbs will freeze at 5°F but are still edible.
- **Inoculant:** Not applicable with brassicas.
- **Planting Times:** In the North, plant in July or early August. In the South, October to November.
- **Seeding Rates:** Alone, broadcast at 3 to 6 lbs./acre; drill at 2½ lbs./acre. In a mix, plant at 1 to 3 lbs./acre. Can be topsown on bare ground prior to a predicted rainfall.
- **Planting Depth:** Best at ⅛- to ¼-inch deep; never deeper than ¼ inch.
- **Companion Mixes:** Does well when planted alone. Can be mixed with cereal grain, rape, kale, or swede.
- **pH Levels:** Prefers *slightly* acidic soil with a pH of 6.0 to 6.5.
- **Soil Preferences:** Turnips prefer moist, fertile, loamy soils.
- **Germination:** Turnips generally germinate in 7 to 10 days at about 50°F. Longer in colder soil.
- **Fertilizer:** At planting use 350 lbs./acre of 19-19-19. Thirty to 60 days later, top dress with 100 to 150 lbs./acre of ammonium sulfate (34-0-0).
- **Crude Protein Content:** Tops provide about 17 to 25 percent protein; bulbs/roots contain from 12 to 15 percent protein.
- **Total Digestibility (TDN):** The roots (bulb) of turnips have an 80 to 85 percent rate.
- **Overgrazing Concerns:** Is generally not an issue after establishment.
- **Extends Grazing Season:** October to January. Deer will paw up bulbs from under several inches of snow.
- **Sunlight:** Prefer full sun.
- **Pollinator Friendly:** Yes.
- **USDA Hardiness Zones:** Zones 2–9
- **Advice:** Best planted in a strip plot between clovers and grains like a winter oat.
- **Caution:** Do not exceed seeding rates as this will stunt the growth of the plants and the bulbs.
- **Level of Maintenance:** Low.

PASJA HYBRID FORAGE TURNIP

Pasja (pronounced Pa-Ja) was developed in New Zealand as a hybrid crossing of a forage turnip with a forage rapeseed. It is an early maturing, high-yielding brassica rich with extremely sweet leaves that produce an exceptional number of leaves—more than other brassicas. Pasja hybrid forage turnip has a root that is longer and more tapered than other turnips. This narrower root can penetrate soils and assist in soil breakup and infiltration. It is also a drought-resistant plant.

Pasja, like other turnips, is a cold tolerant variety. Furthermore, like the entire family of brassicas, Pasja's winter longevity depends heavily on several elements including the location of the planting, planting date, and the stage of the plant's maturity before a heavy killing frost. Pasja turnips are mostly unaffected by an early, light frost but begin dying around 25°F and 10°F temperatures will kill it quicker. However, the more mature the plant is, and the more leaves it retains, the longer the plant will continue to grow into the winter and the better it will tolerate colder temperatures.

Like most hybrid brassicas, good soil fertility will aid in quicker maturity. Pasja matures in 50 to 60 days. Winter hardiness is higher for plants that reach a rosette stage (between 6 to 8 leaves) before the first killing frost.

Pasja was specifically bred for rapid growth and high performance. In the North, Pasja can be planted in spring as an early summer crop or sown in late July or early August for an extended grazing season from October to December. In the South, Pasja can be planted from October to November.

Pasja is mostly used as part of a cover crop mixture that is seeded in August into fallow ground or into

▲ Pasja is a hybrid forage brassica. Its sweet leaves were bred for multiple grazing by both deer and other wildlife as well as livestock. It is a very leafy plant. Photo: Merit Seed

harvested cereal grain stubble. It can be planted into cornfields to provide grazing options for deer and other wildlife after corn is harvested.

Pasja contains an elevated level of energy and digestibility. It is also high in crude protein as well as digestible energy. The turnip averages a crude protein value of 15 percent and a TDN of 73 percent. Those two points alone make Pasja an excellent choice for food plot managers.

What also makes this plant desirable is that it can be used over a much longer period than the traditional turnip and rape cultivars. Pasja has exceptional regrowth ability too, which helps managers to save some money and work.

▲ This photo demonstrates the different shapes and sizes of Pasja (left) and Appin (right). Photo: Welter Seed

Pasja can be used to supplement or extend the grazing season into winter months when other cool-season plantings slow down. Even in summer, Pasja will be a top grazing planting as it performs well in heat when other plantings often become less productive. Like most forage plants, the best palatability takes place before Pasja flowers.

Fertilization of Pasja is important. Nitrogen (N) requirements are from 50 to 100 lbs./acre. Therefore, it should be fertilized at planting.

Pasja turnip seed is available at www.meritseed.com, www.outsidepride.com and other seed sellers.

CONDENSED RECAP
- **Attraction:** Medium to high.

- **Temperature Tolerances:** From summer to late fall/early winter.
- **Inoculant:** Not applicable with brassicas.
- **Preferred pH:** Prefers a slightly acidic pH level between 5.3 and 6.8.
- **Planting Time:** Plant in May for spring/summer or in July/August for fall. Best planted before a predicted rainfall.
- **Soil:** Hybrid brassicas grow best in sandy loam and loamy, fertile soil. Does not do well in wet or poorly drained soils.
- **Seeding Rates:** Alone, broadcast at 8 to 10 lbs./acre; drilled at 4 to 5 lbs./acre; in a mix, 2 to 4 lbs./acre.
- **Seed Depth:** Plant $1/8$ to $1/4$ inches deep; never deeper than $1/4$-inch.
- **Germination:** Germinates in about 7 to 10 days.
- **Fertilizer:** At planting, use 350 to 400 lbs./acre of 19-19-19. Top dress with 100 to 150 lbs./acre of ammonium sulfate (34-0-0) 30 to 45 days later.
- **Maturity:** Managed properly, matures within 50 to 70 days.
- **Crude Protein Content:** 16 percent or more.
- **Total Digestibility (TDN):** Rated at 73 percent.
- **Companion Mixes:** Can be planted alone or with cereal grains, sorghum, pearl millet, or annual rye grass. Like other annual turnips, can be planted with other brassicas, grains, or cool-season clovers.
- **Overgrazing:** Not an issue after established; generally 30 days.
- **Extends Grazing Season:** From fall to early winter.
- **Advice:** Can be seeded into standing corn, cereal rye, annual rye grass, and summer- or winter-type oats.
- **Caution:** Like any plant, soil test should be taken before sowing the seed. Pasja is sensitive to soil fertility. Therefore, for best growth, be sure to adjust pH and lime amounts via a soil test before planting Pasja.
- **Pollinator Friendly:** Yes, Pasja's flowers are attractive to honeybees.
- **Sun:** Prefers full sun.
- **USDA Hardiness Zones:** Can grow anywhere in continental U.S. but check the USDA Plant Hardiness Zone Map for your area.

T-RAPTOR HYBRID FORAGE BRASSICA

T-Raptor is another early maturing hybrid brassica that can be planted in mid-May to early June as a

▲ T-Raptor is an early maturing hybrid cross between a forage turnip and a forage rape. It has a higher leaf-to-bulb ratio. It is an excellent late summer forage planting for deer and other wildlife. Like all brassicas, it is winter-hardy. Photo: Barenbrug

warm-season food plot or, better yet, in late July or the beginning of August for a winter-hardy planting. T-Raptor is a hybrid cross between two of the most successfully planted singular brassicas: forage turnip and forage rape. It has excellent large leaf growth (higher leaf-to-bulb ratio) and it is well-suited to grazing by deer and other wildlife. T-Raptor hybrid forage rape is an impressive multi-graze brassica that produces a small bulb. Hybrid brassicas are exceedingly high in crude protein and energy and low in fiber.

T-Raptor's digestibility is rated as particularly good. T-Raptor is an outstanding late-summer and winter feed source, when other cool-season forages slow in production. Like hybrid and other brassicas, T-Raptor begins to winter-kill around 25°F and at extended 10°F temperatures, it will die more quickly. This turnip has good plant vigor, good clubroot resistance, rapid re-growth, and is widely adaptive throughout the country. It matures in about 50 to 60 days after planting.

T-Raptor, like all brassicas, is susceptible to insect attacks like cabbage beetles, common aphid, and striped flea beetle when planted in the same plot more than 2 years in a row. The effect is dramatic. Plants will be very sparse, or worse, the entire crop will turn black and die in a noticeably short time frame.

T-Raptor seed is available from www.forageseeds. com, www.tecomate.com and other seed companies.

CONDENSED RECAP

- **Attraction:** High to very high.
- **Temperature Tolerances:** Rated as cold or winter-hardy.
- **Inoculant:** Not applicable.
- **Preferred pH:** Tolerates pH levels from 5.3 to 7.5. Prefers 6.5 to 6.8.
- **Planting Time:** As a winter planting, late July or beginning of August in the North and November in the South.
- **Soil:** Prefers moist soil with good drainage.
- **Seeding Rates:** Broadcast alone at 3 to 5 lbs./acre, mix at 1 to 3 lbs./acre, drill at 1½ to 2½ lbs./acre.
- **Seed Depth:** Plant at ⅛-inch deep in a well-prepared seedbed. Can be top-seeded and cultipacked.
- **Germination:** In ideal soil temperatures of a minimum of 45°F and weather conditions, will emerge in about 7 days.

- **Fertilizer:** Like all turnips, in lieu of a soil test, fertilize with 350 to 400 lbs./acre of 19-19-19. Top dress with 100 to 150 lbs./acre of ammonium sulfate (34-0-0) 30 to 45 days later.
- **Maturity:** Hybrid brassicas mature within 40 to 60 days after planting.
- **Crude Protein Content:** Contains 18 to 30% percent and sometimes more.
- **Total Digestibility (TDN):** Is rated at 80 percent.
- **Companion Mixes:** Suggested as a stand-alone planting.
- **Overgrazing:** Generally, not an issue after 30 days of growth.
- **Extends Grazing Season:** Extends grazing season into late winter.
- **Advice:** Do not plant in the same plot more than 2 consecutive years.
- **Caution:** Do not overseed or it will result in stunted plants and bulbs.
- **Pollinator Friendly:** Yes.
- **Sun:** Likes full sun.
- **USDA Hardiness Zones:** Does well in most all northern areas, check your USDA zones before planting.

▲ The deep roots of this groundhog radish plant show the depth at which they can redeposit organic matter into the soil after they die. Photo: Wildlife Perfect

NITROGEN SCAVENGING ABILITY

As radish roots grow, they scavenge between 40 to 100 pounds of nitrogen, a.k.a. N, per acre deep in the soil where it has not been available to shallower-growing plants. The following year, the radish's dead roots leave nitrogen, phosphorus, and calcium in the soil and become available for future plantings, which helps to reduce the amount of fertilizer needed. According to the USDA, "Many cover crop species are nitrogen scavengers, but the roots of radish are able to absorb nitrogen at greater depths, preventing it from leaching into groundwater." Additionally, as radish plants die, they return up to 5 tons—you read that correctly, 5 tons—of organic matter per acre, which further aids in providing better soil for future crops planted in the same spot. "Biomass decomposes quickly and leaves the seedbed ready for planting, without the need to till or remove leftover residue," as noted on the USDA's website.

FORAGE RADISH

Forage radishes are somewhat new as a wildlife food plot crop. They became popular about a decade ago. Before that, radishes were, to some extent, a secret as a wildlife food crop within the family of cold-weather brassicas. Today, managers across the country have learned that although it may take deer a season to discover what forage radishes are, once they do, they quickly become attracted to them.

▲ Forage radishes are extremely fast to sprout and equally rapid to grow. They scavenge nitrogen (N) and other nutrients. Additionally, radishes break-up compacted soil. They are sold under various cultivar names such as Groundhog, Daikon, Nitro, Sodbuster, etc. Photo: L.B. Wannamaker

Radishes are large broadleaf annuals that are regarded as being very tolerant of cold weather. They can withstand temperatures of about 25°F, and it will take a temperature of -20°F to winter-kill them. I have had good success planting a brand called Groundhog Radish. There is a multitude of seed companies that carry Ground Hog radish, or other varieties of radish seed as well. Radishes not only provide forage for deer, but their long, wide root system is a terrific soil builder by "drilling" into the soil and naturally loosening condensed soils. This is a benefit for food plotters, as the radishes break up compacted soil for the next crop.

Forage radishes produce large amounts of root and leaf mass, providing about 200 lbs./ nitrogen per acre in the process. They also capture and recycle soil nutrients. Radishes decompose quickly, helping to allow better water and air infiltration into the soil.

Radishes have large, long, fleshy taproots that can grow up to 18 inches in length and much longer. The actual radish plant has wide, succulent leaves that are soft and palatable. It can grow semi-erect and reach about 1 to 2 feet high above the ground. Radish leaf tops provide high nutrition and excellent production. Radishes are very quick to germinate, often breaking through the soil in a few days.

Radishes are high in protein, more than 20 percent for the root tubers and 25 to 35 percent for the leaves. This offers deer a high source of energy during the strenuous period of the rut and during the hard times of winter. Radishes are also high in vitamin C, digestible fiber, and selenium. They contain manganese, zinc, copper, and boron, which are all important trace minerals for white-tailed deer, elk, mule deer, and other wildlife.

Deer feed heavily on the tender green leaves in fall, dig up the roots and consume them soon after the first few hard frosts, typically into winter. The green leaves grow tall enough to stand above a few inches of snow, making them easy for deer to browse on. Once deer become familiar with radishes, they quickly become fond of their taste. Like other brassicas, radishes convert starches to sugars when cold temperatures occur, making them especially appealing during the late fall and winter.

Radishes have a pungent odor, which helps deer to easily locate them. This often leads to deer nibbling at the radishes and discovering that they like

▲ In a well-prepared and cared-for food plot, you can expect to grow a food plot of radishes that looks like this photo. Radishes are among the easiest plants to grow. Photo: Whitetail Institute

them. Radishes quickly suppress weed competition, too. They germinate fast and grow heartily. They also provide a dry-matter production of 5,000 lbs./acre of top growth plus 2,000 lbs./acre of root dry matter. The forage radish looks like a long green or white or light green carrot, and often reaches lengths of 18 to 24 inches. Deer eat the leaves when they turn green and succulent, unlike other forage crops such as rape, kale, and other brassicas, which deer often ignore until heavy frosts make them more attractive. Radishes can be planted in mid-July to early August in the North and from September to November in the South. I prefer to plant them in mid-July. By doing so, I assure myself that the radishes will be fully mature by mid-October.

This easy-to-grow plant can be sown throughout the Northeast, Southeast, and Midwest. As a brassica, radishes should not be grown on the same ground for more than 2 successive years because of a possible buildup of disease in the soil.

Incidentally, radishes, like swede, turnips, mustard, canola and kale, are also good for human consumption. They can be stir-fried or eaten raw, as they have a crispy, crunchy texture and mild, sweet flavor. They are great in salads and are very nutritious, especially high in calcium, phosphorus, and iron. But don't eat them all—save some for your deer—they will enjoy them too. I have had success with planting different types of radishes such as Ground Hog and Daikon (a.k.a. Winter Radish). Other varieties include Japanese, Oriental, Asian, Ripper, Tillage, Sodbuster, and Trophy radishes. Radish seeds are available at www.wannamakerseeds.com, www.wildlifeperfect.com, www.antlerking.com and a horde of other seed companies.

CONDENSED RECAP

- **Attraction:** Medium to high once deer discover what they are.
- **Temperature Tolerances:** Tolerates winter temperatures down to 15°F.
- **Inoculant:** Not applicable with brassicas.
- **Planting Time:** Forage radish grows best when planted in late August or early September. It germinates very quickly. In the North, plant in early August. In the South, September to October.

- **Seeding Rates:** Broadcast alone at 8 to 12 lbs./acre; mixed 3 to 6 lbs./acre; drill at 2 to 6 lbs./acre. Best planted prior to an expected rainfall within 48 hours. Plant when soil temperatures reach 50°F.
- **Planting Depth:** Plant $1/8$- to $1/4$-inch below the surface, no deeper.
- **Companion Mixes:** Radishes do well as a stand-alone crop, but they can be mixed with other brassicas like kale and rape. When mixed reduce the radish seeding by half.
- **Preferred pH:** Prefers a range of 6.0 to 6.5, but will tolerate low pH levels of 5.3 to 5.9.
- **Soil Preferences:** Will tolerate most soils but does not like wet soils, particularly extended wet ground.
- **Germination:** Very quick to emerge, usually in 3 to 4 days. Daikon radish will germinate at 40°F.
- **Fertilizer:** Without a soil test, at planting use 300 lbs./acre of 19-19-19, 100 lbs./acre of ammonium sulfate (34-0-0) and top off with 1 to 2 lbs./acre of boron.
- **Maturity:** Matures in 40 to 60 days.
- **Crude Protein Content:** Protein levels of the foliage are more than 30 percent; roots and tubers provide more than 20 percent.
- **Total Digestibility (TDN):** The TDN of forage radish is rated as high as 82 to 93 percent.
- **Overgrazing Concerns:** Will be grazed heavily after a few hard frosts turn the starches to sugar.
- **Extends Grazing Season:** From November throughout January.
- **Sunlight:** Full.
- **Pollinator Friendly:** No.
- **USDA Hardiness Zones:** Grows well in all northern areas. Radishes do not have a USDA hardiness zone rating yet.
- **Advice:** As with all brassicas, do not overseed. It will stunt the growth of the plant and the radish bulb.
- **Caution:** Do not plant in the same food plot for more than 2 consecutive years.
- **Level of Maintenance:** Low.

CANOLA (*Brassica rapa or B. napus*)

Canola, a.k.a. rapeseed or double-zero, is a more contemporary kind of rapeseed. It is a fast-growing, high-yielding, quality summer or winter brassica. I heartily recommend planting only the winter variety if attracting deer during the hunting season is a priority. Canola will have a high yield when properly planted. Canola meal is produced from canola seed after the oil is extracted. Canola oil is traditionally produced by crushing the canola seed through an extraction process which is common-place in the oilseed processing industry. Canola is a type of oilseed crop like rape and mustard.

Canola's leaves have a crude protein level of about 20 to 33 percent. When the seed is crushed, it contains about 40 percent vegetable oil. The remaining oilmeal has about 33 percent protein, 10 percent fiber, and about 8 percent fat. Canola's total digestible nutrients (TDN) ranges from 50 to 75 percent and its dry matter ranges from 10 to 18 percent. Canola is distinguished from other forms of rapeseed by its low level of a fatty acid, referred to as erucic acid.

The winter-hardy brassica variety will extend the grazing season from early fall through January. It is a plant that deer find especially attractive when winter temperatures have caused other plantings to go dormant. Deer will feed on both the stems and leaves as soon as it is ready to graze, which is 60 to 90 days after planting it. For that reason, plant canola in plots that are at least one acre or more to prevent deer from overgrazing smaller plots.

Canola is a short-season plant; meaning, the time frame between the last spring frost and the first frost is considered a growing season. Anything less than 120 days is termed as a short-season plant. As a winter-hardy food plot planting in the North, canola can be planted in July and no later than the beginning of August. As a spring plot it can be sown in April or May. Canola takes about 60 to 90 days to mature. It is eagerly sought after by deer from the first hard frost through November and later.

▲ Canola is a must-have food plot. It is a tremendous draw for deer, especially after the first hard frost. Simply put, plant it right, and they will come! Photo: PCFImages

▲ Canola is a winter-hardy annual broadleaf with stand-out disease packages. I have planted it several times on our farm, and I have never been disappointed in how it attracted deer. Photo: NRCSWA

Canola grows best in medium-textured to well-drained soils, but it can also tolerate a wide range of soil types. Optimum pH levels are 6.0 to 7.0. Yields of most canola varieties may be reduced considerably when pH levels are below 5.5. Signs of a pH that is too low will be seen in the fall as crinkled up leaves. That is why it is always wise to test the soil prior to planting it. Canola is also drought and heat tolerant. It prefers a plot that has good drainage. Like all brassicas, it should not be planted more than two consecutive years in the same plot to prevent insect and disease problems.

Although some directions say to plant the canola seed about ¼-inch deep, canola seeds are very tiny. As such, they can be planted successfully at ⅛-inch deep. If possible, plant the seeds prior to an expected rainfall, but be sure the seed is compacted to make good seed-to-soil contact. By planting the seed just prior to a forecasted rainfall, you will greatly enhance the seeds' germination.

Broadcast canola alone at 3 to 5 lbs./acre using a quality hand-operated Harvest Broadcast Spreader or something similar. Compact the soil to make good seed-to-soil contact.

For canola to have the best production, at planting you will need to provide 200 lbs./acre of 19-19-19 or 16-18-19 with 200 lbs./acre ammonium sulfate (34-0-0) or 150 lbs./acre of urea (46-0-0). Other possible fertilizers that may be needed include 2 to 4 lbs./acre of Boron (B), 70 to 140 lbs./acre of magnesium (Mg), and trace amounts of Copper (Cu) and Zinc (Z). It is highly recommended to take a soil test to be sure these elements

▲ A well-fertilized stand of canola can produce up to 2 tons of forage/acre from October to January. Plant canola either the last week of July or early August. If it is planted later, it may not mature. Photo: Ernst Seed

are needed. Remember, that when a plot of canola is fertilized properly, it can provide 20 to 33 percent crude protein levels, and about 2 tons of forage per acre.

Canola can be planted with other brassicas like kale and forage rape. When planting it in a mix with kale and rape, consider planting clovers or other legumes nearby to help divert the deer from over-browsing the canola before October and into December. This plan can save plantings like kale, rape, turnip, and other brassica plots from being overeaten by deer. You will be pleasantly surprised to see how heavily deer will eat canola. It will help resident deer to remain on the property longer and attract transient deer as well especially during the hunting season.

I strongly suggest trying canola as a wildlife food plot for white-tailed deer, mule deer, elk, and other wildlife. Why? Because deer go *berserk-o* for canola. When buying it, remember that there is a wide selection of both spring and winter varieties. For most food plotters, that boils down to choosing a winter variety.

CONDENSED RECAP

- **Attraction:** Once deer become familiar with it, high.
- **Temperature Tolerances:** Can tolerate winter temperatures down to 10°F. Minimum temperatures for growth have been reported to be near 32°F.
- **Inoculant:** None needed.
- **Planting Times:** Plant the winter-hardy variety in late June or July to be ready by deer season. In the South, plant in September. It can also be planted in the North in late August or early September.
- **Seeding Rates:** Alone, broadcast at 5 to 8 lbs./acre; when drilled, 3 to 4 lbs. pounds/acre.
- **Planting Depth:** Can be planted at ⅛-inch, not deeper than ¼-inch. Can be top-seeded prior to a rainfall.

- **Companion Plants:** Sow with other brassicas like kale, turnips, or rape.
- **pH Levels:** Does well 6.5 to 7.0; does best in 6.0; will tolerate 5.5.
- **Soil Preferences:** Prefers medium-textured to well-drained for best growth.
- **Germination:** Canola will germinate and emerge relatively quickly in about 7 to 10 days with soil temperatures at 41°F, but the optimum temperature for germination is 50°F.
- **Fertilizer:** 200 lbs./acre of 19-19-19 or 16-18-19 with 200 lbs./acre ammonium sulfate (34-0-0) or 150 lbs./acre of urea (46-0-0).
- **Maturity:** Matures in 60 to 90 days.
- **Crude Protein Content:** Contains 20 to 30 percent crude protein.
- **Total Digestibility (TDN):** Averages about 50 to 75 percent.
- **Overgrazing:** Once established, not an issue.
- **Extends Grazing Season:** From October to January.
- **Sunlight:** Full sun.
- **Pollinator Friendly:** Yes, rapeseed is a good crop for honeybees, offering both nectar and pollen in early spring.
- **USDA Hardiness Zones:** Can grow anywhere in continental USA but check the USDA Plant Hardiness Zone Map for your area.
- **Advice:** Canola can do very well when it is strip planted with other brassicas next to clover mixes, for the most part in one-acre fields or more.
- **Caution:** Do not plant canola in the same plot more than 2 consecutive years.
- **Level of Maintenance:** Medium.

SWEDE (*Brassica napus ssp. napobrassica*)

Swede, a.k.a. rutabaga, is a root vegetable that is a member of the Brassicaceae family. Swede is also known by other nicknames such as Swedish turnip, neep, and turnip. It originated as a hybrid of the turnip and the cabbage. Swede is characterized by its white, fleshy, broad, elliptical-shaped bulb and red to bronze skin color. It is rated as being a terrific winter-hardy plant for deer that can extend the grazing season from late October through January.

In the United States, swede is thought of as a close relative of rutabaga and turnips but is not officially either one. Forage swede, like other brassicas, is a high-yielding, high-quality, annual crop. The leaves are exceedingly high in energy and low in fiber. It produces large edible bulbs, a.k.a. roots, that are tender and very palatable to deer. In fact, all parts of the plant are eaten by deer including the leaves, stems, and roots. Interestingly, deer eat each part of the plant, like other brassicas, at separate times starting after the first frost, usually in October in the North through January.

▲ This is a variety called Major Plus Swede. Deer love it. This photo was taken only a few weeks after the tiny seeds were planted in July just before a rainfall. Deer love the sweet, tender bulbs (roots). Photo: PCFImages

Additionally, swede's yield is more than that of turnips, but it is slower growing than other bulbous plants like turnips. It can take 150 to 180 days to reach maturity and top production. This plant normally produces a short stem, but it can grow up to 2½ feet long. The leaves and stems normally have 20 to 25 percent crude protein and 65 to 80 percent TDN. The broad elliptical shaped bulbs usually have 10 to 15 percent crude protein and 80 to 85 percent digestibility. Swede is also known for its high yields, excellent disease resistance, and bulbs that are larger than Purple Top turnips. However, the bulbs are much more tender than turnips and are easier for deer to eat.

Since swede seeds are extremely small, it is vital to not overseed the plot. To control this problem, be sure to correctly calibrate the seeder. Because swede is exceptionally sensitive to overseeding, always use the exact recommended seeding rate provided by the seed company supplier. If too much seed is sown, swede plants will suffer greatly. The height of the plants will be much shorter, the leaves will be much smaller, and the bulbs will be tiny. All this will also severely reduce the plant's ability to produce its best protein levels and palatability. This all stems from over competition between individual plants.

Like other brassica seeds, swede can be drilled or broadcasted. The seed should be drill planted at ¼-inch-deep once soil temperatures reach at least 50°F. Never cover it more than ½-inch deep. The tiny seeds can be planted as a stand-alone plot at 4 to 8 lbs./acre. Depending on the type of companion plants used, anywhere from 4 to 6 or 2 to 4 lbs./acre. It can also be drilled at 1½ to 3 lbs./acre.

Swede, like most newly planted tiny seeds, will benefit when sown prior to a forecasted rainfall. Do not grow swede in the same plot for more than 2 consecutive years. Like all brassicas, swede must be rotated every 2 years to prevent soil borne insect infestation. Top choice rotation plants are clovers, legumes, or grains.

In lieu of a soil test, which is always recommended for any planting prior to fertilizing and liming, fertilize swede at planting using 300 to 400 lbs./acre of 19-19-19. About 4 to 6 weeks later, top dress the plot with 100 to 150 lbs./acre of ammonium nitrate. It will increase production and utilization of the plant's leaves and especially its bulb. Boron and/or sulfur may also be needed, but only a soil test can reveal this. Major Plus can also be used as a breakup crop to convert older pastures to different species and newer varieties of plants.

▲ If you plant swede, be especially careful to follow the recommended planting rates. A plot of swede that is overseeded will not grow like this. The leaves will be small and sparse and the bulbs tiny, all due to surpassing the seeding rates. Photo: PCFImages

▲ To have your swede look like this rich green plot, make sure the pH is at least 6.0 and better yet 6.5. Fertilize at planting with 300 to 400 lbs./acre of 19-19-19. About 6 weeks later, use 150 lbs./acre of 34-0-0. Photo: PCFImages

fertile, well-drained soil. Swede requires a firm seed bed. Once the seed is sown, make sure to compact it to ensure good seed-to-soil contact. Swede is quick to germinate, usually within 5 to 7 days. It has proven to be an extremely winter-hardy plant that grows well in cold, moist climates.

Plant swede in early June in the North and in June or July in the South. Swede is a long-season root plant that can be sown to extend a food plot's attractiveness to deer well into winter. It is a desired crop for bowhunters in October and for firearm hunters from November to January, when some other crops have fizzled out.

There are several varieties of swede including Major Plus swede. The variety known as Major Plus is a newer generation swede with high yield potential, with 84 percent of its yield in the bulb. Swede ranks high as one of my favorite brassica plantings.

Swede and other varieties like Winton Swede, Calder, and Sensation are available from www.seedland.com, www.deercreekseed.com, www.welterseed.com, www.preferredseed.com, and other seed companies.

The first plot of swede I planted several years ago was a small test plot (about ¼ acre). The deer avoided eating the leaves in July and August. In late September they nibbled on them. After a couple of hard frosts in mid-October, they began eating the leaves with gusto. They began eating the stems by mid-November. After that, the plot resembled a field of fox holes dug by soldiers as the deer earnestly began digging up and devouring every bulb they could unearth.

Swede, like any brassica, will benefit greatly when the plot is properly prepared prior to being planted. The first step is to use a glyphosate postemergence translocated herbicide that effectively kills turf, grasses, and broadleaf weeds. Wait about 7 to 10 days, or whatever the label states, to plant the seed. Swedes need a supply of moisture to grow well and do well in heavier soils. Sow in an open, sunny site on moist,

CONDENSED RECAP

- **Attraction:** High to very high.
- **Temperature Tolerances:** Endures winter temperatures around 10° to 20°F. Colder temperatures will kill the foliage, but deer will continue to eat the bulbs.
- **Inoculant:** Not applicable.
- **Preferred pH:** Will tolerate 5.8 to 6.2. Ideal pH is 6.0 to 6.5.
- **Planting Time:** In the North, plant in June to achieve full maturity. In the South, plant in July or August.
- **Matures:** Swede requires 150 to 180 days to reach maturity.
- **Soil:** Grows best in loamy, fertile, and slightly acid soils. Does not like wet or heavy clay like soils. Avoid light soils with low water holding capacity.
- **Seeding Rates:** As a stand-alone plot, 4 to 8 lbs./acre. Depending on the type of companion plants used, reduce the seeding rate accordingly. It can also be drilled at 1½ to 3 lbs./acre.
- **Seed Depth:** Plant ⅛- to ¼-inch deep. Can be successfully top-sown in a well-prepared plot before a forecasted rainfall.
- **Germination:** In a well-developed plot, emerges within 7 to 10 days.
- **Fertilizer:** 350 lbs./acre of 19-19-19. About 6 weeks later top off with 150 lbs./acre of 34-0-0.
- **Maturity:** 150 to 180 days.
- **Crude Protein Content:** Leaves provide 15–27 percent protein. Bulbs provide 10 to 15 percent protein.

▲ Once deer become familiar with mustard plants, they eat them heartily. I have never been disappointed in how mustard attracts deer. They can smell the aroma from long distances. Photo: Deposit Photo

- **Total Digestibility (TDN):** Swede's roots (bulb) yield 80 to 85 percent TDN.
- **Companion Mixes:** In reduced rates, mix with other brassicas like kale or turnips.
- **Overgrazing:** Not an issue before a hard frost.
- **Extends Grazing Season:** From October well into January.
- **Advice:** It is super sensitive to being overseeded.
- **Caution:** It has a slow growth rate, and it does not like wet or waterlogged soils.
- **Pollinator Friendly:** Yes. Swede's yellow cross-shaped flowers are attractive to honeybees.
- **Sun:** Prefers full sun.
- **USDA Hardiness Zones:** Grows in zones 2–7. Check your USDA Hardiness Zone first.

MUSTARD (*Brassica rapa var. rapa*)

Forage Mustard, a.k.a. field mustard, is a member of the cruciferous vegetable family. It is also known as common mustard and wild mustard. It is an upright winter annual or biennial. Plants can reach heights of 1 to 4 feet. It has a fleshy, enlarged taproot. Lower leaves can exceed 10 inches long and have large central lobes. The upper leaves are smaller and not lobed. Forage mustard's bright yellow flowers are clustered at the tops. The colorful yellow flower's petals are ¼- to ½-inch long. Mustard is one of the pollinator friendly plants that is often seen wild in fields, or planted as agricultural crops, in orchards, and in wildlife food plots.

Forage mustard helps to prevent erosion, lessen soil compaction, scavenge nutrients, and stifles weeds and soil-borne insects and other pests. Field mustard grows quickly in the fall and has high biomass production. Mustard can be grown as a stand-alone crop or in a blended mix with other brassicas, small grains, or clovers and other legumes. Field mustard can produce 2,000 to 5,000 pounds of dry matter per acre per year.

▲ Mustard is another big leaf brassica. Mustards are perfect to include in any food plot as a stand-alone or a mixed brassica seeded food plot. Each plant can reach up to 24 inches tall and is packed with vitamins A, B, and C. Photo: © Akhtaransa | Dreamstime

Forage mustard is an exceptionally adaptable plant. It will grow in sandy, to heavy clay soils, but grows best when planted in well-drained, moist soils. This plant is so adaptable it can also grow in moderate heat, droughty conditions and even in soils with exceptionally low fertility of about 4.8 pH. Forage mustard grows best in full sun, but it will tolerate moderate shade.

The winter forage mustard varieties are perfect plants to add to any food plot as a stand-alone crop or in a blended mix. Mustard is an aromatic winter leafy broadleaf brassica. Most mustard varieties are fast growing. Mustards are extremely high in vitamins A, B, and C. As the broad deep green leaves become older (larger), the leaves become slightly tough and bitter, but deer don't seem to mind. They will browse on mustard plants from mid-summer into late fall or early winter. Winter varieties are said to tolerate temperatures between 5° and 10°F. When planting mustard as a warm-season crop, sow it 4 to 6 weeks after the last spring frost. As a winter planting, sow mustard 8 to 10 weeks before the first frost.

Mustard and other brassicas planted in small plots that are ½ acre or less (150 feet by 150 feet) should be fenced off from deer and other critters to prevent over-feeding. This can be accomplished using electric fencing or other less expensive forms of wire fencing. Another option is to use liquid-type deterrents like Bobbex Repellent, *Deer* Away® Big Game *Repellent,* and Liquid Fence. All the liquid repellents have helpful reviews on chat websites and score consistently high in studies assessing repellent effectiveness. If repellents are not used, then it is both practical and necessary to plant mustard in larger plots of ½-acre or more to avoid losing the plot to over-browsing.

Mustard seed, like all brassica seeds, is best planted using a drill to develop rows and spacing. When drilled in summer or fall, sow mustard at a rate of 5 to 8 lbs./acre. Field mustard seed can also be broadcast at 8 to 14 lbs./acre into a well-prepared seed bed that is cultipacked after planting. Plant mustard seed at ½ to ¾-inches deep, preferably prior to a predicted rainfall. For quick germination and growth, the soil temperatures for planting mustard should be between 45° to 85°F. Before planting mustard, the soil should be tested to determine the exact amount of fertilizer and lime that may be needed. Add lime as necessary to correct the pH to a level of 5.5 to 6.8. In lieu of taking a soil test, use a NPK mix of 19-19-19.

Field mustard seed is usually attainable from most seed company sources, but I have often found that mustard seed quantities can be limited. So, it may be wise to check with seed suppliers well in advance of planting. A list of mustard seed suppliers can be found at www.hancockseed.com, www.hearneseed.com and others.

Although mustard seed is not as popular a food plot crop as are the more familiar brassica plants, it should not be overlooked by managers who want to experiment with this truly unconventional food plot seed. One good point about planting mustard is that it is more than likely not being grown by other nearby food plotters. I doubt that any food plot manager will be disappointed with the results after planting field mustard.

CONDENSED RECAP

- **Attraction:** Medium to high.
- **Temperature Tolerances:** Winter-type varieties will withstand temperatures as low as 10°F. Non-winter varieties tolerate temperatures around 20° to 25°F.
- **Inoculant:** Not applicable.
- **Preferred pH:** The ideal pH for mustard is between 5.8 to 6.2. Will tolerate 5.5 to 6.8.
- **Planting Time:** Winter varieties should be sown as early as possible, at least 12 weeks before the average date of the first hard freeze.
- **Matures:** Mustard matures in 80 to 85 days. The plant reaches full bloom in 7 to 10 days.
- **Soil:** Grows best in sandy to heavy clay soils. Grows best in well-drained, moist soil, but can tolerate droughty conditions and moderate heat.
- **Seeding Rates:** Alone, broadcast at 5 to 8 lbs./acre; drill at 3 to 5 lbs./acre; mix with other brassicas at lower broadcast rates of 4 to 7 lbs./acre.
- **Seed Depth:** Plant at ½- to ¾-inch deep, followed by cultipacking.
- **Germination:** In soil temperatures from 45° to 85°F, emerges in 7 to 10 days.
- **Fertilizer:** Mustard is heavily dependent upon the soil test results. In lieu of a soil test, use 350 lbs./acre of 19-19-19. About 6 weeks later, top off with 150 lbs./acre of 10-10-10.
- **Maturity:** Varieties range from 80 to 95 days.

- **Crude Protein Content:** Leaves provide 20–25 percent protein.
- **Total Digestibility (TDN):** Contains 80 to 85 percent TDN.
- **Companion Mixes:** In reduced rates with other brassicas, small grains, or legumes.
- **Overgrazing:** Not an issue before a hard frost.
- **Extends Grazing Season:** Into early winter.
- **Advice:** Establish winter crops as early as possible, about 8 weeks before the average date of the first hard freeze.
- **Caution:** Mustard can become weedy or invasive and can displace desirable vegetation if not effectively managed.
- **Pollinator Friendly:** Yes. Mustard's yellow flowers are attractive to honeybees.
- **Sun:** Prefers full sun.
- **USDA Hardiness Zones:** Hardy through zone 7.

GENERAL BRASSICA MATURITY TIMES AFTER ESTABLISHMENT

Canola (rapeseed)—60 to 90 days
Purple Top Turnips—45 to 60 days
Hybrid Turnips:
T-Raptor Hybrid Turnip—42 to 56 days
Pasja Hybrid - 50 to 70 days
Appin Forage Turnip—55 to 80 days
Barkant Turnip—60 to 90 days
Kale - 150 to 220 days
Radish—40 to 60 days
Rape—30 to 90 days.
Swede (a.k.a. rutabaga)—150 to 180 days
Mustard—80 to 85 days

Note: Maturity dates can vary somewhat depending on varieties, soil temperatures, and other factors.

▲ When it comes to deciding what to plant, think about including some crops that are not available in the surrounding properties. Smaller "non-traditional" food plots could be the key to bringing in and holding other bucks. Credit: © Mikael Males | Dreamstime

Chapter Twenty-Two
Additional Plantings

Forage chicory is a deep tap-rooted perennial broadleaf. It is considered a cold-season herb. It will remain green in winter, but its best production takes place from May through October. It is sometimes mistakenly considered a legume, which it is not. Chicory looks like plantain, which is another perennial herb. It is considered a highly nutritious broad-leaved perennial that is part of the sunflower family.

Chicory has numerous qualities that make it an outstanding option to include as a wildlife food plot, particularly for deer. Chicory's long tap root helps it reach moisture that lies deep in the ground, which aids the plant during prolonged dry periods. Chicory can be planted almost anywhere throughout the country. Properly maintained chicory plots can last for several years. Good management requires that you mow this plant before the flower stems get taller than 6 inches.

Forage chicory will withstand heavy grazing pressure, which makes it a good choice in areas with high

▲ Chicory is a winter-hardy perennial forb. It offers deer digestibility, protein, palatability, and nutrition. Chicory needs a high level of soil fertility to grow best. Photo: Tecomate

deer densities. Chicory is one of the finest forages for extracting nutrients from the soil and transferring them to deer to help them grow heavier body weights and larger antlers. Chicory has excellent protein levels.

Chicory is broadly adapted to most climate conditions. It should be planted preferably prior to a predicted rainfall, in July to early August, to help it develop a deep tap root prior to winter. The overall forage production of chicory is rated as "good." It has been reported that yields can provide 4 to 5 tons/acre (dry weight). Its long slender leaves reach 6 inches or more. In summer it produces a deep purple or bright blue flower.

Another benefit of chicory is it can perform well when perennial clovers cannot, due to its ability to tolerate dry conditions in summer. Chicory is slow to establish, but it has excellent resistance to grazing pressure by deer, even in high deer density areas. It will grow in a pH as low as 4.5, but it prefers a pH value of 5.5 for optimal growth.

Planted alone, broadcast chicory at 6 to 8 lbs./acre. In a mix with cold-season clovers, broadcast it at 2 to 3 lbs./acre and sow at about ¼- to ½-inch below the soil's surface. Cultipacking the soil will assure the seeds get the best seed-to-soil contact. Since chicory

▲ Chicory can be planted as a stand-alone food plot. It is also an ideal plant to sow with clovers, other legumes, annual grass, and even small grains. Photo: Whitetail Institute

seeds are very tiny, they can also be top-seeded directly on a well-prepared food plot. I have had good success top-seeding chicory particularly when done within 24 hours of a predicted rainfall.

Chicory can also be planted as a mix with winter-hardy clovers, legumes, small grains, or brassicas. When mixing chicory, reduce the seeding rate to about half. Many wildlife food plot seed companies provide forage chicory blended with other seeds.

It is always best to use a recommended fertilizer after a specific soil test is done. However, I have had good luck using 300 to 400 lbs./acre of 19-19-19 fertilizer in stand-alone plots. Chicory is very responsive to nitrogen fertilization as it requires a high rate of fertility to reach its best production. That's why it is a good plant to blend with other winter-hardy clovers and legumes, as they will add nitrogen into soil to benefit the chicory.

There are many brands of forage chicory. Some of the more popular are Oasis, Forb Feast, and Barenbrug. Chicory is a terrific plant to extend the grazing season. Over the years I have noted deer are attracted to chicory all year long but seek it more enthusiastically in October and into early November. With years of experience planting chicory, I have made it a favorite choice to plant.

A few chicory brands are Whitetail Institute's Imperial Whitetail "Chic" Magnet, featuring WINA-100 perennial forage chicory, which is much more tender and palatable to deer than traditional "waxy" textured chicories, and it provides up to 44 percent more protein for antler building. Moreover, it is cold-tolerant. (www.whitetailinstitute.com). Another favorite brand of chicory is Buck Forage Chicory, which is a terrific protein source as a fall planted chicory plot, www.buckforage.com, Antler King's Chicory www.antlerking.com and Tecomate's Chicory (www.teco-mate.com).

Once you discover how easy it is to grow chicory and how attractive it is to deer, particularly during the deer season, chicory will quickly become one of your favorites and most successful winter-hardy plantings as well. I also like planting Forb Feast Chicory as it has excellent drought resistance and is a cold-hardy variety. Other than the seed companies mentioned above, chicory is available as countless other seed companies.

CONDENSED RECAP

- **Temperature Tolerances:** Chicory can withstand below freezing temperatures but not for extended periods of time.
- **Inoculant:** Not applicable.
- **Planting Time:** No later than July to early August to develop deep roots before winter.
- **Seeding Rates:** Broadcasted alone, plant chicory at 6 to 8 lbs./acre. When drilled, use 3 to 4 lbs./acre. When planted in a mix, reduce the seeding rate of chicory to 2 to 3 lbs./acre
- **Planting Depth:** ¼-inch deep.
- **Companion Mixes:** Mix with cold-hardy clovers and legumes, small grains, and brassicas.
- **pH Levels:** Ideal 6.0 to 7.0; will tolerate 5.0 to 5.5.
- **Soil Preferences:** Chicory is suited to well-drained and/or moderately well-drained soils. It needs a high-level of fertility.
- **Germination:** In a well-prepared food plot, will sprout within 1 to 3 weeks.
- **Fertilizer:** Chicory is very responsive to nitrogen fertilization. Use 300 to 400 lbs./acre of 19-19-19.
- **Crude Protein Content:** Chicory is a superb provider of protein levels that can range from 20 to 25 percent or more. However, that is dependent on soil fertility and its growth stage.
- **Total Digestibility (TDN):** Below 20 percent.
- **Nitrogen Fixation:** None.
- **Overgrazing:** Generally, not an issue after 14 days.
- **Extends Grazing Season:** Into late October or longer.
- **Sunlight:** Full sun.
- **Pollinator Friendly:** Yes.
- **Maturity:** Matures within 30 to 40 days.
- **USDA Hardiness Zones:** Can be planted in all northern zones.
- **Herbicide:** An herbicide for plots of chicory or chicory mixed with other clovers, legumes or broadleaf plants is BioLogic's Weed Reaper.
- **Advice:** Mow at least twice over the summer to discourage bolting (flowering). Responsive to nitrogen after mowing.
- **Caution:** Do not allow flower stems to exceed 6 to 10 inches in height.
- **Level of Maintenance:** Medium.
- **Note:** Once bolting takes place, the plant's production is reduced for the rest of the season or until it is mowed.

▲ This is one of our chicory plots. It is 3 years old. Each season, I keep it well fertilized and mowed to about 6 inches tall. Mowing chicory a few times a season keeps it green and healthy. Photo: PCFImages

SUGAR BEETS (*Beta vulgaris*)

Sugar beets are an ideal planting for the food plotter looking for an exceptional addition to his program. They are often said to be an "ice-cream" type plant to deer—simply meaning that deer rank sugar beets exceedingly high as a preferred food. Sugar beets should be a part of any food plotter's program.

Sugar beets are grown in a wide range of temperate climatic zones throughout the country. It is a biennial vegetable that under ideal conditions can produce XL- to XXL-size storage roots (a.k.a. bulbs). The roots can weigh from 1 to 4 pounds with a dry mass that can produce 25 to 30 percent or more fructose (sugar). The sugar beet energy is converted to fat stores in a deer's body.

The white-colored roots are incredibly attractive to deer and other wildlife. Sugar beets are highly digestible for deer and provide a crude protein content of about 10 percent. One acre of ground may produce as much as 15 tons of this highly nutritious plant. Holy tonnage Batman! Not surprisingly, many animals from rabbits to deer and bears, will chow down on both the tops of sugar beets and the bulbs.

Sugar beets are a robust planting and as such they can adapt to a variety of soils. They can deal with heavy soils if they are in full sun for at least 6 hours a day. More important, they require good drainage. Sugar beets do not handle weed competition well. Therefore, weed control measures must take place prior to planting sugar beets. Weeds can be controlled either through tillage or by using a grass-selective herbicide such as Whitetail Institute's Arrest Max, SelectMax® or Poast®.

Sugar beets also require adequate water. They are not drought-tolerant to any extent and will only produce a

▲ This plot of sugar beets is weed free because once the plants begin to grow, they quickly shade out the weeds. Photo: Buck Lunch

substantial crop if they receive adequate rainfall. Sugar beets should be planted in a medium to heavy loam soil that receives an ample amount of moisture. Be careful about the plot site selection, however. While the beets will need adequate water to germinate, they are vulnerable to drowning if they get too much water when they are immature plants.

▲ Deer eat both the foliage and the roots (bulbs) of sugar beets, which provides high amounts of nutrition. Photo: Deposit Photo

Sugar beets can mature in about 90 to 100 days and grow best when the temperatures are between 60° and 75°F and the evening temperatures do not fall below 40°F. Planting times vary from North to South. In the northern end of their range, sugar beets have a reduced growing season of about 100 days. I have found that they can be planted in late June or early July where I live in upstate New York. I generally plant sugar beets in mid-June, prior to a predicted rainfall. Usually, by the last week of September, they have fully matured. Sugar beets can be planted in early spring and they will continue to grow into fall. Do not mow the tops of the sugar beets when they are growing. It will encourage additional leaf growth, which ends up decreasing the sugar content in the plant's root system, which is the key to attracting deer. Unfortunately, southern states like Florida, Louisiana, southern Alabama, and Georgia are not well-suited for growing sugar beets.

Sugar beet plots can quickly become a prime food source for deer once they undergo a couple of intense frosts. Deer will then enthusiastically and relentlessly visit sugar beet crops even more than they did before, until they have unearthed and devoured every single sugar beet they can find. The plots begin to look like minefields with deep holes dug up throughout them. Eventually, the holes in the plots appear as though they were made with shovels.

Broadcast sugar beets at about 10 to 15 lbs./acre. It is crucial to make sure that the plot is weed-free prior to planting the seeds. This will go a long way to assure a successful crop. Once the plants begin to shoot up, their leaves will sufficiently block out the sun to shade out weed growth and competition.

Before planting sugar beets' it is highly advisable to first take a soil test. Sugar beets' ideal pH is 5.0 to 6.5. At planting, fertilize the beets with 300 to 400 lbs./acre of 19-19-19, and about 20 to 30 lbs./acre of manganese sulfate (if your soil test comes back suggesting you need manganese sulfate). Turn both fertilizers under the soil slightly, about an inch or so to limit disturbing the weed bed. When the plants are almost

▲ I took this buck at 11:30 a.m. in a sugar beet plot during the late muzzleloading season in December. Note: The beets are still being eaten this time of year and the buck was active in the late morning.

fully grown (about 8 weeks later), broadcast about 100 lbs./acre of urea (46-0-0).

Here is an important tip about planting sugar beets: Do not overseed the plot. An overseeded sugar beet plot will result in each plant fighting for the nutrients in the soil. At best, the result will be a food plot of stunted sugar beet plants and bulbs caused by competition. The plot's attractiveness to deer will diminish ten-fold. In the worst-case scenario, overseeding a sugar beet plot could lead to the plot's *total* failure. This is true for all plantings but is especially noticeable for plants that produce bulbs like turnips, swede, radishes, rutabaga and sugar beets.

You can buy sugar beets from www.antlerking.com, www.amazon.com, www.seedland.com or other seed retailers.

CONDENSED RECAP

- **Temperature Tolerances:** Once mature, will tolerate cool to cold temperatures. Extended temperatures under 25°F will damage the beets, but deer will still eat them. A few days of heavy frost will kill the leaf tops.
- **Inoculant:** Not applicable.
- **Preferred pH:** Ideal is 5.0 to 6.5. Will tolerate 7.0 to 7.5.
- **Planting Times:** Plant after all danger of frosts have passed. Plant anytime, with nighttime soil temperatures above 60°F.
- **Soil Preferences:** Prefers heavy soil, but not pure clay.
- **Seeding Rates:** Alone, 8 to 10 lbs./acre. Mixed with turnips, kale, radish, etc., use 5 lbs./acre.
- **Seed Depth:** ½- to ¾-inch deep.

- **Germination:** About 14 days; as long as 3 weeks if it does not rain.
- **Fertilizer:** Needs fertilizer throughout its growth. Use 300 to 400 lbs./acre of 19-19-19 at planting along with 25 to 30 lbs./acre of manganese sulfate. When plants are nearly mature, about 8 weeks later, fertilize with 100 lbs./acre of urea 46-0-0.
- **Maturity:** Sugar beets will reach maturity from 90 to 100 days.
- **Crude Protein Content:** About 10 percent.
- **Total Digestible Nutrients (TDN):** Sugar beets have the highest digestibility of all food plot forage plants, at 90 to 95 percent.
- **Nitrogen Fixation:** Not applicable.
- **Companion Mixes:** Sugar beets are best planted as a stand alone plot.
- **Overgrazing Concerns:** Not an issue once young beets are established.
- **Sunlight:** Prefers at least 6 hours a day of full sun.
- **Extends Grazing Season:** Yes, if the deer haven't eaten them, into November and longer.
- **Pollinator Friendly:** Not applicable.
- **USDA Hardiness Zones:** 2, 3, 4, 5, 6, 7, 8, 9, 10, and 11.
- **Herbicide:** Use a grass selective herbicide such as Arrest Max, Select® or Poast®.
- **Advice:** Pelletized seeds are best for improved germination and emergence.
- **Caution:** Newly emerged plants are susceptible to drowning from too much moisture.
- **Maintenance Level:** Medium to high.
- **Note:** Do not plant sugar beets in pure clay. Eliminate weeds prior to planting.

BUCKWHEAT (*Fagopyrum esculentum Moench*)

Buckwheat is almost a fail-proof planting when grown in a wildlife food plot. It is a warm-season, high-quality annual forb plant. Despite its name, buckwheat has nothing at all in common with wheat, which is a grass. It is a tough-guy type plant. Buckwheat is so adaptable it could be sown successfully throughout the continental United States and even into southern Canada (if it is not planted in areas with extremely low rain, or dry desert-like conditions). It can endure low-fertility.

Buckwheat does well as a stand-alone crop, or it can be mixed with clovers and other legumes and grains. Buckwheat can reach heights of up to five feet. It grows best in cool, moist conditions. It does not do well in heavy, wet soils though. Buckwheat offers a terrific "rotational effect" for follow-up crops. It also makes an excellent smother crop. It can tolerate a wider variety of soil conditions than almost any other forage crop. It is an excellent planting to use for suppressing weeds.

▲ Buckwheat is a terrific crop to attract deer, wild turkeys, all upland birds, and waterfowl. It is a good cover crop that suppresses weeds and attracts beneficial insects and pollinators with its abundant blossoms. Photo: Merit Seed

Buckwheat can be planted after the last frost, depending on where your hunting land is located. If your land is in southern areas, you will have a longer growing season to plant buckwheat—from as early as April to as late as September. In northern regions, plant buckwheat from May through August. Early planted buckwheat may produce 2 to 3 stands during the summer due to its ability to reseed. Buckwheat's resistance to grazing pressure is rated as "fair to good."

▲ Deer are particularly fond of eating the tender shoots of buckwheat. Photo: River Refuge Seed

Deer will eat the leaves, flowers, and often the seed of buckwheat once they discover the food source. The plant makes a good cover crop for idle land, and the flowers are a favorite among beekeepers. The seeds are a high-quality food for doves, wild turkeys, and other upland birds, and waterfowl. It is said by a couple of food plot "pros" on YouTube and outdoor TV shows that deer use of buckwheat is light to none. I don't know what those guys are growing, because someone forgot to send their memo to the deer on my land. Deer enthusiastically eat the blooms and leaves. On occasion they will even eat the mature seeds.

However, it can take deer a season to learn what buckwheat is. Once they do, however, they will eat the leaves and blooms enthusiastically. This will often cause small plots of buckwheat that are less than an acre to be entirely wiped out. Consequently, it is best to plant buckwheat in mixes with other seeds to divert grazing pressure from the primary buckwheat plant. It would even be better to plant in larger plots of an acre or more. Smaller plots less than 1 acre must be protected by using liquid deterrents, electrical fencing, or other types of methods to prevent deer from destroying the planting.

White-tailed deer, mule deer, elk, antelope, and other big game are also highly attracted to buckwheat, as are the critters mentioned above. The profuse white flowers of buckwheat make a field of it quite striking, and the flowers can be produced over several weeks, also providing an extended period of pollen and nectar to support honeybees.

You can buy buckwheat seed from www.seedranch.com, www.greatbasinseeds.com, www.oregonwholesaleseed.com or many other seed retailers.

CONDENSED RECAP

- **Temperature Tolerances:** Buckwheat is sensitive to cold temperatures.
- **Inoculant:** Not applicable.
- **Preferred pH:** Ideal pH is 5.0 to 6.5 but will tolerate pH from 5.5 to 6.0.
- **Planting Times:** After all danger of frost is over, sow in spring or can be sown in mid-summer.
- **Soil:** Grows best in well-maintained moderately fertile soil with good drainage. Does not like heavy clay.

- **Seeding Rates:** Alone, 70 to 90 lbs./acre. When seeded with any companion crops, cut buckwheat's seeding rates to 20 to 25 lbs./acre.
- **Seed Depth:** Plant into a well-prepared seedbed at ½- to 1-inch deep.
- **Germination:** Best when soil is at 80°F, it will germinate between 45° to 100°F.
- **Fertilizer:** In lieu of a soil test, options include 200 lbs./acre of 5-10-15, 300 lbs./acre in a pure stand; and 150 to 300 lbs./acre of 3-12-12 or 100 lbs./acre of 8-24-24.
- **Maturity:** In about 12 weeks.
- **Crude Protein Content:** About 10 to 13 percent.
- **Total Digestible Nutrients (TDN):** About 40 percent.
- **Nitrogen Fixation:** No.
- **Companion Mixes:** Small grains, sun hemp, winter type clovers, corn, tall sorghum, cowpeas, soybeans, Austrian winter peas and other legumes.
- **Overgrazing Concerns:** Occurs in small plots smaller than 1 acre.
- **Sunlight:** Full sun.
- **Extends Grazing Season:** No, it is a warm-season-only planting; is killed after the first frost. In a mixed plot the buckwheat dies off but the clovers and other legumes live on into the winter.
- **Pollinator Friendly:** Incredibly attractive to honeybees.
- **USDA Hardiness Zones:** Zones 3 to 7 until the first frost date September 15 to October 1.
- **Herbicide:** Usually buckwheat shades out weeds.
- **Advice:** Plant no later than 60 days prior to the first frost.
- **Caution:** Sensitive to herbicides, weed control application must be done *prior* to planting.
- **Maintenance Level:** Rated as low.
- **Note:** If possible, avoid tilling by using no-till drill or broadcasting on surface.

SMALL BURNET (*Sanguisorba minor Scop*)

Small burnet is an introduced hardy evergreen perennial forb. As a wildlife food plot, it is noted by the USDA's NRCS as an "excellent" forage. In fact, small burnet is a very desirable forage particularly for elk, but is also a favorite of mule deer, antelope, and white-tailed deer. It is also attractive to all upland birds, and other game. In other words, small burnet is so appealing it is consumed by a wide variety of animals.

Small burnet remains green throughout the growing season, providing a nutritious forage and seed to wildlife well into winter. In areas of low rainfall or droughty conditions it will grow to about 6 inches tall. In areas with adequate rainfall, it will reach 12 to 14 inches. Small burnet has excellent cold tolerance, making it a terrific choice for attracting deer during the hunting seasons.

Small burnet will grow well in the West, upper Midwest, Northeast, New England, and the Southeast. It has even adapted to southern Canada. Basically, small burnet can be grown anywhere that it will receive 14 or more inches of rainfall per year, making it a plant most managers can include in their food plot program.

Small burnet will grow best when planted in well-drained soils. It is not tolerant of areas with poor drainage, flooding, extended standing water, or high-water tables. It will tolerate a wide range of pH levels. Small burnet can be broadcasted or drilled. It should be planted no deeper than 1/2-inch no matter how it is seeded. It can be planted as a stand-alone plot, but it can also be part of a mix with other plants. It is usually seeded in June or July.

Small burnet has an excellent seeding vigor, albeit a slow establisher, making it vulnerable to being overgrazed. Consequently, it should be planted in a mix for no other reason than to divert early grazing pressure by elk, deer, and other animals. It is compatible with many different types of other cold-season plantings including grains, chicory, red or white clovers, some legumes like birdsfoot trefoil. When used as a component of a mix, small burnet's seeding rate should be cut to about 3 to 4 lbs./acre. In lieu of a soil test, apply 300 to 350 pounds/acre of 19-19-19. If clovers and other legumes are included in a mix with small burnet, once a year, fertilize it in late summer or early fall with 0-20-30.

It is drought tolerant and is also considered fire resistant due to leaves and stems staying green with relatively high moisture content. This is noteworthy for food plotters in the western states during the fire season. Small burnet is known for its longevity. A well cared-for plot can last 2 decades, particularly on western rangelands. One way to help its persistence is through continued weed control practices. It prefers full sun but will tolerate semi-shaded conditions.

Small burnet is readily available and not difficult to locate using a simple search on Google. Some seed companies that carry it include Preferred Seed Company (www.preferredseed.com), Pawnee Buttes Seed Inc. (www.pawneebuttesseed.com), and Kester's Wild Game Food Nursery's Inc., (www.kestersnursery.com), and other seed companies.

A variety of small burnet called Delar is a selected release from seed originating in Europe. It was developed by the USDA for exceptional seed and forage production, cold tolerance, and palatability. Just these 3 important factors alone are why managers should include small burnet in their food plot programs.

By the way, small burnet is an excellent food source for humans too. Its leaves are high in Vitamin C and used fresh off the plant in salads, soups, herbal butters, flavored cream cheese, vinegars, or cold drinks. They are said to have a pleasant cucumber-like taste.

▲ Small burnet has excellent forage value for wildlife during all four seasons. It is very winter-hardy and deer will eat it until heavy snows cover it up. Photo: River Refuge Seed

▲ It is not widely known that small burnet is a desirable forage for elk, antelope, deer, upland birds, and waterfowl. They feed on either the herbage or the seed. Photo: River Refuge Seed

CONDENSED RECAP

- **Temperature Tolerances:** Withstands cold temperatures.
- **Inoculate With:** Not applicable
- **Suggested Planting Times:** Early spring to mid-summer, preferably with a predicted rainfall.
- **Seeding Rates:** Alone 20 lbs./acre. In a mix, 3 to 4 lbs./acre.
- **Companion Plants:** Chicory, red or white winter-hardy clovers, small grains, and some legumes like birdsfoot trefoil.
- **Stand-Alone Crop:** For best success, plant in a mix.
- **Seed Depth:** Should be planted ¼ to ¾ of an inch deep.
- **pH Levels:** Has a wide range of pH tolerances from 6.0 to 8.0.
- **Soil Preferences:** Prefers well-drained soils. Will tolerate infertile soils.
- **Germination:** Normally happens the first season with adequate rainfall.
- **Fertilizer:** Without a soil test, use 300 to 350 lbs./acre of 19-19-19. When planted with clovers fertilize in late summer once per year with 0-20-30.

- **Days of Maturity:** With sufficient rainfall, it will emerge within 14 to 21 days.
- **Crude Protein Levels:** Average about 9 percent.
- **Total Digestible Nutrients (TDN):** Rated as "medium."
- **Nitrogen Fixation:** Not applicable.
- **Overgrazing Concerns:** Should be planted in a nurse crop mix to deter deer from overgrazing it.
- **Extends Grazing Season:** Throughout the growing season and into winter.
- **Sunlight Needs:** Prefers full sun, will tolerate partial-shade.
- **Pollinator Friendly:** Yes, attractive to honeybees.
- **USDA Hardiness Zones:** Can be planted in zones 4a, 4b, 5b, 5a, 6a, 6b, 7a, 7b, 8b, 8a.
- **Herbicide Use:** Not applicable.
- **Advice:** Take a soil test before planting to determine exact needs of fertilizer and lime.
- **Caution:** A slow grower that can take time to firmly establish.
- **Avoid:** Do not plant in extended wet areas; may become weedy.
- **Level of Maintenance:** Low.
- **Note:** Is also used for erosion control.

PHACELIA (*Tanacetifolia*)

Phacelia, a.k.a. lacy phacelia, blue tansy, or purple tansy, is a native forb that is winter-hardy down to 18°F. It is also a fast-growing annual broadleaf. Phacelia *Tanacetifolia* is a herbaceous, non-leguminous, flowering annual. It's native to the arid Southwest region of the United States and Mexico. Phacelia's height can range from 6 to 36 inches or more. The foliage looks like a fern, and the flowers are in flat-topped clusters in shades of purple and occasionally white. Spring- and summer-planted phacelia flowers about 6 to 8 weeks after germination and will continue flowering for 6 to 8 weeks more. Phacelia needs a minimum of 13 hours of daylight to initiate flowering.

Mostly used for soil improvement, phacelia's root system is an excellent conditioner of topsoil. Phacelia, like radishes, has terrific root structure for breaking up clay-type soils. It also absorbs excess nitrogen and calcium in soil. Phacelia scavenges nitrogen and calcium and tolerates a wide range of soil pH from 6.4 to 8.6. In addition to its soil benefits, phacelia has another benefit. It is an excellent weed suppressant plant. Phacelia has the potential to produce abundant biomass and does a respectable job at catching excess nitrates before they leach into groundwater.

Over the last several years it has become more and more popular as a good cover crop. Cover crops are plants that are planted to cover the soil rather than for the purpose of being harvested. They manage soil erosion, soil fertility, soil quality, water, weeds, pests, diseases, biodiversity, and wildlife in any system managed and shaped by farmers, food plotters, orchardists, and vineyard managers.

Phacelia is used similarly to buckwheat and other popular cover crops. It is comparable to buckwheat in a lot of ways. Cultural differences are that buckwheat germinates more readily, especially at higher soil temperatures, and phacelia is more tolerant of cold and drought.

Phacelia is hard to beat as a pollinator. It produces ample amounts of lavender-blue fragrant flowers that attract honeybees, bumblebees, and other beneficial bugs. Phacelia is listed by a majority of the major seed sellers as one of the top 20 honey-producing flowers for honeybees. Phacelia's habit of flowering abundantly and for an extended period can increase beneficial insect numbers and diversity, because it provides high quality nectar and pollen.

Food plotters can use phacelia as a cover crop, for erosion control, and as a forage crop in mixes with cold-hardy clovers, and other warm or cold season legumes. Deer can take a season or more to learn phacelia is edible. At first, deer use is generally light but eventually deer consume it more heavily.

CONDENSED RECAP

- **Temperature Tolerances:** Winter-hardy, winter kills at 18°F.
- **Inoculant:** Not applicable.
- **Planting Times:** Plant in spring, summer, or fall.
- **Seeding Rates:** Should be planted in a well-prepared seedbed. Broadcast alone at 6 to 8 lbs./acre; in a mix use 3 to 4 lbs./acre. Solely as a cover crop, use 11 to 18 lbs./acre. Phacelia is a re-seeding annual.
- **Planting Depth:** Plant at ¼-inch deep.
- **Companion Plants:** Compatible with clovers and other legumes.
- **pH Levels:** Prefers 6.5 but will tolerate 6.0 to 8.5.
- **Soil Preferences:** Prefers moist soil, although it will grow well in hot, dry soil. Research reports indicate the optimum soil temperature for germination is between 37° to 68°F. Wet or compacted soils reduced germination success.
- **Germination:** Phacelia seed also requires cool soil temperatures for good germination.
- **Fertilizer:** Phacelia responds to a variety of fertilizers.
- **Crude Protein Content**: Protein content ranges from 7 percent to about 20 percent at the pre-bloom stage.
- **Total Digestibility (TDN):** TDN is rated at about 58 percent.
- **Nitrogen Fixation:** Phacelia does not fix nitrogen but is a very rapidly growing annual nitrogen holder.
- **Overgrazing:** Overgrazing is not an issue in most cases.
- **Extends Grazing Season:** Will be viable in winter temperatures above 18°F.
- **Sunlight:** Prefers as much sun as possible—at least 13 hours of daylight.

- **Pollinator Friendly:** It is an excellent pollinator. Its eye-catching purple flowers are particularly good at attracting honeybees, bumblebees, and other beneficial insects.
- **USDA Hardiness Zones:** Zones 1 to 10.
- **Advice:** Can be used as a cover crop or in a mix as a wildlife food plot.
- **Caution:** Plant at a depth of ¼-inch. Provide maximum daylight.

- **Level of Maintenance:** Low.
- **Maturity:** This non-leguminous forb flowers 45 to 60 days after sprouting and has a flowering period lasting from 6 to 8 weeks.
- **Note:** Deer use of phacelia as a food plot can range from light to medium. Phacelia's residue breaks down quickly.

▲ Phacelia is a top-notch plant with purple flowers that are highly attractive to bees. It is a terrific choice to ensure pollination of food plots, fruit trees, etc. Credit: GO Seed

▲ Phacelia has excellent cold tolerance and will winter-kill at 18° F. It is an excellent nitrogen scavenger and a good weed suppressant. Credit: GO Seed

SUNFLOWER

A mature planting of sunflowers can be jaw-dropping. Sunflowers are mostly planted for doves and other gamebirds. However, other game, including deer, will consume them. They should not be ignored in places where they can be grown. They are extremely high in protein and offer deer a unique food source that, most often, is not being grown by your neighbors. As stated in my first food plots book, planting what the neighbors don't have is the name of the game. Give deer foods to eat they can't get elsewhere.

This warm-season plant is highly attractive for deer, wild turkeys and other wildlife. I've planted sunflowers and have had excellent success with them. Sunflowers should be sown in plots of 1 to 2 acres. To prevent deer over-eating the sunflowers in the vegetative growth stage, sunflowers can be planted with sorghum, corn, cowpeas, lablab, or soybeans. I recommend planting at least 1 to 2 acres at a time, especially if there aren't many early season food sources already available. Begin with a soil test. Sunflowers can be difficult to grow without adequate soil nutrients. If you opt out of a soil test, spread roughly 200 lbs./acre of 10-10-10 or 13-13-13.

One of the more popular varieties is the Peredovik sunflower. Peredovik sunflowers grow 4 to 5 feet tall and provide a nutritious, high-energy food source for wild turkeys and other upland birds. Deer love sunflowers and will eat their leaves throughout their growing stage and will reach up to eat the leaves when the sunflowers reach their maximum height. Once sunflowers begin to drop their seeds, I have seen passing waterfowl drop down to enjoy the bounty.

▲ A sunflower food plot like the one planted on our land here, will attract a host of huntable winged critters including waterfowl, wild turkeys, and upland birds. It's best to plant black-oil sunflower seed. Photo: La Crosse Seed

All types of sunflower seeds originate from the common sunflower, *Helianthus annuus*, although there are many specialized and hybrid flower varieties that offer different benefits like size, stalk height, and seed yield. The seeds they produce are similar, however. Black oil sunflower seeds are meatier and have a higher oil content than striped sunflower seeds. They offer more nutrition and calories in every bite to all wildlife. Black oil seeds also have thinner shells, making them easier for wildlife to crack open.

Sunflowers are a terrific addition to any management program. They can also be planted with millets. An interesting way to invite a wide variety of wildlife to your sunflower buffet is to strip plant them. A strip planting could include Browntop or Japanese millets, sunflowers (in the center), and sorghum (a.k.a. milo). Get ready. You just rang the dinner bell for a host of wildlife. This plant matures in approximately 100 days.

▲ Black oil sunflower seeds have thinner shells and more nutmeat than the striped variety. Deer and bears will invade a plot of sunflowers once the seed ripens to get to the tasty snacks. Photo: PCFImages

Sunflowers can be purchased from www.deercreek-seed.com, www.hancockseed.com, www.johnston-seed.com and other seed retailers.

CONDENSED RECAP
- **Temperature Tolerances:** Can withstand temps as low as 25°F with only minor harm.
- **Inoculant:** No
- **Planting Times:** From May to June
- **Seeding Rates:** Broadcast at 20 to 30 lbs./acre; drill at 10 to 15 lbs./acre.
- **Planting Depth:** ¼-inch.
- **Companion Plants:** Sorghum, corn, milo, cowpeas, lablab, and soybeans.
- **pH Levels:** Ideal 6.0 to 7.0
- **Soil Preferences:** Fertile, well-drained soil; will tolerate sandy and clay soils.
- **Germination:** 2 to 4 weeks.
- **Maturity:** 100 days.
- **Fertilizer:** 10–10–10 13–13–13
- **Crude Protein Content:** 25–30 percent. Provides 28 percent fat, 25 percent fiber, calcium, B vitamins, iron, vitamin E, and potassium.
- **Total Digestible Nutrients (TDN):** 10–12 percent (slightly lower than corn).
- **Nitrogen Fixation:** No.
- **Overgrazing Concerns:** Can be overgrazed when planted in plots smaller than 1 acre.
- **Extends Grazing Season:** Not past a couple of hard frosts.
- **Sunlight:** Full.
- **Pollinator Friendly:** Extremely pollinator friendly.
- **USDA Hardiness Zone:** Can grow throughout most of the country.
- **Advice:** Don't plant in shaded areas.
- **Caution:** Need sufficient soil nutrients for best growth.
- **Level of Maintenance:** Low.
- **Note:** Peredovik is one of the better varieties I have used.

CHUFA (*Cyperus esculentus*)

Chufa is a legume species that produces a tasty underground nut. Deer eat chufa and it can be planted as a food plot solely for them. All too often, however, managers get caught up developing food plots focused on benefiting deer. Instead, to round out a food plot program, managers should also consider particular plantings that target specific species of wildlife groups such as wild turkeys and other upland birds, waterfowl, hogs, and even small game. One of the most popular upland gamebirds hunted throughout the United States is the largest of all upland birds, the wild turkey. The *average* wild turkey hen reaches a weight of 10 to 12 pounds, while an adult longbeard tom can tip the scales from 15 to 20 pounds and more.

So, even if those of you reading this book purchased it primarily to plant food plots for deer, but also are semi-fanatical about hunting wild turkeys, I have included the one failproof food plot favored by turkeys, waterfowl, and upland birds. All food plot managers who hunt wild turkeys should give earnest consideration to planting chufa. If you also like to hunt wild hogs or javelina, chufa is a plant to help you score big time on the little piggies! However, if you don't live in Texas, I strongly recommend not planting chufa for feral pigs.

Chufa, a.k.a. tiger nut, Zulu nut, yellow nut grass, ground almond, edible rush, and rush nut, is a perennial sedge plant that produces a nut-like seed on its root system that is like peanuts. Chufa plants have underground tubers. A single chufa tuber will produce a plant that can grow 15 to 75 additional underground tubers when mature. Once chufa matures, turkeys (and wild hogs and javelina) locate the underground tubers by scratching the surface.

Tubers provide ample amounts of protein and fat, making them particularly nutritious for wild turkeys and their piggy-wiggy brethren and other wildlife both hunted and non-hunted. If turkeys, et-al have never been exposed to chufa, it may take them a season to learn about it. Where it is legal, the quickest way to get wildlife familiar with this planting is to turn the soil over lightly, exposing the tubers. This helps considerably to "teach" wildlife that chufa is an edible plant.

▲ In this strip plot, chufa is the middle plant. Deer, turkeys, and wild hogs are the primary feeders of chufa. Mallards and other dabblers prefer chufa when it is flooded at a depth of 2 to 8 inches. The diving ducks prefer chufa, but like it planted about a foot deep. Photo: Hancock Seed

Chufa is a cold-season perennial bunch grass that can be planted from late April to mid-August. The best experience I have had with planting chufa has been to sow it in April, making it a prime food plot for fall turkey hunting and for spring mating season the following year. For best success, plant at *least* a half-acre plot of chufa.

Chufa plants will grow in a variety of soils. They grow best when planted in well-drained, sandy, or loamy soils. They do not do well in pure heavy clay soil. Usually, chufa will grow anywhere that corn or grain sorghum can be successfully grown. Chufas take about 75 to 125 days to mature and start producing nuts. It can be purchased from www.hancockseed.com or www.seedland.com and other seed companies.

▲ If hunting wild turkeys is your "thing," then planting chufa should be too. Wild turkeys go gobble, gobble bonkers for chufa. Photo: NWTF

CONDENSED RECAP

- **Temperature Tolerances:** Warm and cold season planting. Will tolerate temperatures in the low 20s.
- **Inoculant:** No.
- **Planting Times:** Spring to early summer.
- **Seeding Rates:** Broadcast at 25 to 50 lbs./acre in a well-prepared seed bed, free of weeds and grasses.
- **Planting Depth:** 2 to 3 inches deep when the soil reaches 60°F.
- **Companion Plants:** Best planted alone.
- **pH Levels:** Will tolerate a wide range from 5.5 to 7.0.
- **Soil Preferences:** Does best in moderately well-drained sandy or loamy soils.
- **Germination:** Under ideal conditions 6 days.
- **Fertilizer:** Use 250 lbs./acre of 10-10-10, top dress with urea, 46-0-0, when 6 inches high.
- **Crude Protein Content:** From 10 to 14 percent.
- **Total Digestible Nutrients (TDN):** Good.
- **Nitrogen Fixation:** No.
- **Overgrazing Concerns:** Generally not an issue.
- **Extends Grazing Season:** Into November.
- **Sunlight:** Full sun.
- **Pollinator Friendly:** No.
- **USDA Hardiness Zone:** Zones 3–9.
- **Advice:** Provide chufa plenty of water in the summer. Arrest Max or Poast® can be used to kill grasses prior to seeding.
- **Caution:** May need to expose chufa tubers by digging up some of the soil (where legal).
- **Level of Maintenance:** Low.
- **Note:** Chufa can been cultivated for a wildlife food plot.

PUMPKIN (*Cucurbita pepo*)

Pumpkins are in the plant family known as *Cucurbitaceae*, which consists of various squashes, melons, gourds, cucumber, luffas, and watermelon. Deer do eat pumpkins and other gourds when they are available. One of the main reasons pumpkins are not listed in many wildlife food plot books is because they are not efficient users of tillable acreage. Pumpkins demand a lot of space to grow well.

Pumpkins are rarely, if ever, sold through the traditional types of wildlife seed companies that retail forage seeds for deer and other wildlife. They are primarily sold by seed catalogs and internet sites that retail seeds, including bulk seed purchases. At the end of this section, I have listed seed company sources that sell bulk pumpkin seeds.

I generally plant pumpkins alone. Sometimes, though, I plant them with other gourds. The small types of pumpkins I grow are called Small Sugar Pumpkins (Burgess Seed & Plant Co. www.eburgess.com). They are marketed as pumpkins to make pumpkin pies. I like them because they are small, high in sugar (which provides more energy to deer), and their skin is thinner, making it easier for deer to break them open. They have proven to be successful food plots for me. After a few hard frosts, all pumpkins are easy to break open and deer utilize them as soon as that happens.

I know a few farmers who plant several acres of pumpkins to sell along roadsides to the public for Halloween and Thanksgiving decorations. They have told me that when they are planted as a wildlife food plot, it wouldn't hurt to increase the seeding slightly to have some extra pumpkins to attract deer during the hunting season.

I can assure you that after monitoring how deer on our land reacted to our pumpkin plantings, they are

▲ Deer really like eating the soft pumpkin pulp (a.k.a. guts) more than the outer shell. Pumpkins contain a variety of nutrients including potassium, Vitamin C, fiber, and antioxidants. Surprisingly to some, deer will even eat the pumpkin leaves in summer. Photo: NRCSWA

very fond of eating them. As soon as the pumpkins become overripe and are easy to break open, deer are in the plot smashing open the pumpkins with their front hooves.

What I have learned, however, is that planting pumpkins isn't as difficult as most instructions direct.

One farmer friend of mine, Alex Henderson, told me, "Buying quality pumpkin seed is an all-important first step in order to ensure a high germination percentage, as well as healthy and vibrant plants." Purchase seed with a known variety, and avoid generic seed or VNS (variety not stated).

Plant pumpkins where they will get full sun, at least 6 full hours per day. The vines get quite long (usually 15 to 20 feet) and need room to grow. The site should have good drainage. If a plot allows water to stand, it will not be a suitable selection for planting pumpkins. Weeds can be an issue when growing pumpkins. It

would be wise to sow pumpkins in a well-prepared plot that an herbicide has been applied to at least 2 or more weeks prior to planting the pumpkins. That will go a long way to giving the young plants time to grow their leaves to shade out any potential new weeds.

It is recommended to plant pumpkins into small hills, as they do grow better if that is done. However, the seeds can be broadcast. They germinate in less than 1 week. If the soil temperature reaches 70°F, they will sprout in no more than 10 days. Pumpkins, squash, and other gourds prefer slightly acidic soils. Soils high in acidity should be limed accordingly.

Plant your seeds ½- to 1-inch deep. Pumpkins can be fertilized with Osmocote, which has an NPK of 19-6-12. It is time-released, which makes it less likely you will over-fertilize or burn a young plant. Pests that can attack pumpkins are cucumber beetles, four-line bugs, squash beetles, and aphids. To eliminate bugs

▲ Deer tend to eat the fruit inside pumpkins (a.k.a. pulp, or guts) in late winter when other all other food sources become scarcer. Photo: © Jiri Vaclavek | Dreamstime

from your pumpkin plot you may have to resort to a pesticide. If you need to spray your pumpkins, try to do so in the early evening after the bees have headed back to their hives.

Several herbicides can be used after the pumpkin seeds germinate and begin to grow. Sethoxydim helps control grasses, but can harm pumpkin leaves if applied on hot, sunny days. The herbicide DCPA can be applied once the pumpkin plants have at least 4 to 5 leaves to control grasses and some broadleaf weeds.

As mentioned, it is recommended that pumpkins be planted in rows with small hills at 3 to 6 feet apart. That's a lot of work for most food plot managers, especially without the right equipment. When planted for deer, the plot does not have to look pretty or be grown as a farm crop. My alternative to the recommended type of planting has been to use a pinch bar to poke a shallow hole (½- to 1-inch deep or so) and plant 2 to 3 pumpkin seeds in each hole and then cover it. Once the pumpkin plants begin to grow, thin out 2 of the 3 plants/hole. This method has worked for me well enough to provide an attractive pumpkin plot for deer and other wildlife.

Pumpkin seeds are available from: www.eden-brothers.com, www.bulkseedstore.com, www.harris-seeds.com, www.burpee.com and other on-line seed companies.

CONDENSED RECAP

- **Temperature Tolerances:** Cool-season planting.
- **Inoculant:** No.
- **Planting Times:** Depending on varieties, plant in May or June in the North, later in the South. If practical, space 3 to 6 feet apart.
- **Seeding Rates:** 2 to 3 lbs./acre; use 4 to 5 lbs./acre for bush varieties.
- **Planting Depth:** At ½- to 1-inch.
- **Companion Plants:** Best planted alone. Could be mixed with other gourds.
- **pH Levels:** Grow best when pH is 6.5, will tolerate 6.0 to 6.8.
- **Soil Preferences:** Does best in moderately well-drained, fertile, loamy soils. Will grow in heavier clay soils if they are not wet for extended periods.
- **Germination:** In soil temperatures of 70°F and above, the seed will germinate in 5 to 10 days.

- **Maturity:** Generally, 85 to 120 days, depending upon variety.
- **Fertilizer:** At planting, use a heavy nitrogen NPK like 19-6-12 at 400 lbs./acre. When the plant grows, use 400 lbs./acre of 20-20-20. When flowers bloom, switch to a phosphorous-heavy fertilizer use about 300 to 350 lbs./acre of 10-30-20 or 15-30-50.
- **Crude Protein Content:** 12–18 percent.
- **Total Digestible Nutrients (TDN):** Greater than 72 percent.
- **Nitrogen Fixation:** No.
- **Overgrazing Concerns:** Not an issue.
- **Extends Grazing Season:** Into Thanksgiving and longer.
- **Sunlight:** Full sun.
- **Pollinator Friendly:** Yes, attracts honeybees.
- **USDA Hardiness Zone:** Zones 3 to 7.
- **Advice:** Smaller to medium pumpkins are easier for deer to break open.
- **Caution:** Need room to grow well.
- **Level of Maintenance:** Medium–best to keep weed-free..
- **Note:** After flowers bloom, use a phosphorous heavy fertilizer.

PLANTING TIPS

Pumpkins are very frost-sensitive. They should be planted when the average soil temperatures are at least 65° to 70°F and the last chance of frost has passed. Generally, the best time to plant pumpkins in the North is in May or no later than the first week of June, depending upon where you are in the United States. If you plant any later than late June, large pumpkin varieties won't be mature until after Halloween, and both large and small varieties can be damaged by fall frosts. Most pumpkin varieties take between 85–125 days to mature. Most of the heirloom and larger varieties are on the longer end of the spectrum.

▲ Not only do grasses provide nutrition to wildlife, but they also provide nesting and brooding areas for pheasants, turkeys, and other upland birds. Credit © Mikael Males | Dreamstime

Chapter Twenty-Three

Grasses

The SucraSEED® product line features ryegrasses for wildlife and agricultural livestock that were developed to contain elevated sugar levels. Sweet Spot™ is a seed mix made from High-Sugar Grass (HSG) that was developed by breeders at Go Seed, Inc. High-sugar grasses improve the health of deer and other wildlife. Jerry Hall, President/Seed Breeder of GO Seed Hall said, "SucraSEED® Sweet Spot™ mixes have been thoughtfully formulated utilizing leading edge genetics and vetted by an advisory committee consisting of nationally recognized wildlife nutritionists, Pro-Staff hunting enthusiasts, seed breeders and agronomists. These mixes are regularly evaluated and improved as new genetics become available, new technologies are discovered and as food plot management practices evolve."

▲ Please read this twice. Plant SucraSEED® Sweet Spot™ for deer (repeat). After sowing SucraSEED® Sweet Spot™ you will be one happy plot-head. Sweet Spot™ mixes feature High-sugar grasses. This perennial ryegrass can produce larger antlered bucks with more body weight—as much as 20 percent more. Photo: GoSeed.com

An exclusive mix including High-sugar grasses from SucraSEED® is called Sweet Spot™. Deer cannot process proteins without carbohydrates or sugars. While many other types of plot mixes are packed with high proteins and excellent levels of total digestible

nutrients (TDN), Sweet Spot™ mix delivers necessary sugars to process proteins. Sweet Spot™ is high in both protein and carbohydrates. This mix allows deer to get the optimum nutrition.

Sweet Spot's unique perennial ryegrasses can produce bigger antlers and increase body mass by as much as 20 percent. Deer, elk, and other ruminant animals that eat on HSGs are shown to benefit the environment by emitting up to 24 percent less nitrogen in their urine and feces. What makes Sweet Spot™ even more attractive is that it is a northern perennial wildlife mix that establishes quickly and is winter-hardy.

Sweet Spot™ creates fail-proof food plots with high-sugar grasses that are extremely drought and cold tolerant. It produces higher dry matter intakes. It is a fast-growing grass mix that will effectively shade out weeds, and it doesn't require extra fertilizer. Moreover, food plot managers will benefit from planting Sweet Spot™ because it regenerates each year even after tough weather conditions.

▲ Sweet Spot™ provides deer with high-nutrition. Sweet Spot™ Northern Blend is a unique blend in both protein and carbohydrate, which is more effective on a deer's complex digestive system. Photo: GoSeed.com

Sweet Spot's northern mix contains 55 percent HSG, 10 percent Frosty Berseem clover (which can survive to temperatures of 10°F), 10 percent FIXatioN Balansa clover (which can withstand temperatures as low as -14°F), 10 percent Medium red clover, 7 percent Ladino white clover, 5 percent chicory, and 3 percent Purple Top turnip. The Sweet Spot™ mix contains two of my very favorite winter-hardy clovers: Frosty Berseem and FIXatioN Balansa.

Sweet Spot's southern blend contains 50 percent HSG, 20 percent Frosty Berseem clover, 15 percent FIXatioN Balansa clover, 4 percent Daikon radish, and 3 percent Purple Top turnips. The southern blend was formulated for annual plots.

To establish a successful plot of Sweet Spot™, allow the weeds to grow a few inches before applying a non-selective, post-emergent herbicide before sowing the plot. The plot should have a firm seedbed free of leaves, branches, softball-sized rocks, clods of dirt, and other similar debris. The soil should be packed to retain soil moisture for quick germination. Seeds should be planted no more than ¼- to ½-inch deep. Cultipack for good seed-to-soil contact. Most times the deer will keep the mix grazed. Otherwise, mow it to keep it from growing higher than 5 to 6 inches. It should, however, not be grazed lower than 2 inches. Sweet Spot™ should be planted at 20 lbs./acre. It will do well in pH values ranging from 5.5 to 8.5.

By planting Sweet Spot™ food plot managers ensure creating highly sustainable food plots that reduce the

need to disturb the soil by replanting the plot season after season.

Sweet Spot™ is available from www.outsidepride. com, www.welterseed.com, and other seed sellers. Can also be found at other seed companies.

CONDENSED RECAP

- **Temperature Tolerances:** Cold-hardy.
- **Inoculant:** N/A
- **Planting Times:** In the North, April/May or early October. In the South, late September/early October.
- **Seeding Rates:** Product is packed in 10 lb. bags that plant ½-acre.
- **Planting Depth:** No more than ¼- to ½-inch deep.
- **Companion Plants:** Pre-mixed with winter-hardy clovers, chicory, and turnips.
- **pH Levels:** Prefers 6.5 but will 5.5 to 8.5.
- **Soil Preferences:** Prefers well-drained soil. Will tolerate sandy soil as well.
- **Germination:** Will sprout in 7 to 14 days; the clovers in the mixes will sprout earlier.
- **Fertilizer:** At planting, use 150 lbs./acre of 19-19-19, 16-18-19 or 16-16-16.
- **Sugar Content:** Rated as remarkably high.
- **Total Digestible Nutrients (TDN):** Rated as exceedingly high in well-managed plots.
- **Nitrogen Fixation:** The mixed clovers fix nitrogen.
- **Overgrazing Concerns:** Not an issue once established.
- **Extends Grazing Season:** Depends on the location of the planting. It will go dormant when temperatures drop below freezing for long periods.
- **Sunlight:** Prefers full sun but can tolerate partial shade.
- **Pollinator Friendly:** Yes, the clovers are honeybee friendly.
- **USDA Hardiness Zone:** 4–7
- **Advice:** Start with a well-worked, firm seed bed. A seed bed is firm enough if you can bounce a soccer ball on it. Most plots fail when starting with a cloddy seed bed or one that is too powdery.
- **Caution:** In USDA climate zones lower than 4, Sweet Spot™ may not overwinter. Persistence can be greatly increased if plants are insulated by a snow cover. In climate zones higher than 7, portions of the mix may perform as an annual.
- **Level of Maintenance:** Low to medium.
- **Note:** High-Sugar Grasses (HSG) are extremely drought tolerant.

▲ Sweet Spot™ Northern Blend contains 55 percent SucraSEED® High-Sugar Grass, 10 percent Medium Red Clover, 10 percent Frosty Berseem Clover, 10 percent FIXatioN Balansa Clover, 7 percent Ladino Clover, 5 percent Chicory, and 3 percent Purple Top turnips. There is also a special Southern Blend. Photo: GoSeed.com

TIMOTHY GRASS (*Phleum pratense L.*)

Timothy, a.k.a. herd's grass, meadow cat's tail, *Phleum nodosum,* is considered among the highest quality cool-season perennial bunch grasses. It has a natural adaptation to cool, humid climates. It can reach heights of 2 to 5 feet. It is best fit for fertile, medium to heavy soils of the Northeast, New England, Pacific Northwest, and the Great Lakes states. It can also do well in the northern areas of southern states such as Georgia, North Carolina, and Oklahoma, especially in their higher altitudes. It also grows well on sandy-loam soils that are well-drained. Timothy is very palatable to deer. It is also ideal as nesting and brood-rearing cover. The stiff, erect stems of timothy create good fall roosts for pheasants, wild turkeys, and other upland and non-hunted birds.

▲ Timothy is very palatable to deer and elk. It can be made more attractive in late fall by planting it with cold-hardy clovers like Frosty Berseem, FIXatioN Balansa, and a legume like birdsfoot trefoil, which can withstand severe cold temperatures. Photo: Deposit Photos

Timothy is easy to establish. It is among the quickest germinating bunchgrasses and it matures quickly too. Timothy can be established successfully in spring or late summer. Late summer or early fall plantings are successful because the cool fall weather is more suitable for timothy growth, and weeds are waning and are less problematic. The best stands of timothy are when they are planted no deeper than ½ inch in a well-prepared, firm seedbed. A firm seedbed is vital to the successful establishment of a small-seeded grass like timothy. A firm seedbed allows greater management in seeding depth, it holds moisture better, and it increases seed-to-soil contact.

Timothy can be planted successfully as a stand-alone plot using 10 lbs./acre. A well-managed pure stand of timothy will provide a nutritious, palatable forage for deer for many years. When timothy is planted in a mixture of winter-hardy clovers, however, it produces an even more desirable crop for deer. When the clovers die back after 5 or 6 years, the plot will become a useful pure stand of timothy. A good blend for a timothy and clover planting would be 7 to 8 lbs./acre of timothy, and 5 lbs./acre of FIXatioN Balansa clover or Frosty berseem and 3 lbs./acre of Alice white clover. All clovers are rated as "very winter-hardy" red and white clovers.

If timothy is blended with another grass and other clovers, one blend could include 12 lbs./acre of BG-34 perennial ryegrass, 5 lbs./acre of timothy, 5 lbs./acre of Alice and legacy white clovers. Alice is aggressive enough to compete well with grasses. Another mixture could include 10 lbs./acre of timothy, 6 lbs./acre of Kentucky bluegrass, and 4 lbs./acre of Alice white clover. Kentucky bluegrass is an important forage species for white-tailed deer. It is also an important winter forage grass for western game like elk, mule deer, and even bighorn sheep.

In lieu of a soil test, fertilize timothy at planting with 300 lbs./acre of 19-19-19. After timothy becomes established, it will need some attention. It should be mowed twice a year: once in late May or early June, and again in mid-August, preferably prior to a predicted rainfall to give the new grass growth a moisture boost. If at all practical or possible, remove the cuttings. A couple of weeks later use 200 to 300 lbs./acre of 0-20-30 or 100 lbs./acre of 0-46-0 and 150 lbs./acre of potassium chloride (a.k.a. muriate of potash) 0-0-60.

▲ I plant Climax timothy. It is leafy, fine stemmed, tall, and very palatable. It is used widely in the U.S. and Canada. It performs best in cool, moist conditions. It also matches well with clovers and birdsfoot trefoil. Photo: © Volga 1971 | Dreamstime

Deer will graze on timothy until late spring; then, as green-up takes hold, they move off to forage elsewhere, making timothy's lack of tolerance to intense grazing a non-problem for deer managers. It's for this reason why I like to plant timothy with winter-hardy clovers or legumes such as birdsfoot trefoil or alfalfa. They help to deflect any initial stages of heavy grazing and help to keep the plot attractive throughout the summer and into late fall. For deer managers who want to include a grass within their management program, as the fictional *Star Trek* character Spock would say, timothy "is the most logical choice."

The Barliza and Bart varieties of timothy are both very persistent, high-yielding types that withstand heavy grazing pressure. Climax is my favorite variety. Other varieties consist of Colt, Horizon, Derby, Presto, Clair, Tuukka, and the European types sold by Barenbrug USA. Timothy is available at www.barenbrug.com, www.preferredseed.com and other seed sellers.

CONDENSED RECAP

- **Temperature Tolerances:** Can tolerate late fall temperatures.
- **Inoculant:** Not applicable.
- **Planting Times:** Spring to late summer.
- **Seeding Rates:** In a pure plot, 8 to 10 lbs./acre. In a mix, 5 to 7 lbs./acre depending on the mixture.
- **Planting Depth:** At ¼- to ½-inch and not deeper.
- **Companion Plants:** Clovers, grasses, alfalfa, and birdsfoot trefoil.
- **pH Levels:** Prefers 6.0 and higher, will tolerate 5.5 to 7.0.
- **Soil Preferences:** Prefers finer textured soils, loamy soil, and clay soil.
- **Germination:** In 7 to 14 days.
- **Fertilizer:** In a pure plot, 300 to 350 lbs./acre of 19-19-19. In a mix, a couple of weeks later use 200 to 300 lbs./acre of 0-20-30 or 100 lbs./acre of 0-46-0 and 150 lbs./acre of potassium chloride (a.k.a. muriate of potash) 0-0-60.
- **Crude Protein Content:** Contains 11 percent to 17 percent in vegetative state and 8 percent when mature.
- **Total Digestible Nutrients (TDN):** 62 percent.
- **Nitrogen Fixation:** None.
- **Overgrazing Concerns:** After established, can tolerate heavy grazing, particularly when mixed with clovers.
- **Extends Grazing Season:** From spring to fall.
- **Sunlight:** Prefers full sun. Can tolerate moderate shade.
- **Pollinator Friendly:** No. If mixed with clovers, they will attract honeybees.
- **USDA Hardiness Zone:** Can be planted in the entire United States and much of Canada.
- **Advice:** Timothy is very responsive to the fertilizers above; apply frequently and in ample quantities.
- **Caution:** Stem rust disease causes loss of vigor and forage quality to timothy. Rust-resistant varieties have been developed to control stem rust.
- **Level of Maintenance:** Medium to high.
- **Note:** Timothy is commonly found in wildlife mixtures for nesting, brood cover, and escape.

PERENNIAL RYEGRASS (*Lolium spp*) and ANNUAL RYEGRASS (*Lolium multiflorum*)

Ryegrass is a bunch grass grown throughout the United States. It has two types: annual and perennial. Both the annual and perennial ryegrasses have dark green, shiny, smooth leaves, and grow 2 to 3 feet tall. The annual ryegrasses are chiefly adapted to the South but will grow in the North if they are planted in April or early May.

Ryegrass is a quick-establishing crop. It can tolerate wet, poorly drained soil. Ryegrass has good nutritional value and is known to be palatable to wildlife. It is mainly a pasture crop that provides supplemental feed for wildlife during fall and early spring months when other warm-season grasses are dormant. It grows best on well-drained soils with good water holding capabilities. It can be an attractive forage to deer, especially when it is planted as a mixed seed food plot. It should be planted with cold-hardy clovers or other legumes as companion mixtures. They will improve the stand's quality for deer and other wildlife and lower the plot's nitrogen requirement.

Ryegrass must be managed carefully. Annual ryegrass could become a weed if it's allowed to set seed. It often requires regular mowing to reduce competition. Without proper management and control, ryegrass can quickly become a pain-in-the-grass. Varieties include Linn, Albion Tetraploid, TetraMag, Enhancer Italian, Spring Green, Gulf Annual, Rival Annual, Bruiser Annual, and RG Pasplus-50.

Rye grass is available from many seed companies including www.backwoodsattraction.com, www.pawneebuttesseed.com and www.raganandmassey.com.

▲ Annual ryegrass is a leafy, cool-season grass that is preferred by deer, turkey, rabbits, and other wildlife. It is a popular product for use in overseeding and cover crop programs. Photo: LaCrosse

CONDENSED RECAP

- **Temperature Tolerances:** Vary with location, most often will be viable through October and into early November.

▲ Perennial ryegrass seed is more persistent than annual ryegrass seed. Perennial ryegrass has more leaves in the lower parts of the plant canopy. In the US., perennial ryegrass is used as deer forage mostly in the Midwest and Northeast. Photo: La Crosse

- **Inoculant:** None.
- **Planting Times:** Best time—September. Can also be seeded in April or May, late winter and frost-seeded, too.
- **Seeding Rates:** Alone, 20 to 30 lbs./acre; in a mix, 10 to 15 lbs./acre.
- **Planting Depth:** About $\frac{1}{8}$- to $\frac{1}{4}$-inch deep. No deeper.
- **Companion Plants:** Winter-hardy clovers are best.
- **pH Levels:** Between 6.0 and 7.0; will tolerate to 5.0.
- **Soil Preferences:** Fertile well-drained soils; will tolerate periodic wet soils.
- **Germination:** In about 5 to 10 days in ideal temperatures.
- **Fertilizer:** Highly recommend fertilizing according to a soil test.
- **Crude Protein Content:** Up to 20 percent.
- **Total Digestible Nutrients (TDN):** 70 percent.
- **Nitrogen Fixation:** No.
- **Overgrazing Concerns:** Not a concern once established.
- **Extends Grazing Season:** Into early November.
- **Sunlight:** Full sun.
- **Pollinator Friendly:** No.
- **USDA Hardiness Zone:** All zones
- **Advice:** Best planted with companion winter-hardy clovers.
- **Caution:** As noted, ryegrass can be an aggressive pest without careful management.
- **Level of Maintenance:** High.
- **Note:** Italian ryegrass is like perennial ryegrass, except it is an annual or biennial.

KENTUCKY BLUEGRASS (*Poa pratensis L.*)

Kentucky bluegrass (a.k.a. June grass) is often thought of as only a popular sod-forming grass used on lawns, golf courses, and ski slopes. Kentucky bluegrass is also an important forage species for sheep, cattle, horses, and hunted and non-hunted wildlife.

This may be surprising to some wildlife food plot enthusiasts, but Kentucky bluegrass is an important winter forage grass for deer. It is an essential grass for western big-game animals like elk, mule deer, antelope, and bighorn sheep. They eat the tender plants immediately after growth begins. The leaves remain succulent and green if soil moisture is present. Cottontails, wild turkeys, prairie chickens, and other upland birds also consume the leaves and seeds of Kentucky bluegrass.

Kentucky bluegrass is a cool-season perennial grass that can grow 1 to 3 feet tall. Bluegrass is an excellent forage because it's nutritious, palatable, and tolerant of close grazing. Another reason it is worthwhile as a forage food plot is that Kentucky bluegrass is very winter-hardy.

While Kentucky bluegrass can be grown from the Midwest east, ideally it is a better suited grass in the western areas of the country. As a forage in a food plot program, Kentucky bluegrass will not do well in the deep South. It does not tolerate hot, dry summers found there and becomes low-growing and, therefore, low-yielding.

Kentucky bluegrass pastures are best managed under a grazing system. At the end of the growing season, it becomes less palatable and protein and fiber contents decline. Hence, like timothy grass and perennial rye-grass, Kentucky grass should be sown as a mixture with other cold-hardy clovers and legumes. Once Kentucky begins to get less nutritious to deer, that is when the clovers or other legumes will keep drawing wildlife to the plot.

▲ Elk, mule deer, and bighorn sheep eat Kentucky bluegrass. It is an important winter forage grass for these animals in the West. Photo: © Gerald D. Tang | Dreamstime

▲ In the East, Kentucky bluegrass is mostly planted as pasture for cattle, sheep, and other livestock. Whitetails do eat it, but not nearly as much as they do their favorite grasses like fescue grass, wintergrass, witchgrass, and panic grass. Photo: © Frischschoggi | Dreamstime

There are more than 100 Kentucky bluegrass cultivars readily available from seed companies. Most seeds for sale are not meant for forage. However, some of these cultivars have been developed as forage crops, have disease resistance, and nutritional content for both wildlife and livestock.

If you like to experiment with growing different plants, Kentucky bluegrass is one of the few grasses (other than all the grasses mentioned above) that is nutritionally beneficial for deer and other big game. Other grasses deer eat are consumed only when the grass is young, green, and succulent. Even then, these grasses do not provide them with the type of nutrients they require. That's not the case, however, with all the grasses listed in this chapter.

In wildlife pastures, Kentucky bluegrass should not be grazed shorter than 1½ to 2 inches or it will become weedy and unproductive. When overgrazed, poor root and rhizome development takes place; weeds and shrubs may invade the plot.

CONDENSED RECAP

- **Temperature Tolerances:** Can withstand temperatures into early winter.
- **Inoculant:** Not applicable.
- **Planting Times:** Spring or summer.
- **Seeding Rates:** Alone, 10 lbs./acre.
- **Planting Depth:** At ¼- to ½-inch deep.
- **Companion Plants:** Winter-hardy clovers and legumes.

- **pH Levels:** Good pH values are 6.0 to 7.5.
- **Soil Preferences:** Best adapted to well-drained, fertile, medium-textured soils.
- **Germination:** About 14 days.
- **Fertilizer:** Apply 25 to 30 lbs./acre of nitrogen fertilizer in early spring before green-up.
- **Crude Protein Content:** 12–17 percent.
- **Total Digestible Nutrients (TDN):** 60–75 percent.
- **Nitrogen Fixation:** No.
- **Overgrazing Concerns:** Can withstand close, heavy grazing better than most other grasses. Should not be browsed lower than 1½ inches. Small plots under ½-acre are at risk of being overgrazed.
- **Extends Grazing Season:** From summer to late fall/early winter.
- **Sunlight:** Prefers full sun, but some varieties can tolerate light shade.
- **Pollinator Friendly:** No, unless planted in a mix with winter-hardy clovers or other legumes.
- **USDA Hardiness Zone:** Zones 1,3,4,5,7
- **Advice:** Should be mowed twice a season.
- **Caution:** May become weedy or invasive. Consult your local NRCS Extension Office.
- **Level of Maintenance:** Medium.
- **Note:** Becomes dormant in the heat of summer but regains or at least maintains its green color in fall. Optimum temperatures for forage production are between 60° and 90°F.

MISCANTHUS (Miscanthus *X Giganteus*)

Miscanthus makes an excellent tall habitat (cover) for deer, turkeys, upland birds, and other wildlife. It is not a forage crop. Miscanthus can also be used as heavy screening of neighboring borders, roadsides, and dividing large fields of food plots. At a tall hedge height, but less than 15 feet, miscanthus can be planted with wide spacing so you can sow food plots in between. Another use of Miscanthus is to plant it as a screening to walk to a hunting blind without being seen by deer.

▲ Over the last several years, Miscanthus Giganteus has become exceedingly popular with food plot managers. It works well as a hedge or screening from neighboring properties and as a wildlife cover and habitat. Photo: Maple River Farms

▲ Miscanthus Giganteus is very desirable plant to include in a wildlife landscape. It is a vigorous, fast grower, reaching 12 to 14 feet high. Photo: Maple River Farms

Miscanthus is a "woody" *perennial* grass of Asian descent. Once established, it will grow to at least 11 feet tall. It produces new shoots (stalks) annually that are averagely 3/8 inches in diameter, with a 4-inch average cluster spread. The crop is established by planting pieces of the root (rhizomes), which are generally about 4 inches each in length. Miscanthus is a cold-hardy grass that grows rapidly due to C4 photosynthesis. It has low nutrient requirements, few insect pests, and few diseases. *Miscanthus Giganteous* is a non-invasive grass that can be controlled because it has no viable seeds and runners underground. In the spring, the rhizomes should be sown horizontally into a well-prepared seed bed at about 4 inches deep, and slightly deeper if the soil moisture level is low. Miscanthus can tolerate a wide range of pH values from 5.5 to 7.5. Sandy or free-draining soils only yield well if rainfall is adequate so they should be avoided if possible.

This is a grass that will produce for 15 years or more. Therefore, consider its site selection carefully. Complete proper site preparation, particularly weed control, is essential to ensure vigorous establishment. If practical, water the crop at planting and continue to irrigate it if dry conditions persist. Weeds can slow the growth the first 2 years of establishment. Like corn, miscanthus is in the grass family. Common corn herbicides that have been used successfully on miscanthus are Dual, Atrazine, 2D and 4D. Miscanthus can also be grown as a bio-energy crop. The harvested dry stems can be used as fuel for heat, electricity, or converted to ethanol. You can buy Miscanthus X Giganteus at Maple River Farms–www.mapleriverfarms.com, Lacy Creek Growers–www.lacycreekgrowers.com, Real World Wildlife Products–www.realworldwildlifeproducts.com, and other companies.

▲ Miscanthus Giganteus can provide deer with ideal safety, bedding and fawning areas, or a deep, thick concealment from predators. Photo: Maple River Farms

▲ Millets are easy to grow and its seeds are favorites of not only deer, but also small game, waterfowl, and other gamebirds. Credit © Mikael Males | Dreamstime

Chapter Twenty-Four

The Underrated and Underused Millets

Millet wildlife food plots have become popular with food plotters over the last several years. Some believe that millets are considered cereal grains, but they are different. Millets are a group of highly variable small-seeded grasses, widely grown around the world for human food and forage. There are more than 500 varieties of millets worldwide. As a food plot for wildlife, however, there are about 10 varieties that are highly favored and attractive to a wide range of game. They are unlike the commonly grown grains used for deer and other wildlife such as cereal rye, triticale, wheat, oats, and barley, that all grow best as warm- and cold-season plantings. Millets also differ from other cereal grains by having small, rounded seeds, while most cereal grains have the elongated, pointed seeds.

▲ A flock of Kodak geese about to alight on the water. They will feed on the adjacent millet fields. Geese are prone to dry land feeding in millet grasses, and grainfields, especially with a water body close by. Photo: River Refuge Seed Company

Browntop, Japanese, and white proso millets are the most popular varieties, while Japanese millet probably leads among millets used for waterfowl and Browntop millet being popular for deer, waterfowl, and upland birds. All 6 millets listed in this chapter (browntop, foxtail, proso, pearl, Japanese, and Finger) can be successfully sown as forage food plots to attract a particular species, or a variety of different wildlife. There is a wide array of millets from which to choose, in addition to the ones mentioned.

Millets are easy to grow; even the proverbial black thumb–type grower can sow and grow millets. They tolerate tough growing conditions, make good cover crops, tolerate dry conditions, create summer cover, produce maximum biomass, can withstand wet soils, or temporary flooding conditions, and they are relatively inexpensive and easy to plant. These points among other positive attributes help millets contribute to their ever-growing popularity as diverse stand-alone or mixed seedings. Knowing a little more detail about each type of millet will help you make wiser choices as to which millets you may want to plant and for what game.

Millets are available in many varieties. Before planting any of the millets, I highly recommend contacting local USDA or local NRCS offices for the best recommendations on what varieties will grow best in your area. By doing so, you ensure better success with the planting, and save a lot of time, money, and potential frustration from planting the wrong type of millet. A few of the nurseries that offer millets also provide excellent helpful information on their web sites. This information is included below. Some of the companies will discuss options with you over the phone.

BROWNTOP MILLET (*Urochloa ramose*)

Browntop millet is a warm-season, leafy annual that is attractive to a broad range of wildlife. The flower head of browntop is a cluster of flowers arranged on a stem composed of a main branch or branches. It makes a flower mass with the separate flowers attached along a central stem. It is one of the millets that can be planted and flooded as wildlife food for ducks or planted as food plots on dry areas for deer. When grown erect, it is 2 to 5 feet tall. Its roots can reach 2 feet deep.

Browntop millet grows in rocky, shallow soils from sea level up to an altitude of about 7,500 feet. It is adaptable to almost all upland soil, but it does not grow well in areas with water restrictions, or in droughty conditions. The plant will not survive in temperatures less than 52°F, but ducks, upland birds, and deer will continue to eat the fallen seeds until they are totally consumed. The dropped seeds can remain available until late fall or longer.

As a food plot planting, it is an exceedingly popular millet because it is not only super easy to grow, but it is also popular as feed for waterfowl and other game-birds. In fact, browntop millet can represent from 10 to 25 percent of the diet of both water and land game-birds. Browntop millet is also attractive because it is a prolific seed producer. Its seeds will quickly attract all upland gamebirds, mourning doves, wild turkeys, ducks, deer, and small game like rabbits. Ducks go utterly quacky about browntop millet.

Browntop millet is an early producing and fast-growing millet that can begin to provide its seeds

▲ Browntop millet is planted to mainly attract waterfowl. It can represent 10 to 25 percent of both waterfowl and terrestrial birds. Planted in dry areas, browntop is also consumed by deer. Photo: Serendipity Seeds

about 55 to 60 days after they sprout. It generates copious quantities of seeds for wildlife to eat. Browntop (and other millets) can be planted along lakes, beaver ponds, marsh areas, flooded woods, or any area inhabited by waterfowl. Browntop and other millets really shine when they are sown in places that are prone to seasonal flooding. Plant browntop millet at a depth of ½-inch. The best planting time is from spring to summer.

Browntop millet can tolerate a variety of soils and climates. It can, however, be easily over-seeded as a food plot planting. Browntop millet is used as a companion plant with other grasses. Use at a rate of 25 to 35 lbs./acre, in divided food plots alone or in combination with other crops. Browntop is a non-aggressive, non-invasive plant.

A terrific companion plant with browntop millet is white proso millet. Sown in a mixture, both millets make an excellent food plot for ducks and other waterfowl. When planted in a mix, sow 15 lbs./acre of browntop millet with 15 lbs./acre of proso millet in early July. I learned about these millets from an acquaintance who worked in Lowes. Every time I stopped in the store Anthony would talk to me about duck hunting. During one conversation, he mentioned how he and his buddies, "limited-out over a field of millet." When I asked what kind of millets, he replied, "Browntop mixed with proso." If you are like Anthony, try this combo for ducks. But do not forget that both browntop and proso millets, planted in a combo or alone, are attractive foods for deer as well.

CONDENSED RECAP

- **Temperature Tolerances:** Attracts waterfowl, deer, and upland birds into hunting season.
- **Inoculant:** Not applicable.
- **Planting Times:** Spring to summer. Plant when soil temperatures reach 65°F or warmer.
- **Seeding Rates:** As forage for wildlife, broadcast at 25 to 30 lbs./acre; drill at 14 to 20 lbs./acre.
- **Companion Plants:** Proso millet, grasses, clovers, and other legumes.
- **Planting Depth:** At ¼- to ½-inch deep.
- **pH Levels:** Millet grows best in soil pH ranges between 5.5 to 6.5.
- **Soil Preferences:** Grows best in sandy loam soils; adaptable to a variety of well-drained soils.
- **Germination:** Fast. In ideal conditions, will sprout in 5 days when temperatures reach 63–79°F.
- **Maturity:** Reaches maturity in about 60 days.
- **Fertilizer:** In lieu of a soil test, apply 400 to 600 lbs./acre of 10-10-10.
- **Crude Protein Content:** Slightly higher than corn, generally 6 to 9 percent.
- **Total Digestible Nutrients (TDN):** Rated high in digestibility and deer preference.
- **Nitrogen Fixation:** Yes, capable of setting more than 100 units of nitrogen per acre.
- **Overgrazing Concerns:** Not an issue; tolerates heavy grazing pressure by deer and other game.
- **Extends Grazing:** Will winter kill after a couple hard frosts.
- **Sunlight:** Prefers full sun, will tolerate some shade.
- **Pollinator Friendly:** Yes, its white to pink flowers are attractive to honeybees.
- **USDA Hardiness Zones:** Will kill off after the first hard frost.
- **Advice:** Plant on dry ground to attract deer, mourning doves, turkeys, and other upland birds, and temporary flooded areas for waterfowl.
- **Caution:** Can be weedy or invasive. Consult your local NRCS field Office or your local Cooperative Extension Service office for more information.
- **Level of Maintenance Level:** Rated as low.
- **Notes:** All millets can be grown for summer cover.

JAPANESE MILLET (*Echinochloa esculenta*)

Japanese millet, a.k.a. duck millet, barnyard millet, white millet, alkali millet, water grass, and black millet, is an outstanding annual millet within the group of millets. It is a nutritious, beneficial, and highly preferred food source for a variety of ducks and other winged gamebirds. Japanese millet is ideal for sowing on wet land, food plots in flood areas, or in areas of seasonal flooding. It is a fast-growing millet that can reach 2 to 4 feet. Japanese millet has a group or cluster of flowers on a stem that is comprised of a main branch. It produces a ripe seed in about 45 days.

Japanese millet can not only be planted in wetlands; it can also do well in non-wetland sites in some regions and can grow in sandy soils. It will grow in flooded soils and standing water but *only* if part of the plant remains *above* the water's surface. One of the reasons I grow Japanese millet is because it is better suited to colder conditions and wetter soils than other annual millets like Browntop millet. It will winter kill after a first hard frost. Its seeds will still be eaten by wildlife long after that.

As a wildlife food plot, Japanese millet's attractiveness to wildlife does not begin, or end, with only attracting or being nutritionally beneficial to ducks. Most upland birds will feast on its seeds, particularly when it is planted in non-wetland areas. Deer and wild turkeys will also eat the seeds. Deer prefer eating Japanese millet in its young stage when most palatable. Songbirds are also attracted to Japanese millet. It is popularly known as the "Billion-Dollar Grass," especially to food plot managers who want to attract waterfowl to their property.

It is strongly recommended to take a soil test before planting. The suggested NPK mixes below are recommended only in lieu of taking a soil test. For best results, take a soil test to get the exact NPK mix for each millet.

▲ This is Japanese millet planted by my cousin Attilio on his 114-acre farm. The plot was sown on dry ground between two small ponds. Ducks, geese, and deer ate in it regularly. Photo: PCFImages

▲ Seen in this photo is the entire field of Japanese millet. One of the ponds is in the upper right of the image. Photo: PCFImages

CONDENSED RECAP

- **Temperature Tolerances:** Warm-season planting that has some cold tolerance.
- **Inoculant:** Not applicable.
- **Planting Times:** Sow in the Northeast from mid-June to July, August in the Southeast. Plant when soil temperatures reach 65°F or warmer.
- **Seeding Rates:** Broadcast at 20 to 25 lbs./acre; sow 8 to 12 lbs./acre when mixed.
- **Planting Depth:** At ¼- to ½-inch deep or covered lightly at ¼-inch deep for wildlife food plot plantings.
- **Companion Plants:** Japanese millet grows best alone, without companion plants.
- **pH Levels:** Prefers pH values of 4.6 to 7.4 but tolerates pH levels of 4.5.
- **Soil Preferences:** Grows best in sandy-clay loams.
- **Germination:** Under ideal conditions, it will sprout in less than 1 week.
- **Maturity:** It will mature in 45 to 60 days.
- **Fertilizer:** At planting, needs about 10 lbs./acre of nitrogen, 5 lbs./acre of phosphorus, and 12 lbs./acre of potassium. In lieu of a soil test, use 10-10-10 at 500 lbs./acre.
- **Crude Protein Content:** When cut before heading, the protein can range from 14 to 20 percent.
- **Total Digestible Nutrients (TDN):** Can range from 45 to 55 percent.
- **Nitrogen Fixation:** Not applicable.
- **Overgrazing Concerns:** Not an issue.
- **Extends Grazing Season:** Winter kills after a few hard frosts.
- **Sunlight:** Requires full sun.
- **Pollinator Friendly:** Millets are wind pollinated.
- **USDA Hardiness Zone:** Grows in warm to cool season zones.
- **Advice:** Plant as a stand-alone plot for best results.
- **Caution:** Do not confuse Japanese millet with barnyard grass.
- **Level of Maintenance:** Low.
- **Note:** Japanese millet has the capability of becoming weedy, sometimes establishing itself in fields where it was sown.

▲ Japanese millet is the most popular variety among the millets. Since millets like ample amounts of nitrogen, they should be fertilized between cuttings. Credit: Kauffman Seeds

FOXTAIL MILLET (*Setaria italica*)

Foxtail millet, a.k.a. German, Italian, Italian foxtail, Siberian, foxtail, and bristlegrass, is a warm-season annual. It is from southern Asia and is considered one of the oldest cultivates of all millets. Foxtail can grow from 2 to 5 feet tall. Its root system is shallow, so it has poor tolerance for droughty conditions. The seedheads are dense and bristly and the seed grain can be a variety of colors.

Foxtail millet grows better in cooler regions than the other millets. In the United States foxtail is mostly grown in the northern and western Great Plains, Midwest, Colorado, Wyoming, Kansas, Nebraska, and upper Northeast. Foxtail is generally sown in dry soil, but it can be planted in wetlands. It can grow in sandy to loamy soil. It will grow rapidly in warm weather and can do well in semi-arid conditions. Foxtail does not require a lot of water. But should foxtail undergo droughty conditions, it is hard for it to recover because it has a shallow root system.

Foxtail millet is most often used for wildlife as food plots. It attracts white-tailed deer, elk, mule deer, wild turkeys and other upland game, and doves. However, deer and other ruminants prefer the plant when it is in its early stage producing tender, highly palatable shoots. It is also attractive to ducks, but to a lesser degree than other millets. Foxtail can produce 1 ton of forage on 2½ inches of moisture and requires approximately ⅓ less water than corn. It has an elevated level of tolerance to salinity, produces 1 to 3 tons of dry matter per acre, and it can grow at higher elevations around 5,000 feet as well as in the plains.

CONDENSED RECAP

- **Temperature Tolerances:** Warm-season planting that has a cold tolerance.
- **Inoculant:** Not applicable.
- **Planting Times:** Sow in the Northeast from spring to summer, slightly later in the Southeast. Plant when soil temperatures are at least 65°F before sowing.
- **Seeding Rates:** Broadcast at 20 to 30 lbs./acre, drill at 15 to 20 lbs./acre.
- **Planting Depth:** At ¼- to ½-inch deep.

▲ This is a multi-acre field planted in foxtail millet. All deer, turkeys, and upland birds eat foxtail's tender shoots mostly in its young growth stages. It is not a favorite millet of ducks and geese. Like most millets, it is quite easy to plant. Photo: River Refuge Seed

- **Companion Plants:** Grows best as a stand-alone plot.
- **pH Levels:** Optimum pH values of 5.5 to 6.5.
- **Soil Preferences:** All millets grow best on well-drained loamy soils.
- **Germination:** Under ideal conditions it will sprout in 5 days.
- **Maturity:** Matures in 75 to 90 days.
- **Fertilizer:** Apply phosphorus and potassium according to a soil test. Use 60 to 80 lbs./acre of nitrogen at planting.
- **Crude Protein Content:** Values range from 6 to 8.5 percent.
- **Total Digestible Nutrients (TDN):** Can range from 55 to 65 percent.
- **Nitrogen Fixation:** Produces at least 40 lbs./acre of nitrogen.

- **Overgrazing Concerns:** Not an issue.
- **Extends Grazing Season:** From spring to the first few hard frosts.
- **Sunlight:** Requires full sun.
- **Pollinator Friendly:** Millets are wind-pollinated.
- **USDA Hardiness Zone:** Grows in warm- to cool-season zones.
- **Advice:** Its water efficiency makes it a top crop for semi-arid areas.
- **Caution:** Has the capability of becoming weedy.
- **Advice:** Plant as a stand-alone plot for best results. Like most millets, it can be mixed with other millets.
- **Level of Maintenance:** Low.
- **Note:** Foxtail millet is sown in cooler, droughtier areas than other millets.

▲ Foxtail millet is a warm-season annual that is also known as German, Italian, Siberian, or Bristlegrass. It attracts all species of deer, wild turkeys, and upland game birds. Credit: River Refuge Seed

PROSO MILLET (*Panicum milliaceum var.*)

White proso millet, a.k.a. dove, broomcorn, proso, wild, black seeded proso, panic, broom corn, hog, and common millet, is a warm-season summer annual grass. White proso performs well in mixes for wildlife cover and grows from 1 to 3½ feet tall. There is both a weedy wild proso and a domesticated proso millet. Domesticated proso has yellow or light brown seeds.

It may produce substantial amounts of seeds in a short time frame. White proso performs well in mixes for wildlife cover and matures in 75 days after emergence. Proso is a popular millet for doves, quails, turkeys, and ducks. Can be used as an emergency crop when other primary crops have failed in drought. Proso millet produces well during hot weather conditions. Planting should always be made early enough so seeds mature prior to the first frost yet must be planted after danger of frost has passed.

In the United States, it is mainly grown in the Great Plains states of Nebraska, South Dakota, and Colorado, with limited production in Kansas, Wyoming, and Minnesota. Proso millet grows best in full sun, moist to dry conditions, and can perform well in many soil types. It is found in croplands, fallow fields, roadsides, and disturbed soils. Proso millet is heat and drought-tolerant and is mostly grown in arid type terrains. Its high-water use efficiency allows it to grow in water-limited environments.

Proso millet seed is primarily a millet for doves. Dove proso should be planted within a half-mile of a water supply to encourage more flocks of doves into the plot. A minimum of 5 acres is expected to attract enough doves for a managed hunt. It is also attractive to upland birds such as pheasants, bobwhite and other quail, wild turkeys, and a wide variety of songbirds and other non-hunted fowl. Seedbed preparation should begin long before proso is sown. Prior to planting, the plot site should be firm and have accumulated soil moisture.

The millet seed heads of proso mature from the top of the stalk downward and become so heavy that the seed heads tend to droop over toward the ground, giving gamebirds easy access to the mature seeds even

▲ A large field planted in white proso millet. Proso is a prolific seed producer. Leave it standing dry to attract doves and other upland birds. It is mostly sown to attract doves. Photo: River Refuge Seed

before they fall off. As a food plot it is advisable to mow proso millet fields to provide additional breaking of the seeds for easier consumption by gamebirds. All types of wild birds and fowl will feed on these seeds from the stalk or from off the ground. It is an excellent millet choice for doves, other gamebirds, and fowl, but not so much for ducks and deer.

CONDENSED RECAP

- **Temperature Tolerances:** Warm-season planting that has a cold tolerance.
- **Inoculant:** Not applicable.
- **Planting Times:** Sow in late May to early June. Plant when soil temperatures are at least 55° to 65°F.
- **Seeding Rates:** Broadcast at 20 to 30 lbs./acre. Can be as low as 10 to 12 lbs./acre. Drill at 6 lbs./acre.
- **Planting Depth:** At ¼- to ½-inch deep.
- **Companion Plants:** Winter wheat and sunflowers.
- **pH Levels:** Optimum pH values of 5.5 to 6.5.
- **Soil Preferences:** Adapted to most well-drained, fertile soils.
- **Germination:** Under ideal conditions of 50–100°F, it will sprout in 5 days. However, the optimum soil temperature is 55–65°F.

- **Maturity:** In 60 to 90 days.
- **Fertilizer:** Apply 300 to 500 lbs./acre of 6–12–12 or 8–12–12.
- **Crude Protein Content:** Values range from 6–12 percent.
- **Total Digestible Nutrients (TDN):** Up to 75 percent.
- **Nitrogen Fixation:** Can produce more than 40 lbs./acre of nitrogen.
- **Overgrazing Concerns:** Not an issue.
- **Extends Grazing Season:** September to October.
- **Sunlight:** Grows best in full sun.
- **Pollinator Friendly:** Self-pollinating but can also be wind-pollinated.
- **USDA Hardiness Zone:** Grows best in warm zones.
- **Advice:** Its water efficiency makes it a top crop for semi-arid areas.
- **Caution:** Can be weedy or invasive. It is a rapidly growing, vigorous, prolific seed producer that has developed some herbicide resistance.
- **Level of Maintenance:** Low.
- **Note:** Proso millet does not perform well on coarse sandy soils.

▲ Proso millet is a popular planting for attracting doves, quails, turkeys, and ducks. Credit: River Refuge Seed

PEARL MILLET (*Pennisetum glaucum l.*)

Pearl millet goes by several aliases including bulrush millet, bajra, and babala. It is an introduced warm-season, annual crop. Widely recognized and sown throughout the entire United States for grazing, hay, and as a wildlife seeding. Pearl millet grows 4 to 8 feet tall. Pearl millet has a deep root system that grows reasonably fast. It can be grown throughout the continental United States.

▲ There are 2 types of pearl millet: tall and dwarf varieties. It is generally sown to attract bobwhite quail, doves, wild turkeys, and other upland birds. Photo: © Mrhighsky | Dreamstime

There are 2 types of pearl millet: dwarf and tall. The dwarf variety is leafier and used for grazing. The taller type produces higher seed yields. Pearl millet and all the other millet cultivars should be chosen based on local climates, resistance to local pests, and intended use. It is a good idea to check with a local USDA NRCS office for the best recommendations on adapted cultivars for use in your area. Pearl millet can produce up to 3 to 5 tons of dry matter. It has a high root density and vegetative vigor. Pearl millet does well in mixes. It can be sown with forage legumes like sunn hemp, cowpea, or lablab.

Pearl millet hardly ever grows in wetlands in western arid zones. However, it may sometimes be found in a wetland environment. Pearl grows nicely on sandy and acidic soils. A good way to relate to what type of soil to plant pearl in is to remember that it will grow best in any area of the country where sorghum is grown. Pearl is *the* most drought resistant of the millets, but somewhat oddly for a millet, pearl cannot survive standing water. Pearl will not do well in elevations above 6,000 feet.

▲ A standing field of tall proso millet. Proso can grow to 8 feet tall. Photo: © Mrhighsky | Dreamstime

Pearl millet is the preferred choice for forage when compared to similar warm-season millets such as browntop, Japanese, and proso millets. It is mostly planted by food plotters as a source of seeds for game-birds. Planted as a wildlife food plot it attracts waterfowl and other upland birds including wild turkeys. Pearl millet is used in commercial birdseed mixes. Like all millets, pearl millet has different varieties. Contact your local ag agencies or local USDA/NRCS for the best variety recommendations.

CONDENSED RECAP

*   **Temperature Tolerances:** Warm-season planting that has a cold tolerance.

- **Inoculant:** Not applicable.
- **Planting Times:** Sow in late May to early June, slightly later in the South. Plant when soil is at least 55 to 65°F.
- **Seeding Rates:** Broadcast at 30 to 40 lbs./acre; drill at 12 to 15 lbs./acre.
- **Planting Depth:** At ½ to ¾-inch deep.
- **Companion Plants:** Lablab and cowpea.
- **pH Levels:** Optimum pH values of 5.5 to 6.5.
- **Soil Preferences:** Like all millets, pearl does best in well-drained, loamy soils.
- **Germination:** Occurs at 54 to 55°F; seedlings can emerge in 2 to 4 days.
- **Maturity:** 60 to 90 days.
- **Fertilizer:** Apply 300 to 500 lbs./acre of 6-12-12 or 8-12-12. Add 225 lbs./acre of nitrogen in late season to increase production.
- **Crude Protein Content:** Values range from 8 to 11 percent.
- **Total Digestible Nutrients (TDN):** From 52 to 65 percent.

- **Nitrogen Fixation:** Minimal.
- **Overgrazing Concerns:** Not an issue.
- **Extends Grazing Season:** To first hard frost, but wildlife continues to eat the seeds.
- **Sunlight:** Grows best in full sun.
- **Pollinator Friendly:** Yes. Pearl millet is a cross-pollinated millet.
- **USDA Hardiness Zone:** Grows best in zones 2 to 11.
- **Advice:** Its water efficiency makes it a top crop for semi-arid areas.
- **Caution:** Contact local agricultural extension specialists or county weed specialists to determine if this plant is considered a weed.
- **Advice:** Be careful using herbicides. Glyphosate will kill pearl millet. It is tolerant of the herbicide atrazine.
- **Level of Maintenance:** Low. Pearl millet is a low-input crop with low nutrient demands.
- **Note:** There is little threat of pearl millet spreading naturally.

▲ All millets require a soil temperature above 60°F for several days prior to planting. Severe drought conditions may cause prussic acid poisoning in millets. Credit: © Dilip Khant | Dreamstime.com

▲ Mixed seed plots offer deer plants to forage on with varying maturity dates. The key factor is to either purchase or make a mixed blend with plants that work well together for an extended period. Photo Credit: Whitetail Institute of NA

Chapter Twenty-Five

Advantages of Planting Mixed Seed Plots

Over the last few decades, there has been a super nova–type explosion in the interest of planting food plots for wildlife. Seed companies, particularly those within the outdoor industry, like Whitetail Institute of North America, BioLogic, Antler King, Drop-Tine Seed Co., and countless other companies, have developed a wide variety of state-of-the-art clovers. They have also developed high-tech mixtures of many seed blends. These developments are meant to cultivate a healthier deer herd, better buck antler development, fawn survival, doe lactation, and much more. Today, a well-rounded food plot and deer management plan not only includes planting stand-alone food plots but also plots of different combinations of seeds.

Someone who endorses this latter thought process is Jon Cooner, Whitetail Institute's Director of Special

▲ Jon Cooner, Whitetail Institute's Director of Special Projects. Photo: Whitetail Institute

Projects. Cooner told me, "One reason [for mixed plots] is that it is rare for any single plant to meet every single performance category that Whitetail Institute requires of our forages to perform at the highest levels in food plots for deer. For example, high nutritional content, early seedling establishment and vigor, heat, cold tolerance and of course, attractiveness to whitetails. Generally, blends can provide vastly better performance by overcoming the shortcomings of any one plant type. Also, different plant types can have different maturity rates, and properly formulated blends will use that to your advantage. For example, most Whitetail Institute perennial blends also have some annual clovers in them. These annual clovers emerge very quickly and provide the fastest possible green-up to the plot as well as the cover properties of a nurse crop in the early growth stages of the perennial components. Plants with different maturity rates are also used in Whitetail Institute's annual blends as timing elements to help keep the plot at its most attractive and nutritious throughout the fall and winter. The brassica component in our No-Plow is such an example." I agree with everything John said; as it would be almost impossible to find fault with any of it.

THE BENEFIT OF SEED BLENDS
The first step is to dedicate a percentage of your total food plots to growing either prepackaged seed blends or homemade seed mixes. What makes a mixed seeded plot attractive is that each different forage in the plot, as mentioned earlier, will have a different time that it ripens and reaches its apex attractiveness, nutritional value, and production.

▲ Deer Eating in Mixed Plot of Clover. A benefit of planting mixed seed plots is that there is a variety of plantings from which the deer can feed on from spring through fall. Photo: Whitetail Institute of NA

Generally, we plant about 25 percent of food plots in mixtures of different seed plantings. We generally plant about 35 to 40 food plots a year. The plots vary widely in their sizes. A half dozen are as small as 75 x 75 feet, while several others are 100 x 100 feet, about ¼-acre. Others range from ½-acre to 2-acre plantings. We also plant plots at 3 acre or more. We are fortunate to be able to have this option, as our 192 acres includes about 45 acres of plantable fields. However, it does not matter how small, large, or how many food plots you have, what matters *most* is the blends of seeds you choose to plant in them.

MIXED SEED PLOTS

A point worth repeating about mixed forages is that each blend will attract deer at slightly different times when the various plants reach their best palatability, peak protein levels, and best production. Below is an example of a 1-acre blended seed plot of what I

typically plant. However, this illustration can apply to *any* size plot so long as the amount of each forage is adjusted to the size of the plot. *All the sample seeding rates are based on broadcast seeding ratios.*

Let's say you planted a 1-acre plot with 50 pounds of Buck Forage oats, 50 pounds of Sweet Blue lupine, 2 pounds of Jumbo II ladino white clover, 5 pounds of Dynamite red clover, and 3 pounds of BioLogic chicory. If you are planting ¼ acre, you would reduce all the amounts by 75 percent. The attractiveness of a food plot like this will be sustainable and attractive to deer from summer through the fall and into winter. Each of the oats, lupine, clovers, and chicory, and the winter-hardy oats hits its peak production at separate times.

Another example of a 1-acre planting of a blended seed plot is 2 lbs./acre of Bonar forage rape, 2 lbs./acre of Forb Feast chicory, 5 lbs./acre of Marathon red

▲ This is a planting of Mossy Oak BioLogic Winter Bulbs and Sugar Beets. It is designed as a late-season planting and is a terrific diverse food plot offering. Photo: BioLogic

clover, 30 lbs./acre of a small winter grain like triticale or cereal rye. Use the same formula above for the proper mixture of smaller plots less than 1 acre. As in the first example, as one plant begins to falter another plant comes into its peak production.

Food plotters must decide on what their end goals are for their blended seed plots. The age-old questions come up: Are they for summer crops, to provide summer-type nutrition for antler growth and doe lactation? Or are they being planted as cold-season crops that target late fall and winter hunting seasons? In other words, are you feeding deer in summer, or do you want them there when you want to see them the most—during daylight hours of the hunting season? My bet would be that most of you reading this would opt for the latter choice. Better yet, though, planting

▲ This buck is eating Antler King's Lights Out. It is a Canadian seed mix that is extremely cold tolerant and it will last into the winter. Photo: antlerking.com

some summer mixes *and* more winter mixed seed varieties is a sound idea.

HOMEMADE CONCOCTIONS

For food plotters who are so inclined, it can be fun to invest the time, effort, and research of putting together homemade forage seed mixtures. However, by creating your own mixtures you must be ready to go through a period of trial-and-error to see if your mixed seed choices worked as you hoped they would. If they do, I must admit there is a special feeling of satisfaction that goes along with creating your own seed mixtures.

However, there is a much more practical choice. This is especially the case for many food plotters who are weekend warriors, and simply do not have the luxury of time to create their own mixtures. For them, and even food plotters who do have the time to spare, the most practical choice is to plant the hi-tech, painstakingly researched mixtures of seeds developed by seed companies including huntingplots.com, Whitetail Institute of North America's "Imperial" line of blended forages, Deer Creek Seed, Antler King, Pennington, Frigid Forage, Mossy Oak's Biologic, and a plethora of other companies that provide a line of quality blended seeds.

When I asked Jon Cooner what three brands of WTIONA blended seed mixes he would recommend on a general basis, his answer was helpful and to the point. "I have been asked that question many times. The answer depends on factors related to each specific site, not to general popularity. The reason is that each Whitetail Institute seed product is designed to flourish in all parts of the US where rainfall is sufficient for that product and other factors related to the plot itself are satisfied, such as equipment accessibility, whether the site holds moisture well or not, and whether the customer is looking for a perennial or an annual. For example, we recommend that Imperial Whitetail Clover be planted in good bottomland soils in plots that can be accessed with equipment for seedbed preparation and maintenance each year. In contrast, we recommend that Imperial Whitetail Alfa-Rack PLUS or Extreme are planted in sites that are well-drained and, for best results, plots that can be accessed with equipment. For sites that are not accessible with equipment, we recommend products that are designed

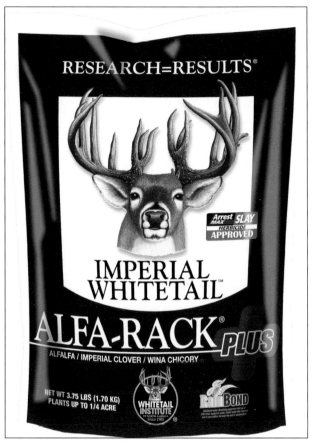

▲ Alfa-Rack Plus is a blend of grazing alfalfas which are high-protein, and drought- and cold-tolerant. Grazing alfalfas have more leaf relative to stem and are more palatable to deer than ordinary hay alfalfas. Photo: Whitetail Institute.

to be planted without tillage such as Imperial Whitetail Secret Spot, BowStand or Imperial No-Plow."

Cooner went on to say, "To get a better idea of how the forage selection process works for Whitetail Institute seed products, go to our website, whitetail-institute.com, and look at the Product Selector link on the home page. It is a short program that takes the important forage-selection factors into account to lead a customer to the right product/s for each site with just the push of a few "yes" and/or "no" answer buttons. Since the characteristics of each plot will be unique, a customer should go through the Product Selector for each site, one site at a time."

At the end of this chapter there is a list of other companies with varieties of blended seeds. Some of these companies like BioLogic, Deer Creek Seed, Merit Seed, Antler King, River Refuge Seed, Drop-Tine Seed

Co., Hancock and Tecomate offer similar assistance on their web sites.

FAILPROOF PLAN

By mixing cool season seeds in a single plot, you are planning for deer to visit the plot throughout the fall and early winter. Another explanation for planting mixtures of seeds relates to taking a page out of Jeopardy champion James Holzhauer's (a.k.a. Jeopardy James) book of wagering; you are hedging your bet. Hedging a bet is a gambling tactic that involves placing a bet on a different outcome to your original wager, to assure a guaranteed profit, regardless of the result of the gamble. Therefore, a hedge bet is generally made to reduce risk.

A hedge bet is an analogy of what happens when planting a mixed blend of seeds. It protects your bet that a stand-alone plot may not be at its best production when you want it to be, or that it could even fail. However, by planting a mixture of seeds in a plot you raise the odds of growing a successful plot—tenfold.

Another way to look at the benefits of a multi-seeded plot is basically like buying an insurance policy. Some of the seeds in a mixture may be more tolerant of drought conditions, excel at dealing with weed competition, or are able to do well in acidic soil. By including a blend of mixed seeds in a food plot you add a factor of flexibility that will provide more success in your blended seed plots rather than a potential catastrophic failure of a single seeded plot.

DUAL SEEDED PLOTS

While many multi-seeded mixtures perform very well, another option is to plant a dual-seeded food plot. In the late 1970s when I was a vegetable garden "junkie," I read a book titled, *Carrots Love Tomatoes*, written by Louise Riotte and published in 1975 by Storey

▲ This mix is a combo of non-native legumes and forbs that attract deer. It is made up of clover, legumes, and sugar beets. Photo: Ernst Seeds

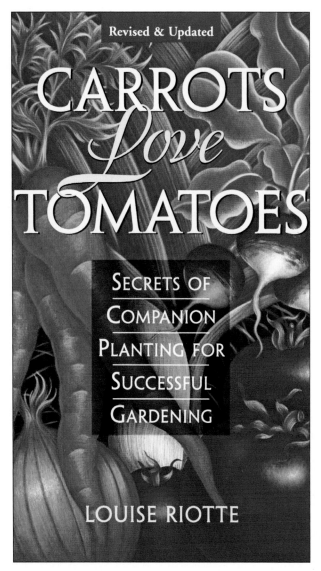

Revised & Updated

CARROTS
Love
TOMATOES

SECRETS OF
COMPANION
PLANTING FOR
SUCCESSFUL
GARDENING

LOUISE RIOTTE

▲ *Carrots Love Tomatoes* is a terrific read for any vegetable garden junkie or wildlife food plotter. Photo: Workman Press

Communications, Inc. The entire book was about how certain vegetable plants grew much healthier, and produced more bountiful veggies, when they were planted alongside other types of vegetables.

So, I offer the following as something to consider regarding planting two-seed mixtures of forages in wildlife food plots. I have been doing this for more than 3 decades. Forage plants that "love" each other, form symbiotic relationships, to assist each other to grow well, increase production, nutrients, height, and, in some instances, even to repel insects. This

knowledge can be applied to planting homemade mixtures or to commercial mixtures that include two different seeds (only after you determine the seeds in the commercial mix "adore" each other).

For instance, here are a few combinations of home-made companion plantings that could be used in your food plot management plan.

- Alfalfa grows better when planted near, of all things, a field of dandelions—a weed.
- Beans go on a bean production rampage when planted with sugar beets, cauliflower, or carrots.
- Radishes grow better when planted with bush beans or pole beans.
- Corn grows better when planted with cowpeas or forage soybeans, because they restore nitrogen into the soil for the corn.
- Oats and vetches (a cool-season legume) do well when planted together.
- When sorghum is planted with soybeans, both will grow exceptionally tall and well.
- Hairy Vetch, a cool-season legume, is an excellent companion plant with all types of turnips: Purple Top, appins, Barkant, Pasja, and swede.

▲ The plot on the right is a mix of warm-season tall-growing forages. It contains grain sorghum, sunflower, sun hemp, lablab, winter peas, and soybeans. It is an excellent long season, high protein food source. Photo: Merit Seed

All the mixtures and dual-seeded companion plants are part of the win-win plant relationships of symbiosis—meaning the intimate association, or union, of two dissimilar organisms for the benefit of both. Examples of other types of beneficial symbiotic relationships include sea anemones and hermit crabs, goby fish and snapping shrimp, and ants and fungi.

However, food plot managers should be sure the mixtures of seeds they choose will "love" each other, as not all symbiotic relationships are beneficial when they are not specifically matched up. For example, sunflowers produce a substance which inhibits nitrogen-fixing bacteria in the soil. Therefore, they hamper any crop like corn (that requires a lot of nitrogen) if it is planted in the preceding sunflower plot.

This is only one comparison to remind food plot managers that not *all* plants "love" other companion plants. Sometimes, plants just want to be left alone in a plot. They do much better when planted in a stand-alone plot than when they are used in certain blended mixtures. I don't want to imply that it is better or even necessary to plant every seed in a mixture. There are benefits to planting stand-alone plots that should not be ignored. So, do your homework when concocting blended homemade mixes.

PERENNIAL/ANNUAL COLD-HARDY MIXTURES

A terrific surefire plot for attracting deer is a companion mixture of annual small grains mixed with perennial winter-hardy clovers or cool-season perennial legumes. A mixture of each one of these plants will provide deer with high levels of protein, palatability, and tender nutritious foliage.

Unfortunately, there is a hiccup with this planting. Some cold-hardy perennial clovers and some legumes (like birdsfoot trefoil, hairy vetch, Sweet Blue lupine, sweetclover, and alfalfa) will carry over nicely to the following spring. All the small grains, however, are rated as cool-season annuals, and usually do not carry over. Grains like rye and triticale seem to have more of a propensity to reseed themselves, although they will not perform as robust as the original planting did. Deer will still nibble on their tender foliage, though.

▲ This is a mix of 3 cold-hardy clovers: Jumbo II ladino, Dynamite red clover, and AberLasting. It is a homemade concoction that worked well to attract deer into the late fall. Photo: PCFImages

The point is the following spring a plot with clovers, legumes, and grains will have *transformed* itself into an entire plot of sumptuous perennial winter-hardy clovers and legumes that were planted a year before. Nice.

A word of caution. Some food plotters choose to plant perennial mixtures of cold-hardy clovers and legumes with perennial grasses like orchardgrass, or Indiangrass. These are not good companion choices with clovers and other legumes and should be avoided. They will compete aggressively with the perennial clovers and legumes and will eventually take over the plot entirely.

If you replace orchardgrass with a much better perennial food plot choice, consider timothy grass. Timothy is a perennial grass that makes an ideal combination perennial nurse crop for clovers and legumes. Another choice is perennial rye grass. A suggested planting of timothy as a companion mixture could include: 6 pounds of Barliza timothy with 15 pounds of Big Daddy perennial ryegrass, 5 pounds of Regal Graze ladino white clover, and 10 pounds of Marathon red clover. The amounts are all based on a 1-acre planting; reduce them according to your food plot's size.

HOMEMADE PERENNIAL MIXES

Below are a few ideas for homemade seed mixtures. I have created several perennial, cool-season, cold-hardy, and summer-type mixtures that I have planted successfully on our farm. These are companion mixes designed for northern zones but can also be used as warm-season plantings and in other areas as well. All seeding rates are based on a 1-acre planting, adjust them according to your food plots' sizes.

▲ Homemade mixtures can be fun and satisfying to create. It takes some experimenting, however, to put the correct percentages of the different seeds together so the entire mix is compatible with each other. That's why buying mixed blends from seed companies is beneficial. Photo: PCFImages

Perennial Winter-Hardy Mix No. 1

- 4 pounds of Alice white clover. Alice is known for its high palatability. It is very winter-hardy.
- 10 pounds of Marathon red clover. Marathon is exceptionally winter-hardy, and can withstand temperatures of 5°F.
- 50 pounds of Forage FX 101 Triticale. Triticale is a hybrid cross of grain rye and wheat. It has protein values of 20 to 25 percent.
- 25 pounds of Buck forage oats that is winter-hardy and has a high protein forage from 10–25 percent. They are drought resistant and designed to provide more tender growth for a longer interval of time.

Perennial Winter-Hardy Mix No. 2

- 4 pounds of Frosty Berseem white clover. Berseem clover tolerates temperatures to -5°F. It has crude protein levels of 18–25 percent and can fix 100 to 150 units of nitrogen per acre.
- 10 pounds of medium red clover. Medium red clover is winter-hardy and has 20–30 percent protein levels. It is a good companion plant for small grains. Red clover is also good for weed suppression.
- 2 pounds of Buck Forage Chicory. Buck Forage can tolerate heavy grazing, low temperatures, and has a protein content of 22–23 percent.
- 30 pounds of winter rye. Winter rye is a small cereal grain. It has protein levels of 10–25 percent. Deer will browse it heavily in fall and winter.

▲ Frosty berseem tolerating frosty conditions. Frosty berseem is an improved cold-tolerant clover. It is much more cold-hardy than other berseem varieties. Frosty Berseem is a must have planting in our wildlife food plot program. Photo: Goseed.com

- 25 pounds of wheat. Check your local Ag Extension office for best varieties to plant in your area. Wheat protein levels run from 10–25 percent.

Perennial Cool-Hardy Grass Mix No. 3
- 6 pounds of Climax timothy grass. Timothy is a cool-season grass that is well suited for the northeastern and north-central climates in the United States. Its deer palatability is rated as "very high."
- 20 pounds of Hancock's perennial ryegrass. It can be used as a cover crop, forage, or nurse crop for clovers and other legumes.
- 5 pounds of Pennington ladino white clover. Pennington clover seed is a cool-season perennial legume. It makes for excellent grazing from fall through early summer. Patriot Clover has 18–28 percent crude protein levels and total digestible nutrients (TDN) ranging from 65–85 percent.

Annual Cold-Hardy Brassica Mixture No. 4
- 4 pounds of Barsica forage rape seed. Barsica is an early maturing forage rape with high yields and excellent cold tolerance.
- 3 pounds of Major Plus swede. Major Plus swede is highly digestible. It is a late maturing swede noted for its high leaf yield, high digestibility, and elevated levels of energy. Major Plus swede has 84 percent of its yield in its bulbs.

- 3 pounds of Ground Hog radishes. Ground Hog is a winter-hardy broadleaf radish. It produces more root mass than oil seed radish or mustards. It is an ideal plant to break up compacted soil.

All the company names mentioned here or anywhere throughout this book are only meant to provide you with a resource and are not in any way my endorsement of any one brand. They are meant to support the variety of products that are mentioned.

THE END-GAME OF COMPANION PLANTING
There are two prominent issues to consider when you use homemade seed mixes: noxious seeds and seed compatibility. Make sure your homemade mixture does not contain noxious seeds. Also be sure that your seed mixtures contain plants that complement one another. This is not a concern when you use commercially blended brands. However, when you purchase commercially made seed mixtures, make sure to buy them from long-standing, reliable seed companies. Remember the more compatible each plant is with the other seed or seeds in the mixture, the better your food plot planting results will be. Again, reputable seed companies have already taken care of these two issues through careful research and in-field trials.

Blended or companion seed planting is necessary to accomplish a well-rounded food plot and deer management plan. One last thought: Using seed mixtures

▲ A food plot mix of Buck's Banquet mix from La Crosse seed. It contains clovers, leafy rape, turnips, radish, and chicory. Once the colder temperatures arrive, this mix becomes sweet and succulent to deer and other wildlife. Photo: Lacrosseseed.com

from reputable companies leads to some amazingly successful food plots. Below is a "baker's dozen" list of seed companies that produce quality, researched, seed mixtures. A more comprehensive listing of wildlife seed companies can be found in Appendix B: Food Plot Seed Company Sources.

1. Antler King—www.antlerking.com
2. Buck Forage Products—www.buckforage.com
3. Deer Creek Seed Company—www.deercreek.com
4. Elk Mound Seed Company—www.elkmoundseed.com
5. Evolved Harvest - www.evolved.com
6. Ernst Seeds—www.ernstseed.com
7. Frigid Forage—www.sunrichfarm.com
8. Hancock Seed Co.—www.hancockseed.com
9. Preferred Seed Company—www.preferredseed.com
10. Seedland. Inc.—www.seedland.com
11. Thunder Ridge's www.huntingplots.com
12. Welter Seed & Honey Co.—www.welterseed.com
13. Whitetail Institute of North America—www.whitetailinstitute.com

▲ A planting of Ridgeline Summer Draw on our land. Ridgeline is a high-protein annual blend of forage soybeans, sunn hemp, peas, sunflower, forage buckwheat, and Teosenti (a Mexican grass) from huntingplots.com. It is a highly attractive warm-season planting from May into early fall. Photo: PCFImages

▲ Companies like Whitetail Institute, Mossy Oak, Antler King, Huntingplots.com, and many others provide seed mixes with different maturity rates to provide apex attractiveness, nutritional value, and production. Photo: Whitetail Institute

▲ Many of the crops often planted in food plots to attract deer also attract geese and other waterfowl. A few of these crops include corn, several varieties of millets, and grasses like timothy. Credit: PCFImages

Chapter Twenty-Six

Plantings for Wild Turkeys, Waterfowl, and Upland Birds

Most of the plantings included to this point have *primarily* focused on crops for whitetails and other species of deer. There are many other plantings you can add to your wildlife management program to attract other types of game such as wild turkeys, the largest and most popular hunted upland bird, most other upland birds, and waterfowl. Below are some plants that these gamebirds prefer.

WILD TURKEY

The wild turkey (*Meleagris gallopavo*) has a firm grip on North American hunters. As any turkey hunter will confess, hearing a longbeard gobbling from a ridgetop to a hen in the valley below can send goosebumps along a grown man's arm.

There are many crops that draw wild turkeys to food plots in the spring and fall. They include chufa, corn,

▲ If you hunt wild turkeys, you are among about 2.5 million hunters who pursue them. In fact, the wild turkey is the second-most sought-after game after whitetails. Sow what they like most, and they will come! Photo: Arrow Seed

sorghum, all the small grains, sunflowers, cowpeas, millets, buckwheat, nuts, acorns, and even fallen ripe fruits. Of these plants, there are a few that are highly sought after by wild turkeys and are magnets to draw them to your land.

CHUFA

Chufa is a perennial sedge plant that produces a nut-like seed on its root system that is like a peanut. It also is among the most preferred forage foods of wild hogs. Chufa plants have underground tubers, which are the part of the plant that turkeys eat. A single chufa tuber will produce a plant that can grow 15 to 75 additional underground tubers.

Once chufa matures, turkeys locate the underground tubers by scratching the surface to get at them. Tubers provide considerable amounts of protein and fat, making them particularly nutritious forage for turkeys. So, this plant is a prime choice for wildlife managers who want to manage and attract turkeys to their lands.

Sometimes it may take turkeys a season to discover that they like chufa. The quickest way to get turkeys familiar with this planting is to turn the soil over lightly, exposing the tubers. This helps to "teach" wildlife the benefits of eating this valuable plant. Always check your game laws first, before turning the soil to expose the chufa tubers. This tactic may not be legal in some states.

Chufa can be planted from late April to mid-August throughout the country. Some say the plant will reseed, making it a potential biennial planting. The best experience I have had with planting chufa, however, has been to replant it each spring. For best success, plan to sow at least ½-acre or more.

Chufa can grow in a variety of several types of soils, but it performs best when planted in well-drained, sandy, or loamy soils. Clay soil can support chufa but only when it is not pure heavy clay soil. Generally, chufa will grow anywhere that corn or grain sorghum (a.k.a. milo) can be successfully grown. Chufa also benefits ducks and deer. The Condensed Recap of chufa can be found in Chapter 22, "Additional Plantings."

Other plantings that are highly sought after and preferred by turkeys include sunflowers, buckwheat,

▲ The plant in the middle is chufa. It will attract wild turkeys on a day-to-day basis from spring until late fall. Chufa ranks as the number one choice planting for wild turkeys (followed closely by corn, sorghum, any of the other small grains, buckwheat, sunflowers, and millets). Photo: Hancock Seed

▲ Once chufa matures, it turns brown. That is when turkeys eat it most. Wild turkeys feed on it throughout late fall and winter. Chufa should be replanted each year, but it is possible to get a second year's growth, but only if the turkeys do not eat it all. Photo: NWTF

all the small grains, including the summer and winter varieties of wheat, barley, oats, triticale, and cereal rye. Other good choices for turkeys include spring and winter-hardy plantings of bird's-foot trefoil, red and crimson clover, alfalfa, and other legumes. Turkeys also go bonkers for all types of wild berries, as well as any type of ripe fruit that falls to the ground.

In the fall, they will actively seek out standing or cut corn, forage sorghum, and soybean fields. They will peck at the corn cob while it is on the plant or peck up all the leftover kernels, seeds, or beans on the ground after harvest. They will also consume the heads of milo on or off the plant. Wild turkeys will remain close by any harvested grainfield and visit it daily, sometimes 3 or 4 times a day, until they have consumed every kernel of corn, sorghum seed head, sunflower seed, etc.

However, while chufa and the other plants mentioned are preferred by turkeys, one of their most sought-after of all food stuffs are berries. Any land and wildlife manager looking for a plant specifically to attract turkeys should be sure to plant the highly nutritious and incredibly attractive berry bushes. Wild turkeys will come from all points of the compass to browse on berry-type plants including blackberry, raspberry, bayberry, elderberry, highbush, and cranberry. Any type of berry is an important planting that will help to complete even the most inclusive food plot program. An excellent source to purchase berry plants is the Willis Orchard Company.

OTHER UPLAND GAMEBIRDS

Almost all the other smaller upland gamebirds—including pheasants, quail, grouse, partridges, chukars, doves, and even rock pigeons—are attracted to most of the same wildlife food plot plantings that wild turkeys find appealing. Each species does have a favorite plant that it finds more attractive than others, though. Following are some favorite foods of the other upland birds.

Ring-necked Pheasant—Other than the wild turkey, the most widely hunted upland gamebird in the United States is the ring-necked pheasant. Recent figures show hundreds of thousands of licensed pheasant hunters took 829,500 of these cackling beauties in crop fields across the country during autumn and winter. Flushing a ringneck from a standing field of corn can weaken even the most experienced upland hunter's knees, and have him whispering, "Come to me, come to me!"

▲ While pheasants will eat anything they can peck at, they are attracted to the short varieties of corn, sorghum, and black sunflowers. Any of these three crops will draw in pheasants as regular diners. Photo: PCFImages

Some of the ring-necked pheasant's favorite foods are tall grain sorghum and the short WGF sorghum varieties, tall and short varieties of corn and sunflowers (as one group), all the other small grains, and buckwheat. Truth be told, pheasant food consists of anything they can peck at, even if the food is not good for them. If you are a dedicated pheasant hunter, you may want to join Pheasants Forever to support their conservation of pheasants and quail. Their website has custom blends for pheasants, doves, turkeys, upland birds, waterfowl (and even deer). www.pheasantsforever.org. It's a terrific organization that deserves support from all hunters.

▲ Grouse are birds of the woodlands. To improve grouse hunting, prune and fertilize wild bramble bushes. If you do not have a lot of wild berry shrubs, plant some, as grouse are attracted to all types of berries. They also favor corn, sorghum, and fallen ripe fruits. Photo: © Shawn Milne | Dreamstime

Grouse—Favorite food plot plantings are grains, millets, and fallen ripe fruits.

Quail—Brown and Japanese millet, sorghum, buckwheat, and sesame.

Dove—Among their favorite foods are dove proso millet, black sunflowers, Japanese millet, Browntop millet, and sorghum.

Partridge—All grains, particularly wheat and corn, sunflower, and sorghum.

Chukar—Perennial grasses, sunflower, and all lightheaded sorghums.

WATERFOWL

According to the U.S. Fish and Wildlife Service, in 2020 there were 989,500 active waterfowl hunters in the United States. Hunting for ducks and geese has become an immensely popular pastime for hunters. Calling back a flock of passing ducks is exhilarating, but even more exciting is watching a retriever jump into a frigid body of water to bring back a fallen duck. Both ducks and geese have their preferred foods, and they share some of the favorite plantings listed below.

▲ Millets are popular plants to sow to attract waterfowl. The two best varieties are Japanese and browntop millets. They are relatively inexpensive and easy to grow. Corn is also a top choice as it provides waterfowl quick amounts of energy, particularly in frigid temperatures. Photo: PCFImages

Ducks—Wild rice, Japanese, Browntop, and other millets, smartweed, buckwheat, and lightheaded sorghum.
Geese—Corn, all grains—particularly barley; smartweed, German, Browntop, Japanese and foxtail millets, and grasses, especially timothy.

WILD RICE (*Zizania palustris L*)

Wild rice is often thought of as a grain, but it is not. It is a North American long-grain marsh grass. Wild rice is an incredibly attractive food plot planting for all game including waterfowl, upland birds, and even deer. Mallards, pintails, teal, and geese will fly long distances to a wild rice marsh or food plot. In the fall the ducks find the ripened seed that has fallen into the water. The wild rice also provides a hiding place among the plant's tall growth. A pond planted with wild rice

▲ The absolute best plant to attract ducks is wild rice. Ducks will fly in from every direction to dine on wild rice. It creates a permanent feeding area that attracts ducks and geese until they have consumed the entire planting. Photo: River Refuge Seed

can be a permanent feeding area for waterfowl. As a food plot for waterfowl there is nothing that attracts ducks and geese more than wild rice. It produces more than 2,000 lbs./acre of seed for ducks and other gamebirds to eat.

While wild rice is mostly planted in water, it can just as easily be planted on dry land to attract game. This versatile food plot seed can be sown into a prepared seedbed. So, if it is ducks, particularly mallards, you are after, you will do best by sticking with one of the most popular wet-soil crops around—wild rice. Wild rice seed typically matures in 75 days.

As favorite foods of the above birds, all the plantings discussed will attract them to your property on a regular basis in the fall. Many of these plants can be sown as pure stands. However, many seed companies have developed proprietary blends specific to the bird species.

With more than 75 varieties of native wetland seeds, River Refuge Seed is my go-to source for waterfowl and upland bird food plot plantings—www.riverrefugeseed.com. Other seed companies with gamebird

blends include Nature's Seed (www.naturesseed.com); Hancock Seed (www.hancockseed.com); Deer Creek Seed (www.deercreekseed.com); Kester's Wild Game Food Nurseries, Inc., www.kestersnursery.com; Pheasants Forever (www.pheasantsforever.com) and Seedland (www.seedland.com). The fact is many seed companies today carry mixed blends of seeds to either attract waterfowl or upland birds.

POTHOLES

When it comes to attracting waterfowl, all other upland birds, small game and all big game, if practical and affordable, it is highly beneficial to create a small pond when developing a wildlife management plan. If it is not in your budget, however, an alternate plan would be to build several small potholes in different areas on your property. The most cost-effective way to do this is to hire a backhoe operator for a half-day. You will be amazed how many potholes a skilled backhoe operator can dig in that amount of time. Another option is to rent a tiny backhoe and dig your own small pothole-sized watering holes. If you don't know how to operate a

▲ This is a pond we put in as part of Natural Resources Conservation Service (NRCS) and the U.S. Department of Agriculture (USDA). The ponds were part of the wetland program which provides funds to build large or small ponds as waterfowl habitat. Photo: PCFImages.

backhoe, it doesn't take much to learn how to dig out several 12 by 12 by 2 foot deep or larger potholes.

A watering pothole doesn't have to be large to supply a water source for upland birds, small game, waterfowl, and deer. Potholes are nothing more than depressions in the ground with the sides draining to a slightly deeper center area. They fill from rainwater, water that is just below the surface, and from springs. A wildlife pothole that is about 3 feet in diameter and 6 to 12 inches deep will attract different types of wildlife. Of course, if you can double the size of the diameter and the depth, your potholes will be even more attractive to all sorts of amphibious wildlife, too. Small potholes also attract waterfowl, particularly wood ducks.

The best locations to place tiny watering potholes are in areas where the soil tends to hold water more effectively. To prevent potholes from filling with soil or

getting too many nutrients in them, it is important to build them in places where they won't receive direct runoff from surrounding areas. This is particularly true for larger-sized potholes than mentioned above. By simply planting grass around the edges of the pothole and letting it grow, the grass will act as a filter and remove sediment and unwanted nutrients, helping to keep the pothole water clean and clear.

CREATE FOOD AND COVER
Create thick, low cover throughout your property by planting a variety of shrubs. One choice is highbush cranberry, which is valued by game- and non-game-birds alike. Another good choice is elderberry, which not only provides an excellent food source, but also grows in thick clusters and up to 15 feet tall. Bristly locust is a fast-growing shrub that reaches heights

▲ Even a small, shallow, hand-dug, ten-by-ten-foot watering hole will provide water for deer. Many times, wood ducks use small waterholes, especially if they are made in the woods. Photo: © Mikael Males | Dreamstime

of 10 to 12 feet. Its bristly branches and pods make excellent cover. Lespedeza bicolor is a large, leguminous shrub that grows to about 10 feet high. It will provide food and shelter for pheasants, grouse, quail, and other gamebird species as well as deer and small game. There are many more types of shrubs to choose from as well.

▲ A variety of elderberry called Nova makes a thick compact bush. It produces fruits sweeter than other elderberry varieties. It is said to be self-fertile, but I have noticed that it grows denser and produces heavier crops when planted with another variety for cross pollination. Photo: © Wirestock | Dreamstime

By including the recommendations in this chapter, you will enhance your upland gamebird, small game, waterfowl habitat, and natural propagation exponentially. You will also ensure yourself top-quality hunting opportunities for these game animals for many years to come.

▲ To consistently attract adult bucks to your property, create as much cover as is practical. Photo: Deposit Photos

▼ Where the variety of forage is available, deer can eat several hundred different plant species over the course of a year. When supplementing the natural forage on your land, be sure to select varieties that are native to your area. Photo Credit: Canstock Photo

Chapter Twenty-Seven

Brambles, Shrubs, and Vines for Food and Cover

Believe it or not, an important food plot strategy is locating and identifying naturally growing native plants that deer prefer on your property. Big-game animals live predominantly in woodlands. They need 4 elements: water, food, cover, and land to roam. As a food plot and land manager you can provide nutritious plantings to a wide diversity of animals. Whether you have a couple of acres or 1,000 or more acres, you can enhance existing or buy new inexpensive brambles, shrubs, and vines on your land to improve your wildlife's habitat.

All species of deer browse on brambles, shrubs, and vines. All upland birds, waterfowl, and small game animals also eat these types of plantings. This can be done mostly with the brambles, but also with some wild grape and other vines and shrubs. When these wild-growing forages are improved by fertilizing and pruning, it creates a complete and attractive food plot program for deer and other wildlife.

▲ All types of big game, including elk like this bull, eat berry-producing brambles. Photo: Fiduccia Ent

For instance, over the last 21 years I have planted at least one or more berry brambles a year to complement the wild berry brambles on my land. This single tactic is a key component to successful deer hunting, mostly because these types of plants can be grown along the edges of woods and even within woodlots. Therefore, it is important to understand the preferred naturally growing forages deer eat that are available on your property.

Deer eat about 10 pounds of different foods a day. What can be revealing is that deer food research has documented that deer eat several hundred plant species over the course of a full season. Many deer foods are eaten by deer regardless of the time of the year. Other foods are sought by deer during specific times, and some are only eaten when food sources are scarce.

Some favorite wild-growing foods include well-known items like acorns, fruits, nuts, herbs, forbs, grasses, sedges, leaves, twigs, mushrooms, and many types of agricultural crops. But what often goes overlooked is that all species of deer browse heavily on different brambles, shrubs, and vines. They use these plants mostly for food, but also for cover. Cover protects deer from predators and foul weather elements. Plantings that provide food as well as cover for deer and other wildlife are top-grade plantings.

WHAT ARE SHRUBS, VINES, AND BRAMBLES?
A shrub is also known as a bush (the latter term is generally used as a gardening phrase). But often the terms are interchangeable. A shrub is generally characterized as a woody plant that has several perennial stems and generally does not exceed about 12 feet in height. A shrub's stems usually do not get bigger than 3 inches in diameter. Part of the shrub group also includes what

▲ This shrub grows to about 15 feet tall. Deer do not eat the arrowwood fruit but use the shrub for cover and bedding. Credit: © Gerald D. Tang | Dreamstime

is termed dioecious shrubs, which include smaller growing trees.

Vines are any plant with a climbing growth habit. It generally is a woody-stemmed plant with runners usually of the grape family. Wild grape vines make excellent forage for deer. Other vines include greenbrier. They do best when planted in areas with a lot of second-growth (young) trees. The grape vine sends up a main stem that branches out and uses the young tree as a trellis. Grape vines grow into the tops of trees by growing up with the tree or by growing into the canopy from a neighboring tree. If you plant grape vines or manage wild ones, make sure you prune them to improve the grape production and to prevent them from overcoming the tree. Keep the vine at a practical height to avoid it growing so tall that it eventually becomes impractical to prune it.

A bramble is any rough, tangled, prickly plant generally within the genus *Rubus*. There are so many berries that fall into this grouping that it staggers the imagination. Some sources refer to the bramble fruits containing more than 200 species. The more popular bramble fruits include raspberries, dewberries, cloudberries, boysenberries, and blackberries. There are many varieties including Darrow berry, Blue Ray berry, Duke raspberry, Spartan blueberry, and more. As discriminating feeders, whitetails choose these wild-growing native plants with discerning selectiveness. Brambles are my favorite wild plants to fertilize and prune. I try to create thickets of diverse types of brambles to attract deer to certain areas. I also plant a few new brambles every

year to compliment the wild brambles on my land. Extra care goes into my wild and nursery planted brambles because I know deer love eating their fruit berry, *berry* much.

Many wild plants like wild grapes, blackberry, red raspberry, dewberry, and blueberry bushes, can be found in abundance on some properties. With a little pruning and fertilizing (NPK 4-3-4), these wild, edible vines, bushes, and brambles will produce substantial crops of nutritious, highly preferred forage for deer.

When a property does not include these types of wild berry plants, adding extra nursery-grown varieties will help to create an ecological explosion of food items. Each of the berries have different varieties as well. Do not buy the miniature varieties as they will only grow a few feet tall. Non-miniature types of berry bushes can grow up to 12 feet tall, albeit most peak at about 8 feet. In the spring, clusters of blossoms are pollinated by honeybees.

▲ Most berry bushes are favorite foods of deer and a wide variety of other hunted and non-hunted animals. They eagerly seek out elderberries, blackberries, holly berries, blueberries, winterberries, mulberries, and other berry-producing plants. Photo: Deposit Photo

When planning this type of habitat project, it is always better to include species that are native to a specific area. Native plants tend to grow better than introduced species because they have evolved under local growing conditions. They are also less prone to diseases, and once established, they require less attention than non-native species. Remember that you are not planting a landscape around your home. It is a habitat improvement design you are seeking. This means that they should be sown in a random arrangement. You can include a diverse array of shrubs, bushes, small cover type trees, vines, grasses, and even wildflowers. A valuable group within these plantings will be to include all the major fruiting brambles like bayberry, elderberries, blackberries, boysenberries, dewberries, and other types of berries.

Most deciduous shrubs, vines, and brambles can also be planted along the edges of fields, riparian zones, and brushy areas. These versatile plantings can be purposely grown by food plotters along the edges of woodlots, in deep woods near treestands, in clear cuts, logged zones, burned-out areas, and other landscapes.

No matter where you sow many of these plantings across the country, all species of deer, wild turkeys, bears, other big game, waterfowl, upland birds, small game, and a wide variety of other wildlife eat most of the flowering or fruiting shrubs, vines, and brambles listed here.

▲ Many of the shrubs are used by deer primarily for food. However, they commonly use some mostly for cover, bedding, and for fawning. Photo: © Gerald Tang | Dreamstime

Do not forget that one of the most crucial elements to planting brambles, vines, and shrubs is to also create cover. The denser the cover you create, the better it will serve your hunting purposes. By including these types of plants in your food plot program, not only will you provide all the benefits mentioned, but you will also experience a dramatic uptick in the numbers of deer you see on your property.

American Holly (*Ilex opaca*): The American holly's fruit is eaten mostly by gamebirds and songbirds. It does not rank high on the list of deer-preferred shrubs. Therefore, hollies are browsed by deer mostly when winter limits other available foods. However, this plant makes excellent cover for deer and larger game as it grows as understory in woodlands. The height of American holly (and most of the 6 other types of holly) ranges from 25 to 60 feet. A shorter multi-tipped trunked form may grow when holly is planted in lower-light areas. This is an ideal plant to create as a hedge, to make a windbreak tall hedge, or a thick area for cover for deer and other game. It also makes a particularly good protective shelter as well. It typically grows as an understory tree in forests. American holly is rare in the north of its range in southern Connecticut, southeastern New York, and isolated areas of Cape Cod. The branches are short and slender. The roots are thick and fleshy. It will even grow in swampy soil, but it does so slowly. Holly likes soils that are 6.0 and higher. The flowers are pollinated by bees and other insects. The berries are said to be poisonous to humans but are important as a survival food for upland game and song-birds that eat the berries after other food sources are exhausted. The tree also forms a thick canopy that offers protection for birds from predators and storms. Since deer *don't* eat any part of holly, it should only be considered as a cover type plant that deer can use to get out of inclement weather, to hide from predators, to bed in, and as a windbreak. USDA planting zone rating 5–9.

▲ Like this American holly, many of the brambles and shrubs provide food, shelter from the elements, and cover from predators. Photo: Deposit Photo

Arrowwood Viburnum (*Viburnum dentatum*): A multi-stemmed, rounded shrub that grows 6 to 15 feet with a comparable spread. It forms dense thickets and provides excellent cover for deer and nesting sites for birds. Birds consume the abundant fruits. Deer do not eat the fruit of arrowwood but use the shrub for cover and as bedding. It has creamy white late spring or early summer flowers. Arrowwood leaves are lustrous, dark green in the summer, changing to yellow to glossy red and reddish- purple in the fall. Flowers are followed by ½-inch blue-black berries that ripen in early fall. It prefers well-drained soils and full sun to partial shade. USDA Hardiness Zones 3–9.

Azalea (*Rhododendron*): The evergreen azaleas are ornamental plantings that people often use with their landscaping around the house. But azalea can also be used by food plotters to attract deer to woodland areas. They grow from 4 to 10 feet tall. Fortunately, azalea shrubs are very desirable to deer, even though the plant is poisonous when eaten in substantial amounts to most mammals. Pinxter bloom (also a rhododendron) is also edible to deer despite it being poisonous to mammals. Although there are many deer-resistant flowering shrubs, azaleas are not one of them. In fact, azaleas are a go-to snack for deer, particularly white-tailed deer. Evergreen azaleas are rated as "frequently severely damaged" by deer, according to Rutgers University. Deciduous azaleas are slightly less delicious to deer. That is mostly because deciduous azaleas do not retain their tasty leaves throughout the winter. Deer also use groves of rhododendron to hide and bed down in. Planting a dozen or so azaleas can quickly attract deer as a source of food, shelter, safety, and bedding. USDA Hardiness Zones 5–8.

Bayberry (*Myrica pensylvanica*): The mature height of the bayberry is 6 to 9 feet. Very aromatic, it will grow in a wide variety of site conditions from sandy, poor soils to heavy clay soils. These are plants that enjoy extremes, as they also prefer bogs, marshland, and wet woodlands. They grow in areas along roadsides, on sand dunes near mid-Atlantic beaches, and in old, abandoned fields. Although deer don't find the bayberry fruit attractive, it is a good choice to plant as cover for deer and other wildlife. Bayberry bushes

▲ Bayberry is a deer-resistant shrub. Its fragrance deters deer from eating the fruit. However, bayberry's growth habit is rounded, and the branches fill in densely, providing excellent cover for deer and other wildlife. Photo: Deposit Photo

are tough, hardy plants that have pleasantly scented foliage and berries. They are native to the continental United States and grow vigorously along the eastern coast and throughout the South. Bayberry shrubs are also known as candleberry, tallow shrub, waxberry, and tallow berry. They make excellent hiding, bedding, and cover for deer and other wildlife. USDA Hardiness Zones 3a—8b.

Blackberry (*Rubus fruticosus*): This is a favorite berry of humans, deer, and other wildlife. Deer will eagerly consume the tasty, purplish-black fruit of the blackberry even though the bush is covered with tiny, sharp thorns. Deer can still pick every berry from the plant. Blackberries are quick growing. They like at least 6 hours of full sun. Some species of blackberries are said to be aggressive, and have consequently been placed on certain states' invasive species list. Blackberries provide outstanding health benefits from the fruits they produce for deer and other wildlife. The delicious fruits contain a lengthy list of desirable nutrients such as vitamins, minerals, anti-oxidants, and dietary fibers. Blackberries are easy to grow and will grow very well in acidic soils. Therefore, for best growth and fruit production, be sure to plant them in soils with acidic pH levels. They also thrive and produce best in well-drained soils. Most blackberry plants are thorny, although some plant nurseries, like Nature Hills, offers thornless varieties, making it easier for both humans

▲ Even though the stems of blackberry bushes are covered in sharp thorns, animals carefully pick the fruit from the plant. Deer, elk, moose, Rocky Mountain sheep, and goats all consume the succulent, purplish-black fruit of the blackberry bush. All species of bears are particularly fond of blackberries. Photo: Deposit Photo.

and deer to pick off the berries. A few examples of thornless species of plants are Chester, Arapaho, and Triple Crown. Blackberries are self-fertile, so they do not need another pollinator to produce fruit. Since blackberries are great plants, plant several as your deer and other wildlife will feast on them until every single berry is exhausted. USDA Hardiness Zones 5–10.

Black Chokeberry (*Aronia melanocarpa*): Black Chokeberry is a cold-hardy, small to medium deciduous shrub that produces clusters of small white flowers that are attractive to deer, gamebirds, small mammals, songbirds, and honeybees. The berries are rich in antioxidants and they ripen into a black color in late summer. USDA Hardiness Zones 3–8.

Blueberries (*Vaccinium corymbosum*): Highbush blueberries can grow up to 6 to 12 feet tall. There are a few different varieties of blueberries, but highbush grow the tallest. Their height makes them an excellent choice for wind breaks and so on. Deer feed on blueberry shrubs with gusto. Blueberry bushes are high in essential vitamins, such as vitamin C. Deer relish these high-energy fruits and are known to deplete the berry crop, post haste. While deer tend to eat only the fruit of blueberry bushes, they will eat young plants if particularly hungry and cause damage to mature plants when they rub the branches. Blueberries will serve as an excellent food-plot-type plant, a wind breaker and a plant that will provide some cover for deer if several shrubs are planted near each other. USDA plant hardiness zones 5–8.

Blueberry Elder (*Sambucus canadensis*): Deer feed on nearly every variety of berries. One fruit that they sometimes eat is the blueberry elder, a wild plant that can also be purchased from greenhouses and online nurseries. It prefers full sun and moist soil and spreads quickly. Plants can grow up to 12 to 15 feet tall, making them the king of all berry shrubs as far as height goes. This is truly a shrub that is meant for the wild. Blueberry elder bushes should be planted in long rows to offer the maximum in cover for deer. Native to eastern North America, the blueberry shrubs thrive in moist, acid soil. USDA Hardiness Zones 3–11.

Beach Plum (*Prunus maritima*): A native shrub of the Atlantic coastal region, the beach plum is a round, dense bush that grows 4 to 10 feet tall. It prefers sandy, well-drained soils and full sun, and has edible fruit that grows 1 to 1½ inches long. It is a good cover plant. Beautiful white blossoms cover the branches of this shrub-like tree in the spring. The blossoms develop into colorful fruits that all wildlife will eat, including deer, bears, turkeys, and upland gamebirds. The fruit is popular among people who gather it to make delicious jams and jellies. It may be bluish purple, red, or even yellow when it ripens in September. The beach plum flourishes in the poorest soils imaginable. It is so hardy that it tolerates long droughts, sub-zero cold, and most diseases. It is a plant that will work well in

▲ Beach plum is a favorite fruit of deer. The taste is a cross between a plum and a prune with a heady tang and an especially deep flavor. It prefers sandy soil. Deer, bears, turkeys, and other upland birds eat the fruit. Photo: © Maria1986nyc | Dreamstime

any management program. Usually, it bears its fruit the year following its planting. USDA Hardiness Zone 3a–8a.

Beautyberry (*Callicarpa americana var. lacteal*): This shrub typically grows 4 to 5 feet tall and wide, although it has been known to reach 9 feet in height. It's known for its bright purple berries that grow around the plant's stems in plump clusters. In some parts of the South beautyberry is an important deer food. Whitetails will eat the plant's stems, leaves, and fruit particularly when preferred foods start to become less available. Beautyberries remain on the shrub well into winter. American beautyberry is useful as a large understory shrub with a naturally loose form. Deer will also use clusters of this shrub to hide and bed down in. It is useful as a screen in swampy or wooded locations or under larger shade trees in woodland settings. A single shrub can be left to mature naturally into a tall woody shrub. This plant is a native of the southern United States. It grows fast in full sun or partial shade, is tolerant of different soils, and is reasonably drought tolerant. This fruit is an important food for many species of non-hunted birds including robins, brown thrashers, cardinals, towhees, mockingbirds, finches, and woodpeckers. Other animals that also eat the fruit include bears, foxes, raccoons, squirrels, opossum and, of course, deer. USDA Hardiness Zones 3–11.

▲ Beauty Berry ranks high on the list as an important deer food. White-tailed deer eat the plants stems, leaves, and fruit. One reason the berries are a valuable food source is because they remain on the shrub well into winter. Photo: © Dan Rieck | Dreamstime

Boyne Raspberry (*Rubus idaeus*): The Boyne raspberry may be a top performer when it comes to its berry production. Boyne produces massive crops, but it also boasts superb disease resistance. It thrives despite the cold and comes back in the spring ready to bear a large crop of brilliant berries. Plant these highly productive berries along your fence lines, or at the edge of an impenetrable wooded area. The Boyne raspberry thrives in full sun or partial shade. It is an early ripening berry. This boisterous berry ripens in early summer and tastes amazing to both deer, bears and other wildlife as well as humans. Each berry is remarkably sweet and aromatic. Luckily, the Boyne raspberry produces a lot of berries. By the way, save some of these raspberries to eat at home. They are super delicious.

Common Buttonbush (*Cephalanthus occidentalis*): Common buttonbush is a wetland shrub that grows in swamps, floodplains, marshes, bogs, and ditches. It can even tolerate growing underwater for part of the year, or in areas with intermittent flooding. Waterfowl and shorebirds consume the seeds of common buttonbush. White-tailed deer browse foliage in the northeastern United States. Wood ducks use the plant's structure for protection of brooding nests. Butterflies, bees, and hummingbirds are attracted to common buttonbush for its nectar. This is a large, woody shrub, 6 to 12 feet tall,

that has a flower that forms a ball-like seed cluster that is approximately 1 inch in diameter. Showy flowers and fruit make common buttonbush a popular choice for use in native shrub borders. USDA Hardiness Zones 5 to 9.

Dewberries (*Rubus trivialis*): Dewberry plants grow like shrubs. The berries of dewberry plants are purplish red, like raspberries. Growing dewberry plants

▲ Dewberries have smaller fruit and grow with trailing stems along the ground, Deer will eat the berries, and browse the new plant growth in the spring when the leaves and stems are tender. Photo: © Annalevan | Dreamstime

attain a height of only about 2 feet or so and have slender thorns. Grown in the wild, dewberries tend to be slightly more acidic than other berries. Dewberries make good plantings for bears and deer because they have large lateral growing root systems that spread and interconnect, creating perennial thickets. They need several hours of direct sun each day. Dewberries will grow best when planted along the edges of fields near woods or overgrown areas. In a few short years they develop into thick patches of thickets that will offer wildlife cover and a nutritious food source. Like other shrubs, dewberry plants can be obtained as seedlings or cuttings from a local nursery, or from your wild patch of dewberries after a couple of years. USDA Hardiness Zones 3–7.

Eastern Dogwood (*Cornus florida*): This is a valuable shrub for wildlife because its high calcium and fat content makes it palatable. In May, the copious white flowers are stunningly attractive. Eastern dogwood is an extremely hardy species. It can succeed in any soil of good or moderate fertility and can withstand temperatures down to –13°F. The wood is heavy, strong, and extremely shock-resistant. The fruits, seeds, flowers, and twigs of this tree are an extremely valuable food source to many species of wildlife, including deer, black bears, turkeys, grouse, pheasants, rabbits, beavers, squirrels, and many other non-hunted species of birds and other wildlife. However, the seeds of this tree are poisonous to humans. Dogwood provides excellent shelter and habitat for deer and other game. USDA Hardiness Zones 5–8.

Eastern Red Cedar (*Juniperus virginiana*): This is a columnar-shaped tree that, when grown in groups, can reach heights of 30 to 50 feet. Eastern Red Cedar prefers open, well drained sites. Its twigs and foliage are readily eaten by all species of deer. The tree bears a small blue berry on females, providing food for all types of game and non-hunted animals. Male trees bear a tiny cone. Cedar provides important nesting and security coverage for deer and other wildlife. Their dense foliage protects deer and other game from foul weather and cold temperatures and helps them escape detection from predators, especially in large stands of cedar. Oftentimes, male deer prefer to rub their antlers on cedar tree trunks. USDA Hardiness Zones 2–9.

Elderberry (*Sambucus nigra*): Elderberry is a native shrub of North America that grows up to 15 to 20 feet in height in moist, organic soils. The fruit is dark purple to black and about 1/8-inch in size. Elderberries are relished by many gamebirds, deer, bears, and other mammals. Deer also eat the twigs and leaves. Elderberry is a fast grower and aggressive competitor with weeds and herbaceous species. Individual plants don't live exceptionally long; however, root masses produce new shoots quickly. Elderberry as a wildlife plant should not be pruned or cut. Pruning will prevent it from growing wild and gnarly, which creates the type of coverage deer and other wildlife use as security. This forest species will grow in full sun if the soil is well-tilled and watered. It can be planted as a hedge or alone. Elderberry provides effective erosion control on moist sites. The berries grow in clusters and its large, flat-topped, white flowers are edible for humans and used for making jams, pies, or wine. Deer and other wildlife seek this plant out for both food and cover. **WARNING:** Elderberry plant parts are toxic to humans and animals; they are especially dangerous for children. USDA Hardiness Zones 3–8.

Gray Dogwood (*Cornus racemose*): Gray dogwood is a very adaptable, native shrub that is excellent for establishing in difficult riparian areas of pond and stream banks. Its suckering, spreading habit makes it practical for a wildlife planting as shrub borders and useful as a general mass planting. It is a wide upright shrub that grows from 10 to 15 feet high, creating large thickets. Gray dogwood grows in full sun in wet or dry sites but does better in well-drained soils. It is tolerant of heavy shade, which makes it a candidate for planting in the woods as excellent cover for deer. It is also a terrific plant as a screen or to use along ponds and stream banks. Creamy white clusters of flowers in May are followed by white berries in late summer that are quickly eaten by nearly 100 species of gamebirds. It forms a dense thicket, providing cover and nesting sites for wildlife. Deer will use its thickets and mass for bedding sites, shelter, and seclusion from predators. USDA Hardiness Zones 3–8.

▲ Upland gamebirds feed heavily on the fruit and foliage of elderberry. Bears are highly attracted to eating elderberry fruits. Whitetails, elk, and moose browse mostly on the stems and foliage. Photo: © Mike Nettleship | Dreamstime

Highbush Cranberry (*Viburnum trilobum*): This is a favorite choice planting of mine. Highbush cranberry is a large, hardy, deciduous shrub with a growth rate of up to 3 feet per year. The plant will typically grow 10 to 15 feet tall and 8 to 10 feet wide with arching stems and a very dense, rounded form. These are all attributes that make highbush cranberry a popular wildlife landscaping choice for use as a screening hedge. The berry-like fruit can remain on the branches well into mid-winter. It is tolerant of frost. It does well in sun or semi-shaded areas. Highbush cranberry tolerates most soil types but does better in well-drained, moist soils that are rich and loamy. Established plants can tolerate drought, but not for extended periods of time. It will grow to create food, bedding, and cover large areas that will keep deer on your property. It bears a bright red, edible fruit in the fall that lasts well into winter. The fruit is eaten by many species including deer,

▲ High bush cranberry red fruits often last throughout the winter. It is said they may not be especially palatable for wildlife. However, they are known to be eaten by deer and moose, upland birds, and many small game animals. Photo: Deposit

bears, turkeys, rabbits, grouse, pheasants, squirrels, and many other non-hunted animals. Highbush cranberry prefers moist, well-drained, open sites. USDA Hardiness Zones 2–7.

Honeoye Strawberry (*Fragaria spp.*): Deer are extremely fond of all strawberries, be they wild or nursery-grown varieties. Honeoye strawberry is a top variety to plant for deer and other wildlife (including people). After the second year of planting, it produces a large-sized berry. They are so big that deer have no problems plucking them off the plant. Honeoye strawberries produce high yields over a long fruiting season.

Juneberry (*Amelanchier*): Juneberry is more commonly known as Saskatoon berry. Saskatoon berry is planted to produce fruit. Many cultivars are commercially available. You can select them for a desirable plant and/or fruit characteristic. **Human Alert**: The fruits are used in pies, jams, and fruit rolls and for making jelly and syrup. **Double Human Alert**: Juneberry makes a delicious wine. Native Americans ate the berries fresh and dried, often mixed with other foods for sweetening and flavor. But what about wildlife? Saskatoon is an attractive shrub. It is an important species for reclamation and to a lot of wildlife like deer, bears, wild turkeys and other upland birds, rabbits, squirrels, and a host of other non-hunted animals.

A typical juneberry is 18 percent sugar and about 80 percent water. Juneberries have relatively high amounts of calcium, natural fiber, proteins, carbohydrates, and lipids in them. It is said they are an excellent source of iron (about 23 percent RDA for iron—almost twice as much iron as blueberries). They contain elevated levels of phenolic compounds, particularly anthocyanins, and they provide healthy amounts of potassium, magnesium, and phosphorous. Juneberries have about as much vitamin C, thiamin, riboflavin, pantothenic

▲ Juneberry (a.k.a. Saskatoon berry, service berry) fruits are highly nutritious for deer and other wildlife. This shrub-like tree produces edible berries that look like blueberries. Juneberry berries are ideal to make jellies and jams. Photo: © Mykola Ohorodnyk | Dreamstime

acid, vitamin B-6, folate, vitamin A, and vitamin E as blueberries, and trace amounts of biotin. All this makes them an extremely healthy berry for wildlife and humans alike.

Native shrubs grow 23 feet high, forming thickets or clumps. They make great cover for deer and other wildlife when several are planted nearby each other. The underground portions include an extensive root system. Juneberries leaves are deciduous. The flowers are short and dense. The fruit is small, smooth, purple-black, and slightly gray-blue. The pulp is fleshy and sweet. Juneberries, like apples, are eaten by a lot of wildlife including songbirds, squirrels, wild turkeys, and, of course, deer love them. Even your dog will love eating Juneberries. USDA Hardiness Zones 4–8 (or 9 depending upon species).

Mulberry (*Morus rubra*): A.k.a. the fabled mulberry, this was cultivated deliberately for human use. Mulberry trees are found in many parts of the world and throughout most of the United States. Deer LOVE mulberries. They simply can't resist mulberry leaves and the tasty fruit. Deer will hone in on areas where

▲ Deer can't resist mulberry bushes. They will eat the leaves, green twigs, and the berries. When planting a mulberry bush (tree), it must be fenced off to prevent deer from stripping it bare. After a few years, the shrub will better tolerate browsing by deer and other wildlife. Photo: Nativ Nurseries

mulberry bushes or trees grow. Wildlife mulberry bushes and trees are also well liked by bears, elk, moose, wild turkeys, and other upland gamebirds and some waterfowl. The US Fish and Wildlife Service reports that mulberry is so well-liked by wildlife, that wildlife that many state game departments and other agencies have planted them in many wildlife refuges throughout the country. Mulberry bushes make an ideal berry bush or tree for any wildlife food plot program. Deer seem to crave the deep purple/black variety but will eat any color mulberry they find with gusto.

Mulberry is best grown in rich, moist, well-drained soils. It prefers full sun but will tolerate light shade. Mulberry should be pruned in late fall or winter for a good spring/summer crop. *Morus rubra*, commonly known as red mulberry, is a medium-sized, deciduous tree that typically grows 35 to 50 feet tall. It is native to rich woods, bottomlands, and wood margins from Massachusetts, southern Ontario, and Minnesota south to Florida and Texas. It is noted for its often-lobed leaves, milky sap, reddish-brown bark, and edible fruits. Trees are monoecious or dioecious. Lobed leaves are more frequently found on new shoots, while unlobed leaves are more frequently found in tree crowns. Their leaves turn yellow in the fall. Unisexual greenish flowers in small catkin-like spikes appear in early spring with male and female flowers usually appearing on separate trees (dioecious). Trees with only male flowers obviously never bear fruit. Fertilized female flowers are followed by sweet blackberry-like edible fruits (to 1 inch long) that are reddish to dark purple in color. Mulberries are sweet and juicy and may be eaten off the tree.

Nannyberry (*Viburnum lentago*): Nannyberry is a native understory shrub-like tree that can reach a height of 18 feet. It is a hardy, upright growing shrub with green foliage that turns reddish-purple in fall. The white flower clusters in spring mature into small blue-black fruit from September to October. They provide winter food for many types of birds and mammals. The nannyberry's twigs, bark, and leaves are eaten by deer and beaver. It is a thicket-forming shrub that provides important cover for deer and other wildlife. Nannyberry shrub can also be used for windbreaks, hedges, or as a screen. It prefers at least part sun and will tolerate shady sites. Nannyberry prefers loam soil with ample moisture. USDA Hardiness Zones 2 to 8.

Poison Ivy (*Toxicodendron radicans*): Many animals eat the plant and use it for shelter. When poison ivy flowers blossom, they attract many insect pollinators as well. Deer and black bears browse the leaves and stems of poison ivy. Deer depend on poison ivy leaves as an additional food source. For obvious reasons, food plotters pass on planting poison ivy. However, it may pay to leave a naturally growing bush or two on your land.

Prairie Willow (*Salix humilis*): Although this plant does not grow tall, it does grow thick. It is a medium-sized shrub, 3 to 9 feet tall. It will grow well on dryer sites in full sun. It prefers sandy, well-drained, open sites, but will tolerate partial shade. The best aspect of this plant is that it grows in thick clusters and makes exceptionally good visual barriers from the neighbors' place or along roads. It is also an excellent choice to create bedding areas for deer and other wildlife. USDA Hardiness Zones 4–6.

Pussy Willow (*Salix cinerea*): Pussy willow is a thin-branched, medium-sized shrub that will grow up to 20 feet tall. Pussy willows are versatile trees that thrive in poor soil and soggy ground. Although you can purchase a plant from nurseries, it is simple and more cost effective to grow a shrub from a cutting. Pussy willows grow rapidly and can become enormous making them good cover for deer. Pussy willows like wetter areas—marshes, stream banks, flooded ditches, or wet bottomlands—and are good for erosion control. Grown in thick, heavy stands, deer will use pussy willows as cover. Select a site for pussy willow that will attract deer. Keep in mind that the shrub can become quite large, and the roots spread rapidly. They make an ideal cover plant when establishing a refuge. USDA Hardiness Zones 4–8.

Raspberry (*Rubus leucodermis*): Black raspberries are native to North America. There are more than 200 species of raspberries with red, purple, black, yellow, and orange fruits. Raspberry bushes generally reach

heights of 4 to 6 feet, with 24- to 36-inch spreads. To maximize the berry harvest, the shrub should be regularly pruned. Deer, bears, and other wildlife are very fond of eating raspberries. Even though the stems of raspberry are covered in sharp thorns, deer can still carefully pick the fruit from the plant. The new growth on thorny varieties is palatable to deer. Once the thorns have hardened up, deer will still browse on the leaves, which do not have the big thorns. Deer are mostly interested in the soft new growth and tender leaves. All raspberries are self-fertile, so you only need one bush to produce fruit. Raspberry bushes are naturally inclined to grow in cooler climates. They grow best in a sunny position but, unlike many fruits, they will also grow successfully in a partially-shaded spot. The more sun, the more fruit. The planting site needs rich and well-drained soil. Avoid planting them in wet areas, as well as windy spots. Raspberries contain antioxidants and are rich in vitamin C. It is not a shrub to plant in woodlands or as cover for deer. Like all traditional food plot plants, it is simply another plant for deer to eat and benefit from. Raspberries will do best when planted at the edges of fields bordering woods, so long as they receive plenty of sunlight. If you plant raspberries, establish at least a few shrubs

▲ Deer are particularly fond of eating the tender new growth and the leaves of raspberry plants. They also dine on the berries. Bears, on the other hand, eat just the raspberries. Photo: PCFImages

per year in different areas. Within a few short years you should have several thick patches. **Human Alert**: Raspberries are very tasty as fresh fruit, and they make excellent jams, jellies, pies, and dessert toppings. You may find yourself fighting off the deer and bears for this yummy berry. Like the strawberry, the raspberry is not a berry at all. But again, deer will not care. USDA Hardiness Zones 5–10.

Red-Osier Dogwood (*Swida sericea*): This is a medium-sized shrub with numerous stems that grow between 3 to 19 feet tall. The fruit is preferred mostly by ruffed grouse, but turkeys will eat it as well. It is well-suited for wetter, open areas. It is good for erosion control, stream shade, and windbreaks. Deer will seek out dense stands of this plant for food and cover. USDA Hardiness Zones 2–8.

Rhododendron (*Rhododenron ferrugineum*): As anyone who has ever planted rhododendron around their house knows, deer love eating rhododendron. Once rhododendron matures, it creates thick stands of cover. Most rhododendron prefer to be near streams and in moist woodlands. Like other specific types of rhododendrons, they are all favorite shrubs for deer to browse in winter. Thick stands of rhododendron make particularly good hiding cover and bedding areas for deer. USDA Hardiness Zones 4–8.

Sandbar Willow (*Salix exigua*): This is a medium-sized shrub that offers terrific height, as it grows to 20 feet. It is often used for stream bank stabilization and riparian area restoration. It is a good plant for both food and cover for deer. The fruits of the sandbar willow provide important winter sustenance and shelter for deer, small game, and other wildlife. It can be planted almost anywhere and in any type of soil. The sandbar willow's red fruit is mostly eaten by wildlife throughout winter when they remain on the shrub. The fruit provides a needed food source when more desirable foods are scarce or dormant. Deer and rabbits eat the bark, fruits, and stems. Gamebirds such as grouse and turkeys rely heavily on the fruits, as do many winter songbirds. USDA Hardiness Zones 2–7.

▲ Sandbar willow provides superb shelter for many gamebirds and forage for deer. Credit: © Gerald D. Tang | Dreamstime

Canadian Serviceberry (*Amelanchier canadensis*): There are 9 species of serviceberry trees and shrubs. It is a woody, deciduous shrub native to the US. Shadbush is its common name since its flowering coincides with the annual migration of shad in Northeast and New England rivers. Serviceberry is an understory tree, often found growing in clumps in swamps, lowlands, and thickets at the edges of forests. In the Northeast, it is found growing in association with tupelo, speckled alder, poplar, hazel shrubs, white oak, red cedar, choke cherry, and bayberry. It has several smooth, gray trunks that grow to approximately 26 feet tall and 15 to 20 feet wide. They have berries that resemble blueberries and are consumed by deer, birds, and humans. The fruit is purplish-black, juicy, and sweet. It is technically a pome (like an apple or pear). Because serviceberry is an early blooming plant, it plays a vital role as a food source for pollinators like bees and butterflies. The fruit is eaten by songbirds, wild turkeys, squirrels, and deer. USDA Hardiness Zones 4–7.

▲ Canadian serviceberry is eaten by wild turkeys, other upland birds, rabbits, squirrels, and deer. Photo: © Nadmak2010 | Dreamstime

Silky Dogwood (*Cornus amomum*): The silky dogwood is a dense shrub. The stems and leaves of the silky dogwood are a favorite food source for deer, especially in the winter. Rabbits also eat the twigs. A variety of gamebirds, including wild turkeys, grouse, and wood-cock, eat the berries all winter long. The fruit stays on the tree for months after maturing. Migrating songbirds seek out the fruit too. Because it is so dense, the shrubs work well as windbreaks, or as thick screens of cover when planted in a row. Silky dogwood is good for riparian areas to control streamside erosion as well. USDA Hardiness Zones 5–8.

Snowberry (*Symphoricarpos*): Snowberry is a berry-producing shrub that attracts a lot of different wildlife other than deer. Hummingbirds love the flowers. Snowberries produce hummingbird- and butterfly-attracting tubular-shaped blooms that are followed by white, waxy berries. In the fall the white berries

▲ Snowberries remain on the branches almost the entire winter. They are an important source of food for wild turkeys and other upland birds, rabbits, and squirrels. Big game like deer, elk, and bears mostly eat the leaves of snowberry. Photo: © Jana Scigelova | Dreamstime

are an excellent food for other gamebirds like wild turkeys and grouse—and even songbirds. The berries hang on all season offering winter foods to wildlife. Snowberries grow to about 6 feet tall and provide cover from the elements for small game. White snowberry is a dense, twiggy shrub that spreads by suckers underground. This plant tolerates any type of soil. It should be planted where it can get sunlight part of the day. USDA Hardiness Zones 2–7.

Speckled Alder (*Alnus rugosa*): This is a clump-forming shrub or small tree that thrives in wet areas but will grow in upland soils if it has adequate moisture. If left to grow naturally, it forms a dense thicket which can be used as protective shelter by deer, moose, and rabbits. USDA Hardiness Zones 2-6.

Sumac (*Smooth Sumac-Rhus glabra and Staghorn Sumac—Rhus typhina*): This is a shrub commonly found in old fields and forest openings. It can grow to 20 feet high. Sumac has heavy, stiff, brown twigs and branches. The leaves are 12 to 16 inches long. They exude a white, sticky sap. In fall, sumac leaves turn bright red. The bark of the sumac is grayish brown and has rough and raised pores. Sumac flowers from May to July. The male and female flowers are found in dense bunches among branched clusters, mostly at the end of new growth. Sumac's fruit usually ripens in August or September. As young shrubs, many types of birds and small mammals use sumac to nest in or to hide their young. Sumac fruit is eaten by songbirds as well as gamebirds. Deer and cottontail rabbits also eat the bark and twigs. Deer use dense patches of sumac to seek shelter from inclement weather and to hide from predators. Most are hardy to USDA Hardiness Zone 3.

Thimbleberry (*Rubus parviflorus*): This berry bush grows to about 3 to 4 feet high, but when fertilized and pruned it can get as tall as 8 feet. Planting a few of them near each other can create good cover for deer. It is the soft-stemmed cousin of the blackberry bush. Thimbleberry thrives in shaded and moist areas and produces pink or white fragrant blooms. It can tolerate occasional flooding but tends to spread if not controlled. The brambles rank at the very top of summer foods for wildlife, especially upland and song-birds

and are highly sought after by deer, bears, and other mammals. Additionally, the leaves and stems are eaten extensively by deer and rabbits. The flowers are usually pollinated by insects. USDA Hardiness Zones 2–10.

Wild Grape (*Vitis vinifera*): While they prefer to be planted in rich woods and along stream banks, wild grape will grow almost anywhere it can get decent soil and 10 to 12 hours of sunlight. The more sun, the better. I like to make thick stands of this plant in overgrown fields and second-growth stands of woods. The fruit is favored by most wildlife including deer, wild turkeys, bears, and grouse. USDA Hardiness Zones 4–10.

▲ Whether wild or cultivated, grapes are a favorite of all deer and a wide variety of wildlife. I have seen foxes eating grapes. As part of a wildlife food plot, nursery grape vines must be managed with fencing for the first few years to give them a chance to mature so they can withstand deer browsing them. Photo: © Irina88w |Dreamstime

Wild Strawberry (*Fragaria vesca*): Strawberries are a delicious fruit highly sought after by deer and other wildlife. In fact, strawberries are the most popular berry of all the berries grown for wildlife—so much so that it is generally a hard plant to get started and one that is even more difficult to keep from being demolished by deer. If you grow strawberries for deer, you have too much time on your hands. Few things, however, are as attractive to deer as strawberries. Oh, by the way, strawberries are not berries. But deer don't care about that. I included them here because deer love to eat them. If you do grow them, you will have to fence off the entire strawberry patch for at least a couple years for the strawberry's runners to establish and overtake the fenced-in area. Even then, my bet is as soon as the fence is removed, so too will the strawberries be removed by deer, bears, wild turkeys, upland birds, gorillas, and anything else that has a mouth. USDA Hardiness Zones 5–10.

Winterberry (*Ilex verticillate*): Winterberry is a slow-growing shrub with a rounded upright growth habit. The leaves are dark green and elliptical, about 2 to 3 inches long. Winterberry shrubs typically grow in wetland areas, although they can be successfully cultivated elsewhere. However, if your land has some wet areas, you should take advantage of this shrub's native predisposition and plant it in such areas where it is difficult to grow most other plantings. Winterberry holly prefers acidic soils. It can be grown in partial shade or full sun.

▲ Winterberry is an attractive bright-red fruit eaten mostly by wild turkeys and other gamebirds. The leaves and stems of winterberry are not a preferred source of browse. Deer, moose, cottontail rabbits, and snowshoe hares also utilize this plant. Photo: © Virginialovejoy | Dreamstime

More sunlight will increase its berry production. The attractive red fruit of winterberry is eaten by small mammals and dozens of species of birds including upland birds. The leaves and stems of winterberry are not a preferred source of browse, but white-tail deer, moose, bears, cottontail rabbits, and snowshoe hares do occasionally browse on this plant. If you do plant winterberries, protect them for the first year until they get large enough to withstand getting browsed. It helps to plant a large group of winterberry plants. As a dioecious species, you will need both male and female cultivars that bloom at the same time to produce fruit. It is possible to use 1 male plant to 4 to 5 female plants in a group setting. It typically grows 3 to 15 feet tall and uses its suckers to form large thickets in woodlands and/or border screens making it an important consideration for food plotters. It is a terrific addition to any wildlife landscape plan. USDA Hardiness Zones 3–9.

Witch Hazel Shrub (*Hamamelis virginiana*): This shrub is known as common witch hazel. It grows 20 to 30 feet tall and wide in an oval shape. In the Finger Lakes of my home state of New York, this is a common species. It provides both food and shelter for deer and other animals. Deer, rabbits, birds, and other wildlife eagerly seek out the seeds after they have fallen. Browsing by deer does not hurt this shrub, in fact it helps it by making it grow thicker. It is a fall blooming deciduous shrub (small tree) that is native to woodlands, wilder natural areas, forest margins, and even riparian areas along stream banks. The fruits are greenish seed capsules that become woody as they get old and eventually turn light brown. Witch Hazel's bright-yellow flowers bloom in mid to late fall. The leaves turn a golden yellow in fall as well. The flowers are slightly fragrant. If the plant is fertilized, its flowers will form fruit over a long period and will extend through winter and into the following growing season. In the fall the capsule will open and blast 1 to 2 seeds up to 30 feet away. USDA Hardiness Zones 5–7.

Zereshk Barberry (*Berberis vulgaris*): Zereshk barberry, also known as common barberry or European barberry, is one of the most widely utilized barberry species. The thorny branches and dense growth have made it a top choice as a planting for providing deer

▲ Barberries are easy-to-grow shrubs that are great for adding heavy cover, especially in a wildlife refuge. These tough bushes are deer and disease resistant, salt tolerant, and low maintenance. Photo: © Andris Tkacenko | Dreamstime

and other wildlife food and cover, particularly as a plant in a refuge. It has bright-yellow flowers that appear in spring and are also a tangy and delicious treat to both wildlife and humans. Zereshk barberry is a deciduous shrub but before going dormant for the winter it puts on a psychedelic display of bright red foliage that is accented by any of the deep red berries that might have gone unharvested. Barberries like 10 to 12 hours of full sun and well-drained soil. Barberries are self-fertile. They have a winter hardiness to -40°F. Moreover, they will bear fruit 2 years after planting that will ripen in September. Barberry is not bothered by pests and diseases. USDA Zone: 3–9.

By including a few or more of these shrub plantings in your management program, you will increase the number of deer and other wildlife you attract within your property. These plants also encourage deer to use them as cover, food, and protection from predators throughout the entire year. This increases the chances of housing deer on your land to the nth degree.

NOTE: BEAR BERRY ALERT

Even though it is well-established that deer eat berries, they don't come close to a bear's preference for berries as a wild forage. All bears are professional berry-pickers (eaters of berries). It has been well-documented by biologists and bear researchers that when there is a heavy crop of berries, bears will eat up to 30,000 of them per day. You didn't mis-read that. Not 3,000—but 30,000! Bears can also be called the "Johnny Berry Seed" of the wild. As they can deposit unbroken seeds in their scat to serve as seed dispersers.

▲ All fruits are loaded with vitamins, minerals, proteins, carbohydrates, folic acid, copper potassium, fiber, and vitamin C. Both bucks and does enthusiastically seek out all types of fruits. Credit: Canstock Photo

Chapter Twenty-Eight
Fruit Trees Are Food Plots Too!

When creating a food plot program, plant diversity is an all-important factor. Like a well-rounded investment portfolio, a food plot program should have a wide variety of different plantings. When there is variety in your plantings, there is less risk of having all your eggs in one basket so to speak. Deer have a greater selection of plantings from which to eat than just a few. Thus, it increases the odds of attracting deer and other wildlife to your land.

Traditional lush plantings of clovers, legumes, small grains, brassicas, and other plants are not the end-all choices to offer deer. Another option is to plant fruit trees. With a variety of several types of fruit trees, you will hit paydirt and will have trees with ripened fruit throughout the entire deer season—and longer.

When planting a variety of fruit trees, you not only add a wider choice of energy-packed fruits for deer, but you will also be adding long-lived plantings that can last decades. Fruit trees will initially cost more up front, but the long-term payoff and ease of maintenance is worth it. The types of fruit trees planted are the key in creating a more all-inclusive food plot planting strategy.

No matter where you live, you can add different fruit trees to your food plot program. When choosing fruit trees, keep in mind that not all varieties are suitable for cold climates or timing of when their fruits fall. The first important consideration is to know if the tree will grow well within the USDA Hardiness Zone of your land. Other important points include a tree's disease resistance, ripening date, height, soil requirements, preferred pH levels, and the month the fruit will begin to fall (a.k.a. drop-time). By paying strict attention to these factors, you will enhance your success when selecting and planting fruit trees.

ALL DEER EAT FRUIT

Not only do white-tailed deer eat nutritious fruits, so do elk, mule deer, bears, moose, and other big-game animals. Other wildlife fruit lovers include turkeys, other upland birds, some waterfowl, and most small game critters. By having both traditional and non-traditional food plot plantings, you add a unique variety that provides substantial amounts of sugar-packed energy to wildlife. Additionally, you add one of the most important variants: the time of year when certain fruit tree varieties drop their bounty.

Commonly, when food plotters plant fruit trees, it is often done as an afterthought. The fact is that fruits should be considered as *must-have* plantings. It would be a colossal

▲ The trunk of this Gala apple tree shows that it is young fruit tree. It produced several apples in only its third year Photo: PCFImages

▲ By planting just four- 2- to 3-year-old fruit trees per year, in 10 years you can create a few small orchards that will produce heavy bounties of fruit to attract deer and other wildlife. Photo: Fiduccia Enterprises

▲ Deer love to eat persimmon's orange fruit. Persimmons ripen after the first frost. They are high energy sources for deer that help them build body reserves for winter. Photo: Nativ Nurseries

mistake to not include a variety of fruit trees within a food plot plan. They will not only round out a food plot program, but they will also enhance it significantly.

Furthermore, planting fruit trees only requires a one-time planting of the trees and minimal maintenance. The trees go on to produce their fruit for decades to come. If this makes sense to you, it's time you seriously consider planting a variety of fruit trees. It will take your food plot program to a higher level of success.

NUTRITIONAL BENEFITS

Every food plot plan that includes fruit trees, no matter how small or large the acreage, will enable deer and other wildlife to benefit tremendously from different types of nutritional fruits. Fruit trees supply deer with valuable high-energy calories, sugar, water, protein, fiber, carbohydrate, fat, and several important vitamins. That's more nutrition in one food item than most other types of seeded plants can provide.

All these nutrients help build critical fat reserves leading into the rut and the oncoming winter. For instance, persimmons are an excellent source of

thiamin (B-1), riboflavin (B-2), folate, magnesium, and phosphorus. They are also loaded with fiber. Pears are rich in protein, carbohydrates, folate (folic acid), copper, potassium, fiber, and vitamin C. Apples and other fruits provide similar nutrients.

The fruit of fruit trees is termed soft-mast. Deer eat all varieties of fruits. Some top-choices among food plotters are generally pears, apples, persimmons, several varieties of crabapples and peaches. These types of fruit trees can be grown almost anywhere in the country. The most popular fruit tree planted, though, is the common apple tree. There are many other equally good choices of fruit trees from which to choose. For instance, it isn't a well-known fact, but white-tailed deer often prefer pears over apples.

THE KEY COMPONENT

It's important to have fruit trees that attract deer throughout the archery, regular firearm, and late-season bow and muzzleloading seasons. To accomplish this, plant fruit trees that drop their fruit late, from mid-October through December and even later. This will increase the numbers of deer you see and kill during these timeframes.

When planting distinct types of fruit trees, 25 percent should be early dropping fruit (August to September). The remaining 75 percent should be late-dropping varieties of fruit trees (like pears, apples, persimmons, crabapples, etc.). This plan will result in deer browsing on late-dropping fruits even during the daylight hours of hunting season.

▲ This is another Gala apple tree on our land. It is only 3 years old. Gala apples generally ripen in September, making them a good tree for early bow season. Gala are self-fertile trees. Yields increase when cross-pollination occurs from other apple trees, including crabapples. Photo: PCFImages

Unbelievably, there are even a few species of late-dropping fruit trees that will hold fruit into *January*. Late-dropping fruit trees not only keep resident deer from straying off your land during hunting season, but they also help to keep your neighbor's and transient deer visiting your property much more regularly. Eventually, some of them will set up temporary homesteads on your land until all the fruit is consumed. By including a variety of late-dropping fruit trees you will raise the bar even higher. If the neighbors have fruit trees, they are more than likely growing early dropping apples and pears which their deer will have eaten by early October.

MATCH TREES TO LOCATIONS

A critical factor to planting fruit trees successfully is to plant them only in the USDA Hardiness zones that they are meant to grow best in. Be vigilant in your research about this point. Many of the USDA Hardiness Zone map websites allow you to enter your zip code to get the exact Hardiness Zone/s for your land.

POLLINATION

Pollination happens when the pollen is transferred from the male part of the flower to the female part. Some types of fruit trees may be pollinated with their own pollen and are called self-fruitful (may need another tree of same variety) or self-pollinating (no need for a separate pollinizer). Other types of trees require pollen from a different variety of the same type of tree and are considered self-unfruitful or self-incompatible. The transfer of pollen from one variety to a different variety of the same type of tree is called cross-pollination. Cross-pollination is vital for apples and pears. Apples, pears, and other fruit trees grow better when they are planted with at least two different varieties, as cross-pollination will ensure that the trees consistently bear fruit. In the spring, both varieties should bloom at about the same time and include pollen that is compatible. Simply check fruit tree catalogs or talk to nursery growers for more detailed information about this. It is often recommended that an accompanying cross-pollinating tree be planted within 40 to 50 feet. However, the spacing distance depends on what the size of the tree will be when it reaches maturity. Check with the grower or the directions that come with most trees.

▲ Some fruit trees are self-pollinating but most need to be cross-pollinated. Honeybees do an excellent job of pollinating fruit trees. This honeybee is pollinating a flower on an apple tree. Photo: © Nailia Schwarz | Dreamstime

Dwarf trees can be planted closer, while standard-size trees should be planted farther away from one another. When planting standard-size fruit trees, it is recommended to plant at least 2 compatible-pollen varieties within 45 to 50 feet of one another, which is considered an ideal spacing for pollination. Early dropping fruit trees need to be pollinated, but here is yet another benefit of planting many varieties of late-dropping dwarf fruit trees: they are self-pollinating.

Fallen fruit quickly draws in deer much like a magnetar star draws in matter (a.k.a. Neutron star) which are the universes' *most* powerful magnetic fields—up to 1 quadrillion gauss. That's 1,000 trillion times stronger than Earth's magnetic field you are in while reading this. A magnetar's magnetic field is so strong, it draws in matter at up to 2/3 the speed of light (186,282 miles per second). So, a magnetar attracts matter at 124,188 miles per second! So, now you know how quickly deer will come in to your late-dropping fruit.

▲ A magnetar has huge magnetic fields. If you are unlucky enough to be within 100,000 miles from one, the magnetic force would rip apart iron in your bloodstream and you as well. That's the type of magnetism fruit has on deer. Fruit is a powerful attractant! Photo: © Pitris | Dreamstime.

Seriously, during the hunting season deer will abandon most other food items and quickly switch to eating late-falling ripe pears, apples, and other fruit. As soon as the fruit begins to hit the ground, deer often come trotting in to eat it. The fruit will remain a preferred deer food source until it is completely exhausted.

SIZES OF FRUIT TREES

Fruit trees, potted and bare root, are available in dwarf, semi-dwarf, and standard sizes. Nearly all popular fruit trees—like apple, pear, cherry, peach, plum, persimmon, and crabapple—are available in each of these

▲ The fruit from black cherry (and all other varieties of cherry trees) is eaten by deer, black bears, wild turkeys, upland birds, and many other animals. The black cherry tree has a rapid growth rate and produces fruit at an early age. Photo: Nativ nurseries

proportions. Each size has its own benefits and some negative aspects that should first be considered before purchasing them.

Dwarf Trees

Dwarf trees, a.k.a. spur-type trees, mature when they are about 8 to 10 feet tall and equally as wide. Dwarf trees will often mature and produce fruit in 3 to 4 years. They are ideal for small properties with limited acreage to plant. Dwarf fruit trees tolerate high winds much better than standard or semi-dwarf varieties. On the negative side, their small size limits the amount of fruit they can produce. Because of their limited height, deer can reach their fruit while it is still hanging on the tree. With dwarf trees, be aware that deer can eat all the fruit early in the season.

Semi-Dwarf Trees

Most semi-dwarf fruit trees grow 12 to 15 feet tall and almost as wide. Their extra height enables them to almost double the amount of fruit they produce when compared to a dwarf variety. Semi-dwarf trees take slightly longer to mature and also produce fruit in 3 to 4 years. They, too, are easy to care for and maintain,

▲ This is a semi-dwarf size apple tree on our land. It ripens in late October, making it ideal for both archery and firearm season. I bought the variety because we wanted an apple tree with sweet fruit to eat for ourselves. Photo: PCFImages

although they do require a little more space than dwarf trees.

Standard-Size Trees

Standard-size trees grow much taller and wider than dwarf or semi-dwarf varieties, reaching heights of 25 feet and more. While standard-size fruit trees can be planted on small properties, you won't be able to plant as many as you would if you were planting dwarf or semi-dwarf trees. Therefore, they are ideal for food plotters with larger tracts of property of 50 acres or more. Generally, standard-size fruit trees will mature and produce fruit in about 5 years. Their fruit production is many times greater than the other two smaller varieties, and their life span is much longer too. Standard-size fruit trees do require more work when it comes to pruning. Because of their height, they are more vulnerable to wind damage.

All types of dwarf, semi-dwarf, and standard fruit trees—are available in both early- and late-dropping varieties. Large box stores like Lowes, Home-Depot, Tractor Supply, and Walmart usually sell the semi-dwarf or standard-size trees. Some, if not most, local nurseries will carry these size trees too. The semi-dwarf trees can range in price from about $25 to $45 a tree, and are about 5 to 6 feet tall, depending on where you buy them. The standard trees cost about $50 or more per tree, depending on the circumference of the tree's trunk and its height.

LOCATION, LOCATION, LOCATION

When it comes to growing fruit trees that will produce heavy bounties of fruit, selecting the right planting sites is as critical as selecting the best spot to open a successful restaurant—which, by the way, is a good analogy as both serve food. The fundamental component

▲ Iain Wallace is the C.E.O. of Chestnut Hill Outdoors. Chestnut Hill is known for its founder, Dr. Robert T. Dunstan, who worked to stop the complete devastation of the American chestnut tree by breeding a blight-resistant hybrid called the Dunstan chestnut. Photo: Chestnut Hill Outdoors

for a fruit tree to grow to its maximum potential is to plant it in a place where it can receive a minimum of 6 to 8 hours per day of direct sunlight. The more sunlight, the better the tree will do.

In a conversation about providing full or partial sunlight to fruit trees with the C.E.O. of Chestnut Hill Outdoors, Iain Wallace, he said, "Ultimately, all fruiting and flowering trees prefer full sun. Partial sun will work, but it can hinder the plant's vegetative and mast (fruit) growth. We [Chestnut Hill Outdoors], in some instances, say to provide partial sun to a Baldwin pear tree on our website because it is possible to grow a Baldwin pear in partial sunlight. However, it will be better for even a Baldwin pear tree to receive full sunlight, if it is at all possible."

Planting fruit trees in open areas that offer full sunlight is the most advantageous for maximum growth. Field edges that border sanctuaries or open areas leading to known bedding areas are also excellent planting choices. Open types of areas usually provide better soil quality (pH levels) than shaded areas or areas within the woods. Fruit trees do best when planted in well-drained soils that have pH levels between 6.0 to 7.0. Before planting any fruit tree, treat it like any other traditional food plot planting, and take a soil test first.

AVOID COMMON ERRORS

Not all food plotters have success growing fruit-bearing trees. Most times it is due to simple mistakes. For instance, some food plotters either ignore or forget the advice just mentioned above. They fail to take a soil test

▲ Taking a soil test is the first step to growing the best food plots possible. Without taking a soil test, you run the risk growing stunted, under-performing plants. Photo: NRCS

before planting the trees. Or they do not dig a hole at least twice the size of the root ball. This is a common slip-up. Yet another oversight is neglecting to precisely follow all the planting directions. A major mistake after planting a fruit tree is not providing at least some supplemental watering until the tree can depend on rainfall for its watering needs. But the most egregious of errors is not paying attention to the USDA Hardiness Zone on the tree's tag to make sure it is suitable for your land.

When the above components are paid attention to, fruit trees will grow to their utmost potential. In the best-case scenario, not properly planting a fruit tree severely reduces its chances of growing quickly and it will take more years to produce fruit. In the worst-case scenario, the tree's chances of surviving decrease as quickly as ripe fruit falls from a healthy tree. To avoid these problems, carefully read and follow the planting instructions that come with each fruit tree.

GRAFTED TREES

Some fruit trees are sold only as grafted stock. The term "grafting" refers to a technique that joins two plants into one. Many fruit trees today are grafted onto rootstock. Besides imparting specific characteristics to a resulting tree, it is a faster and more dependable method of procreating plants that do not grow true to their type from seed.

Instead of cross-pollinating two plants and producing a hybrid seed, grafted trees use the roots and the bottom portion of one plant (rootstock) and attach it to a tender shoot (scion) from the top portion of another plant. This combines the best characteristics of both plants. For example, a grafted fruit tree could have a trait to hold onto its fruit for a long period of time. In fact, many grafted types of fruit trees are unique and patented.

During a conversation about grafting with Ryan Haines, the owner of Blue Hill Wildlife Nursery in Selinsgrove, Pennsylvania, Haines said, "Most of our pear tree varieties are those that I found and began grafting myself. Through grafting, I was able to bring the exact varieties back to my nursery. I had to find and develop my late-dropping pears through grafting. I wanted a pear that attracted deer, had a great taste, was very productive and vigorous, and showed strong resistance to fire blight."

Fire blight is the most serious and potentially deadly pear disease in the eastern part of the country. It is caused by the bacterium *Erwinia amylovora*. In fruit trees, the disease can attack and kill blossoms, shoots, limbs, tree trunks, and fruit.

◀ Ryan Haines is the founder and owner of Blue Hill Wildlife Nursery. Haines' grafting techniques have resulted in an impressive variety of "late-dropping" fruit trees. Photo: Blue Hill Wildlife Nursery.

Haines went on to say, "Most importantly, I wanted to develop drop-times of fruit when I wanted pears hitting the ground the most—in November and December. Through proper grafting techniques I developed my different late-dropping pear varieties. Most all my pears are from central Pennsylvania to the New York border."

Haines's comments make it clear about the importance and benefits of developing specific desired characteristics through grafting techniques, like developing pear trees that hold on to their fruit into November and December.

BUYING LATE-DROPPING FRUIT TREES

Not all nurseries carry late-dropping fruit trees, mostly because many nurseries sell fruit trees to provide customers with tasty and wholesome early-dropping varieties as tablefare. Therefore, it takes a little research to locate nurseries that sell late-dropping varieties. Recently, however, more nurseries have begun to realize that there is an ample market for late-dropping fruit trees.

No matter where you live in the country, and whether you hunt white-tailed deer, elk, moose, bears, or mule deer, planting late-dropping fruit trees will enable you to unlock a door that leads to significantly more deer and other big-game sightings, and therefore increase your kill ratio hunting success. It will also contribute to making your overall food plot and deer management program a considerably more well-rounded plan. Truth be told, fruit trees are food plots too!

▲ This is a young three-year-old pear tree on our land. We plant 25 percent of our fruit trees in different varieties of pears. Some fruit tree growers have told me that in their observations, deer prefer pears to apples. Credit: Fiduccia Enterprises

When it comes to planting fruit trees, the following is good advice: Plant pollinating companions (pear, apple, persimmons, crabapple, and other fruit trees) every year for at least 3 to 5 years in a row. For example, plant two apple trees one year, two pear trees the next, etc. In just a few noticeably short years, you will be astonished by the successful results of this surefire food plot game plan.

There are many places to purchase fruit trees from big box stores to large and small local nurseries. Additional fruit tree sellers are in the Fruit Tree Sources section. The web is another source that will provide information on buying fruit trees.

CHESTNUT HILL OUTDOORS

LATE-DROPPING PEARS

In a conversation about late-dropping fruit trees with C.E.O. Iain Wallace of Chestnut Hill Outdoors, Wallace said, "To increase the numbers of deer you attract during the deer season, hordes of deer in fact, you want your fruit to start falling in November and December and not only in September or October." To me, and I think to any hunter, this is very practical advice. Most if not all hunters who plant food plots do so predominately to attract deer during the hunting seasons.

The following late-dropping fruit tree descriptions are abbreviated to include them within this chapter. For more detailed information on each of the important late-dropping trees below, visit the websites of the growers listed. There you will find all the information you need for each variety.

Thanksgiving Pear: Chestnut Hill Outdoors sells several varieties of late-dropping pear, apple, and persimmon trees. One pear variety is called the Thanksgiving pear. This grafted tree grows 20 feet or more and has a spread of 10 to 20 feet. Depending upon which state it is planted in, it can bloom as early as February or March and drops its fruit from late October into December. Thanksgiving pears are hardy with a sweet, crisp flavor. This variety of pear ripens in late fall and will hold the fruit on the tree until about Thanksgiving. The Thanksgiving pear is disease resistant. According to Chestnut Hill Outdoors, it bears fruit in 3 to 5 years. The Thanksgiving pear prefers a soil pH from 6.0 to 7.0. It grows best when it is provided full sunlight. Plant a Thanksgiving pear about 30 to 40 feet from a different variety of pear to increase your yields of pears on each tree. When varieties are not self-fertile, they need a pollination partner. The partner has to be a different variety of the same fruit species. Two trees of the same variety will not pollinate each other. Otherwise choose a self-fertile variety. But, when you plant self-fertile trees, it is still best to plant two to increase the fruit production.

Thanksgiving pear trees can be planted in upland, well-drained, or sandy clay or loam. This tree can tolerate wet soil but only seasonal wet ground and only if it is well drained. Its USDA Hardiness Zone is 5–9.

▲ Fruit from the Thanksgiving pear tree ripens in late fall and holds on the tree until Thanksgiving. It is disease resistant. The fruit is excellent for deer and other wildlife and it will attract them throughout the hunting season Photo: Chestnut Hill Outdoors

Wallace also told me, "Newly planted fruit trees should be watered regularly. This is the most critical step in the establishment of any newly planted fruit tree. Do not fertilize the trees at planting. Once the trees are established, though, you can fertilize in March or April as its growth begins. Do not fertilize in the fall, which could promote late-season tender growth that can be damaged by early frosts. To care for pear trees properly, they should be pruned annually in the winter when they are dormant." You can refer to the Chestnut Hill Outdoors pruning section on their website under "How to Plant and Grow" and how to water trees in their "Learning Center."

Dr. Deer Pear: Another late-dropping pear tree offered by Chestnut Hill Outdoors is called Dr. Deer Pear.

▲ This pear was discovered by Dr. James Kroll. It ripens in late fall and holds on the tree until Thanksgiving. Dr. Deer pears have small fruit in clusters and tend to hold onto them well into late fall. Photo: Chestnut Hill Outdoors

Please do not confuse Dr. Deer, my friend Dr. James Kroll, with me—The Deer Doctor. Dr. Kroll discovered this pear, *not I*. Dr. James Kroll found this variety of pear in Texas. This wildlife pear ripens in late fall and hangs on the tree until late-November. The real benefit to using a Dr. Deer Pear tree is that it produces small fruit in clusters. The fruit is excellent for deer and other wildlife and attracts them throughout the hunting season. The Dr. Deer Pear is grafted and thus self-fertile, though you will see better fruit production when you plant this tree with other similar pollinators.

I planted 8 Dr. Deer Pear trees on my land. They all developed fruit within a few years of planting. I live in upstate New York and we have some severe winters. All my Dr. Deer Pear trees have weathered the harsh winters very well.

This pear tree grows from 20 to 30 feet and has a spread of 10 to 15 feet. It does best when planted where it will receive full sunlight for at least 6 hours per day. Space this tree about 20 to 30 feet from another Dr. Deer Pear tree. It does not need to be fertilized at planting. The USDA recommended Hardiness Zones are 5–9.

CHESTNUT HILL'S LATE-DROPPING APPLE TREES

Arkansas Black Apple: Chestnut Hill Outdoors offers an apple variety called Arkansas Black Apple which ripens extremely late, in November and December, making it an excellent choice for attracting deer

and other big game during the hunting seasons. It is an apple variety that has been around since 1870. Arkansas Black apple is disease resistant, including a resistance to cedar apple rust. The tree can reach heights of 15 to 20 feet and has a spread of 5 to 10 feet. Arkansas Black apple trees require full sunlight, a pH of 6.0 to 6.5, and well-drained soil. It is necessary to plant two different varieties for cross pollination. The USDA Hardiness Zones for this tree are 5 to 8.

▲ This is an orchard of Arkansas Black apples. Arkansas needs at least two apple varieties to cross-pollinate. According to Chestnut Hill Outdoors, it will usually bear fruit in 2 to 3 years. Photo: Chestnut Hill Outdoors

Pink Lady Apple: This tree is a self-fertile grafted apple tree. It is a late-dropping fruit tree. The Pink Lady loses its fruit from October through December. It is

▲ Pink lady is a cross between Golden Delicious and Lady Williams apples. It will thrive in summer heat if ample soil moisture exists. It does best with a pollinator. It ripens late September, making it a good choice for archery and firearm seasons. Photo: Chestnut Hill Outdoors

another choice of late-dropping apple trees that will attract deer and other wildlife into winter. The Pink Lady apple is a cross between Golden Delicious and Lady Williams apple varieties. The apples are oblong and green that turn yellow when they are mature. This tree thrives during the summer heat if it has ample soil moisture. The tree will reach heights of 15 to 20 feet and a spread of 5 to 15 feet. It prefers full sun, well-drained soil, and pH levels of 6.0 to 6.5. As with all fruit trees, plant another variety of the same fruit for pollination and fruit. The USDA Hardiness Zones for Pink Lady are 6–9.

CHESTNUT HILL'S LATE-DROPPING PERSIMMON TREES

Grafted Persimmons: The two persimmon varieties offered by Chestnut Hill Outdoors are Deer Magnet (late dropping) and Deer Candy (early dropping). The Deer Magnet holds its fruit until October and drops through November. The Deer Candy variety begins dropping fruit in August through October. Iain Wallace suggests planting both varieties together for good pollination and extended fruit production from August through November. Both varieties are grafted females, which means every tree will produce fruit, unlike wild persimmons that can be male (non-producing trees) or female. These grafted varieties were also selected because they are heavy producers. The USDA Hardiness Zones for both are 5–9.

Deer Magnet Persimmon: Chestnut Hill Outdoors offers 12 different early persimmon trees and one that is an extremely late-dropping persimmon—The Deer Magnet. The Deer Magnet is a grafted "American female persimmon." Deer find the fruit of this persimmon tree highly attractive. In fact, according to Chestnut Hill Outdoors' CFO, Dunstan Wallace, "Bucks will guard Deer Magnet's fruit in order to prevent other deer eating this special food supply."

Deer love the sweet nutty flavor of this late-dropping persimmon tree. It loses its fruit late in October through December, depending on the USDA zone and

▲ Deer will find these trees and bucks will "guard them to protect this special food supply." They love the sweet nutty flavor. This persimmon ripens late and drops its fruit starting in late October through December (depending on the USDA zone and climate where planted). Photo: Chestnut Hill Outdoors

▲ Deer will seek out persimmons from long distances away. Deer Candy Persimmons are grafted American female persimmons and will bear fruit in 2 to 3 years depending on the climate and the care they receive. Photo: Chestnut Hill Outdoors

climate where it was planted. A Deer Magnet persimmon tree will bear fruit in 2 to 3 years, depending on the climate and the care it receives. The fruit of a medium-sized persimmon is about 1¼ to 1½ inches long. The Deer Magnet persimmon tree is termed to be a heavy bearer of fruit. It can reach heights of 30 to 50 feet with a spread of 20 to 35 feet.

The Deer Magnet persimmon tree is adapted to upland, well-drained, sandy clay, or loamy soils. It can tolerate seasonal wet soil if the soil is well-drained. It requires full sunlight and prefers a soil pH level between 6.0 to 7.0. The Deer Magnet needs a pollinator for fruit production. Chestnut Hill Outdoors suggests a second Deer Magnet, a Deer Candy, or Native American persimmon variety as a good companion pollinator tree for the Deer Magnet persimmon. The USDA Hardiness Zones are 6–9.

Chestnut Hill Outdoors' website has an enormous amount of helpful information. Dunstan Wallace told me, "Chestnut Hill's Learning Center is a living library for planting, food plotting, maintenance, and much more. We update this library regularly with the knowledge our customers need and want to enrich their land and ensure that their trees and plants thrive for many years to come. If any of your readers don't find what they are looking for on our website or at the Learning Center's library, they can call us. We're always happy to talk about trees, wildlife, and habitat with folks." Nice.

▲ Persimmons can be considered as candy to deer and most other wildlife. Credit: Chestnut Hill Outdoors

BLUE HILL WILDLIFE NURSERY

Blue Hill Wildlife Nursery has developed a variety of grafted, late-dropping fruit trees that are good choices for hunters who plant food plots. Many of Blue Hill's grafted trees are unique and are trademarked. For bow-hunters, Blue Hill offers fruit trees that drop their boun-ties in September, October, and into early November. For regular season firearm and late-season muzzle-loader and archery hunters, Blue Hill offers a wide variety of fruit trees that drop their fruits in November, December, and some even into January.

▲ This grafted applecrab tree produces heavy crops of large 2-inch applecrabs that hold well to the tree and drop from October into winter; a late dropper for the bow and firearm hunter. Photo: Blue Hill Wildlife Nursery

According to Blue Hill Wildlife Nursery's website (www.bluehillwildlifenursery.com), their late-dropping trees begin to produce fruit when the tree reaches between 3 to 5 years old. To ensure pollination, Blue Hill recommends planting at least two different variet-ies within proximity to each other. When purchasing trees from Blue Hill, remember to check all the plant-ing instructions for their trees on their website.

Listed below are Blue Hill Wildlife Nursery's selec-tions of their late-dropping fruit trees. A few of Blue Hill's offerings are trees that were not created by owner and grower Ryan Haines but were developed by other plant enthusiasts or nurseries.

As I mentioned earlier, when including fruit trees within a food plot plan, it is a wise idea to plant about 25 percent of them in early-dropping fruit trees and 75 percent in late-dropping fruit trees. By planting both early- and late-dropping fruit trees, you're assuring that deer will have nutritious fruits to eat from August through December or longer. More important, if you follow this plan, you can plant them strategically so that you know what trees are dropping their fruits at various times of the hunting seasons and plan your hunting accordingly.

BLUE HILL'S LATE-DROPPING GRAFTED PEAR TREES

Rifle Deer Pear™ This grafted Blue Hill tree produces an abundance of extremely sweet pears that begin to ripen in mid-November. According to owner Ryan Haines, "The original parent tree is huge for a pear tree. It has greater than a 6 foot circumference at the bottom, stands well over 60 feet tall, with zero signs of ever having fire blight. Even in Pennsylvania's heavily pressured rifle deer season in mid-November, there would be deer under this tree."

▲ The Rifle Pear tree produces an abundance of super-sweet pears that begin ripening on the tree in mid-November. This tree is an excellent choice for regular firearms seasons. Photo: Blue Hill Wildlife Nursery

Rifle Deer Pear™ only drops its fruit for a few short weeks, making this a powerful draw for deer that typically ends by the first week of December. This tree produces an abundance of pears annually. The Rifle Deer Pear™ tree is a highly desirable pear to deer. It tolerates low temperatures down to -22°F, placing it in USDA's Hardiness Zone 4. However, according to owner Ryan Haines, "This tree is a solid pear tree for Plant Hardiness zones 5 to 8." Rifle Deer Pear™ will reach a mature height of at least 20 feet. As a bonus, it is an excellent pear for making jams and jellies.

Malus Pear™ Is yet another late-dropping fruit tree from Blue Hill. It drops its fruit mostly in November with some fruit hanging into early December. The Malus Pear™ has a USDA Hardiness Zone rating of 4–7.

Winter Deer Pear™ This late-dropping pear tree provides deer and other wildlife with a nutritious winter food source. According to Blue Hill's website, the drop time of the Winter Deer Pear™ is from January to March. Winter Deer Pear™ is an excellent choice for food plotters who want to provide their deer and other game an extremely late winter food source. USDA Hardiness Zones are 4–7.

Sweet Advent Pear™ Begins to drop its fruit in early to mid-November and will continue to drop its pears into December. USDA Hardiness Zones are 5–8.

Korean Giant Pear: Drops its fruit in mid-October into November. USDA Hardiness Zones are 4b–8.

Marble Hill Pear: A late-ripening pear. Marble Hill drops its pears from mid-October into mid-November. USDA Hardiness Zones are 4–7.

PEAR PLANTING INFO
Plant all pear trees in moist, but well-drained soil. The optimum pH level for most pear trees is between 5.5 to 7.2. All pear trees require at least 6 hours of full sunlight for fruit production and yearly growth. Space the trees about 20 to 30 feet apart. Fence off each tree with wire fencing that is 4 to 5 feet high and supported by metal stakes to protect the trees from deer, rabbits,

and other animals for the first few years. This applies to all fruit and different types of nut trees.

Plant at least two different pear varieties within close proximity to each other to ensure pollination. The varieties of grafted Blue Hill Nursery's pears will blossom and overlap each other providing "excellent pollination." For more detailed information on Blue Hill's grafted pear trees, visit their website at www.bluehillwildlifenursery.com.

BLUE HILL'S LATE-DROPPING APPLE TREES
Blue Hill Wildlife Nursery also offers a wide selection of bare-root, late-dropping apple trees. Owner Ryan Haines, told me the varieties of apple trees I have listed below "are some of my best apple trees to plant for deer. They will grow well, and as claimed, as long as the trees are planted according to the directions that come with them."

▲ Like so many other tree nurseries, Blue Hill Wildlife Nursery sells its trees as bare root stock. Photo: Blue Hill Wildlife Nursery

Canisteo Apple Tree: Canisteo red apple trees begin dropping fruit in January and continue into March. This is ideal for deer hunters with food plots in the northern regions of the southern states like Texas, Alabama, and Georgia. Even after many freeze and thaw cycles through mid-February, the hanging apples of the Canisteo don't become rotten. The Canisteo apple is an invaluable fruit tree for the food plotter who wants to provide nutritious sustenance for deer after the deer season has ended. USDA Hardiness zones for the Canisteo apple tree are 5–8.

Arkansas Black Apple: This grafted dark red apple will begin dropping a few apples in late October and continue through November. This variety is a top choice for hunters who plant food plots that include fruit trees. Arkansas Black is a very productive apple tree annually producing ample amounts of apples. USDA Hardiness Zones are 5–8.

Grafted Keener Seedling: This tree produces yellow apples that ripen extremely late. The fruit is said to hang on the tree into December. The Keener is another terrific choice throughout most firearm deer hunting seasons in the Northeast, New England, and Midwest regions of the country. Blue Hill's website states the Keener Seedling has proven to be an exceptional apple tree. USDA Hardiness Zones 4–7.

Yates Apple: This apple tree drops its red fruit from mid-October well into December. The Yates grafted apple tree yields an annual dense number of apples.

◀ Yates apple is a grafted applecrab tree. It will thrive well in temperatures down to -25°F, making this tree a solid applecrab tree into USDA Zone 4. Photo: Blue Hill Wildlife Nursery

This is a point worth noting as it will continue to have ample amounts of fruit throughout the archery and firearms seasons. USDA Hardiness Zones 4–8.

BLUE HILL'S APPLECRAB TREES

For some food plot managers, applecrab may be a new term. Simply put, the fruit of an applecrab tree is larger than the fruit of a small crabapple. But, it is not as large as a traditional apple. Applecrabs are various hybrids between crabapples and apples. They are bred for varying reasons, including disease resistance and use in cold climates because they are often hardier than standard apple trees and their fruit has good eating qualities. Because they are bred to be not only cold-hardy but also have late-dropping fruit, they are included in this chapter.

Big Lou Applecrab: This grafted applecrab tree holds its fruit well. The applecrabs will begin to drop starting in mid-December and continue to fall into early March. You read that correctly, December to early March!

▲ Big Lou™ applecrab is a grafted tree that is a heavy annual producer of 2-inch apple crabs. It begins dropping some of its fruit in November, December, and January in the Northeast. Most of its fruit falls in January and even February. This tree is a must-have for any deer hunter. Photo: Blue Hill Wildlife Nursery

According to Ryan Haines, "The applecrabs that fall from this tree in January have a nutty flavor. Even in this time of year, the flesh is still very intact, yet soft and palatable. The integrity of the flesh of this fruit is the best I have ever seen on an applecrab after it has undergone freezing and thawing many times over." He went on to say, "The deer sign in and around this tree is always very impressive." This indicates the tree provides a steady preferred food source for deer. A video posted on their website was taken with snow on the ground and fresh-looking applecrabs were still hanging from the tree.

Big Lou applecrab is said to be a late, heavy-bearing applecrab tree that bears fruit annually. It has also proven to have a strong resistance to fire blight. Big Lou applecrab comes from a parent tree with a USDA Hardiness Zone 5a rating located in Northwest, PA.

With its very late-dropping of applecrabs, Big Lou applecrab is a top candidate as a must-have fruit tree for any food plotter who wants to provide deer and other wildlife a healthy and beneficial food source during the tough times of the winter months. USDA Hardiness Zones 4b - 7.

Big Dog Applecrab: The Big Dog applecrab is a grafted tree that will begin dropping its red apples from mid-October through mid-January. This tree is very productive, producing abundant crops of 2-inch size applecrabs. Its USDA Hardiness Zones 3–7.

▲ Big Dog, a grafted applecrab tree, is a heavy producing tree with good disease resistance in a no-spray situation. It shows strong signs of resistance to cedar apple rust, apple scab, powdery mildew, and fire blight. It begins dropping in mid-October and will continue into mid-January. Photo: Blue Hill Wildlife Nursery

BLUE HILL'S CRABAPPLE TREES

Ryan Haines told me, "All the varieties of Blue Hill's crabapple trees are an amazing food source for white-tailed deer." Haines' bare root crabapple trees, of which there are more than 20 different varieties, are all grafted to standard rootstock. This one factor produces vigorous and fast-growing apple trees that can reach mature heights of 22 feet or more.

Acorn Pippen: This grafted tree is a prolific crabapple that produces a heavy annual bounty. The fruit ripens and falls from the tree throughout October and into November. Acorn pippen is resistant to apple scab, fire blight, and powdery mildew, making it an exceptional tree for deer and other wildlife. However, it is moderately susceptible to cedar apple rust. Acorn pippin will reach a mature height of at least 20 feet. USDA Hardiness Zones 5a - 8.

Buckman Crab Crabapple: A grafted red crabapple that is very cold-hardy and productive. It produces exceptionally large 2-inch crabapples. The Buckman's crabapples start dropping in October and last through winter. A few apples may still be hanging on the tree into March. USDA Hardiness Zones 3–8.

Dolgo Crabapple: Dolgo is a grafted crabapple that is cold-hardy. Dolgo is very productive and it will bear its red fruit at an "incredibly" early age. This tree begins dropping in late August and its apples will persist on the tree until December. It is said to be one of the most widely planted crabapples planted for white-tailed deer. USDA Hardiness Zones 3–8.

Golden Hornet Crabapple: The Golden Hornet crabapple is known to be a late-dropping crabapple tree. It produces a consistent annual crop of yellow apples. Unlike many other crabapples, the 1 to 1½-inch Golden Hornet crabapples are edible for people. It typically starts dropping at a fast rate after the first few frosts in mid- to late October and will retain good amounts of apples into winter. This tree is self-fertile and an excellent pollinator. USDA Hardiness Zones 4–7.

Kerr Crabapple: Kerr red crabapple is a cross between the dolgo and harlson crabapples. This tree produces

1- to 2-inch crabapples. It is a very cold-hardy tree. This tree will begin dropping its fruit in October and crabapples will persist on the tree through winter. USDA Hardiness Zones 3–8.

October Crab Apple: This tree produces red 1 to 1½-inch crabapples. It begins bearing a lot of fruit at a noticeably immature age, typically the same year it is planted. It drops a lot of apples at a heavy rate through the month of October, making this tree very desirable for bow hunters. October Crab™ is a favorite crabapple of deer. USDA Hardiness Zones 5–8.

▲ October Crab™ is a grafted tree that produces 1 to 1½-inch crabapples. It begins bearing a lot of fruit early, often the same year you plant it! October Crab™ has good disease resistance to fire blight, powdery mildew, or cedar apple rust in no spray cultivation. Photo: Blue Hill Wildlife Nursery

BLUE HILL'S PERSIMMON TREES

Deer Magnet Persimmon: According to Blue Hill Wildlife Nursery's web site, this persimmon tree is self-fruitful. It was chosen for its ability to hold persimmons on the tree longer than other persimmons. Deer Magnet typically does not begin dropping fruit until around December 1st, as the freezing weather of winter moves in. This extremely late-dropping persimmon is a top draw for deer during late-season hunting. Deer Magnet trees begin producing fruit in about their third year. USDA Hardiness Zones 5–8.

Deer Candy Persimmon: Deer Candy persimmons, according to Blue Hill Wildlife Nursery's web site, drop from the first week in October through November. This tree produces large 2-inch persimmons. I have been told that deer will dig up and eat Deer Candy persimmons that are snow covered. USDA Hardiness Zones 5–8.

Full Draw™ Persimmon: A self-fruitful tree that produces large 2-inch persimmons annually. The fruit begins falling free from the tree in mid-September and it will continue to drop fruit into winter. It is a very cold-hardy persimmon tree. Full Draw™ is one of the best persimmon trees to grow for whitetails and other big game. USDA Hardiness Zones 5–8.

Meader Persimmon: This tree is yet another grafted self-fruitful persimmon. It is widely grown in colder climates because it is very cold-hardy to -25°F. This tree begins to drop fruit in early October and continues into November and into later winter months. Meader produces annually, making it an excellent choice for attracting white-tailed deer all season long. USDA Hardiness Zones 5–8.

Deer Luscious™ Persimmon: This is Blue Hill's grafted persimmon, which is self-fruitful. This tree produces sweet 2-inch persimmons. The fruit drops free from the tree beginning in September and, according to Blue Hill's website, it continues to drop fruit well into December. USDA Hardiness Zones 5–8.

The Blue Hill Wildlife Nursery products are so popular that most items sell out as soon as they are posted. Check the site regularly to find out when they are listed for sale.

See Blue Hill Wildlife Nursery's "Drop Time Chart" info below.

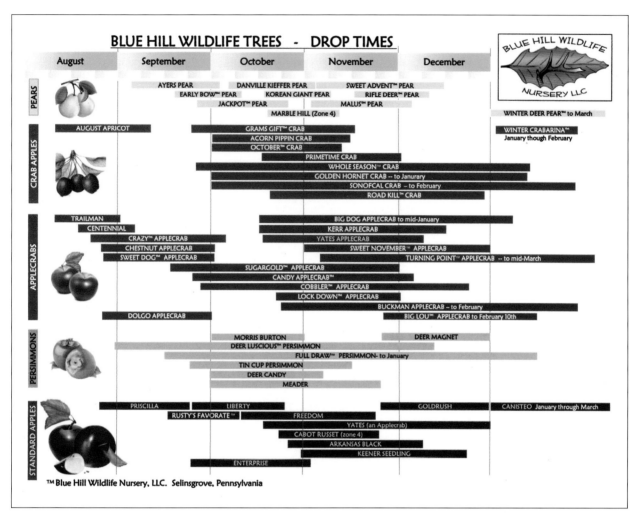

BLUE HILL WILDLIFE TREES - DROP TIMES

| August | September | October | November | December |

PEARS
- AYERS PEAR
- EARLY BOW™ PEAR
- JACKPOT™ PEAR
- DANVILLE KIEFFER PEAR
- KOREAN GIANT PEAR
- MARBLE HILL (Zone 4)
- SWEET ADVENT™ PEAR
- RIFLE DEER™ PEAR
- MALUS™ PEAR
- WINTER DEER PEAR™ to March

CRAB APPLES
- AUGUST APRICOT
- GRAMS GIFT™ CRAB
- ACORN PIPPIN CRAB
- OCTOBER™ CRAB
- PRIMETIME CRAB
- WHOLE SEASON™ CRAB
- GOLDEN HORNET CRAB -- to Janurary
- SONOFCAL CRAB – to February
- ROAD KILL™ CRAB
- WINTER CRABARINA™ January though February

APPLECRABS
- TRAILMAN
- CENTENNIAL
- CRAZY™ APPLECRAB
- CHESTNUT APPLECRAB
- SWEET DOG™ APPLECRAB
- BIG DOG APPLECRAB to mid-January
- KERR APPLECRAB
- YATES APPLECRAB
- SWEET NOVEMBER™ APPLECRAB
- TURNING POINT™ APPLECRAB -- to mid-March
- SUGARGOLD™ APPLECRAB
- CANDY APPLECRAB™
- COBBLER™ APPLECRAB
- LOCK DOWN™ APPLECRAB
- BUCKMAN APPLECRAB – to February
- DOLGO APPLECRAB
- BIG LOU™ APPLECRAB to February 10th

PERSIMMONS
- MORRIS BURTON
- DEER LUSCIOUS™ PERSIMMON
- DEER MAGNET
- FULL DRAW™ PERSIMMON- to January
- TIN CUP PERSIMMON
- DEER CANDY
- MEADER

STANDARD APPLES
- PRISCILLA
- RUSTY'S FAVORATE™
- LIBERTY
- FREEDOM
- YATES (an Applecrab)
- CABOT RUSSET (zone 4)
- ARKANSAS BLACK
- KEENER SEEDLING
- ENTERPRISE
- GOLDRUSH
- CANISTEO January through March

™ Blue Hill Wildlife Nursery, LLC. Selinsgrove, Pennsylvania

BLUE HILL WILDLIFE NURSERY LLC

▲ This is a Drop-Time Chart for fruit trees grown by Blue Hill Wildlife Nursery (BHWN). Photo. BHWN.

CUMMINS NURSERY
(Fruit Trees, Scion Wood, and Rootstocks)

Cummins nursery has a wide selection of different varieties of bare root apple, pear, peach, cherry, plum, nectarine, and apricot fruit trees. They also offer a variety of wildlife fruit tree plantings. You can choose disease-resistant varieties, which lowers the maintenance of the trees. Trees within the wildlife group also hold their fruit longer, into late October and some into January. Cummins Nursery has a shop-online website that is very user friendly and highly informative. Fruit trees are shipped annually in March and April. Cummins Nursery ships nationwide. They are in Ithaca, New York. Visit them at www.cumminsnursery. com.

LATE-DROPPING APPLE TREES

Grafted Goldrush Apple: GoldRush is a very late-dropping apple tree that can hold its fruit well into December. At the time of this writing (February 2022),

▲ This is a bare-root late-ripening (and dropping) Gold Rush apple tree from Cummins Nursery. The roots are long and healthy, which help the tree to take root faster and produce a healthier and stronger tree. Photo: PCFImages

Gold Rush apples are still hanging on the trees in Cummins Nursery. Gold Rush is field immune to scab, highly resistant to powdery mildew, and moderately resistant to fire blight. It is, however, susceptible to cedar-apple rust. The tree will survive temperatures down to -22°F. It shouldn't be grown north of zone 5, as the season will be too short for ripening. GoldRush's disease resistance and easy growing habits make it an excellent choice for wildlife food plotters. The fruit ripens late October through mid-November in upstate NY, but extremely high-sugar levels help protect it from freezing.

▲ Grafted Gold Rush will survive temperatures down to -22°F. The fruit ripens late October through mid-November in upstate New York. Its high-sugar levels help protect it from freezing. It is a good choice for both bow and firearms hunters. Photo: Cummins Nursery

Enterprise Apple: You didn't think I would overlook a late-dropping apple tree for food plotters who are also *Star Trek* "Trekkies," did you? The Enterprise apple tree is one of the best and most widely planted apple trees for deer, and for good reason. It ripens at a perfect time during late October and continues to drop its fruit well into November.

Enterprise is an attractive, highly disease-resistant apple, ideal for food plotters. Enterprise is the perfect apple for no-spray cultivation. It is field immune to scab, and resistant to mildew and fire blight. This grower-friendly tree is vigorous, spreads rapidly, and is reliably productive. Enterprise apples generally begin

making fruit at 3 to 5 years of age. Beam one to me, Scotty! USDA Hardiness Zones 4b - 8.

▲ Enterprise Apple ripens in late October and is a viable choice for bowhunters in the Northeast. It is field immune to scab, and resistant to mildew and fire blight. This grower-friendly tree is vigorous, spreads rapidly, and is reliably productive. Photo Cummins Nursery

Grafted Freedom Apple: This Freedom red apple is annually productive and produces an abundance of apples that ripen in mid-September and drop from the tree during October and November. It is disease-resistant, highly resistant to scab, and moderately resistant to fire blight, cedar-apple rust, all types of canker, and mildew. It is precocious, productive, vigorous, and hardy. Freedom is a terrific apple tree choice for wildlife food plotters. Freedom has a double dose of genetic scab resistance. Freedom derived its name from the breeders for its "freedom" from this affliction. USDA Hardiness Zones 4b–8.

LATE-DROPPING FRUIT TREE SOURCES

Blue Hill Wildlife Nursery—www.bluehillwildlife nursery.com
Canyon View Nursery—www.canyonviewnursery.com
Chestnut Hill Outdoors—www.chestnuthilloutdoors .com
Cummins Nursery—www.cumminsnursery.com
Edward Fort Nurseries—www.edwardfortnurseries .com
Fast Growing Trees - www.FastGrowingTrees.com

Grandpa's Orchard—www.grandpasorchard.com
Morse nursery—www.morsenursery.com
Real Tree Nursery - www.realtreenursery.com
Smith Nursery Company—www.smithnursery.com
Stark Brothers—www.starkbros.com
The Nursery at TyTy—www.tytyga.com
Willis Orchard Co.—www.willisorchard.com

APPLE SCAB PREVENTION

Apples succumb to the disease called "apple scab," a frequent problem in wet climates. To avoid this disease, select resistant varieties such as Pristine, Enterprise, Freedom, Liberty or Crimson. Other varieties have partial resistance to apple scab, Honeycrisp, Hudson's Golden Gem, and Wolf River. For more information about Apple Scab, refer to the following PDF from Cornell University—http://plantclinic.cornell.edu/fact-sheets/applescab2B.pdf

For more information on varieties with resistance to scab, refer to this section from the University of Maine https://extension.umaine.edu/fruit/growing-fruit-trees-in-maine/varieties/

USDA HARDINESS ZONES

The USDA Hardiness Zones offer a general guide to where fruit trees will grow best in particular climate zones. Each zone matches the minimum winter temperatures experienced in each area. Make sure that your USDA Hardiness Zone lies within the zone compatibility range before purchasing a fruit tree. A United States Department of Agriculture's (USDA) *Plant Hardiness Zone Map* divides the United States into zones according to the expected coldest winter temperature. Zone 1 is the coldest and Zone 11 the warmest. Within Zone 6, winter temperatures are expected to get as cold as -10°F. Most tree fruits can survive in Zone 5, but peaches, sweet cherries, and Asian plums will suffer from winter injury in colder years. More northern and western regions fall within Zone 4, which is expected to get as cold as -30°F. This is too cold for peaches, nectarines, apricots, cherries, Asian plums, and European plums. Some varieties of pear and plum will tolerate winter in Zone 4. The most northerly regions are within Zone 3, and only a few varieties will survive the cold in this region.

▲ These 4-year-old peach trees are in our orchard in USDA Hardiness Zone 5. Photo: PCFImages

FERTILIZERS FOR FRUIT TREES

Fruit trees need the right nutrition to grow healthy so they can produce bountiful fruit year after year. Using the proper types of fertilizer for fruit trees is the best way to make sure your trees are getting exactly what they need. Some recommended fertilizers are listed below:

• Jobe's Organics Fruit & Citrus Fertilizer with Biozome—3–5–5
• Jobe's Fruit and Citrus Tree Fertilizer Spikes—9–12–12
• Urban Farm Fertilizers Apples & Oranges Fruits and Citrus 4.5–2.0–4.2
• Espoma CT4 Citrus-Tone Plant Food 5–2–6
• Southern Ag Chelated Citrus Nutritional Spray Fe 1.2% Zn 1.7% Mn 1.2% Mg 1% S 4.1%
• JR Peters Inc 52524 Jacks Classic Citrus Food Fertilizer 20–10–20
• Miracle-Gro Fruit & Citrus Fertilizer Spikes 10–15–15
• Others include an NPK of 12–0–0, 15-0-0, and 16–0–0 which are all high nitrogen fertilizers. And one that I use is 12–7–10, which fertilizes fruit trees and shrubs.

▲ Deer readily gobble up Wild Deer Pear. This variety does not require nearly as much maintenance or special attention as other pear trees planted for deer. Photo: Nativ Nurseries

▲ Like all nuts, chestnuts can pack the pounds on bucks and does. By including chestnuts in your food plot management program, you will be able to offer nutritious sustenance to deer and other wildlife year after year with minimal maintenance. Photo Credit: Ted Rose

Chapter Twenty-Nine

The Extraordinary Chestnuts

All wildlife instinctively prefer high-energy food sources which help them gain weight quickly. Nuts and acorns influence the winter survival rate, physical condition, reproductive success, and the overall size of the population rates as well, especially for female deer and other female wildlife.

CHESTNUT (*Castanea*)

Over the last decade, interest by food plotters to plant chestnut trees to attract deer and other game animals has grown exponentially. Chestnuts belong to a group of deciduous trees and shrubs. Their nuts are encased in spine-covered burrs. They are highly sought out by deer and innumerable other game animals because they are sweet-tasting. Once the spiny burr falls to the ground, it opens. Deer and other wildlife easily break open the thin soft shell to eat the nuts. Chestnuts have a high amount of starch (complex carbs) that is greatly beneficial to wildlife's metabolism. Chestnut trees

▲ If this photo does not inspire you to plant chestnut trees, nothing I can write about them will either. Photo: Missouri State University

bear their nuts from September to November. The nuts contain 40 percent carbohydrates, 10 percent protein, along with vitamin C and other nutrients.

Many chestnut varieties are cold-hardy. They can grow in a wide climatic range from USDA Hardiness Zones 4 to 8. Many chestnut varieties can be grown throughout the United States, particularly in the eastern part of the country. However, there is also a genetic variation in the climatic tolerance of chestnut trees, especially when it comes to cold hardiness. Therefore, it is vital to buy varieties of chestnut trees adapted to your climate. Chestnuts do best in areas that have hot, humid summers. They do not like consistently wet soil, as they are susceptible to root-rot.

Some of the most common varieties of chestnut trees include American, Chinese, European, Japanese, and Chinquapin. However, there are many other types of chestnut trees (see varieties listed below). Steer clear of species like horse or buckeye chestnuts; they are toxic species to animals. Chestnuts contain no bitter-tasting tannins like many red and other oak nuts.

AMERICAN CHESTNUT (*Castanea dentata*)

The American chestnut tree is native to eastern North America. It is a large, deciduous, broad tree that grows rapidly, but it needs room to grow. It can grow 12 to 24 inches per year once established. When mature it can reach 60 to 80 feet tall and have a 30 to 40 foot spread. American chestnut trees are self-incompatible, which means any two trees of any member of the genus Castanea are required for pollination. This tree produces small but highly tasty nuts for wildlife.

I planted two American chestnut trees on our farm in 2012. I chose grafted bare-root hybrid varieties because they produce large nuts and are resistant to chestnut blight. They are also cold-hardy. Where I live in central New York, the temperatures can plummet

▲ American chestnut trees are cold-hardy and can generally take temperatures to -20 F. An excellent variety is called Colossal, the one I chose to plant. Photo: © Mizet1 | Dreamstime

to -25°F, especially at the 1,756 feet elevation of our land. The variety I chose was Colossal, as it produces the largest, most abundant nuts at the youngest age.

American chestnut trees do best in full sun. The burrs open and fall to the ground later than some other chestnut varieties, usually near the first frost of the season. Each burr contains at least 3 nuts.

CHINESE CHESTNUT (*Castanea mollissima*)

The Chinese chestnut is gaining in popularity. Its nuts are sweet-tasting to wildlife. The tree does best in hot dry climates and can reach 40 to 60 feet tall. It is said to grow at a "slow to medium" rate. The spiny husk ranges from 2 to 3 inches or more, and each husk contains 1 to 4 chestnuts. The large chestnuts are said to be "meaty, crisp, and sweet" but are "less sweet than the American chestnuts."

▲ Chinese chestnut trees are easy-to-grow and are cold-hardy. They produce up to 4 chestnuts per husk. Chinese chestnut trees are disease-resistant to chestnut blight. To pollinate, plant two seedlings or a grafted chestnut variety. Photo: Blue Hill Wildlife Nursery

Chinese chestnut trees need at least 6 hours of full sunlight per day, and full sunlight throughout the day would be better. The Chinese chestnut will grow in acidic, moist, loamy sandy, well-drained, and even clay soils. These trees are said to produce nuts within 3 to 4 years. Planted nursery stock will bear nuts sooner. Chinese chestnut trees produce a ripened nut crop from early September to the end of October. Each bur contains 2 to 3 nuts. They can grow well in USDA Hardiness Zones 4–8.

To ensure pollination, it is recommended to plant Chinese chestnuts in cultivars of one or even groups of trees. In ideal growing conditions, it will produce a heavy viable wildlife crop in about 3 to 5 years, and 5 to 6 years in less ideal conditions. They are generally sold as bare-root tree stock, but some nurseries offer them as containerized trees. There are available at many online nurseries and in local garden nurseries.

JAPANESE CHESTNUT (*Castanea crenata*)

Japanese chestnuts, a.k.a. Korean, have some of the largest nuts of all, growing to 2 inches in size and weighing about 1 to 1½ ounces. Although they have a resistance to chestnut blight, there can be some genetic differences in their resistance tolerances. They should be grown in moist, deep, well-drained loams in full sun. They are tolerant of heat and humidity. Established trees do well in dry conditions. They dislike consistently wet soils. More than one tree

▲ Japanese chestnut trees produce the largest nuts, at 2 or more inches. With good soil fertility, they begin to produce chestnuts within 2 to 3 years. They need another chestnut variety tree for cross-pollination. The nuts ripen in August, earlier than most other chestnut varieties do. Photo: Deposit

facilitates cross-pollination which helps to produce a more abundant crop. Single trees are close to being self-sterile.

The Japanese chestnut burrs grow in a mass of spines that interlock in a thatched arrangement. Japanese chestnuts are an excellent source of copper, magnesium, and manganese. The nuts are also a reliable source of vitamin C (which is an antioxidant) and they also contain some potassium, fiber, iron, and phosphorus.

Japanese chestnuts are usually not as cold-hardy as American, Chinese, and European chestnut species. Nevertheless, Japanese chestnut trees generally begin bearing nuts at a much younger age than other varieties. Japanese chestnuts are large and edible, have a slightly bitter flavor from tannin content, but are still sweeter than acorns to deer. Japanese chestnut is noted for having resistance to chestnut blight. The tree reaches a maximum height of 35 to 50 feet. Each large burr contains 2 to 3 nuts, yet some Japanese varieties contain up to 7 nuts per burr. USDA Hardiness Zones 4–8.

EUROPEAN CHESTNUTS (*Castanea sativa*)

The European chestnut, a.k.a. Spanish chestnut or sweet chestnut, is a tall deciduous tree that can reach 100 feet in height. Like all chestnut trees, it belongs to the beech family. Oddly, European chestnut trees are not native to Europe but rather to western Asia—go figure. Although each European chestnut tree has male and female flowers (catkins), they produce better nuts when more than a single tree is planted.

European chestnuts are not as blight resistant as the three other common varieties (American, Chinese, and Japanese). It can grow up to 36 inches per year and live up to 150 years. A mature European chestnut tree can spread to 50 feet wide and twice that in height. Sweet chestnuts are flexible, will grow in sun or partial shade, and will accept clay, loamy, or sandy soil. They also accept acidic or slightly alkaline soil. Each burr contains 2 to 3 nuts. USDA Hardiness Zones 5–7.

DUNSTAN CHESTNUTS™

Today we hear a lot about the loss of a species, mass extinctions, and most recently the virus called Covid-19 and its Omicron subvariant. But less than 100 years

▲ This 4-year-old Dunstan™ chestnut tree is one of fifty in this particular orchard. It is not uncommon for a young chestnut tree to produce the kind of bounty seen on this tree. Photo: PCFImages

ago, there was a mass extinction on an unimaginable scale throughout North America, which for the most part has either been forgotten or unknown. The event was awfully close to being a near-extinction of the American chestnut tree, a magnificent and valuable tree once found throughout all forests of the eastern United States and Canada. It is estimated that between three and four *billion* (that's a "B" as in billion) trees perished from a blight during the first part of the twentieth century.

The "good news" about the chestnut extinction is that it seemed that all was lost, but it wasn't. In the 1950s the chestnut enthusiast James Carpentar, from Salem, Ohio, found a large, still-living American chestnut tree in an area filled with dead trees. Carpentar realized the tree could have immunity to the deadly fungus. He sent some branches to a fellow enthusiast and plant breeder, Dr. Robert T. Dunstan. To preserve the genetics of the tree, Dr. Dunstan grafted it onto chestnut roots and found the trees grew well. Dr. Dunstan knew that to strengthen the resistance of the tree he needed to bring in some of the protective genes that the Asian chestnut had. So, Dr. Dunstan decided to cross-pollinate James Carpentar's trees with some of

his top-quality Asian varieties. Over the next 30 years, Dr. Dunstan crossed and re-crossed his trees, always using the healthiest ones, and those with the healthiest and sweetest nuts. Eventually Dr. Dunstan created a strain of trees that combined American and Asian characteristics and that has now lived for 50 years without showing sign of the fungal disease. These trees became known as Dunstan chestnuts.

Dunstan chestnut trees are fast-growing trees that are easy to grow across most of the country. They grow well in a wide range of soils, and once established, they are drought resistant. Most important, after decades of healthy growth, they appear to be immune to the blight disease. Unlike some other kinds of chestnuts, Dunstan trees produce a heavy crop in fall, and begin to bear chestnuts within a few years of planting. It is necessary to plant at least 2 different chestnut trees for cross-pollination, but the good news is that both trees will bear nuts, so you double your harvest. Their green, spiny case breaks open to reveal inside several large shiny nuts. Unlike other wild chestnuts, the Dunstan chestnut is naturally sweet and makes great eating for humans, deer, and other wildlife.

Dunstan chestnuts™ are part of the fastest growing group of "true" nut trees, which includes American

▲ There are many varieties of chestnut trees. This one is a hybrid of American, Chinese, European, and Japanese. Photo: Mossy Oak Nativ Nurseries

hazelnut, Chinese chestnut, walnut, almond, and pecan. I have planted more than 100 Dunstan chestnut™ trees over the last 5 years. Most of them were 2- to 3-year-old containerized nursery stock, while several were 4-year-old potted trees. Unlike most oak trees, the 2-year-old trees produced chestnuts with 2 seasons. The 3-year-old trees all produced chestnuts the following year, and the 4-year-old trees made chestnuts the same year I planted them. One of the most valuable reasons for planting chestnut trees is that you do not have to wait 15 to 20 years for them to start bearing nuts, like many oak trees.

Through personal experience, I can say my Dunstan chestnut™ trees perform exceedingly well. They are an excellent choice to consider planting. (Dunstan chestnuts™ are available at www.chestnuthillnursery.com).

Other varieties of chestnut trees include the following:

- Belle Epine—a French cultivar of pure European ancestry.
- Bisalta #2 - a consistent producer of chestnuts.
- Bisalta #3—can tolerate colder growing seasons.
- Bouche de Betizac—is a very upright growing chestnut tree.
- Colossal—produces the largest, most abundant nuts starting at a young age, usually the second year. Cold-hardy to -20°F.
- Marrone di Marradi—flavorful, sweet, and rated as one of the best chestnut trees.
- Marrone di Susa—an Italian chestnut that grows well in the cool areas of the Pacific Northwest.
- Marigoule—hybrid from France. Resistant to root rot. Winter cold-resistant to -30°F.
- Marsol—resistant to root rot. Nuts are large. Winter cold-resistant to -30°F.
- Maraval—pollinates trees 150 feet away. Resistant to root rot. Winter cold-resistant to -30°F.

- Okie—large nuts and good pollinator. A hybrid of chinquapin and Japanese chestnut trees.
- Precoce—excellent pollen producer. Upright growth habit. Winter cold-resistant to -30°F.
- Regina Montis (ExJ)—good growth vigor. Makes nuts in 2 years. Winter cold-tolerant to -30°F.

The above listed varieties can be found at www.washingtonchestnut.com and some other chestnut nurseries.

Chestnut trees are an essential element to include in your nut tree food plots. There are two very good reasons to include chestnuts: one, to attract wildlife, and two, to enhance your land stewardship.

It is important that you carefully research any variety you want to plant, as each different cultivar has its positive and negative aspects. This is true when you are trying to limit negative characteristics such as blight, root rot, fungus, mold, etc.

▲ Dunstan chestnuts grow in groups, as seen here. Each burr usually contains 3 chestnuts. Photo: Chestnut Hill Outdoors

▲ There is absolutely no doubt that nuts are highly sought after by deer. They provide protein and fat, making them an excellent food for deer. Credit © Mikael Males—Dreamstime

Chapter Thirty

Nut Trees in a Nutshell

It is likely a key hunting strategy of our early nomadic ancestors was a lie-in-wait tactic. Hunters lurked in cover awaiting prey animals that browsed the ground under trees that dropped acorns or other nuts. Acorns were surely a keenly valued and nutritious food source that both hunters and prey binged on as soon as the nuts became available. They provided both species large amounts of protein, fiber, carbohydrates, fats, vitamins, and minerals like calcium, phosphorus, and potassium. In fact, acorns and other nuts have been a healthy food staple for both humans and animals, ever since man hurled his first spears at prey.

▲ It is reasonable to presume early humans quickly learned they had more success killing game by ambushing them at areas where animals gathered to eat during different seasons. One such apparent location would have certainly been where game flocked to eat nuts or acorns. Photo: Pond 5

Today, acorns and other types of nuts are still used by hunters as a food source to ambush prey. Acorns play a significant role in the white-tailed deer's diet. As quickly as acorns and other nuts start to drop in September, deer seek them out. The minerals they contain, particularly calcium and phosphorus, contribute to the bone growth of deer. These minerals help both

female and male deer to develop healthier skeletal structures and buck antlers. As the rut approaches, mast crops become even more important for deer to eat as the carbohydrates help them to put on weight.

THE ELEMENTS

Deer require protein to develop muscles, nerves, and antlers. The pedicle and antler are structurally comprised of fibrous tissue, bone, cartilage, nerves and blood vessels. Proteins, which are organic molecules made up of carbon, hydrogen, oxygen, and nitrogen, are vital elements for deer. A 3½-ounce portion of acorns provide deer with more than 40 different elements, including 6 grams of protein, 40 grams of carbohydrates, 23 distinct types of fat, 18 different proteins, 8 distinctive vitamins, 9 minerals, and 27.9 grams of water. All these elements are needed for general good health. As deer prepare for the rigors of the rut and the oncoming winter, they use acorns and other types of nuts as a significant source of energy. Deer need to convert the energy from acorns into carbohydrates, fats, and all the other elements, vitamins, minerals, and proteins mentioned above.

MINERALS

Many research studies have documented that calcium and phosphorus are the two most common minerals in deer antlers. Calcium and phosphorus, however, are only a portion of what is needed for the most advantageous antler growth. The remaining minerals (macro and micro) must also contribute to the deer's diet when they are growing or developing their antlers. That is why mineral supplements prior to and during antler growth are beneficial.

At the end of fall, when deer and other wildlife have eaten most of the acorn crop, deer will eat every leftover acorn they discover, even if they must dig them up from under the snow. They scavenge for uneaten acorns to help them gain back some of the weight they lost during the breeding season. This is particularly the case for deer that do not have access to agricultural or food plot winter-hardy crops. It becomes easy to see that acorns, and other types of nuts, are important foodstuffs that deer need.

ACORNS AND OTHER MAST

The simple fact is that all types of nut-producing trees provide the nutrients deer require to improve their overall health, antler development, fawn survival, and winter subsistence. Therefore, all food plot and deer managers, novices and experienced alike, should be highly motivated to enhance their food plot and deer management programs by planting, growing, and managing a variety of different acorn- and other nut-bearing trees. Adding a variety of different types of traditional oaks, and other non-traditional nut trees, will enhance the overall well-being of your deer herd and help you see and bag more deer.

▲ All types of hard mast, including oaknuts (acorns), provide deer with significant amounts of energy. Nature delivers this bounty in fall, which helps deer put on fat prior to the onset of the rut and the rigors of winter. Photo: © Motorolka |Dreamstime

THE PLAN

Plan A is to diversify and enhance your food plot and deer management program by improving the numbers and varieties of nut-bearing trees on your property. This means caring for existing mature acorn-bearing oak trees and planting and managing other new nut trees. Planting varied species of nursery-raised nut trees will

help to deliver a reliable and higher-quality hard mast crop to your deer herd.

Consider this: Deer will temporarily shift from eating other food items and concentrate on acorns and other nuts as soon as they ripen and fall to the ground. Deer consume substantial amounts of acorns. Biologists state that acorns may constitute up to 25 percent or more of a deer's diet in autumn. On lands with food plots or farms with agricultural crops, the percentage of acorns eaten by deer in the fall is said to be slightly lower.

▲ The white acorns seen here are a favorite oaks nuts of deer due to their low content of tannins. However, deer will eat all types of acorns, even when they contain high amounts of tannins. Photo: © Ricard Coomber |Dreamstime

Most properties throughout the country include native varieties of oak trees that bear acorns. If a food plotter adds several types of nursery nut-bearing trees that will drop their bounty, it will dramatically help to draw in deer regularly. Nursery nut trees other than oaks are generally referred to as "true" nut trees. **There is no Plan B.**

OAK TREES

Some food plot pros say deer will only seek out acorns from white oak trees because of their low tannins. They also claim deer will not seek out other acorns until all the white oak acorns are gone. My feeling is *that's crazy nuts*! Yes, deer do prefer one acorn type over another mostly, if not primarily, due to the various levels of tannic acid that dissimilar acorns contain. Basically, it boils down to the less tannic acid contained in an acorn, the more deer prefer that type of acorn. But even when acorns contain medium and even elevated levels of tannins, deer will still eat them. In areas where there are a variety of white and red acorns, deer will inevitably eat the sweetest tasting acorn first: white acorns. After eating the sweeter acorns, deer will not ignore an acorn because it might taste bitter. I have never heard of, nor have I observed, during my five-plus decades of hunting and studying deer behavior, any oak acorn not being perceived by deer as a principal food item.

Acorns provide all species of deer, turkeys and other upland birds, bears, wild pigs, and countless other hunted and non-hunted animals with all the healthy nutrients mentioned earlier. Instinctively, deer realize that. Deer also recognize that acorns are a digestible and palatable food source. Therefore, I can state unequivocally that no food plotter will go wrong by including a variety of oak trees as part of the overall food plot and deer management program, whether they are white or red oak.

There are a few important considerations. One of the most important factors to research is the length of time various oak trees need to produce acorns. Some will produce acorns in several years. Most others will take decades. Another matter to investigate is to make sure the oak tree's winter-hardiness zone is viable for your land's location. Other factors worth considering are the types of soil they need, their preferred pH, and how much sunlight is required.

Red oak acorns contain higher levels of tannic acid, making their acorns considerably more bitter than acorns from other oaks. But guess what? Even at that, deer still eat them. They won't eat them as eagerly as other acorns, but they will still consume them—high tannic acid and all. In the end, it is better to have a few red-acorn-producing trees with acorns containing tannins than no red oak trees at all. On the flip side, a wise food plotter will plant a variety of white, red, and other types of oak trees including scrub oaks. By doing so you will see and kill more deer.

Oak trees grow worldwide. North America is home to the widest variety of diverse types of oak species. In the United States, there are said to be about 90 or more distinct types of native oak trees. Many of them

▲ The most bitter acorn belongs to the red oaks. They contain higher levels of tannic acid. Even though it is bitter tasting to deer, they will not pass up an opportunity to eat them. That speaks highly for how acorns are such a preferred food source for deer. Photo T. Rose

are categorized as either white or red oaks. However, as they are related to food plots, this section will focus on the more common native oak trees. When it comes to planting oak trees, hunters with food plot and deer management programs often become hades-bent on only planting white oak trees as they are a deer "fav" as far as acorns go. This is a good idea, but only if the food plotter is young enough to see seedling white oaks (less than 3 feet tall) develop a significant and reliable acorn crop from year-to-year. Generally, it'll be at least 20 years. The key words here are "reliable crop."

There is an adage about planting white or red oak trees that a food plotter should heed. It says, "One doesn't plant oak trees chiefly for themselves. Rather, they are planted for upcoming generations." While that is true of many of the slow-growing oaks, the adage does not apply to all the other varied species of acorn and/or other types of nut-producing trees, especially the nursery-raised traditional and non-traditional acorn and other nut species.

Below is a list of traditional oak trees in no order of preference for your consideration and information. I have only included the more popular oak species.

White Oak (*Quercus alba*): If you are fortunate enough to have several *mature* white oaks on your hunting property you have hit the jackpot lotto of acorn Heaven. White oaks are stately trees that can reach heights of 80 to 100 feet. They grow throughout most of the eastern United States, central Michigan, southeastern Minnesota, western Iowa, eastern Kansas, Oklahoma, Texas, and even as far south as northern Florida and Georgia. White oaks prefer moist upland soils. They like full sun to partial shade. White oak acorns have the least amount of tannic acid of all oak acorns. Because of this, white oaks are the number one acorn food choice not only of deer, but also bears, wild turkeys, upland game-birds, squirrels, and any other acorn-eating animals. White oaks drop their fruit from September to early November, providing food for deer and other wildlife into early winter.

Now comes the only glitch. The white oak only begins to bear a reliable and nutritious acorn crop after it is a decade or two old. They hit peak production at around 50 years old. Even then, white oak trees only produce heavy acorn crops irregularly, about every 4 to 10 years. If you have white oaks on your land, you should be grateful. If you don't and you are young enough to see a white oak bear its acorns, then you should consider planting several on your land. It is an oak tree that should never be left out of a wildlife program unless it will not grow in your area. USDA Hardiness Zones 4 to 8.

▲ White oaks provide oaknuts with the least amounts of tannins, making them quite palatable to deer. Unfortunately, the white oak produces its first acorns after 20 years of age, and its peak crop after 50 years. Hence, they are best planted by food plotters in their twenties. Photo: © Sandra Lund | Dreamstime

Swamp Chestnut Oak (*Quercus michauxii*): The swamp chestnut oak, a.k.a. cow oak, closely resembles the chestnut oak *Quercus prinus*. It is a larger, stately white oak tree that grows best in richer soils. It typically grows to around 60 to 80 feet high. Do not let the name of this tree fool you. It can grow well from New York to southern Florida. It will not tolerate poor drainage or long periods of flooding. The swamp chestnut oak produces an exceptionally large acorn that is 1 to 1½-inches long, ovoid, and covered about ⅓ of its length in a thick cup with rough scales. Its acorns are low in tannin, making them prized by white-tailed deer, wild turkeys, other upland birds, waterfowl, squirrels, and hogs. But here is the hiccup that many of the white oak trees have: the swamp chestnut oak begins to bear acorns between 20 and 25 years of age, with its best production around 40 years. USDA Hardiness Zones 6 to 9.

▲ Do not let the "swamp" part of this tree's name mislead you. It will not tolerate poor drainage or lengthy periods of flooding. Swamp chestnut oak acorns are very palatable. They are eaten by deer, black bears, all upland birds, waterfowl, wild hogs, and squirrels. Photo: Mossy Oak Nativ Nurseries

Swamp White Oak (*Quercus bicolor*): The swamp white oak is a large, relatively moderate to fast growing tree. It has a mature height of 50 to 60 feet and can live longer than 300 years. It has large leaves with rounded lobes, and a scaling bark. The white oak likes swampy situations, prefers acidic soil (pH 5.0 to 6.5, with 6.0 to 6.5 ideal), is drought tolerant, and survives in a variety of habitats. Growth in alkaline soils may cause iron chlorosis. The mast usually grows in pairs on long stems. They are oval, about 1-inch long with about $\frac{1}{3}$ of their length encased in the cup. The acorns are sweet and are eaten by deer, bears, wild turkeys, other upland birds, squirrels, ducks, and non-hunted song-birds, and other animals. Its large acorns are heavily favored because of their low tannin content. However, the swamp white oak only begins to bear acorns after it is 20 to 30 years old. Even then, its mast crops are only

produced every 3 to 5 years. The acorns drop from October to November. USDA Hardiness Zones 4 to 8.

▲ Swamp oak is another variety of white oak. It can take a decade or two to bear its first acorn crop. But after that, deer will be rewarded with its bounty. Photo: Mossy Oak Nativ Nurseries

Burr Oak (*Quercus macrocarpa*): This tree has several other common names including mossy cup oak, blue oak, and burly oak. It is a species of oak in the white oak section. When mature, it can reach heights of 70 to 80 feet. It is a slow-growing oak with height increases of only a single foot per year, but it is one of the most massive oaks with a trunk diameter of up to 10 feet at maturity. It is native to North America in the eastern and midwestern United States and southcentral Canada. It grows best in well-drained sandy loam with full sun, although it can tolerate partial shade. The burr oak acorns are exceptionally large and can grow to be 2 inches long and 1½ inches broad. They are high in tannic acid but are still eaten by wildlife. Black bears eat the burr oak's acorns and so do other animals like wild turkeys, squirrels, and rabbits. Deer will eat burr oak acorns. However, their high tannin levels don't put this acorn on a deer's preferred oaknut list. If there are other acorns more easily available, deer usually eat the burr oak acorn as a last choice. USDA Winter Hardiness Zone 4 to 8.

▲ Burr oak is yet another variety of white oak. It doesn't produce its first acorn crop until it is about 35 years old. Photo: Mossy Oak Nativ Nurseries

Chestnut Oak (*Quercus prinus*): Also known as the mountain chestnut oak, this species of oak lies within the white oak group. It is also known as the rock oak because it is generally found in mountainous elevations. It is native to the eastern United States. It is one of the most abundant trees of the mountainous ridges of the Appalachian Mountains, extending from Maine to Georgia. The chestnut oak is particularly well suited to rocky upland forest and ridges. It is a small tree due to the nutrient deficiency of the environment in which it grows, and only reaches a height of about 55 to 80 feet. The tree grows at a medium growth rate. The chestnut oak is the shorter cousin of the venerable white oak. The acorns of the chestnut oak are prodigious, growing to a length of more than an inch with a girth nearly as large. They are among the largest acorns of all the American oaks. However, good crops of chestnut oak acorns are relatively rare. Chestnut oak acorns production is very erratic, and heavy crops take place only once every 4 or 5 years, as compared to most other oak mast cycles of 2 to 3 years. Chestnut oak acorns are not a favorite acorn of deer because the acorn contains high tannin levels, making them bitter. In fact, chestnut oak acorns have been measured to contain 10.4 percent

tannins, making them the most tannic acid acorn found in North America. That doesn't mean deer won't eat them. Despite the bitterness of the chestnut oak's acorns, deer will feed on them, especially if other acorns are not available. The chestnut oak's acorns are an important food source to many other animals, including bears, wild turkeys, upland birds, and other small hunted and non-hunted mammals. USDA Winter Hardiness Zone 4.

▲ Chestnut acorns are large. Depending on their species, it can take 20 to 30 years before they produce their first acorns. Even then, acorn production is not consistent from year to year. Credit—© Andrey Khokhlov | Dreamstime.com

Chinkapin Oak (*Quercus muehlenbergii*): Chinquapin, also spelled chinkapin, is any of several species of trees in various genera of the beech family (*Fagaceae*). Chinkapin oaks, a.k.a. yellow chestnut oak, are found on dry, limestone outcrops in the wild and perform well in alkaline soils (7.0 pH and higher). The chinkapin oak prefers full sun and should get at least 6 hours of direct, unfiltered sunlight per day. This tree grows at a slow to medium rate, with annual height increases of about 1 to 2 feet per year. Chinkapin oaks can reach heights of about 65 to 80 feet. The trunk diameter can reach 2 to 3 feet. Chinkapin oak is native to eastern and central North America, ranging from Vermont west to Wisconsin and south to South Carolina, western Florida, New Mexico, and northeastern Mexico. The acorns are dark colored, oval, and about ³⁄₄-inch long. They are encased about halfway into the cup. The 1-inch-large acorns are overly sweet, much like the white oak acorn. They contain much less tannic acid than most other oak tree acorns. Chinkapin oaks produce acorns in a single season, making them more productive than almost any other oak tree. They are highly attractive to deer, bears, wild turkeys, upland birds, squirrels, and many other types of wildlife. Chinkapin acorns are at the top of the food preference list for deer. If a food plotter is going to grow oak trees, the chinkapin oak should be a top choice to consider. USDA Winter Hardiness Zones 4–7.

▲ The chinkapin oak prefers alkaline soil. It is a dependable grower. Its acorns are small but sweet, and possibly more preferred by deer than white oak nutoaks. As a bonus, its chestnut-like leaves turn very colorful in fall. Photo: treesandshrubsonline.org

Gobbler Sawtooth Oak (*Quercus acutissima*): Gobbler sawtooth oak is the same tree as the sawtooth oak. It is a species of white oak. The only difference is that the gobbler sawtooth oak produces smaller acorns, up to ⅝- to ¾-inch long. By comparison, the sawtooth oak's acorns are huge oaknuts at about 1½ inches long. They are among the favorite acorns of wildlife. The gobbler sawtooth oak is one of the fastest growing of the oak trees. It can reach heights of 40 to 75 feet and can have an equal canopy (the length between its furthest branches). They are cold-hardy trees that do well in northern climates as far as Canada. Typically, a sawtooth oak produces acorns at an early age, when the tree is about 4 to 6 years old. Once a gobbler sawtooth or a sawtooth tree reaches 12 to 15 years old, it is said to produce 1,000 to 1,300 pounds of acorns in a year. That and the other benefits mentioned makes it a top choice for food plot and deer managers. With proper care, they can produce acorns within 4 years. This is considerably faster than most other oak trees that historically take anywhere from 20 to 30 years to produce their first acorn crop. In alternate years, the acorn production will be heavier than the preceding year. The acorns contain slightly more tannin than the white oaks, but less than a lot of other oak tree acorns. Gobbler sawtooth oak nuts are highly favored by all deer species, bears, wild turkeys, upland birds, small mammals, and a host of other hunted and non-hunted animals. In fact, some ducks, like woodies and mallards, eat this acorn too. Deer managers should give this oak earnest consideration. USDA Winter Hardiness Zones 5–9.

Northern Red Oak (*Quercus ruba*): Red oaks are found in many forested areas with other hardwoods and conifers, particularly pines. Their bristle-tipped leaves turn red in the fall. Red oaks grow best in deep, fertile, well-drained but moist soils. They are cold-hardy, semi-fast-growing trees putting on 2 feet per year during their first 10 years. Northern red oaks can reach heights of more than 65 to 75 feet. They are used in the restoration of wildlife habitat and degraded sites, particularly in areas with acidic soil conditions (pH from 5.0 to 6.9). Northern red oaks are one of the largest oaks and can produce enormous amounts of ¾- to 1-inch-long acorns. The acorns are near the top of the oaknut preference of deer, black bears, wild-turkeys, grouse, other birds, squirrels, and small mammals. Deer will also browse the buds and twigs of northern red oaks in wintertime. In the absence of white oaks and a few other sweet acorn-bearing trees, red oak acorns are heavily eaten by white-tailed deer, even as

▲ Like most species of oaks, red oaks begin producing acorns at about 20 years old. Peak production generally takes place at 50 to 80 years old. Some red oak trees produce more acorns than other red oak trees, a condition that deer hunters should keep a close eye on. Photo: © Aga7ta | Dreamstime

a secondary choice. Northern red oaks often produce a reliable and abundant crop of acorns on a yearly basis. However, they occasionally can skip a year of production. They are advantageous choices to be included in a woodlot management agenda as well as a deer management program. USDA Hardiness Zones 3 to 8.

Overcup Oak (*Quercus lyrata*) is an oak within the white oak group, meaning it has sweeter tasting oaknuts than red and other types of oak trees. It is native to lowland wetlands in the southeastern United States from Delaware to southern Illinois and down to northern Florida and southeast Texas. The tree can reach heights of 60 to 90 feet, but most will be smaller. Overcup oaks are a white oak that typically begin to produce acorns at about 25 years of age. In good soil and in full sunlight they will produce acorns at a younger age. Their acorns range in size from ¾- to 1½-inch. Overcup oaks produce good white acorn crops every 3 to 4 years. The acorns drop from late October through November. Like most other white oak acorns, the overcup oak's acorns are attractive to deer, bears, and a host of other wildlife. Its acorns take between 6 and 24 months to mature. The time it takes for this tree to make acorns makes it only a good choice if the food plotter is young enough to see the benefits of the overcup oak's acorn production. If I planted an overcup oak this fall, I would be 99 years old before I saw an acorn from this tree—ugh. USDA Hardiness Zones 5–9.

Post Oak (*Quercus stellata*) is sometimes called iron oak. The post oak is in the white oak family and is a slow-growing oak that lives in dry, poor soils, and is resistant to rot, fire, and drought. It is a medium-sized tree abundant throughout the southeastern and south-central United States. It is a slow-growing oak that is considered drought resistant. The range of post oak extends from southeastern Massachusetts, Rhode Island, southern Connecticut, and extreme southeastern New York (including Long Island); west to southeastern Pennsylvania and West Virginia, central Ohio, southern Indiana, central Illinois, southeastern Iowa, and Missouri; south to eastern Kansas, western Oklahoma, northwestern and central Texas; and east to central Florida. The acorns mature in one growing season and drop soon after ripening during September through November. The acorns are sessile or short-stalked, born solitary, in pairs, or clustered. As a white oak acorn, they are highly sought after by deer, bears, wild turkeys, upland gamebirds, squirrels, and a host of other small mammals. The acorns are about ½- to ¾-inch long, oval-shaped, broad at the base, and set in a cup ⅓ to ½ their length. In common with many other oaks, post oak begins to bear acorns when it is about 20 years old. After that, good acorn crops are produced at 2- to 3-year intervals. USDA Winter Hardiness Zones 4–8.

▲ Post oak is a slow-growing oak. It generally takes about 20 years before it makes acorns. However, it is resistant to fire, drought, and rot; thus, the nickname iron oak. Photo: © Larry Metayer | Dreamstime

Black Oak (*Quercus velutina*) a.k.a. yellow barked oak. It is a quite common oak in the eastern forests. It can attain heights of 50 to 80 feet and generally has a trunk diameter of about 4 feet when it matures. Black oak is a member of the red oak group. The acorn is rounded, rust-colored, and is about ½- to ¾-inch long. It is encased up to half its entire length in a bowl-shaped cup. This tree requires full sun and grows best in well-drained, slightly acidic soil (6.0 to 6.5 pH). It will not do well in shade. A mature black oak tree produces an acorn crop every other year. The acorns of the black oak are rated as having medium to high tannic acid levels. If white oak acorns are available to deer, they will eat them first and then eat the acorns of black oak. If the deer's range only includes black oak acorns, deer will readily gobble them down. The USDA Hardiness Rating Zone 3.

▲ Depending on their species, the trees of a black oak are 20 to 30 years old when they produce their first acorns. Acorn production is not reliable from year to year. Photo: © Gerald D. Tang | Dreamstime

Blackjack Oak (*Quercus marilandica*): Also known as sand oak or upland willow oak, this is a small oak compared to other oaks. It is a member of the red oak group. It has a moderate growth rate. Its thick, black bark is deeply divided into rough, nearly square plates. Blackjack oak is a tree common of the Old South. It appears from southeastern New York into Oklahoma and Texas. Its acorns are small, less than ½-inch to about ¾-inch in length. It has a deep cup that covers the nut to about half its length. Like other red oaks, its acorns take 18 months to mature. The blackjack oak's tannin level is rated as high. All types of wildlife, from rodents to all types of birds and mammals, eat the acorns. Blackjack oak acorns rank low on the white-tail's preference list of acorns to eat. USDA Winter Hardiness Zone 3a–9b.

Laurel Oak (*Quercus laurifolia*), a.k.a. swamp laurel oak, diamond-leaf oak, water oak, and obtusa oak. Laurel oak is in the red oak section and is a fast-growing, acorn-producing deciduous tree. It is among one of the most cold-hardy evergreen oaks. An evergreen oak keeps its old leaves until new leaves appear. Trees growing in Cincinnati indicate the laurel oak may be hardy even farther north than previously thought, tolerating temperatures lower than -20°F and surviving into zone 5. It can reach heights of 60 feet with a dense canopy. Laurel oak grows scattered with other hardwoods in well-drained soils near the edges of streams and rivers. It grows throughout the coastal plain from southeastern Virginia to central Florida and west to southern Texas. Laurel oak is abundant in Florida and in other parts of the South. It produces solitary acorns, but sometimes they are in pairs with large crops of small ½-inch-long acorns with saucer-shaped cups. The acorns are high in tannin but, despite their bitter taste, they are eaten by deer. Acorn production is often heavy, enhancing the laurel oak's value to wildlife. It produces its acorns regularly, making it a good tree for wildlife food plot managers to consider. It is an important wildlife food resource for white-tailed deer, turkeys, ducks, squirrels, upland and other birds, and other wildlife. USDA Hardiness Zones 6–9.

Live Oak (*Quercus virginiana*): Live Oak is a red oak tree that will do well for deer and food plot managers in southern areas. Live oak ranges from the coastal plains to southern Florida and west into Texas. It is often found in a variety of habitats including grasslands, forested areas, and savanna-type terrain. Often, live oak is mixed with other hardwoods, pines, and junipers, and it is frequently decorated with Spanish moss. This species of trees can grow to 50 feet in height. It develops a short, solid trunk that supports many of its huge, nearly straight, wide-spreading branches that form the tree's dense crown. Live oak needs plenty of room to develop and does best when it is planted in large open areas. It is not susceptible to many diseases or insects unless it is stressed by fire or other damage. The live oak produces an abundant amount of small- to medium-sized sweet acorns low in

▲ A bountiful crop of live oak acorns by a tree that is 20 years old. Live oak is tough and can live for an amazing several hundred years if planted correctly. It is vulnerable to the fatal oak wilt disease, spread by insects, however. Photo: © Elba Cabrera | Dreamstime

tannins. Its mast is highly prized by deer, turkeys, and other birds and mammals. It can produce ¾- to 1-inch acorns as early as age 5, making it one of the fastest-growing oak-producing trees. For managers in southern zones, live oak is a splendid choice to provide quality mast for deer and other wildlife. It is hardy in areas as cold as USDA Hardiness Zone 7 even though it is native to Zones 8–10. However, it is susceptible to damage from freezes for extended periods.

Nuttall Oak (*Quercus nuttalli*) is a species in the red oak group. It is commonly found in the mid-southern states bordering or close to the Mississippi River. Nuttall red oaks grow quickly, up to two to four feet per year. They tolerate wet soil as well as moderate drought and prefer moist bottomland soils. They can grow 60 to 90 feet tall and have stout trunks 4 feet or more in diameter. Nuttall oaks prefer full unfiltered

▲ If a nuttall oak receives lots of nutrients, sun, and water, it can start to make acorns as early as 7 to 10 years old. This is an oak even an old guy like me can plant and live long enough to see the bounty. Photo: Chestnuthillnursery.com

sun for at least 6 hours per day. They can produce acorns at an early age, 7 to 10 years. Nuttalls produce acorns every year and can begin making heavy crops of acorns from year 10 on. More important, nuttall oak trees drop their acorns in winter, from November through February, providing deer with a late-season acorn food source after most other acorns have already been eaten by deer or have decayed on the forest floor. It doesn't matter that their acorns have more tannin than some other oaks. Because nuttall acorns drop in winter, deer eagerly seek them out and eat them. The late-dropping aspect alone should make this oak a top-shelf choice for food plot managers who have hunting property within the nuttall oak's restricted growing area. Providing deer with winter acorns is a huge asset to any manager's deer herd. The oblong acorns are about 1-inch long and have a thick deep cup. If nuttall oaks are within your planting zone, order them directly after reading this. USDA Hardiness Zones 5–9.

Pin Oak (*Quercus palustris*): Pin oak is a red oak found from southwestern New England, west through extreme southwestern Ontario, to northern Illinois, southwest to northeastern Oklahoma, and east to Virginia. It is a moderately fast-growing tree that can reach heights of about 50 to 75 feet and live about 150 years. It needs a spot in full sunlight to produce its best acorn crop and it is partial to moist soils. Don't plant a young tree in a wet area, as the roots must be established for the pin oak to survive in wet conditions. After several years, when a pin oak is well-established, it can then tolerate even being in standing water for weeks at a time. The pin oak requires a pollinator. The pin oak thrives in acidic soils (pH 5.0 to 6.5) The brown acorns mature in the second year and are about ½-inch long, nearly round, and about ⅓ is enclosed in a very shallow cap. They drop in September and October. The mast is small but favored by birds and small animals. The pin oak's acorns are highly sought after by ducks and wild turkeys. Of course, where there are acorns, they will attract deer too. USDA Hardiness Zones 5–8.

Scarlet Oak (*Quercus coccinea*): This tree falls into the red oak group. It is a medium-growing red oak that tolerates a wide range of soils except alkaline soil. It is rated as a medium-growing oak that grows about 1 to 2 feet each year. It can reach heights of 70 to 80 feet. Scarlet oak trees can take decades to mature; in fact, the trees are 20 to 30 years old when they produce their first acorns. Even then, the acorn production is not consistent from year to year. A scarlet oak's acorns are usually about ¾- to 1-inch long. They are oval shaped and ½ to ⅓ of their length is encased in a deep, basin-like cup. The end that sticks out is usually marked with circular lines. Scarlet oak acorns are higher in tannin than the acorns from the white oaks, but they are still an important food source to deer, upland birds like grouse, squirrels, large songbirds, and other animals. USDA Hardiness Zones 4–9.

Shumard Oak (*Quercus shummardii*): The Shumard oak is a fast-growing, drought-tolerant red oak. It will do well in alkaline, acidic, loamy well-drained soils (from pH 7.0 to 8.0). It can grow 14 to 24 inches a year and can reach 40 to 60 feet in height. It prefers well-drained soil. After reaching about 25 years, it will begin making acorns. Once it does, it will produce an acorn crop every 2 to 4 years. They are known to be a long-lived tree with some reaching at least 450 years

of age. Shumard oak's small acorns are highly sought after by deer, upland birds, squirrels, and other birds and mammals. It is native to the more southern states of the eastern United States, even reaching into the northernmost areas of Florida. The acorn is ¾ to 1¼ inches long, oval, and has a thick, rough cup that is flat and saucer-like. Most of the acorn fruit sticks out of the cup. What makes the shumard oak an attractive planting is that it drops its acorns in October and November. USDA Hardiness Zones 5–9.

Southern Red Oak (*Quercus falcata*): Southern red oak, a.k.a. Spanish oak, is a tree in the red oak group. Despite its name, it is not just a southern tree. It is native to the eastern and south-central United States. This tree grows in southern New York to central Florida and west to southern Missouri and eastern Texas. It is a medium-sized tree reaching 50 to 80 feet tall, with a trunk that's 2 to 3 feet wide. The tree's growth rate is rated as medium. Southern red oaks can usually be found growing in the wild in poor soils on slopes and hilltops. The acorns are short, bright orange-brown, and enclosed for ⅓ to ½ of their length in a flat cup. The ½-inch-diameter acorns are popular with wildlife.

▲ Shumard oaks are super-fast acorn producers, generally making large acorns in 2 to 3 years. Shumards are drought tolerant, grow amazingly fast, and produce beautiful fall colors. Photo: Mossy Oak Nativ Nurseries

▲ Do not be fooled by the name of this tree. Although it thrives in the South, the southern red oak will do well growing from New York to south Florida. Photo: Mossy Oak Nativ Nurseries

Like most species of oak trees, the southern red oak takes about 20 to 25 years to produce its first crop of acorns. However, this tree does not reach its peak acorn production until about 50 to 80 years old. Therefore, managers need to plant this tree for their children. The southern red oak's acorns are bitter due to their medium tannin level. With that said, deer, bears, wild turkeys, and squirrels will readily eat the acorns. USDA Hardiness Zones 7–9.

Willow Oak (*Quercus phellos*): The willow oak is a North American species of a deciduous tree in the red oak group. It is native to the eastern and central United States, from Long Island Sound south to northern Florida and west to southernmost Illinois, Missouri, Oklahoma, and eastern Texas. The willow oak grows at a medium rate. It prefers full sun and soil

▲ Willow oaks thrive in floodplains and near streams and marshes. However, they are also remarkably drought tolerant as well. Photo: © Callum Redgrave Close | Dreamstime

that is medium-textured, silty, or loamy, contains some organic matter, and is acidic (pH 4.5 to 5.5). Willow oaks can regularly reach heights of 60 to 70 feet, with trunk diameters of about 3 to 4 feet. The round acorns are small, only growing about ½-inch long with a thin, flat, scaly cup. A willow oaks takes about 2 years to mature. It is noted for its rapid growth and long life. However, it can take more than 20 years before the first acorn crop. The willow oak falls into the red oak group, which makes its acorns bitter tasting from tannins. Although they are bitter, the acorns are still an attractive food preference for white-tailed deer, wild turkeys, some upland birds. Wood ducks and mallards also eat the acorns when stands of willow oak are near ponds or flooded areas. USDA Hardiness Zones 5–9.

OTHER TYPES OF DEER NUT FAVS

My wife Kate, our son Cody, and I manage our food plot program on our 192 acres. Our program includes a variety of 35 or more food plots, traditional forage plants, early and mostly late-dropping fruit trees, acorn-bearing white and red oak trees, and other types of nut-bearing trees. Without a doubt we have reaped the benefits of these plantings over the 20 years that we have owned our farm. We are always looking for new types of plantings to keep all our food plot options open, as our supplemental feedings have helped the fawn production, doe lactation, and the antler growth of the bucks.

About 6 years ago, we began planting 2- to 3-year-old Dunstan chestnut trees, and have had excellent

▲ These are the ripe chestnuts that have fallen from one of our Dunstan chestnut trees. Many of our 2-year-old Dunstan chestnut trees produced nuts in their third year. Dunstan chestnuts prefer to be planted in well-drained soil. Photo: Chestnut Hill Outdoors

success from those plantings. At this writing, we have planted more than 100 Dunstan chestnut trees. These trees produce medium to heavy crops of chestnuts yearly, depending on the tree's age. The deer have reaped what we have sown. (There is more detailed information about Dunstan and other chestnut trees in Chapter 29, The Extraordinary Chestnuts.)

A few years ago we started thinking about what other types of nut trees would be beneficial for both deer and people. We started planting almond trees and have been adding other types of nut trees that are loaded with protein and fat.

THE NUTLET TREES

I want to wrap up this chapter with bona-fide nut trees that produce meaty nuts consumed by a vast assortment of wildlife and humans. In botany, these types of nut trees are referred to as "nutlet" or "real nut" trees. The term explicitly refers to a pyrene, which means "joined or packed together"—a seed that is covered or encased by an outer layer. An example would be an almond. The meaty nut is covered by an inedible skin or shell. Some of the trees I am referring to are almond, pecan, hazelnut, walnut, pistachio, and cashew nuts are all tree nuts, a.k.a. "nutlets" or "true nuts." Depending on your USDA Hardiness Zone, these nut trees can grow throughout the lower 48 states.

They are nuts under some definitions but are also referred to as drupaceous (hanging) nuts. They are not part of the oak tree acorn-producing oaknuts. The nut trees listed below can be grown within a food plot program as either a small orchard or as random plantings. When planning to buy nutlet trees, pay incredibly careful attention to the USDA Hardiness Zone recommendations for each species. Planting these types of nutlets in the proper hardiness zones will ensure that the trees will not only grow to their best ability, but nut production will also be hastened. Generally, many of these types of nutlet trees will produce bountiful crops of nuts within 4 to 6 years but, again, only if they are properly planted in the recommended hardiness zones.

A wide variety of wildlife feed on these types of nuts, squirrels being the most obvious nut eater. Nutlets are also eaten by some waterfowl, many upland birds, wild turkeys, and numerous songbirds. Not so surprisingly,

white-tailed deer, mule deer, elk, moose, and black bears gorge themselves on nutlets in the fall. There are several native nut-producing trees in North America. They include hickories, beech, almond, pecan, walnut, hazel, and pine nuts. All these nut trees are prized by a wide array of wildlife.

▲ This ol' bruiser of a bear is lazily eating walnuts that have dropped from the walnut tree behind it. Walnuts are part of the part of the "nutlet" or "real nut" type nut trees. A wide variety of hunted and non-hunted animals eat nutlets. Photo: ©Betty 4240 | Dreamstime

When planting these types of nut trees, food plot and deer managers should consider planting a few diverse types of nursery-raised nut trees. They can be purchased as bare-root or as potted stock. I prefer buying bare root stock as they often take off more quickly than trees in containers.

Below is a list of suggested nut trees you can plant either in small orchard-type settings of 6 to 12 trees per mini-orchard (like fruit or chestnut trees), in larger orchards of 24 or more trees, or even in random groups of 2- to 4-tree settings. These types of nut-bearing trees also do well as random plantings along field edges, in overgrown fields that are reclaimed, and in field plots that are used for traditional food plots. Again, to be clear, what I am referring to are nut trees that do not produce acorns; rather they produce nuts that most people eat.

The variety of nut trees below can be grown in various locations from coast to coast. Nowadays, though, some of these nut trees have been scientifically created by agronomists as "frost-resistant" stock. Some varieties are available to northern areas where they couldn't be grown before. Each of these trees can provide copious bounties of nutlets that are highly nutritious food sources for deer. They are sweet and very palatable to deer and other wildlife because they are generally free of any noticeable tannins.

(See the accompanying sidebar from Department of Nutrition, Food & Exercise Sciences, Florida State University, Tallahassee, Florida. Moreover, like ice-cream is to most people, nuts are to deer.)

WILDLIFE GOES NUTTY FOR NUTLETS

American Beech (*Fagus grandifolia*): The American beech, a.k.a. North American beech, is native to the eastern United States and lower southeast Canada. This

▲ Beechnuts are mostly eaten by wood and black ducks, wild turkeys, some upland birds, rabbits, and squirrels. Black bears love them. Deer find them less palatable than other "true nuts." Photo: treesandshrubs.com

tree grows from a slow to medium rate with increases in height from 1 to 2 feet per year and can reach heights of 50 to 80 feet. Ideally the American beech needs 6 hours of unfiltered sunlight per day. It likes moist soils, is very shade tolerant, and grows well in a wide range of soil types. Beech trees are unisexual, with male and female flowers growing on a single tree. The hard-brown nuts are ½- to 1-inch in diameter and contain about 50 percent fat and 20 percent protein. Like other nuts eaten by humans, beech nuts are edible but have a slight tannin taste. Eating a few raw beech-nuts is okay, but don't eat too many. Beechnuts contain the toxin saponin glycoside, which can cause gastric issues. The safer approach is to cook them. Luckily, wildlife does not have that problem with beechnuts. Even though they are slightly bitter, they are a favorite food of black and wood ducks, wild turkeys, upland birds, black bears, rabbits, and squirrels. Deer will eat beechnuts, but generally don't browse on their twigs or leaves. Plant this tree mostly for other huntable game. USDA Winter Hardiness Zones 4–9.

Butternut (*Juglans cinerea*): The butternut, a.k.a. the white walnut, is the hardiest of the walnut species, growing widely across eastern North America from New Brunswick in the East to Minnesota in the Midwest and southward to northern Georgia. The tree is rated as a "slow grower" and only puts on about 12 inches of height per year. When it matures, a butternut tree can reach 40 feet in height and spread. Generally, a butternut tree takes about 5 to 10 years to bear nuts. It is an alternate bearing tree (meaning it will be abundant one year and less the next). The butternut's fruit ripens in late October. The tree is self-fertile. Yet, it is better to plant 2 trees to ensure a better crop. The nuts are oblong and tapered at about 1½ to 2½ inches in diameter. The butternut has a thick, brown, corrugated inner shell that contains the nut kernel, which has a sweet buttery flavor. It is a valuable wildlife food source for deer, bears, birds, and small mammals. USDA Hardiness Zones 3–7.

Almond (*Prunus amygdalus*): Like some other nutlet trees today, the almond tree has been genetically engineered by agronomists to be planted in northern areas. The almond is an excellent nut tree for foo plots.

Surprisingly, the almond is related to apples, pears, and peaches. It grows best in hot, dry climates in locations such as California's Great Central Valley. Today with the cold-hardy varieties they can be grown in northern areas like New York. Almonds are relatively fast-growing and can reach heights of about 30 feet and produce nuts within 3 to 5 years. They, too, need 2 or more trees for cross pollination. Almonds adapt to most soils if they are well-drained. They produce best where summers are hot, long, and dry. Almonds are delicious and nutritious for deer. USDA Hardiness Zones 5–9.

▲ Almonds are a favorite nutlet of deer and other wildlife. Deer like them so much they often can't wait until they fall to the ground. Instead, they stand on their hind legs and eat them directly from the tree. Photo: © Barmalini–Dreamstime

Cashew Nuts (*Anacardium occidentale*): Anyone who has ever eaten a cashew nut knows how tasty they are. Cashews are chock full of healthful benefits for both wildlife and people. A mature cashew tree grows to about 45 feet. Dwarf varieties grow 12 to 20 feet in height. It is extremely adapted to hot lowland areas. Cashew trees take 3 years from planting before starting production. They prefer 6 hours per day of unfiltered sunlight. Cashews are rated as fast-growing trees. Important to food plot managers, cashews mature from November to January. They are exceptionally durable and adaptable. Under favorable conditions, cashew trees will grow well and thrive, bearing nuts in just 2 years. Cashew trees can tolerate poor soil, are drought resistant, and self-fertile. Thus, they are an easy tree for food plot managers to grow in their USDA Hardiness Zones. Cashew trees are cold sensitive and grow best in warmer climates. With cashew nut trees as part of your food plot plan, you will be able to harvest some cashews from your trees and leave the rest for deer and other animals. Cashew trees grow best in USDA Winter Hardiness Zones 10 and 11 but can also survive in warmer parts of USDA Zone 9.

Chestnut (*Castanea dentata*): The fruit of the chestnut tree securely holds first place in all categories of planting, managing, and providing the most desirable nut to deer and other wildlife. There is so much to say about the distinct types of chestnut trees, there is a dedicated chapter on them. (See Chapter 29 for detailed information about the American, Chinese, Japanese, European, and Dunstan chestnut trees.)

Filbert Nuts: See Hazelnuts.

Hazelnut (*Corylus sp.*): A.k.a. the American filbert, the hazelnut tree is a rather unique selection. It is native to the entire northeastern half of North America. Hazelnut trees are also found from Louisiana and Georgia in the south to Manitoba and Quebec in Canada. Food plotters will not have to wait long for the hazelnut tree to bear its bounty of nuts. It is a medium- to fast-growing species. Their nuts mature from September to October and drop their bounty into November making them an ideal nut tree selection to include in a food plot program. Generally, they will begin bearing nuts in their second to third year. After that, they will produce heavy yields of nuts from when they are 6 years old forward. The tree can be grown as a bushy shrub that reaches heights from 8 to 12 feet. Grown as a tree, it can reach a height of 16 feet or more and can be equally as wide. The tasty nuts are a favorite of deer, and any other mammal that walks, flies, hops, or crawls.

An interesting note for food plotters is that the hazelnut tree can also serve as a windbreak, visual screen block, or a bedding area for deer and other wildlife. Many hunters who grow hazelnut trees claim that deer love to eat hazelnuts as they do not find it hard to crack the shell of this small nut. It is important to note that at least two other trees or two different compatible layered cultivars are required to produce nuts. There are a varied number of different seedlings to choose from including the New York hazelnut seedling as well as the Grimo, Gamma, Turkish, Yamhill, Jefferson, and Gene varieties. The American hazelnut adapts easily to all soil types and thrives in full sunlight. Once established, hazelnut trees are tolerant of variances in rainfall from year to year. The nuts have sweet kernels that are rich with a wide combination of antioxidants and nutrients that deer benefit from. If the deer and other wildlife do not eat them, which would be highly unlikely, that will leave more nuts for you. When growing hazelnuts in the coldest part of their range, choose the American hazelnut variety, which is more tolerant than European types in cold climates and temperatures below 15°F. USDA Hardiness Zones 4–8.

▲ The American hazelnut has a higher nutritional value to deer and other wildlife than traditional acorns and even some nutlets. Deer, elk, wild turkeys, and other upland birds as well as squirrels, foxes and non-hunted birds all eat hazelnuts. Photo: NITKA Hazelnut Zs Nutty Ridge

English Walnut (*Juglans*): For the food plotter, there is one top-notch option when planting walnut trees for deer and other wildlife, and that is the Franquette

English walnut, a.k.a. English walnut. Franquette is one of the most widely planted English walnuts for commercial production. It produces delicious, sealed, thin-shelled nuts. Its thin shell is what makes this walnut a top choice, as the nut is easier for deer to crack open, unlike the rigid and extremely tough shell of a black walnut. While deer do not eat walnuts as much as they do other nuts, they do occasionally eat them. The nut's flavor and other attributes make it an ideal planting within a wildlife food plot fruit and nut tree program. Because this is a larger tree with more developed branching and roots, the Franquette English walnut bears its nuts faster than other walnut varieties. It is also cold-hardy down to -10°F, making it an ideal choice for food plotters in more northern areas of the country. Although the Franquette English walnut can be self-fertile, to ensure a hefty crop, plant it with another variety like Manregion English walnut (Manregion English walnut is a very hardy form of English walnut that is prized for its large, easy-to-crack open, delicious nuts). Plant walnut trees in a small group of 2 to 4 trees in open, full-sun, well-drained areas. Try a loose group for a natural grove, varying the planting distance from 20 to 30 feet. These walnut

▲ Once the green husk of a walnut ripens it opens much like a chestnut burr, revealing the soft shell of the walnut that encases the nut itself. Deer do not have trouble breaking a walnut open. Photo: © Kutizoltan | Dreamstime

trees are easy to care for, as they are rugged. Plant on a hill or create a raised bed to improve soil drainage. For the first season, don't allow the tree's roots to dry out. Provide a moderate amount of water on a regular basis. After the tree is established in your soil, it requires less supplemental watering. Apply a layer of mulch around the trunk, but don't let it touch the bark. Keep the root system cool and slowly improve the quality of your soil with mulch. Franquette English walnuts ripen later in October making this walnut highly attractive to deer. But deer aren't the only wildlife that enjoys eating walnuts. Elk, moose, black bears, and a host of other large and small mammals are big fans of eating walnuts. USDA Winter Hardiness Zones 6–9.

Hickory (*Carya laciniosa*): Hickory trees are in the walnut, or Juglandaceae, family. In eastern North America, there are about 18 different hickory species. Hickories are also known as pecan trees. That is because hickory and pecan are the same genus, although they are distinct species. Hickory is self-pollinating and pecan requires a cultivar. Hickory trees are deciduous hardwoods; the most known are shagbark, shellbark, mockernut, and pignut. All hickory trees are known for their hard nuts. They make excellent trees for use in a wildlife landscape and are a terrific provider of nuts. They produce yellow-green catkins in spring. The hickory nut is oval shaped, about 1 to 2 inches long and enclosed in a husk that splits open when ready to release the nut. You've seen how this is done if you have ever watched any of the "Alien" movies.

▲ Some say deer do not eat hickory nuts. Yes, they do. They favor the pignut and bitternut species. They avoid eating shagbark or mockernut due to their hard shells, but that does not mean they will not eat them if they are hungry enough. Photo: Grimo Nuts.

The nuts of some hickory species are very palatable, while others are slightly more bitter. Deer have been observed eating hickory nuts. However, the only species of hickory deer are known to eat are the pignut and bitternut varieties of hickory. They are not known, or have not been observed, to eat shagbark or mockernut nuts because of how hard the shells are. But as deer they will eat almost anything, so it does not mean they will not eat other hickory varieties if they are hungry enough. The nuts attract deer, bears, wild turkeys, other upland birds, squirrels, other small mammals, and birds. Hickory trees thrive in wet soils but will tolerate most other soil types. Shagbark and shellbark hickory are said to be some of the finest nut-bearing trees. What also makes the hickory a terrific nut tree

choice for food plotters, is that it will produce a yearly nut crop. If your hunting land is in the northern areas of the country, hickory trees are for you, as the tree does well in northern zones. It takes the tree some time to develop a strong tap root and is rated as slow-growing. After the tap root takes hold, though, hickory trees begin to grow quickly. Most times, hickory trees take about 5 years or so to begin bearing nuts. That is a lot faster than a white or red oak tree. They produce small, sweet nuts that are housed in sturdy shells that deer don't have too much trouble cracking open. Deer prefer hickory nuts mostly because of the palatability of the large nut kernel with a buttery flavor. To get a quicker nut crop from a hickory tree, there is a practical option, although it costs a little more money.

Instead of planting a seedling or a 1 to 2-year-old tree, purchase 4- to 5-year-old trees from a reliable tree nut nursery. Many grafted varieties grow somewhat faster and yield more crops. They are extremely cold-hardy and, as such, make excellent choices for northern areas. Dwarf varieties are a good option for any fruit or nut tree. USDA Hardiness Zones 4–8.

Peanuts (*Arachis hypogaea*): Peanuts are not actually nut trees; they are classified as a legume. Deer are attracted to peanuts (a.k.a. ground nut and goober). Because they are often referred to as real nuts or nutlets, I included them in this section, even though they are not trees, but plants that grow from 12 to 20 inches tall. If you are lucky enough to live in a zone where peanuts can grow, they are worth considering as a wildlife planting. Peanuts are high in protein and fat, making them a top food source for deer and other wildlife. This combination can be especially important during the post-rut, when both does and bucks need to replace weight lost during the breeding season. Depending on your property, you may want to plant a peanut food plot for white-tailed deer. Peanuts like sandy loam-type soil. They are limited to specific areas of the country and can be an expensive wildlife food plot to establish. The USDA Plant Hardiness Zones for peanuts are 5b -10b; but peanuts are said to be adaptable to a range of climates, and prefer full sun. While it is safe to say they prefer warm weather and are drought tolerant, peanuts are surprisingly frost tolerant, and it has been reported they are able to grow in areas with an average low winter temperature of -15°F. Peanuts reach their peak growing performance in soil temperatures between 70° and 80°F.

▲ Deer love to eat peanuts. They are high in protein and fat, making them terrific food for deer, bears, wild turkeys, and other upland birds. Photo: © Lovelyday12 | Dreamstime

Pecan (*Carya illinoinensis*): The deciduous pecan does not get a lot of positive press. That's because some say deer love them and others say deer only eat them when they have nothing else to eat. The pecan is a good choice as a nut tree for deer, however. In fact, many pecan orchard growers state deer really like eating pecan nuts. Some orchard growers in Georgia, Missouri, and South Carolina say that pecan orchards are the most desirable hunting leases. Pecan trees can reach 70 or more feet high, have a 40- to 60-foot spread, and can live up to 70 years. They do best when planted in full sun. Pecan trees are adaptable to a wide variety of soils. They require a moderate amount of moisture to grow well. They also add to the splendor of fall when their green leaves turn bright yellow. Pecan nuts are a favorite among deer, bears, and a wide range of other wildlife. Deer are attracted to pecan nuts because they can easily crack open the pecan's thin shell and eat the delicious nut. Though an abundant producer, some faster-growing varieties of pecan trees can take 3 to 5 years or so to produce nuts. The nuts have a thin husk that splits into 4 sections when ripe. Some nut tree nurseries offer specific northern-zone species of pecan trees. Choices include the ultra-northern pecan available from Grimo Nursery and the hardy pecan, available from Nature Hill Nursery. These trees are known for their adaptability to cold northern climates. The pecan tree is a terrific choice as a wildlife nut tree planting, as it produces highly nutritious and palatable nuts. The hardy pecan is a native of the United States, primarily found in the Mississippi River Valley regions and its tributaries. Although the tree does not need a cultivar, it is recommended to plant a hardy pecan with a second tree to increase pollination to improve the pecan harvest. According to Nature Hill nursery, for best nut production you'll want to plant two of them and consider adding another variety. USDA Winter Hardiness Zones 5–9.

Another variety of pecan is called the ultra-northern. They were established as a distinct strain of northern pecan. The best ultra-northern pecans produce nuts the size of typical wild trees found further south. These northern species can be purchased from a nursery in Ontario Canada called Grimo Nut Nursery. Grimo's grafted ultra-northern pecan trees are grown on 3-year-old rootstocks in containers for two more years to encourage fibrous rooting for best transplant success and growth. Pecan trees do best with long hot summer conditions to fully fill the nutmeat. Leafhopper insects are a problem in the first two years with pecan trees. They can cause the leaves to wrinkle and turn black on the edges. Spray the pecan tree with a fruit tree insecticide in late June and again in July to get the best results to kill leafhoppers. They will do well in USDA Winter Hardiness Zones 5b - 8.

▲ It is often said that deer mostly eat the pecan tree's buds, twigs, and leaves, and only lightly consume the nuts. Pecan orchard owners would argue that claim. They say deer eat pecan nuts heavily. Photo: © Karen Foley | Dreamstime.com

Pistachio Nuts (*Pistacia vera*): Pistachio nuts are rich in phytosterols, antioxidants, unsaturated fat carotenoids, vitamins, minerals, and fiber. Pistachios have a long juvenile stage, and they won't typically produce many nuts for the first 5 years. While they do produce nuts after year 5, their *peak* nut production is reached when they are about 10 years old. Another characteristic of pistachios is their tendency to biennial cropping, alternately bearing lots of nuts one year, and fewer nuts the following year. These trees have deep root systems which allow them to draw water from the water table. This adaptation allows pistachios to survive prolonged periods of drought. They are also more tolerant of briny water than many other nut tree species. Both are attributes that go along with a tree that grows mostly in arid semi-desert areas. Pistachios do better in soil conditions with a pH close to neutral (7.0). The biggest issue with growing pistachios for deer and other wildlife is that they require long, hot, dry summers and moderate winters. That leaves out most of the northern

states within the country. However, if you are growing wildlife food plots in warm areas like California, Arizona, Nevada and southern Utah, pistachio trees will do well for you.

The reality about growing pistachio trees is that prospective food plotters need to come to grips with the fact that there are very few places that are hot enough in summer and cold but mild enough in winter to grow pistachio nut trees successfully. Growing pistachios is recommended where winter temperatures are no colder than 5°F and where they get 850 or more hours of temperatures between 34° and 45°F in the fall and winter. Otherwise, they won't bear their delicious nuts. But if you can grow them, they will draw in deer and a host of other animals to your land. USDA Hardiness Zones 7–10.

▲ Deer will eat any nut they can break open. A pistachio shell is easily opened by deer. When it comes to pistachio nuts, it is more about where they can be grown successfully, rather than how much deer favor them. Photo: © Sergio Boccardo | Dreamstime

EDIBLE PINE NUTS

More than a dozen species of evergreen pines produce edible pine nuts, or pinons, that deer and humans eat. But not all evergreen pines produce edible nuts. Factually, pine nuts are not considered nuts, but are thought of as seeds. Below are some seed-bearing pine trees that a wide variety of wildlife eat, including deer. Pines that produce edible nuts for wildlife can not only be grown in areas where these trees are native, but also by any food plotter who would like to experiment in areas that are compatible to their USDA Hardiness Zone. An example of this would be the Jeffrey pine that is native to southwest Oregon and the eastern mountains of California. It grows in USDA Hardiness Zone 8.

A study in Florida discovered that slash pine nuts made up to 0.6 percent of white-tailed deer rumens. Although pine nuts don't rank as favorite nut foods of white-tailed deer, when the nuts are available, they will eat them. Pine nuts are more desired and sought out by mule deer and elk. Because pine seeds are available year-round, they provide all deer a continual source of protein.

▲ Pine nuts are highly attractive to elk, mule and white-tailed deer, wild turkeys, bears, and Rocky Mountain upland gamebirds. When grown in eastern states, pine nuts quickly become favorite foods of deer and other wildlife. Photo: © Baloncici | Dreamstime.com

Pine nuts can be grown in any area of the United States that is conducive to the USDA's hardiness recommendations for each pine tree. Many sweet, edible pine nuts are mostly found in the Southwest and parts of the Rocky Mountains. Pine nuts are favorite foods to many small Rocky Mountain mammals like pika, chipmunks, squirrels, yellow-bellied marmots, rabbits, and hares. They are also regular staples to larger big game including elk, mule deer, white-tailed deer, and bears. All upland Rocky Mountain gamebirds, wild turkeys and other upland birds, wood ducks, and most other non-hunted birds consume them. When grown in eastern states, pine nuts quickly become a favorite staple for deer and other wildlife once they discover what they are.

Jeffrey Pine (*Pinus jeffreyi*): Jeffrey pine looks like the closely related Ponderosa pine. It occupies much of California and southwestern Oregon, western Nevada,

and northern Baja California. Its maximum height at maturity is about 150 feet. Edible seed cones can be a foot long. Its small pine nuts are eaten by deer and other wildlife. Winter Hardiness Zones 4–9.

Pine Nut (*Pinus koraiensis*): This needled evergreen is a species of pine commonly known as the Korean pine. Its large nuts are about ¾-inch long, like the size of pistachio nuts. The large pine nuts make this tree an excellent choice for any food plot managers across the country who wants to supplement their program with pine nuts. It is a member of the white pine group. It reaches a height of 100 or more feet. It requires full sun and a moderate amount of water throughout its lifetime.

It grows best in moist, well-drained loams, but tolerates a wide range of soils including sandy, acidic, clay, and even poor soils. Avoid planting it in poorly drained wet soils. The Korean pine prefers cool summer climates and generally does not like a lot of heat and humidity. The Korean pine has an excellent tolerance for cold winter temperatures. Nut production starts at about 6 to 7 years of age. Cones can average about 70 nuts each. Like other pine nut trees, deer, bears, wild turkeys, gamebirds, and other animals seek out the Korean pine's large nuts. USDA Winter Hardiness Zones 2–9.

Pinyon Pine (*Pinus edulis*): Otherwise known as the Colorado pinyon, two-needle piñon, pinyon pine, or simply piñon, this is a slow-growing pine in the pinyon pine group. Like a white or red oak, this tree is planted for the benefit of younger generations. The pinyon pine's range includes Colorado, southern Wyoming, eastern and central Utah, northern Arizona, New Mexico, western Oklahoma, southeastern California, and far western Texas. The trees are well-suited to dry, warm, sunny climates. Pinyon pines grow at altitudes of 5,200–9,800 feet but rarely below 4,600 feet. The piñon pine is a small- to medium-size tree reaching about 35 to 65 feet tall, but it rarely gets taller than that. The cones are about 1¼ to 2 inches long. The nut seeds are small, generally smaller than ½-inch and have thin shells. Nut production is slower than other nut seeds from evergreen trees taking 10 or more years. The nuts are edible and considered a delicacy for human consumption. Their delicate flavor makes the seeds an important wildlife food for mule, coues, and white-tailed deer, black bears, upland birds (particularly quail), squirrels, chipmunks, and other small mammals and songbirds. Cold hardiness limit between -10° and -20°F. USDA Hardiness Zones to Zone 5.

▲ Food plotters in the Rocky Mountains and West will do well with planting pinyon trees. Mule deer, bears, wild turkeys, and other upland birds all consume pinon nuts. Even white-tailed deer in the West eat pinyon nuts. Photo: Cone © Heather Mcardle | Dreamstime

Russian Cedar (*Pinus siberica*): This tree can withstand very cold temperatures. When it is mature, it can reach 100 feet in height. The Russian cedar is noted for the thin shell of its nut. It can be easily cracked open by most wildlife or between a person's fingers. It is remarkably like Korean pine, but it is narrower in its appearance. Nut production of its cones usually begins around 6 years. The Russian cedar's seeds are larger than Swiss stone pine, but the thinness of its shell makes it a valuable type of nut for all types of wildlife large and small. Deer, bears, upland birds, and many small mammals and birds seek out the tasty nuts of this tree. USDA Winter Hardiness Zones 1–9.

Swiss Stone Pine Nut (*P. Cembra*): This is the largest seeded of the northern-hardy edible nut pines. It is a small evergreen that is very hardy and perfect for wildlife food plot managers with smaller properties. It is tailor-made to plant in rocky areas. Requiring full unfiltered sun for best growth, the Swiss stone pine nut tree produces a gourmet nut for humans and wildlife that is slightly smaller than a pistachio nut. The cones take 3 years to mature. Each year new cones are formed,

ensuring a continuous nut crop once they reach nut bearing age. To adapt the Swiss pine nut tree to your soil, use soil from under a mature pine tree to inoculate the tree with the mycorrhiza live bacteria that they need to survive. The Swiss pine nut tree produces it edible fruit within 5 to 7 years. Like other pine nut trees, its nuts are sought out by deer and other wildlife. USDA Winter Hardiness Zones 2–9.

Nut-producing pine trees offer an alternate source of protein for white-tailed deer. Throughout the Rockies and West, nuts from pine trees are a primary source of protein for elk, coues and mule deer, as well. What makes them a good choice within a wildlife food plot program is that they are easy to plant, withstand winter temperatures, and need little care once established. Pine nuts are available from September through October, which makes them an ideal protein source during the bowhunting season. Pine trees also provide secondary benefits. They can be used as wind breaks or natural dividers between open areas. Additionally, no matter where they are planted, they provide a decorative touch to any food plot program. They are sources of nutrition that can be grown throughout the U.S. Once deer become accustomed to eating pine nuts, they will enthusiastically seek them out. They provide protein and oil, both beneficial to deer.

▲ Swiss stone pine nuts are tailor-made for food plotters in the West. They even do well on small properties. Mule deer, elk, bears, and western whitetails eat Swiss stone pine nuts. Photo: © Amelia Martin | Dreamstime

There you have the lowdown on the many diverse types of acorns, nutlet (a.k.a. real nut), and pine nut trees that can be successfully planted as food plots. They will all attract hunted and non-hunted wildlife and provide them with a highly nutritious food source. You can be assured that no matter what part of the country you live in, or what type of game you hunt, oaknuts, nutlets, and pine nuts will draw in deer and a wide variety of big game, small game, upland birds, some waterfowl, and lots of wild turkeys, as well as a host of other non-hunted animals.

◄ As a food plotter, you cannot go wrong planting all types of oaknuts, chestnuts, nutlets, and pinion pine nuts. They are all consumed by a surprisingly large amount of big game including whitetails, mule deer, blacktails, Coues deer, elk, moose, forest caribou, Rocky Mountain goats, bighorn sheep, black, brown, and grizzly bears, wild boars, and javelinas. Additionally, all upland birds, some waterfowl, and most small game animals eat nuts. Credit for elk—© Bobby J Norris | Dreamstime.com; Credit for Goat—© Jesse Kraft | Dreamstime; Credit for Bighorn Sheep—PCFImages; Credit for wild boar–© Zagrosti | Dreamstime

Some Nut Tree Nurseries (for additional nurseries, see Appendix C—Fruit, Chestnut, Nut & Acorn Tree Sources for additional information)

Blue Hill Wildlife Nursery—www.bluehillwildlifenursery.com

Burnt Ridge Nursery and Orchards—www.burntridgenursery.com

Chestnut Hill Nursery—www.chestnuhilltreefarm.com

Conifer Kingdom—www.coniferkingdom.com

Greenwood Nursery—www.greenwoodnursery.com

Grimo Nut Nursery layered and seedling trees—www.grimonut.com

Mossy Oak Nativ Nurseries—www.nativnurseries.com

Northern Ridge Nursery—www.northernridgenursery.com

Oikos Tree Crops seedling trees—www.oikostreecrops.com

Raintree Nursery www.raintreenursery.com

Stark Brothers www.starkbros.com

Twisted Tree Farm www.twisted-tree.net

Wildlife Heritage Tree Nursery—www.wildlifeheritagetreenursery.com

Z's Nutty Ridge layered and seedling trees—www.znutty.com

The accompanying USDA Plant Hardiness Zone Map is a valuable agricultural and horticultural reference. (Neither this writer, the publisher, nor the USDA, NCRS, as a whole, are responsible for pinpoint accuracy of this map.) The USDA Plant Hardiness Zone Map is a product of the USDA Agricultural Research Service (ARS), with the assistance from the Prism Climate Group at Oregon State University—http://planthardiness.ars.usda.gov. Each zone is determined by the average minimum winter temperatures of each. Nut trees that are ideal for Zone 5 include walnuts, chestnuts, hazelnut, and hickory nuts.

TANNINS

According to the USDA Forest Service, tannins are complex chemical substances derived from phenolic acids (sometimes called tannic acid). They are classified as phenolic compounds, which are found in many species of plants in all parts of the world. They are large molecules that bind readily with proteins, cellulose, starches, and minerals. These resulting substances are insoluble and resistant to decomposition. Tannins occur in many species of coniferous trees and in the acorns of oak trees. The water in the soil becomes rich with tannins and seeps into the ground water or drains into lakes and streams. These waters become brown in color and look like tea.

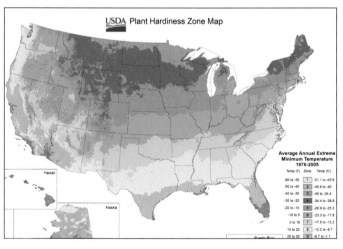

▲ Credit: Oregon State University

▲ All too often trees are not correctly planted. This can result in slow development of the tree. If it's a fruit or nut tree, improper planting techniques can reduce the size and volume of fruit. In the worst-case scenario, it could also kill a tree. Photo Credit: Canstock Photo

Chapter Thirty-One

Guidelines to Plant Trees Successfully

Planting a tree in an undersized hole or planting it improperly may end up killing it. Planting a tree the proper way will also save you time and money. More important, it will save you frustration and disappointment. Fruit and nut trees that are not planted correctly will either end up with delayed development or, worse, die. The initial planting process, therefore, is critical to a tree's long-term success. It is also important to the timing of when the tree will eventually bear its fruit or nuts.

▲ If you buy a potted tree, make sure you water it thoroughly (as seen here) prior to planting it. It should also be watered regularly after it is planted until the tree gets established. Photo: PCFImages

After buying new trees or other wildlife plantings in spring, summer, or fall, I place them in a sunny location and water them thoroughly. I do not plant them immediately. Instead, I keep them for a week or so in full sunshine and let them acclimate after the stress of being transported. I continue to water them daily unless it has rained. Each day, I check the soil in the pot, to see if it feels dry. I probe into the soil with my finger down to about 1 inch. If the soil is not damp, I water the tree. Most times, it is dry. I have found the best time to water trees is in the morning. If I miss that time frame, I water them in the early evening just after the heat of the day has subsided. Be cautious not to over water the trees during this resting period from pot to soil. Too much watering can cause leaf browning at the tips or edges and lead to the same problems as not watering the plants enough.

This method helps to get the trees physically fit and ready for planting. This temporary staging preparation strategy allows the trees to recover faster from the stresses of being transplanted from pot to soil. In tests I have carried out, the trees that I have not set aside for a week, and planted within a day or two, displayed a slower recovery to being transplanted into a newly dug hole in the soil.

Fertilizers are not needed after planting a new tree. Most nurseries already include slow-acting fertilizers in the soil of the pots.

SOAKING POTTED TREES

Shortly before I plant a tree, I soak it with water while it is in the pot. By the time the hole is dug out and the tree is finally set in the ground, the roots will still be damp. Most trees I have used this tactic with have acclimated quicker than if they were only watered after they were put into the soil. The latter watering, however, is not only helpful, but also it is crucial. Just don't over-soak the tree, before or after planting.

PROPER DISTANCING

The 3 principal elements of spacing are the size of the tree, sunlight, and pollination. For instance, if trees are planted too far apart, inefficient pollination may occur. If planted too close, they will not receive adequate water, sunlight, and nutrients as they continue to grow. If you plant trees too closely, it will affect their fruit or

▲ This aerial shot is of one of our orchards. It shows about 80 trees of the 100 trees planted in it. There are several dozen Dunstan chestnut trees, and a mix of almond, peach, apple, pear, cherry, persimmon, and blueberry brambles—many of which are making fruit in the third and fourth years. Photo: PCFImages

mast production. Trees must be spaced so that they get plenty of sun and air circulation to prevent fungal issues. Both soft and hard mast trees like full sun. If you have robust soil, a little extra spacing should be given since the tree will grow out wider.

If you are planting a small orchard section, which we have done on our farm, you can create an organized row setting that has the look associated with commercial orchard plantings. Don't fuss over how straight the rows are or how precisely the trees are planted next to one another compared to a commercial orchard. The proper food plot orchard-type spacing is mostly dependent on whether the trees are standard, dwarf, or semi-dwarf sizes.

Another way to plant nut and fruit trees is to plant them in a more unorthodox arrangement rather than using an orchard plan. You still must take into consideration spacing. No matter what pattern you choose to plant your trees, follow the recommendations on each tree's planting information tag.

SIZE OF THE HOLE

Begin by digging a hole at least twice as wide as the container the tree came in, as this helps the roots grow outward without crowding them. The hole should be slightly shallower than the root ball. Roughen the sides and bottom of the hole with a narrow-bladed shovel or hand-held spade so that roots can penetrate the soil deeper and more easily. The more you "work" the dirt of the hole, the easier it will be for the roots of the tree to expand into the surrounding soil.

▲ This is a planting of blueberry bush. Note the size and depth of the hole. Photo: © Helinloik | Dreamstime

CONTAINER REMOVAL

When planting fruit and nut trees, it pays big dividends to buy trees that are at least 2 to 3 years old and sold in pots or bare-root. Potted trees should be removed *carefully* in order not to stress the tree or damage the root system. Gently remove the tree from the container, keeping in mind to keep the soil around the roots intact. It helps to tap the outside of the container to loosen the edge. Then slowly slide the tree from the container. Never yank or pull the tree out of the container. By doing so, you can separate the roots from the tree. If there are any tightly circled roots, gently

separate and spread them with your fingers before planting.

▲ The easiest and safest way to remove a tree from a pot is to gently roll the pot with your hands. When you use this technique, the tree can be easily slipped out of the pot. Photo: © Oleg Kopyov | Dreamstime

Another way to remove the tree is by rolling the container gently in your hands several times while applying pressure to the sides. This will help free the tree from the container when you are ready to remove it. Lay the tree on its side with the container end near the planting hole. Tap the bottom and sides of the pot until the root ball is totally loosened. Then slowly and carefully lift the tree out of the container.

If you notice that the roots wind tightly in a circle at the bottom of the root ball, again, use your fingers to gently separate the roots. If a tree comes in a burlap wrapping, it is unnecessary to completely remove the burlap bag. But, it is advisable to loosen the bag, if it is tightly wrapped. If you notice an exceptionally long root or two, trim them and guide the shortened roots downward and outward so they will quickly establish themselves into the soil. This is necessary because root tips die quickly when exposed to light and air.

PLANTING POTTED TREES

Plant potted trees at the same height they were grown in the container. This should be down at the crown where the bark changed from green to brown, with plenty of room for the roots. Partially fill the planting hole with the native soil first. Set the tree in the middle

PLANTING BARE-ROOT STOCK

Many nurseries sell fruit and nut trees as bare-root stock. Bare-root trees are grown in rows or beds for up to 3 years; they are not grown in pots. They are usually shipped without any soil. Planting a bare-root tree is different than planting a potted tree.

First, it is ideal to store a bare-root tree that was shipped by a nursery at a temperature of about 40°F. With that said, anything under 60°F can work for a short period of time. This method will help keep your bare-root plants and trees dormant so you can safely delay planting for up to a week.

▲ When planting bare-root trees, let the roots soak in water for an hour or so prior to planting the tree. Photo: © Mikhail Dmit… | Dreamstime

When the tree is ready to be planted, allow a bare-root tree's roots to soak in water an hour or two before planting. Do not soak the roots for more than 24 hours, though. The planting hole will need to be large enough to fit the tree's root system comfortably, meaning the roots should not be tight in the hole, they should have a little extra room to grow into. Before placing the roots in the hole, carefully spread them out in an out-ward growth pattern. This means keeping the roots as vertical as is possible when placing them in the hole. They should be perpendicular to the ground. This helps the tree to grow straight. Keep the graft union (the vis-ible bump in the lower trunk) 2 to 3 inches above the ground.

Place the soil that was removed as well as any addi-tional soil as needed, back into the hole and cover

▲ This is a Dunstan chestnut tree. The tree will be planted in the hole at the same height it was when it was in the pot. Photo: PCFImages

of the hole, again allowing for plenty of room for the roots. Avoid planting the tree too deeply. Using some soil, secure the tree in a straight position, then fill with native soil and firm the soil around the lower roots making sure there are no air pockets. Keep backfill-ing and gently packing down the soil until the soil is level with the root collar. Do not add soil amendments such as compost, peat, or bark, as they can cause root fungus. Do not use fertilizer or chemicals on your young trees. Then thoroughly water the tree as often as needed to keep the soil from drying out.

the roots. Once the hole is filled, gingerly tap down around the entire hole to eliminate any potential air pockets. Then thoroughly water the tree. Finally, use tree stakes to promote straight tree growth. This is especially important with dwarf-type rootstocks planted in windy areas.

After the tree is planted, create a water-holding basin around the hole. Water slowly at the drip line. After the water has soaked in, spread a protective layer of 2 to 4 inches of mulch deep around the trunk. Make sure that you remove the mulch at least a few inches away from the trunk of the tree. You can use leaf litter, hay, shredded or fine bark as mulch. Another viable choice is to use weed mats to prevent weed competition and reduce water evaporation.

▲ After a tree is planted, it is imperative to water it regularly, at least twice a week, until the tree gets established. If it rains a couple of times over a week, the tree does not need any additional water. Photo: © Yzqblyxy | Dreamstime

The trees will need to be watered regularly, at least twice per week as temperatures rise throughout the summer growing season, and more often during dry spells. I use my tractor to do this. I fill up the tractor's bucket and then use a 5-gallon bucket to scoop out the water. You can also fill several 5-gallon buckets with water, cap them, and drive up to the trees to water them. The amount of water and the times they need to be watered is dependent on your soil, temperatures, and rainfall. I water newly planted trees for at least a few weeks after planting them. But remember, it is critical that newly transplanted trees be watered regularly as described. If they can be watered regularly during their first summer of growth, that would be even better. Watering the trees regularly is the most crucial factor to ensure the successful start of newly transplanted nut and fruit trees.

FERTILIZING

Professional nursery growers do not recommend fertilizing trees at planting. Most growers use slow-release fertilizers on their tree stock in spring at the nursery. Therefore, you should not fertilize the tree until the following spring. Use a time-released fertilizer with balanced micronutrients, such as Scotts Osmocote Indoor-Outdoor fertilizer 19-6-12. You can also use Espoma Holly Tone or Tree Tone Organic Fertilizer. Newly planted trees do not grow rapidly during their first year. The trees put most of their energy into new root production during their first year after being planted. Once the roots are established, though, they will make rapid growth in the following years. You can purchase tree fertilizers at any farm supply store. Check with them to see what fertilizers work best for the type of tree you are planning to plant.

STAKING THE TREE

Keep the pot stake attached to the tree for one season; you can remove it after that. If the tree appears stable, you do not have to stake the tree at all. If staking is necessary, however, hold the trunk with one hand to find the height at which the unsupported top can stand up on its own and it will spring back to a vertical position when it is gently flexed. Allow the tree to have a slight amount of flex rather than holding it rigidly in place. Tree straps should be made of material that will not injure the trunk of the tree. If injury from a strap occurs, it will damage the tree, especially once it begins to bear nuts or fruit. An injury then will cause the fruit to not grow normally. If you use grow tubes, you eliminate having to stake the tree. You will, however, need to attach a stake to the grow tubes.

GROW TUBES

We use grow tubes for tree plantings. Grow tubes act like mini-greenhouses, recycling moisture from leaf transpiration to nurture growth of young trees

▲ When I plant fruit or nut trees, I always use quality tree protectors called Plantra® Jump Start® Grow Tubes. They are designed to provide both greenhouse benefits and protection to the tree's trunk. Photo: Plantra.com

until the tree is big enough to depend on only rainfall. Grow tubes also provide protection against deer rubbing the trunk or rodents and rabbits eating and chewing the lower bark. They also provide a barrier against herbicide drift if herbicide is used to control nearby weeds. Keep in mind that herbicide will kill a young tree lickety-split. Do not use black plastic drainpipe or tubing as tree shelters, as they will damage your trees. Weeds compete for water and fertilizer, so weed control is important. I use weed mats to help keep weeds down around the base of young nut and fruit trees.

In the process of planting well over 100 fruit and nut trees, I have had remarkable success using Plantra's Grow Tubes. Plantra's Jump Start™ Grow Tubes are designed to be used with their Trunk Builder™ staking system. Staking trees is crucial to their survival and healthy growth. Trunk Builder™ is the first stake ever purposely built to support a grow tube or tree tube while helping the growing tree develop a stronger stem faster. Trunk Builder™ U-Stakes flex when the wind blows but are engineered to stand tall with built-in super strong "memory" to return to a straight position even on the windiest sites. Trunk Builder™ stakes deliver benefits with a grow tube for wildlife plantings. Many young tree plantings do not survive from either being eaten or rubbed on by deer. Bucks can cause severe damage when they rub trees. Always protect the trunk of a newly planted tree, particularly if it is a seedling.

PRUNING

Generally, there is no need to prune newly transplanted trees. Pruning should be done only in the first several years to shape the tree to its proper form—central leader, open leader or modified leader. Pruning with a central leader is when a tree is created with a single vertical central leader. Pruning with an open leader is when the central leader is cut back and the outline of the tree resembles a goblet. Pruning with a modified leader is a combination of the two previous methods. See the sidebar below.

Most nut trees grow naturally with a straight trunk (central leader) with only a little pruning required. Occasional pruning is necessary to open the center of the tree for greater light and air penetration. Light

▲ A newly planted tree generally does not have to be pruned until the following year. One exception to this rule is if the tree's branches have been damaged or snapped. In that case, the damaged area should be pruned to prevent the injury from damaging the tree further. Photo: © Deviddo | Dreamstime

annual pruning of dead wood or an out-of-place branch helps older trees by rejuvenating growth and promoting better fruit production.

Proper care for planting a tree is so much more than placing it in a hole in the ground. It requires paying attention to all the elements mentioned above to ensure it has the best chance for survival and subsequent fruit or nut production. The better you take care of the initial planting steps, the better your tree will thrive.

▲ Understanding the different degrees of sunlight is an important factor to growing successful food plot crops or nut and fruit trees. Credit © Mikael Males | Dreamstime

Chapter Thirty-Two

Shedding Light on Sunlight

All seeds and nut and fruit trees sown in a food plot program come with abbreviated instructions regarding the sunlight needed for healthy growth and maximum production. Many of them read something like this: "Light Requirements: Sun, Part Sun, Part Shade, or Shade." Unfortunately, the directions do not define exactly what each term means. For instance, a plant may be tolerant of partial shade, or a fruit tree may require full sunlight. Understanding sunlight exposure or sun and shade examples can get confusing and frustrating. This chapter will help explain these terms better. Therefore, let's shed some light on this subject.

FULL SUN

Full sun is the easiest term to understand. Full sun means a plant needs *direct* summer sun for 6 or more hours per day. For food plotters, that would mean planting in fields, meadows, prairies, or other open spaces that receive at least 6 hours of direct sunlight per day. Where it becomes more difficult is everything sandwiched between full sun and various levels of shade.

SHADE

Shade is more complicated. It's about varying degrees of respite from full sun. Different measures of shade are easier to understand when they are broken down into four groups ranging from full sunlight to dense shade.

LIGHT SHADE, PARTIAL SHADE, OR PARTIAL SUN

These terms often describe a spot that receives about 3 to 5 hours of direct sunlight a day—or it is said to be shaded for at least half of the day. There is a difference between morning and afternoon sun and its effects on

▲ This orchard receives full sun. Full sun means a plant or tree receives at least 6 hours of direct sunlight a day. However, some plants, like vegetables, need 8 to 10 hours of direct sunlight per day. Photo: © Ilona Tymchenko | Dreamstime

▲ When it comes to plants that can tolerate shade, it is important to know just how much shade they can endure. Shade can range from light to full. Photo: © Andreistanescu | Dreamstime

▲ This is image represents dense shade. For the food plotter, planting anything in dense shade is not applicable. © Taya Johnston | Dreamstime

plants that can tolerate shade. Partial shade is good for many flowering and non-flowering natural-growing wildlife plants, shrubs, trees, and bushes. Partial shade can also be found under or around trees, or in areas that only receive morning sun for a few hours and little or no hot afternoon sun. For instance, morning sun is cooler and less intense, and therefore it is easier on shade-loving food plot plants than the hot afternoon sun, which can stress them. Plants that receive too much intense light can become dry.

FULL SHADE

Full shade areas only get fewer than an hour or so of direct sunlight each day. It can also be filtered or diffused sunlight that comes through a tree canopy for most of the day. Full shade is not just a result of trees, but also fences that cast shadows, block direct sun rays, tall trees, or even plants, like corn, which provides partial shade to companion plants like soybeans.

DENSE SHADE

Dense shade means no direct sunlight and little indirect light seldom reaches the ground. This can be seen from the light under evergreen trees or overhanging heavy branches of mature trees, including but not limited to oaks, maples, and full-size fruit and nut trees, which are along the edges of food plots. Dense shade can be under shrubs, bushes, and other thick-growing natural vegetation and forage. The soil beneath them is usually dry and dark from lack of light. Dense shade is the most difficult and limiting growing condition for almost all food plot plants, trees, shrubs, and bushes. Dense shade rarely, if ever, grows any type of food plot.

Understanding the sun and shade patterns of all plantings within wildlife food plots is only part of the equation. The second part is understanding a plant, tree, bush, or shrub's needs. This can be confusing, as some food plot plants can adapt to several light levels. But keep in mind the adaptation is related in many ways to the intensity of the sunlight. Remember, morning sun is cooler and less intense, so it does not result in leaf scorch and overall plant stress. Some plants can tolerate a lot more morning sun as opposed to the hot, scorching afternoon sun.

Understanding sun and shade patterns becomes a little easier once you comprehend the nuances. With a little thought, you can figure out what is right for your favorite food plot plants, trees, shrubs, and bushes. Almost every seed bag, tree or shrub's tag provides sun and shade recommendations. In this compendium, every plant tree and shrub described includes its sunlight requirements in each recap section.

▲ Knowing what the different ranges of sun are and the amount of sunlight plants require is an important aspect to growing the best plants possible. Photo: © Nikolay Denisov

▲ Providing deer with minerals and other nutrients can help with body weight, antler size, and overall health. Of course, this should be done only where it is legal to do so. Credit: Canstock Photo

Chapter Thirty-Three

Supplemental Feeding

Bucks and does need minerals, and they need to be supplied to deer at the proper times of the year, as well as in the right quantities. For example, deer seek out minerals most often during green-up in spring and carbohydrates beginning in early fall. Most deer managers create food plot programs to produce a healthier deer herd, enhanced fawn survival, improved doe lactation, and so on. However, the foremost reason for starting a food plot program often focuses around improving the age and size of bucks' antlers. The natural minerals most often found in the soils in Wisconsin, Illinois, Michigan, Iowa, and Kansas are primarily responsible in helping bucks grow very impressive sets

of antlers in that part of the country. Of course, not all managers live in areas where the soil contains the correct combination of minerals to enhance antler quality.

By contrast, most soils in the Northeast don't contain the necessary primary macronutrients such as Nitrogen (N), Phosphorus (P), Calcium (Ca), Potassium (K), Magnesium (Mg), and Sulphur (S). Nor do these soils have the number of other micro elements such as Iron (Fe), Manganese (Mn), Copper (Cu), Zinc (Zn), Boron (B), Molybdenum (Mo), and Chlorine (Cl) that are required to improve a healthier deer herd, or for bucks to grow large sets of antlers. For a buck to grow a set of antlers like they do in the areas I just mentioned, these

▲ Bucks need high contents of the macro- and micro-nutrients found in soil to develop large antlers. In soils lacking such minerals, supplemental minerals can be immensely helpful. Photo: © Bruce Macqueen | Dreamstime

macro and micro elements must be available to them in sufficient quantities. Other factors include genetics, age, and prime nutrition, which include taking in all the necessary minerals needed to develop superior antlers.

THE AGE FACTOR

For a buck to grow his best set of antlers in an effectively managed deer herd, the buck must reach adulthood. Most biologists agree a white-tailed buck reaches maturity status at 4½ years of age. With that said, the reality is there are always exceptions to any rule. Therein lies one of the most crucial aspects of creating a deer management program that centers on improving the size of antlers of bucks on a particular property. To aid bucks to achieve their maximum antler potential, managers should abide by a commonsense concept. They should not shoot bucks that are between 1½ and 2½ years old. Judging the age of a buck on the hoof can be confusing, however. Therefore, it is often better to simply let spikes, fork horns, and small basket-rack 8-points (inside spread of 12 to 14 inches or less) live a couple of more seasons, so they can get old enough to grow larger sets of antlers. Here again, let me emphasize that this guideline is only for those who are focused on growing bucks with bigger antlers.

▲ To grow a set of antlers this large, bucks need excellent genetics, quality nutrition, and longevity. Photo: © Sandra Burm | Dreamstime

I'm paraphrasing here, but the phrase created and used by the National Deer Association (NDA), "Let him go—to let him grow," should be the call-to-action catchphrase for any determined deer manager who wants to see and kill larger-antlered bucks. For that

matter, it should be the same slogan for any buck hunter who wants to see and take bigger-antlered bucks. Food plotters and deer managers can improve the antler size of any age-class buck from a yearling on by providing the type of complete nutrition, minerals, carbohydrates, vitamins, and proteins bucks require during their initial stages of life.

GENETICS

When it comes to a buck growing large antlers, it could be said that it is all in the genes. Genetics is the movement that launched the whitetail industry to new heights for a few decades. The aura about bucks growing bigger antlers has been the force behind the popularity of deer hunting seminars, quality deer management (QDM), deer hunting television shows, magazine articles, books, websites, and so on. The increased fascination with the size of a buck's antlers has also led to more research about genetics. Often, genes contributed by the doe are not taken into consideration into the antler-size equation. Many hunters do not realize the genes passed on by the doe are as important as genes passed on by the buck. The fact is, a doe can contribute an added genetic impact on her buck fawns, more so than a buck can.

Let's say the area you traditionally hunt produces larger antlered bucks than another area a few miles away with similar terrain and food sources. The reason for this could be linked to the fact that your female deer have superior antler-growth genes than the other area's female deer. Where such a scenario develops, it would be wise to protect older does so they can continue to pass on their exceptional antler-growing genes to their fawns. The most recent research suggests that it is better to kill the sub-adult does to preserve the dominant does that bear larger and stronger fawns with better antler development genes. However, at this writing there is still not any concrete evidence that taking sub-adult female deer rather than older does is a strategy that has been conclusively proven. But it seems that many biologists support the theory, and the consensus that such a tactic should still help to increase the odds in favor of growing larger antlered bucks on a piece of property.

Because antler development is soundly based on genetics (as well as age and nutrition), it should be

▲ Research about killing female deer indicates that hunters should take sub-adult does rather than older mature does. Healthy mature does are capable of bearing fawns with better antler development genes, and female fawns with the same genetic potential. Photo: © Justinhoffmanoutdoors | Dreamstime

clear that not all deer have the same good or bad genetic potential. The genes a fawn buck inherits from the doe and buck are inescapably linked to many factors of the fawn buck's body size, hair color, weight, behavior, and, inevitably, the size and shape of the male fawn's future antlers. The bottom line is that if a buck fawn is not born with the type of superior genes that he needs to achieve large antlers during his lifetime, he will not grow impressive sets of antlers. There is not much that can be done to change that fact, even if the buck reaches a mature age and is provided high-quality nutrition. However, nutrition does play a key role in allowing a buck to reach his maximum genetic potential antler size no matter what that size ends up being. In other words, if a buck ends up with genes to produce a set of antlers that fall within a specific size range, improved nutrition will almost always help to reach the best potential of an average set of antlers.

Because of this, it is important for those who manage their land and deer herd to establish the absolute best buck-to-doe ratio that they can. Although the apex buck-to-doe ratio is 1:1, few managers will achieve this in the wild. Even a 3:1 ratio is out of reach for most managers. A somewhat more achievable ratio is 4:1. Mother Nature will take care of the natural selection process. The more bucks there are for a given number of does, the more they compete for the chance to breed. Button bucks get pushed out and the older bucks have more chances to pass on their genes.

Consequently, as mentioned above, it is important to manage the does on your land to keep the buck-to-doe ratios at appropriate levels. That is why game departments' doe management permits are "golden" to serious-minded deer managers.

NUTRITION

Nutrition, which includes quality foodstuffs and enough intake of a variety of quality minerals, vitamins, crude proteins, carbohydrates, and so on, is as important as age and genetics. In fact, there are some biologists who state that nutrition is as important as age and genetics. Many studies claim that aside from genetics, quality nutrition, and more important, premium mineral supplements, often produce bigger antlers within the shortest period—in some cases, as quickly as the first year. Nutrition, therefore, seems to be the easiest factor to enhance. By providing quality mineral supplements to your deer herd, you will help increase the size of any size antlers. The formula is quite simple: To produce better antlered bucks, you must provide high-quality nutrition, provide the correct amounts of supplements (minerals, vitamins, carbohydrates, crude protein, etc.) and reduce the numbers of female deer on your land to achieve a more balanced buck-to-doe ratio. Many researchers and studies have documented that quality habitats that produce larger antlered bucks have all these factors in common.

▲ Providing quality foods like this field of Imperial PowerPlant forage will allow deer to take in a variety of quality minerals, vitamins, crude proteins, and carbohydrates. Photo: Whitetail Institute

MINERALS

When I lived in Colorado, I had several friends who raised beef cattle. It was standard operating procedure to provide their cattle with free-choice minerals in addition to the forage provided on the grasslands they grazed. The term "free choice" minerals came about from the need to decrease over-consumption of liquid types of supplements containing phosphoric acid, protein, other minerals, and even molasses. Research showed that the liquid supplements were being used too much by cattle managers as a source of phosphorous. It was discovered that a better option was to give cattle or other animals the choice to consume phosphorous—hence the term "free choice"—rather than providing liquids in their daily diet. That spurred the concept to other vitamins and minerals as well. Instead of being fed liquid minerals and vitamins daily, cattle were able to choose when they wanted phosphorous, calcium, and other minerals and vitamins.

▲ Providing deer "free choice" minerals like this salt block Mr. Bullwinkle is licking, in addition to natural forages, allows deer to choose when they need to supplement their diets. Photo © Lindamore | Dreamstime

As any food plot manager who also raises cattle will attest to, a lot of wildlife, particularly deer, will select to feed at the mineral feeders established for beef or dairy cattle. When starting a mineral and vitamin program for a deer herd, the number one factor is to first check with your state game departments to find out if providing minerals or vitamins for deer is legal. In some states it is **illegal** to feed deer minerals or vitamins in liquid or any other form. If your state allows you to provide deer minerals and vitamins, then it is certainly a practice to consider for your deer herd, to aid in the deer's nutrition including the development of larger antlers.

Today there are many companies that offer quality mineral mixes designed specifically for deer. They are said to provide benefits that can range from a good to even a significant improvement in a deer herd. Many hunters consider providing minerals, again where it is legal to do so, as a major factor in deer herd management on a yearly basis. To avoid buying supplements that are high in salt and low in other minerals and vitamins, carefully read the labels. Make sure you are getting not only enough calcium and phosphorus and other macro and micronutrients but vitamins as well.

PROVIDE MINERALS ACCORDING TO WHAT DEER NEED

"Deer start growing their antlers, especially the farther north you go, at the worst time of the year," said Steve Scott, formerly of Whitetail Institute. "Snow and ice are still on the ground; things haven't greened up. Research has shown that if there is stunted antler growth earlier, there is no compensatory gain down the road. The pregnant does also need the minerals. Most mineral products are hit hard in the spring and summer and the deer back off them in the fall and winter. Deer nutritional needs change and Mother Nature provides differently at that time of the year." Many other biologists feel that the greatest shortfall of mineral and vitamin programs is making the same minerals available to deer throughout the entire year.

▲ Female deer need quality minerals and nutrients to produce healthy fawns. Managers should scrutinize what a deer's physical needs are during different times of the year. Photo: © Robhainer | Dreamstime

Managers who do this are simply not monitoring the deer's physical needs during different times of the seasons. Although the term physiological cycle sounds complicated, it really is not difficult to grasp.

For instance, in the spring, during the time known as "green-up," plants have their highest content of moisture. That is the primary time of year when deer need and desire a high amount of salt. As the summer progresses, depending on rainfall, the moisture content and vegetation decreases substantially. Then deer require less salt and a more concentrated source of minerals. Calcium and phosphorus are the two keys, but a lot of other minerals are also involved. Calcium and phosphorus, however, are common; the other minerals are more site-specific. If you take care of the calcium and phosphorus, you will be covering most of what deer need.

A good beginning program would be to provide a mixture of about 75 percent salt and 25 percent of other needed minerals in spring. This method aids in two ways. Deer receive the salt they need. As the season moves to June, perhaps a mixture of 50 percent salt and 50 percent minerals is called for. Then, during late summer, when many plants lose some to a lot of moisture, changing your plan to include 75 percent minerals and vitamins and 25 percent salt is a more appropriate plan. The reason is to keep the mineral flow being absorbed by the deer's skeletal system. Deer store calcium and phosphorus in their bones and bucks activate it for antler development and female deer assemble it for healthier lactation.

PROVIDING YEAR-ROUND MINERALS

As mentioned, the three most critical factors for bucks to produce larger antler growth are age, genetics, and healthy nutrition. It is difficult to control the first two, but it is quite possible to supplement nutrition, with minerals (and vitamins). By doing so, in some areas, it is said with the proper minerals during the right periods of time, a deer manager can increase a spike or 4-point buck to having a small 6- or even 8-point rack over a season or two of application. Minerals can also increase the general health and body size of your deer herd if used properly in a good wildlife management program.

Minerals are not a cure-all; they must be used in combination with a sound food plot management

▲ Studies have documented that providing the proper minerals at the right times of year can increase a small 4-point set of antlers to a larger 6-point set. Photo: © Josh Zaring | Dreamstime

program that includes plenty of year-round crude protein and other macro and trace elements. Minerals and blocks are available in two forms: those specifically designed as mineral and vitamin supplements and those with added aromatic attractants. A combined program using minerals as a free-choice option throughout the year and mineral and protein blocks available from midwinter through late summer make for an extremely effective mineral and vitamin program. For instance, Pennington Seed suggests using its RackMaster Deer Mineral Salt Lick and RackMaster Deer Mineral/Nutrition Block together.

No matter which brand of minerals you choose to use, always follow the manufacturer's directions that come with the product. The one primary mistake when using minerals (where it is legal) is that some believe they will work to attract deer or provide supplements when they are put out only days before the hunting season. That is a plan that can be called, "Too little . . . too late."

A good supplemental feeding program includes both food plots and minerals. The combination is very beneficial to a deer herd mostly in spring. I would recommend providing deer minerals from about April 1st and continuously throughout the summer. Each mineral site should be replenished about 4 to 6 times per year, depending on how often the deer eat the minerals. Providing deer minerals in the fall and winter is unnecessary as they simply do not provide them with that much of a benefit at that time of year.

WHAT MINERALS TO PROVIDE

Phosphorus and calcium make up most of a buck's antler-growth mineral requirements, with fewer amounts of other minerals and various vitamins also needed. Female deer also need phosphorus and calcium during pregnancy and for milk production. Not every area has enough of these minerals naturally available, however. The fact is that in most parts of the country, deer need a supplemental program that addresses these diet deficiencies.

One supplemental program that landowners sometimes use is an ordinary livestock salt mix, which contains trace minerals. One reason they do this is because animals are attracted to salt. These economical salt mixes are useful for cattle producers, and they can be used for deer herds, but, in most instances, they will not provide deer with enough calcium and phosphorus. Period, end of story. The point is to always check the "guaranteed analysis" on the mineral mix bag to determine exactly what is included in the product.

Most mixes contain about 50 percent salt, as salt attracts deer to the minerals. Other ingredients should include Calcium (Ca) and Phosphorus (P), as well as Magnesium (Mg), Potassium (K), Sulfur (S), Manganese (Mg), Zinc (Zn), Iron (Fe), Copper (Cu), Boron (B), Molybdenum (Mo), and other trace minerals. Some mixes also include trace amounts of vitamins such as A and D. Vitamin E is also important in immune function and in the integrity of cell membranes.

MANUFACTURER SUGGESTIONS

Imperial Whitetail 30–06 Mineral/Vitamin Supplement. Antler Up D3 30–06 Mineral/Vitamin Supplement delivers essential macro and trace minerals along with vitamins A, D, and E needed for a healthy herd and for bucks to reach more of their genetic potential in antler growth. This supplement is a true, professionally

▲ Female deer need phosphorus and calcium to produce healthier milk for their fawns. It is wise to provide does a supplement that addresses such needs—where it is legal to do so. Photo: © David Kay | Dreamstime

▲ When it comes to providing minerals, stick with any of the well-known brand names. Photo: Whitetail Institute

formulated, high-quality mineral and vitamin supplement—not a glorified salt lick. Its exclusive scent and flavor enhancer draws in deer quickly and consistently. Professionally formulated specifically for the needs of deer during the spring and summer, it includes necessary vitamins and specific minerals in correct forms and ratios for antler growth, pregnancy, and lactation. Antler Up D3 increases calcium and phosphorus uptake to promote growth and development of antlers. It also promotes heavier body weights and improves the overall health of deer.

Antler Up D3 contains scent and flavor attractants and enhancers. It is simple to use. Just rake or shovel an area 2 to 3 feet in diameter and mix with the soil. CAUTION: 30–06 Mineral/Vitamin Supplement is such a powerful attractant that some states consider it bait. Consult your local game laws before using.

Antler King Trophy Deer Mineral. The original Antler King product that is still a top-selling deer mineral after 30 years on the market and several enhancements. It contains 27 different proven antler growing vitamins,

minerals, and other additives. AK Trophy Deer Mineral contains a special yeast culture to help deer better digest their food. This formula is comprised of highly digestible chelated minerals. According to the manufacturer, deer will have their greatest consumption from February through September. Just pour the contents onto the ground or just off a deer trail. According to Antler King's studies, the deer consumption will vary from 1 to 5 ounces per head per day.

Evolved Habitat Deer Cane. According to Evolved Habitat, Deer Cane is their most popular mineral product. Deer are highly attracted to the odor and especially the taste of this mineral. The original Deer Cane® formula reacts with moisture to release vapors that will bring deer to a created mineral site. In a short time, it will turn the site into a high traffic area and a highly active mineral site. The powder is a super-dense mineral concentration formula that covers more area than brick and liquid forms do.

In addition to mineral supplements, protein supplements are also extremely important. Several companies produce protein blocks or mixes including Hi Protein Big Buck Block by Antler King, Mossy Oak's BioLogic BioRock (contains 50 minerals) and Imperial 30–06 "Plus Protein" by Whitetail Institute. A more comprehensive listing of companies that produce protein blocks, powder or liquid minerals, and protein supplements can be found on-line.

When used properly, minerals cannot hurt and only help the deer. It is worth repeating, before using any

▲ Other top-selling minerals include Mossy Oak's BioLogic BioRock, Imperial Whitetail 30–06, Big Tine Mineral Brick, Lucky Buck, Antler King Trophy Deer Mineral, and Hunter Specialties' NUFUZ Protein Block. Photo: Mossy Oak Bio-Logic.

▲ According to Evolved Habitat, the Deer Cane® formula reacts with moisture to release vapors that attract deer to the mineral site. Photo: PCFImages

mineral, salt, protein, or any type of supplement for deer, be sure that it is legal to do so in the state you deer hunt.

PROTEIN SUPPLEMENTS

Last, but far from least, protein is also an important building block for antler growth. It helps establish the cartilage-like framework and the blood-rich velvet to distribute the elements needed to form antler makeup to the structure. To help bucks develop bigger antlers, protein should be made available as early as February in the South and March in the North—or at least before bucks begin to develop the first sign of new antler growth. Protein supplements will help to quickly kick off the process of antler development and provide bucks with a vigorous start to growing their new set of antlers. Protein supplements are mostly available in pellet form. They can be specifically prepared by feed and grain stores to your exact specifications. Or they can be purchased already prepared in bags from a variety of sources that also make minerals.

A supplemental mineral, vitamin, and protein feeding program, particularly in regions where the natural soil lacks the amount of nutrients bucks need to grow larger antlers, is a good and useful management tool and addition to any deer management program. Minerals, vitamins, and protein supplements will provide deer with a more complete nutritional diet than some natural ranges can provide. A long-term mineral, vitamin, and protein supplement plan will help not only in larger antlers for the bucks, but also in an increase to the overall health of the deer herd (where such programs are legal).

▲ Another way to provide deer vital minerals is to sow plants that provide high protein, macro and micro minerals, and vitamins. Photo: Whitetail Institute

THE FUNCTION OF MINERALS IN WILDLIFE AND EFFECTS OF DEFICIENCIES

THE MAJOR MINERALS

Major Mineral	Function in Wildlife	Effects of Deficiency
Calcium	Growth of bones and teeth and antlers	Abnormal bone and antler development, function of muscles, loss of muscle tone and nerves
Phosphorus	Growth of bones, teeth, and antlers, and energy metabolism and enzyme systems, proper protein utilization	Poor feed efficiency and weight gain, abnormal appetite, lower reproductive performance, abnormal bone and antler development
Potassium	Function of nerves, part of enzyme systems, maintains water and minerals balance	Poor growth and feed efficiency
Sulfur	Essential part of some proteins	Poor growth
Sodium	Function of muscles and nerves, maintains water balance	Poor feed efficiency, abnormal appetite
Chloride	Forms hydrochloric acid in abomasums (the 4th stomach), aids in breakdown of protein	Poor feed efficiency
Magnesium	Involved in almost all body processes	Poor feed efficiency and weight gain

THE MICRO MINERALS

Trace Mineral	Function in Wildlife	Effects of Deficiency
Manganese	Essential for good bone development and feed utilization	Anemia, poor growth, and feed efficiency
Copper	Needed for blood and for proper feed utilization	Anemia, poor growth, and feed efficiency
Zinc	Influences rate of nutrient absorption	Poor growth
Iodine	Component of thyroid hormone which controls body temperature and rate of metabolism	Poor feed efficiency
Selenium	Needed for growth and reproduction, involved in enzyme system	Poor growth
Cobalt	Necessary component of Vitamin B-12 and enzymes that digest food	Poor growth
Iron	Component of red blood cells	Anemia, poor growth

THE FUNCTION OF VITAMINS IN WILDLIFE

Vitamin	Function in Wildlife
Vitamin A	Necessary to support growth, vision, reproduction, and involved in bone development and antler growth. Aids in controlling infections.
Vitamin D	Necessary for the mineralization of bone development and antler growth. Also helps maintain proper functioning of muscles, nerves, blood clotting, and cell growth.
Vitamin E	Involved in the enzyme system, acting as antioxidants at the cellular level. It also has a significant role in selenium metabolism.
Vitamin B-1	A catalyst in carbohydrate metabolism, enabling carbohydrates to release energy. Also acts as a natural insect repellent.
Vitamin B-2	Acts as a critical cofactor or coenzyme in the metabolism of fats, carbohydrates, and amino acids.
Vitamin B-3	Is critical to cellular respiration and essential for the metabolism of carbohydrates and fats.
Vitamin B-5	Is required in the metabolism of fat, protein, and carbohydrates. Plays a leading role in many cellular enzymatic processes.
Vitamin B-6	Is required in the synthesis and metabolism of protein and amino acids. It also plays a role in the formation of red blood cells.
Vitamin B-12	Is critical to normal nerve cell activity, DNA replication, and the development of red blood cells.
Vitamin C	Functions as a powerful antioxidant, is a key factor in collagen. Helps protect vitamin A, E, and some B vitamins from oxidation.
Biotin	Serves as a critical cofactor in the metabolism of carbohydrates, proteins, and fats. Also aids in antler growth.
Folic Acid	Plays a key role in the synthesis of the genetic material DNA and RNA.

Special thanks to GSM Brands/Hunter's Specialties Vita Rack 26.

CRUDE PROTEIN REQUIREMENTS

According to biologists, deer should have a bare minimum of 6 to 7 percent crude protein in their diet to maintain healthy rumen function. A diet of less than 10 percent protein will result in less healthy animals and poor antler development. Deer require a daily diet of 12 to 16 percent crude protein for the best development of bone and muscle.

▲ This buck has obviously received the proper proteins and other nutrients to develop its impressive antlers and body size. Photo: © Tony Campbell | Dreamstime

▲ Trophy Rock and other similar products provide deer a variety of mineral supplements, electrolytes, and trace minerals. Where it is legal to use them, place a rock on a tree stump where they will last longest. Otherwise, place them at the base of a tree. As they slowly dissolve, they will create a natural mineral hole at the tree's base. Credit: PCFImages

▲ The most effective refuges include cover, water, and total security from human trespass. Credit: © Twildlife | Dreamstime

Chapter Thirty-Four

Creating a Successful Refuge

A ll food plotters should give thoughtful consideration to creating a safe zone. Most people use the word sanctuary to describe a safe-haven area. The word refuge, however, is a more proper term for a no-hunting area for deer. A sanctuary offers shelter from pursuit, but it does so with limitations. A refuge, though, is defined as providing shelter from pursuit without any restrictions whatsoever. Refuge is described as "A condition of being *totally* sheltered from pursuit; an area of total safety; free of all danger,

▲ The large, unmarked area in the middle of our property depicts our refuge. Since it was established in 2001, we have never entered it. Map and Photo: PCFImages

trespass, or trouble; a place where no harm can come to its occupants, anyplace providing entirely safe spaces without any restrictions; a place of *total* protection."

Whether you own or lease 10 or 1,000 acres, creating a refuge will benefit your overall food plot and deer management program. When a refuge is available to deer, they will quickly come to understand that a certain portion of their range is undisturbed by human scent or presence and, consequently, it provides the best safety. Hence, the prerequisite of making a section of land into a refuge is to create a secure area for deer that remains totally undisturbed, year-to-year, from *any* type of human encroachment.

Before committing to creating a refuge, a food plotter must make a self-imposed unbreakable pledge to commit to treat the refuge as what it is meant to be: **a place of *total* protection.** There can be no wavering from that principle. Merely setting aside a portion of acreage and calling it a refuge, but not treating it as such, is pointless. It is not worth the effort of making a refuge in the first place. So, once established, all who hunt the property must never enter it.

▲ This is a sign a friend created to post around his refuge, which he refers to as a sanctuary—which is fine if it is treated as the dictionary defines a refuge. Photo: Monti Loomis

This is the only way a refuge, sanctuary, safe haven, safety zone, or whatever word you choose to refer to it as, allows deer to feel categorically comfortable and secure enough to consistently seek shelter in it. Hopefully, I have made my point emphatically clear by now. If not, let me repeat: once you establish a portion of your land as a refuge, from that point on, everyone who hunts the property MUST stay out of it!

This single rule is the number one component required to create a refuge that will regularly entice deer, including mature bucks, to seek its safety. Once they become accustomed to the refuge, deer will use it steadily to seek protection from human predation. I have emphasized this point because statistically, hunters who create a refuge end up eventually ignoring the most important caveat of forever staying out of it. By ignoring this rule, hunters quickly put to an end the refuge's ability to consistently attract deer. And once deer realize the refuge is not totally free of human odor and presence, they will treat it as just another area of the property.

The total amount of land dedicated to creating a refuge can be as little as one percent on small properties, and as high as 10 percent or more on large tracts of land. If at all practical, a refuge should be created smack dab in the middle of a property. When you finally select an area in which to create a refuge, the entire plan must be carefully considered. Make a written "Things-To-Do" list. The tasks must be totally completed within the area *before* declaring it (with posters) as your refuge. The refuge must include enough cover for deer to hide in. If it doesn't, you can plant additional cover. It should also include a few natural food sources, water, and shelter from inclement weather. Therefore, even a small dense stand of evergreens is a plus within a refuge. It will protect the deer from

▲ Even a small refuge of an acre or two will draw deer into it to seek safety and cover. The success to any size refuge—large or small—solely depends on it NEVER being entered into once it is established. The only reason to enter a refuge is to recover a wounded or dead deer within the guidelines noted in this chapter. Photo: Dreamstime

snow, wind, ice, and other extreme weather. A wet area or even a small bog is also a suitable location, as deer often seek dry land within wet marsh areas where many hunters avoid going.

If practical, a refuge should offer deer a natural source of fresh water. If it doesn't, it would be a good plan to make few dug-out potholes that are about 5 x 5 x 2 feet deep. Better yet, rent a mini backhoe to create a few that are larger and deeper (10 x 10 x 3 feet deep). Both will collect rainwater, runoff, and underground seepage. Mini backhoes are readily available at stores like Home Depot and other tractor and agricultural-type stores for rent. Another option is to hire someone to create a few potholes.

▲ This pothole, at the edge of our refuge, is 2 feet deep. Small ponds or man-made potholes in a refuge provide deer access to water in a safe zone free of human pressure. Dehydrated or exerted bucks often use the water to drink or cool themselves down during the big chase of the rut. Photo: PCFImages

The refuge should also include natural forage like a few mature oaks of white or red acorns, crab apple trees, and other natural browse. If there aren't any cra bapple trees, plant some late-dropping varieties (see the fruit tree chapter for recommendations). Also plant a few late-dropping pear and persimmon trees within the refuge area.

The most functional and successful refuges have other nutritious food sources growing close to their borders. This includes a variety of traditional food plots

like winter-hardy grains, clovers, legumes, brassicas, etc. Also add some quick-growing shrubs within the refuge. The Zereshk barberry grows 8 to 12 feet high, bears fruit after 2 years, and is hardy to -40°F. Highbush cranberry, as the name suggests, reaches heights of 10 to 15 feet. Sandbar willow grows up to 20 feet and is an excellent deer forage. Adding sumac and dogwood will also help create cover and food. Another plant that provides plenty of cover is Gigantus miscanthus. Deer will eat and bed in all these types of plantings.

▲ This small food plot is bordered by our refuge at the top and right. Food plots bordering a refuge add an extra element of attraction to deer. Photo: PCFImages

Another way to create superb cover and food is to hinge-cut existing oak, birch, maple, and crabapple. The fall leaves of these trees are sought after as an excellent food source. The leaves provide deer with carbohydrates and sugar. They will even eat them after the leaves lose their autumn color and turn brown. The trunks of the hinged-cut trees provide cover slightly off the ground, which helps to hide deer. If there is a potential refuge site in the middle of your property, but it lacks some of the essential elements mentioned above, do not let this stop you.

Taking the time to enhance a refuge in the middle of your property far outweighs creating one elsewhere. However, if the middle doesn't work, choose another location. Having a refuge not in the middle of your property is better than not having a refuge at all. The end goal is to provide abundant cover that will protect deer from the eyes of natural predators and from human scent and hunting pressure.

When a refuge is created properly, deer quickly learn to retreat to it for full security. Once that happens, they seldom need or desire to leave the refuge to seek cover on other properties. This is especially the case when the other properties contain good cover—but it is not treated as a refuge and is still hunted. The only time all bets are off regarding keeping deer consistently using a refuge, even under heavy hunting pressure, is during the rut.

I can say with total confidence and frankness that creating a refuge in the middle of our 192 acres has helped considerably to attract and keep deer in it throughout the entire year. Our totally non-hunting, no-trespassing refuge zone has been the single-most effective strategy to increase our daytime sightings of deer, including adult bucks. We are fortunate that we have enough land to create our 21-acre refuge, which occupies 11 percent of our total property. It had sufficient natural cover and most of the other elements within it. What it didn't have we added in before declaring it off-limits. After establishing our refuge in 2001, we have never stepped one foot into the area again for any reason. While I am very curious about what the interior area looks like now, the benefit of creating a complete year-round off-limits refuge far outweighs trespassing into it to satisfy my inquisitiveness.

Over the 35-plus years of providing food plot and deer hunting strategies seminars, I have talked with

▲ This 1/4-acre mixed-brassica plot is planted along the borders of a refuge. If this buck is spooked, he would only be a few seconds from the safety of the refuge. Photo: WINA

thousands of deer hunters and food plotters. They often relate stories to me about their "sanctuaries." An overwhelming number of the conversations inevitably turns to why they "had to" enter their sanctuaries. One of the primary justifications, believe this or not, was to look for shed antlers. The second-most popular excuse was to check for deer sign. Another totally unbelievable justification was to count the number of deer that were jumped while walking through the refuge. This is a ridiculous reason for entering a refuge. Lastly, I have even heard advice from some "pros" that they entered their refuge to hunt an adult buck that was caught entering the refuge on a trail camera. What? This excuse beats it all!

There is only one reasonable and ethical reason to go into a refuge: to look for a wounded or dead deer. Even then, specific rules must be established and followed without exception. Our rules for this situation are steadfast. We have been extremely fortunate that we have never had to look for an injured or dead deer in our refuge. At one point or another, though, it is likely to happen. When it does, we have developed specific guidelines about searching the refuge for a wounded or dead deer.

▲ One of the most nonsensical reasons for entering a refuge is to look for shed antlers. Enter it and you will have defeated the entire purpose of creating a refuge. Photo: © Ruhuntn | Dreamstime

- It must first be firmly established via a blood trail that a deer has entered the refuge. Once this is confirmed, then the refuge's other borders must be slowly and carefully checked by the hunter who wounded the deer, to determine if the deer left a blood trail coming out of the refuge.
- If no blood is found exiting the refuge, the assumption is the deer is still within it. But if blood is found leaving the refuge, the deer can be tracked without disturbing the refuge.
- If no blood is found outside the refuge, and there is still legal shooting light, the only ethical option left is to enter it. But first, and if practical, hunters should be posted along each border in case the deer emerges while the hunter who shot it is searching inside the refuge.

Since we established the refuge 21 years ago, it has developed into a high-traffic deer area. Throughout the year, countless deer funnel in and out of it. Adult does have taught their fawns that it offers safety and, in turn, those fawns went on to teach their offspring. No matter what happens outside of our refuge, deer now know they are *completely* safe from pursuit within it, because they have **NEVER** been disturbed within our safe-haven refuge zone by human presence or scent.

We have also documented that, during the bowhunting season and more so during the firearm season, transient deer also seek safety in our refuge. As early as the third day of firearm season the number of deer existing in our refuge swells considerably. This has been proven by the increased number of deer we see in the fields.

Soon after a refuge is established, it will attract groups of adult female deer and their yearlings and fawns. It is not unusual for us to sit in one of our blinds during the late summer and see 25 to 30 deer feeding in our food plots. Of that number, we have established that at about ⅓ of them have repeatedly enter our food plots from different points of our refuge.

Inherently, female deer living in the refuge, or at least using it as a sanctuary on a regular basis, will be live decoys that attract bucks into the refuge during the rut. That fact has been proven to us many times over the years. Frequently at least one buck is shot that we have never seen on the property or captured on our trail

▲ Before hastily entering a refuge to search for a wounded deer that entered it, first confirm if there is a blood trail leading out of the refuge. Carefully check all outside borders for blood. If blood is found *leaving* the refuge, there is no reason to enter it. Photo: PCFImages

cameras. So, it becomes clear that the does that seek safety in our refuge are luring in bucks from surrounding properties.

The key element for our refuge's success is entirely attributed to steadfastly enforcing strict off-limits policies. This is worth repeating. For 21 years we have never stepped one foot into our refuge—not to look for rubs, scrapes, tracks, shed antlers, or to count the deer, and certainly not to hunt a buck. What sense does that make? It's certainly not a refuge after hunting it!

Here is the nitty-gritty of this entire chapter. Create a refuge. Treat it exactly as the word is defined and you will see a noticeable increase in the numbers of

▲ One of the best aspects of a refuge is that it is highly attractive to female deer. During the rut, estrus does will be live decoys for drawing bucks into your refuge. Many times, an estrus doe has lured a buck from our refuge into a food plot in broad daylight during the rut. Photo: © Mikael Males | Dreamstime

deer on your land in one season. The excitement and anticipation of establishing a refuge are a bonus as well. A refuge results in better odds for a hunter to be in the right stand at the right time, when an estrus doe unknowingly coerces a buck from the security of the refuge into one of your food plots in broad daylight. Her estrus scent will act as an invisible rope tugging him out of the refuge and into the sights of your bow or firearm. Then, and only then, will you realize the importance and practicality of creating a refuge that

is a place of total safety and is never disturbed from human scent or presence for any reason.

Our refuge signs read **"Sanctuary—Keep Out."** I bought them not only to alert our invited friends who hunt our property about entering our refuge, but also to remind Kate, Cody, and me about the absolute importance of never penetrating our refuge. By the way, at the time, I could not find signs that had the word "Refuge."

▲ A vital point in attracting bucks from neighboring properties is to plant crops or fruit and nut trees that the neighbors don't have. Photo Credit: PCFImages

Chapter Thirty-Five

Attracting Neighboring Bucks to Your Property

I would not be surprised if you turned to this chapter first as it would be understandable. After all, the end game, for most deer hunters, is to draw bucks from all points of the compass to the lands they hunt. One of the most often-asked questions I receive is, "How can I hold bucks on my land?" Most times, the person is taken aback by my reply, "I am sorry to say, you absolutely cannot 'hold' a buck on any given piece of land indefinitely."

The reason is simple, at least according to the definition of the word *hold*, even if it is a large tract of property, and especially if it is a small piece of land. This concept is generally conveyed by well-meaning professional outdoor communicators who are unintentionally using improper deer hunting terminology to make a point. Sometimes, professional writers, seminar speakers, or television hosts don't realize what they say or write is often perceived as the Golden Rule. Please understand that I am not only criticizing other outdoor professionals; I, too, have been guilty on occasion of misusing hunting tactic terms that could have been much better defined.

The fact about this question is straightforward. The odds of holding a buck, particularly an adult buck, on a piece of property permanently or even for any extended amount of time is not realistic. This is even more so during the rut. It's just as farfetched as saying you could keep a herd of African wildebeest on a single piece of grassland indefinitely. The snag lies in the use of the word "hold." Hold is defined by the Merriam-Webster dictionary as "to keep, retain, imprison, restrain, confine, or lock up." None of these terms apply to "holding" a buck on a piece of property. Well-meaning professionals who use such emphatic phrases only end up confusing hunters and food

▲ While it is certainly possible to draw bucks to your land regularly, particularly when you grow food plots, it is also impossible to "hold" a buck on any given piece of land indefinitely. Photo: © Tony Campbell | Dreamstime

plotters (particularly novices), with whom they are trying to share their legitimate deer hunting information and opinions.

A classic example of the misuse of a concept is when outdoor professionals convey that "bucks go totally nocturnal." The key misnomer about that statement lies in the misuse of the word *totally*. It is the single-most common example of a misused adverb when applied to bucks. There isn't a buck in North America that becomes a *totally* nocturnal deer. Even more so, a mature buck won't go totally nocturnal, even during heavy hunting pressure. You probably just said to yourself, "What the heck did he just say?!" I understand your surprise. The fact is, however, there are simply too many variables to make such a categorical statement.

Think about this. Isn't it possible that a mature buck can get jumped from its bedding area by another deer hunter? Basically, the answer is that it is not only possible; it happens often. Bucks also move about during daylight simply to get up and stretch their muscles. A

▲ Despite the long-held belief that bucks go totally nocturnal, they don't. This is especially true during the rut. A buck could get up to check a scrape, it could catch the scent of an estrus doe, even chase one, or it could be jumped by a hunter or predator. There are too many variables to unequivocally claim bucks go totally nocturnal. Photo: © Mikael Males | Dreamstime

buck could also leave its bed and move about during daylight to check nearby scrapes or to freshen a rub. Another factor that prevents bucks from becoming totally nocturnal is the breeding season. A bedded buck could be coerced to move during daylight because a nearby estrus doe just got up and moved. The reality is a doe in estrus could easily lure a buck into following her right past a hunter on stand during daylight. Furthermore, a buck may be enticed to leave his bed during the day to follow the wafting odor of fresh estrus scent. Additionally, during extreme winter weather all deer instinctively move about, albeit it may only be in short distances. They do so to feed and generate enough energy from forage to keep their body temperature up. Moreover, a buck could be chased out of its hiding spot by a coyote in daylight. And, of course, there is daytime naturally occurring movement by male deer that happens even under heavy hunting pressure.

Therefore, to unconditionally suggest bucks go "totally" nocturnal because of hunting pressure, and that they will not move about at all during the day, is a far-reaching statement.

THE BRAIN GAME

Whether it is holding a buck on the property you hunt or claiming that a buck goes totally nocturnal, there are simply too many random circumstances that can come into play that could end up placing a buck in the crosshairs during legal hunting hours. Therefore, these unpredictable circumstances that occur could certainly end up with you field-dressing a buck you killed during daylight hours. Don't give up and stay home or, equally as bad, sit in a stand convinced that you're not going to see a buck. There is an old saying, "If a man convinces himself he is going to die, he'll probably figure a way to make it happen." The same negative thinking applies to deer hunting. If you convince yourself you won't see a buck, you'll figure a way to make it happen. In doing so, you are commanding your brain to not pick up, see nor sense obvious signs of a buck passing by your stand. Negative thoughts are processed by the brain, and it reacts to them accordingly. In a situation like this, the brain will fire off electrical signals to make its owner distracted by dampening his or her alertness to support the order given it, "I am not going to see a buck."

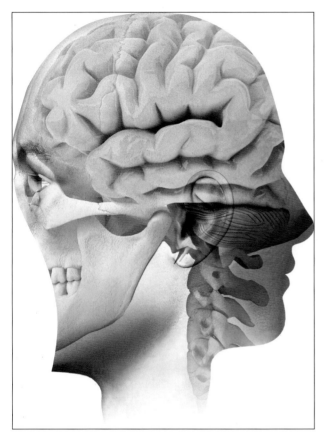

▲ When you instruct your brain not to see a buck, it will automatically follow your instructions. It will do whatever it can to prevent you from seeing what you asked it not to have you see. Photo: © Leonello Calvetti | Dreamstime

If you still don't believe that the odds are stacked against bucks, especially adult bucks, becoming nocturnal, consider this: Outdoor Life and the National Deer Association released a deer take press release in late January 2022. It stated that hunters across the nation killed a total of 6.3 million whitetails during the 2021 deer season. Of the 6.3 million deer taken, 3 million were bucks. It would not be inconceivable that a fair share of the 3 million bucks included adult bucks. Therefore, the press release further supports my point about the exaggerated statement that bucks go "totally" nocturnal once hunting pressure is detected by them. So, I ask this question, "If, as it is often mis-stated, bucks go totally nocturnal soon after undergoing hunting pressure, how then, were 3 million bucks killed?"

Even Star Trek's Commander Spock would have to admit, "If one was to believe the claim that all bucks restrict themselves to only traveling in total darkness,

then the only logical answer, Captain, would have to be that 97.0033419 percent of bucks nationwide were all shot at night." Obviously, this hypothetical conjecture is in no way intended to be factual. The 3 million bucks legally killed poke a large hole in the misused statement that bucks go "totally nocturnal" when undergoing heavy hunting pressure. Get my point?

What really takes place is this: Bucks become more secretive and instinctively recognize it is far safer to remain hidden in cover for longer periods of the day. They will often let a hunter pass within feet of them rather than to reveal themselves by running off. They also change their movement patterns, moving less at dawn and dusk. However, they do move more during the off hours of the day (about 11 a.m. to 1 p.m.), even if the movement is strictly limited to a confined area. The fact is that bucks are up and about and are not totally nocturnal. Again, this is especially the case during the weeks of the four phases of the rut (false-rut, big-chase phase, primary rut, and post-rut).

What I'm really conveying here are two points. First, don't become disheartened when buck sightings drop, even considerably. They have NOT gone totally nocturnal. Adjust your hunting times and you will discover daylight buck movement. The second point is that it is possible to keep resident bucks from straying off your land *less* often and attract bucks from other areas *more* frequently to your land. Even by growing food plots, however, you won't be able to *indefinitely* "hold" bucks on any piece of property. It just isn't possible to do so.

ESSENTIAL ELEMENTS

So, setting aside all the finer distinctions of terms and phrases for now, just how do deer managers entice and increase the numbers of bucks, including adult bucks, into repeatedly using their land? It isn't all that problematic to achieve, so long as you don't try to over-complicate how to get it done.

The short answer to this dilemma is to make sure your land is attractive during the entire year to *female* deer. Keep that point uppermost in your overall food plot and deer management plan. Although having does on your land is a crucial factor in attracting bucks, it isn't the only piece of the puzzle. There are several other factors that will enable you to achieve the goal

▲ Draw bucks to your land by making your property exceptionally attractive to female deer during the entire year. Female deer are live decoys. They will often draw bucks into a food plot during daylight, especially in secluded food plots. Photo: WINA

of attracting bucks on to your land on a regular basis, and even have one or two adult bucks call your land "home." In no special order of importance, some of the essential elements include:

- Natural water sources like a pond, stream or even a creek.
- Small man-made watering potholes.
- Nutritious summer and winter-hardy clovers, other legumes, grains, brassicas, etc.
- A variety of soft mast like sugar-packed peaches, persimmons, and late-dropping pears and apples, etc.
- An assortment of shrubs, wild grapes, and berry bushes.
- Hard mast trees including chestnuts other nutlet producing trees and oak nuts.
- A totally secure and never-penetrated refuge.
- A healthy buck-to-doe ratio.
- Lower impact hunting pressure.
- A variety of secure undercover.

- A thick stand of softwood pines not planted in rows but planted unevenly.
- Hinged-cut trees for both food and cover.

These elements and others will help make your piece of ground more attractive to bucks and does. I mention this because I want to be clear that just planting food plots isn't enough. You must develop an overall management *plan* that provides all the elements needed to attract the general population of deer and to make bucks feel safe.

▲ A lush field of clover is an ideal piece of the puzzle to draw does to your property. By consistently attracting does to your food plots, you raise the odds of drawing in resident and transient bucks to your land. Photo: Arrow Seed

Think of your deer management and food plot program as having many parts of an overall puzzle. While they are important single puzzle pieces, alone they cannot complete the entire puzzle. But when all factors of a well-thought-out and implemented food plot and management program come together, they will work rather smoothly to achieve your overall hunting goals. Always keep the puzzle analogy in mind while developing your program. Leave any one piece out of your food plot and deer management plan and it, like a puzzle missing a piece, remains incomplete.

Something else to keep in mind, is that bucks and does have established home ranges that generally encompass about a square mile, or 640 acres. (This is not written in stone though. Sometimes the amount of acreage is smaller and other times larger). That's a large amount of property, especially considering the average hunter who owns property has about 50 to 100 acres. That leaves another 590 to 540 acres for your deer to roam. Within a deer's home range, however, bucks generally establish a few core areas. They use each core area during different times of the year, and under different types of hunting pressure. Generally, biologists say the average core area is about 40 or so acres. In some rare instances, core areas can range from as little as 5 percent up to 25 percent of a buck's total home range. Bucks that have survived several hunting seasons reduce their core areas considerably during the peak of hunting season. Biologists also state that adult bucks spend about 70 to 80 percent of their time within their core areas.

THE VALUE of WATER

One of the principal elements in developing a complete deer and habitat management program is having both natural and man-made water sources on your land. Water availability for deer often gets overlooked. As any biologist will tell you, deer that live in areas other than arid regions get most of their daily intake of water by extracting it from the plants they eat. However, a deer that has access to fresh water via ponds, creeks, streams, and even man-made potholes that collect fresh water from rain, runoff, or underground springs, will readily visit these watering sites. This is mainly true during the big chase phase of the rut when bucks become dehydrated by chasing hard after estrus does, sometimes over long periods of time. They use ponds, streams, and potholes not only to drink water, but also to wade into to cool down their body temperature.

On our land, we have several potholes, 3 ponds, and a tiny seasonal creek. When a buck seeks out a home range, he will almost always make sure it includes at least one reliable fresh water source, and that will be generally within his core area.

FOOD SOURCES

Over the last 35 years, I have used two mantras about planting food plots in books, seminars, and on our T.V. show: "Plant it *right* and they *will* come," and, "You reap what you sow." Both are promotional motivating statements. Basically, they are my attempt to enlist more hunters into becoming food plotters, deer managers, and habitat improvement gatekeepers. There is no doubt that food plots are a valuable element to hunting success.

Plant it *right* and they *will* come! Remember that planting food plots, like any of your hunting strategies, is a valuable hunting tool. But to consistently attract all age classes of bucks (and does), food plots must be combined with the other bits and pieces of the puzzle. I can't emphasize this enough: Food plots should not be thought of as the only silver bullet a hunter has to kill a buck. On the flip side of the coin, food plots will improve your sightings and kill ratios dramatically.

As anyone who has hunted lands planted with food plots quickly learns, there are times when food plot plantings are not a deer's first choice. In early fall, deer

▲ There is no question that developing a pond or creating small potholes that hold water will attract deer. Bucks often use a small pond or watering pothole to cool off or to get a drink after chasing does during the rut. Photo: © Mikael Males | Dreamstime

▲ Even the most sumptuous food plots do not draw in deer consistently. When acorns, chestnuts, nutlets, and fruit ripen, deer will gorge on them and only intermittently browse food plots until the other foods are exhausted.Credit: Deposit Photos

often browse quickly through food plots as they head to more preferred food sources. Deer will eat acorns until they begin to lose their nutritional value. But they will concentrate on consuming them most in early fall when deer focus on loading up on carbs.

Carbohydrates are terrific sources of energy for deer. Food plot managers can provide high-energy carbohydrates to deer by planting corn, soybeans, wheat, oats, turnips, chestnuts, and other nuts to help deer get through the tough times of winter.

Mother Nature also plays a role. She provides acorns as building blocks of protein, carbohydrates, and fats. Acorns are low in protein, but they are exceedingly high in carbs and fats. These are two elements that help put body weight and fat on deer to prepare them for winter. In the fall, deer will also concentrate on eating late-dropping pears, apples, and persimmons. These sugar-packed, soft masts are also rich with high carbohydrates. At one point, however, when deer are done with "carbo-loading," they quickly and enthusiastically return to eating in food plots and in agricultural farm fields. The point is that food plots and agricultural crops have a definite short "down time" when deer temporarily browse through them more lightly in favor of other natural or planted vegetation.

A deer manager's end goal when planning and developing a food plot program should be to lure deer, especially bucks, into using their property to feed and bed in as much as possible. As I have said, this is often achieved by planting a few warm-weather crops (like huntingplots.com's Ridgeline Summer Draw, Biologic's Alfalfa, Full Draw Clover from Sinclairville Seed, Chicory from LaCrosse, and Imperial Whitetail Fusion). More important, add a higher percentage of extreme winter-hardy plantings (like AberLasting, Frosty Berseem or FIXatioN Balansa clovers) that are more nutritionally attractive to deer during the firearm seasons from November through January. Bucks will be instinctively drawn to choose their core areas in places offering reliable, naturally available food sources. In farming areas, look for core zones that include nearby staple agricultural foods. Therefore, planting a separate food plots of warm-season and winter-hardy food plantings on your land, within a convenient distance of a buck's core area, can significantly raise the bar to attract bucks to your plots more dependably.

▲ This doe is eating Full Draw white and red clovers plus chicory. It is a seed mix deer eat throughout the year, particularly in October and November. With the proper maintenance, it will last 3 to 4 years. Photo: Sinclairville Seed

While it is important to include nutritious year-round plantings, it is even more practical and crucial to provide plantings that are more palatable and nutritious from October through January. The longer the food plots are available, the more a buck becomes accustomed to, dependent on, and comfortable feeding in them. That is why we plant at least 60 percent of our food plots with winter-hardy plantings.

REFUGES

To make my point yet again about creating bona fide refuges, I will compare it to an episode of *Seinfeld*. In the show, Jerry is at the counter of a rental car company to pick up a vehicle that he reserved. The woman at the counter tells Jerry she doesn't have a single car to rent him. Jerry tells her, "But I made a reservation!" Once again, the rental agent states that there aren't any vehicles available. Jerry then tells the woman (paraphrased here), "Anyone can just *taaaaake* a reservation, but you have to know how to *hoooold* the reservation!"

The same point applies to creating a refuge on your hunting property. Anyone can just *create* a refuge. But you must know how to *treat* it like a refuge. As I have mentioned, a genuine refuge provides the occupants within it a total safe haven. A refuge for deer is a place where they can find asylum; it's meant to provide your deer with shelter from human danger, a zone of complete safety from hunting pressure. When you create a refuge, you must treat it as such, or it will never truly be a place of absolute refuge for deer and especially for mature bucks. Once you establish an authentic refuge, never enter it for any reason whatsoever, except to recover a dead or wounded deer.

▲ A genuine refuge provides deer a safe haven where they can find total asylum. Whether your signs read sanctuary or refuge, give deer total protection from human trespass year-after-year, for the life of the refuge. Photo: PCFImages

THE DOE DYNAMIC

On one hand, it is advisable to encourage does through a variety of management techniques to feel as if your piece of property offers them all the elements they require to survive. There are, on the other hand, two theories regarding having too many breeding does on a piece of land. One camp says having enough female propagating does will be beneficial in attracting and seeing more bucks, including transient bucks, during the rut.

The second camp believes that you can never have enough does on a property. They restrict the killing of does. This camp strongly believes in the practice of letting does live so they can have more fawns. This belief is generally held by old-time hunters. It doesn't make much sense, to me, as a healthy deer herd must have a good buck-to-doe ratio. Therefore, doe populations must be kept in check.

Having a healthy population of does on our land is better than having an over-population. The key issue about how many does you have on your land relates to the buck rutting activity levels. With a healthy buck-to-doe ratio (ranging from a 1:1 ratio to a maximum of 1:5 buck to doe) will create a dynamic, if not vigorous, breeding season throughout all four phases of the rut. It will also dramatically increase the number of rubs and scrapes on the property.

REDUCE YOUR HUNTING FOOTPRINT

No matter where you hunt or what tactics you use to pursue white-tailed deer, your hunting activity creates human presence. Deer relate to excess human intrusion as predator pressure. If you trespass into a mature buck's core bedding area more than a few times during the hunting season, the buck will adjust his movements and habits to your presence. He will move to a more secluded, undisturbed area within his home range (640 acres). Note that I did NOT say an adult buck will leave his home range if he is disturbed. He will not. *Instead*, he will adjust to another area within his home range.

The quick fix to this dilemma is to reduce your footprint within your property throughout the year (as is practical). The first step to keeping your deer feeling secure is to create trails that run alongside your property's borders. Once you establish these trails, set up tree stands and blinds or use portable climbers to hunt along the fringes of your land, leaving the interior as undisturbed as practical. The more stands you have, the more you will keep the bucks from associating the stands with human presence.

Another tactic to reduce your intrusion during hunting season is to enter and exit your deer stands as carefully and as quietly as possible, and from different entry and exit directions as often as practical.

On our 192 acres, we have a combination of 45 wooden and metal tree stands, and 11 enclosed hunting blinds. Some stands are intentionally close to one another to take advantage of different convection, thermal and prevailing wind directions. Others are only used during the archery or firearm seasons. Some stands are used to capitalize on uncommon wind directions and thermal and convection currents, while others take advantage of drives put on by surrounding neighbors. Having that many stands allows us almost unlimited flexibility and options. It also permits us to change from a morning stand to a stand that is hunted from 11 a.m. to 1 p.m., and then another stand for the afternoon post. Keep 'em guessing; it puts meat in the freezer.

In all, our stands help us to significantly reduce our human presence, as most are not set up in the interior of the property. I'm not suggesting everyone needs a lot of stands on their land. Having more rather than fewer stands, though, provides more options from which to choose. It also helps keep your presence down which, in turn, helps to keep your bucks from looking for a safer area within their home range.

CREATE COVER, COVER, AND MORE COVER

Creating cover is another piece for completing the entire wildlife food plot and deer management puzzle. One way to figure out if the cover on your land isn't appealing to deer is to use stealth cameras. If your cameras are only capturing buck images at night, you can be assured that your property is lacking in the type of cover bucks feel secure in. Or, that there is too much of a heavy hunting footprint happening on your land. That could be attributed to too much ATV use, too much interior use (instead of along the borders), too much day-to-day activity, or one of the worst culprits—over-scouting the property.

If your land does not have a variety of secure cover for deer to use as protection and bedding, take the

▲ This is Big View blind. It looks out over 5 acres of fields planted in food plots. There is another enclosed blind and 7 tree stands covering the same 5-acre area. Photo: PCFImages

▲ Cover is an all-important element for deer, particularly bucks who learn at an early age that thick cover translates into survival. Photo: © Michael Tatman | Dreamstime

necessary steps to change it. That may mean planting several types of shrubs and other plants to create secure cover. To keep bucks on your land more consistently, you must pay attention to this essential element. It may require hiring a food plot and deer management consultant to come in and provide you with the type of advice you need to add the elements of thick, secure cover to your land.

IT'S A WRAP

All the suggestions mentioned above will help you attract transient bucks and keep resident bucks using your property more often. Remember, a buck is genetically programmed to cruise over its home range and even outside of it at times. A buck can even leave its 640-acre home range for some far-flung outskirt areas to find better food, a more reliable water source, better cover, and most often, to locate receptive does. By using the above advice, you will increase the number of bucks that you attract and frequent your land. But, as the saying goes, particularly during the rut, "It's hard to hold an old boy down."

▲ No matter how much food, cover, or security is provided to an adult buck, during the rut he may be inclined to seek out does elsewhere.
Photo: Ted Rose

▲ The bottom line about comprehensive record-keeping is this: It makes a land manager a more informed hunter.
Photo Credit: © Steven Oehlenschlager | Dreamstime

Chapter Thirty-Six

The Vital Importance of Keeping Records

All enthusiastic wildlife managers should understand the impact of keeping accurate, long-term records about their food plot and deer management program. With Mother Nature at the helm and no guarantee that every single planting will turn up as expected, keeping accurate records will help you improve your food plots with the same or different plantings. All it takes is a mindset to commit to accurately document everything going on within your food plot and deer management program. When you can refer to a history of records to either solve a potential problem, check a fact, or any other important element—accurate record keeping will come to the forefront as a significant tool. You are probably thinking that recordkeeping requires more time and effort. Yes. It does. But I assure you it will be a worthwhile endeavor.

WHAT'S IN A NAME?
I learned early on to record the exact name of each plant or plants we seeded in a plot, along with the food plot's name and location. Additionally, instead of just a number or single letter, each plot is given a descriptive name that can be easily remembered and identified. For instance, some names of our plots include Finger Field, Big View Plot, The 3-acre Field, Hot-Stuff, etc. I stay away from labeling plots (or soil tests) with numbers; using numbers never fails to create confusion or the possibility of having a brain-freeze and forgetting what a number represents. Plot names should mean something. They are much easier to remember when the plot can reflect information that relates to where it is. We have a plot called Big Oak Lane. It's a long narrow plot near a huge old oak tree in the woods. Another plot is called Instant Doe. A doe was taken from the blind shortly after we put it up. These types of monikers are hard to forget. Like each treestand and blind on our property, every individual food plot gets a name. So, to answer my own question, "What's in a name?" The simple answer is everything.

(Use pencil or permanent marker)

Quality Deer Management Association
P.O. Box 160, Bogart, GA 30622
800-209-3337

DEER NUMBER: _0040_   DATE HARVESTED: _11 / 18 / 17_
           MO   DAY   YEAR

HUNTER'S NAME: _KATE_   PROPERTY: _WEOWNIT_

WEAPON: ☑Rifle ☐Shotgun ☐Muzzleloader ☐Bow ☐Other_____

SEX: ☑Buck ☐Doe   Milk Present? ☐Yes ☐No

Live Weight: _240.66_ lbs.   Dressed Weight: _191_ lbs.

Age: _4.5_   Inside Spread: _____ in.

Number Antler Points: Left _4_   Right _4_

Beam Circumference: Left _5.5"_ in.   Right _5.5"_ in.

Beam Length: Left _21_ in.   Right _20 3/4_ in.

Comments: _SEE BACK OF CARD_

▲ We keep detailed computer records of every deer killed on our land. Additionally, each hunter must fill out a data card that includes a hand-written recounting on the back of the card of how the deer was taken. Photo: PCFImages

NAME OF PLOT	Disc	Herb	Date	SEEDS PLANTED	COMMENTS
				2019 Food Plot Plantings -- Page 1	
B.V. E.WID. LONG MIDDLE PLOT #2				Marathon Red & White Clovers	2017 is 3rd year needs to b reseeded in Spring 2019
B.V. S.E. WID. NARROW ANGLE PLOT #3				Marathon Red Clover	2017 is 3rd year orginally planted 6/9/2015
B.V. N.E.WINDOW PLT JUST BELOW B.V.					2017 is 3rd year orginally planted 6/1/2015
B.V.E.WINDOW LONG-ASS PLOT				Freedom Marathon Red & Domino Clovers (nearest E. Window)	2017 clvers doing well in lower plt. Upper needs reseeding 2015 & Fert.
B.V.N-W " FARM RD PLOT	N		6/9	Apin Tunrips & Rape hand seeded (by farm road)	20' w X 184'L = 3,680 sq ft = (tilled and hand seeded in late August)
B.V. WEST WID. PLOT-#1				50% Jumbo Ladino/25% Domino/25%Freedom Red	40' W x 175'L = 7,000 sq ft = 1/7 acre Planted 6/19/2017
BEHIND THE BARN LONG NARROW PLOT	Y		6/19	Rape & Berseem Clover (planted late August 2017)	30 x 200 = 6,000 sq feet = 2/10ths A
B.V. FAR S. PLOT #4 (NEAR BLUEMAN)	Y			Chicory & Balansa clover (planted 9-5-16)	Tilled & compacted with drag chain.
SLANTED HILL PLT				Chicory (stand alone plot)	Planted last few days of July 2017 (fertilize ASAP)
CODY'S STAND PLOT				Red clovers	**Plot is 4 yrs old - needs to be reseeded & measured in 2019**
COYE BROOK ROAD-3 ACRE PLOT	Y			Wtr Wheat, Rape, O.Chicory, Radish, Oats, Marathon red, Alice,	Berseem, B.F.Tfoil, Nordic Trefoil, & Barenbug clvr- planted 9-3-16!
FINGER FIELD				Red & Kura Clover	**Plot has to be sprayed, disced & reseeded in 2019**
POND BLIND N. PLOT #2				Rape & Berseem Clover (plot has potential to flood)	Planted in late August 2017
FIVE POINT TREESTAND PLOT #1				NOT PLANTED IN 2019 DUE TO WEATHER	**Plot has to be sprayed, disced & reseeded in 2019**
HORSE-SHOE PLOT BELOW & N. OF B.V.				Swede & little G.H. Radish & Purple Top Turnips	Planted late Aug 2017 W. end of plot taken over by weeds
KATE'S WOODS N. E. PLOT #1				Alice clvr & Chicory	**5th year in 2017 Plot needs to be reseeded & measured in 2019**
KATE'S WOODS S. E. PLOT #2	Y			Marathon Red Clover & Chicory	**5th year in 2017 plot needs to be reseeded & measured in 2019**
KATE'S WOODS N. WEST PLOT				Red & Ladino White Clvrs w/Chicory	5th year in 2017 plot doing ok org. plnted 2015 fertilize 2/T-19
LITTLE VIEW CHESTNUT TREE PLOT				Dunstan Chestnut Trees & Marathon Red Clover	**Replace dead D. Chestnuts w/American Chtnuts as test in 2019**
LITTE VIEW "SHORTY" PLOT	Y			PLANTED MISPLACED INFORMATION	100' x 160' 16,000 sq ft = 1/3 acre **Herb/mow/disc & plant**
LITTLE VIEW S. WID (Furthest Plot) #2	Y			Purple Top Turnips	Planted in late August 2017 (as a late planted test plot)
L. VIEW MAIN S WID (neartest Plot) #1	Y			Rape & Berseem & crimson clover	Planted in late August 2017 (as a late planted test plot)
LITTLE VIEW Plot #3 "L" PLOT				Ground Hog Radish	Planted in late August 2017 (as a late planted test plot)
FIVE PT FRUIT & CHESTNUT TREE PLOT	Y			D. Chestnuts, Pears, Persimmons	55'W x 185' L = 10, 175 sq ft =0.23358 of an acre
CHESTNUT ORCHARD PLOT				Chstnts, Pears, Hale Haven Peaches, Apples, fruit trees	64' W x 126' L = 8,064 sq ft =
B.V. FAR W. CHSTNT, FRUT & CLVR PLOT	Y			D. Chestnuts, Pears, Apple, Peache Trees w/M Red Clover	20' W x 110' L = 2,200 sq ft =
FIVE POINT CHESTNUT & PEAR PLOT #3					
WOUNDED DOE HILL PLOT #-1	Y	YES	5/29	1.5 PLbs of Fixation Balansa Clover w/Nitro Coat	Planted 2015 (overtaken by too many weeds- replant spring 2019)
W. SIDE BORDER MTL STAND N.PLOT #-2	Y	YES	5/29	Oasis Chicory (not coated) 1.5 lbs.	Doing okay but weedy. Reseed w/more chicory in spring 2019
W.SIDE BORDER MTL STAND N. #-3			SAME	Forage Rape (as a stand-alone)	Overtaken by weeds do the severe drought in 2017 reseed in 2019
POND BLIND N. NUT&FRUIT TREE PLOT #2				Pear, Persimmon & Apple fruit trees	
STUCK-TRUCK PLOT				Swede & a little ground-hog radish (planted late Aug 2017)	Tilled and planted late Aug as test plot.
WEEPING WILLOW PLOT #1	Y			Alice Clover (3nd year in 2017)	11 x 313 = 3,443 sq feet = 2/10 A
VEGGIE GARDEN PLOT				Marathon Red Clover & Chicory	3 year in 2017
NARROW PLOT #1				Chicory & White clover (just below Santed Hill Plot)	
			2019	PLANTED TWO GALA APPLE & TWO HALE HAVEN PEACH IN AUG	I APL & 1 PCH IN CHSTNUT ORCH /SAME IN B.V.F.W. FRUIT & NUT PLOT
			2019	PLANTED THREE PEAR LOWER ORCHARD JUNE	
			2019	PINK COUSA DOGWOOD & CLVELD SELECT FLOWERING PEAR	NOTE: BOTH TREES ON SALE 1/2 PRICE PD $15 EA. LOWES

▲ This is a typical data form we create to record seeds planted each year. It contains the name of the plot, what was seeded in it, comments, and other pertinent information on the back. Photo: PCFImages.

GATHERING DATA

We have about 45 plantable acres on our farm, but not all are planted. By the end of the 2021 planting season, we planted no less than 25, varying in size from tiny to large, scattered throughout different fields. I can tell anyone what I planted in Finger Field since 2001 to the present year. My records include the year, month, day, weather condition, soil temperature and condition, the pH level, how the soil in the plot was prepared, what seed was planted in it, the seeding rates used, if the soil was dry, damp, or recently rained on, when the seed germinated, when the plot was fertilized and with what type of NPK mix, if the soil had to be amended, and of course how a particular seed grew.

Additional data includes management of each plot; for example, which clovers were mowed and how many times they were cut over the season. Of all the plantings, I also want to know which of them deer prefer most and what time of the season they are preferred. For instance, I have discovered that Swede, which has a lush, large, deep green broadleaf and a sweet turnip-like bulb, is basically ignored by deer until a few hard frosts, which generally occurs by late

October. Then deer will exit the woods, run past other plots—including corn, clovers, soybeans, triticale, grain rye, and other brassicas—to go to the Swede plots first. That's an example of what keeping data will provide a food plotter. It eliminates the guesswork.

▲ Our food plots are pinned with a GPS unit. That way we know the exact location and the size of each plot. One benefit is that it helps to prevent overseeding issues. Photo: PCFImages

We take notes afield mostly with a notebook, yet we also plug-in temporary data into our phones. Each plot's location (as well as each treestand or blind) is pinned and recorded on a GPS unit. Notes taken on the phone or on paper can be entered into a notebook or put on the computer. But I like to keep them in a notebook because it is easier to refer to it, if necessary, when I am in the field. I don't leave much of our food plots and deer sighting information to memory. If I did, I would have a very thin memory file, with little pertinent information.

CORRECTING MISTAKES

Recordkeeping also helps to significantly reduce the chances of making the same mistakes more than once. If you have made a correction to a problem with a planting, and the process was accurately entered into the records, you know exactly what to do should the problem repeat itself. There is no waste of time or frustration about trying to recall what you did. Your data will tell you exactly what steps you took to find the solution.

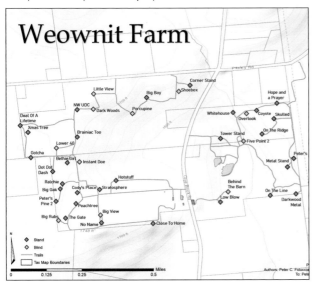

▲ A GPS is used to pin all our stands on a master map. It helps us when we assign stands. After a stand has been assigned, a quick look at the map helps plan a better approach regarding wind direction. Photo: PCFImages

IT'S A MIX OF ERRORS

There is one major error that is often made by food plotters. I know because when I first started planting food plots, I made the same mistake several times. The mistake is when food plotters mix different seeds into a single planting of a plot and don't record the details of the mix. Additionally, you may not think this next point is important, but it is. Record the brands used. You will discover that some brands may work better in your soil than others.

That's why it is important to always buy quality brand mixes like Whitetail Institute's Imperial Whitetail, Mossy Oak's Biologic, Antler King, Frigid Forage, Pennington, Buck Forage, huntingplots.com's Ridgeline 5 Star blends, and many other reliable seed companies.

THE BOTTOM LINE

What recordkeeping all amounts to is having accurate rock-solid information about your entire food plot and deer management program to refer to at your fingertips. After all, planting food plots boils down to being a farmer, of sorts. As a farmer, good recordkeeping information helps to project realistic forecasts on many related factors. Additionally, you will know exactly which types of fertilizers work better on plants than others. It will also provide you with accurate information about how much fertilizer was used on different plantings and if lime was used, how much, and how it improved the pH. Another key point is that recordkeeping helps keep track of changes in seed prices, fuel costs, weather, equipment purchases and repairs, and similar information from year to year.

It becomes easy to see how many benefits are derived by documenting not only the progress of all your plantings but also your deer management efforts. Record-keeping is not guaranteed to put meat in the freezer or antlers on the wall, but it pays off by saving you time, money, and frustration. For any food plotter, recordkeeping pays big dividends in the long run.

▲ Recordkeeping can include information gathered by cell phone photos, written information, trail camera images, drone images, and boots on the ground. Photo: PCFImages

▲ The only way to accurately determine the age of a deer is to have a laboratory perform cementum annuli tooth analysis. Photo Credit: PCFImages

Chapter Thirty-Seven

Aging Deer Scientifically

Most hunters develop a food plot program to attract deer to their lands during the hunting seasons. The goals are to grow and kill adult bucks with larger antlers and create a healthier deer herd. Consequently, it is imperative to keep vital data about all deer culled on your property. Maintaining a comprehensive list of deer-kill records will help take an average deer management plan to a much higher, useful, and illuminating level. Keeping such information is especially critical when the plan is focused on specifically growing older bucks with larger antlers and healthier adult breeding female deer.

DEVELOPING A DATA SYSTEM

Most information on this subject is relatively easy to gather, record, and analyze. Even so, the information often isn't recorded accurately, which is an unfortunate miscalculation, as it is essential to keep long-term, accurate data about deer killed on your lands. Keep in mind that the ultimate goal is to improve the *age* classes of bucks and does on your property.

If that is the goal, then you must faithfully adhere to developing a long-term recordkeeping system. Your program must document the key elements about the *age* and the *live* and *field-dressed weights* of each buck and doe taken.

When such information is unfailingly kept from year-to-year, the data will form a comprehensive log detailing the success, or shortcomings, of the deer management segment of an overall management program. Plans like this will enable you to determine if your food plot and deer management strategy is working, or if it isn't performing as hoped.

Copyrighted 1999

Quality Deer Management Association
P.O. Box 160, Bogart, GA 30622
800–209–3337

(Use pencil or permanent marker)

DEER NUMBER: _0038_ DATE HARVESTED: _12_ / _20_ / _16_
  MO DAY YEAR

HUNTER'S NAME: _Peter_ PROPERTY: _WEOWNIT_

WEAPON: ☐ Rifle ☐ Shotgun ☑ Muzzleloader ☐ Bow ☐ Other_____

SEX: ☑ Buck ☐ Doe Milk Present? ☐ Yes ☐ No

Live Weight: _225.54_ lbs. Dressed Weight: _179.5_ lbs.

Age: _EST. 4.6 - CONF. 5.5_ Inside Spread: _18 3/4_ in.

Number Antler Points: Left _6_ Right _6_

Beam Circumference: Left _5'/8_ in. Right _5.0_ in.

Beam Length: Left _17.'/4_ in. Right _16.5_ in.

Comments: _Taken in "Behind the Barn" blind._
  OVER...

▲ Recordkeeping helps greatly when you're trying to recall specifics of a buck taken. This is particularly true when aging deer. Comparing age stats from year-to-year can often reveal surprising similarities. Photo: PCFImages

Determining the accurate age of a buck or doe killed on hunting grounds should not be limited just to those who have food plot and deer management programs, however. All hunters should keep detailed records on this subject, if for no other reason than to satisfy their curiosity.

HOW TO AGE DEER ACCURATELY

Unfortunately, there are far too many old wives' tales about how to accurately age deer. The methods used run the gamut from aging a buck by the number of tines on its antlers, to the amount of gray hair on the deer's muzzle, or the gait of its walk, the sway in its back, or the droop in its belly. These are all inaccurate methods of aging a deer. While it is said that some of these methods can determine an *approximate* age, for me, they amount to nothing more than pure guesswork.

▲ Some of the old adages about how to age a deer on the hoof can be associated with this mule deer buck. They run the gamut from counting tines, looking at the sway in its back, the droop in its belly, and the amount of grey in its face. These "signs" might give an estimate of age, but these methods always boil down to guesswork. Photo: © Thomas Torget | Dreamstime

AGING BY TOOTH WEAR

There are better ways to approximate the age of a deer, even though they will not be the most accurate way to do so. One process includes examining and counting the exact number of teeth in the deer's mouth. This technique is often referred to as the tooth replacement and wear method (TRW). The TRW method has a high degree of accuracy, but only when it is applied to young deer and attributed to the tooth replacement portion of the method. From the time a white-tailed deer is born until it is about 20 months of age, it obtains new permanent teeth that replace what are known as "milk" teeth in a gradual manner. Tooth observation and counting, by experienced biologists and technicians, is what designates deer into three age categories: fawn deer, 18 months old, and 30 months old. This method is relatively accurate, but only up to the above figures.

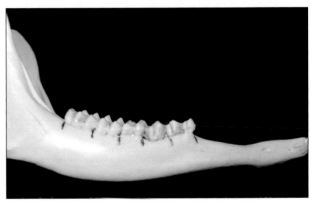

▲ Counting the number of teeth in a deer's jaw is often used to determine the age. While it provides a good guideline, it is not the most accurate method to determine a deer's age. Photo: PCFImages

Side Note: Some biologists say that the TRW method is more accurate than the Cementum Annuli (CA) Tooth Analysis when aging deer *only* up to 2½ years old. The CA tooth analysis method is said the be the most reliable and accurate method of aging *after* a deer reaches 3½ years—bar none. More on CA shortly.

The TRW method is referred to as the "eruption aging" process. This method of counting the deer's teeth works best when the deer is between 2½ and 3½ years old. But once a deer reaches 3½ years of age, there is no longer an absolute way to determine its precise age by counting its teeth. Game department biologists can reliably age deer to 6 months (fawns), 18 months (yearlings), and 30-plus months (2½ years or older). Those with years of experience may venture a *guess* beyond 2½ years old, but this is more of an art than a science.

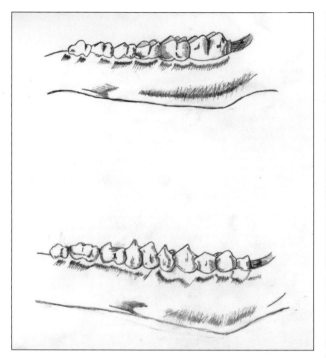

▲ This drawing depicts the tooth replacement and wear method (TRW). It has a good degree of accuracy when it is applied to aging deer, but only up to 30 months or so. Drawing: Max Dawson

The Pennsylvania Game Commission (PGC) has a link to a 7-minute video on its website. The video demonstrates the methods used to identify deer that fall into the three age brackets mentioned above. You can review the video at the PGC's website (www.pgc. state.pa.us).

Dr. Christopher Rosenberry is the PGC's deer and elk management section supervisor. He said, "Looking at the teeth is the best method of aging a white tailed deer. Antler points and amount of gray of the muzzle are not reliable methods of aging deer." Dr. Rosenberry is spot-on about antler points and the gray in a deer's muzzle.

An additional method is to analyze the deer's teeth in the lower jaw and determine the age entirely by the wear and loss of teeth, along with the amount of dentine that appears on them. However, many other wildlife biologists acknowledge this method is also not as reliable as the Cementum Annuli Tooth Analysis (CA) method. Therefore, it should only be used as a *general* guideline for estimating a deer's age.

▲ To get a reliable and accurate age of a deer, remove the front two center incisors (seen here) and send them to a laboratory to perform a Cementum Annuli Tooth Analysis. Photo: PCFImages

SCIENTIFIC ANALYSIS SYSTEM

So, where does that leave us? Well, there is only one completely accurate and reliable way to age a deer that is at least 3½ years old. That is by removing the two center incisors from the lower jaw. It is crucial to include the roots of the teeth. Then send them to a specialized forensic laboratory that uses a process known as Cementum Annuli Tooth Analysis (CA). This method verifies the precise age of a deer.

A certified laboratory technician cuts thin slices of the root of the tooth at the micron level, then stains the roots, places them on a slide, and, using a microscope, counts the layers of the cementum. The method sounds like aging a tree after it has been cut and counting the tree's number of rings.

The number of layers is equal to the number of years the tooth has been in the deer's jawbone. As any biologist will confirm, deer and all other mammals deposit cementum on the surface of the tooth below the gum line. Cementum forms annuli, or aging rings, like the oval bands found inside the trunk of a tree. When the analysis takes place at a specialized histological laboratory, it provides the most accurate method used to precisely determine the age of a deer. Experts in the field state emphatically that no other aging method can provide this type of scientific exactness.

▲ Lab manager AJ Stephens mounts teeth to a slide in preparation of counting the aging rings. This is like counting the rings on a tree. Photo: Matsons Laboratory

▲ The only reliable way to age a buck is via Cementum Annuli Tooth Analysis (CA) performed by a certified laboratory. Here Sarah Marsh, a technician at Matson's Lab, in Manhattan, Montana, slices deer teeth. Photo: Matson's Laboratory

There are two laboratories that I am familiar with that perform Cementum Annuli Tooth Analysis. Both are in Montana.

Carolyn Nistler is the owner at Matson's Laboratory and Arthur Stephens is the manager (www.matsonslab.

▲ Matson's Laboratory in Manhattan, Montana is owned by Carolyn (a certified Wildlife Biologist) and Matt Nistler. The lab has aged more than 2½ million teeth from wildlife including deer, bears, elk, and so on. Another lab in Montana is Wildlife Analytical Laboratories owned by Heather Marlatt-Stevens. Photo: Matsons Laboratory

com), 135 Wooden Shoe Lane, Manhattan, MT 59741. He can be reached at 406-258-6286; email- doScience@matsonslab.com. Matson's Laboratory has ample experience with having aged more the 2½ *million* teeth from wildlife such as deer, bears, elk, and many other hunted and non-hunted animals. Visit their website for more detailed information on how to submit teeth, how to extract teeth from the lower jaw, costs, turnaround time for receiving the tooth analysis, etc. Some products that Matson's offers include a Certificate of Age Analysis, Pre-printed Envelopes and Adhesive Labels, and even gift cards.

Wildlife Analytical Laboratories™ (www.deerage.com). Heather Marlatt-Stevens is the principal of Wildlife Analytical Laboratories™. She can be reached via email at customerservice@deerage.com or 512-756-1989. Results of your teeth aging analysis are posted on their customer portal.

If you are ready to totally remove the guessing game out of aging your deer, remember there is only one surefire way to get an accurate age of a deer older than 3½ years, remember this phrase: "If you want the truth, cut the tooth." Send your deer teeth to a laboratory for accurate analysis.

Sending a deer's teeth out for aging is a worthwhile investment. All hunters should keep track of the accurate age of every deer—buck or doe—killed on their land.

CONCLUSION
Aging your deer is essential to your program's overall success. When aging records are kept reliably, from year-to-year, they form a comprehensive log detailing the overall success or shortcomings of the food plots planted and the deer culled within your wildlife management program.

Early in the morning, approximately 7AM, Cody saw two bucks (not specifically identifiable) up the ridge to the west / southwest. They were moving from the direction of Deer Doctor Trail toward UDC field. They disappeared from view within ten minutes. Over the next hour, there was movement of several deer (unidentifiable) across the ridgeline and within the woods between Porcupine and Deer Doctor Trail. At approximately 8:30AM Cody noticed a movement directly in front of the blind, which he identified as this buck. The buck was feeding on browse at the pine tree directly in the main shooting lane forward of the blind. The buck was also quickly identified as an 8-point, mature deer. Initially, the buck was quartering toward Cody and did not present a clear shot. The buck continued browsing, and Cody waited in order to afford a better shot. Approximately 15 minutes passed before the buck picked up its head, seemingly in response to a curious sound. Upon noticing the buck turning to leave, Cody produced a social blat sound using his mouth, at which point the buck turned and presented a slightly angled broadside shot. After firing, the buck ran to the southeast into the thick underbrush on a diagonal toward Deer Doctor Trail. Cody waited approximately 15 minutes before attempting retrieval. Upon leaving the blind, a strong blood trail was found near the impact site, which led into the thick brush. The buck had expired approximately 35 yards from the impact site, where a well-placed heart / lung shot was observed.

▲ On the back of every stat card, we enter a brief and detailed re-cap of the hunt. As years pass, the details may be forgotten, but the stat cards ensure the information remains accurate. Photo: PCFImages

▲ When growing food plots, it is important to keep accurate weight records on all deer killed on the property. Photo Credit: ©Fiduccia Enterprises

Chapter Thirty-Eight

What Did That Deer Weigh?

Another recordkeeping matter of importance that goes hand-in-hand within a food plot and deer management program is to take the live and field-dressed weights of all deer killed each season. This step should not be skipped.

Attaining the live weight of a dead deer may seem unachievable, as most deer have already been field-dressed before they are brought to a scale. There are tools that make getting the live and field-dressed weights rather easy to do, however. When purchasing a scale to weigh deer, don't skimp by buying an inexpensive one. Instead, purchase a quality unit that will read weights *accurately*. Digital scales are at the high-end of prices, but they tend to provide more accurate readings.

HANGING WEIGHT

The most common method of hanging and weighing deer is called the "hanging weight" system. It applies to weighing a field-dressed deer or other big-game animal on any type of sturdy, non-wobbling game pole. A field-dressed weight should be taken with the head,

hooves, and hide still attached to the deer. Leaving the hooves, head, and hide on the deer will correspond to a more realistic live weight calculation. All the deer's innards must be removed, however.

The hanging weight technique calculates the live weight of a deer by multiplying its field-dressed weight by a coefficient. This method simply allows a hunter to multiply the field-dressed weight by a factor of 1.26 to get the deer's live weight. As an example, during the 2017 deer season my wife, Kate, shot a 4½ -year-old slammer of a buck. We weighed the deer using this method. It was weighed on a calibrated Cabela's 330-pound digital scale (not a plug—just a fact) and witnessed by several of our hunting companions.

The heavyweight buck's field-dressed weight was 191 pounds. Therefore, to attain the buck's live weight we simply multiplied 191 x 1.26 to get a live weight figure of 240.66 pounds. The buck was a genuine heavyweight. This method is a reliable method of determining the live weight from the field-dressed weight of a deer. If you remove the hide and legs, multiply the hanging weight number by 1.33 to get a better estimate of the deer's live weight.

MEASURING THE CHEST GIRTH

Another way to calculate the live weight of a dead deer is to use a chest girth measuring tape, which is a flexible tape that is generally made of a sturdy waterproof material. The Pennsylvania Game Commission (PGC), via its website, offers free tools to guide hunters in determining the answer to one of the most-often asked questions by hunters: "How much did my deer weigh?" The PGC tape includes inches from zero to 55 inches; abbreviations including the following LV (Live weight), DW (Dressed Weight), and EM (the amount of Edible Boneless Meat).

▲ My wife Kate shot this buck in 2017. Its field-dressed hanging weight (taken on an industrial calibrated scale and witnessed by several hunters) was 191 pounds. By multiplying the dressed weight by a coefficient of 1.26, its estimated live weight was 240.66 pounds. Photo: PCFImages

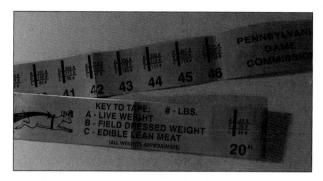

▲ Another method to estimate the live weight of a buck is to use a chest girth measuring tape. This can help to determine the answer to one of the most often asked questions, "What did that buck weigh?" Photo: PCFImages

Once the girth of the deer's chest is determined, which is measured in inches just behind the front legs, the chart will help hunters estimate a deer's live and field-dressed weights, as well as the weight of edible boneless meat. For example, a deer with a girth of 35 inches at the chest has an estimated live weight of 126 pounds, an estimated field-dressed weight of 99 pounds, and will yield around 57 pounds of edible venison. This chart is available on the PGC's website (www.pgc.state.pa.us).

CHEST GIRTH CHART

Below is a table to estimate just the deer's live weight using a Chest Girth measurement.

Girth (in inches)	Estimated Live Weight (in pounds)
24	55
25	61
26	66
27	71
28	77
29	82
30	90
31	98
32	102
33	110
34	118
35	126
36	135
37	146
38	157
39	169
40	182
41	195
42	210
43	228
44	244
45	267
46	290
47	310
48	340

By keeping accurate notes of the live and field-dressed weights of deer taken, you will begin to draw a detailed picture of what your deer generally weigh according to their age. It will also offer a more accurate summary of what your food plots are providing deer in nutrition, which should result in heavier bodies from year

▲ Live and field-dressed weights provide a graph of the average weight of deer on your land from year to year. This will also help determine an overview of how your food plots are helping to bulk up your deer. Photo: PCFImages

to year. Additionally, log entries divulge insights to the type of antlers to expect from the different weight classes of male deer. These measuring tapes are an alternate tool for keeping records on weights of deer, albeit they be estimated.

If you begin to get wide variations up or down from year-to-year in the weights of your deer, it should send up a red flag of alert, or at least an orange flag of interest. If you begin to see lower than usual weights, it could indicate something in the food plot plan is off-kilter. With this pertinent information, you can take whatever actions are necessary to amend the issues causing the loss of weight in your deer.

On the opposite side of the scale (pun intended), should the field-dressed and live weights be higher from year-to-year, it would substantiate that all is well with your program. The plants are providing the type of high protein and other nutritional values for your deer, causing them to steadily gain weight as they age. Good nutrition also promotes larger antlers. With collected information like this from season-to-season, you can quickly see if things are going well or not. It enables you to react and take whatever steps are necessary to correct an issue or continue along the path you are going.

I am an absolute believer in aging and weighing both the live and field-dressed weights of all the deer taken on our farm. I feel this information is an integral part of both the hard work and diligence put into my food plot program as well as providing interesting data. Begin aging and weighing your deer this season

if for no other reason than to win some bets from your hunting companions who guess the weight of the deer through less reliable methods. In other words, cheat. Measure your deer with the tape before weighing it. I am kidding, or am I? Maybe.

Knowing how to accurately determine the weights (live and field dressed) of your deer will make your hunting more interesting and satisfying. More important, it will provide you with crucial management information about the deer you hunt.

▲ It may seem superfluous to record both live and field-dressed weights, but that is an incorrect assessment. The bottom line is recording both weights is among other important elements that go along with developing a comprehensive food plot and habitat program. Photo: PCFImages

▲ It is important to use predator control on any hunting property in order to keep deer numbers stable. Photo Credit © Mikael Males | Dreamstime

Chapter Thirty-Nine

Predator Control—Essential to Deer Management

There is an inherent reality related to undertaking a wildlife management program. Many predators lurk in dark corners and other shadowy places. They will take any opportunity to kill "your" deer after you have invested so much time, sweat equity, care, and money. The worst of these predators, however, does not always walk on four legs.

FOUR-LEGGED PREDATORS

Depending upon where a land manager's property is, he/she must regularly deal with a variety of critters found across the country—like coyotes, bobcats, wolves, mountain lions, and bears. Additionally, even feral dogs can predate on fawns. Depending on the source, in a healthy turkey population, it is said cats

▲ Feral and house cats can kill up to 20 percent of turkey poults, and up to 1.4 to 3.7 billion song and other birds. Reduce this figure by neutering house cats and trapping feral cats and bringing them to animal shelters that will neuter them, often free of charge. Photo: © Brenda Denmark | Dreamstime

can kill up to 20 percent of turkey poults each year. More startling, in *Nature Communications*, an open access journal that publishes high-quality research, it was written that in the United States feral cats kill between 1.4 to 3.7 *billion* song birds, other birds, and an untold number of game birds each year. The American Bird Conservancy reported that in a study conducted by scientists from the University of Georgia and the National Geographic Society's Crittercam program, that the lead author of the study, Kerrie Anne Loyd said, "If we extrapolate the results of this study across the country and include feral cats, we find that cats are likely killing more than 4 billion, billion not million, animals per year." So it should not be startling that they can kill a sizeable number of turkey poults across the nation. Feral cats also decimate the populations of baby ducklings, goslings, rabbits, and squirrels. They are also responsible for destroying the nesting sites of rabbits, turkeys, gamebirds, waterfowl, and songbirds.

The point of controlling feral cats and dogs, or even domestic pets that are allowed to run free, is complicated. The best course of action regarding pets is to approach the owners and plead your case about the damage they could be causing to the deer and other wildlife in the area. Politely, but firmly, request they keep their animals from roaming on your property.

COYOTES

There are other predators that will be problematic at times. Coyotes, especially when hunting in packs numbering sometimes a half-dozen or more, can easily run down deer in deep snow in the winter. In spring, they can also reduce the fawn population, as they make quick work of fawns if they can get close enough. Otherwise, whether they are individuals or in packs, they are opportunistic killers snuffing out an endless variety of game and non-game species.

Believe this or not, in many states (including my home state of New York), there is a fixed hunting season for coyotes. They are not treated as vermin. During the open season for coyotes, we kill them whenever the opportunity presents itself, merely to keep their numbers in check. We don't want to eradicate them. Part of the relationship a steward of the land enjoys with wildlife is the balance of nature and the vital

role of legitimate natural predator-prey relationships that nature has intended. "Balance" is the key word. Keeping coyotes and other similar predators' numbers in balance reduces their ratios considerably.

We reduce the numbers of coyotes hunting on our land during the deer season by using two simple strategies. First, we don't invite them to dinner. Second, we don't use dead deer as bait to attract coyotes.

After field dressing deer, we *never* leave the entrails in the field. We all carry large plastic garbage bags in our daypacks. After shooting and field-dressing a deer, we place the entrails in the bag and remove the bag from the field. With the type of scent receptors that a canine or large feline has, it doesn't take long for a coyote or other predator to get a whiff of deer entrails. Deer gut aroma is like ringing a dinner bell. Removing the innards from the field prevents unnecessarily drawing in coyotes to your property.

▲ Coyote are somewhat less damaging to wildlife than cats, but they still kill a noteworthy number of fawns, poults, deer, and other game. Unfortunately, in most states coyote hunting can only be done in provided seasons. Photo: © Renate Hartland | Dreamstime

The second way to reduce coyote presence on your property is by not inviting them through baiting. Many food plot managers have told me after deer season they use deer carcasses as bait for coyote hunting. Here's some things to consider. I am confounded why anyone would want to set out deer carcasses just to kill a couple of coyotes? All that accomplishes is training the coyotes and bobcats to know where they can find deer meat. The Alpha and Beta coyotes then teach the rest of the pack, "This is where our free lunch is." Killing a few coyotes won't stop other coyotes from coming to your property. Hunger will override their need to be cautious, particularly in winter. If you hunt coyotes on your property, you may want to consider an alternate method other than baiting with dead deer, like calling and decoying. I want to be perfectly clear here that I am not disparaging those food plot managers who use deer as bait to kill coyotes. I am just offering another option.

BEWARE OF THE TWO-LEGGED, GREEN-EYED, ENVIOUS PREDATOR

When it comes to having a successful food plot, deer, and habitat management program you can count on, the fact is that there will be green-eyed serpents watching and slithering nearby. Sadly, they will be waiting to strike when the moment is right. As a food plot manager, you must be ready, willing, and able to report law breakers. This includes reporting trespassers, poachers, illegal spotlighters, or road hunters to local law enforcement, starting with the game warden.

When possible, avoid personal confrontations; instead, if you see a trespasser, try to locate his/her vehicle, jot down the license plate number, and note the time of day. Take photos and pass the information along to local game department authorities. As a bit of additional insurance, place a non-confrontational, but firm note on the vehicle's windshield, informing the owner that he/she has been trespassing on private property and the vehicle's license number has been turned over to local authorities for their reference. If you do that, though, be ready for either an apology or a possible irate confrontation at your front door.

▲ Another predator is not a wild animal. It is a human predator that trespasses on private properties. Report all trespassing to local police agencies. If possible, take a photo of the trespasser on your land and get a license plate number of his/her vehicle. Photo: © Pavel Rodimov | Dreamstime

Appendix A

Glossary of Food Plot Terms

Acidic Soil: On a pH scale of chemistry (0 to 14), soil that has a pH test reading below the neutral measurement of 7.0 is considered acidic. An abundant number of plants do well in soils between 6.0 to 6.5, however. There are four major reasons for soils to become acidic: rainfall and leaching, acidic parent material, organic matter decay, and harvest of high-yielding crops. Wet climates have a greater potential for acidic soils.

Acorns: Acorns are a highly preferred food source of deer, bear, upland birds, and other wildlife. Acorns contain substantial amounts of protein, carbohydrates, fats, minerals, calcium, phosphorus, potassium, and niacin. Deer can digest acorns easily and therefore they can eat many of them per day. In the fall, acorns constitute up to 25 percent of a deer's diet.

Acre: A parcel of land, containing 4,840 square yards or 43,560 square feet.

Adjuvant: Any substance in an herbicide's formulation or added to the spray tank to improve herbicidal activity or application characteristics.

Agronomy: The science of crop production and soil management.

Aldo Leopold: Leopold is widely regarded as the father of the American wilderness system and the science of wildlife management. He was an icon in conservation circles worldwide. The Leopold collection contains the raw materials that document not only Leopold's rise to prominence, but also the history of conservation and the appearance of the field of ecology in the early 1900s until he died in 1948. Shortly before his death, Leopold contended that it was vitally important to protect wilderness for *both* wildlife and humans.

Alfalfa: A leguminous agricultural crop sought after by deer. It is incredibly attractive to deer when planted as a wildlife forage food plot.

Alkaline: A pH scale reading of soil chemistry ranging from 7.1 and higher is considered alkaline (a.k.a. sweet soil).

Allophane: An amorphous to poorly crystalline hydrous aluminum silicate clay mineraloid. This is another mineral that deer seek out when it is lacking in their diets.

Alsike Clover: Alsike is a top choice to plant in wet areas. This is an upright, short-lived perennial legume that does well in low, poorly drained acidic soils. Alsike is a clover to plant in areas with short-term standing water.

Amending Clay Soils: This term refers to a process for some heavy or 'dead'-type clay soils that can be improved by adding a lot of organic matter. Once amended, a minimum amount of disking can continue to help improve the soil. Crops such as corn, sorghum, and radishes, with their extensive root systems will also help to improve the soil.

Annual: A variety of plants that typically grow, produce seed, and die within the same growing season.

Antler Genesis: The annual formation or growth of antler tissue in a white-tailed buck.

Backhoe: A tractor implement used to dig holes, trenches, and ditches, the backhoe is made up of two arms and a bucket connected by hydraulic cylinders. A backhoe is a useful tool for food plotters with extensive parcels of land.

Balanced Fertilizer: Contains NPK (Nitrogen—Phosphorous—Potassium) in equal amounts like 19-19-19 or 10-10-10, etc. As opposed to a non-balanced fertilizer such as 16-18-19.

Bare-root Tree: A term used for plants dug up from the ground while they are still in a dormant state (leafless/budless). A bare-root tree does not include soil. The roots are generally longer and healthier than those of containerized trees. They should be planted as soon as possible. Many times, they are shipped with a slurry to keep the roots moist.

Basic Fertilizer: Simple fertilizer contains only one major nutrient and two minor ones—examples: 16–18–19, 24–4–12, and 20–2–6.

Biennial Cropping: A biennial cropping for nut or acorn trees is when a tree produces a heavy crop one year and less of a crop the following year.

Biomass: A profusion of lush plant life that dominates and crowds out other lower-growing plant life.

Biome: A biome is a substantial region of Earth that has a certain climate and specific types of living things. The largest biomes include vast areas of grasslands, forests, tundra, deserts, and to some extent glaciers. The plants and animals and other living things of each biome have traits that help them to survive in their biome (a.k.a. environment). Every biome has a vast number of ecosystems.

BNF: This is the abbreviation used to describe Biological Nitrogen Fixation (BNF). It is a term used to describe the process in which nitrogen gas (N2) from the atmosphere is incorporated into the tissue of certain plants. Only a select group of plants can obtain nitrogen gas in this manner via the help of soil microorganisms.

Bole: Another word used to describe the trunk of a tree.

Bolting: Bolting is a term that refers to when a plant's flowering stem or stems produce seeds. At this point, the plant is less palatable to deer and other wildlife.

Keep clovers, other legumes, chicory, etc., mowed to prevent bolting/flowering.

Bonehead: A term of endearment coined by Peter Fiduccia, a.k.a. the Deer Doctor, to describe any big-game hunter who is passionately preoccupied with deer antlers, or the antlers of other big game, to the point of being zealous or fanatical. Boneheads are completely unashamed of their obsession, and often will constantly express their views on all things about antlers. Sometimes Boneheads can be insufferable.

Broadcast Spreader: Any spreader or seeder, mechanical or used by hand, to dispense seed, fertilizer, or lime by spreading it indiscriminately onto a prepared food plot bed or ground.

Broadcast Spreading: A method of dispensing seed or fertilizer by either throwing handfuls of seed onto the surface or the ground, or by using the more effective and better controlled ways of using a handheld spreader or PTO-operated broadcast spreader attached to a tractor.

Browse: Deer browse is defined as the leaves, twigs, and buds of woody plants. White-tailed deer are classified as browsers. Eating browse is an important part of what deer do, especially during the winter months when food is hard to come by. Often, browse may be the only food source available during much of the winter. White-tailed deer have an extremely diverse diet eating more than 600 different plants.

Brush Hog: A brush hog is a rotary cutter attached to a tractor to cut up to 3-inch saplings, brush, bushes, weeds, and other natural undergrowth.

Buck-to-Doe Ratio: The ratio of male to female deer in any given herd. Frequently the buck-to-doe ratio is 1–4 or 1–5, but in a well-balanced herd it should be nearer to 1–2 or optimally 1–1.

Bushel: A unit of dry measure (one cubic foot) for grain, fruit, etc. Most large and small grains are usually sold by the bushel. For instance, oats weigh 32 pounds per bushel, barley weighs 46 pounds per bushel, and corn weighs 56 pounds per bushel.

Carrying Capacity: The number of animals a particular habitat can realistically support without harm to either the species or the habitat.

Catkin: A long, droopy, slim, cylindrical flower cluster with unobtrusive petals. They are male parts of a tree that produce and release pollen. They appear on chestnuts, hickory, hazelnuts, etc.

Cellulose: A component of plant cell walls that is not digestible by most animals.

Certified Seed: Seed grown from pure stock that meets the standards of a certifying organization, usually a state government agency. Certification is based on germination, freedom from weeds and disease, and authenticity to variety.

Chisel Plow: A tractor implement that is used for shallow plowing to disrupt or break up the soil's surface. It is used in place of a conventional plow that is meant to deeply plow soil.

Clay Soils: Soil textures that have a high clay content include clay, silty clay, sandy clay, clay loam, silty clay loam, and sandy clay loam. The three textures with the word "loam" in their name usually contain about 20 to 40 percent clay and have varying amounts of sand and silt associated with their names.

Colloidal Materials: Are used to incorporate additional properties to a solution. A colloid can be defined as a microscopic substance that is suspended in another medium, usually a liquid. Colloidal materials can remain evenly distributed in the solution without settling to the bottom or dissolving.

Compaction: The compression of air spaces in the soil by using a compactor implement heavy enough to compress the soil to make good seed-to-soil contact.

Compound Fertilizer: Provides two or more major nutrients.

Concentrate Selector (a.k.a. browser): Deer and other animals are referred to as "concentrate selectors" because they can select the highly nutritious parts of a plant that are low in fiber, like leaves or buds. This requires very selective lips that allow the deer, particularly mule deer, to nibble with precision.

Cooperative Extension Service: A nationwide system for disseminating agricultural knowledge to farmers and food plotters. The system is closely affiliated with the USDA, 4-H, and the nation's land-grant universities.

Corn: Corn, belonging to the grass family, provides deer with carbohydrates and fat, the high-energy food they need before winter. Standing corn also provides deer with cover for bedding, travel lanes, and protection from cold winds.

Corn Ears: A corn ear is the part of a corn plant containing the corn cob, husk, and kernels.

Corn Husk: The leaf-like layer on the outside of corn ears, also known as a shuck. Deer eat the foliage and ears of corn (kernels) and browse the husk.

Cover Crop: A specific plant grown primarily to benefit the soil rather than the crop yield. Cover crops are commonly used to suppress weeds, manage soil erosion, build and improve soil fertility, control diseases and pests, and promote biodiversity. Common cover crops include annual ryegrass, sorghum, buckwheat, hairy vetch, crimson clover, oats, radishes, cereal rye, and other small grains.

Cross Pollination: The term used when one plant pollinates a plant of a similar variety. The two plants' genetic materials combine with each other and the ensuing seeds from a certain pollination will inherit characteristics of both varieties to become an entirely new variety.

Cultipacker: An implement used after disking to press small seeds tightly into the soil's surface to create better seed-to-soil contact.

Cultivar: A cultivar is a plant that is produced and maintained by horticulturists. Although some cultivars can occur naturally in nature due to plant mutations, a majority of cultivars are developed by plant breeders and are called hybrids.

Cultivate: A process used to improve the soil by plowing, disking, compacting, liming, and fertilizing.

Cultivator: A piece of equipment designed to disturb the surface soil. It is used to control weeds between row crops such as sorghum, corn, and other grains.

Cyclone Spreader: A cone-shaped tractor or ATV implement that is either operated by the PTO of the tractor or the battery of the ATV. It is used to uniformly spread either seed, fertilizer, or lime by a spinning disk on its underside.

Dibble: Also called a "planting bar," this is a shovel-like hand tool with a beveled arrow-pointed head, used to open narrow slots in the ground in the planting of conifers and other small 5- to 18-inch trees and shrubs.

Disk: A tractor or ATV implement used to break up surface soil or to break up large furrows of plowed ground. A disk has numerous thin, round, sharp, plate-size wheels with serrated edges.

Disking: A soil preparation practice that generally follows the plowing process, whether it is deep or shallow soil tillage. Plowing cuts, granulates, and inverts the soil, creating furrows and ridges. Disking, however, breaks up clods and surface crusts, thereby improving soil granulation and surface uniformity.

Digestibility: Is a quantity of the forage that is ingested and retained in the body versus being passed as poop.

Diploid: Ryegrass, red clover, and brassicas happen in nature as diploids, meaning each cell of the plant contains 2 sets of chromosomes.

Dominant Soil Order/Suborder: Is identified as the soil order/suborder which the soil possesses.

Dormancy: A period when a plant's growth, development, and activity are temporarily stopped. This minimizes metabolic activity and helps plant life, as resting and not actively growing will conserve energy.

DRI: Is the abbreviation for Disease Rating Index, which can be applied to any plant but is mainly for the six alfalfa diseases—the higher the rating, the more resistant the alfalfa is.

Dry Farming: Any agricultural planting that relies solely on rainfall and moisture stored in the soil, as opposed to irrigation. An overwhelming majority of food plotters fall into this category.

Dry Matter: Dry matter is what remains after all of the water is evaporated out of a forage.

Dwarf Species: A smaller or miniature size description of a plant or tree. Most often used in reference to the size of fruit trees that mature at about 8 to 10 feet tall, it is also used to describe hardwoods and plants like sunflower, corn, and sorghum.

Eating Dirt: Many animals eat dirt. Deer sometimes eat dirt purposely. There are several hypotheses about why deer consume soil. The prevalent theory is that they eat dirt to replenish mineral deficits. The official scientific word for dirt eating is geophagy.

Edge Feathering: The act of creating a gradual transition between two habitat types. It is done by cutting or mowing existing vegetation, or by planting shrubs and grasses of varying heights. Edge feathering is a conservation practice used to make edges more attractive to deer and other wildlife.

Energy: Plants transform the sun's light energy into chemical energy through photosynthesis. The energy within the plant then passes on to other organisms that eat the plants. For example, deer receive energy by eating plants like clovers and other food plot plantings.

Eon of Time: An eon is a really, really, extremely-long, length of geological time. The word eon originates from the Greek word aiōn, meaning "age." An age is not easy to measure, and neither is an eon. Both are just really lengthy periods of time, but in science an eon is about a billion years.

Erosion: The wearing away of topsoil by water, wind, intensive farming, and even overgrazing by domestic or wild animals.

Fallow Soil: A term used to describe fallow soil or ground that has been left unplanted or unused for a period, generally one season to another. In other words, fallow crop land is generally left to rest to regenerate itself. In farming, a field or several fields are taken out of crop rotation for a specific period, usually 1 to 5 years, depending on the crop.

Fawn Recruitment: The number of fawns per doe that survive to 6 months of age. Source: The National Deer Association.

FD: A commonly used rating abbreviation to represent the term "fall dormancy." It is used mostly by large seed distributors that sell a wide variety of seeds to farmers, agriculturalists, and food plotters. For example, the FD of alfalfa is used to rate how soon it will go dormant in the season. The lower the number on the scale, the earlier in the season alfalfa will go dormant. So, food plotters in cold climate areas should not use any plant with a low FD value. The higher the number on the rating scale, the later a plant will continue to grow into the fall.

Feldspars: Are a group of rock-forming tectosilicate minerals that make up about 41 percent of the Earth's continental crust by weight. Feldspars crystallize from magma as veins in both intrusive and extrusive igneous rocks and are also present in many types of metamorphic rock.

Fencing: A planting practice used by food plot managers to surround a crop on all sides with a fence that protects the crop from being eaten by deer and other wildlife. The fence is generally high enough to prevent deer from sticking their heads over it to browse.

Ferrihydrite: Is a widespread hydrous ferric oxyhydroxide mineral (Fh) at the earth's surface, and a likely constituent in extraterrestrial materials. It forms in several types of environments, from fresh water to marine systems, aquifers to hydrothermal hot springs and scales, soils, and areas affected by mining.

Fertility: Is a term used to describe the ability of the soil to produce healthy crops or plants.

Fertilizer: Organic chemical compounds that, when absorbed by plants, help them germinate and grow faster and healthier. The three main growth nutrients of fertilizer are nitrogen, phosphorus, and potassium: NPK. Calcium can also be part of a fertilizer. These organic compounds bond to acidic elements in the soil, blending them together in different percentages in accordance with the needs of different plantings.

Fixation: The ability of clovers and other legume plants to extract nitrogen (N) from the air and attach it to the root nodules for the plant's use. Plants with excellent fixation eliminate the need for fertilizers with high nitrogen content.

Fixing: In the nitrogen cycle, it is the process of nitrogen changing into a less mobile and more usable form by combining with hydrogen to make ammonia.

Flail: A wooden bar with a wooden handle used for removing grain or seeds from stalks.

Fodder Crops: Crops that are cultivated primarily for animal feed. Natural grasslands and pastures are included whether they are cultivated or not. Fodder crops are generally categorized as either temporary or permanent crops and are cultivated and harvested like any other crop.

Food Plot: See **Wildlife Food Plots**.

Food Plotter: A term coined by the author in the early 1980s. It describes a hunter, naturalist, photographer, or wildlife viewer who plants food plots, nut or fruit trees, shrubs, or any other type of edible forage to attract deer and other wildlife and/or to enhance the health and condition of wildlife. Food plotters can also be referred to as plotheads.

Forage Brassicas: Plants that are members of the brassica family include a variety of turnips, rape, kale, swede, radish, rutabaga, canola, broccoli, Brussel sprouts, cauliflower, mustard, and cabbage. Food plot managers most often plant the first 7 listed plants for deer and other wildlife.

Forb: An herb other than grass.

Frost Seeding: This is a method used in the North, whereby the seed is applied to dry ground or a thin layer of snow when the snow is melting. The freezing and thawing process works the seed into the soil, resulting in a seed that eventually reaches the necessary planting depth required for germination. Frost seeding is an excellent way to help a stand of clover remain as thick as possible.

Geophagy: See **Eating Dirt**.

Germination: The moment when the live portion of the seed (germplasm) erupts from the outer shell and begins to grow. Proper soil temperature, planting depth, and amount of moisture activate a plant's seed to germinate.

GMO: An acronym for "genetically modified organism." GMO seeds are bred in a laboratory using modern biotechnology techniques like gene splicing.

Grafting: Grafting is a technique that combines two different plants into one new variety. Instead of cross-pollinating two plants and producing a hybrid seed, grafted plants use the roots and the bottom portion of one plant (rootstock) and attach it to a tender shoot (scion) from the top portion of another plant. Grafting is a customary practice in fruit trees.

Grains: A cereal crop including wheat, triticale, oats, barley, rye, sorghum, and corn.

Grass: A type of plant with jointed stems, slender flat leaves, and spike-like flowers such as corn and wheat.

Gravity Spreader: A device pulled behind an ATV or tractor to scatter seed, fertilizer, or lime in consistent application depending on the width of the spreader.

Grit: The inside of a corn kernel exposed after the outer covering, or hull, is removed.

Growing Media: The materials that plants grow in. Growing media is specifically designed to support plant growth and can either be a solid or a liquid. Several types of growing media are used to cultivate various plants. Growing media may also be known as grow media, culture medium, or substrate.

Habitat and Land Management: Managing the habitat and land to address the food, bedding, shelter, and water needs of whitetails and other wildlife by planting food plots and caring for natural plants.

Hand Spreader: A shoulder-bag or hand-held cloth and plastic device used to uniformly dispense seed or fertilizer by using a hand crank.

Hard Edges: A sudden change in the habitat type. For example, the edge of a crop field and the start of a mature woodlot, with no transitional area separating the two.

Harvest: To gather a ripe crop after it finishes growing (hence—hunters do not "harvest" deer).

Herb: A seed-producing annual, biannual, or perennial that does not develop persistent woody tissue but dies down at the end of a growing season.

Herbicide: Any type of chemical solution used to kill unwanted vegetative or woody growth. Some types of herbicides are "selective," meaning they target only specific plant species but do not affect, harm, or kill others. Other types of non-selective herbicides kill all growth. Some herbicides are foliar or "emergent" and act by burning the above-ground plant growth. Other herbicides are classified as "pre-emergent" and act by killing seeds or otherwise preventing them to germinate. Still other herbicides are "systemic" and act by traveling through the stem and root system to kill the plant growth.

Herbicide-Tolerant: Crops that have been genetically engineered to tolerate herbicide spray, so that the spray kills only the weeds, not the crop; primarily associated with Monsanto's Roundup Ready line of seeds. Corn and soybeans are examples of herbicide-tolerant plants.

Herbivore: An animal that eats plant life almost exclusively.

Honey Hole Food Plots: These small plots are generally placed in secluded areas where mature bucks feel comfortable entering in daylight hours. They can be "L" or "S" shaped and they can connect through a narrowing lane into much larger plots. It is best for the plot to be surrounded on three sides by substantial cover (the fourth side is the narrow gap leading to the larger plot). A mature buck is most comfortable feeding in a food plot that he can exit in haste with just a few jumps. c

Horizons: The capital letters H, O, A, L, B, C, and R represent the master horizons and layers of soils. The capital letters are the base symbols to which other characters are added to complete the designation. Most horizons and layers are given a single capital letter symbol, but some require two.

Horizon A: The A horizon is the top layer of the mineral soil horizons, often referred to as "topsoil."

Horizon B: Commonly described to as the subsoil, horizon B is a zone of accumulation deposited out of percolating waters. The A and B horizons together are called the soil solum.

Horizon C: Refers to a zone of little or no humus accumulation or soil structure development. The C horizon is composed often of unconsolidated parent material from which the A and B horizons have formed.

Horizon E: Is a mineral horizon near the surface. Typically, it is only present in forested areas. It underlies an O or A horizon and is above a B horizon. It is a light colored, leached horizon.

Horizon H (a.k.a. Layers): Horizon H layers are dominated by organic material, formed from accumulations of undecomposed or partially decomposed organic material at the soil surface, which may be underwater. All H horizons are saturated with water for prolonged periods or were once saturated but are now artificially drained.

Horizon O (a.k.a. humus or organic): Mostly organic matter such as decomposing leaves. The O horizon is thin in some soils, thick in others, and not present at all in others.

Horizon R (a.k.a. bedrock): A mass of rock such as granite, basalt, quartzite, limestone, or sandstone that forms the parent material for some soils, if the bedrock is close enough to the surface to weather. This is not soil and is located under the C horizon.

Horsepower (HP): The amount of energy it takes to lift 550 pounds one foot in one second.

Humus: The sticky, brown part of the soil that comes from dead plants and animals and contains many nutrients.

Hydraulic Hose: Hydraulic hoses are used for two primary reasons: to allow movement between two port locations or to reduce the effects of vibration. It is used anywhere in a hydraulic system on a tractor that requires a flexible connection between two fluid ports.

Hydroponic: A plant grown in water without the use of soil. For instance, rice can be grown as a hydroponic or aeroponic seed.

Hydrostatic Transmission: Allows an engine's power to be multiplied and operated to drive a tractor forward and backward. It's a revolutionary device. The hydrostatic transmission allows a tractor to convert mechanical energy into hydraulic power and then back to mechanical energy.

Idle Acres: Sections of a property, mostly planted ground, which are not currently being used to plant or for any other specific purpose.

Idle Land: A section of dormant land that is currently uncultivated or planted.

Illuvial: Illuvium is material displaced across a soil profile, from one layer to another one, by the action of rainwater. The removal of material from a soil layer is called eluviation.

Imogolite: An aluminum silicate clay mineral that occurs in soils formed from volcanic ash. This is another mineral that deer will seek out from the soil if it is lacking in their diet.

Inoculants: The most used soil inoculants are rhizobacteria that live symbiotically with clovers and other legumes like peas, beans, etc. The bacteria live within specialized nodules on the root systems of clovers and other legumes, where they process atmospheric nitrogen (N) into a form available for the plants to use. Soil inoculants are mycorrhizal fungi that attach to the roots of plant species to help conduct water and nutrients for the plant's use.

Insect Infestation: There are countless insects that can invade and kill brassicas, grains, and other plants grown in food plots. Most often, it is the soil-dwelling larval stage of insects like wireworms, black cutworms, white grubs, and army worms that cause the damage.

Insecticide: Larval stage insects, like wireworms and others, eat the roots of the plants, eventually killing them. There are a variety of pesticides that can be used to control such infestations, including Force® 6.5G, which is a high-load granular insecticide that controls corn rootworm and other soil-dwelling insect pests. Pyrethrin and other pesticides can also be used.

Junk Trees: A term used mostly by lumberjacks and foresters to describe less desirable tree species that have little to no wildlife or commercial value.

Kaolinite: A layered silicate clay mineral that forms from the chemical weathering of feldspar or other aluminum silicate minerals. Deer naturally seek it out when it is lacking in their diet to prevent toxins from being absorbed into their bloodstream. These spots are known as mineral licks because deer "lick" the soil.

Legumes: Generally, plants that grow seeds in a pod such as peas and beans. Legumes are of the genus Trifolium, which is made up of 300 or more annual and perennial species having three leaflets (a trifoliate) and flowers in dense heads. Clovers are also referred to as legumes. They are highly palatable to deer and high in protein, phosphorus, and calcium, providing valuable nourishment. Most true legumes have symbiotic nitrogen-fixing bacteria in structures called root nodules.

Leopold Landscape Alliance: Works on landscape scale conservation in the Iowa/Illinois Mississippi River region. Aldo Leopold's two childhood homes in Burlington, Iowa are also owned by the Leopold Landscape Alliance.

Lessee/Lessor: A lessor is the owner of property that is leased, or rented, to another person, party, or group, known as the lessee. Lessors and lessees enter a binding contract, known as a lease agreement, which spells out the terms of their arrangement for hunting or planting food plots.

Lime: The most usual form of agricultural lime is limestone rock ground to almost the consistency of powder. When applied to the soil, lime helps neutralize the pH, allowing more fertilizer to be used by plants in the food plot.

Lock Out: See **Nutrient Lock Out**.

Logarithmic Scale: An important consideration of pH is that soil pH is measured and conveyed in a logarithmic scale. A change in pH of one numeric unit represents a ten-fold change in the soil's acidity or alkalinity. For example, a pH of 6.0 is ten times more acidic than a pH of 7.0 and a pH of 5.0 is one hundred times more acidic than a pH of 7.0.

Long-Season Plant: Anything more than 120 days is termed as a long-season plant.

Mast: There are two types of mast: hard and soft. Hard mast includes acorns from oak trees. Soft mast describes the fruit from fruit trees. It is not widely publicized, but mast also includes seeds and fruits of all other plants such as grasses, herbs, forbs, pines, hardwoods, and fungi.

Micronutrients: The micronutrient group includes small or trace amounts of elements that are vital to healthy plant growth. They include iron (Fe), manganese (Mn), copper (Cu), zinc (Zn), boron (B), molybdenum (Mo), and chlorine (Cl). All plant growth requires these elements in various degrees in the soil to grow well.

Moraines: A moraine is a mass of rocks or sediment or any collection of debris deposited by a glacier. It is sometimes called a glacial till. It can be brought down by either a glacier or even an ice sheet. A moraine can also be a thick-headed person.

Mother: Any plant species which acts as a host by sending out above-ground or below-ground stringers, vine-like roots or appendages that foster the growth of surrounding offspring plants of the same species.

National Deer Association (NDA): Formerly Quality Deer Management Association (QDMA), the NDA is a leading whitetail organization dedicated to conserving deer, deer hunting, and the industry. www.deerassociation.com.

Natural Strategy: Is when a deer hunter, naturalist, photographer, or even an observer of wildlife maintains the existing deer herd without implementing any type of deer management, food plots, habitat enhancement, or population control. This tactic is sometimes referred to as the "do nothing strategy."

Nitrogen Fixation: Any natural process that results in free nitrogen (N2), which is available in the atmosphere, to combine chemically with other elements to form more-reactive nitrogen compounds such as ammonia, nitrates, or nitrites.

No-Till Drilling: No-till drilling is a method used to place seeds into the soil (like corn or soybeans) without going through steps like disking, plowing, and compacting the soil. No-till drills save time, work, and money. A no-till drill is regarded as one of the best ways to plant seeds with minimal soil disturbance while maximizing a plant's germination and growth. It is said that the Hancock Seed Company originated the concept of "No Till" wildlife food plot planting.

No-Till Planting (a.k.a. Zero tillage): The action of seeding on top of bare ground. When planting with the no-till technique, the top layer of soil is developed without breaking it up and turning it over. Existing decaying vegetation is left on top of the ground and the root systems hold the top layer together. It is also a process that returns nutrients to the soil.

NPK: This abbreviation stands for Nitrogen (N), Phosphorus (P), and Potassium (K)—the three nutrient elements that are combined in various proportions in fertilizers. The letters NPK are usually included on fertilizer packages.

NRCS: Natural Resource Conservation Service: A government department that provides helpful information which includes aerial and topographical maps to landowners.

Nurse Crop: A crop sown with another plant that will shelter it from competition with weeds or other undesirable plants.

Nutrients: There are at least 17 essential nutrients of plants. In relatively substantial amounts, the soil supplies nitrogen, phosphorus, potassium, calcium, magnesium, and sulfur; these are often referred to as the macronutrients. The remaining nutrients are called micronutrients. See micronutrients.

Nutrient Lock Out: Nutrient lockout is when plants are unable to intake the nutrients that are being fed to them. Nutrient lockout occurs when a chemical reaction takes place between the nutrient solution and the growing media (materials that plants grow in), whereby the nutrients in the solution are not able to enter the plant's roots.

Nutrition: To deliver adequate amounts of nutrients to white-tailed deer as a food plot crop, forages must produce ample amounts of tonnage, palatability, and digestibility.

Omnivore: An animal that eats both plant and animal life.

OMRI: The abbreviation for the Organic Materials Review Institute (OMRI), an international nonprofit organization that determines which input products are allowed for use in organic production and processing. OMRI Listed® products are allowed for use in certified organic operations under the USDA National Organic Program.

One-Point Hitch: A ball mounted on a drawbar extension at the rear of a tractor or ATV to attach the receiver of a pull-behind implement.

Open-Pollinated: A horticultural term meaning that the plant will produce seeds naturally. Open-pollination happens by wind, fowl, insects, or other natural occurrences. Open-pollinated plants are more genetically diverse.

Over-Seeding: It can refer to top-seeding to minimize soil disturbance. Over-seeding can also be used to describe the planting of seeds without regarding the seed manufacturer's suggested seeding rates. Over-seeding can also refer to a technique used to place small seeds over the top of a thinning or existing crop.

Over-Seeding Food Plots: This refers to not following the seed manufacturer's recommended seed rate for any given plant. Too much seed will drastically reduce the potential growth of a food plot. There is only so much space and nutrient content in the soil. When you plant too much seed, you overcrowd the plants.

Palatability: The texture and taste of a plant to a deer. Both soil quality and plant maturity are major elements affecting a forage's palatability. Cold temperatures can reduce a plant's palatability.

Parent Material: The underlying geological material (generally bedrock or a superficial or drift deposit) in which soil horizons form.

Perennial: The perennial plants are varieties that germinate, grow, may or may not produce seed, and go dormant at the end of the growing season. Perennials will come back and continue to grow the following growing season, unlike annual plants.

Pesticide: A chemical solution that is used to kill insects harmful to plants in either their larval or adult stages.

pH: Soil pH is a measure of the amount of hydrogen (H+) ions present in the soil that can react with other elements. pH is "power of the hydrogen" and is generally referred to as soil acidity.

Photosynthesis: The process by which green plants use light energy from the sun to produce sugar from water and the air.

Planting Zones: A geographic area of the United States where most plant life experiences similar temperatures, rainfall, and length of sunlight. There is a Northern Planting Zone, Transitional Planting Zone, and a Southern Planting Zone.

Plow: An implement used to turn over soil or sod to a depth from 4 to 12 inches or so. Plows used in food plots generally have 1 to 2 blades. Large agricultural plows are multi-bladed.

Pollinate: A process to fertilize plants by transferring pollen from the anther to the stigma of a flower.

Post Hole Digger: A hand-held tool used to dig holes in the ground for fence posts or building piers, or to dig shallow holes for trees or shrubs. It can also be a PTO-driven auger.

Pounds Per Acre (PPA): A unit of measure for seeding rates. It can also be written as lbs./acre.

Preference: Is a choice or selection deer make when they eat one plant rather than another when they are given alternate food choices.

Pre-inoculated: Pre-inoculated seed has been coated with variable mixtures of the appropriate bacteria, peat, minerals, limestone, and a coating to hold the mixture together on the seed. Many seed companies supply forage seeds that come already inoculated (pre-inoculated).

Protein: One of the most important components of deer forage; deer need at least 16 percent protein overall in their diet to help their bodies to reach their full potential.

Power-Take-Off: A power-take-off (PTO) device is most often located on the rear of a tractor. It is a rotating gear shaft driven by the engine and used to transmit power via a driveshaft to an implement such as a seed spreader, mower, or brush-hog.

PTO-Post Hole Digger (a.k.a. Auger): A Three-Point PTO-operated post hole digger is designed to fit any standard tractor PTO. The steel unit drills holes using either a 6, 9, or 12-inch auger.

QDM (Quality Deer Management): The knowledge-able practice of implementing wildlife and habitat management benchmarks and plans to promote healthier deer and better land stewardship.

QDMA: See **National Deer Association**.

Refuge: A refuge is the more appropriate word for a sanctuary. A refuge is a dedicated piece of ground created by the landowner to provide deer and other wildlife an absolute safe haven. By extension, the term has come to be used for any place of total and unlimited safety—not to be entered into or trespassed on for any reason.

Rhizobium: Living bacteria in nodules on the roots of leguminous plants capable of removing nitrogen (N) from the air and soil, "fixing" it into forms that plants utilize for growth.

Rhizome (a.k.a. a creeping rootstalk): A subterranean horizontal underground plant stem capable of producing the shoot and fleshy root systems of a new plant. Rhizomes store starches and proteins and enable plants to survive in harsh conditions. They have many growing points that can be compared to the "eyes" of potatoes.

Riparian: A zone that is referred to as a boundary between land and a waterway. Plant habitats along waterways like river margins and banks are called riparian vegetation.

Rocks: See **Weathering of Rocks**.

Root Disease in Brassicas: Root disease and other pest problems like wireworms (the larval stage of the click beetle) are generally caused by sowing crops in the same plot for two consecutive years or more.

Rotary Cutter: A three-point hitch implement commonly used to cut pastures.

Rotation: The changing of a specific planted crop in one place to another from year to year.

Row Crops: Crops that are cultivated usually by a no-till drill (like a Brillion, Kasco, or Esch, etc.), planted in orderly rows. Row crops have a greater percentage of seeds that grow into a healthy plants, providing more nutrition for deer.

Sanctuary: See **Refuge**.

Scarification: Seeds with hard coats may need to be scarified (or scratched), a process in which the seed coat is modified so that moisture can enter and allow germination to begin.

Seed Drill: A tractor- or ATV-drawn implement used to sow seed into the ground at a precise depth and spacing. The ground does not have to be disked when drilling seed.

Seedling Tree: Seedlings are qualified as trees that are less than 3 feet tall. When planting seedlings, a different planting method is used than when planting containerized trees.

Semi-Dwarf Tree: Trees that reach a mature height of about 12 to 15 feet tall and most times nearly as wide.

Share Cropping: In a food plot program, share cropping is a cooperative planting effort between a landowner and a farmer. A share-cropping arrangement can be done in several ways. For example, the most common arrangement is when a farmer plants the crop and harvests it for his own use. Or the landowner and the farmer share all costs for planting and the farmer leaves a set amount of crop standing and harvests it after the deer season. Another example is when the food plotter buys the seeds, herbicide, fertilizer, and fuel in exchange for the farmer using his equipment to plant, fertilize, herbicide, and harvest the crop/s. There are many variations that can be arranged in share cropping.

Sheet Water: Also referred to as standing water, sheet water is on the ground's surface and is permanent, such as a pond, lake, or stream.

Shooter Buck (a.k.a. Trophy-Class, Slammer, etc.): Most often a mature buck that meets the age, body size, antler mass, and other criteria that a hunter would consider a trophy-class buck. This can vary with each hunter's personal benchmark. A shooter buck is generally considered a buck of at least 3½ years old with antlers having 8 or more points.

Short-lived: The term refers to the life cycle of a plant before it needs to be reseeded or completely replanted. For example, some clovers can last 4 to 8 years, while others are short-lived varieties and will only survive for a couple years. The term does not refer to its life cycle in a single season.

Short-Season Plant: Anything less than 120 days is termed as a short-season plant.

Silage: Grass, grains, or other green fodder compacted and stored in airtight conditions, typically in a silo, without first being dried. It is then used as animal feed throughout the winter months.

Smother Crop: Crops like buckwheat, phacelia, small grains, etc. sown for the main purpose of suppressing persistent weeds.

Soft Edges: Include a combination of thick, brushy shrubs, woody plants and vines that form a row between the smaller cover in the fields and in older wooded forests.

Soil Conservation: The vigilant preservation or protection of soil.

Soil Fertility: Refers to the ability of soil to withstand agricultural plant growth to provide plant habitat and results in sustained and consistent yields of high quality.

Soil Horizon: A layer of soil material approximately parallel to the land surface which differs from adjacent genetically-related layers in color, structure, texture, or consistence. It also differs in biological and chemical characteristics.

Soil Test Probe: Generally, a tubular metal bar made of stainless steel that is probed into the ground to remove a sample of soil. It is an ideal tool to remove a prescribed amount of dirt. Soil probes are mostly used for taking pH tests of soil or for more detailed analysis of a tested soil sample to determine the soil's nutrient content, composition, and other characteristics.

Soil Texture: Refers to the coarseness, fineness, or other textures of a soil. It is determined by the relative proportion of various sized particles (sand, silt, and clay) in a soil.

Soil Type: A finer subdivision of a soil series. It includes all soils of a series which are similar in all characteristics, including texture of the surface layer. The 6 soil types include sand, sandy loam, loam, silt loam, clay loam, and clay.

Specialty Crop: Usually denotes the planting of something other than a traditional food plot plant. Generally, it refers to planting a variety of different types of fruit or nut trees, shrubs, hedges, or bushes. It can also refer to planting vegetables like sugar beets, rutabaga, cabbage, etc. The term is also often used as a catch-all term for any planting that is not considered a commodity crop.

Spodic: Soils that refer to a diagnostic subsurface horizon defined by the illuvial accumulation of organic matter. Iron oxide can be present or absent, and the soil is generally derived from a sandy parent material.

Sprayer: A steel or plastic tank used to apply liquid fertilizer, herbicides, or water. Most often, food plotters use it for spraying herbicide or pesticide to eliminate unwanted weeds and other growth. The 25- to 50-gallon tanks with widespread boom arms can be mounted at the rear of an ATV or tractor. Smaller tanks (a.k.a. backpack sprayers) can be used to dispense chemical solutions via a hand-held metal wand with a single spray nozzle.

Springs: A water spring is the result of an aquifer being filled to a level where water overflows onto the surface or just slightly below the surface of the land. Springs (a.k.a. seeps) vary in size from intermittent seeps, which flow only after a heavy rain, to huge pools flowing millions of gallons daily. Springs can be found above or below the Earth's surface.

Standard-Size Tree: A standard-size tree usually grows to be 15 to 30 feet tall or taller.

Stewardship: A landowner's or lessee's responsibility to exercise care and attention of the property owned, leased, or entrusted.

Stolon: A creeping horizontal plant stem or runner that takes root at points along its length to form new plants.

Stop Plots: Generally, small food plots up to a ¼-acre in size that are planted in strategic areas within view of tree stands or hunting blinds. The plot is designed to have deer pause for a short period to browse the planting before moving on to eat in larger food plots. It gives hunters enough time to draw the bowstring or put the deer in the crosshairs of a scope.

Strip Cropping: Growing crops in long narrow strips with food plots. This is often done with grain, rye, or other small grains. It is also done in some dry areas to conserve moisture and reduce the hazards of wind erosion.

Subsoiling: Refers to the breaking up of compact subsoils without inverting them deeply. Subsoiling can be done with a box tiller set at a shallow depth or a special narrow cultivator shovel and/or blade, which is pulled through the soil at a specific depth and at spacings from 2 to 5 feet.

Subterranean Clover (a.k.a. Sub-Clover): A suitable clover to plant in shaded areas, including thinned stands of pines. It also makes an excellent weed suppressor.

Superweed: A weed that has developed strong resistance to herbicides. It has been documented that the increased use of herbicides, following the introduction of herbicide-tolerant GMO crops, has led to a proliferation of superweeds.

Surfactant: In herbicides, a surfactant is a wetting agent with 80 percent non-ionic surfactant for increasing the penetration, coverage, and overall effectiveness of almost any herbicide. Surfactants for herbicides can be used with almost all herbicide sprays, including Trimec, Atrazine, Brush Killer, and 2, 4-D Amine. Surfactants reduce the surface tension so that the herbicide gets more coverage on the weed.

SWCD: Soil and Water Conservation District. A government department that advises landowners on soil and water conservation and can also provide topographic maps and aerial photos of tracts of land in each county.

Sweet Soil: See **Alkaline**.

Take It to the Deer-Hunting Bank: A catchphrase coined by the author Peter Fiduccia, a.k.a. the Deer Doctor, to illustrate a particular piece of deer hunting advice he believes is exceptional; therefore, it should be deposited in a deer hunter's strategy "bank vault" for future reference and tactic success.

TDN: The sum of all nutrients in a food that are digested by the animal. As plants mature, continuous polymerization (CP) usually decreases. Total digestible nutrients (TDN) are an indicator of the concentration of available energy and/or provides an estimate of digestible forage, expressed as caloric value. TDN is not measured directly but is calculated from acid detergent fiber (ADF).

Tectosilicate: A polymeric silicate in which the silicon-oxygen tetrahedral groups are linked by sharing their oxygen atoms with other such groups to form a 3-D structure or network.

Three-Point Hitch: Generally found at the back of a tractor. It is attached to a pull-behind planting or other implement via two sidearms, one to either side, and one upper point which provides a rigid connection to stabilize a heavier implement and prevent side-to-side swaying.

Three-Point Spreader: A cone-shaped metal or plastic implement mounted on a tractor to uniformly spread seed, fertilizer, or lime on the ground via a spinning disk operated by a PTO. Plastic spreaders save time and money as metal spreaders rust more quickly from fertilizers.

Tilth: The physical condition of soil as related to its simplicity of tillage, its condition as a seedbed, and its support of seedling germination and sufficient root penetration. It also acts as an valuable gauge of soil quality.

Topsoil: The layer of soil used for cultivation, which usually contains more organic matter than underlying soil materials.

TSI: An acronym used to denote timber stand improvement.

Turnip Bulbs: A turnip root, or bulb, commonly called a root vegetable.

Viticulture: The practice of vine growing; for example, grapes. Some food plotters grow grapes for deer to forage on.

VNS: In the world of seeds, VNS means Variety Not Stated. The manufacturer of the seed hasn't gone through the assessment and expense of classifying it as a certain variety of seed.

Water Table: The upper limit of the part of the soil or underlying rock material that is wholly saturated with water.

Weathering of Rocks: Over extended periods of time, weathering breaks down and dissolves rocks. Once a rock has been broken down, erosion transports the bits of rock and its minerals into the soil. Water, ice, acids, salts, plants, animals, and changes in temperature are all agents of weathering.

Weed: Any unwanted or obnoxious plant, especially those that crowd out or compete for nutrients of more desirable plants used in wildlife food plots.

Well-prepared Seed Bed: A well-prepared seed bed has had all the unwanted vegetation eliminated with a herbicide. It should also have had a soil test and, if necessary, has been amended accordingly with lime and fertilizer. All softball-sized rocks and larger, large twigs and branches, and other dead vegetation debris is removed. The plot should also undergo careful disking to eliminate clods or clumps of soil and have a fine texture prior to planting. It also requires the plot being lightly compacted before seeding.

Wetland: Any ground that remains totally or partially covered with water for much of the year and attracts wildlife, particularly waterfowl, turtles, amphibians, and the like.

Wild Game Food (WGF): WGF is an abbreviation for Wild Game Food. It is often used to describe milo or sorghum. WGF milo/sorghum is shorter in height than traditional sorghum. It also is early maturing and is a heavy grain producer. WGF sorghum is bitter tasting to predatory birds during its early stages, yet tastier to wild gamebirds during the fall and winter months.

Wildlife Food Plot: Is mostly comprised of clovers, other legumes, grains, grasses, brassicas, and other plantings including fruit and nut trees. The choice of plantings is meant to provide food primarily for all deer species, but also for a variety of wildlife including turkeys and other upland birds, waterfowl, and small game.

Windbreak: Generally, a windbreak is a straight planting of evergreen, other similar type trees, or tall grasses like Miscanthus, sown tightly next to one another to allow their branches to interlock to block prevailing winds, usually from the North, West, or Northwest. Windbreaks can be used to protect food plot plantings of young fruit or nut trees from a strong gusting wind, driving rain, sleet, ice, or blowing snow.

Wireworms: Roughly 1/16-inch in size, the newly hatched larvae will grow to reach sizes of ¾-inch in length before pupation. This process can take 2 to 3 years. While they are not particularly damaging to plants in their first year, the older larvae can devour the roots of plants, causing wilting and plant death.

WSI: This abbreviation stands for Winter Survival Index. The rating scale is measured from 1 to 6, with 1 being superior winter survival.

Yield: Is best measured in tonnage per acre of digestible forage produced.

Zero-Till Drills (a.k.a. No-Till Drills), Zero-Till Seeding (a.k.a. No-Till Seeding): A method of planting forage crops directly into the soil of a field.

Zero-Till Farming Practices: Zero-till farming is an eco-friendly and efficient way to plant seeds. No-till farming restores and builds organic matter, which is an essential component of soil fertility.

Additional Sources: nesoil.com, NRCS, USDA, Cambridge Dictionary, Wikipedia, The Merriam-Webster Dictionary, National Deer Association, Google Dictionary, Dictionary.com, Oxford Dictionaries, American Bird Conservancy, The Wildlife Society, University of Georgia, National Geographic Society's Crittercam Program, Britannica.com, Clemson.edu, noble.org, bookbuilder. cast.org, Cornell University, Wageningen University and Research Center, maximumyield.com, advancednutrients.com, farmersweekly.co.za, forestry.usu.edu, time.com, extension.psu.edu, omri. org, gardeningknowhow.com, uoregon.edu.

▲ Credit: Dustine Meads Dreamstime

Appendix B

Food Plot Seed Company Sources

The companies listed in this section supply a wide variety of retail seeds and other food plot products and services. I have also included a few wholesale companies that strictly sell seeds to retail seed companies. These types of companies license some special and engineer (create) seed varieties primarily for the agricultural market. Many of the varieties they develop are also sold to retail seed companies for wildlife food plot marketplaces. The odds are good that no matter what type of blended or pure seeds, or other types of plants, products, and services you may be interested in, the retail companies listed here most likely offer them. The many company listings (here and within the body of this book) are solely included for informational purposes. In most places they are listed alphabetically, hence no partiality. When they are not, there is still no favoritism implied.

Agassiz Seed & Supply Co.—701-282-8118; West Fargo, ND, and Eagan, MN. Wildlife seed mixtures, brassicas, upland game mix, chicory plus wildlife mix, clovers and other legumes, native grasses, wildflowers, nurse crops, and annual forages. www.agassizseed.com

Antler King—715-284-9547/888-268-5371; Upper Sandusky, OH. An extensive line of food plot seeds, minerals, soil conditioner products, soil test kits, and attractants. Website has valuable information including a video on planting wildlife food plots. www.antlerking.com

Arrow Seed Co.—800-622-4727; Broken Bow, NE. Arrow Seed has a wide assortment of mixed wildlife blends, as well as alfalfa, grasses, grains, and other forages. Their mixed blends are specifically designed for deer and upland game. Arrow Seed offers a proprietary unique blend called The Shade Mix Food Plot. It excels in areas that are mostly shaded. Their website is easy to navigate and offers a direct contact to their food plot division. www.arrowseed.com

Backwoods Attraction—662-746-5155; Yazoo City, MS. Wide variety of custom-blended brassicas, clovers, other legumes, timber blends, food plot seeds, sugar beets, attractants, and minerals. www.backwoodsattraction.com

Bass Pro Shops®—800-BASSPRO; nationwide. Offers a complete line of branded wildlife seeds, minerals, attractants, feed, game feeders, and more food-plot-related items. www.basspro.com

Best Forage, LLC—888-836-3697; Hudson, IN. Full line of forage seeds, clovers, other legumes, brassicas, chicory, grasses, vetches, and more. www.bestforage.com

Big Tine®—800-989-4178; Rockville, IN. Offers a line of several food-plot mixed seeds including Buck Brunch and Last Stand. Also sells attractants and provides soil tests. www.bigtine.com

BioLogic—West Point, MS. Has a complete line of deer and other wildlife food plot seeds including a wide variety of clovers, other legumes, brassicas, large grains, chicory, sugar beets, chufa, and substantial selection of mixed seed offerings for deer, turkeys, upland birds, and waterfowl, plus food-plot wildlife seeds. Also offers soil tests, fertilizer, and food plot management services. www.plantbiologic.com and www.mossyoakbiologic.com

Blue Hill Wildlife Nursery—570-259-2171; Sellinsgrove, PA. This nursery offers a terrific line up of late dropping fruit trees, and a wide selection of nut trees. BHWN also offers Main Attraction clover, a custom blend of Mammoth and Bearcat red clovers and Endure chicory. www.bluehillnursery.com

Boss Buck—877-269-8490; Irving, TX. This nursery offers Boss Buffet Full Season Forage and Boss Blend No-Till Seed. www.bossbuck.com

Buck Forage Products—800-299-6287 or 501-367-8035; Roland, AR. Offers Buck Forage oats (cold-hardy), Buck Forage peas, Buck Forage chicory, Buck Forage clover, electric fencing. www.buckforage.com

C.M. Payne & Son Seed Co.—863-385-4642 or 863-385-3080; Sebring, FL. Sells a variety of branded wildlife forage seeds. www.farmranch.org

Cabela's®—800-237-4444; nationwide. Sells a full line of branded wildlife seeds, minerals, attractants, feeds, game feeders, and more food-plot-related items. www.cabelas.com

Cisco Farm Seed—800-888-2986; Indianapolis, IN. Offers a good selection of forage plantings including cereal grains, brassicas, clovers and other legumes, grasses, and forage mixes. Also has some hard-to-find plants like phacelia, sun hemp, etc. www.ciscoforage.com

Cooper Seed Co.—877-463-6697; 770-963-6183; Lawrenceville, GA. Offers a diverse line of wildlife seeds including clovers, other legumes, brassicas, grains, wildflowers, and a variety of seeds for ducks, doves, upland birds, wild boars, and bears. Also offers fertilizers, inoculants, wildlife feed, deer repellent, wildlife feeders, and accessories. www.airag.com or www.cooperseeds.com

Deer Creek Seed Co.—877-247-3736; Windsor, WI. Has an enormous selection of a wildlife seeds, wildlife mixtures and straight seed products. Sold by the bag or by the pound. Offers inoculants and soil test kits. Has an informative and helpful website that provides tips, articles, and other useful information. www.deercreekseed.com

Drop-Tine Seed Co.—570-204-4064; Bloomsburg, PA. Is a consumer direct brand. Offers individual species and varieties, a complete line of regenerative and soil health seed blends, clovers, soybeans, brassicas, chicory, perennials, annuals, corn grans, and pollinators. Has screening and cover, food plot fencing, nitro liquid kelp minerals, and specialty crop roller crimp-terminate blends. www.droptineseed.com

East Texas Seed Co.—800-888-1371 or 903-597-6637; Tyler, TX. Offers a robust line of wildlife seeds. Provides lots of seed and other information on their website. www.easttexasseedcompany.com

Elk Mound Seed—800-401-7333 / 715-879-5556; Elk Mound, WI. Has Monsterbuck Wildlife Blended Seed products along with a variety of food plot straight seeds, forage blends, inoculants herbicides, fertilizer, wildflowers, and soil test kits. www.elkmoundseed.com

Ernst Seeds—800-873-3321 or 814-3362404; Meadville, PA. Offers wildlife habitat and seed mixes, individual species, many grasses, millets, clovers, other legumes, woody trees, shrubs, and vines. www.ernstseed.com

Evolved Harvest®—800-847-8269; New Roads, LA. Carries a numerous variety of wildlife forage seeds including clovers, brassicas, legumes, and grains. Also offers minerals and feeds. www.evolved.com

Frigid Forage—218-444-5255; Bemidji, MN. Has annual and perennial mixed blends, pure trophy clover, and a proprietary, visual barrier seed called Plot Screen. Also offers accessories. www.frigidforage.com

GO Seed—503-566-9900; Salem, OR. GO Seed, Inc. is a breeder, producer, and provider of an immense range of seed products as well as information. GO Seed evaluates more than 4,000 unique lines of multiple species annually. GO Seed is the developer of my three absolute favorite extreme winter-hardy clovers: AberLasting White X Kura, FIXatioN Balansa, and Frosty Berseem. That is just a drop in the bucket compared to what GO Seed offers in the way of forage seeds for deer and other wildlife. It is truly a leader in seed development and offerings. No matter what type of brassicas, grasses, clovers, or legumes or other forage plants you are looking for in your area, GO Seed probably offers it to seed sellers across the country. Find a dealer who offers GO Seed forage plants for deer, elk, gamebirds, and waterfowl at www.goseed.com. Their website provides a tab, "Find a Dealer."

Grassland Oregon—503-566-9900; Salem, OR. Offers forage seeds and cover crops. www.grasslandoregon.com

Great Basin Seeds—435-283-1411; Ephraim, UT. Carries a distinctive line of mixes, blends, cover crops, and wildlife forage seeds, including seeds for sage grouse habitat. www.greatbasinseeds.com

Hancock Seed Company—800-552-1027; Dade City, FL. Retails an huge selection of wildlife seeds. Hancock also offers a complete line of its own line of mixed seeds and its website is very thorough and helpful. It is easy to find information on the wide variety of different types of seeds they sell. www.hancockseed.com

Hearne Seed Co.—831-385-5441; King City, CA. Has various selections of seeds for deer and other wildlife including alfalfa, barley, beans, chicory, grasses and native grasses, buckwheat, clovers, trefoil, sweet corn, cover crops seed, cowpeas, and more. www.hearne-seed.com

Huntingplots.com—386-963-2080 or 717-989-6239; Parkesburg, PA. Offers Ridgeline seed blends and Real-World wildlife seed, Eagle seeds, Nature's Trophy blend, and fertilizer. Planting equipment sales and rentals, soil testing and analysis. Provides consulting services. www.huntingplots.com.

Kester's Wild Game Food Nurseries, Inc.—800-558-8815; Omro, WI. Excellent source for waterfowl seeds. Spring & Fall seeds for deer and other wildlife. Wild rice seed, wetland plants, upland plantings, annual & perennial seeds, native grasses, and consulting services. www.kestersnursery.com

Killer Food Plots—616-550-8483; Muskegon, MI. Offers a line of wildlife food plot seeds. Also sells soil treatments and more. www.killerfoodplots.com

La Crosse Seed—800-356-7333; La Crosse, WI. This company has a comprehensive selection of premium seeds of cover crops, clovers, other legumes, brassicas, grains, sugar beets, sunflowers, grasses, and a wide-ranging selection of mixed seeds for wildlife. Their website is a one-stop shop for educational information, technical guides, and useful tips. www.lacrosseseed.com.

Main Street Seed & Supply—866-229-3276; Bay City, MI. Offers many different varieties of wildlife food-plot seeds including clovers, other legumes, grains, brassicas, buckwheat, chicory, etc. Also sells a variety of wildlife food plot seed mixes. www.mainstreetseed-andsupply.com

Maple River Farms—989-743-4344; Owosso, MI. Unique offering for buying Miscanthus X Giganteus Rhizomes; a cold-hardy grass that grows to 11½ feet. Makes the perfect barricade screening. www.mapleriverfarms.com

Merit Seeds—330-893-3196; Berlin, OH. Offers a substantial line of seeds for deer and other wildlife. Their line includes wildlife clover other legumes, sorghum, millet, wildlife soybeans, native grasses, waterfowl food plot seeds, and ag seeds, seeders, and sprayers. Merit's website is a terrific source of information. www.meritseed.com

Missouri Southern Seed—573-364-1336; Rolla, MO. Offers a variety of wildlife seed including blended wildlife seed mixes. www.missourisouthernseed.com

Mossy Oak Nativ Nurseries—662-494-4326: West Point, MS. Nativ Nurseries carries a line of a wide variety of oaks and hybrid oaks, crab apples, berries, persimmon, pawpaw, plum, chestnuts, and other varieties. The website provides a lot of information on tree varieties and planting tips. www.nativnurseries.com

Outside Pride Seeds—800-670-4192; Salem, OR. Carries a line of wildlife forage seeds including clovers, other legumes, brassicas, Sweet Spot™, wildflowers, and supplies. www.outsidepride.com

Pawnee Buttes Seed—970-356-7002; Greeley, CO. Sells more than 500 species of seeds. Wetland species, forbs, shrubs, grasses, etc. Has native blended mixes as well. www.pawneebuttesseed.com

Pennington Seeds—800-285-7333; Easton, PA. A diverse line of wildlife seeds including blended mixes or single seeds for deer and other wildlife. They offer RACKMASTER® for deer and WINGMASTER® Game Bird Mix to attract multiple gamebird species. www.penningtonseed.com

Pheasants Forever and Quail Forever Habitat—877-773-2070 or 651-773-2000; St. Paul, MN. Offers designer mixes from their biologists for quality habitat for upland birds, deer, and other wildlife. All proceeds go directly to support their mission. www.pheasantsforever.org

PlotSpike®—800-264-5281; Ponchatoula, LA. Sells a variety of forage seed mixes and straight seeds for deer and wild turkeys including wheat, oats, ryegrass, peas, clovers, brassicas, and more. PlotSpike is a division of Ragan and Massey. www.raganandmassey.com

Preferred Seed—716-895-7333; Buffalo, NY. Has food plot wildlife seeds, wildlife blends, and single seeds like brassicas, clovers, alfalfa, and timothy. Also offers specialty custom blends. Broad variety of seeds, inoculants, excellent resource in their free Power Point Deer Plot presentation that includes basic information on planting food plots and deer nutrition. Their website includes how to read a seed identity tag. www.preferredseed.com

Purina®—877-773-2070; Gray Summit, MO. Purina Animal Nutrition, Purina AntlerMax Premium Deer Mineral. Deer Block. www.purinamills.com

Ragan and Massey—www.raganandmassey.com See PlotSpike®.

Real World Wildlife Products—217-994-3721; Arthur, IL. Has a full line of food plot seeds, cover and bedding seeds, Maximizer Plus supplement, concentrate, additive, and minerals. Also offers Giant Miscanthus rhizomes. www.realworldwildlifeproducts.com

River Refuge Seed—541-466-5309; Brownsville, OR. Specializes in plantings designed specifically to attract ducks and geese. River Refuge is a family-run business that is heavily involved in waterfowl and wetland conservation. Hence, they have nearly 70 varieties of native wetland seed and several introduced varieties to attract waterfowl. Plantings include wild rice, wild and white proso millet, shortawn foxtail, hard pea, buckwheat, and golden millet. They also have 17 different designer waterfowl seed mixes. Upland seed offerings include wet prairie sunflower, small burnet, short corn, poco barley, and 5 different custom upland seed mixes. They also offer seed for deer food plots. Provides complimentary consulting services via phone or email. www.riverrefugeseed.com

Roundstone Native Seed—270-531-3034; Upton, KY. Offers 300 individual species, 125 standard seed mixes, native grasses, and wildflowers, and custom mixes. www.roundstoneseed.com

Ruffed Grouse Society—570-420-9042; Marshalls Creek, PA. Offers a line of branded RGS seed. Trail and Food Plot Mix. All proceeds go to support the RGS mission. www.ruffedgrousesociety.org

Rural King®—800-561-1752; 125 stores in several states. Offers a line of Federal Hybrids seed corn, soybeans, herbicides, farm equipment, etc. www.ruralking.com

Seed Barn—813-540-2000; Tampa, FL. Carries a line of other companies' branded seeds. www.seedbarn.com

Seed Ranch/Seed World U.S.A.—850-733-7777; Odessa, FL. Both Seed Ranch and Seed World USA offer complete lines of wildlife seeds, blends, from alfalfa to sunflower. Herbicides, fertilizers, inoculants, sprayers, surfactants, spreaders. Also offers branded food-plot seeds. www.seedranch.com or www.seedworldusa.com

Seedland, Inc.—386-963-2080; Wellborn, FL. Extensive line of forage seeds for deer, turkeys, waterfowl, and upland birds. Food plot seed blends and individual seeds. Seed spreaders, minerals, and game feeders. www.seedland.com

SEEDWAY®—800-836-3710; Hall, NY. Offers SEEDWAY® Wildlife Genetics™ Brand seed products. Also sells a full line of forage wildlife seed in blends or single seeds. www.seedway.com

Seedworld USA—813-540-7777; Odessa, FL. Offers a variety of clovers, other legumes, vetches, brassicas, grains, millets, grasses, and other seeds. Also offers herbicides, fertilizers, and inoculants. www.seedworld usa.com

Sinclairville Seed Co., LLC—716-499-8720; Sinclairville, NY. Sinclairville Seed specializes in a variety of seeds to plant for deer and other wildlife. It offers a variety of unique blends including Wallhanger, Clover Candy, Buck Magnet, Full Draw, and more. Custom blending is also available. Sinclairville Seed carries clovers, brassicas, large and small grains, Peredovic sunflowers, and chicory. Other than offering its own line of seed, Sinclairville Seed Company retails Real World Wildlife Seeds and Eagle Seeds. Also offers other products. www.sinclairvilleseed.com.

Smith Seed Services—541-369-2831; Halsey, OR. Produces *wholesale* bulk seed for retail seed companies worldwide. Smith Seed Services is a supplier of a wide variety of turfgrass, forage, cover crop, and wildlife seeds. www.smithseed.com

Southern Seed & Feed—662-726-2638; Macon, MS. Offers a branded complete line of seeds for deer and other wildlife food plots. They also sell deer and wild turkey feed, mineral attractants, and liquid fertilizers. www.southernseedfeed.com.

Sportsman's Guide®—Nationwide. Offers a thorough line of branded wildlife seeds, minerals, attractants, feed, game feeders, and a lot more. www.sportsman-sguide.com

Tecomate—717-628-3617; Lancaster, PA. This company offers a vast selection of single and mixed seeds for deer, turkeys and other wildlife. Tecomate also offers a wide variety of seed mixes in their bulk line of seeds called Managers Line. Additionally, Tecomate carries a complete line of mixed seed for upland birds, an attracting scent, a mineral/vitamin supplement, soil test kits, and branded items. www.tecomate.com.

Tractor Supply®—Nationwide. Offers a line of different branded forage seeds, deer feed, protein blocks, minerals, feeders, herbicides, ATV and tractor implements, and tractor parts. www.tractorsupply.com

Wannamaker Seeds, Inc.—803-707-1112; Saluda, NC. Offers wildflowers, buckwheat, sunn hemp, sesame, millet, sorghum, cowpeas, black Peredovik sunflowers and spring ultimate cover crop mix (deer food plot mix). www.wannamakerseeds.com

Welter Seed & Honey Co.—800-470-3325; Onslo, IA. Extensive selection of wildlife and ag seeds sold by the bag and by the pound. Sells clovers, other legumes, brassicas, grains, grasses, trefoils, millets, vetches, chicory, sugar beets, and much more. Helpful staff are always eager and quick to reply to questions sent to info@welterseed.com. Their complete catalog of seed products is listed on their website. www.welterseed.com.

Whitetail Institute of North America—800-688-3030; Pintlala, AL. Offers a major line of perennial and annual spring and fall plantings including clovers, other legumes, brassicas, sunn hemp, chufa, beets, oats, and other seeds. Sells a complete line of mixed seeded products. Also offers herbicides, attractants, minerals, feed and supplements, soil amendments, soil test kits, hand seeders, soil probe, and sampler packs. The website and magazine provide excellent information including planting dates and more. www .whitetailinstitute.com

Wildlife Perfect Seed—541-928-1651; Tangent, OR. Offers 4 primary deer and other wildlife seed mixes, including Big Buck Perennial, Big Buck Annual, Big Buck Brassica, and Sweet Spot™. Also has single seeds for sugar beets, sainfoin, oats, Peredovic sunflowers, and Small Burnett. www.wildlifeperfect.com

Wildlife Seed Supply—989-763-1051; Sumner, MI. Variety of brassicas, seed mixes, and straight seeds including many clovers, legumes, grains, buckwheat, millet, and grasses. www.wildlifeseedsupply.com

▲ Whether you are an experienced or novice food plotter, the go-to seed that has stood the test of time is clover. Credit: WINA.

Appendix C

Fruit, Chestnut, Nutlet, and Acorn Tree Sources

Most of the fruit and nut tree nurseries that ship trees and shrubs sell them as "dormant bare root" stock. Some, however, also ship containerized trees, but there is a difference in cost. According to Cornell University's Creating the Urban Forest: The Bare Root Method, a bare root tree "has about 200 percent more roots than the same tree sold in a pot or balled-and-burlapped." Both the pot and balled-and-burlapped trees are usually tightly packed in soil around the roots, which can limit their growth.

Furthermore, nurseries raise more selections of bare-root trees than potted mostly because they take up less room and are more effective to mail-order to customers. By purchasing bare-root stock, you will have a greater selection from which to choose for fruit, nut, and other trees that provide food for deer and other wildlife.

Bare-root stock costs are considerably less than container-grown tree stock of the same size. Moreover, they are extremely easy to plant compared to planting a containerized tree. Here's the key for food plotters, however. Bare-root trees most often will grow more quickly because their roots are not making the adjustment from the soil in the pot to the new soil. Because bare-root trees are generally planted in dormancy, it allows them several more weeks of root growth than potted trees.

The downside of bare root trees is that they must be planted during dormancy, meaning before buds emerge. Therefore, your planting window will vary depending on when you can obtain bare-root trees. They need to be planted as soon as possible after they arrive. Another issue with bare-root stock is that nurseries only sell them for a short window of time.

Bare-root trees also take about a year longer to start bearing fruit than containerized fruit and nut trees. Finally, remember that when you're ordering bare-root trees, the nursery selects the trees you will receive. So, even though bare-root trees are the most economical way to purchase fruit and nut trees, not every tree will be perfect. If you buy bare-root or potted trees from local nurseries, Tractor Supply, Lowes, Home Depot, Walmart, etc., here are some helpful tips to consider when selecting your trees.

- Make sure the trunks are straight and do not include dramatic curves or bends.
- If there are branches (some trees come without branches), they should be evenly spaced along throughout the trunk, spreading in all directions.
- The trunk should be free of any wounds.
- The more roots the tree has, the better. They should have a full spread in all directions. The roots should be firm and moist, not soft.
- If the roots are packaged, the packing should be moist and heavy, not dry, or feel light to the touch.

Some Tree Company Sources.

Adams County Nursery—717-677-8105; Aspers, PA. Services mostly commercial customers selling about one million trees a year. They also "reserve" a percentage of their inventory to fill smaller non-commercial orders. They sell 2-year-old bare-root fruit trees including but not limited to apple, pear, nectarine, apricot, peach, plum, hybrids, etc. www.acnursery.com

Arbor Day Foundation—888-448-7337; Lincoln, NE. The Foundation offers a significant variety of various size dormant bare-root fruit and nut trees. Also sells shrubs and evergreens. www.arborday.org

Big Horse Creek Farm—336-384-1134; Lansing, NC. Specializes in apples, heirloom apple varieties of Appalachian Mountains, as well as other apple varieties. www.bighorsecreekfarm.com

Blue Hill Wildlife Nursery—570-259-2171; Selinsgrove, PA. Focuses on offering an extensive selection of dormant bare-root *late-dropping* apple, pear, persimmon, crabapple, and applecrab trees that drop fruit from November into January. They also have early-dropping fruit trees. The website has valuable information and is easy to navigate. www.bluehill-wildlifenursery.com

Chestnut Hill Outdoors—855-386-7826; Alachua, FL. Although Chestnut Hill Outdoors offers a selection of fruit trees, many of which are late-dropping varieties. They sell both dormant bare-root and potted trees. They have many varieties of apple, pear, persimmon, and mulberry trees. Their website is extremely informative, helpful, and quite easy to navigate. They ship nationwide from Alachua, FL. www.chestnuthillout-doors.com

Chief River Nursery Co—800-367-9254; Grafton, WI. Sells bare-root tree stock. They have apple trees including Fuji, Gala, Granny Smith, Honeycrisp, Jonathan, McIntosh, red and yellow Delicious. All their varieties will pollinate one another. www.chiefrivernursery.com

Cummins Nursery—607-269-7664; Ithaca, NY. Cummins Nursery has dozens of bare-root cold-hardy fruit trees including apple, pear, peach, cherry, plum, and apricot fruit trees. They also have a variety of wildlife fruit tree plantings that are disease-resistant for less maintenance, and which hold their fruit into late October and longer. They ship nationwide. Visit them at www.cumminsnursery.com

Edible Landscaping—800-524-4156; Afton, VA. Offers apple, pear, Jujubes, persimmon, plum, peach, cherry, and apricot fruit trees. www.ediblelandscaping.com

Elgin Nursery—623-936-1100; Phoenix, AZ. Carries a line of fruit trees for western areas, including arid zones. Varieties include apricot, apple, jujube, nectarine, peach, pear, pomegranate, avocado, mango, papaya, and tropical passion fruit. www.elginnursery.com

Grimo Nut Tree—905-934-6887; Ontario, Canada. Grimo is an "Ultra Northern Nut Nursery" that also sells a wide variety of fruit trees. Grimo Nut Nursery sells nut trees that include heartnut, butternut, walnut, hazelnut, chestnut, pecan, pine nut and hickory. The company also sells Pawpaw, mulberry, quince and persimmon trees. www.grimonut.com.

Hallman Farms—803-345-0061; Little Mountain, SC. Hallman Farms has a line of late-dropping fruit trees. Their line includes mulberry, pawpaw, plum, persimmon, pear, apple, and crabapple trees and several other varieties of late-dropping fruit trees. www.hall-manfarms.com

Mossy Oak Nativ Nurseries—662-494-4326; West Point, MS. Mossy Oak Nativ Nurseries is an excellent source of oak trees, offering 23 different varieties from burr oak to willow oak and everything in between. They also offer a line of fruit trees including wild deer pear, American persimmon, Chickasaw plum, Mexican Plum, pawpaw, Blackgum, mulberry black cherry, and more. Additionally, they have a line of hybrid oaks. You will also find tree protection and supplies products on their website. Mossy Oak Nativ Nurseries website is easy to navigate and provides a lot of solid information. Visit it at www.nativnurseries.com

Northern Ridge Nursery—715-324-6114; Pembine, WI. Sells American persimmon, American persimmon jumbo, chokecherry, downy serviceberry, and hardy apricot. They also offer several shrub-like trees. www.northernridgenursery.com

One Green World—877-353-4028; Portland, OR. Offers an extensive line of fruit trees, with some unique varieties. For instance: Angelo rosso azarole is hardy to 15°F. Other varieties include che, myrtle berry, Chinese haw, jujube, loquat, wineberry, mayhaw, medlar, quince (fruiting), strawberry (tree) pawpaw, peach, pear, apple, and nectarine. www.onegreen-world.com

Southmeadow Fruit Gardens—616-422-2411; Baroda, MI. Sells apple, pear, quince, apricots, nectarines, plums, cherries, currants, and crabapple trees. www.southmeadowfruitgardens.com.

Stark Bro's Nursery—800-325-4180; Louisiana, MO. Offers pear, peach, plum, apple, and cherry fruit trees. www.starkbros.com

Winter Cove Farm—207-478-8759 or 207-852-9088; Winterport, ME. Has cold-hardy bare-root fruit trees, including apple, cherry, Euro pear, Asian pear, and plum. www.wintercovefarm.com

CHESTNUT TREE SOURCES

Chestnut trees can produce copious quantities of delicious and nutritious nuts that deer and other wildlife, including humans, love to eat. Chestnuts bloom in early summer and ripen in mid fall. They form very prickly husks that are hard and wildlife-proof until they fall ripe from the trees. Dunstan (hybrid), American, Chinese, European, and a dozen other chestnut varieties are highly sought out by deer and a wide variety of other animals. Chestnuts need a sunny location with good soil drainage. Grafted trees initially tend to have a stronger root system than layered trees. Layered trees can re-sprout true to name should anything happen to the top. Grafted and layered trees bear much sooner than seedlings. Generally, chestnut trees will bear fruit within 2 to 5 years depending on varieties, good soil conditions, weather, water, and the correct planting methods. Always order two or more to achieve good cross-pollination.

Below is a list of nurseries that offer chestnut trees.

Blue Hill Wildlife Nursery—570-259-2171; Selinsgrove, PA. Sells a variety called Woodland Chestnut tree. www.bluehillwildlifenursery.com

Burnt Ridge Nursery & Orchards—360-985-2873; Onalaska, WA. This nursery has a variety of common to unique chestnut trees: Bergantz, Bisaltano No.3, Bracalla, Chinese, Colossal, Layeroka, Maraval, Marigoule, Marrisard, Marron Comballe, Marron di Chuisa Pesio, and Marron di Val Susa chestnut trees. www.burntridgenursery.com

Chestnut Hill Outdoors—855-386-7826; Alachua, FL. Dunstan chestnut trees. A result of cross-breeding American and Chinese varieties, the Dunstan produces the large, sweet nut of the American chestnut, and holds the blight-resistant qualities of the Chinese chestnut. Nutrient-dense chestnuts serve as the primary mast source for a wide range of wildlife—bears, turkeys, squirrels, hogs, and especially white-tailed deer. Chestnut Hill's Dunstan Chestnut trees are sold in select Walmart and Rural King stores across the country (at this writing). You can find out the various locations by checking their website. Bare-root trees are available in the spring and container trees are shipped in the fall through their mail order site. www.chestnuthilloutdoors.com.

Chestnut Ridge Nursery—716-725-8043; Buffalo, NY. Sells dormant bare-root chestnut trees mixed in a special hydrogel slurry that protects the root system during shipment. www.chestnutridgenursery.com

Chief River Nursery—800-367-9254; Grafton WI. Sells dormant, bare-root American and Chinese chestnut trees. www.chiefrivernursery.com

Morse Nursery—269-979-4252; Lafayette, IN. Offers American/Chinese hybrid, Chinese, Colossal/Okei hybrid, Layeroka, and dwarf Korean chestnut trees. www.morsenursery.com

Mossy Oak Nativ Nurseries—662-494-4326; West Point, MS. Has a cold-season-variety chestnut tree from a grafted orchard of many different blight-resistant and tolerant strains. The cultivars are grown in USDA hardiness zone 6a, just a few miles from zone 5b. www.nativnurseries.com

Northern Ridge Nursery—715-324-6114; Pembine, WI. Sells bare-root stock of Chinese chestnut trees (a two-pack). Does not ship to AK, AZ, CA, HI, or WA. www.northernridgenursery.com

Planting Justice Nursery—510-756-6965; Oakland, CA. Planting Justice is a non-profit organization. It offers the following 14 varieties of chestnut trees: American, Chinese, European, Nevada, Pandora, Skookum, Szego, Torakuri, Precoce, Gillet, Marissard, Marsol, Colossal, and Bergantz. Different varieties grow best in various parts of the country. Check your USDA hardiness zone for the variety that will do best in your area. www.plantingjustice.org

Stark Brothers—800-325-4180; Louisiana, MO. Carries Chinese chestnut trees. www.starkbros.com

The Nursey at Ty Ty—888-758-2252; Ty Ty, GA. Offers Colossal, Revival, Chinese and American chestnut trees from 2 to 3 feet to 8 to 9 feet. www.tytyga.com.

Willis Orchards—866-586-6283; Cartersville, GA. Carries American, Chinese, Colossal, and Nevada chestnut trees. They sell both dormant bare-root stock as well as balled and burlapped (B&B) trees. The roots are much less disturbed with B&B transplanting process. www.willisorchards.com

Z Nutty Ridge—607-310-1318; McGraw, NY. Offers bare-root hardy Chinese, Chestnut Missouri HARC seedlings, 2-year-old ZCC seedlings, and Colossal chestnut trees. www.znutty.com

NUT AND ACORN TREE SOURCES

Chestnut Hill Outdoors—855-386-7826; Alachua, FL. Carries Shumard oak, nuttall oak, chinkapin oak, swamp chestnut oak, swamp white oak, gobbler sawtooth oak, pin oak, and white oak. www.chestnuthill-outdoors.com.

Garland Truffles—919-732-3041; Hillsborough, NC. Truffle trees, disease-resistant filbert trees, and oak seedling trees. www.garlandtruffles.com.

Grimo Nut Nursery—905-934-6887; Niagara-on-the-Lake, Ontario, Canada. Heartnut, buartnut, hican, butternut, walnut, hazelnut hybrids northern, hickory, pecan, ultra-northern beech, pine nut trees, ginkgo, and oak. www.grimonut.com

Gurney's Seed & Nursery Co.—513-354-1491; Greendale, IN. Offers hazelnut, hardy pecan, black walnut, butternut, shellbark hickory, Hall's hardy almond trees. www.gurneys.com

Heather Farms Nursery—931-635-2826; Morrison, TN. Pignut hickory, nuttall oak, chestnut oak, chinkapin oak, white walnut, and black walnut. www.heather-farmsnursery.com

Ison's Nursery and Vineyards—770-599-6970; Brooks, GA. Hazelnut, almond, walnut, and pecan trees. www.isons.com.

Morse Nursery—269-979-4252; Lafayette, IN. Sells American hazelnut containerized. From 1- to 2-year-old trees. Also offers American hazelnut seedlings. www.morsenursery.com

Mossy Oak Nativ Nurseries—662-494-4326; West Point, MS. Has a variety of 2-foot oaks like ShuWillow, Beadles, Bimundors, Compton, Northern red X Willow, Rainmaker, Scarlet X, ShuWater, Water X Nuttall. www.nativnurseries.com

Musser Forest Inc.—724-465-5685; Indiana, PA. Butternut, hickory, hazelnut, and black walnut. www.musserforests.com

RainTree Nursery—800-391-8892; Morton, WA. Almonds, hazelnuts, gingko, and walnut trees. www.raintreenursery.com

Stark Bro's Nursery—800-325-4180; Louisiana, MO. Stark® Kwik-Krop® Walnut, Starking® Hardy Giant® Pecan, Starking® Southern Giant Pecan, Stark® Bountiful™ butternut, filbert hazelnut, and self-pollinating pecan trees. www.starkbros.com

Useful Plants Nursery—828-669-6517; Black Mountain, NC. Hazelnut, European filbert, and maidenhair tree (gingko biloba). www.usefulplants.org

The Wildlife Group—800-221-9703; Tuskegee, AL. Offers both bare-root and containerized trees. Nutall, swamp white, Shumard, Chinquapin and Sawtooth oaks. www.wildlifegroup.com

Appendix D

Food Plot Consulting Services

Wildlife consulting services provide tailored advice specific to your property about all aspects of planting forage seeds and habitat management for deer and other wildlife. A consultant will provide a customized evaluation of your property, resources, equipment, deer herd, etc., and will set realistic goals that will further improve your food plot endeavors.

Additionally, state wildlife agencies can put you in touch with local wildlife professionals. Moreover, a state wildlife agency may also provide voluntary incentive programs to landowners to improve their wildlife habitat. They can also direct you to federal programs such as the USDA's Environmental Quality Incentives Program (EQIP). For example, EQIP provides technical and cost-sharing assistance to help landowners establish and improve both wildlife and fish habitat. For waterfowl hunters, it may wise to investigate the USDA's Wetlands Reserve Program (WRP). This is a voluntary program that offers landowners the opportunity to protect, restore, and enhance wetlands on their property. Lastly, non-profit organizations like National Deer Association (NDA– formerly QDMA), National Wild Turkey Federation, Pheasants Forever, Ducks Unlimited, Ruffed Grouse Association, and many others provide service to help landowners better manage their wildlife and lands.

Below I have included some food plot and land management consultants and organizations from across the country for your consideration. I listed them alphabetically in order to avoid any conflict of interest or favoritism.

- **1101 Southern Wildlife & Land Consultants—** 502-330-9025; Georgetown, KY. www.southern-wildlife.com
- **American Forest Foundation—**202-765-3660; Washington, D.C. Info@forestfoundation.org.
- **Custom Game Land Services—**608-212-4622; Madison, WI. Bryan at glservices@yahoo.com. Website: www.customgamelandservices.com

- **Drop-Tine Wildlife Consulting—**570-204-4064; Bloomsburg, PA. Certified Wildlife Biologist, jason@droptineseed.com, jason@droptinewildlife.com
- **Habitat Pro LLC—**Detroit Lakes, MN. habitaprollc@gmail.com
- **Huntingplots.com—**717-989-6239; Parkesburg, PA. john@huntingplots.com
- **Kent Kammermeyer Wildlife Consulting, LLC—** 706-878-6159; Certified wildlife biologist. Published more than 300 articles, mostly on deer and deer food plants. Kentk49@yahoo.com. An editor of *Quality Food Plots* with Karl V. Miller and Lindsay Thomas Jr., published by National Deer Association.
- **Kester's Wild Game Food Nurseries, Inc.—**800-558-8815; Omro, WI. pkester@vbe.com
- **Milliken Forestry Company—**803-788-0590; Columbia, SC. staff@millikenadvisors.com
- **Reed's Custom Food Plots—**715-218-2888; Mosinee, WI. matt@foodplotting.com
- **River Refuge Seed—**541-466-5309; Brownsville, OR. Specializes in complimentary food plot consulting services via phone or email. Contact Chris Rogers at www.riverrefugeseed.com
- **Tecomate—**601-480-5197; Meridian, MS. Chris@tecomate.com
- **The Ward Burton Wildlife Foundation—** 434-476-7038; Halifax, VA. www.twbwf.org
- **Whitetail Food Plots USA—**716-796-4820; East Aurora, New York. paul@whitetailfoodplotsusa.com
- **Whitetail Habitat Solutions—**507-730-2321; Munising, MI. jeff@whitetailhabitatsolutions.com
- **Whitetail Strategies—**607-783-2055; South New Berlin, NY. peterfiduccia@outlook.com, www.deerdoctor.com

- **Whitetail Obsession Outdoors**—443-790-4250; Baltimore, MD. daverichmond@whitetailobsessionoutdoors.com
- **Whitetail Plans**—www.whitetailplans.com. Whitetail Plans Team—Steve Bartylla Site Co-Founder, Jay and Wyatt Gregory, Ethan Welscher.

Disclaimer: All seed data provided as well as all the other planting information reflects the author's earnest efforts to interpret a complex body of scientific research, and to translate it into practical wildlife food-plot planting practices and guidelines within this compendium. Following the guidance provided throughout this volume does not assure the reader any or all the information written by the author will imply any steadfast assurances of planting success. As with any farming practice, the planting, management thereof, and successful growing of plants are totally dependent on weather conditions and many other factors.

A personal note from the author:
Throughout this book I mention company names and product brands, including some that I use. I did not include them to suggest in any way that readers should purchase the brands I use or cited. I strongly believe the choice of buying products is left solely up to the reader and should not be swayed by any unintended influence by me. To my best ability I tried to be fair by including a variety of brands, companies, and products.

Additional Sources: nesoil.com, NRCS, USDA, Cambridge Dictionary, Wikipedia, The Merriam-Webster Dictionary, National Deer Association, Google Dictionary, Dictionary.com, Oxford Dictionaries, American Bird Conservancy, The Wildlife Society, University of Georgia, National Geographic Society's Crittercam Program, Britannica.com, Clemson.edu, noble.org, bookbuilder.cast.org, Cornell University, Wageningen University and Research Center, maximumyield.com, advancednutrients.com, famersweekly.co.za, forestry.usu.edu, time.com, extension.psu.edu, www.omri.org, gardeningknowhow.com, www.uoregon.edu.